AMC WHITE MOUNTAIN GUIDE

Twenty-fourth edition

AMC WHITE MOUNTAIN GUIDE

Twenty-fourth edition

A Guide to trails in the mountains of New Hampshire and adjacent parts of Maine

Appalachian Mountain Club
BOSTON, MASSACHUSETTS

AMC WHITE MOUNTAIN GUIDE
Copyright © 1987

EDITIONS

First Edition 1907, Second Edition 1916
Third Edition 1917, Fourth Edition 1920
Fifth Edition 1922, Sixth Edition 1925
Seventh Edition 1928, Eighth Edition 1931
Ninth Edition 1934, Tenth Edition 1936
Eleventh Edition 1940, Twelfth Edition 1946
Thirteenth Edition 1948, Fourteenth Edition 1952
Fifteenth Edition 1955, Sixteenth Edition 1960
Seventeenth Edition 1963, Eighteenth Edition 1966
Nineteenth Edition 1969, Twentieth Edition 1972
Twenty-First Edition 1976
Twenty-Second Edition 1979
Twenty-Third Edition 1983
Twenty-Fourth Edition 1987

**Due to changes in conditions, use of the
information in this book is at the sole risk
of the user.**

Cover photograph by Ron Paula
Cover design by Outside Designs
Composition by Shepard Poorman Communications Corp.
Production by Renée M. Le Verrier

ISBN 0-910146-61-6

5 4 3 2 1   87 88 89

CONTENTS

LIST OF MAPS

MAPS FOLDED IN BACK COVER POCKET

1. Mt. Monadnock
2. Mt. Cardigan
4. Chocorua - Waterville
5. Franconia
6. Mt. Washington Range
7. Carter - Mahoosuc
8. Pilot Range

Maps 1 and 2 are on back of 7. Map 8 is on back of 5. There is no map number 3.

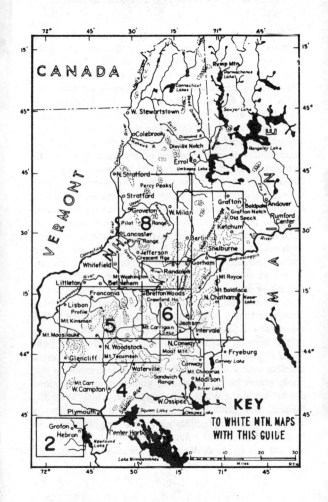

To the Owner of this Book

The White Mtns. are an ever-changing area, and a guidebook to this region can never be more than a record of the way things were at a given moment in time. While every care has been taken to make this book as accurate as possible, changing conditions may render almost any trail difficult to follow, and use of the information in this book is at the sole risk of the user. The various maintaining organizations, including the AMC, reserve the right to discontinue any trail without notice, and expressly disclaim any legal responsibility for the condition of any trail. Trails can be rerouted or abandoned or closed by landowners. Signs are stolen or fall from their posts. Storms may cause blowdowns or landslides, which can obliterate a trail for an entire climbing season or longer. Trails may not be cleared of fallen trees and brush until late summer, and not all trails are cleared every year. Logging operations can cover trails with slash and add a bewildering network of new roads. Momentary inattention to trail markers, particularly arrows at sharp turns, or misinterpretation of signs or guidebook descriptions, can cause one to become separated from all but the most heavily traveled paths. So please remember that a guidebook is an aid to planning, not a substitute for observation and judgment. We request your help in keeping this book accurate; new editions are published at intervals of about four years. If you encounter a problem with a trail, or with a map or description in this book, please let us know. Any comments or corrections can be sent to the White Mountain Guide, AMC, 5 Joy St., Boston, MA 02108. The comments of a person who is inexperienced or unfamiliar with a trail are often particularly useful. This book belongs to the entire hiking community not just to the AMC and the people who produce it.

TRIP PLANNING

The descriptions in this book are intended to apply approximately from Memorial Day to Columbus Day. In some years snowdrifts may remain into the spring, and there will certainly be some severe weather in the early fall. Many trails are far more difficult to follow (or even dangerous) when snow or ice is present. Spring and fall are particularly dangerous seasons in the mountains, since the weather may be pleasant in the valleys and brutal on the summits and ridges. A great portion of the serious incidents in the mountains occur in the spring and fall. Wintry conditions can occur above treeline in any month of the year. Even in midsummer, hikers above treeline should be prepared for cold weather with a wool sweater, hat, mittens, and a wind parka, which will give comfort on sunny but cool days and protection against sudden storms.

Plan your trip schedule with safety in mind. Consider the general strenuousness of the trip: the overall distance, the amount of climbing, and the roughness of the terrain. Get a weather report. Be aware of the fact that most forecasts are not intended to apply to the mountain region, and a day that is sunny in the lowlands may well be inclement in the mountains. The National Weather Service in Concord NH (603-225-5191) issues a recreational forecast for the White Mtn. region and broadcasts it each morning; this forecast is posted at Pinkham Notch Camp at about 8 AM. Plan to finish your hike with daylight to spare (remember that days are shorter in late summer and fall). Hiking after dark, even with flashlights (which frequently fail), makes finding trails more difficult and crossing streams hazardous. Let someone else know where you will be hiking, and do not let inexperienced people get separated from the group. Many dirt roads are not passable until about Memorial Day, and the WMNF closes many of its roads with locked gates from November to May; many trips are much longer when the roads are not open.

FOLLOWING TRAILS

Hikers should always carry a compass and carefully keep track of their approximate location on the map. The best compass for hiking is the protractor type: a circular compass that turns on a rectangular clear plastic base. Excellent compasses of this type, with leaflets which give ample instructions in their use, are available for less than $10. Such a compass is easily set to the bearing that you wish to follow, and then it is a simple matter of keeping the compass needle aligned to north and following the arrow on the base. More sophisticated and expensive compasses have features designed for special applications which are not useful in the woods; they are normally harder to use and apt to cause confusion in an emergency situation. Directions of the compass given in the text are based on true north instead of magnetic north, unless otherwise specified. There is a deviation of 16 to 17 degrees between true north and magnetic north in the White Mtns. This means that true north will be about 17 degrees to the right of (clockwise from) the compass's north needle. If you take a bearing from a map, you should add 17 degrees to the bearing when you set your compass. On the maps included with this Guide, the black lines that run from bottom to top are aligned with true north and south. Diagonal light-brown lines, as on the Mt. Washington map, point to magnetic north.

In general, trails are maintained to provide a clear pathway while protecting and minimizing damage to the environment. Some may offer rough and difficult passage. Most hiking trails are marked with paint on trees or rocks, or with axe blazes cut into trees. The trails that compose the Appalachian Trail through the White Mtns. are marked with vertical rectangular white paint blazes throughout. Side trails off the Appalachian Trail are usually marked with blue paint. Other trails are marked in other colors, the most popular being yellow. Except for the Appalachian Trail and its side trails, and trails maintained by certain clubs such as the CMC and WODC, the color of blazing has no significance and may change without notice. Above timberline, cairns (piles of rocks) mark the trails. Where hikers have trodden out the vegetation, the footway is usually visible except when it is covered by snow or by fallen leaves. In winter, signs at trailheads and intersections and blazes also are often covered by snow.

If a trail is lost and is not visible to either side, it is usually best to backtrack right away to the last mark seen and look again from there. Trails following or crossing logging roads require special care at intersections in order to distinguish the trail from diverging roads, particularly since blazing is usually very sparse while the trail follows the road. Around shelters or campsites, trodden paths may lead in all directions, so look for signs and paint blazes.

If you become separated from a trail in the White Mtns., it is not necessarily a serious matter. Few people become truly lost; a moment's reflection and five minutes with the map will show that you probably know at least your approximate location and the direction to the nearest road, if nothing else. Most cases in which a person has become lost for any length of time involve panic and aimless wandering, so the most important first step is to take a break, make an inventory of useful information, decide on a course of action and stick to it. (The caution against allowing inexperienced persons to become separated from a group should be repeated here, since they are most likely to panic and wander aimlessly. Make sure also that all party members are familiar with the route of the trip and the names of the trails to be used). In many instances, retracing your steps will lead you back to the point of departure from the trail. If you have carefully kept track of your location on the map, it will usually be possible to find a nearby stream, trail, or road to which a compass course may be followed. Most distances are short enough (except in the North Country north of NH 110) that it is possible, in the absence of alternatives, to reach a highway in half a day, or at most in a whole day, simply by going downhill, skirting the tops of any dangerous cliffs, until you come upon a river or brook. The stream should then be followed downward.

WHAT TO CARRY

Good things to have in your pack for a summer day hike in the White Mountains include maps, guidebook, water bottle (plastic soft drink bottles work well), compass, knife, rain gear, windbreaker, wool sweater(s), hat, waterproof matches, enough food plus extra high-energy foods in reserve (such as chocolate or candy), first-aid supplies (including personal medicines, aspirin, adhesive bandages, gauze, and antiseptic), needle and thread, safety pins, nylon cord, trash bag, toilet paper, and a (small) flashlight with extra batteries. Wear comfortable hiking boots. Blue jeans are popular but once wet, dry out very slowly. Most fabrics dry faster than cotton, and wool keeps much of its insulation value even when wet.

EMERGENCIES

For emergencies call the toll-free New Hampshire State Police number (1-800-852-3411) or Pinkham Notch Camp (603-466-2727).

Hypothermia, the most serious danger to hikers, is the loss of ability to preserve body heat because of injury, exhaustion, lack of sufficient food, and inadequate or wet clothing. Most of the dozens of deaths on Mt. Washington have resulted from hypothermia. The symptoms are uncontrolled shivering, impaired speech and movement, lowered body temperature, and drowsiness. The result is death, unless the victim (who will not understand the situation, due to impaired mental function) is rewarmed. In mild cases the victim should be given dry clothing and placed in a sleeping bag, perhaps with someone else in it to provide body heat, then quick-energy food, and, when full consciousness is regained, something warm (not hot) to drink. In severe cases only hospitalization offers hope for recovery. It is not unusual for a victim to resist treatment and even combat rescuers. It should be obvious that prevention of hypothermia is the only truly practical course. Most cases occur in temperatures above freezing; the most dangerous conditions involve rain, with wind, with temperatures below 50° F. Uncontrollable shivering should be regarded as an absolute evidence of hypothermia; this shivering will eventually cease on its own, but that is merely the sign that the body has given up the struggle and is sinking toward death.

Other Hazards

Mosquitoes and black flies are frequently encountered by hikers. Mosquitoes are worst in low, wet areas, and black flies make their most aggressive attacks in June and early July. There are no poisonous snakes or other dangerous animals in the mountains. Deer-hunting season is in November, when you'll see many more hunters than deer. Bears tend to keep well out of sight, but are a nuisance at some popular campsites.

BROOK CROSSINGS

Rivers and brooks are often crossed without bridges, and it is usually possible to jump from rock to rock; a hiking staff or stick is a great aid to balance. Use caution; several fatalities have resulted from hikers (particularly solo hikers) falling on slippery rocks and drowning in relatively small streams. If you need to wade across (which is often the safer course), wearing boots, but not necessarily socks, is recommended. Note that many crossings, which may only be a nuisance in summer, may be a serious hazard in cold weather when one's feet and boots must be kept dry. Higher waters, which can turn innocuous brooks into virtually uncrossable torrents, come in the spring as snow melts, or after heavy rainstorms, particularly in the fall when trees drop their leaves and take up less water. Do not plan hikes with potentially hazardous stream crossings during these high-water periods. Rushing current can make wading extremely hazardous, and several deaths have resulted. If you are cut off from roads by swollen streams, it is better to make a long detour, even if you need to wait and spend a night in the woods. Flood waters may subside within a few hours, especially in small brooks. It is particularly important not to camp on the far side of a brook from your exit point if the crossing is difficult and heavy rain is predicted.

DRINKING WATER

The pleasure of quaffing a cup of water fresh from a pure mountain spring is one of the traditional attractions of the mountains. Unfortunately, in many mountain regions, including the White Mtns., the presence of cysts of the intestinal parasite giardia lamblia is becoming more and more common. It is impossible to be completely sure whether a given source is safe, no matter how clear the water or remote the location. The safest course is for day hikers to carry their own water, and for those who use sources in the woods to treat the water before drinking it. A conservative practice is to boil water for 20 minutes or to use an iodine-based disinfectant. Chlorine-based products, such as Halazone, are in-

effective in water that contains organic impurities and they
deteriorate quickly in the pack. Remember to allow extra
contact time (and use twice as many tablets) if the water is
very cold. The symptoms of giardiasis are severe intestinal
distress and diarrhea. The principal cause of the spread of
this noxious ailment is careless disposal of human waste.
Keep it at least 200 ft. away from water sources. If there are
no toilets nearby, dig a trench 6 to 8 in. deep (but not below
the organic layer of the soil) for a latrine and cover it completely after use. The bacteria in the organic layer of the soil
will then decompose the waste naturally.

DISTANCES AND TIMES

The distances and times that appear in the tables at the
end of trail descriptions are cumulative from the starting
point at the head of each table. Estimated hiking times are
denoted by est. Small disagreements due to rounding will
occasionally be observed in measured distances. The distances given will sometimes be found to differ from those
on trail signs; we provide the most accurate distances
available to us. There is no reliable method for estimating
hiking times; in order to give inexperienced hikers some
basis for planning, the times given in this book have been
calculated by allowing a half-hour for each mile or 1000 ft.
of climbing. These times may be very inadequate for steep
or rough trails, for hikers with heavy packs, or for large
groups, particularly with inexperienced hikers. In winter,
times are even less predictable: on a packed trail, times may
be faster than in summer, but with heavy packs or in deep
snow it may take two or three times the summer estimate.

FIRE REGULATIONS

Campfire permits are no longer required in the WMNF,
but hikers who build fires are still legally responsible for
any damage they may cause. During periods when there is a

high risk of forest fires, the Forest Supervisor may temporarily close the entire WMNF against public entry. Such general closures apply only as long as the dangerous conditions prevail. Other forest lands throughout NH or ME may be closed during similar periods through proclamation by the respective governors. These special closures are given wide publicity so that local residents and visitors alike may realize the danger of fires in the woods.

PROTECTING THE BEAUTY OF THE MOUNTAINS

Please use special care above timberline. Extreme weather and a short growing season make these areas especially fragile. Just footsteps can destroy the toughest natural cover, so please try to stay on the trail or walk on rocks. And, of course, don't camp above timberline.

Once every campsite had a dump, and many trails became unsightly with litter. Now visitors are asked to bring trash bags and carry out everything—food, paper, glass, cans—they carry in. Cooperation with the "carry in/carry out" program has been outstanding, resulting in a great decrease in trailside litter over the past few years, and the concept has grown to "carry out more than you carried in." We hope you will join in the effort. Your fellow backcountry users will appreciate it.

A FINAL NOTE

Hiking is a sport of self-reliance. Its high potential for adventure and relatively low level of regulation have been made possible by the dedication of most hikers to the values of prudence and independence. This tradition of self-reliance imposes an obligation on each of us: at any time we may have to rely on our own ingenuity and judgment, aided by map and compass, to reach our goals or even make a timely exit from the woods. While the penalty for failure rarely exceeds an unplanned and uncomfortable night in the woods, more serious outcomes are possible. Most hikers find a high degree of satisfaction in obtaining the knowledge and skills that free them from blind dependence on the next blaze or trail sign, and enable them to walk in the woods with confidence and assurance. Those who learn the skills of getting about in the woods, the habits of studious acquisition of information before the trip and careful observation while in the woods, soon find that they have surely earned "the Freedom of the Hills."

The AMC earnestly requests that those who use the trails, shelters, and campsites heed the rules (especially those having to do with camping) of the WMNF, NHDP, and SPNHF. The same consideration should be shown to private owners. In many cases the privileges enjoyed by hikers today could be withdrawn if rules and conditions are not observed.

The trails that we use and enjoy are only in part the product of government agencies. Many trails are maintained by one dedicated person, or a small group. Funds for trail work are scarce, and unless hikers contribute both time and money to the maintenance of trails, the variety of trails available to the public is almost certain to experience a sad decline. Every hiker can make some contribution to the improvement of the trails. (Write to AMC Trails, Pinkham Notch Camp, Box 298, Gorham, NH 03581, for information.) Trails must not be cut in the WMNF without the approval of the Forest Supervisor, nor elsewhere without consent of the owners and without definite provision for maintenance.

Introduction

According to Ticknor's *White Mountains,* published in 1887, the higher peaks "seem to have received the name of White Mountains from the sailors off the coast, to whom they were a landmark and a mystery lifting their crowns of brilliant snow against the blue sky from October until June."

This book aims for reasonably complete coverage of hiking trails located in the northern half of New Hampshire and in immediately adjoining parts of Maine, and of the more important trails in southern New Hampshire. No attempt is made to cover any kind of skiing (alpine, downhill, or cross-country), although several cross-country (ski-touring) trails are mentioned where they happen to cross hiking trails. Because of extreme hazards to inexperienced or insufficiently equipped climbers or groups, rock climbs are not described in this book. Rock climbing requires special techniques and equipment, and should not be undertaken except by roped parties under qualified leaders.

CLIMATE AND VEGETATION

The climate gets much cooler, windier, and wetter at higher elevations. The summit of Mt. Washington is under cloud cover about 55% of the time. On an average summer afternoon, the high temperature on the summit is only about 52° F (11° C); in the winter, about 15° F (−9° C). The record low temperature is −46° F. Average winds throughout the day and night are 26 mph in summer and 44 mph in winter. Winds have gusted over 100 mph in every month of the year, and set the world record of 231 mph on April 12, 1934. During the storm of February 24-26, 1969, the observatory recorded a snowfall of 97.8 in. Within a

24-hour period during that storm, a total of 49.3 in. was recorded, a record for the mountain and for all weather observation stations in the United States. Other mountains also have severe conditions, in proportion to their height and exposure.

The forest on the White Mtns. is of two major types: the northern hardwoods (birch, beech, and maple), which are found at elevations of less than about 3000 ft., and the boreal forest (spruce, fir, and birch), which is found from about 3000 ft. to the timberline. At lower elevations oaks and white pines may be seen; red pines and (rarely) jack pines may be seen at up to about 2000 ft. in ledgy areas. Above the timberline is the "krummholz," the gnarled and stunted trees that manage to survive wherever there is a bit of shelter from the violent winds, and the tiny wildflowers, some of which are extremely rare. Hikers are encouraged to be particularly careful in their activities above treeline, as the plants that grow there already have to cope with the severity of the environment. For information about these trees and plants, consult *Trees and Shrubs of Northern New England,* published by the SPNHF, and the *Field Guide to Mountain Flowers of New England* and *At Timberline,* both published by the AMC.

MAPS

The published topographic quadrangles of the USGS cover all of NH and ME. Many areas are covered by the more recent and detailed 7.5 min. quads. New metric maps are being produced; they are now available only for the Presidential Range and nearby areas, but more should be released in the next few years. Although topography on the newer maps is excellent, some recent maps have been inaccurate in showing the locations of trails. Index maps to USGS quads in any state (specify states) and pamphlets concerning USGS maps are available free from the Branch of Distribution, USGS, 1200 South Eads St., Arlington, VA 22202.

Extra copies of AMC maps may be purchased at the AMC's Boston and Pinkham Notch offices and at some book and outdoor equipment stores.

Other maps of specific areas of the White Mtns. are mentioned in the relevant individual sections of this Guide.

CAMPING

Those who camp overnight in the backcountry tend to have more of an impact on the land than day hikers do. In the past some popular sites suffered misuse and began to resemble disaster areas, with piles of trash and surrounding trees devastated by campers gathering firewood. For this reason backpacking hikers should take great care to minimize their effect on the mountains by practicing low-impact camping and making conscious efforts to preserve the natural forest. One alternative is to camp in well-prepared, designated sites; the popular ones are supervised by caretakers. The other alternative has come to be called "clean camping": to disperse camping over a wide area, out of sight of trails and roads, and to camp with full respect for wilderness values. The objective of clean camping is to leave no trace of one's presence, so that the site will not be reused before it has a chance to recover. Repeated camping on one site compacts the soil and makes it difficult for vegetation to survive.

There are more than fifty backcountry shelters and tent sites in the White Mountain area, open on a first-come, first-served basis. Some sites have summer caretakers who collect an overnight fee to help defray expenses. Most sites have shelters, a few have only tent platforms, and some have both. Shelters are overnight accommodations for persons carrying their own bedding and cooking supplies. The more popular shelters are often full, so be prepared to camp off trail with tents or tarps at a legal site. Make yourself aware of regulations and restrictions prior to your trip.

If you camp away from established sites, look for a spot more than 200 ft. from the trail and from any surface water, and observe local RUA rules. Bring all needed shelter, including whatever poles, stakes, ground insulation, and cord are required. Try to choose a clear, level site on which to pitch your tent. Use a compass, and check landmarks carefully to find your way to and from your campsite. Do not cut boughs or branches for bedding. Avoid clearing vegetation and never make a ditch around the tent. Wash your dishes and yourself well away from streams, ponds, and springs. Heed the rules of neatness, sanitation, and fire prevention, and carry out everything—food, paper, glass, cans, etc.—that you carry in (and whatever trash less-thoughtful campers may have left). In some areas you may have to hang your food from a tree to protect it from raccoons and bears.

In some camping areas, a "human browse line" where people have gathered firewood over the years is quite evident: limbs are gone from trees, the ground is devoid of dead wood, and vegetation has been trampled as people scoured the area. The use of portable stoves is practically mandatory in popular areas, and is encouraged elsewhere to prevent damage to vegetation. Operate stoves with reasonable caution. Campfire permits are no longer required in the WMNF but campers are legally responsible for damages caused by any fire that they build. On private land, you need the owner's permission to build a fire, and fires are generally not permitted on state land except at campgrounds. Wood campfires should not be made unless there is ample dead and down wood available near your site;

never cut green trees. Such fires must be made in safe, sheltered places and not in leaves or rotten wood, or against logs, trees, or stumps. Before you build a fire, clear a space at least 5 ft. in radius of all flammable material down to the mineral soil. Under no circumstances should a fire be left unattended. All fires must be completely extinguished with earth or water before you leave a campsite, even temporarily. Campers should restore the campfire site to as natural an appearance as possible before leaving the campsite.

Roadside Campgrounds

The WMNF operates a number of roadside campgrounds with limited facilities; fees are charged. No reservations can be made, and many of these campgrounds are full on summer weekends. Consult the WMNF offices for details. Several NH state parks also have campgrounds conveniently located for hikers in the White Mtns. and other parts of the state. At these also no reservations can be made. For details on state parks, contact the Office of Vacation Travel, Box 856, Concord, NH 03301 (603-271-2665).

Camping Regulations

Trailside camping is practical only within the WMNF, with a few limited exceptions, such as the campsites on the Appalachian Trail. The laws of the states of ME and NH require that permission be obtained from the owner to camp on private land, and that permits be obtained to build campfires anywhere outside the WMNF, except at officially designated campsites. Camping and campfires are not permitted in NH state parks except in campgrounds.

Overnight camping is permitted in almost all of the WMNF. To limit or prevent some of the adverse impacts of concentrated, uncontrolled camping, the USFS has adopted regulations for a number of areas in the WMNF that are threatened by overuse and misuse. The objective of the Restricted Use Area (RUA) program is not to hinder backpackers and campers, but to disperse their use of the land so that people can enjoy themselves in a clean and attractive environment without causing deterioration of natural resources. By protecting the plants, water, soil, and wildlife of the White Mountains, these areas should help to provide a higher quality experience for the visitor. Because hikers and backpackers have cooperated with RUA rules, many trails once designated as RUAs are no longer under formal restrictions. However, common sense and self-imposed restrictions are still necessary to prevent damage.

In summary, the 1986 RUA rules prohibit camping and wood or charcoal fires above timberline (where trees are less than 8 ft. in height); or within a specified distance of certain roads, trails, streams, and other locations, except at designated sites. Stoves are permitted, even for day use. Contact the USFS in Laconia NH (603-524-6450), or any Ranger District office for up-to-date information, including a current RUA map.

WINTER CLIMBING

Snowshoeing and cross-country skiing on White Mtn. trails and peaks have steadily become more popular in the last decade. Increasing numbers of hikers have discovered the beauty of the woods in winter, and advances in clothing and equipment have made it possible for experienced winter travelers to enjoy great comfort and safety. The greatest danger is that it begins to look too easy and too safe, while snow, ice, and weather conditions are constantly changing, and a relatively trivial error of judgment may have grave, even fatal, consequences. Conditions can vary greatly from day to day, and from trail to trail, thus much more experience is required to forsee and avoid dangerous situations in winter than in summer. Trails are frequently difficult or impossible to follow, and navigation skills are hard to learn in adverse weather conditions (as anyone who has tried to read a map in a blizzard can attest). "Breaking trail" on snowshoes through new snow can be strenuous and exhausting work. Some trails go through areas which may pose a severe avalanche hazard. In a "white-out" above treeline, it may be almost impossible to tell the ground from the sky, and hikers frequently become disoriented.

Winter on the lower trails in the White Mtns. may require only snowshoes or skis and some warm clothing. Even so, summer hiking boots are usually inadequate, flashlight batteries fail quickly (a headlamp with battery pack works better), and water in canteens freezes unless wrapped in a sock or sweater. The winter hiker needs good physical conditioning from regular exercise, and must dress carefully in order to avoid overheating and excessive perspiration, which soaks clothing and soon leads to chilling. Cotton clothes are useful only as long as they can be kept perfectly dry (an impossible task, thus the winter climbers' saying, "cotton kills"); only wool and some of the newer synthetics retain their insulating values when wet. Fluid intake must increase, as dehydration can be a serious problem in the dry winter air.

Above timberline, conditions often require specialized equipment, and skills and experience of a different magnitude. The conditions on the Presidential Range in winter are as severe as any in North America south of the great mountains of Alaska and the Yukon Territory. On the summit of Mt. Washington in winter, winds average 44 mph, and daily high temperatures average 15°F. There are few calm days, and even on an average day conditions will be too severe for any but the most experienced and well-equipped climbers. The Mt. Washington Observatory has often reported wind velocities in excess of 100 mph, and temperatures are often below zero. The combination of high wind and low temperature has such a cooling effect that the worst conditions on Mt. Washington are approximately equal to the worst reported from Antarctica, despite the much greater cold in the latter region. Extremely severe storms can develop suddenly and unexpectedly. But the most dangerous aspect of winter in the White Mtns. is the extreme variability of the weather: it is not unusual for a cold, penetrating, wind-driven rain to be followed within a few hours by a cold front which brings below-zero temperatures and high winds.

No book can begin to impart all the knowledge necessary to cope safely with the potential for such brutal conditions, but helpful information can be found in *Don't Die on the Mountain*, a booklet by Dan H. Allen ($1, available from the AMC), and *Winter Hiking and Camping* by John A. Danielson (1982, Adirondack Mountain Club). Hikers who are interested in extending their activities into the winter season are strongly advised to seek out organized parties with leaders who have extensive winter experience. Each year the AMC and Adirondack Mountain Club operate a week-long winter school which exposes participants to the techniques and equipment of safe winter travel. The AMC and several of its chapters also sponsor numerous workshops on evenings and weekends, in addition to introductory winter hikes and regular winter schedules through which participants can gain experience. Information on such activities can be obtained from the AMC information center at the Boston headquarters.

WHITE MOUNTAIN NATIONAL FOREST

Most of the higher White Mtns. are within the White Mountain National Forest (WMNF), which was established under the Weeks Act and now comprises about 750,000 acres, of which about 47,000 acres are in ME and the rest in NH. It is important to remember that this is not a national *park*, but a national *forest*; parks are established primarily for preservation and recreation, while national forests are managed for multiple use. In the administration of national forests the following objectives are considered: recreation development, timber production, watershed protection, and wildlife propagation. It is the policy of the USFS to manage logging operations so that trails, streams, camping-places, and other spots of public interest are protected. Mountain recreation has been identified as the most important resource in the WMNF. The boundaries of the WMNF are usually marked wherever they cross roads or trails, usually by red-painted corner posts and blazes. Hunting and fishing are permitted in the WMNF under the state laws; state licenses are required. Much informational literature has been published by the WMNF and is available free of charge at the Forest Supervisor's Office in Laconia, the Ranger District offices (list below), and other information centers.

The National Wilderness Preservation System, which included the Great Gulf, was established in 1964 with passage of the Wilderness Act. The Presidential Range–Dry River Wilderness, the Pemigewasset Wilderness, and the Sandwich Range Wilderness have since been added to the system. It should be noted that wilderness areas are established by an act of Congress, and not merely by WMNF administrative action. The USFS has established nine scenic areas in the WMNF to preserve lands of outstanding or unique natural beauty: Gibbs Brook, Nancy

Brook, Greeley Ponds, Pinkham Notch, Lafayette Brook, Rocky Gorge, Lincoln Woods, Sawyer Pond, and Snyder Brook. Camping is restricted in many areas under the Restricted Use Area (RUA) program to protect vulnerable areas from damage. To preserve the rare alpine flora of the Mt. Washington Range and to assure that the natural conditions on the upper slopes of the WMNF are maintained, removal of any tree, shrub, or plant without written permission is prohibited.

WMNF Offices and Ranger Districts (R.D.'s)

The Androscoggin and Saco Ranger District offices have been open seven days a week in the summer, sometimes with evening hours. Otherwise, the offices are open during normal business hours.

Forest Supervisor, PO Box 638, Laconia, NH 03247. (on North Main St., across railroad tracks from downtown section).

Tel. 603-524-6450.

Ammonoosuc R.D., Trudeau Rd., Bethlehem, NH 03574

(just north of US 3 opposite Gale River Rd.).

Tel. 603-869-2626.

Androscoggin R. D., 80 Glen Rd., Gorham, NH 03581 (at south end of town along NH 16).

Tel. 603-466-2713.

Evans Notch R. D., RD #2, Box 2270, Bethel, ME 04217 (on US 2).

Tel. 207-834-2134.

Pemigewasset R. D., 127 Highland St., Plymouth, NH 03264

to west of town, between Hatch Plaza on NH 25 and hospital).

Tel. 603-536-1310.

Saco R. D., RFD 1, Box 94, Conway, NH 03818
(on Kancamagus Highway just west of NH 16).
Tel. 603-447-5448.

THE APPALACHIAN TRAIL (AT)

This footpath runs over 2000 mi. from Springer Mtn. in Georgia to Katahdin in ME, and traverses the White Mtns. for about 170 mi. in a southwest to northeast direction, from Hanover NH to Grafton Notch in ME. Its route traverses many of the major peaks and ranges of the White Mtns., following many historic and scenic trails. Except for a few short segments between Hanover and Glencliff, the trails that make up the AT in the White Mtns. are all described in this book. In each section of this Guide through which the AT passes, its route through the section is described in a separate paragraph near the beginning. (South to north, the trail passes consecutively through Sections 6, 5, 3, 1, 2, 1 again, 9, and 12.) Persons interested in following the AT as a continuous path may also consult the Appalachian Trail Conference's *Guide to the Appalachian Trail in New Hampshire and Vermont*. Information on the Appalachian Trail and the several guidebooks which cover its entire length can be secured from the Appalachian Trail Conference, PO Box 236, Harpers Ferry, WV 25425.

With the passage of the National Trails System Act by Congress on October 2, 1968, the Appalachian Trail became the first federally protected footpath in this country and was officially designated the Appalachian National Scenic Trail. Under this act the Appalachian Trail is administered primarily as a footpath by the Secretary of Interior in consultation with the Secretary of Agriculture and representatives of the several states through which it passes. In addition, an Advisory Council for the Appalachian National Scenic Trail was appointed by the Secretary of Interior. It includes representatives of each of the states and the several hiking clubs recommended by the Appalachian Trail Conference.

SOCIETY FOR THE PROTECTION OF NEW HAMPSHIRE FORESTS

This organization has worked since 1901 to protect the mountains, forests, wetlands, and farm lands of NH, and to encourage wise forestry practices. It owns Lost River in Kinsman Notch, a substantial reservation on Monadnock, and a number of other lands. In cooperation with the AMC, it protects and maintains the Monadnock - Sunapee Greenway. Its headquarters building in Concord NH was designed as a showcase in the latest techniques of energy conservation. For membership information, contact the SPNHF, 54 Portsmouth St., Concord, NH 03301 (603-224-9945).

NEW ENGLAND TRAIL CONFERENCE

The New England Trail Conference was organized in 1917 to develop the hiking possibilities of New England and to coordinate the work of local organizations. The Conference serves as a clearinghouse for information about trail maintenance and trail use both for organized groups and for individuals. The annual meeting of this organization is held in the spring, when representatives of mountaineering and outing clubs from all over New England come together for a full day and evening program of reports, talks, and illustrated lectures on mountain climbing, hiking, and trails and shelters. All sessions are open to the public. The work of the Conference is directed by the chairman, who is elected by the executive committee. For information, con-

tact the chairman, Forrest House, 33 Knollwood Drive,
East Longmeadow, MA 01028.

ABBREVIATIONS

The following abbreviations are used in trail descriptions.

hr.	hour(s)
min.	minutes(s)
mph	miles per hour
in.	inch(es)
ft.	foot, feet
km.	kilometer(s)
yd.	yard(s)
est.	estimated
AMC	Appalachian Mountain Club
AT	Appalachian Trail
CMC	Chocorua Mountain Club
CTA	Chatham Trails Association
CU	Camp Union
DOC	Dartmouth Outing Club
HA	Hutmen's Association
JCC	Jackson Conservation Commission
MMVSP	Mt. Madison Volunteer Ski Patrol
NHDP	New Hampshire Division of Parks
PEAOC	Phillips Exeter Academy Outing Club
RMC	Randolph Mountain Club
SLA	Squam Lakes Association
SPNHF	Society for the Protection of New Hampshire Forests
SSOC	Sub Sig Outing Club
USFS	United States Forest Service
USGS	United States Geological Survey
WMNF	White Mountain National Forest

WODC   Wonalancet Outdoor Club
WVAIA   Waterville Valley Athletic and Improvement Association

The Nancy Pond Trail is currently maintained by Camp Pasquaney and Camp Mowglis maintains several trails in the Cardigan area.

WHITE MOUNTAIN GUIDEBOOK COMMITTEE

Editor
Eugene S. Daniell III

Philip Levin, *ex-officio*
T. Walley Williams, *ex-officio*

D. William Baird	Angus McEachern
Iris Baird	John McHugh
Lawrence R. Blood	Doris Meyer
Helen Cawood	Avard Milbury
Gordon Cawood	Kenneth E. Miller
Debra Y. Clark	Paul A. Miller
Eugene S. Daniell IV	Robert Nesham
Daniel DeHart	William Nichols
Sharon DeHart	Christopher Northrup
Kathleen Donaghue	Faith Northrup
Richard M. Dudley	Herbert G. Ogden Jr.
George Dussault	Anne Peterson
David O. Elliott	Frank L. Pilar
Terrence P. Frost	David H. Raymond
Hal Graham	Tom W. Sawyer
Samuel Hagner	Diane D. Sawyer
Joseph J. Hansen	Roioli Schweiker
Mary Hansen	Roy R. Schweiker

Robert C. Hansen
Alice A. Johnson
Timothy Kennedy
Allen Krause
Albert LaPrade
James R. Lindsley
Forrest Mack
Tom Maguire

Kimball Simpson
Vera V. Smith
Dennis Spurling
Audrey Sylvester
Thomas F. Vallette
Guy Waterman
Laura Waterman
David F. Wright

Mount Washington and the Southern Ridges

This section includes the summit of Mt. Washington and the major ridges which run south from it, which constitute the southern portion of the Presidential Range. It is bounded on the north by the Mt. Washington Cog Railway and the Mt. Washington Auto Rd., on the east by NH 16, on the south by US 302, and on the west by US 302 and the Base Rd. The northern portion of the Presidential Range, including Mts. Clay, Jefferson, Adams, and Madison, and the Great Gulf, is covered in Section 2. Many of the trails described in Section 2 also provide routes to Mt. Washington. The AMC Mt. Washington Range map (map 6) covers this entire section.

Three major ridges run southwest or south from Mt. Washington, separated by deep river valleys from each other and from the ranges to the west and east. The most impressive ridge is formed by the Southern Peaks, which run southwest from Mt. Washington, comprising (from northeast to southwest) Mts. Monroe, Franklin, Eisenhower, Pierce (also known as Clinton), Jackson, and Webster, ending abruptly above Crawford Notch at the cliffs of Mt. Webster. On the northwest, the headwaters of the Ammonoosuc River (a Connecticut River tributary) flow across the Fabyan Plain between the Southern Peaks and the much lower Dartmouth Range. The Dry River begins in Oakes Gulf high on Mt. Washington, and runs to the Saco River below Crawford Notch through a deep ravine between the Southern Peaks and the Montalban Ridge. The Montalban Ridge is the longest of all Mt. Washington's subsidiary ridges, extending about 15 mi. from the summit; it first runs south over Boott Spur, Mt. Isolation, Mt. Davis, Stairs Mtn., Mt. Resolution, and Mt. Parker, then

1

swings east to Mts. Langdon, Pickering, and Stanton, the low peaks above the intervales of Bartlett and Glen near the confluence of the Rocky Branch and Saco River. The Bemis Ridge is a significant spur running from Mt. Resolution southwest over Mt. Crawford, then south to Hart Ledge, which overlooks the great bend in the Saco. East of the Montalbans lies the Rocky Branch, and to the east of the Rocky Branch rises the Rocky Branch Ridge, a long, wide-spreading assortment of humps and flat ridges running south from Boott Spur via Slide Peak, with no outstanding summit except Iron Mtn. at the far south end. Still farther east the Ellis River flows down from Pinkham Notch, with NH 16 running through the valley and the ridges of Wildcat Mtn. on the opposite side.

In this section the Appalachian Trail follows the entire Webster Cliff Trail from Crawford Notch to its intersection with the Crawford Path near the summit of Mt. Pierce, then follows the Crawford Path to the summit of Mt. Washington. From there it descends to the Gulfside Trail (see Section 2) via the Trinity Heights Connector. On the way it crosses the summits of Mts. Webster, Jackson, Pierce, and Washington, and passes near Mts. Eisenhower, Franklin, and Monroe. Then, after passing over the Northern Peaks (although it misses most of the summits) and through the Great Gulf (areas covered in Section 2), it returns to Section 1 at the Mt. Washington Auto Rd., following the Old Jackson Road to Pinkham Notch Camp and NH 16.

SUMMIT BUILDINGS

No hotel or overnight lodging for the public is available on the summit of Mt. Washington. From Columbus Day to Memorial Day no buildings are open to hikers for shelter or refuge. The new summit building named in honor of former NH Governor Sherman Adams and operated by the NH Division of Parks and Recreation during the summer season (mid-May to mid-October) has food service, pack room, souvenir shop, public rest rooms, telephone, and a post office. It houses the Mt. Washington Observatory, the Mt. Washington Museum, and facilities for park personnel.

The Yankee Building was built in 1941 to house transmitter facilities for the first FM station in northern New England. It is now leased by WMTW-TV and houses two-way radio equipment for various state, federal, and local organizations. This building is closed to the public.

The transmitter building and powerhouse for WMTW-TV and WHOM-FM, built in 1954, provides living quarters for station personnel and houses television and microwave equipment. The structure, built to withstand winds of 300 mph, is not open to the public.

The Stage Office, built in 1975 to replace a similar building constructed in 1908, is owned by the Mt. Washington Auto Road Company and used only in connection with their operation.

The first Summit House on Mt. Washington was built in 1852. The first Tip Top House hotel, built in 1853, suffered a fire in 1915. It is now owned by the State of New Hampshire and is part of the Mt. Washington State Park. Plans call for restoring this ancient stone building at a future date. Its eventual use has not yet been decided. At present it is closed to all but park use. The second Summit House, 1873–1908, was destroyed by fire.

MOUNT WASHINGTON OBSERVATORY

There has been a year-round weather observatory on Mt. Washington from 1870 to 1886 and from 1932 to the present. The present observatory is operated by a nonprofit corporation, and individuals are invited to become members. For details contact the Mt. Washington Observatory, Membership Secretary, 1 Washington St., Gorham, NH 03581.

THE MOUNT WASHINGTON AUTO ROAD

This road, constructed in 1855–61 and long known as the "Carriage Rd.," extends from the Glen House site on NH 16 to the summit. Automobiles are charged a toll at the foot of the mountain. With long zigzags and an easy grade, it climbs the prominent northeast ridge named for Benjamin Chandler, who died of exposure on the upper part in 1856. Hiking on the road is not forbidden, but despite easier grades and smoother footing than hiking trails, the distance is long and the competition with automobile traffic is annoying and potentially dangerous. In winter ruts from snow vehicle traffic and severe icing and drifting make it a less pleasant and more difficult route than might be anticipated. The emergency shelters that were formerly located along the upper part of the road have been removed.

Because of the continual theft and destruction of trail signs, they are often placed on the trails at some distance from the Auto Rd. The names of some trails are painted on rocks at the point where they leave the road.

The Auto Rd. leaves NH 16 opposite the Glen House site (1600 ft.) and crosses the Peabody River. The Appalachian Trail crosses just above the 2-mi. mark after sharp curves right and then left. To the south, the Appalachian Trail follows the Old Jackson Road (a foot trail), past junctions with the Nelson Crag Trail and the Raymond Path, to Pinkham Notch Camp. To the north it follows the Madison Gulf Trail toward the Great Gulf and Madison Hut. Lowe's Bald Spot, a fine viewpoint about 0.3 mi. from the road, is reached by an easy hike on the Madison Gulf Trail and a side path. The site of the Halfway House (3840 ft.) is on the right at treeline. Just above, where there is a fine view to the north, the road skirts a prominent shoulder, known as the Ledge. A short distance above this point the Chandler Brook Trail to the Great Gulf leaves right. Just above the 5-mi. mark, on the right and exactly at the sharp turn, there are some remarkable folds in the strata of the rocks beside the Auto Rd. At this point, near Cragway Spring, the lower section of the Nelson Crag Trail enters left, and a few yards above, the upper section diverges left. At about 5.5 mi. the road passes through the patch of high scrub in which Dr. B. L. Ball survived two nights in a winter storm in October 1855. A short distance above the 6-mi. mark, the Wamsutta Trail descends right to the Great Gulf, and the Alpine Garden Trail diverges left. The trenchlike structures near the road are the remains of the old Glen House Bridle Path, built in 1853. Just below the 7-mi. mark the Huntington Ravine Trail enters left. Just above, in the middle of a lawn known as the "Cow Pasture," the remains of an old corral are visible. A little beyond on the right are the Cog Railway and the Lizzie Bourne monument at the spot where Bourne perished in September 1855 at the age of 23 (the second recorded fatality on the mountain). The summit is reached at approximately 8 mi. (13 km.).

THE MOUNT WASHINGTON COG RAILWAY

The Mt. Washington Cog Railway, an unusual artifact with a fascinating history, was completed in 1869. Its maximum grade, 13.5 in. to the yd., is equaled by only one other railroad (excluding funicular roads), that on Pilatus in the Alps. The location of the Base Station is called Marshfield, in honor of Sylvester Marsh, an inventor of meat-packing machinery who was the promoter and builder of the railway, and Darby Field. When the cog railway is in operation, walking on the track is not permitted; at other times it is a poor walking route. A new public parking area is located on the Base Rd. about 0.5 mi. west of Marshfield. Hikers who wish to visit the Base Station itself should expect to pay an admission fee.

The cog railway ascends a minor westerly ridge in a nearly straight line to the treeline near Jacob's Ladder (4800 ft.). This trestle, at its highest point about 30 ft. above the mountainside, is the steepest part of the road. After crossing the shoulder toward Mt. Clay, the line curves right and crosses the Westside Trail close to the edge of the Great Gulf. Between the Great Gulf and the cog railway lies the Gulfside Trail, which soon turns right and crosses the tracks. From the Gulf Tank (5600 ft.) there is a fine view across the Gulf toward the Northern Peaks. It is 3 mi. from Marshfield to the summit, and trains ascend in about 1 hr. 10 min.

SKIING IN THE MOUNT WASHINGTON AREA

A number of cross-country ski trails have been constructed in the vicinity of Pinkham Notch Camp, which has become a center for the pursuit of this sport. In addition, a number of the summer trails are suitable for ski-touring. Information on these trails can be obtained at the camp's Trading Post.

The slopes of Tuckerman Ravine and the snowfields on and near the summit cone are justly famous for the opportunities they offer for alpine skiing. The skiing season on the Tuckerman headwall starts about the beginning of March and may last into June in some seasons. The ravine area and the John Sherburne Ski Trail (see below) are patrolled by the USFS and the Mt. Washington Volunteer Ski Patrol. Sections that are unsafe because of ice or possible avalanches are posted in the shelter area. Skiing areas in the ravine, in the Gulf of Slides, or on any other part of the mountain above timberline are subject to wide temperature variations within short periods of time. The difference between corn snow and ice or bathing suits and parkas may be an hour, or even less, when clouds roll in or the afternoon sun drops behind a shoulder of the mountain. Skiers should prepare accordingly. There is a sun deck at Hermit Lake, but no longer a warming room open to the public.

The John Sherburne Ski Trail (WMNF) permits skiers to descend from Tuckerman Ravine to Pinkham Notch Camp. The Tuckerman Ravine Trail affords a good ascent route on foot, as it is normally well packed, but downhill skiing on the Tuckerman Ravine Trail is prohibited since it would endanger persons walking on the trail. The Sherburne Trail is named for John H. Sherburne, Jr., whose efforts contributed greatly to the establishment of this trail. It leaves the south end of the parking lot at Pinkham Notch Camp in company with the Gulf of Slides Ski Trail, and ascends to the Little Headwall of the ravine by a zigzag course, keeping at all times left (south) of the Tuckerman Ravine Trail and the Cutler River. Just below Hermit Lake a short side trail leads right to the Hermit Lake Shelters. From the top of the Little Headwall to the floor of the ravine the trail lies on the north of the stream. It is 10 to 50 ft. wide, and although the slope is suitable for expert and intermediate skiers at some points, even less expert skiers can negotiate this trail because of its width.

The Gulf of Slides, which is situated somewhat similarly to Tuckerman Ravine, receives a large volume of snow that remains in the ravine, so open-slope skiing is possible well into the spring (April and May). Its slopes, though less severe than those in Tuckerman, are more uniform and avalanche frequently. The Gulf of Slides Ski Trail (WMNF) leaves the south end of the parking lot at Pinkham Notch

Camp in company with the John Sherburne Ski Trail, and ascends west 2200 ft. in about 2.5 mi. to the bowl of the Gulf of Slides. Although wet in places, it is used as a hiking trail to the Gulf of Slides in summer.

The Mt. Washington Auto Rd. is not usually suitable for skiing on account of icy spots, windblown bare spots, and ruts from snow vehicle traffic. The areas between the top of the Tuckerman headwall and the summit cone, and Chandler Ridge near the 6-mi. mark on the Auto Rd., afford good spring skiing at all levels of experience, but are hard to reach because of their elevation. The Old Jackson Road is a good run for all levels. It drops 650 ft. and can be run in 30 min. The ascent takes 1 hr. Skiers should use the old trail instead of the relocation; enter the Old Jackson Road below the 2-mi. mark, about 0.2 mi. below where the relocation and the Madison Gulf Trail meet at the Auto Rd. The Raymond Path is not a ski run, but it affords a route between Tuckerman Ravine Trail and the Auto Rd. It is wide on the level sections, but narrow and difficult on the steep pitches. In deep snow, the trail is often obscured. It drops, not uniformly, about 1100 ft. toward the north and east.

MOUNTAIN SAFETY

Caution. Mt. Washington has a well-earned reputation as the most dangerous small mountain in the world. Storms increase in violence with great rapidity toward the summit. The highest wind velocity ever recorded at a surface weather station (231 mph on 12 April 1934) was attained on Mt. Washington. Judged by the wind-chill temperatures, the worst conditions on Mt. Washington are approximately equal to the worst reported from Antarctica, although actual temperatures on Mt. Washington are not as low. If you begin to experience difficulty from the weather, remember that the worst is yet to come, and turn back, without shame, before it is too late. (This warning applies to all peaks above timberline, particularly the Northern Peaks.) Each hiker should carry, as a bare minimum, a good rain suit with a hood (or equivalent outfit) which will also protect from wind, an extra sweater, wool hat, and mittens.

Ascents of the mountain in winter are sometimes easy enough to deceive inexperienced hikers into false confidence, but the worst conditions in winter are inconceivably brutal and can materialize with little warning. Safe ascent of the mountain in winter requires much warm clothing, some special equipment, and experienced leadership. From Columbus Day to Memorial Day no building is open to provide shelter or refuge to hikers.

Inexperienced hikers sometimes misjudge the difficulty of climbing Mt. Washington by placing too much emphasis on the relatively short distance from the trailhead to the summit. To a person used to walking around the neighborhood, the trail distance of 4 mi. or so sounds rather tame. But the most important factor in the difficulty of the trip is the altitude gain of 4000 ft., give or take a few hundred, from base to summit. To a person unused to mountain trails, and in less than excellent physical condition, this unrelenting uphill grind can be grueling and intensely discouraging. If you are not an experienced climber or a trained athlete, you will almost certainly enjoy the ascent of Mt. Washington a great deal more if you build up to it with lesser climbs.

The visitor who ascends the mountain on foot should carry a compass and should take care to stay on trails. The hiker who becomes lost from the trail above treeline in a cloud or "white-out," particularly if the weather is rapidly deteriorating, is in a grave predicament. There is no completely satisfactory course of action in this situation, since the object is to get below treeline, with or without a trail, and the weather exposure is generally worse to the west, while cliffs are more prevalent in the ravines to the east. If you know where the nearest major trail should be, then it is probably best to try to find it. If you have adequate clothing, it may be best to find a scrub patch and shelter yourself in it. In the absence of alternatives, take note that the cog railway on one slope and the Mt. Washington Auto Rd. on another make a line, although a very crooked one, from west to east. Remember which side of the mountain you are on, and go north or south, as the case may be, skirting the heads of ravines; sooner or later you will approach the road or the railroad, landmarks that cannot be missed in the darkest night or the thickest fog, except in winter when they may be obliterated by snow. Given a choice, avoid the railroad, as it is on the side of the mountain facing the prevailing winds.

Whether Mt. Washington has the worst weather in the world, or in North America, is subject to debate. But the dozens of people who have died on its slopes in the last century furnish adequate proof that the weather is vicious enough to kill those who are foolish enough to challenge the mountain at its worst. This appalling and needless loss of life has been due almost without exception to the failure of robust but incautious hikers to realize that wintry storms of incredible violence occur frequently, even during the summer months. Winds of hurricane force exhaust even the strongest hiker, and rain driven horizontally by the wind penetrates clothing and drains heat from the body. The temperature may or may not drop below freezing, but temperatures just above freezing are every bit as dangerous as those below, although sleet and freezing rain on rocks may obstruct a belated attempt to return to safety. As the victim's body temperature falls, brain function quickly deteriorates; this is one of the first, and most insidious, effects of excessive heat loss (hypothermia). Eventually the victim loses coordination, staggers, and then falls, numb and dazed, never to rise again. At this point, even immediate access to the best medical treatment obtainable will not assure the victim's survival. Prevention is the only sure cure. Most of those who misjudge conditions and their own endurance get away with their mistakes, and thus many are lulled into carelessness. The mountain spares most fools, but now and then claims one or two without mercy.

All water sources in this heavily used area should be suspected of being unfit to drink; the safest course is to avoid drinking from trailside sources. Water is available at the Sherman Adams summit building during the months that it is open.

GEOGRAPHY

Mt. Washington (6288 ft.), the highest peak east of the Mississippi and north of the Carolinas, was seen from the ocean as early as 1605. Its first recorded ascent was in June 1642 by Darby Field, of Exeter NH, and two Native Americans, who probably made the ascent by way of the Ellis River valley and Boott Spur. The mountain has had several hotels, a road and a railway, a weather observatory, a daily newspaper, a radio station and a television station, and has been the site of auto, foot, and ski races. *The Story of Mt. Washington* by F. Allen Burt treats the fascinating (and frequently unusual) human history of the mountain in great detail, while Peter Randall's *Mount Washington* is a much shorter and less detailed handbook of human and natural history.

Mt. Washington is a broad, massive mountain with great ravines cut deeply into its steep sides, leaving buttress ridges which reach up through the timberline and support the great upper plateau. The timberline occurs at an elevation of 4500 to 5000 ft., depending on the degree of exposure to the mountain's fierce weather. The upper plateau, which varies in elevation from 5000 to 5500 ft., bears comparatively gentle slopes interspersed with "lawns"—wide grassy areas strewn with rocks; the summit cone, covered with fragments of rock and almost devoid of vegetation, rises steeply above the plateau. The upper part of the mountain has a climate similar to that of northern Labrador, and its areas of alpine tundra support a fascinating variety of plant and animal life, species adapted to the extreme conditions of the alpine environment. Many of these species are found only on other high mountaintops or in the tundra many hundreds of miles farther north, and a few are found only or primarily on the Presidential Range. The plant species in particular have attracted many professional and amateur botanists (including Henry David Thoreau), and many of the features of the mountain are named for early botanists, such as Manasseh Cutler, Jacob Bigelow, Francis Boott, William Oakes, and Edward Tuckerman. Great care should be exercised not to damage the plant life in these areas, as their struggle for survival is already sufficiently severe. Hikers should avoid unnecessary excursions away from the trails, and should step on rocks rather than vegetation wherever possible. The AMC publishes the *AMC Field Guide to Mountain Flowers of New England,* an illustrated guide to all plants which normally grow above or near treeline, and *At Timberline,* a handbook that covers geology and animal life as well as plants. The NH Department of Resources and Economic Development (PO Box 856, Concord, NH 03301) publishes geological booklets intended for the general public; the Presidential Range area is covered by *The Geology of the Mt. Washington Quadrangle* and *The Geology of the Crawford Notch Quadrangle* ($2.50 and $2.00, respectively, in 1986).

The slopes of Mt. Washington are drained by tributaries of three major rivers: the Androscoggin, the Connecticut, and the Saco. The high, massive Northern Peaks continue the rocky alpine terrain of Mt. Washington to the north and northeast in an arc which encloses the Great Gulf, the largest glacial cirque in the White Mtns. Moving clockwise from the Great Gulf toward the east side of the mountain, Chandler Ridge (which is ascended by the Mt. Washington Auto Rd.) and the low peak of Nelson Crag form the northern boundary of a lawn called the "Alpine Garden," and divide the Great Gulf from the great ravines of the east face: Huntington Ravine, the Ravine of Raymond Cataract, and Tuckerman Ravine. The latter is one of the finest examples of the glacial cirque.

Raymond Cataract falls through a series of wild and beautiful cascades in the Ravine of Raymond Cataract. Brush has covered a former footway, so the Cataract can only be reached by those intrepid explorers who are skilled in off-trail travel. Easier to visit is Glen Ellis Falls, reached from NH 16 by a gravel path with rock steps and handrails, which leaves the parking area 0.8 mi. south of Pinkham Notch Camp, passes under the highway through a tunnel, and reaches the falls in 0.3 mi. (This path is not described as a hiking trail in this guide.) The main fall is 70 ft. high, and below it are several pools and smaller falls.

Boott Spur, the great southeast shoulder of Mt. Washington, forms the south wall of Tuckerman Ravine and the north wall of the Gulf of Slides, and the flat ridge connecting it with the cone of Mt. Washington bears Bigelow Lawn, the largest of the Presidential Range lawns. Both the Montalban Ridge and the Rocky Branch Ridge descend from Boott Spur and quickly drop below treeline, continuing south in thick woods with occasional open summits. Oakes Gulf, at the headwaters of the Dry River, lies west of Boott Spur and east of Mt. Monroe. The Southern Peaks, running southwest from Mt. Washington, form the second most prominent ridge in the range (after the Northern Peaks), dropping to the treeline slowly and rising above it again several times before the final descent into the woods below Mt. Pierce. The Mt. Washington Cog Railway ascends the unnamed ridge between the less spectacular ravines of the western face, Ammonoosuc Ravine and Burt Ravine, which lie between the Southern Peaks and the Northern Peaks.

Day trips to the summit of Mt. Washington can be made by several different routes, but the vast majority of climbers use only a very few trails. From the west, the mountain is ascended from a parking area (2500 ft.) on the Base Rd. near the Cog Railway by the Ammonoosuc Ravine Trail and the Crawford Path, or by the Jewell and Gulfside trails (see Section 2), or by a loop using both routes. The Ammonoosuc Ravine Trail has a long, very steep section but offers the shelter of Lakes of the Clouds Hut, just above treeline, if a storm arises. The Jewell Trail provides an easier ascent or descent, but reaches the Gulfside Trail on the slope of Mt. Clay, a more dangerous place in bad weather. Both of these trails are used heavily. Because of the very high elevation of its trailhead (3000 ft.) on the Jefferson Notch Rd., the Caps Ridge Trail is frequently used for a one-day hike to Mt. Washington, in combination with the Gulfside Trail and the Cornice (see Section 2). It offers fine scenery and the opportunity to also climb Mt. Jefferson with little extra effort, but this longer, rougher route to Mt. Washington is more exposed to bad weather and saves no exertion. The Boundary Line Trail (see Section 2) connects the Base Rd. parking area with the Jefferson Notch Rd., and thus makes possible loop trips involving the Caps Ridge Trail and the Ammonoosuc Ravine or Jewell trails.

Most hikers ascend from the east. The Tuckerman Ravine Trail from Pinkham Notch Camp (2000 ft.) is by far the most popular route, affording what is probably the easiest ascent of Mt. Washington, with moderate grades for most of its length and spectacular views of the ravine. It also provides easy access to Crystal Cascade, a beautiful waterfall not far from Pinkham Notch Camp. In the spring and fall this trail is often closed by the WMNF on account of dangerous snow or ice conditions; notice of its closure is posted at the top and bottom. In this case the Lion Head Trail is usually the best alternative. The Lion Head Trail runs along the prominent and aptly named ridge north of Tuckerman Ravine; an older route of this trail, closed for summer hiking, is the most popular and least dangerous route of ascent in winter. Routes other than the Tuckerman Ravine Trail are all somewhat longer, or steeper, or both, but have good views and are less crowded.

The Southern Presidentials form a great ridge that extends about 8 mi. southwest from the summit of Mt. Washington to the Webster Cliffs above Crawford Notch. The Ammonoosuc River lies to the northwest, and the Dry River to the southeast. The summits on this ridge decrease steadily in elevation from northeast to southwest.

Mt. Monroe (5384 ft.), the highest, is a sharply pointed pyramid rising abruptly from the flat area around the Lakes of the Clouds, with a secondary summit, a small crag sometimes called Little Monroe (5207 ft.), on its west ridge. It is completely above treeline, and affords fine views of the deep chasm of Oakes Gulf on the east, the beautiful Lakes of the Clouds, and the nearby summit of Mt. Washington. The flats between Mt. Monroe and the Lakes of the Clouds support a bountiful number of alpine plants, making it the most significant, and most vulnerable, habitat in the White Mtns. Part of this area is closed to all public entry due to damage caused in the past by hikers coming to admire these plants, which can withstand the full violence of above-treeline weather but not the tread of hikers' boots. Sadly, we can now pay homage to some of these rare survivors only from a distance. The summit of Mt. Monroe is crossed by the Mount Monroe Loop.

Mt. Franklin (5004 ft.) is a rather flat shoulder of Monroe, which appears impressive only when seen from below, in the Franklin—Pleasant col. The exact location of the summit is not obvious, but the summit does exists and lies a short distance off the Crawford Path.

Mt. Eisenhower (4761 ft.), formerly called Mt. Pleasant, was renamed after the former President's death. While there is a good deal of scrub on the lower slopes of this dome-shaped mountain, the top is completely bald. Its summit is crossed by the Mount Eisenhower Loop.

Mt. Pierce (4310 ft.) was named for Franklin Pierce, the only President born in NH, by act of the NH Legislature in 1913. Although this name appears on all USGS maps it was not universally accepted, and the mountain's former name, Mt. Clinton, persists in the Mt. Clinton Rd. and the Mount Clinton Trail, which ascends the southeast slopes of the mountain. Mt. Pierce is wooded almost to the top of its flat summit on the west, but a broad open area on the east side affords fine views. Its summit lies on the Webster–Cliff Trail, just off the Crawford Path.

Mt. Jackson (4052 ft.), named for NH State Geologist Charles Jackson and not for President Andrew Jackson, has a square, ledgy summit with steep sides and a flat top, and possibly the finest views overall of all the Southern Peaks. Its summit is crossed by the Webster Cliff Trail and is also reached by the Jackson branch of the Webster–Jackson Trail.

Mt. Webster (3910 ft.), once called Notch Mtn., was renamed for Daniel Webster, the great US Senator and Secretary of State, an illustrious orator who was probably the best-known native of NH. The summit is crossed by the Webster Cliff Trail, which is intersected by the Webster branch of the Webster–Jackson Trail not far from the top.

To the southeast of the Southern Peaks lies the Dry River, running down the central valley of the Presidential–Dry River Wilderness Area. This river has also been called the Mt. Washington River, but Dry River has won the battle, possibly because of the ironic quality of the name. The Dry River runs from Oakes Gulf to the Saco through a deep, narrow, steep-walled ravine. Though in a dry season the flow is a bit meager, with lots of rocks lying uncovered in the stream bed, its watershed has extremely rapid runoff, and its sudden floods are legendary. It has killed hikers. No other logging railroad ever constructed in the White Mtns. has ever had as many river crossings in so short a distance as the railroad which was built up this valley, and no other logging railroad has ever had all its trestles swept away so quickly after ceasing operations.

Access to the Dry River area has always been somewhat difficult, and ascents of the Southern Peaks from this side have always been relatively arduous, but since the Wilderness Area was established and the number of wilderness-seeking visitors increased sharply, the WMNF has made access somewhat easier by eliminating many river crossings through trail relocations and the construction of a bridge. It is still an area where visitors need to keep a careful watch on the weather, including that of the last few days.

The Montalban Ridge extends southward from Boott Spur, forming the longest subsidiary ridge in the Presidential Range, running for about 15 mi. between the Rocky Branch on the east and the Dry River and Saco River on the west. At Mt. Resolution the main ridge curves to the east along the Saco valley, while the short Bemis Ridge carries the line of the upper ridge south to the great bend in the Saco. The peaks of the Montalban Ridge, in order from the north, include Mt. Isolation (4005 ft.), Mt. Davis (3840 ft.), Stairs Mtn. (3460 ft.), Mt. Resolution (3428 ft.), Mt. Parker (3015 ft.), Mt. Langdon (2423 ft.), Mt. Pickering (1942 ft.), and Mt. Stanton (1748 ft.). The peaks of the Bemis Ridge include

Mt. Crawford (3129 ft.), Mt. Hope (2520 ft.), and Hart Ledge (2040 ft.). Cave Mtn. (1460 ft.), a low spur of the range near Bartlett village, is much better known for the cave on its south face than for its summit.

East of the Montalban Ridge, across the Rocky Branch and west of the Ellis River, lies the Rocky Branch Ridge. This heavily wooded ridge runs south from Gulf Peak, and is sharply defined for only about 3 mi., then spreads out and flattens. It has no important peaks. Iron Mtn. (2716 ft.), near Jackson, is the most significant summit on the ridge between the Rocky Branch and the Ellis River, but the Rocky Branch Ridge ceases to be a prominent ridge long before it reaches Iron Mtn.

The views from the summits of Mts. Isolation, Davis, and Crawford are among the finest in the White Mtns., and Mt. Resolution and Mt. Parker also offer excellent outlooks. The Giant Stairs are a wild and picturesque feature of the region, offering a spectacular view from the top of the cliff that forms the upper stair. These two great steplike ledges at the south end of the ridge of Stairs Mtn. are quite regular in form, and are visible from many points. A third and somewhat similar cliff, sometimes called the "Back Stair," lies east of the main summit, but there is no trail. Mt. Stanton and Mt. Pickering are wooded but have frequent open ledges which afford interesting views in various directions. Iron Mtn. has a fine north outlook, and a magnificent open ledge at the top of the south cliffs.

All of the peaks named above are reached by well-maintained trails, except Mt. Hope and Hart Ledge. Mt. Hope is heavily wooded, pathless, and very seldom climbed. The fine cliff of Hart Ledge rises more than 1000 ft. above the meadows at the great bend in the Saco River just above Bartlett and affords commanding views to the east, west, and south. There is no regular trail, but intrepid bushwhackers may follow the roads west along the north side of the river, passing under the cliffs, then climb up the slope well to the west of the cliffs.

HUTS, SHELTERS, AND CAMPING

Note: No hotel or overnight lodging for the public is available on the summit of Mt. Washington. No camping is permitted above treeline between 1 May and 1 November.

HUTS

Pinkham Notch Camp (AMC)

Pinkham Notch Camp is a unique mountain facility in the heart of the WMNF. This camp, originally built in 1920 and greatly enlarged since then, is located on NH 16 practically at the height-of-land in Pinkham Notch, about 20 mi. north of Conway and 11 mi. south of Gorham. It is also 0.8 mi. north of Glen Ellis Falls and 1 mi. south of the base of the Wildcat Mtn. Ski Area. Pinkham Notch Camp offers food and lodging to the public throughout the year and is managed similarly to the AMC huts. The telephone number is 603-466-2727. Concord Trailways offers daily bus service to and from South Station in Boston, and the AMC operates a hiker shuttle bus during the summer.

The Joe Dodge Center, which accommodates over a hundred guests in rooms with two, three, or four bunks, also offers a library that commands a spectacular view of the nearby Wildcat Ridge, and a living room where accounts of the day's activities can be shared by an open fireplace. The Center features a 65-seat conference room equipped with audiovisual facilities.

The Trading Post, a popular meeting place for hikers, has been a center of AMC educational and recreational activities since 1920. Weekend workshops, seminars, and lectures are conducted throughout the year. The building houses a dining room, and an information desk where basic equipment and guidebooks are available. The pack-room downstairs is open 24 hours a day for hikers to stop in, relax, shower, and repack their gear.

Pinkham Notch Camp is the most important trailhead on the east side of Mt. Washington, and free public parking is available, although sleeping in cars is not permitted. The Tuckerman Ravine Trail, the Lost Pond Trail, and the Old Jackson Road all start at the camp, giving access to many more trails, and a number of walking trails have been constructed for shorter, easier trips in the Pinkham vicinity. Among these are the Crew-Cut Trail, Liebeskind's Loop, and the Square Ledge Trail. There are also several ski-touring trails; for information consult personnel at the Camp Trading Post.

Crawford Notch Hostel (AMC)

Low-cost, self-service lodging is available in historic Crawford Notch. The main hostel holds thirty people in one large bunkroom. There is also a kitchen, bathrooms, and a common area. Three adjacent cabins accommodate eight persons each.

The hostel is open to the public. AMC members receive a discount on lodging. Overnight lodging is available year-round. Reservations are encouraged. Guests must supply food and sleeping bags; stoves and cooking equipment are provided. The hostel is an excellent choice for families and small groups and offers a wide range of hiking and outdoor experiences.

Lakes of the Clouds Hut (AMC)

The original stone hut, greatly enlarged since, was built in 1915. It is located on a shelf near the foot of Mt. Monroe about 50 yd. west of the larger lake at an elevation of about 5050 ft. It is reached by the Crawford Path or the Ammonoosuc Ravine Trail, and has accommodations for ninety guests. The hut is open to the public from mid-June to mid-September, and closed at all other times. Space for backpackers is available at a lesser cost. A refuge room in the cellar is left open in the winter for emergency use only.

Mizpah Spring Hut (AMC)

The newest of the AMC huts was completed in 1965 and is located at about 3800 ft. elevation, on the site formerly occupied by the Mizpah Spring Shelter, at the junction of the Webster Cliff Trail and the Mount Clinton Trail, near the Mizpah Cutoff. The hut accommodates sixty guests, with sleeping quarters in eight rooms containing from four to ten bunks. This hut is open to the public from mid-June to mid-October. There are tentsites nearby (caretaker, fee charged).

For current information on AMC huts, Pinkham Notch Camp, or Crawford Notch Hostel, contact Reservation Secretary, Pinkham Notch Camp, Box 298, Gorham, NH 03581 (603-466-2727).

CAMPING

Presidential Range–Dry River Wilderness

In this area, camping and fires are prohibited above treeline, and within 200 ft. of any trail except at designated sites. No campsite can be used by more than ten persons at any one time. Many shelters have been removed, and the remaining ones will be removed when major maintenance is required; do not count on using these shelters.

Restricted Use Areas

The WMNF has established a number of Restricted Use Areas (RUA's) where camping and wood or charcoal fires are prohibited from 1 May to 1 November. The specific areas are under continual review, and areas are added to or subtracted from the list in order to provide the greatest amount of protection to areas subject to damage by excessive camping, while imposing the lowest level of restrictions possible. A general list of RUA's follows, but one should obtain a map of current RUA's from the WMNF.

(1) No camping is permitted above treeline (where trees are less than 8 ft. tall). The point where the restricted area begins is marked on most trails with small signs, but the absence of such signs should not be construed as proof of the legality of a site.

(2) No camping is permitted within one-quarter mile of most facilities, such as huts, cabins, shelters, or tentsites, except at the facility itself.

(3) No camping is permitted within 200 ft. of certain trails. In 1986, designated trails included the Ammonoosuc Ravine Trail, Edmands Path, the Crawford Path from US 302 to Mt. Pierce, and those parts of the Webster Cliff Trail and Webster–Jackson Trail which are not in the State Park (where camping is absolutely prohibited).

(4) In Tuckerman and Huntington ravines (Cutler River drainage), camping is prohibited throughout the year except at the Hermit Lake Shelters; the Hermit Lake tentsites are available in winter only. The Hermit Lake Shelters are lean-tos open to the public. Tickets for shelter space (nontransferable and nonrefundable) must be purchased at Pinkham Notch Camp in person (first come, first served) for a nominal fee, for a maximum of seven consecutive nights. Overnight use is limited to the 86 spaces in the shelters. Ten tentsites for forty people are available between 1 December and 1 April. Fee is $1.75 per person per night. Users may no longer kindle charcoal or wood fires; people intending to cook must bring their own small stoves. Day visitors and shelter users alike are required to carry out all their own trash and garbage. No receptacles are provided. This operating policy is under continual review, so it can

change from time to time. Information is available at the caretaker's residence. There is no warming room open to the public, and refreshments are not sold.

Crawford Notch State Park

No camping is permitted in Crawford Notch State Park, except at the public Dry River Campground (fee charged).

Established Trailside Campsites

Mizpah Tentsite (AMC) has seven tent platforms at Mizpah Spring Hut. There is a caretaker, and a fee is charged in summer.

Lakes of the Clouds Hut (AMC) has limited space available for backpackers at a substantially lower cost than the normal hut services.

Rocky Branch Shelter #1 and Tentsite (WMNF) is located near the junction of the Rocky Branch and Stairs Col trails, just outside the Presidential Range–Dry River Wilderness.

Mt. Langdon Shelter (WMNF) is located at the junction of the Mount Langdon and Mount Stanton trails, at the edge of the Presidential Range–Dry River Wilderness.

Rocky Branch Shelter #2 (WMNF) is located at the junction of the Rocky Branch and Isolation trails, within the Presidential Range–Dry River Wilderness. Following the established policy for management of wilderness, this shelter will be removed when major maintenance is required.

Dry River Shelter #3 (WMNF) is located on the Dry River Trail, 6.3 mi. from US 302, within the Presidential Range–Dry River Wilderness. This shelter will be removed when major maintenance is required.

Resolution Shelter (AMC) is located on a spur path which leaves the Davis Path at its junction with the Mount Parker Trail, within the Presidential–Dry River Wilderness.

The water source is scanty in dry seasons. This shelter will be removed when major maintenance is required.

LIST OF TRAILS   MAP

THE TRAILS

Tuckerman Ravine Trail (WMNF)

This trail is the most popular route of ascent on Mt. Washington. From Pinkham Notch Camp to the floor of Tuckerman Ravine it uses a rocky tractor road. It is a well-graded path from there to the top of the headwall, steady but not excessively steep. Its final section ascends the cone of Mt. Washington steeply over fragments of rock. In the spring and fall the WMNF often closes the section of trail on the headwall because of snow and ice, and notice is posted at the top and bottom. In these circumstances, the Lion Head Trail is usually the most convenient alternative route. In the

winter this section is often impassable except by experienced
and well-equipped snow and ice climbers, and it is frequently
closed even to such climbers by the WMNF.

The trail leaves the west side of NH 16 behind the Trading Post at Pinkham Notch Camp. Be careful to avoid
numerous side paths in this area. In 0.3 mi. it crosses a
bridge to the south bank of Cutler River, and soon climbs
to a side path 20 yds. right to the best viewpoint of the
Crystal Cascade. At a curve to the right 0.4 mi. from
Pinkham Notch Camp, the Boott Spur Trail leaves left.
After two long switchbacks, the path continues west, ascending by steady grades. At 1.3 mi. the Huntington Ravine Trail diverges right. At 1.5 mi. the trail crosses a
tributary, then at 1.6 mi. the main branch, of the Cutler
River. Soon the Huntington Ravine Fire Rd., which is the
best route to Huntington Ravine in winter, leaves right. At
2.1 mi. the Raymond Path enters right, at a point where the
Tuckerman trail turns sharply left. At a crossroads at 2.3
mi. the Boott Spur Link turns left, and directly opposite
the Lion Head Trail turns right.

In another 0.1 mi. the trail reaches the buildings in the
floor of Tuckerman Ravine near Hermit Lake. The cliff on
the right is Lion Head, so called because of its appearance
from the Glen House site. The more distant crags on the
left are the Hanging Cliffs of Boott Spur.

The main trail keeps to the right (north) of the stream
and ascends a well-constructed footway into the floor of
the ravine, and finally, at the foot of the headwall, bears
right and ascends a steep slope where the Snow Arch can
be found on the left in the spring and early summer. In the
spring the snowfield above the Snow Arch usually extends
across the trail, and the trail is often closed. Some snow
may persist in the ravine until late summer. The arch
(which does not always form) is carved by a stream of snow
meltwater which flows under the snowfield. **Caution.** Do

not approach too near the arch and under no circumstances cross or venture beneath it: one death and some narrow escapes have already resulted. Sections weighing tons may break off at any moment. When ascending the headwall, be careful not to start rocks rolling, since such carelessness may put others in serious danger.

Turning sharp left at the top of the debris slope and traversing under a cliff, the trail emerges from the ravine and climbs almost straight west up a grassy, ledgy slope. A short distance above the top of the headwall, the Alpine Garden Trail diverges right. At Tuckerman Junction, at the top of the plateau, the Tuckerman Crossover leads almost straight ahead (southwest) to the Crawford Path near the Lakes of the Clouds Hut; the Southside Trail leads west and northwest, skirting the cone to the Davis Path; and the Lawn Cutoff leads left (south) toward Boott Spur. The Tuckerman Ravine Trail turns sharp right and ascends the steep rocks, marked by cairns and paint on ledges. About a third of the way up the cone, at Cloudwater Spring, the Lion Head Trail enters right. The Tuckerman trail continues to ascend to the Auto Rd. a few yards below the lower parking area, just below the summit.

Tuckerman Ravine Trail (map 6:F9)
Distances from Pinkham Notch Camp
- *to* Boott Spur Trail: 0.4 mi., 20 min.
- *to* Huntington Ravine Trail: 1.3 mi., 1 hr. 10 min.
- *to* Raymond Path: 2.1 mi., 1 hr. 50 min.
- *to* Lion Head Trail and Boott Spur Link: 2.3 mi., 2 hr. 5 min.
- *to* Hermit Lake shelters: 2.4 mi., 2 hr. 10 min.
- *to* Snow Arch: 3.1 mi., 2 hr. 50 min.
- *to* Tuckerman Junction: 3.6 mi., 3 hr. 30 min.
- *to* Mt. Washington summit: 4.1 mi. (6.6 km.), 4 hr. 15 min.

Lion Head Trail (AMC)

The Lion Head Trail follows the steep-ended ridge that forms the north wall of Tuckerman Ravine. It begins and ends on the Tuckerman Ravine Trail and thus provides an alternative route, although it is much steeper in parts. It is especially important as an alternative when the Tuckerman Ravine Trail over the headwall is closed on account of snow or ice hazard. An older route of the trail, closed to summer hiking, is considered the least dangerous route to Mt. Washington in winter conditions, and is the most frequently used winter ascent route. The signs and markings are changed at the beginning and end of the winter season to ensure that climbers take the proper route for prevailing conditions.

This trail diverges right from the Tuckerman Ravine Trail 2.3 mi. from Pinkham Notch Camp and 0.1 mi. below Hermit Lake, opposite the foot of the Boott Spur Link. Running north, it passes a side path left to one of the Hermit Lake shelters and crosses the outlet of Hermit Lake. In 0.1 mi. the winter route diverges left, and the summer trail soon begins to climb the steep slope by switchbacks, scrambling up several small ledges with very rough footing, and reaches treeline at 0.4 mi. It then bears left, ascends the open slope to the left, and the winter route rejoins at 0.7 mi., just below the lower Lion Head. (The winter route is 0.2 mi. shorter.) The trail continues to the upper Lion Head at 0.9 mi., then runs mostly level, with impressive views from the open spur, until it crosses the Alpine Garden Trail at 1.1 mi. After passing through a belt of scrub, it ascends to the Tuckerman Ravine Trail, which it enters at Cloudwater Spring about a third of the way up the cone of Mt. Washington.

Lion Head Trail (map 6:F9)
Distances from lower junction with Tuckerman Ravine Trail
  to Alpine Garden Trail: 1.1 mi. (1.8 km.), 1 hr. 15 min.

to upper junction with Tuckerman Ravine Trail: 1.6 mi. (2.5 km.), 1 hr. 45 min.

Distance from Pinkham Notch Camp
to summit (via summer route): 4.3 mi. (7.0 km.), 4 hr. 20 min.

Huntington Ravine Trail (AMC)

Caution. This is the most difficult trail in the White Mtns. Many of the ledges demand proper use of handholds for safe passage. Although experienced hikers who are comfortable on steep rock probably will encounter little difficulty when conditions are good, the exposure on several of the steepest ledges is likely to prove extremely unnerving to novices and to those who are uncomfortable in steep places. Do not attempt this trail if you tend to feel queasy or have difficulty on ledges on ordinary trails. Persons encumbered with large or heavy packs may experience great difficulty in some places. This trail is very dangerous when wet or icy. Extreme caution must be exercised at all times. Descent by this trail is strongly discouraged. Since retreat under unfavorable conditions can be extremely difficult and hazardous, one should never venture beyond the "Fan" in deteriorating conditions or when weather on the Alpine Garden is likely to be severe. During late fall, winter, and early spring, this trail (and any part of the ravine headwall) should be attempted only by those with full technical ice-climbing gear and training. In particular, the ravine must not be regarded as a viable "escape route" from the Alpine Garden in severe winter conditions.

The trail diverges right from the Tuckerman Ravine Trail 1.3 mi. from Pinkham Notch Camp. In 0.2 mi. it crosses the Cutler River and, at 0.3 mi., the brook that drains Huntington Ravine. At 0.5 mi. it goes straight across the Raymond Path, a junction that might not be well signed. Above this junction it crosses the brook and the Huntington Ravine Fire

Rd. several times, and care should be used to distinguish the trail from the road. At 1.3 mi. it reaches the first-aid cache in the floor of the ravine. Just beyond here there are some interesting boulders near the path whose tops afford good views of the ravine. Beyond the scrubby trees is a steep slope covered with broken rock, known as the "Fan," whose tip lies at the foot of the deepest gully. To the left of this gully are precipices, the lower known as the "Pinnacle." After passing through the boulders the path ascends the left side of the Fan for about 60 ft. It then turns right, and, marked by yellow blazes on the rocks, crosses a stream and ascends the north (right) side of the Fan to its tip at 1.8 mi. The trail then climbs the rocks to the right of the main gully. The first pitch above the Fan—a large, steeply sloping slab—is probably the most difficult scramble on the trail. The trail now climbs about 650 ft. in 0.3 mi. The route follows the line of least difficulty and should be followed carefully over the ledges, which are dangerous, especially when wet. Above the first ledges the trail climbs steeply through scrub and over short sections of rock, with some fairly difficult scrambles. About two-thirds of the way up it turns sharp left at a promontory with a good view, then continues to the top of the headwall where it crosses the Alpine Garden Trail at 2.1 mi. From this point it ascends moderately, crossing the Nelson Crag Trail at 2.3 mi., and reaches the Mt. Washington Auto Rd. just below the 7-mi. mark, 1.1 mi. below the summit.

Huntington Ravine Trail (map 6:F9)
Distances from Tuckerman Ravine Trail
   to Raymond Path: 0.5 mi., 30 min.
   to first-aid cache in ravine floor: 1.3 mi., 1 hr. 15 min.
   to Alpine Garden Trail crossing: 2.1 mi., 2 hr. 20 min.
   to Auto Rd.: 2.4 mi. (3.8 km.), 2 hr. 35 min.

Distance from Pinkham Notch Camp
  to Mt. Washington Summit (via Nelson Crag Trail): 4.3
  mi. (6.9 km.), 4 hr. 20 min.

Nelson Crag Trail (AMC)

This trail leaves the Auto Rd. on the left in common with
the Old Jackson Road and Raymond Path, just above the
2-mi. mark and opposite the Madison Gulf Trail. It soon
diverges right and bears southwest, then almost due west,
climbing steadily with some sharp ascents. After about 1
mi. it rises steeply out of the scrub, emerging on a watershed ridge from which there is an unusual view of Pinkham
Notch in both directions. From here on it is above treeline
and very exposed to the weather. It then bears slightly
north, climbs moderately over open ledges, and joins the
Auto Rd. near Cragway Spring, at the sharp turn about 0.3
mi. above the 5-mi. mark. A few yards above, the trail
again diverges left from the Auto Rd. and climbs steeply to
the crest of the ridge. It travels over Nelson Crag, crosses
the Alpine Garden Trail, then swings left and follows a
newly relocated route across the Huntington Ravine Trail
and up the rocks to Ball Crag (6106 ft.), then runs to the
summit, crossing the Auto Rd. and the Cog Railway.

Nelson Crag Trail (map 6:F9)
Distances (est.) from two-mile mark on Auto Rd.
  to its middle junction with the Auto Rd.: 1.6 mi., 1 hr.
  40 min.
  to the summit of Mt. Washington: 3.7 mi. (6.0 km.), 3
  hr. 40 min.

Boott Spur Trail (AMC)

This trail runs from the Tuckerman Ravine Trail near
Pinkham Notch Camp to the Davis Path near the summit
of Boott Spur. It follows the long ridge that forms the
south wall of Tuckerman Ravine and affords fine views.

The trail diverges left from the Tuckerman Ravine Trail at a sharp right turn 0.4 mi. from Pinkham Notch Camp, about 150 yd. above the side path to Crystal Cascade. It crosses the John Sherburne Ski Trail, bears right, soon crosses a small brook, bears sharp left at the base of a rocky ledge, and, a short distance beyond, makes a sharp right turn and ascends an old logging road for about 0.3 mi. Descending slightly, the trail shortly makes a sharp right turn, where a side trail (left) leads in 50 yd. down to a restricted view east. The trail then passes through some interesting woods, ascends to the south side of a small wooded ridge, crosses a south outlook and turns right. It soon reaches a short moist area and ascends northwest up a steep slope. Halfway up the slope a side trail leads left 100 yd. to a brook (last water). At the top of this slope, at 1.0 mi. from the Tuckerman Ravine Trail, a side trail leads right (east) 25 yd. to an interesting outlook. At this junction the trail turns left, continues upward at moderate grades, heads more north, and shortly makes a sharp left turn. Turning more to the west, the trail ascends steadily, and at 1.7 mi. a short side trail right leads in 30 yd. to Ravine Outlook, with a view of Tuckerman Ravine, and of Lion Head directly in front of the summit of Mt. Washington.

The main trail emerges from the trees at 1.9 mi., soon bears left and slabs the ridge to Split Rock, which you can pass through or go around, at 2.2 mi. The trail then turns right, rises steeply over two minor humps to a broad, flat ridge, where, at 2.2 mi., Boott Spur Link descends on the right to the Tuckerman Ravine Trail near Hermit Lake. Above this point the trail follows the ridge, which consists of a series of steplike levels and steep slopes. The views of the ravine are excellent, particularly where the path skirts the dangerous Hanging Cliff, 1500 ft. above Hermit Lake. After passing just right (north) of the summit of the Spur, the trail ends at the Davis Path.

Boott Spur Trail (map 6:F9)

Distances from Tuckerman Ravine Trail
   to Ravine Outlook: 1.7 mi., 1 hr. 45 min.
   to Split Rock: 2.0 mi., 2 hr.
   to Boott Spur Link: 2.2 mi., 2 hr. 20 min.
   to Davis Path junction: 2.9 mi. (4.7 km.), 3 hr.

Distances from Pinkham Notch Camp
   to Davis Path junction: 3.4 mi., 3 hr. 25 min.
   to Mt. Washington summit (via Davis and Crawford paths): 5.5 mi. (8.9 km.), 5 hr.

Boott Spur Link (AMC)

This trail diverges south from the Tuckerman Ravine Trail 2.3 mi. from Pinkham Notch Camp and 0.1 mi. below Hermit Lake, opposite the foot of the Lion Head Trail. It immediately crosses two branches of Cutler River and the John Sherburne Ski Trail, then runs straight up the side of the ridge very steeply through scrub until it tops the ridge, and ends in a few yards at Boott Spur Trail.

Boott Spur Link (map 6:F9)

Distance from Tuckerman Ravine Trail
   to Boott Spur Trail: 0.6 mi. (1.0 km.), 45 min.

Glen Boulder Trail (AMC)

This trail runs from NH 16 to the Davis Path 0.4 mi. below Boott Spur. It is rough in parts, but reaches treeline and views relatively quickly.

The trail leaves the west side of NH 16 at the parking area near Glen Ellis Falls. It ascends gradually for about 0.4 mi. to the base of a small cliff. You can go up the cliff via the rather muddy and unappealing Chimney Route or, preferably, take the Chimney Bypass, which goes around to the right of the cliff. The Bypass makes a short, steep climb and then meets the Direttissima, which enters from the right (north) from Pinkham Notch Camp. The Chimney Bypass swings south, the Chimney Route enters left, and then a short branch trail leads left to an outlook on the brink of a cliff, which commands a fine view of Wildcat Mtn. and Pinkham Notch. The main trail turns west, rises gradually, then steepens. At 0.8 mi. it crosses the Avalanche Brook Ski Trail, which is marked with blue plastic markers and is not suitable for hiking. The Glen Boulder Trail soon reaches the north bank of a brook draining the minor ravine south of the Gulf of Slides. After following the brook, which soon divides, the trail then turns southwest and crosses both branches. It is level for 200 yd., then rapidly climbs the northeast side of the spur through evergreens, giving views of the minor ravine and spur south of the Gulf of Slides. Leaving the trees, it climbs over open rocks and, at 1.6 mi., reaches the Glen Boulder, an immense rock perched on the end of the spur, which is a familiar landmark for travelers through Pinkham Notch. The view is wide, from Chocorua around to Mt. Washington, and is particularly fine of Wildcat Mtn.

From the boulder the trail climbs steeply up the open spur to its top at 2.0 mi., re-enters high scrub and ascends moderately. At 2.3 mi. a side trail descends right about 60 yd. to a fine spring. The main trail continues to Gulf Peak (sometimes called Slide Peak), the rather insignificant peak heading the Gulf of Slides, at 2.6 mi. It then turns north, descends slightly, soon leaves the scrub, and runs entirely above treeline—greatly exposed to the weather—to the Davis Path just below a minor crag.

Glen Boulder Trail (map 6:F9)
Distances from Glen Ellis Falls parking area on NH 16
   to Chimney: 0.4 mi., 20 min.

to Avalanche Brook Ski Trail: 0.8 mi., 45 min.

to Glen Boulder: 1.6 mi., 1 hr. 40 min.

to Slide Peak: 2.6 mi., 2 hr. 45 min.

to Davis Path junction: 3.2 mi. (5.2 km.), 3 hr. 15 min.

to Boott Spur Trail (via Davis Path): 3.7 mi., 3 hr. 35 min.

to Mt. Washington summit (via Davis and Crawford paths): 5.8 mi. (9.3 km.), 5 hr. 5 min.

The Direttissima (MMVSP)

For hikers desiring access to the Glen Boulder Trail from Pinkham Notch Camp, this nearly level trail eliminates a road walk on NH 16. It begins just south of the highway bridge over the Cutler River near Pinkham Notch Camp, indicated by a sign at the edge of the woods. Marked by paint blazes, the trail turns sharp left about 10 yd. into the woods and follows a cleared area south. It turns slightly west at the end of this clearing and winds generally south, crossing a small brook, skirts through the upper (west) end of a gorge, and then crosses the New River. The trail continues past an excellent viewpoint looking down the Notch, climbs alongside a cliff, crosses another small brook, and ends on the Chimney Bypass near its upper junction with the regular (Chimney) route of the Glen Boulder Trail.

The Direttissima (map 6:F9-G9)
Distance (est.) from Pinkham Notch Camp

to Glen Boulder Trail: 0.6 mi. (1.0 km.), 35 min.

Alpine Garden Trail (AMC)

This trail leads from the Tuckerman Ravine Trail through a grassy lawn called the Alpine Garden to the Mt. Washington Auto Rd. It forms a convenient connecting link between the trails on the east side of the mountain. Although its chief value is its beauty, it also affords various combinations of routes to those who do not wish to visit the summit. It is completely above treeline and exposed to bad weather, although it is on the mountain's east side, which is usually more sheltered.

The tiny alpine flowers here are best seen in late June. Especially prominent in this area are the five-petaled white Diapensia, the bell-shaped pink-magenta Lapland Rosebay, and the very small pink flowers of the Alpine Azalea. (See the AMC's *Field Guide to Mountain Flowers of New England* and *At Timberline: A Nature Guide to the Mountains of the Northeast*.) No plants should ever be picked or otherwise damaged. Hikers are urged to stay on trails or walk very carefully on rocks so as not to kill the fragile alpine vegetation.

The trail diverges right from the Tuckerman Ravine Trail a short distance above the ravine headwall, about 0.1 mi. below Tuckerman Junction. It leads northeast, bearing toward Lion Head, and crosses the Lion Head Trail. Beyond the crossing the trail leads north, its general direction until it ends at the road. It traverses the Alpine Garden and crosses a tiny stream, which is the headwater of Raymond Cataract. (This water is unfit to drink: it consists largely of drainage from the summit buildings.) The trail soon approaches the top of Huntington Ravine and crosses the Huntington Ravine Trail. Here, a little off the trail, there is a fine view of this impressive ravine. Rising to the top of the ridge, the trail crosses the Nelson Crag Trail, then descends and soon enters the old Glen House Bridle Path, constructed in 1853, whose course is still plain although it was abandoned about a century ago. In a short distance the Alpine Garden Trail leads left and in a few yards enters the Auto Rd. a short distance above the 6-mi. mark and opposite the upper terminus of the Wamsutta Trail.

Alpine Garden Trail (map 6:F9)
Distances (est.) from Tuckerman Ravine Trail
    to Lion Head Trail: 0.3 mi., 10 min.

to Huntington Ravine Trail: 1.3 mi., 45 min.
to Nelson Crag Trail: 1.5 mi., 50 min.
to Auto Rd. junction: 1.8 mi. (2.9 km.), 1 hr.

Southside Trail (AMC)

This trail forms a link between Tuckerman Ravine and the Crawford Path and Westside Trail. It diverges right (west) from Tuckerman Crossover about 10 yd. southwest of Tuckerman Junction and, skirting the southwest side of the cone of Mt. Washington, enters the Davis Path near its junction with the Crawford Path.

Southside Trail (map 6:F9)
Distance (est.) from Tuckerman Junction
to Davis Path: 0.2 mi. (0.3 km.), 10 min.

Tuckerman Crossover (AMC)

This trail connects Tuckerman Ravine with Lakes of the Clouds Hut. It is totally above treeline, and crosses a high ridge where there is much exposure to westerly winds. It leaves the Tuckerman Ravine Trail left (southwest) at Tuckerman Junction, where the latter trail turns sharply right to ascend the cone. It rises gradually across Bigelow Lawn, crosses the Davis Path, then descends moderately to the Crawford Path, which it meets along with the Camel Trail a short distance above the upper Lake of the Clouds. Turning left on the Crawford Path, the Lakes of the Clouds Hut is reached in 0.2 mi.

Tuckerman Crossover (map 6:F9)
Distances from Tuckerman Junction
to Crawford Path: 0.8 mi. (1.3 km.), 25 min.
to Lakes of the Clouds Hut (via Crawford Path): 1.0 mi. (1.6 km.), 30 min.

Lawn Cutoff (AMC)

This trail provides a direct route between Tuckerman Junction and Boott Spur. It is entirely above treeline. It leaves the Tuckerman Ravine Trail at Tuckerman junction and leads south across Bigelow Lawn to the Davis Path about 0.5 mi. north of Boott Spur.

Lawn Cutoff (map 6:F9)
Distance from Tuckerman Junction
  to Davis Path: 0.4 mi. (0.6 km.), 15 min.

Camel Trail (AMC)

This trail, connecting Boott Spur with the Lakes of the Clouds Hut, is named for ledges on Boott Spur which resemble a kneeling camel when seen against the skyline.

The trail is the right of the two that diverge right (east) from the Crawford Path 0.2 mi. northeast of Lakes of the Clouds Hut (the Tuckerman Crossover is the left of the diverging trails). It ascends easy grassy slopes, crosses the old location of the Crawford Path, and continues in a practically straight line across the level stretch of Bigelow Lawn. It aims directly toward the ledges forming the camel, passes under the camel's nose, and joins the Davis Path about 100 yd. northwest of the Lawn Cutoff.

Camel Trail (map 6:F9)
Distance from Crawford Path
  to Davis Path: 0.6 mi. (1.0 km.), 30 min.

Westside Trail (WMNF)

This trail was partially constructed by pioneer trailmaker J. Rayner Edmands; many segments are paved with carefully placed stones. It is wholly above timberline, and is very much exposed to the prevailing west and northwest winds. By avoiding the summit of Mt. Washington, it saves nearly 1 mi. in distance and 600 ft. in elevation between points on the Northern Peaks and on the Crawford Path.

The trail diverges left from the Crawford Path, where the latter path begins to climb the steep part of the cone of Mt. Washington. It skirts the cone, climbing for 0.6 mi. at an easy grade, then descends moderately, crosses under the Mt. Washington Cog Railway, and soon ends at the Gulfside Trail.

Westside Trail (map 6:F9)
Distance from Crawford Path
to Gulfside Trail: 0.9 mi. (1.4 km.), 30 min.

Trinity Heights Connector (NHDP)

This newly constructed trail allows the Appalachian Trail to make a loop over the summit of Mt. Washington. From the true summit (marked by a large sign) it runs approximately northwest to the Gulfside Trail, not far from its junction with the Crawford Path.

Trinity Heights Connector (map 6:F9)
Distance (est.) from true summit of Mt. Washington
to Gulfside Trail: 0.2 mi. (0.3 km.), 5 min.

Raymond Path (AMC)

This old trail leaves the Auto Rd. along with the Old Jackson Road and the Nelson Crag Trail just above the 2-mi. mark, opposite the Madison Gulf Trail, and extends to the Tuckerman Ravine Trail about 0.3 mi. below Hermit Lake. Its grades are mostly easy to moderate.

It is the second trail to diverge right from the Old Jackson Road just south of the Auto Rd. (the first one is the Nelson Crag Trail). It crosses several streams—first a branch of the Peabody and then branches of the Cutler River. It crosses the Huntington Ravine Trail near the largest stream (this junction may not be well signed), then soon crosses the brook that drains the Ravine of Raymond Cataract, and ends about 0.4 mi. beyond at the Tuckerman Ravine Trail.

Raymond Path (map 6:F9)
Distances from Old Jackson Road

to Huntington Ravine Trail: 1.8 mi., 1 hr. 20 min.

to Tuckerman Ravine Trail: 2.4 mi. (3.9 km.), 1 hr. 50 min.

to Hermit Lake (via Tuckerman Ravine Trail): 2.7 mi., 2 hr.

Old Jackson Road (AMC)

This trail runs north from Pinkham Notch Camp to the Mt. Washington Auto Rd. It is part of the Appalachian Trail and is blazed in white. It diverges right from the Tuckerman Ravine Trail about 50 yd. from the camp. After about 0.3 mi. it begins to ascend steeply and steadily and the Crew-Cut Trail leaves right (east). At about 0.6 mi. the Blanchard Loop Ski Trail crosses. Upon reaching the height-of-land, where the George's Gorge Trail leaves right (east), the Old Jackson Road descends slightly, crosses several brooks, and at a large one takes a sharp left uphill. After a short, steep climb it slabs the slope, and the Raymond Path enters left, several small brooks are crossed, and then the Nelson Crag Trail enters left. Continuing north the trail climbs slightly, continues through an old gravel pit and meets the Auto Rd. just above the 2-mi. mark, opposite the Madison Gulf Trail.

Old Jackson Road (map 6:F9)
Distance from Pinkham Notch Camp

to Mt Washington Auto Rd.: 1.8 mi. (2.9 km.), 1 hr. 15 min.

Crew-Cut Trail (MMVSP)

The Crew-Cut Trail starts at the Old Jackson Road, leaving right about 0.3 mi. from Pinkham Notch Camp, after a stream crossing near where the abandoned section of the old road enters on the right from NH 16, as the Old Jackson Road starts to climb steeply. It is called "Brad's Trail" on some signs. After crossing a stony, dry brook bed it runs generally east-northeast, crossing two small brooks. On the east bank of the second brook, at 0.2 mi., the George's Gorge Trail leaves left.

The Crew-Cut Trail continues its same general line, rising gradually through open woods in a long slabbing of the slope and crossing several gullies. It skirts southeast of the steeper rocky outcroppings until it reaches the base of a cliff. At this point the main trail turns sharply right (south) while a very short side trail leads straight ahead and directly up to a lookout, "Lila's Ledge." From this ledge you can look straight in at the Wildcat ski-trail complex, down Pinkham Notch over the AMC buildings, and up at Mt. Washington over Huntington Ravine.

The main trail makes a sharp turn around the nose of the cliff and then resumes its generally east-northeast direction. In about 50 ft., and 0.5 mi. from the Old Jackson Road, Liebeskind's Loop enters left, coming down from the knob at the high point on the George's Gorge Trail. The Crew-Cut Trail continues its descent over a few small ledges and through open woods until it passes east of a small high-level bog formed by an old beaver dam. Shortly thereafter, it goes through open woods again, emerging at the top of the grassy slope on NH 16 almost exactly opposite the south end of the Wildcat Ski Area parking lot.

Crew-Cut Trail (map 6:F9-F10)
Distances (est.) from Old Jackson Road
   to George's Gorge Trail: 0.2 mi., 5 min.

to Liebeskind's Loop: 0.5 mi., 25 min.
to NH 16: 0.7 mi. (1.1 km.), 35 min.

Liebeskind's Loop (MMVSP)

Liebeskind's Loop makes possible a loop hike (using the Crew-Cut, George's Gorge, Loop, and Crew-Cut trails) without resorting to returning either by NH 16 or by the steep section of the Old Jackson Road. This loop hike is best made in the direction described, since the Gorge is more interesting on the ascent and the Loop is more interesting on the descent.

Liebeskind's Loop leaves right (east) near the top of the George's Gorge Trail 0.2 mi. from Old Jackson Road, just before George's Gorge Trail makes the final short ascent to the knob. From this knob a short spur to the left (south) leads to an excellent view of Wildcat Mtn. and Huntington and Tuckerman ravines. Liebeskind's Loop descends to a swampy flat, then rises through a spruce thicket to the top of a cliff, where there is a fine lookout with a good view down Pinkham Notch. Here the trail turns left and runs along the edge of the cliff, finally descending by an easy zigzag in a gully to a beautiful open grove of birches. The trail continues east, descending through two gorges and skirting the east end of rises until it finally climbs a ridge and descends 50 yd. on the other side to join the Crew-Cut Trail just east of Lila's Ledge. The Crew-Cut Trail can then be followed back to the starting point.

Liebeskind's Loop (map 6:F9-F10)
Distance (est.) from George's Gorge Trail
to Crew-Cut Trail: 0.5 mi. (0.8 km.), 15 min.

George's Gorge Trail (MMVSP)

This trail leaves the Crew-Cut Trail to the left on the east bank of a small brook 0.2 mi. from the Old Jackson Road, and leads up the brook, steeply in places, passing Chuda-coff Falls. Liebeskind's Loop enters right at 0.6 mi., and in a very short distance George's Gorge Trail passes a spur path right (south) to an excellent view of Wildcat Mtn. and Huntington and Tuckerman ravines. From here it descends west to the Old Jackson Road in its upper, flat section, about 1 mi. from Pinkham Notch Camp.

George's Gorge Trail (map 6:F9-F10)
Distances (est.) from Crew-Cut Trail
   to Liebeskind's Loop: 0.6 mi., 40 min.
   to Old Jackson Road: 0.8 mi. (1.3 km.), 45 min.

Crawford Path (WMNF)
Caution. Parts of this trail are dangerous in bad weather. Below Mt. Eisenhower there are a number of ledges exposed to the weather, but they are scattered and shelter is usually available in nearby scrub. From the Eisenhower–Franklin col it lies completely above treeline, exposed to the full force of all storms. The most dangerous part of the path is the section on the cone of Mt. Washington, beyond Lakes of the Clouds Hut. Several lives have been lost on the Crawford Path through failure to observe proper precautions. Always carry a compass and study the map before starting. If trouble arises on or above Mt. Monroe, use the Lakes of the Clouds Hut or go down the Ammonoosuc Ravine Trail. If the path should be lost in cloudy weather, go northwest if you are below Mt. Monroe, west if you are above, descending into the woods and following water. On the southeast, toward the Dry River valley, nearly all the slopes are more precipitous, the river crossings potentially dangerous, and the distance to a highway is much greater.

This trail is considered to be the oldest continuously maintained footpath in America. The first section, a footpath leading up Mt. Pierce (Mt. Clinton), was cut in 1819 by Abel Crawford and his son Ethan Allen Crawford. In 1840 Thomas J. Crawford, a younger son of Abel, converted the footpath into a bridle path, although it has not been used for horses for many decades. The trail still follows the original path, except for the section between Mt. Monroe and the Westside Trail. From Mt. Pierce to the summit of Mt. Washington, the Crawford Path is part of the Appalachian Trail, and so it is blazed in white.

The path leaves US 302 opposite the Crawford House site, just south of the parking area near the junction with the Mt. Clinton Rd. It passes a short side trail to a view of a small flume in Gibbs Brook, and at 0.2 mi. from US 302 a side trail leads left to Crawford Cliff. This side path immediately crosses Gibbs Brook and follows it to a small flume and pool. It climbs steeply above the brook, then turns left at an old sign, becomes very rough, and reaches a ledge with an outlook over Crawford Notch and the Willey Range, 0.4 mi. (20 min.) from the Crawford Path.

There are plans to build a short link path to the Webster–Jackson Trail from this vicinity. The main trail continues along the south bank of Gibbs Brook, and at 0.4 mi. a side path leads 40 yd. left to Gibbs Falls. Soon the trail passes an information sign for the Gibbs Brook Scenic Area, and climbs moderately but steadily. At about 1 mi. from US 302 the trail climbs away from the brook and slabs the side of the valley. At 1.7 mi. the Mizpah Cutoff diverges east for Mizpah Spring Hut. The Crawford Path continues to ascend at easy to moderate grades, crossing several small brooks, then reaches its high point on the shoulder of Mt. Pierce and runs almost level, breaking into the open with fine views, and at 2.9 mi. reaches its junction with the Webster Cliff Trail, which leads right (south) to the summit of Mt. Pierce in about 0.1 mi.

From Mt. Pierce to Mt. Eisenhower the path runs through patches of scrub and woods with many open ledges that give magnificent views in all directions. Cairns and the marks of many feet on the rocks indicate the way. The path winds about fairly near the crest of the broad ridge, which is composed of several rounded humps. The general direction in ascending is northeast. At 3.6 mi. the trail crosses a small brook in the col, then ascends mostly on ledges to the junction with the Mount Eisenhower Loop, which diverges left at 4.1 mi. The trip over this summit adds only 0.2 mi. and 300 ft. of climbing to the trip, and the view is excellent in good weather. The Crawford Path continues right and slabs through scrub on the southeast side of the mountain; this is the better route in bad weather. In the col between Mts. Eisenhower and Franklin the path passes close to the right of stagnant Red Pond, and just beyond the Mount Eisenhower Loop rejoins the Crawford Path on the left. In another 100 yds., at 4.7 mi., the Edmands Path also enters left, and at 4.8 mi. the Mount Eisenhower Trail from the Dry River enters right.

The trail then begins the ascent of the shoulder called Mt. Franklin, first moderately, then steeply for a short distance near the top. At 5.3 mi. the trail reaches the relatively level shoulder and continues past an unmarked path at 5.8 mi. which leads in 130 yds. to the barely noticeable summit of Mt. Franklin, from which there are good views. At 6.1 mi. the Mount Monroe Loop diverges left to cross both summits of Monroe, affording excellent views. It is about the same length as the parallel section of the Crawford Path but requires about 350 ft. more climbing. The Crawford Path is safer in bad weather, as it is much less exposed to the weather. The Crawford Path continues along the edge of the precipice that forms the northwest wall of Oakes Gulf, then follows a relocated section, passing an area that has been closed to public entry to preserve an endangered species of plant. The area between the two ends of the Mount Monroe Loop is one of great botanical importance and fragility. To protect this area, the most scrupulous care is required on the part of visitors. At 6.7 mi. the Mount Monroe Loop rejoins on the left, and the path descends easily to Lakes of the Clouds Hut.

The Ammonoosuc Ravine Trail diverges left at the corner of the hut and in another 30 yd. the Dry River Trail diverges right. The Crawford Path crosses the outlet of the larger lake and passes between it and the second lake, where the Camel Trail to Boott Spur and the Tuckerman Crossover to Tuckerman Ravine diverge right. The path then ascends gradually, always some distance below (northwest) the crest of the ridge. The Davis Path, which here follows the original location of the Crawford Path, enters at 7.7 mi., at the foot of the cone of Mt. Washington. In another 50 yd. the Westside Trail to the Northern Peaks diverges left. The Crawford Path turns straight north, switching back and forth as it climbs the steep cone through a trench in the rocks. At the ridge top it meets the Gulfside Trail at 8.0 mi., then turns right, passes through the pen in which saddle horses from the Glen House used to be kept, and from there ascends to the summit, marked by frequent cairns. (Descending, the path is on the right (north) side of the railroad track. Beyond the buildings it leads generally northwest, then swings west. Avoid random side paths toward the south.)

Crawford Path (map 6:G8-F9)
Distances from US 302 near Crawford House site
   to Mizpah Cutoff: 1.7 mi., 1 hr. 20 min.
   to Webster Cliff Trail: 2.9 mi., 2 hr.
   to south end of Mount Eisenhower Loop: 4.1 mi., 2 hr. 45 min.
   to Edmands Path: 4.8 mi., 2 hr. 55 min.
   to Mt. Franklin summit: 5.8 mi., 3 hr. 45 min.

>   *to* south end of Mount Monroe Loop: 6.1 mi., 4 hr. 5 min.
>   *to* Lakes of the Clouds Hut: 6.8 mi., 4 hr. 30 min.
>   *to* Westside Trail: 7.7 mi., 5 hr. 20 min.
>   *to* Gulfside Trail: 8.0 mi., 5 hr. 50 min.
>   *to* Mt. Washington summit: 8.2 mi. (13.2 km.), 6 hr.

Mount Eisenhower Loop (AMC)

This short trail parallels the Crawford Path and crosses over the bare, flat summit of Mt. Eisenhower, which provides magnificent views. It diverges from the Crawford Path 4.1 mi. from US 302 at the south edge of the summit dome, climbs easily for 0.1 mi., then turns sharp left in a flat area and ascends steadily to the summit at 0.4 mi. It then descends moderately to a ledge overlooking Red Pond, drops steeply and passes through a grassy sag just to the left of Red Pond, and finally climbs briefly to rejoin the Crawford Path on a small, rocky knob.

Mount Eisenhower Loop (map 6:G8)
Distances from south junction with Crawford Path

>   *to* summit of Mt. Eisenhower: 0.4 mi., 20 min.
>   *to* north junction with Crawford Path: 0.8 mi. (1.2 km.), 35 min.

Mount Monroe Loop (AMC)

This short trail runs parallel to the Crawford Path and passes over the summits of Mt. Monroe and Little Monroe. The views are fine but the summits are very exposed to the weather. The trail diverges from the Crawford Path 6.1 mi. from US 302 and quickly ascends the minor crag called Little Monroe and descends into the shallow, grassy sag beyond. It then ascends steeply to the summit of Mt. Monroe at 0.3 mi., follows the northeast ridge to the end of the shoulder, and drops sharply to the Crawford Path 0.1 mi. south of Lakes of the Clouds Hut.

Mount Monroe Loop (map 6:F9)
Distances (est.) from south junction with Crawford Path
   to summit of Mt. Monroe: 0.3 mi., 20 min.
   to north junction with Crawford Path: 0.6 mi. (1.0 km.), 30 min.

Ammonoosuc Ravine Trail (WMNF)

The Ammonoosuc Ravine Trail runs from the Base Rd. to Lakes of the Clouds Hut, following the headwaters of the Ammonoosuc River with many fine falls, cascades, and pools, and affords fine views from its upper section. It is the most direct route to Lakes of the Clouds Hut, and the best route in bad weather, since it lies in woods or scrub except for the last 200 yd. to the hut. The section above Gem Pool is extremely steep and rough, and is likely to prove quite arduous to many hikers; it is also somewhat unpleasant to descend this section, on account of the steep, often slippery rocks. Together with the upper section of the Crawford Path it provides the shortest route to Mt. Washington from the west. It can also be reached on foot from the Jefferson Notch Rd. via the Boundary Line Trail (see Section 2).

The trail begins at a newly constructed parking lot on the Base Rd. about 1 mi. east of its junction with the Mt. Clinton Rd. and the Jefferson Notch Rd. It follows a newly cut path through the woods, crossing Franklin Brook at 0.3 mi., then passing over a double pipeline as it skirts around the Base Station Area. It joins the old route of the trail at the edge of the Ammonoosuc River at 1.0 mi., after a slight descent, and bears right along the river, following the old trail for the rest of the way. It ascends mostly by easy grades, with some rough footing, crosses Monroe Brook at

1.7 mi., and at 2.1 mi. crosses the outlet of Gem Pool, a beautiful pool at the foot of a cascade.

Now the very steep, rough ascent begins. At 2.3 mi. a side path (sign) leads right about 80 yd. to a spectacular viewpoint at the foot of the gorge. Above this point the main brook falls about 600 ft. down a steep trough in the mountainside at an average angle of 45 degrees. Another brook a short distance to the north does the same, and these two spectacular waterslides meet at the foot of the gorge, forming a pool at the base. The main trail continues its steep ascent, passes an outlook over the falls to the right of the trail, and continues to the main brook, which it crosses at 2.5 mi. on flat ledges at a striking viewpoint at the head of the highest fall. The grade now begins to ease, and the trail crosses several brooks as ledges become more frequent and the scrub becomes smaller and sparse. At 3.0 mi. the trail emerges from the scrub and follows a line of cairns directly up some rock slabs (which are slippery when wet), passes through one last patch of scrub, and reaches the Crawford Path at the south side of Lakes of the Clouds Hut.

Ammonoosuc Ravine Trail (map 6:F8-F9)
Distances from the Base Rd. parking lot

to Gem Pool: 2.1 mi., 1 hr. 30 min.

to brook crossing on flat ledges: 2.5 mi., 2 hr. 10 min.

to Lakes of the Clouds Hut: 3.1 mi. (5.0 km.), 2 hr. 55 min.

Edmands Path (WMNF)

The Edmands Path leads from the Mt. Clinton Rd. to the Crawford Path in the Eisenhower–Franklin col. It provides the shortest route to the summit of Mt. Eisenhower, and an easy access to the middle portion of the Crawford Path. The last 0.2 mi. segment before the Crawford Path junction is very exposed to northwest winds and, although short, could pose problems in bad weather. J. Rayner Edmands, the pioneer trailmaker, relocated and reconstructed this trail in 1909. The rock cribbing and paving in the middle and upper sections of the trail testify to the infinite pains that Edmands expended to construct a trail with constant comfortable grades in rather difficult terrain. Most of his work has survived the weather and foot traffic of many decades well, and the trail retains what is probably the best grade and footing of any comparable trail in the White Mtns. The trail is nearly always comfortable, and almost never challenging.

The path leaves the east side of the Mt. Clinton Rd. 2.3 mi. north of the Crawford House site. It runs nearly level across two small brooks, then at 0.4 mi. it crosses Abenaki Brook and turns sharp right onto an old logging road on the far bank. At 0.7 mi. the trail diverges left off the old road and crosses a wet area. Soon it begins to climb steadily, undulating up the west ridge of Mt. Eisenhower, carefully searching out the most comfortable grades. At 2.2 mi. the trail swings left and slabs up the hillside on a footway supported by extensive rock cribbing, then passes through a little stone gateway. At 2.5 mi. it crosses a small brook running over a ledge, and soon the grade becomes almost level as the trail contours around the north slope of Mt. Eisenhower, affording excellent views out through the trees. At 2.8 mi. it breaks into the open, crosses the nose of a ridge on a footway paved with carefully placed stones, and reaches the Crawford Path after a slight descent.

Edmands Path (map 6:G8)
Distances from Mt. Clinton Rd.

to stone gateway: 2.3 mi., 2 hr. 10 min.

to Crawford Path junction: 3.1 mi. (4.9 km.), 2 hr. 45 min.

Webster–Jackson Trail (AMC)

This trail connects US 302 at the Crawford Depot information center with the summits of both Mt. Webster and Mt. Jackson, and provides the opportunity for many interesting loop trips from this vicinity. The two summits are linked by the Webster Cliff Trail.

The trail, blazed in blue, leaves the east side of US 302 0.1 mi. south of the Crawford Depot and 0.1 mi. north of the Gate of the Notch. The trail runs through a clearing, enters the woods, and passes the side path leading right to Elephant Head at 0.1 mi. from US 302.

Elephant Head is an interesting ledge forming the east side of the Gate of the Notch, with veins of white quartz in the gray rock providing a remarkable likeness to an elephant's head. The path runs through the woods parallel to the highway at an easy grade, then ascends across the summit of the knob and descends 40 yd. to the top of the ledge—which overlooks Crawford Notch with fine views— 0.2 mi. (10 min.) from the Webster–Jackson Trail.

The main trail runs above Elephant Head Brook, then turns right, away from the brook, at 0.2 mi. There are plans to construct a short trail from this point to the lower part of the Crawford Path. The trail continues up the slope, crosses Little Mossy Brook at 0.3 mi., and continues in the same general direction, nearly level stretches alternating with sharp pitches. At 0.6 mi. from US 302 a side path leads right 60 yd. to Bugle Cliff, a massive ledge overlooking Crawford Notch, where the view is well worth the slight extra effort required; if there is ice present, exercise extreme caution. The main trail rises fairly steeply and crosses Flume Cascade Brook at 0.9 mi. At 1.4 mi., within sound of Silver Cascade Brook, the trail divides, the left branch for Mt. Jackson and the right (straight ahead) for Mt. Webster.

Mount Webster

The Webster (right) branch immediately descends steeply to Silver Cascade Brook, crosses it just below a beautiful cascade and pool, bears left and climbs the bank steeply. The trail then climbs steadily south 1.0 mi., meeting the Webster Cliff Trail on the high plateau northwest of the summit of Mt. Webster, 2.4 mi. from US 302. The ledgy summit of Mt. Webster, with an excellent view of Crawford Notch and the mountains to the west and south, is 0.1 mi. right (south); turn left for Mt. Jackson.

Mount Jackson

The Jackson (left) branch ascends easily until it comes within sight of the brook and begins to climb steadily. About 0.5 mi. above the junction, it crosses three branches of the brook in quick succession. At 1.0 mi. from the junction it passes Tisdale Spring (unreliable, often scanty and muddy), a short distance below the base of the rocky cone. The trail climbs, soon ascending steep ledges to the open summit, 2.6 mi. from US 302.

Webster–Jackson Trail (map 6:G8)
Distances from US 302

to Elephant Head side path: 0.1 mi., 5 min.

to Bugle Cliff: 0.6 mi., 35 min.

to Flume Cascade Brook: 0.9 mi., 45 min.

to Mt. Webster–Mt. Jackson fork: 1.4 mi., 1 hr. 10 min.

to Webster Cliff Trail (via Webster branch): 2.4 mi., 2 hr. 15 min.

to summit of Mt. Webster (via Webster Cliff Trail): 2.5 mi. (4.1 km.), 2 hr. 20 min.

to summit of Mt. Jackson (via Jackson branch): 2.6 mi. (4.2 km.), 2 hr.

for loop trip over summits of Webster and Jackson (via Webster Cliff Trail): 6.5 mi. (10.5 km.), 4 hr. 30 min.

Webster Cliff Trail (AMC)

This trail, a part of the Appalachian Trail, leaves the east side of US 302 opposite the road to Willey House Station, about 1 mi. south of the Willey House Recreation Area at the Willey House site. It ascends along the edge of the spectacular cliffs which form the east wall of Crawford Notch, then leads over Mts. Webster, Jackson, and Pierce to the Crawford Path 0.1 mi. north of Mt. Pierce.

From US 302, it runs nearly east 0.1 mi. to a bridge across the Saco River. Then the trail climbs steadily up the south end of the ridge, winding up the steep slope, growing steeper and rougher as it approaches the cliffs and swinging more to the north. At 1.8 mi. from US 302 it reaches the first open ledge, and from here on, as the trail ascends the ridge with easier grades, there are frequent outlook ledges giving ever-changing perspectives of the notch and the mountains to the south and west. At 2.4 mi. a ledge affords a view straight down to the State Park buildings, and at 3.3 mi. the jumbled, ledgy summit is reached.

The trail then descends north, and in 0.1 mi. the Webster branch of the Webster–Jackson Trail from Crawford Depot on US 302 enters left. The Webster Cliff Trail swings east and crosses numerous wet gullies, finally ascending the steep, ledgy cone of Mt. Jackson, reaching the summit at 4.7 mi., where the Jackson branch of the Webster–Jackson Trail enters left.

The trail leaves the summit of Mt. Jackson toward Mt. Pierce, following a line of cairns running north, and descends the ledges at the north end of the cone quite rapidly into the scrub, then enters and winds through open alpine meadows. At 5.2 mi., where a side path leads right 40 yd. to an outlook, the trail turns sharp left and drops into the woods. It continues up and down along the ridge toward Mt. Pierce, then descends gradually to the junction at 6.3 mi. with the Mizpah Cutoff, which leads left (west) to the

Crawford Path. At 6.4 mi. Mizpah Spring Hut (which also has tentsites) is reached, and the Mount Clinton Trail to the Dry River diverges right (southeast) diagonally down the hut clearing. Continuing west of the hut, the trail ascends very rapidly, passes an outlook toward Mt. Jackson, and reaches an open ledge with good views at 6.6 mi. The grade lessens, and after a sharp right turn in a ledgy area the trail reaches the summit of the southwest knob of Mt. Pierce, which affords a view of the summit of Mt. Washington rising over Mt. Pierce. The trail descends into a sag, ascends easily through scrub to the summit of Mt. Pierce at 7.2 mi., where it comes into the open. It then descends moderately in the open in the same direction (northeast), to its junction with the Crawford Path.

Webster Cliff Trail (map 6:G8)
Distances from US 302
   to first open ledge: 1.8 mi., 1 hr. 50 min.
   to summit of Mt. Webster: 3.3 mi., 3 hr.
   to summit of Mt. Jackson: 4.7 mi., 4 hr.
   to Mizpah Spring Hut: 6.4 mi., 5 hr. 10 min.
   to Crawford Path: 7.3 mi. (11.7 km.), 5 hr. 35 min.

Mizpah Cutoff (AMC)
This short trail provides a direct route from US 302 near the AMC Crawford Notch Hostel to Mizpah Spring Hut. It diverges right (east) from the Crawford Path 1.7 mi. from US 302, climbs the ridge at a moderate grade, passes through a fairly level area, and descends slightly to join the Webster Cliff Trail 0.1 mi. south of Mizpah Spring Hut.

Mizpah Cutoff (map 6:G8)
Distance from Crawford Path
   to Mizpah Spring Hut: 0.7 mi. (1.1 km.), 30 min.

Distance from US 302
   to Mizpah Spring Hut (via Crawford Path and Mizpah Cutoff): 2.4 mi. (3.9 km.), 1 hr. 50 min.

Saco Lake Trail (AMC)

This very short trail makes a loop around the east shore of Saco Lake, beginning and ending on US 302. It starts opposite the AMC Crawford Notch Hostel and ends after crossing the dam at the south end of Saco Lake. In addition to being an attractive short walk, it provides an alternative to part of the road walk between the Crawford Path and Webster–Jackson Trail.

Saco Lake Trail (map 6:G8)
Distance (est.) from north junction with US 302
   to south junction with US 302: 0.4 mi. (0.6 km.), 15 min.

Dry River Trail (WMNF)

The Dry River Trail is the main trail from US 302 up the valley and through Oakes Gulf to Lakes of the Clouds Hut, with access to Mt. Washington, the Southern Peaks, and the upper portion of the Montalban Ridge. The first 5 mi. roughly follows the route of an old logging railroad, although the river and its tributaries have eradicated much of the old roadbed, and the relocations cut to eliminate the numerous, potentially hazardous river crossings have bypassed much of the remaining grade. The few river crossings that remain can be very difficult when water is high. The trail is somewhat rougher than most similar valley trails elsewhere in the White Mtns. This trail is almost entirely within the Presidential Range-Dry River Wilderness. Dry River Shelters #1 and #2 have been removed; Dry River Shelter #3 will be removed whenever major maintenance is required.

The trail leaves the east side of US 302, 0.3 mi. north of the entrance to Dry River Campground. From the highway the trail follows a wide wood road, generally northeast, for 0.5 mi. to its junction with the bed of the old logging railroad. From here the trail follows the railroad bed, passes the Wilderness Area boundary at 0.7 mi., and leaves the railroad grade sharp left at 0.9 mi, staying on the west side of the river (the railroad crossed it). Just downstream from this point there is a pleasant pool. The trail turns left and climbs over a low bluff, rejoins the roadbed, then leaves it again and climbs over a higher bluff, where there is a restricted but beautiful outlook up the Dry River to Mt. Washington, Mt. Monroe, and the headwall of Oakes Gulf. At 1.7 mi. the trail crosses the Dry River on a suspension bridge, and continues up the east bank, occasionally using portions of the old railroad grade. At 2.9 mi. the Mount Clinton Trail diverges left to ascend to Mizpah Spring Hut. At 4.2 mi. the trail makes a sharp turn away from the river, then turns left and continues along the bank at a higher level. At 4.9 mi. the trail crosses Isolation Brook, turns right along the bank, and in 60 yd. the Isolation Trail diverges right.

The Dry River Trail continues straight along the high river bank on a recently cut path, passes a cleared outlook over the river, and at 5.2 mi. the Mount Eisenhower Trail diverges sharp left and descends the steep bank on a former section of the Dry River Trail. Now back on the older route, the trail continues along the east bank, passing at 5.4 mi. a side path (sign) that leads down left 40 yd. to the pool at the foot of Dry River Falls, a very attractive spot. The top of the falls, with an interesting pothole, can also be reached from here. At 5.6 mi. the trail crosses the river to the west side; the crossing is fairly easy, but could be a problem at high water. At 6.3 mi. Dry River Shelter #3 is passed; it will be removed when major maintenance is required. In 60 yd. the trail crosses a major tributary of Dry River at the confluence, and continues along the bank, gradually rising higher above the river.

At 7.4 mi. it begins to swing away from the river, which has been at least audible to this point, and gradually climbs into Oakes Gulf. After crossing a small ridge and descending sharply on the other side, views begin to appear, although the trail remains well sheltered in the scrub. At 8.7 mi. there is a good outlook perch just right of the trail. The trail climbs out of the scrub, turns left and crosses a small brook at a right angle. At 9.1 mi. the trail turns sharp right from its former route, where signs forbid public entry into the area formerly crossed by the trail. The closed area is the habitat of an endangered plant species. The trail continues to climb, passing the Wilderness Area boundary sign in a patch of scrub, and reaches the height-of-land on the southwest ridge of Mt. Washington at 9.4 mi. It then descends to the larger of the Lakes of the Clouds, follows its south edge, and ends at Lakes of the Clouds Hut.

Dry River Trail (map 6:H8-F9)
Distances from US 302
  to suspension bridge: 1.7 mi., 1 hr. 5 min.
  to Mount Clinton Trail: 2.9 mi., 1 hr. 50 min.
  to Isolation Trail: 4.9 mi., 3 hr. 15 min.
  to Mount Eisenhower Trail: 5.2 mi., 3 hr. 25 min.
  to Dry River Shelter #3: 6.3 mi., 4 hr. 15 min.
  to Lakes of the Clouds Hut: 9.6 mi. (15.5 km.), 7 hr.

Mount Clinton Trail (WMNF)

This trail connects the lower part of the Dry River to Mizpah Hut and the southern part of the Southern Peaks. The crossing of Dry River near its junction with the Dry River Trail can be impassable in high water. This trail is almost entirely within the Presidential Range-Dry River Wilderness.

The trail diverges left from the Dry River Trail 2.9 mi. from US 302, and immediately crosses the Dry River. This crossing can vary from an easy skip over the stones to a waist-high ford in a torrent, and there may be no safe way across. On the west side of the river it follows a short stretch of old railroad grade, then swings left up the bank of a major tributary, following an old logging road at a moderate grade much of the way. At 0.5 mi the trail crosses this brook for the first of seven times, and scrambles up a washed-out area on the other bank. At 1.2 mi. the trail turns sharp left off the road and descends to the brook, crosses at a ledgy spot, and soon regains the road on the other side. It follows close to the brook, crossing many tributaries as well as the main brook, to the seventh crossing at 1.8 mi. Above an eroded section where a small brook has taken over the road, the walking on the old road becomes very pleasant, and the Dry River Cutoff Trail enters on the right at 2.5 mi. From here the trail ascends past a large boulder to the Wilderness Area boundary at 2.9 mi., and soon enters the clearing of Mizpah Spring Hut, where it joins the Webster Cliff Trail.

Mount Clinton Trail (map 6:G8)
Distances from Dry River Trail
   to Dry River Cutoff: 2.5 mi., 2 hr.
   to Mizpah Spring Hut: 3.0 mi. (4.8 km.), 2 hr. 35 min.

Mount Eisenhower Trail (WMNF)
This trail connects the middle part of the Dry River valley to the Crawford Path at the Eisenhower–Franklin col. Its grades are mostly easy to moderate and it is only above treeline for a short distance on the ridge top. This trail is almost entirely within the Presidential Range–Dry River Wilderness.

The trail diverges left from the Dry River Trail about 5.2 mi. from US 302, and descends rather steeply on a former route of the Dry River Trail through an area with many side paths; care must be used to stay on the proper trail. The trail crosses Dry River (may be difficult or impassable at high water), and follows the bank downstream. At 0.2 mi. it joins its former route, and bears right up a rather steep logging road. The Dry River Cutoff Trail diverges left at 0.3 mi., and soon the grade eases. The Mount Eisenhower Trail generally leads north, keeping a bit to the west of the crest of the long ridge that runs south from a point midway between Franklin and Eisenhower. At 1.3 mi. it passes through a blowdown patch with views of Mt. Pierce, and from here on there are occasional views from the edge of the ravine to the west. At 1.8 mi. it turns sharp right, then left, and soon ascends more steeply for a while. At 2.4 mi. the trail finally gains the crest of the ridge, and winds among rocks and scrub, passing the Wilderness Area boundary 50 yd. before reaching the Crawford Path, 0.1 mi. north of the upper terminus of the Edmands Path in the Eisenhower–Franklin col.

Mount Eisenhower Trail (map 6:G8)
Distances from Dry River Trail
 to Dry River Cutoff Trail: 0.3 mi., 15 min.
 to Crawford Path: 2.7 mi. (4.3 km.), 2 hr. 15 min.

Dry River Cutoff Trail (AMC)
This trail connects the middle part of the Dry River valley to Mizpah Spring Hut and the southern section of the Southern Peaks. Grades are mostly easy with some moderate sections. This trail is almost entirely within the Presidential Range–Dry River Wilderness.

The trail diverges left from the Mount Eisenhower Trail 0.3 mi. from the latter trail's junction with the Dry River Trail. In 0.1 mi. it crosses a substantial brook after a slight descent, then turns sharply left and climbs the bank, crosses a tributary, then swings back and climbs above the bank of the tributary. It crosses several branches of the tributary and gains the height-of-land on the southeast ridge of Mt. Pierce at 1.3 mi., then runs almost on the level to its junction with the Mount Clinton Trail at 1.7 mi. Mizpah Spring Hut is 0.5 mi. to the right from this junction via the Mount Clinton Trail.

Dry River Cutoff Trail (map 6:G8)
Distance from Mount Eisenhower Trail
  to Mount Clinton Trail: 1.7 mi. (2.8 km.), 1 hr. 15 min.

Davis Path (AMC)

The Davis Path, constructed by Nathaniel P. T. Davis in 1844, was the third bridle path leading up Mt. Washington. It was in use until 1853 or 1854, but soon after became impassable, and eventually went out of existence. It was reopened as a foot trail in 1910. The sections leading up Mt. Crawford and Stairs Mtn. give some idea of the magnitude of the task Davis performed. The resolution that enabled Davis to push forward with this apparently hopeless task was the inspiration for the naming of Mt. Resolution. This trail is almost entirely within the Presidential Range–Dry River Wilderness.

This path leaves US 302 on the west side of the Saco River at a paved parking lot, and follows the bank of the river about 100 yd. upstream to the suspension footbridge (Bemis Bridge). Beyond the east end of the bridge, the trail passes through private land. Continue straight east across an overgrown field and a small brook and turn southeast on an embankment. Ignore other branching paths and blazes, which relate to new housing. At about 0.3 mi. the path turns east and enters the woods (WMNF and Wilderness Area) on a logging road. It then crosses a dry brook and, leaving the logging road at the foot of a steep hill 0.8 mi. from US 302, soon enters the old, carefully graded bridle path and begins to ascend the steep ridge connecting Mt. Crawford with Mt. Hope. Attaining the crest, the Davis Path follows this ridge north, mounting over bare ledges with good outlooks.

At 2.3 mi. from US 302, at the foot of a large, sloping ledge, a side trail diverges left and climbs to the bare, peaked summit of Mt. Crawford, from which there is an magnificent view of Crawford Notch, the Dry River Valley, and the surrounding ridges and peaks, at 0.3 mi. (15 min.).

From this junction the path turns northeast, descends slightly to the col between the peak of Mt. Crawford and its ledgy, domelike east knob (sometimes called Crawford Dome), and resumes the ascent. It soon passes over the ledgy shoulder of Crawford Dome and dips to the Crawford–Resolution col. Leaving this col, the path runs north, rises slightly, and keeps close to the same level along the steep west side of Mt. Resolution. The Mount Parker Trail, which diverges right (east) at 3.8 mi., leads in about 0.6 mi. to open ledges near the summit of Mt. Resolution. A trail that branches left at this junction descends a short distance to the AMC Resolution Shelter, an open camp with room for eight, situated on a small branch of Sleeper Brook. (WMNF policies call for removal of this shelter whenever major maintenance is required.) Ordinarily there is water just behind the shelter, but in dry seasons it may be necessary to go down the brook a short distance. In most seasons, this is the first water after starting up the grade of Crawford and the last before the site of the former Isolation Shelter.

At 4.1 mi. the path passes just west of Stairs Col, the col between Mt. Resolution and Stairs Mtn. Here the Stairs Col Trail to the Rocky Branch diverges right. The path now veers northwest, passing west of the precipitous Giant Stairs, ascending gradually along a steep mountainside, then zigzagging boldly northeast toward the flat top of

Stairs Mtn. Shortly before the path reaches the top of the slope, a branch trail leads right a few steps to the "Downlook," a good viewpoint. At the top of the climb, 4.5 mi. from US 302, a branch trail leads right (southeast) 0.2 mi. past the summit to the top of the Giant Stairs, where there is an inspiring view.

The Davis Path continues down the north ridge of Stairs Mtn. for about 1 mi., then runs east in a col for about 0.1 mi. Turning north again (watch for this turn), it passes over a small rise and descends into another col. The path next begins to ascend the long north and south ridge of Mt. Davis, keeping to the west slopes. At 8.5 mi. a branch trail diverges right (east) 0.2 mi. to the summit of Mt. Davis, with the finest view on the Montalban Ridge, and one of the best in the mountains.

The main path now descends to the col between Mt. Davis and Mt. Isolation, then ascends the latter. At 9.8 mi. a spur path (which is signed, but easily missed) diverges left, leading in 125 yd. to the summit of Mt. Isolation. The open summit provides magnificent views in all directions.

At 10.6 mi. the path leads past the site of the former Isolation Shelter and at 10.7 mi. the east branch of the Isolation Trail enters right from the Rocky Branch valley. Water can be obtained by going down the Isolation Trail to the right (east); decent water (which is nevertheless unsafe to drink without treatment) may be some distance down. The path continues to climb steadily, and the west branch of the Isolation Trail descends left to the Dry River valley at 11.0 mi. The trail passes over a hump and runs through a sag at 11.6 mi., then ascends steadily to treeline at 12.2 mi. From here the trail is above treeline and completely exposed to the weather. At 12.6 mi. the Glen Boulder Trail joins on the right just below a small crag, and at 13.1 mi. the path passes just west of the summit of Boott Spur (5500 ft.), and the Boott Spur Trail to AMC Pinkham Notch Camp diverges right (east).

Turning northwest, the path leads along the almost level ridges of Boott Spur and crosses Bigelow Lawn. At 13.7 mi. the Lawn Cutoff diverges right to Tuckerman Junction, and a short distance farther on, the Camel Trail diverges left (west) to the Lakes of the Clouds Hut. At 14.1 mi. the Davis Path begins to follow the original location of the Crawford Path, crosses the Tuckerman Crossover, and in about 0.3 mi. is joined on the right by the Southside Trail. Soon the Davis Path enters the present Crawford Path, which climbs to the summit of Mt. Washington.

Davis Path (map 6:H8-F9)
Distances (est.) from US 302

to Mt. Crawford spur path: 2.3 mi., 2 hr. 5 min.
to Mount Parker Trail: 3.8 mi., 3 hr.
to Stairs Col Trail: 4.1 mi., 3 hr. 10 min.
to Giant Stairs spur path: 4.5 mi., 3 hr. 35 min.
to Mt. Davis spur path: 8.5 mi., 6 hr.
to Mt. Isolation spur path: 9.8 mi., 6 hr. 40 min.
to Isolation Trail, east branch: 10.7 mi., 7 hr. 20 min.
to Isolation Trail, west branch: 11.0 mi., 7 hr. 45 min.
to Glen Boulder Trail: 12.6 mi., 8 hr. 55 min.
to Boott Spur Trail: 13.1 mi., 9 hr. 20 min.
to Lawn Cutoff: 13.7 mi., 9 hr. 35 min.
to Crawford Path: 14.6 mi (23.5 km.), 10 hr. 10 min.
to Lakes of the Clouds Hut (via Camel Trail): 14.6 mi., 10 hr.
to Mt. Washington summit (via Crawford Path): 15.1 mi. (24.1 km.), 10 hr. 45 min.

Stairs Col Trail (AMC)
This trail connects the Rocky Branch valley with Stairs Col on the Davis Path, providing, in particular, the easiest

route to the Giant Stairs. Note that there is water along this trail, but very little on the Davis Path. This trail is almost entirely within the Presidential Range–Dry River Wilderness.

It leaves the Rocky Branch Trail left opposite the Rocky Branch Shelter #1 area, and follows an old railroad siding 50 yd. It then turns sharp left, crosses a swampy area, and climbs briefly to a logging road where it enters the Dry River Wilderness Area. From here nearly to Stairs Col, the trail follows a logging road along the ravine of a brook, crossing it about halfway up the valley. The last part is rather steep. The trail crosses Stairs Col and continues down the west side a short distance to meet the Davis Path. For the Giant Stairs turn right.

Stairs Col Trail (map 6:H9)
Distance from Rocky Branch Trail

to Davis Path junction: 1.9 mi. (3.1 km.), 1 hr. 45 min.

Rocky Branch Trail (WMNF)

The valley of the Rocky Branch of the Saco River lies between the two longest subsidiary ridges of Mt. Washington: the Montalban Ridge to the west and the Rocky Branch Ridge to the east. In the upper part of the valley the forest is still recovering from fires which swept the slopes in 1914–16. The lack of mature trees, particularly conifers, is evident in many areas. The northeast terminus of the trail is at a paved parking lot on NH 16 about 5 mi. north of Jackson, just north of the highway bridge over the Ellis River. The Jericho (south) trailhead is reached by following the Jericho Rd. (FR 27), which leaves US 302 just east of the bridge over the Rocky Branch, 1 mi. west of the junction of US 302 and NH 16. The Jericho Rd. is asphalt for about 1 mi., then a good gravel road for another 3.4 mi. to the beginning of the trail. From NH 16, the trail ascends moderately, mostly on old logging roads, to a pass in the Rocky Branch Ridge, then descends easily to the old logging railroad grade in the valley, and follows the railroad grade on its gradual descent to the south terminus. After reaching the valley, the trail crosses the Rocky Branch several times; these crossings are wide, and are difficult and possibly dangerous at high water.

At the northeast terminus, the trail leaves the north end of the parking lot (avoid a gravel road that branches left just below the parking lot) and climbs moderately on an old logging road. At about 0.5 mi. a ski-touring trail enters from the left and shortly leaves right. At 1.3 mi. the trail swings left away from the bank of a small brook, and continues to ascend, then turns sharp left and follows an old, very straight road on a slight downhill grade. After about 0.5 mi. on this road, it swings gradually right and climbs moderately, following a brook part way, and reaches the Dry River Wilderness Area boundary just east of the ridge top. Passing the almost imperceptible height-of-land at 2.8 mi., the trail follows a short bypass left of a very wet area and runs almost level, then descends easily, with small brooks running in and out of the trail. At 3.5 mi. the trail begins to swing left, descends to the Rocky Branch, follows it downstream for a short distance, then crosses it at 3.7 mi. This crossing may be very difficult. (*Note.* If you are climbing to Mt. Isolation from NH 16, and the river is high, you can avoid two crossings by bushwhacking along the east side of the river upstream for 0.4 mi., since the Isolation Trail soon crosses back to the east bank.) On the west bank is the junction with the Isolation Trail, which diverges right (north), following the river bank on the old railroad grade.

The Rocky Branch Trail follows the old railroad grade left at this junction, and passes Rocky Branch Shelter #2 in 60 yd. (USFS Wilderness policies call for removal of this shelter whenever major maintenance is required.) The trail then runs generally south along the west bank for about 2.0 mi., at times on the old railroad grade, then follows the grade, crossing the river four times. These crossings are difficult at high water, but it may be possible to avoid some or all by bushwhacking along the west bank. Passing out of the Wilderness Area, the trail reaches a junction at 8.1 mi. with the Stairs Col Trail right and a spur path 60 yd. left to WMNF Rocky Branch Shelter #1 and tentsite. Continuing south along the river and railroad grade, it crosses the river on a logging road bridge just before reaching the south terminus.

Rocky Branch Trail (map 6)
Distances from parking lot off NH 16
to height-of-land: 2.8 mi., 2 hr. 20 min.
to Isolation Trail: 3.7 mi., 2 hr. 50 min.
to Stairs Col Trail: 8.1 mi., 5 hr.
to Jericho Rd.: 9.8 mi. (15.8 km.), 5 hr. 50 min.

Isolation Trail (WMNF)

This trail links the Dry River valley (Dry River Trail), the Montalban Ridge (Davis Path), and the Rocky Branch valley (Rocky Branch Trail). It is entirely within the Presidential Range-Dry River Wilderness.

The trail diverges from the Rocky Branch Trail just north of Rocky Branch Shelter #2 (which will be removed when major maintenance is required), at the point where the Rocky Branch Trail swings east to cross the river. The Isolation Trail follows the river north on what is left of the old railroad grade, crossing the river at 0.4 mi. At 0.7 mi. the trail turns sharp right off the railroad grade, climbs briefly, then follows a logging road that runs high above the river. The trail crosses the river three more times; the next two are only 70 yd. apart. The last crossing comes at 1.7 mi., after which the trail climbs easily along a tributary, reaching the Davis Path at 2.6 mi. after passing through an area of confusing side paths where the trail must be followed with care.

Coinciding with the Davis Path, it climbs steadily north for about 0.3 mi., then turns left off the Davis Path, runs level for 0.2 mi., then descends moderately southwest into the Dry River valley. At 4.3 mi. the trail reaches a branch of the Dry River and follows its northwest bank on an old logging road, ending at the Dry River Trail, 4.9 mi. from US 302.

Isolation Trail (map 6:G9-G8)
Distances from Rocky Branch Trail

   to fourth crossing of the Rocky Branch: 1.7 mi., 1 hr. 10 min.

   to Davis Path, south junction: 2.6 mi., 1 hr. 50 min.

   to Davis Path, north junction: 2.9 mi., 2 hr. 10 min.

   to branch of Dry River: 4.3 mi., 2 hr. 50 min.

   to Dry River Trail: 5.3 mi. (8.6 km.), 3 hr. 20 min.

Distances from Rocky Branch Trail at parking area on NH 16

   to Isolation Trail: 3.8 mi., 2 hr. 50 min.

   to Davis Path, south junction: 6.4 mi., 4 hr. 40 min.

   to Mt. Isolation (via Davis Path): 7.3 mi. (11.8 km.), 5 hr. 15 min.

Mount Langdon Trail (WMNF)

This trail runs from Bartlett village to the Mt. Langdon Shelter, meeting both the Mount Parker Trail and the Mount Stanton Trail, and thus giving access to both the higher and lower sections of the Montalban Ridge. It should be noted that this trail does not get particularly close to the summit of Mt. Langdon, which is crossed by the Mount Stanton Trail.

From the four corners of the junction of US 302 and the Bear Notch Rd. in Bartlett village, follow the road that leads north across a bridge over the Saco to an intersection at 0.4 mi. The trail begins almost straight ahead; there are two entrances which very soon converge (no sign). The trail follows a fairly recent gravel logging road, and at 0.3 mi. the path to Cave Mtn. diverges left, marked by the word "cave" painted on a rock, which is hard to see unless you are looking for it. The road gradually becomes older and less evident. The trail crosses a good-sized brook at 1.0 mi. and climbs more steadily, bearing sharp right twice as the road fades away.

The Mount Langdon Trail crosses Oak Ridge at 2.2 mi. and descends, sharply at times, to the Oak Ridge–Mt. Parker col, where it bears right at 2.5 mi. at the junction with the Mount Parker Trail. The Mount Langdon Trail then descends gradually to the WMNF Mt. Langdon Shelter, capacity eight, where this trail and the Mount Stanton Trail both end. Some care is required to follow the trail near the shelter. Water may be found in a brook 60 yd. from the shelter on the Mount Stanton Trail, although in dry weather the brook may have to be followed downhill.

Mount Langdon Trail (map 6:H9)
Distances from the road on the north bank of the Saco River

to Mount Parker Trail: 2.5 mi., 2 hr.

to Mt. Langdon Shelter: 2.9 mi. (4.7 km.), 2 hr. 15 min.

to Mt. Langdon (via Mount Stanton Trail): 3.7 mi., 2 hr. 55 min.

Mount Parker Trail (SSOC)

This trail passes some excellent viewpoints, and provides access from Bartlett to Mt. Parker, Mt. Resolution, the Stairs Col area, and the upper Montalban Ridge. There is no sure water.

This trail begins in the Oak Ridge–Mt. Parker col 2.5 mi. from Bartlett, continuing straight ahead to the north where the Mount Langdon Trail turns right (east). It swings right, then sharp left as it joins an old graded path at a switchback. It follows this, climbing easily with many switchbacks, to an open spot with good views to the southwest. It then slabs to the east of the ridge through beech and oak woods until it reaches the base of some cliffs, where a side path leads left up through a gully to a good viewpoint. Continuing, the trail descends right with a switchback before turning left and climbing steeply onto the main ridge. Heading generally northwest, the trail climbs easily to an outlook to the southwest, then turns right and levels off before the last short, steep climb to the open summit of Mt. Parker, where there are excellent views.

Continuing north, the trail descends to the long ridge between Mt. Parker and Mt. Resolution and passes over three bumps, alternating between spruce woods and open ledges with good views. It then slabs the west and south sides of the remainder of the ridge until it reaches the southeast corner of Mt. Resolution, where it turns sharp right and zigzags steeply up to the col between the main summit ridge and a southerly knob. Here a short branch trail leads left over this open knob, where there are fine views, and rejoins the main trail in about 100 yd. Beyond this junction the trail winds along the flat top of Mt. Resolution until it reaches a large cairn on an open ledge with excellent views. The true summit is about 0.1 mi. east-northeast, very slightly higher, with excellent views north but no path. From the cairn the trail descends sharply into a gully where it crosses a brook (water unreliable), then heads northwest down past several ledges, and finally drops steeply to the Davis Path, opposite the branch trail to Resolution Shelter.

Mount Parker Trail (map 6:H9)
Distances (est.) from Mount Langdon Trail
   to summit of Mt. Parker: 1.3 mi., 1 hr. 15 min.
   to branch trail to open southerly knob: 3.0 mi., 2 hr. 20
     min.
   to high point on Mt. Resolution: 3.5 mi., 2 hr. 40 min.
   to Davis Path junction: 4.2 mi. (6.8 km.), 3 hr.

Mount Stanton Trail (SSOC)

This trail passes over the low eastern summits of the
Montalban Ridge, and affords many views from ledges. For
the east trailhead (the west trailhead is at Mt. Langdon
Shelter), leave the north side of US 302, 1.8 mi. west of its
junction with NH 16 in Glen, and a short distance east of
the bridge over the Saco River. Follow a paved road west
about 0.2 mi., then bear right on Oak Ridge Dr., and
almost immediately turn sharp right on Hemlock Dr. At a
crossroads 0.6 mi. from US 302 turn right, and trailhead is
on left of this road (limited parking). This is an area of
new home construction; the turns at road junctions are
well marked with unobtrusive signs. In 100 yd. it passes a
red-blazed WMNF boundary corner to the left of the trail,
and at 0.3 mi. turns sharp left with yellow blazes where the
red-blazed WMNF boundary continues straight ahead. The
trail climbs steeply at times, but there are gentler sections,
and the outlooks from White's Ledge begin at 0.8 mi. The
trail climbs steeply again after passing a large boulder on
the right of the trail, and at 1.2 mi. the trail turns sharp
right on a ledge as climbing becomes easier. At 1.4 mi. the
trail passes within 15 yd. of the summit of Mt. Stanton.
The summit area is covered with a fine stand of red (norway) pines and there are good views from scattered ledges
near the summit.
   The trail descends to the Stanton–Pickering col, ascends
steadily, crosses a ledgy ridge and descends slightly, then

climbs again and at 2.1 mi. passes 30 yd. to the right of the summit of Mt. Pickering. The trail then leads to ledges on a slightly lower knob, where there are excellent views. The trail descends to a minor col, then crosses over several interesting small humps sometimes called the Crippies. These humps have scattered outlook ledges, and the best view is from the fourth and last Crippie, which is crossed at 3.3 mi.

From the last Crippie the trail descends somewhat along the north side of the ridge toward Mt. Langdon, then climbs north moderately with a few steep pitches, passing an outlook to Carter Dome, Carter Notch, and Wildcat. At 4.5 mi. the trail passes about 35 yd. to the right of the summit, which is wooded and viewless, then descends easily to a gravel slope, turns right and descends to a brook that is crossed 60 yd. east of Mt. Langdon Shelter, where the Mount Stanton Trail ends.

Mount Stanton Trail (map 6:H10-H9)
Distances from the trailhead off Hemlock Drive
to Mt. Stanton summit: 1.4 mi., 1 hr. 15 min.
to Mt. Pickering summit: 2.1 mi., 1 hr. 50 min.
to fourth Crippie: 3.3 mi., 2 hr. 35 min.
to Mt. Langdon summit: 4.5 mi., 3 hr. 35 min.
to Mount Langdon Trail at Mt. Langdon Shelter: 5.3 mi. (8.5 km.), 4 hr.

Cave Mountain Path
This mountain, remarkable for the shallow cave near its wooded summit, is easily reached from Bartlett via a path that leaves the Mount Langdon Trail for 0.3 mi. to a left fork signed only by a rock with the word "cave" painted on it (watch carefully). In less than 0.5 mi. this branch trail leads up a steep gravel slope to the cave. A faint trail to the right of the cave leads, after a short scramble, to the top of

the cliff in which the cave is located, where there is an excellent view of Bartlett.

Cave Mountain Path (map 6:H9)
Distances (est.) from Mount Langdon Trail
    to cave: 0.5 mi., 25 min.
    to Cave Mtn. summit: 0.8 mi. (1.3 km.), 45 min.

Winniweta Falls Trail (WMNF)

This trail provides easy access to an interesting waterfall. It leaves the west side of NH 16, 3 mi. north of the bridge over the Ellis River in Jackson. It fords the wide bed of the Ellis River, normally a rather shallow stream but difficult to cross at high water, turns right, and follows a logging road up the north bank of Miles Brook. At an arrow, the path turns left from the road and soon reaches the falls.

Winniweta Falls Trail (map 6:G10)
Distance (est.) from NH 16
    to Winniweta Falls: 1.0 mi. (1.6 km.), 40 min.

Iron Mountain Trail (JCC)

The summit of this mountain is wooded, with somewhat restricted views, but an outlook on the north side and the fine south cliffs provide very attractive views for relatively little effort. A prominent easterly ridge, on which there was once a trail, descends almost to NH 16, ending in a cliff called Duck's Head, near the Iron Mtn. House. To the east of the cliffs are some abandoned iron mines. The trail is reached by leaving NH 16 in Jackson, next to the golf links and nearly opposite the red covered bridge, and following a road prominently signed Green Hill Rd. At 1.2 mi. the pavement ends, and at 1.4 mi. FR 325 bears right. Bear left here, as the road (FR 119) becomes fairly steep, a bit rough, and very narrow (be prepared to back up if required for other cars to pass). At 2.7 mi. from NH 16, swing left at a sign as the road ahead becomes very poor, and park in a small designated field behind the house of the Hayes Farm (now a summer residence).

The trail crosses the field, passes through a narrow band of trees, and crosses a second field, entering the woods at the top edge. The path climbs steadily and the footing is good. At 0.6 mi. there is a side path right 20 yd. to a fine outlook up the Rocky Branch valley to Mt. Washington, with the Southern Presidentials visible over the Montalban Ridge. The main trail continues to the summit at 0.8 mi., where there are remains of the former fire tower and a rickety wooden tower. The trail descends steadily along a rocky ridge, dropping about 300 ft., then crosses several humps in thick woods. At 1.5 mi. a side path descends left 0.2 mi. and 250 ft. to the old mines (tailings, water-filled shaft), and the main trail ascends shortly to ledges and the edge of the cliffs, where wide views to the south and west are obtained.

Iron Mountain Trail (map 6:H10)
Distances from Hayes Farm
 to summit of Iron Mtn.: 0.8 mi., 50 min.
 to south cliffs: 1.6 mi. (2.6 km.), 1 hr. 15 min.

The Northern Peaks and the Great Gulf

This section covers the high peaks of Mt. Washington's massive northern ridge, which curves north and then northeast like a great arm embracing the magnificent glacial cirque called the Great Gulf. This ridge runs for 5 mi. with only slight dips below the 5000 ft. elevation, and each of the three main peaks rises at least 500 ft. above the cols. The AMC Mt. Washington Range map (map 6) covers the entire area. The RMC map of the Randolph Valley and Northern Peaks, with a larger scale useful for the dense trail network on the north slopes, is available on plastic-coated paper for $2; the guidebook *Randolph Paths*, 1977 edition, is available for $1.50 (map not included) from the Randolph Mountain Club, Randolph, NH 03570.

In this section, the Appalachian Trail follows the Gulf-side Trail, from its junction with the Trinity Heights Connector near the summit of Mt. Washington, to Madison Hut. It then follows the Osgood Trail over Mt. Madison and down into the Great Gulf, proceeding to the Auto Rd. via the Osgood Cutoff and Madison Gulf Trail.

GEOGRAPHY

Mt. Clay (5541 ft.) is the first peak on the ridge north of Mt. Washington. Strictly speaking it is only a shoulder, comparable to Boott Spur on the southeast ridge of its great neighbor, since it rises barely 150 ft. above the connecting ridge. But it offers superb views from the cliffs, which drop away practically at the summit to form the west side of the Great Gulf headwall.

Mt. Jefferson (5712 ft.) has three summits a short distance apart, in line northwest and southeast, with the highest in the middle. Perhaps the most striking view is down the Great Gulf with the Carter Range beyond; the best views of the gulf are obtained from points on the Gulfside Trail to the north of the summit. There are other fine views, most notably those to Mt. Washington and the other Northern Peaks, to the Fabyan Plain on the southwest, and down the broad valley of the Israel on the northwest. The Castellated Ridge, sharpest and most salient of the White Mtn. ridges, extends northwest, forming the southwest wall of Castle Ravine. The view of the "Castles" from US 2 near the village of Bowman is unforgettable. The Ridge of the Caps, similar in formation but less striking, extends to the west. The two eastern ridges—Jefferson's "knees"—truncated by the Great Gulf, have precipitous wooded slopes and gently sloping tops. South of the peak of Mt. Jefferson is a smooth, grassy plateau called Monticello Lawn (5400 ft.). Jefferson Ravine, a glacial gulf tributary to the Great Gulf on the northeast side of the mountain, and Castle Ravine, a cirque to the north, are divided by the narrow ridge which runs from Jefferson through Edmands Col to Mt. Adams.

Mt. Adams (5774 ft.), second highest of the New England summits, has a greater variety of interesting features than any other New England mountain except Katahdin: its sharp, clean-cut profile; its large area above treeline; its inspiring views, the finest being across the Great Gulf to Mts. Washington, Jefferson, and Clay; its great northern ridges, Durand sharp and narrow, Nowell massive and broad-spreading; its four glacial cirques, King Ravine and the three that it shares with its neighbors, the Great Gulf, Madison Gulf, and Castle Ravine. It has several lesser summits and crags, of which the two most prominent are Mt. Sam Adams (5594 ft.), a flat mass to the west, and Mt. Quincy Adams (5410 ft.), a sharp, narrow shark-fin ridge to the north.

Mt. Madison (5367 ft.) is the farthest northeast of the

high peaks of the Presidential Range, remarkable for the great drop of over 4000 ft. to the river valleys east and northeast from its summit. The drop to the Androscoggin at Gorham (4580 ft. in about 6.5 mi.) is probably the closest approach in New England, except at Katahdin, of a major river to a high mountain. The views of nearby mountains south and southwest, and into the Great Gulf, are very fine. The distant view is cut off in these directions only, though Chocorua can be seen.

Pine Mtn. (2410 ft.) is a small peak lying to the northeast, between Mt. Madison and the great bend of the Androscoggin River at Gorham. Though low compared to its lofty neighbors, it is a rugged mountain with a fine cliff on the southeast side, and offers magnificent, easily attained views of the mountains and of the river valleys to the north and east.

The Great Gulf is the largest cirque in the White Mtns., lying between Mt. Washington and the Northern Peaks and drained by the West Branch of the Peabody River. The headwall, bounded on the south by the slopes of Mt. Washington and on the west by the summit ridge of Mt. Clay, rises from 1100 to 1600 ft. above a bowl-shaped valley that is enclosed by steep walls that extend east for about 3.5 mi. The gulf then continues as a more open valley about 1.5 mi. farther east. The Great Gulf and its tributary gulfs, Madison Gulf and Jefferson Ravine, were hollowed out by the action of glaciers, mainly before the last ice age. The views from its walls and from points on its floor are among the best in New England, and steep slopes and abundant water result in a great number of cascades. The first recorded observation of the Great Gulf was by Darby Field in 1642, and the name probably had its origin in 1823 in a casual statement of Ethan Allen Crawford, who, having lost his way in cloudy weather, came to "the edge of a great gulf." The region was visited in 1829 by J. W. Robbins, a botanist, but was little known until Benjamin F. Osgood blazed the first trail, from the Osgood Trail to the headwall, in 1881.

Caution. The peaks and higher ridges of this range are nearly as exposed to the elements as Mt. Washington, and should be treated with the same degree of respect and caution. Severe wintry storms can occur at any time of the year. Many lives have been lost in this area from failure to observe the basic principles of safety. In addition, all of the major peaks are strenuous climbs by even the easiest routes. The distances quoted may seem short to a novice, but there is only one route to a major peak, the Caps Ridge Trail to Mt. Jefferson, that involves less than 3000 ft. of climbing; and that route is not at all easy, being rather short and steep, with numerous scrambles on ledges which a person unfamiliar with mountain trails might find daunting. Most routes to the summits involve 4000 to 4500 ft. of climbing, roughly equal to the ascent of Mt. Washington, due to the lower elevations of the major trailheads. The substantial amount of effort required to attain these goals, together with the threat of sudden and violent storms, should make the need to avoid overextending oneself quite apparent.

The upper part of the mass of the Northern Peaks is covered with rock fragments. Above 5000 ft. there are no trees and little scrub. Ridges and valleys radiate from this high region on the north and west sides, the most important being, from north to south: on Mt. Madison, the Osgood Ridge, Howker Ridge, Bumpus Basin, Gordon Ridge, and the ravine of Snyder Brook, which is shared with Mt. Adams; on Mt. Adams, Durand Ridge, King Ravine, Nowell Ridge, Cascade Ravine, the Israel Ridge, and Castle Ravine, which is shared with Mt. Jefferson; on Mt. Jefferson, the Castellated Ridge and the Ridge of the Caps; and an unnamed but very salient ridge extending westerly from Mt. Clay. Bumpus Basin, King Ravine, and Castle Ravine are glacial cirques. Two small cirques, Jefferson Ravine and Madison Gulf, branch off from the Great Gulf, and the two Jefferson knees are prominent ridges, abruptly truncated by the Great Gulf.

Edmands Col (4930 ft.), between Mt. Adams and Mt. Jefferson, is named after pioneer trailmaker J. Rayner Edmands. Sphinx Col (4970 ft.) lies between Mt. Jefferson and Mt. Clay. The col between Mt. Adams and Mt. Madison has an elevation of 4890 ft. Thus there is a range of only 80 ft. between the lowest and highest of the three major cols on this ridge. In the unnamed Adams–Madison col lies Star Lake, a small, shallow body of water among jagged rocks with impressive views, particularly up to Mt. Madison and Mt. Quincy Adams.

The first trail on the Northern Peaks was probably cut about 1850; in 1860 or 1861 a partial trail was made over the peaks to Mt. Washington, of which some sections still exist. Lowe's Path was cut in 1875–76, the branch path through King Ravine was made in 1876, and the Osgood Path was opened in 1878. Many trails were constructed between 1878 and the beginning of lumbering in about 1902, but this network was greatly damaged by lumbering, and some trails were obliterated. The more important ones have since been restored.

HUTS, SHELTERS, AND CAMPING

HUTS

Madison Hut (AMC)

In 1888, at Madison Spring (4800 ft.), a little north of the Adams–Madison col, the AMC built a stone hut that was later demolished. The present hut, rebuilt and improved after a fire in 1940, accommodates fifty guests on a coed basis and is open to the public from mid-June to mid-

September. It is 6.0 mi. from the summit of Mt. Washington via the Gulfside Trail, and 6.8 mi. from Lakes of the Clouds Hut via the Gulfside Trail, Westside Trail, and Crawford Path. In bad weather the best approach (or exit) is via the Valley Way, which is sheltered to within a short distance of the hut. Nearby points of interest include the Parapet, a crag overlooking Madison Gulf, and Star Lake.

For current information contact Reservation Secretary, Pinkham Notch Camp, Box 298, Gorham, NH 03581 (603-466-2727).

CAMPING

Great Gulf Wilderness

Overnight use will be limited to 75 individuals per night, with a maximum stay of four nights, between 15 June and 15 September. Permits are free and may be reserved no more than thirty days in advance through the Androscoggin District Ranger, Gorham, NH 03581 (603-466-2713). They may be picked up at the WMNF Ranger Station on US 2 near Gorham or at Dolly Copp Campground. Camping is prohibited above treeline, within 200 ft. of any trail except at designated sites, and within one-quarter mile of Spaulding Lake. No campsite may be used by more than ten persons at any one time. All former shelters have been removed.

Restricted Use Areas

The WMNF has established a number of Restricted Use Areas (RUA's) where camping and wood or charcoal fires are prohibited from 1 May to 1 November. The specific areas are under continual review, and areas are added to or subtracted from the list in order to provide the greatest amount of protection to areas subject to damage by excessive camping, while imposing the lowest level of restrictions possible. A general list of RUA's follows, but one should obtain a map of current RUA's from the WMNF.

(1) No camping is permitted above treeline (where trees are less than 8 ft. tall). The point where the restricted area begins is marked on most trails with small signs, but the absence of such signs should not be construed as proof of the legality of a site.

(2) No camping is permitted within one-quarter mile of most facilities such as huts, cabins, shelters, or tentsites, except at the facility itself.

(3) No camping is permitted within 200 ft. of certain trails. In 1986, designated trails included the Valley Way.

Established Trailside Campsites

The Log Cabin (RMC), built about 1890, and totally rebuilt in 1985, is located at a spring at 3300 ft. altitude, beside Lowe's Path at the junction with the Cabin–Cascades Trail. The cabin is partially enclosed, and is open to the public at a charge of $2 per person per night. There is room for about ten. It has no stove, and no wood fires are permitted in the area. Guests are requested to leave the cabin clean and carry out all trash.

The Perch (RMC) is an open log shelter located at about 4300 ft. on the Perch Path between the Randolph Path and Israel Ridge Path, but much closer to the former. It is open to the public and accommodates eight. There are also four tent platforms at the site; the caretaker at Gray Knob often visits to collect the overnight fee—$2 for use of the shelter, $1 for tent platforms.

Crag Camp (RMC) is situated at the edge of King Ravine near the Spur Trail at about 4200 ft. It is open to the public at a charge of $2.50. It is an enclosed cabin, supplied with cooking utensils and a gas stove in the summer, with room for about fourteen. During July and August it is maintained by a caretaker. Wood fires are not allowed in the area. Hikers are required to limit groups to ten and stays to two nights. All trash must be carried out.

Gray Knob (Town of Randolph and RMC) is an enclosed, winterized cabin on Gray Knob Trail at its junction with Hincks Trail, near Lowe's Path, at about 4400 ft. It is open to the public at a charge of $2.50 per person per night. Gray Knob has room for about twelve and is supplied with a gas stove and cooking utensils in the summer. There is a caretaker year round. Rules are the same as for Crag Camp.

These RMC shelters are all Restricted Use Areas, and no camping is allowed within one-quarter mile except at the shelters and tent platforms. Fees should be mailed to the Randolph Mountain Club, Randolph, NH 03570, if not collected by the caretakers. Any infraction of rules or acts of vandalism should be reported to the above address.

Osgood Campsite (WMNF) is located in the Great Gulf Wilderness, near the junction of the Osgood Trail and Osgood Cutoff (which is on the Appalachian Trail). Permits are not required.

Valley Way Campsite (WMNF) is located off the Valley Way above its junction with the Watson Path, 3.1 mi. from US 2 at the Appalachia parking area.

ACCESS ROADS AND PARKING

Important access roads in this section are the Pinkham B Rd. (also called Dolly Copp Rd.), Jefferson Notch Rd., and the Base Rd. Pinkham B Rd. runs from US 2 at the west foot of the great hill between Gorham and Randolph, over the notch between Pine Mtn. and Mt. Madison, to NH 16 about 4.5 mi. south of Gorham. Dolly Copp Campground is on the road near NH 16. Jefferson Notch Rd. runs from the Valley Rd. in Jefferson (which in turn runs between US

2 and NH 115), through the notch between Mt. Jefferson and the Dartmouth Range, to the Base Rd., which runs from US 302 at Bretton Woods to the Base Station of the Cog Railway at Marshfield. Directly across the the Base Rd. is the Mt. Clinton Rd., which runs south to the Crawford House site. Jefferson Notch Rd., a good gravel road, is open in summer and early fall, but since it reaches the highest point of any public through road in NH (3008 ft. at Jefferson Notch), snow and mud disappear late in the spring and ice returns early. Drive with care, since it is winding and narrow in places, and watch out for logging trucks. The southern half is in better condition than the north, which is sound but very rough. The high point in the notch is about 5.5 mi. from the Valley Rd. on the north, and 3.4 mi. from the Base Rd. on the south.

The most important parking areas are at Pinkham Notch Camp; at a newly constructed area on NH 16 1.5 mi. south of Dolly Copp Campground; at Randolph East, on Pinkham B (Dolly Copp) Rd. near its junction with US 2; at Appalachia, on US 2 about 1 mi. west of Pinkham B Rd.; at Lowe's Store on US 2 (nominal fee charged); and at Bowman, on US 2 about 1 mi. west of Lowe's Store. (Randolph East, Appalachia, and Bowman owe their names and locations to their former status as stations on the railroad line.) The highest points from which to climb the Northern Peaks, not including the summit of Mt. Washington, are Jefferson Notch Rd. at the Caps Ridge Trail (3008 ft.), the parking lot on the Base Rd., 1.1 mi. east of the Jefferson Notch Rd. for the Jewell Trail (2500 ft.); and the Pinkham B Rd., also called Dolly Copp Rd., at the Pine Link (1650 ft.).

LIST OF TRAILS   MAP

Trails on the Main Ridge

Trails on Mount Jefferson

Trail on Mount Clay

Trails on Pine Mountain

Pleasure Paths on the Lower North Slopes of the Range

THE TRAILS

Gulfside Trail (WMNF)

This trail leads from Madison Hut to the summit of Mt. Washington. It threads the principal cols, avoiding the summits of the Northern Peaks, but offers extensive and ever-changing views. Its altitudes range from about 4800 ft. close to the hut, to 6288 ft. on the summit of Mt. Washington. The name Gulfside was given by J. Rayner Edmands who, starting in 1892, located and made the greater part of the trail, sometimes following trails that had existed before. All but about 0.8 mi. of the trail was once a graded path, and parts were paved with carefully placed stones—a work cut short by Edmands's death in 1910. The whole length is part of the Appalachian Trail, except for a very short segment at the south end.

The trail is well marked with large cairns, each topped with a yellow-painted stone, and, though care must be used, it can often be followed even in dense fog. The trail is continuously exposed to the weather, and dangerously high winds and low temperatures may occur with little warning at any season of the year. If such storms threaten serious trouble on the Gulfside Trail, do not attempt to ascend the cone of Mt. Washington, where conditions are usually far worse. If you are not close to the huts at Madison Spring or at Lakes of the Clouds, descend into one of the ravines on a trail if possible, or without trail if necessary. A night of discomfort in the woods is better than exposure on the heights, which may prove fatal. Slopes on the Great Gulf (southeast) side are more sheltered, but generally steeper and farther from highways. It is particularly important not to head toward Edmands Col in deteriorating conditions; there is no easy trail out in bad weather, and the emergency refuge was removed in 1982. There is no substitute for studying the map carefully before setting out on the ridge.

Part I. Madison Hut–Edmands Col

The trail begins about 30 yd. from Madison Hut, leads southwest through a patch of scrub, then aims to the right (north) of Mt. Quincy Adams and ascends a steep, open slope. At the top of this slope, on the high plateau between King Ravine and Mt. Quincy Adams, it is joined from the right by the Air Line, which has just been joined by the King Ravine Trail. Here there are striking views back to Mt. Madison, and into King Ravine at the "Gateway" a short distance down on the right. The Gulfside and Air Line coincide for a few yards, then the Air Line branches left toward the summit of Mt. Adams. Much of the Gulfside Trail for about the next 0.5 mi. is paved with carefully placed stones. It rises gently southwest, curving a little more south, then steepens, and at 0.9 mi. from the hut reaches a grassy lawn in the saddle (5520 ft.) between Mt. Adams and Mt. Sam Adams.

Here, where several trails intersect at a spot called Thunderstorm Junction, there is a massive cairn about 10 ft. high. Entering the junction right is the Great Gully Trail, coming up across the slope from the southwest corner of King Ravine. Here also, the Gulfside is crossed by Lowe's Path, ascending from Lowe's Store on US 2 to the summit of Mt. Adams. A few yards down Lowe's Path, the Spur Trail branches right for Crag Camp. The summit of Mt. Adams is about 0.3 mi. from the junction (left), via Lowe's Path; a round trip to the summit requires about 25 min.

A cairned trail, known as the "White Trail," runs from Thunderstorm Junction over the summit of Mt. Sam Adams and along its south ridge to the Gulfside at the point where the Israel Ridge Path comes in from Bowman. This is not an official trail, and should not be used in bad weather, since it is more exposed to the wind.

Continuing southwest from Thunderstorm Junction and beginning to descend, the Gulfside Trail passes a junction on the left with the Israel Ridge Path, which ascends a short distance to Lowe's Path and thence to Mt. Adams. For about 0.5 mi. the Gulfside Trail and Israel Ridge Path coincide, passing Peabody Spring (unreliable) just to the right in a small, grassy flat, and more reliable water is just beyond at the base of a conspicuous boulder just to the left of the path. Soon the trail climbs easily across a ridge, then the Israel Ridge Path diverges right at 1.5 mi. from Madison Hut. Near this junction in wet weather there is a small pool called Storm Lake. The Gulfside bears a bit left toward the edge of Jefferson Ravine, and, always leading toward Mt. Jefferson, descends southwest along the narrow ridge that divides Jefferson Ravine from Castle Ravine, near the edge of the cliffs, from which there are fine views into the gulf. This part of the Gulfside was never graded. The trail reaches Edmands Col at 2.2 mi. from the hut, with 3.5 mi. to go to Mt. Washington.

At this col (4930 ft.) is a bronze tablet in memory of J. Rayner Edmands, who made most of the graded paths on the Northern Peaks. The emergency shelter once located here has been dismantled. From Edmands Col the Randolph Path leads north into the Randolph valley. The Edmands Col Cutoff leads south about 0.5 mi. to the Six Husbands Trail, affording the quickest route to shelter in bad weather. Branching from the Randolph Path about 0.1 mi. north of the col are the Cornice, leading west to the Castle Trail, and the Castle Ravine Trail. Gulfside Spring (reliable) is 30 yd. south of the col, and Spaulding Spring (reliable) is about 0.2 mi. north near the Castle Ravine Trail.

Part II. Edmands Col–Sphinx Col

South of Edmands Col the Gulfside Trail ascends steeply southwest over rough rocks, with Jefferson Ravine on the left. It passes flat-topped Dingmaul Rock, from which there is a good view down the ravine, with Mt. Adams on the left. A few yards beyond, the Mount Jefferson Loop branches right, and leads 0.3 mi. to the summit of Mt. Jefferson (5715 ft.). The loop is about the same distance, but involves about 300 ft. of extra climbing and about 10 min. more hiking time than the parallel section of the Gulfside. The views from the summit are excellent, and the extra effort relatively minor.

The path now turns southeast and rises less steeply. It crosses the Six Husbands Trail and soon reaches its greatest height on Mt. Jefferson, 5400 ft. Curving southwest and descending a little, it crosses Monticello Lawn, a comparatively smooth, grassy plateau. Here the Mount Jefferson Loop rejoins the Gulfside in about 0.3 mi. from the summit. A short distance southwest of the lawn the Cornice enters right from the Caps Ridge Trail. The Gulfside continues to descend south and southwest. From one point there is a view of the Sphinx down the slope to the left. A few yards north of the low point in Sphinx Col, the Sphinx Trail branches left (east) into the Great Gulf, through a grassy passage between ledges.

Part III. Sphinx Col–Mount Washington

From Sphinx Col the path leads toward Mt. Washington, and soon the Mount Clay Loop (a rough trail) diverges left to climb over the summits of Mt. Clay, with impressive views into the Great Gulf. It adds about 300 ft. of climbing and 10 min.; the distance is about the same. The Gulfside Trail is easier and passes close to water, but misses the most impressive views. It bears right from the junction with the Mount Clay Loop, runs south and rises gradually, slabbing the west side of Mt. Clay. In about 0.3 mi. a loop leads to water a few steps down to the right. The side path continues about 30 yd. farther to Greenough Spring (more reliable), then rejoins the Gulfside farther up. The Gulfside continues its slabbing ascent, and the Jewell Trail enters from the right, ascending from the Base Rd. From this junction the ridge crest of Mt. Clay is a short scramble up the rocks without trail. The Gulfside swings southeast and descends slightly to the Clay–Washington col (5380 ft.), where the Mount Clay Loop rejoins it from the left. A little to the east is the edge of the Great Gulf, with fine views, especially of the east cliffs of Mt. Clay.

The path continues southeast, rising gradually on Mt. Washington. About 0.1 mi. above the col, the Westside Trail branches right, crosses the Cog Railway, and leads to the Crawford Path and Lakes of the Clouds Hut. The Gulfside continues southeast between the Cog Railway on the right and the edge of the gulf on the left. If the path is lost, follow the railway to the summit. At the extreme south corner of the gulf, the Great Gulf Trail joins the Gulfside from the left, 5.4 mi. from Madison Hut. The Gulfside turns sharp right, crosses the railway, and continues west. It passes a junction with the Trinity Heights Connector, a link in the Appalachian Trail, which branches left and climbs for 0.2 mi. to the true summit of Mt. Washington. In a short distance past this junction the Gulfside joins the Crawford Path just below (north) of the old corral, and the two trails turn left and coincide to the summit. (Descending from the summit, the Gulfside Trail turns sharp right from the Crawford Path just below the old corral.)

Gulfside Trail (map 6:F9)
Distances from Madison Hut

   to Air Line: 0.3 mi., 20 min.

   to Thunderstorm Junction: 0.9 mi., 50 min.

   to Israel Ridge Path, north junction: 1.0 mi., 55 min.

   to Israel Ridge Path, south junction: 1.5 mi., 1 hr. 5 min.

to Edmands Col: 2.2 mi., 1 hr. 30 min.

to north end, Mount Jefferson Loop: 2.4 mi., 1 hr. 40 min.

to Six Husbands Trail: 2.6 mi., 1 hr. 50 min

to south end, Mount Jefferson Loop: 3.0 mi., 2 hr. 5 min.

to Cornice: 3.1 mi., 2 hr. 10 min.

to Sphinx Trail: 3.7 mi., 2 hr. 25 min.

to north end, Mount Clay Loop: 3.8 mi., 2 hr. 30 min.

to Jewell Trail: 4.5 mi., 3 hr.

to south end, Mount Clay Loop: 4.8 mi., 3 hr. 15 min.

to Westside Trail: 5.0 mi., 3 hr. 25 min.

to Great Gulf Trail: 5.4 mi., 3 hr. 50 min.

to Trinity Heights Connector: 5.7 mi., 4 hr. 5 min.

to Crawford Path: 5.7 mi. (9.2 km.), 4 hr. 5 min.

to Mt. Washington summit (via Crawford Path): 6.0 mi. (9.7 km.), 4 hr. 20 min.

to Lakes of the Clouds Hut (via Westside Trail and Crawford Path): 6.8 mi., 4 hr. 25 min.

Mount Jefferson Loop (AMC)

This trail diverges right (west) from the Gulfside Trail about 0.2 mi. south of Edmands Col, and climbs steeply. Just below the summit, the Six Husbands Trail enters on the left, then the Castle Trail enters on the right, and soon the junction with Caps Ridge Trail is reached at the base of the summit crag. The high point is a few yards right (west) on the Caps Ridge Trail. The Mount Jefferson Loop then descends to rejoin the Gulfside Trail on Monticello Lawn.

Mount Jefferson Loop (map 6:F9)
Distances (est.) from north junction with Gulfside Trail

to summit of Mt. Jefferson: 0.3 mi., 25 min.

to south junction with Gulfside Trail: 0.6 mi. (1.0 km.), 35 min.

Mount Clay Loop (AMC)

This trail diverges left (east) from the Gulfside Trail about 0.1 mi. south of Sphinx Col, and ascends a steep, rough slope to the ragged ridge crest. The views into the Great Gulf from the brink of the east cliffs are very fine. After crossing the summit, and passing over several slightly lower knobs, the trail descends easily to the flat col between Mt. Clay and Mt. Washington, where it rejoins the Gulfside Trail.

Mount Clay Loop (map 6:F9)
Distances (est.) from north junction with Gulfside Trail
to summit of Mt. Clay: 0.5 mi., 35 min.
to north junction with Gulfside Trail: 1.0 mi. (1.6 km.),
   55 min.

Edmands Col Cutoff (RMC)

This important link, connecting the Gulfside Trail and Randolph Path at Edmands Col with the Six Husbands Trail, makes a quick descent possible from Edmands Col into the Great Gulf, the fastest way to shelter in bad weather. It is on the lee side of Mt. Jefferson, and scrub provides plentiful shelter. It is almost entirely within the Great Gulf Wilderness.

Leaving Edmands Col, the trail shortly passes a fine spring, then rises slightly and begins a rough scramble of about 0.5 mi. over rocks and through scrub, marked by cairns. The trail is mostly level, with only a few rises and falls over gullies, and good views to the south and the Great Gulf. It ends at the Six Husbands Trail about 0.5 mi. below that trail's junction with the Gulfside Trail.

Edmands Col Cutoff (map 6:F9)
Distance from Edmands Col
to Six Husbands Trail: 0.5 mi. (0.8 km.), 20 min.

Cornice (RMC)

This trail leads west from the Randolph Path in Edmands Col, 0.1 mi. north of the Gulfside Trail, crosses the Castle Trail and the Caps Ridge Trail, and returns to the Gulfside at Monticello Lawn. From Edmands Col to the Caps Ridge Trail it is extremely rough, with a large amount of tedious and strenuous rock hopping. It is very hard on knees and ankles. It may take considerably more time than the estimates below. As a route from Edmands Col to the Caps Ridge Trail, it saves a little climbing compared to the route over the summit of Jefferson, but is much longer, requires more exertion, and is just as exposed to the weather. This makes its value as a bad weather route very questionable. It does offer some interesting views, and it does provide a good shortcut from the Caps Ridge Trail to the Gulfside south of Mt. Jefferson.

The Cornice leaves the Randolph Path and climbs moderately over large rocks, slabbing around the north and west sides of Mt. Jefferson. It crosses the Castle Trail above the Upper Castle and enters the Caps Ridge Trail above the Upper Cap. It then turns left (east) up the Caps Ridge Trail about 20 yd., diverges right (south), and climbs gradually with improved footing to the Gulfside Trail on Monticello Lawn.

Cornice (map 6:F9)
Distances (est.) from Randolph Path

to Castle Trail: 0.5 mi., 30 min.

to Caps Ridge Trail: 1.5 mi., 1 hr. 5 min.

to Gulfside Trail junction: 2.0 mi. (3.2 km.), 1 hr. 30 min

Randolph Path (RMC)

This graded path extends southwest, from the Pinkham B (Dolly Copp) Rd. near Randolph Village, over the slopes of Mt. Madison and Mt. Adams, to the Gulfside Trail in Edmands Col between Mt. Adams and Mt. Jefferson. In addition to providing a route from Randolph to Edmands Col, it crosses numerous other trails along the way, and thus constitutes an important linking trail between them. It was made by J. Rayner Edmands from 1893 to 1899; parts of it were reconstructed in 1978 as a memorial to Christopher Goetze, active RMC member and former editor of *Appalachia*, a journal published by the AMC.

The path begins at the parking space known as Randolph East, 0.2 mi. south of US 2 on the Pinkham B Rd. and 0.3 mi. west of the Boston and Maine Railroad crossing. It coincides with the Howker Ridge Trail for approximately 80 yd. west, turns south, crosses the railroad, and 30 yd. beyond diverges right (west); the Howker Ridge Trail continues left (southeast). The Randolph Path keeps south of the power line for about 0.3 mi., where it enters the old location. It then turns southwest, crosses the Sylvan Way in about 0.5 mi., and in about another 0.8 mi. reaches Snyder Brook, where the Inlook Trail and Brookside diverge left. The Brookside and the Randolph Path cross the brook at the same place, then the Brookside diverges right and leads down to the Valley Way. A few yards beyond the brook it is crossed by the Valley Way, coming up from Appalachia. The Randolph Path soon joins the Air Line, coincides with it for 20 yd., then branches right. At 2.0 mi. the Short Line, a shortcut (1.3 mi.) from Appalachia, comes in on the right.

The Short Line coincides with the Randolph Path for 0.4 mi., then branches left for King Ravine. The Randolph Path descends slightly and crosses Cold Brook on Sanders Bridge, where the Cliffway diverges right. At 3.0 mi. it crosses the King Ravine Trail at its junction with the Amphibrach, a junction called the "Pentodoi." The Randolph Path crosses Spur Brook and in about 100 yd. the Spur

Trail leads left and the Randolph Path climbs around the nose of the ridge. Soon two short side paths descend right to the RMC Log Cabin. At about 3.9 mi. from Pinkham B Rd., Lowe's Path is crossed.

The grade on the Randolph Path now moderates. Slabbing the steep west side of Nowell Ridge for about 0.8 mi., the path passes Franconia Spring, where there is a view of Mt. Lafayette. At about 4.9 mi. the Perch Path crosses, leading right (southwest) to The Perch and Israel Ridge Path and left (east) to the Gray Knob Trail. There is water on the Perch Path a few yards west of the Randolph Path.

Above this junction the Randolph Path rises due south through scrub. Water is usually found at a spring left. In about 0.5 mi. the scrub ends, and the Gray Knob Trail from Crag Camp and Gray Knob enters left. In a short distance the Israel Ridge Path enters right (west), ascending from Bowman. For a few yards the paths coincide, then the Israel Ridge Path branches left for Mt. Adams. From this point the Randolph Path is nearly level to its end at Edmands Col, curving around the head of Castle Ravine. The path is above treeline, much exposed to the weather, and visible for a long distance ahead. Near the col, right, is Spaulding Spring (reliable water). The Castle Ravine Trail comes in from the right (northwest) and the Cornice leads west to Castle Trail. In about 0.1 mi. more the Randolph Path joins the Gulfside Trail in Edmands Col.

Randolph Path (map 6:E9-F9)
Distances (est.) from Randolph East (parking area)

to Short Line: 2.0 mi., 1 hr. 30 min.
to King Ravine Trail: 3.0 mi., 2 hr. 20 min.
to Lowe's Path: 3.9 mi., 3 hr. 5 min.
to Perch Path: 4.9 mi., 4 hr.
to Israel Ridge Path: 5.4 mi., 4 hr. 30 min.

to Edmands Col and Gulfside Trail: 6.0 mi. (9.7 km.), 4 hr. 50 min.

to Mt. Washington summit (via Gulfside Trail and Crawford Path): 9.8 mi., 7 hr. 45 min.

The Link (RMC)

This path "links" the Appalachia parking area and the trails to Mt. Madison with the trails ascending Mt. Adams and Mt. Jefferson. It connects with the Amphibrach, Cliffway, Lowe's Path, and Israel Ridge Path, and the Castle Ravine, Emerald, Castle, and Caps Ridge trails. The section between the Caps Ridge and Castle trails, although rough, makes possible a circuit of the Caps and the Castles from Jefferson Notch Rd. It is graded as far as Cascade Brook.

The Link, with the Amphibrach, diverges right from the Air Line about 40 yd. south of the junction of the Air Line and Valley Way and 100 yd. south of Appalachia. It runs west about 0.6 mi. to where the Beechwood Way diverges left, and just east of Cold Brook, Sylvan Way enters left. Cold Brook is crossed on the Memorial Bridge, where there is a fine view of Cold Brook Fall, which is reached by Sylvan Way. West of the brook, after 50 yd., the Link diverges right from the Amphibrach.

The Link then follows old logging roads southwest for about 1.5 mi. It enters the WMNF 1.2 mi. from Appalachia, and at 2.0 mi. the Cliffway leads east to viewpoints on Nowell Ridge. At about 2.1 mi. the Link turns left and runs south to Lowe's Path, which it crosses at about 2.8 mi. Continuing south about 0.4 mi., it crosses the north branch of the Mystic, and, turning a little to the right, crosses the main Mystic Stream at 3.3 mi. It soon curves left, rounds the western buttress of Nowell Ridge, and running southeast nearly level, enters Cascade Ravine on the mountainside high above the stream. It crosses a slide and keeps the same general direction at nearly the same altitude until it approaches Cascade Brook.

The Israel Ridge Path comes up right from Bowman and, just above its junction with the Cabin–Cascades Trail, unites with the Link at 4.0 mi. from Appalachia. The trails coincide for 30 yd., then the Israel Ridge Path branches left for Gulfside Trail and Mt. Adams, and the Link crosses Cascade Brook, at 4.1 mi. On the stream, a little below and a little above the Link, are the first and second cascades. The Link continues southeast for 30 yd., then crosses a slide, rounds the tip of Israel Ridge, and turns south and southeast into Castle Ravine, uniting at 5.1 mi. with the Castle Ravine Trail, with which it coincides for about 0.3 mi. The two trails pass Emerald Trail and cross Castle Brook. Then, at 5.4 mi., the Link turns right and ascends west, slabbing the southwest wall of Castle Ravine. In about 0.6 mi. it crosses the Castle Trail below the first Castle at about 4050 ft. It then descends slightly, crosses three small brooks and continues southwest over sections of treacherous roots and hollows for 2.0 mi., slabbing a rough slope, then ascends somewhat to the Caps Ridge Trail, which it enters 1.0 mi. above the Jefferson Notch Rd., just above a ledge with potholes and a fine view up to Jefferson.

The Link (map 6:E9-F8)
Distances (est.) from Appalachia parking area
    to Cold Brook Fall: 0.8 mi., 25 min.
    to Cliffway: 2.0 mi., 1 hr. 25 min.
    to Lowe's Path: 2.8 mi., 2 hr.
    to Cascade Brook: 4.1 mi., 2 hr. 50 min.
    to Castle Ravine Trail, lower junction: 5.1 mi., 3 hr. 25 min.
    to Emerald Trail: 5.3 mi., 3 hr. 40 min.
    to Castle Trail: 5.9 mi., 4 hr. 20 min.
    to Caps Ridge Trail: 7.9 mi. (12.7 km.), 5 hr. 30 min.

Great Gulf Trail (WMNF)

This trail runs from the new parking area on NH 16 (1.5 mi. south of Dolly Copp Campground), follows the West Branch of the Peabody River through the Great Gulf, climbs up the headwall, and ends at a junction with the Gulfside Trail 0.6 mi. below the summit of Mt. Washington. Ascent on the headwall is steep and rough. Except for approximately the first mile it is in the Great Gulf Wilderness.

Leaving the new parking lot, the trail descends slightly to cross the Peabody River on a bridge, then ascends to a junction at 0.1 mi. with the former route from Dolly Copp Campground—now called the Great Gulf Link Trail. The Great Gulf Trail turns left and follows a logging road south on the west bank of the Peabody River until the West Branch forks from the main river, then continues northwest of the West Branch. At 1.7 mi. the Osgood Trail diverges right; Osgood Campsite is about 0.8 mi. from here via the Osgood Trail. The Great Gulf Trail soon approaches the West Branch and runs for about 0.3 mi. close to the north bank. Then, diverging from the stream, it ascends to the Bluff, where there is a good view of the gulf and the mountains around it. The trail follows the edge of the Bluff, and descends sharply left to Parapet Brook, where the Madison Gulf Trail enters right. The trails cross Parapet Brook on a bridge, continue over the crest of the little ridge that separates Parapet Brook from the West Branch, and descend to cross the West Branch on a suspension bridge. After ascending the steep bank, the Madison Gulf Trail branches left, while the Great Gulf Trail branches right, up the south bank of the river.

At 3.8 mi. the Great Gulf Trail crosses Chandler Brook, and on the far bank the Chandler Brook Trail diverges left and ascends to the Mt. Washington Auto Rd. The Great Gulf Trail continues close to the river for more than 0.5

mi., passing in sight of the mouth of the stream that issues from Jefferson Ravine on the north, to join the Six Husbands (right) and Wamsutta (left) trails at 4.5 mi. The Great Gulf Trail continues on the southeast bank, then in the bed of the stream, to the foot of a waterfall. Scrambling up to the left of this fall, it crosses a large branch brook and passes left of a beautiful cascade on the main stream. The trail soon crosses to the northwest bank, and in a short distance crosses the brook that descends from the Clay–Jefferson col. At this point the Sphinx Trail, leading to the Gulfside Trail, diverges right. The Great Gulf Trail soon crosses again to the southeast bank of the West Branch, passing waterfalls, including Weetamoo, the finest in the gulf. There are remarkable views down the gulf to Mt. Adams and Mt. Madison. The trail crosses an eastern tributary and, after a slight ascent, reaches Spaulding Lake (4250 ft.) at 6.4 mi. from NH 16 and about 1.4 mi. by trail from the summit of Mt. Washington.

The Great Gulf Trail continues on the east side of the lake, and a little beyond begins to ascend the steep headwall. The trail runs south and southeast, rising 1600 ft. in about 0.5 mi., over fragments of stone, many of which are loose. The way may be poorly marked, because snow slides may sweep away cairns, but paint blazes probably will be visible on the rocks. The trail curves a little left until within a few yards of the top of the headwall, then, bearing slightly right, emerges from the gulf and ends at the Gulfside Trail near the Cog Railway. It is 0.6 mi. to the summit of Mt. Washington by the Gulfside Trail and Crawford Path.

Great Gulf Trail (map 6:F10-F9)
Distances (est.) from new parking area on NH 16
    to Osgood Trail: 1.7 mi., 1 hr. 10 min.
    to Madison Gulf Trail: 2.8 mi., 1 hr. 55 min.

to Six Husbands and Wamsutta trails: 4.5 mi., 3 hr. 10 min.

to Sphinx Trail: 5.5 mi., 3 hr. 55 min.

to Spaulding Lake: 6.4 mi., 4 hr. 40 min.

to Gulfside Trail junction: 7.2 mi., 6 hr.

to Mt. Washington summit (via Gulfside Trail and Crawford Path): 7.8 mi. (12.6 km.), 6 hr. 25 min.

Great Gulf Link Trail (WMNF)

This trail was formerly a segment of the Great Gulf Trail. It leaves Dolly Copp Campground at the south end of the main camp road, just before reaching the site of the old bridge crossing. The trail follows a logging road south, on the west bank of the Peabody River, to its junction with the Great Gulf Trail, which comes in from the new parking lot on NH 16.

Great Gulf Link Trail (map 6:F10)
Distance (est.) from Dolly Copp Campground

to Great Gulf Trail: 0.7 mi., 20 min.

Madison Gulf Trail (AMC)

Caution. The section of this trail on the headwall of Madison Gulf is one of the most difficult in the White Mtns., going over several ledge outcrops, bouldery areas, and a chimney with loose rock. The steep slabs may be slippery when wet, and several ledges require scrambling and the use of handholds—hikers with a short reach may have a particular problem. Stream crossings may be very difficult in wet weather. The trail is not recommended for the descent, in wet weather, or for hikers with heavy packs. Allow extra time, and do not start up the headwall late in the day. The ascent of the headwall may require several hours more than the estimated time; parties frequently fail to reach the hut before dark on account of slowness on the headwall.

This trail begins on the Mt. Washington Auto Rd. a little

more than 2 mi. from the Glen House site, opposite the
Old Jackson Road, and descends gently to the West
Branch, where it meets the Great Gulf Trail. It then ascends along Parapet Brook to the Parapet, a point 0.3 mi.
from Madison Hut. With the Old Jackson Road, it provides the shortest—but far from the easiest—route from
Pinkham Notch Camp to Madison Hut. It is well marked,
well protected from storms, and has plenty of water. For
most people, particularly those with heavy packs, the
routes via the Osgood Trail (in good weather) or the Buttress Trail (which is almost as well sheltered), though
longer, are a better choice. From the Auto Rd. to Osgood
Cutoff the Madison Gulf Trail is part of the Appalachian
Trail, and therefore blazed in white; the rest is blazed in
blue. It is almost entirely within the Great Gulf Wilderness.

The trail leaves the Auto Rd. above the 2-mi. mark,
opposite the Old Jackson Road junction. In a short distance, a side path branches right in a little pass west of
Lowe's Bald Spot and climbs to this summit, an excellent
viewpoint, in 0.1 mi. The Madison Gulf Trail bears left and.
ascends about 75 ft. over a ledge with a limited view, descends rapidly for a short distance, then gently, crossing
several water courses. The trail comes within sound of the
West Branch of the Peabody River and continues along on
contour until it meets the Great Gulf Trail on the south
bank at 2.3 mi. The Madison Gulf Trail turns sharp right
and, coinciding with the Great Gulf Trail, descends the
steep bank to the West Branch.

Both trails cross a suspension bridge to the north bank,
pass over the crest of the little ridge that divides Parapet
Brook from the West Branch, and cross a bridge to the
northeast side of Parapet Brook. Here the Madison Gulf
Trail turns left up the stream, as the Great Gulf Trail
diverges right. Soon the Osgood Cutoff continues ahead,
leading in 0.5 mi. to the Osgood Trail for Mt. Madison and

Madison Hut. The Madison Gulf Trail swings left and continues up the stream, soon crosses to the southwest side, and diverges from the brook, to which it later returns, crossing a small branch brook and turning sharp left just before it reaches the main stream. It soon crosses again to the northeast bank, follows that for a little way, then turns right, ascending steeply with good views. The trail next turns left, slabbing the mountainside high above the brook, which it approaches again at the mouth of the branch stream from Osgood Ridge. It ascends rapidly between the two brooks, crosses to the west bank of the main stream, then recrosses, and, climbing more gradually, gains the lower floor of the gulf, crosses again, and soon reaches Sylvan Cascade, a fine fall.

The Madison Gulf Trail then ascends to the upper floor of the gulf, where it crosses four brooks. From the floor it rises gradually to Mossy Slide at the foot of the headwall, then ascends very rapidly by a stream. The trail now turns left, continues near a brook partly hidden among the rocks, then ascends very steeply on the headwall of the gulf. Ultimately it reaches the scrub, emerges on the rocks, and ends at the Parapet Trail. Turn left for the Parapet (0.1 mi.) and Madison Hut (0.3 mi.), and right for the Osgood Trail.

Madison Gulf Trail (map 6:F9)
Distances (est.) from Mt. Washington Auto Rd.
  to Great Gulf Trail: 2.3 mi., 1 hr. 10 min.
  to foot of Madison Gulf headwall: 4.0 mi., 2 hr. 50 min.
  to Parapet Trail: 4.5 mi., 3 hr. 30 min.
  to Madison Hut (via Parapet and Star Lake trails): 4.8 mi. (7.7 km.), 3 hr. 40 min.
Distance (est.) from Pinkham Notch Camp
  to Madison Hut (via Old Jackson Road and Madison Gulf, Parapet, and Star Lake trails): 6.8 mi. (10.9 km.), 5 hr.

Chandler Brook Trail (AMC)

This trail runs from the Great Gulf Trail 3.8 mi. from NH 16 to the Auto Rd. above the Halfway House site. It is almost entirely within the Great Gulf Wilderness. It diverges south from the Great Gulf Trail just west of Chandler Brook, and follows the brook rather closely, crossing three times. Fine waterfalls can be seen from the trail. From the last crossing the course is southeast, rising over a confused mass of stones and keeping west of interesting rock formations. The trail enters the Auto Rd. near a ledge of white quartz slightly less than 0.5 mi. above the 4-mi. post, at the bend above the Halfway House. (Descending, look for this white ledge, which is close to the Auto Rd. The trail is marked by cairns here and is visible from the road.)

Chandler Brook Trail (map 6:F9)
Distance (est.) from Great Gulf Trail
  to Mt. Washington Auto Rd.: 1.0 mi. (1.6 km.), 1 hr. 10 min.

Wamsutta Trail (AMC)

This trail begins on the Great Gulf Trail opposite the Six Husbands Trail, 4.5 mi. from NH 16, and ascends to the Auto Rd. just above the 6-mi. mark, opposite the Alpine Garden Trail, with which it provides routes to Tuckerman Junction, Lakes of the Clouds Hut, and other points to the south. It is almost entirely within the Great Gulf Wilderness. The trail got its name from Wamsutta, the first of six successive husbands of Weetamoo, a queen of the Pocasset Indians, for whom a beautiful waterfall in the Great Gulf is named.

Leaving the Great Gulf Trail, the trail runs southwest to a small stream, then ascends gradually. Soon it climbs the very steep and rough northerly spur of Chandler Ridge. Passing a quartz ledge on the right, the trail continues steeply to a small, open knob on the crest of the spur, which offers a good view. It then ascends gradually through woods, passing a spring on the right. Continuing along the crest, the trail emerges at treeline and climbs to the top end of the winter shortcut of the Auto Rd. After turning right, it ends in a few yards at the Auto Rd.

Wamsutta Trail (map 6:F9)
Distance from Great Gulf Trail
   to Mt. Washington Auto Rd.: 1.7 mi. (2.7 km.), 1 hr. 55 min.

Sphinx Trail (AMC)

This trail runs from the Great Gulf Trail below Spaulding Lake to the Gulfside Trail in Sphinx Col, between Mt. Jefferson and Mt. Clay. The trail is important because it affords the quickest escape route for anyone overtaken by storm on Mt. Clay or on the south part of Mt. Jefferson. It diverges east from the Gulfside Trail 40 yd. north of the Clay–Jefferson col, through a grassy rock-walled corridor, and descends to the Great Gulf Trail. Once below the col, the hiker is protected quickly from the rigor of west and northwest winds. The trail's name is derived from the profile of a rock formation seen from just below the meadow where water is found. It is almost entirely within the Great Gulf Wilderness.

The trail branches northwest from the Great Gulf Trail near the crossing of the brook that descends from between Mt. Clay and Mt. Jefferson, 5.5 mi. from NH 16. It ascends through forest, first gradually, then very steeply. It follows the brook rather closely, using the bed for about 0.3 mi., and passes several small cascades. At 0.6 mi. the trail turns southwest, leaves the brook, and scrambles to a sloping shelf or plateau, partly covered with scrub, through which the trail is cut. It crosses a small meadow, where there is usually water under a rock north of the trail. After ascending slightly farther, the Sphinx Trail joins the Gulfside Trail on a level area a little north of the col.

Sphinx Trail (map 6:F9)
Distance (est.) from Great Gulf Trail
  to Gulfside Trail: 1.0 mi. (1.6 km.), 1 hr. 10 min.

Six Husbands Trail (AMC)

This spectacular trail diverges from the Great Gulf Trail at 4.5 mi. from NH 16, opposite the Wamsutta Trail, and climbs up the north knee of Jefferson, crosses the Gulfside, and ends at the Mount Jefferson Loop a short distance northeast of the summit. It is very steep and is not recommended for descent except to escape bad conditions above treeline. Up to the Gulfside Trail junction, it is entirely within the Great Gulf Wilderness. The name honors the six successive husbands of Weetamoo, queen of the Pocasset Indians.

Leaving the Great Gulf Trail, it descends northwest for a few yards, and crosses the West Branch; in times of high water go upstream to a better crossing. The trail bears right away from the West Branch, then ascends gently north until it comes close to the stream that flows from Jefferson Ravine, which it ascends on its southwest bank. At 0.6 mi. the Buttress Trail branches right and crosses the stream. The Six Husbands Trail continues a little farther beside the brook (last sure water), turns west and leads under two huge boulders. It ascends by ladders made of two-by-fours and passes near a cavern (10 yd. to the left), where snow and ice may be found even in August. The trail soon comes to an overhanging ledge and leads along under its edge for a short distance, ascending again by ladders. It then leads to a crag affording a good view up the gulf, continues to ascend steeply, and keeps close to the crest of the ridge until it comes out on the north knee of Jefferson (view), where the ascent becomes easier. Across the bare stretches the trail is marked by cairns. The Edmands Col Cutoff branches right, leading in 0.5 mi. to Edmands Col. Beyond, the trail becomes steeper, begins to climb the cone of Mt. Jefferson, and leads past a snowbank that often lasts well into July. Marked by cairns, the trail crosses the Gulfside Trail and continues west toward the summit of Mt. Jefferson, joining the Mount Jefferson Loop 100 yd. below the summit.

Six Husbands Trail (map 6:F9)
Distances from Great Gulf Trail junction

to Buttress Trail: 0.6 mi., 25 min.

to Gulfside Trail: 1.9 mi., 2 hr. 5 min.

to Mount Jefferson Loop: 2.2 mi. (3.5 km.), 2 hr. 25 min.

Buttress Trail (AMC)

This trail leads from the Six Husbands Trail to the Star Lake Trail near Madison Hut. It is the most direct route from the upper part of the Great Gulf to Madison Hut, as well as the easiest route from the gulf to the hut. It is well sheltered until it nears the hut, and grades are moderate. In bad weather, or for hikers with heavy packs, or for descending, it is probably the best route from the gulf to the hut, in spite of the greater length. It is almost entirely within the Great Gulf Wilderness.

The trail begins in the ravine between Mt. Adams and Mt. Jefferson, leaving the north side of the Six Husbands Trail at a point 0.6 mi. northwest of the Great Gulf Trail. It immediately crosses the brook (last sure water) flowing out of Jefferson Ravine, bears right (east) in 0.1 mi., and climbs diagonally across a steep slope of large, loose, angular fragments of rock—some are easily dislodged, so care must be taken. The trail continues in the same direction, rising gradually along a steep, wooded slope. At the top of this slope, 0.6 mi. from the start, the trail turns north across a gently sloping upland covered with trees. There is a spring (reliable water) on the left, at about 1.0 mi. As the trail nears treeline, it passes under a large boulder. At about 1.3 mi. the trail reaches the foot of the steep, rock-covered peak of Mt. Adams. Here, a little left of the trail, a small, ledgy summit provides a fine view.

The trail runs nearly level northwest and then north, passing through patches of scrub, across patches of rock fragments, and crossing two brooks. Then, rising slightly through scrub, it passes through a gap between the Parapet and Mt. Quincy Adams and enters Star Lake Trail just southwest of Star Lake, 0.2 mi. from Madison Hut.

Buttress Trail (map 6:F9)
Distances from Six Husbands Trail junction

    to Parapet: 1.9 mi. (3.1 km.), 1 hr. 45 min.
    to Madison Hut (via Star Lake Trail): 2.1 mi. (3.4 km.),
        1 hr. 50 min.

Osgood Trail (AMC)

This trail runs from the Great Gulf Trail, 1.7 mi. from the new Great Gulf Wilderness parking area on NH 16, up the southeast ridge to the summit of Mt. Madison, then down to Madison Hut. Made by B. F. Osgood in 1878, this is the oldest trail now in use to the summit of Mt. Madison. Above the Osgood Cutoff it is part of the Appalachian Trail. The section of the trail that formerly ran from the Great Gulf Trail to the Mt. Washington Auto Rd. has been abandoned. The Osgood Trail begins in the Great Gulf Wilderness, but for most of its length it is just outside the boundary (in fact, it constitutes the northern section of the eastern boundary of the Great Gulf Wilderness).

The trail leaves the Great Gulf Trail about 0.2 mi. west

of the previous intersection of the two trails, 1.7 mi. from the new parking lot, and proceeds at an easy to moderate grade, rejoining the old route at 0.3 mi. It continues a moderate climb, crosses a small brook, and soon begins a steeper ascent. At 0.8 mi. the Osgood Cutoff comes in from the left, and a spur path leads right about 100 yd. to Osgood Campsite and to a spring which is the last sure water. From this junction to Madison Hut the Osgood Trail is part of the Appalachian Trail. (The former Madison Gulf Cutoff has been abandoned.)

The steep ascent continues to treeline at 2.3 mi., where the trail emerges on the crest of Osgood Ridge. Ahead, on the crest of the ridge, ten or twelve small, rocky peaks curve to the left in a crescent toward the summit of Mt. Madison. Cairns mark the trail over these peaks; keep on the crest of the ridge. The Daniel Webster–Scout Trail enters right at Osgood Junction, ascending from Dolly Copp Campground. Here, at 2.8 mi. from the Great Gulf Trail, the Parapet Trail diverges left, slabbing the south side of the cone of Madison, a rough but sheltered route to Madison Hut. As the Osgood Trail nears the last prominent hump below the summit and bears more west, it is joined on the right by the Howker Ridge Trail. It continues west over the summit of Mt. Madison, where the Watson Path enters, follows the crest of the ridge past several large cairns, drops off to the left (south) and continues west just below the ridge crest—above steep slopes falling off into Madison Gulf on the left. Soon it recrosses to the north side of the ridge and descends steeply, meeting the Pine Link, which enters right 30 yd. before the Osgood Trail reaches Madison Hut.

Osgood Trail (map 6:F10-F9)
Distances (est.) from Great Gulf Trail
  to Osgood Cutoff: 0.8 mi., 40 min.

to Osgood Junction: 2.8 mi., 2 hr. 55 min.
to Mt. Madison summit: 3.3 mi., 3 hr. 25 min.
to Madison Hut: 3.8 mi. (6.1 km.), 3 hr. 40 min.

Osgood Cutoff (AMC)

This link runs nearly on contour east from the Madison Gulf Trail to the Osgood Trail at its junction with the spur path to the Osgood Campsite. It is entirely within the Great Gulf Wilderness. The cutoff is part of the Appalachian Trail, and provides a convenient shortcut from Pinkham Notch Camp to the summit of Mt. Madison via the Osgood Trail.

Osgood Cutoff (map 6:F9)
Distance from Madison Gulf Trail
to Osgood Trail: 0.5 mi. (0.8 km.), 15 min.

Daniel Webster–Scout Trail (WMNF)

This trail, cut in 1933 by the Boy Scouts, leads from Dolly Copp Campground to Osgood Junction on the Osgood Trail, about halfway between the timberline and the summit of Mt. Madison. It begins on the main campground road about 0.8 mi. south of the campground entrance on the Pinkham B (Dolly Copp) Rd. It makes several zigzags not apparent on the map, though the approximate location is correct. The trail is steep and quite rough through the scrub and above timberline.

Daniel Webster–Scout Trail (map 6:F10-F9)
Distances (est.) from Dolly Copp Campground
to Osgood Junction: 3.5 mi., 3 hr. 30 min.
to Mt. Madison summit (via Osgood Trail): 4.0 mi., 4 hr.

Parapet Trail (AMC)

This trail, marked with blue paint, starts from Osgood Junction, where the Daniel Webster–Scout Trail joins the

Osgood Trail, and leads west to Madison Hut, running nearly on a contour on the south side of the cone of Madison. It meets the Madison Gulf Trail where the latter leaves the scrub at the head of the gulf, and continues beside the Parapet to join the Star Lake Trail to Madison Hut. Although above timberline and extremely rough in its eastern one-third, in bad weather the Parapet Trail is sheltered from the northwest winds. The rocks can be very slippery, the trail may be hard to follow if visibility is poor, and the extra effort of rock-hopping more than expends the energy saved by avoiding the climb of about 500 ft. over the summit of Mt. Madison. Therefore it is probably a useful bad-weather route only if strong northwest or west winds are the problem.

Parapet Trail (map 6:F9)
Distances (est.) from Osgood Junction
  to Madison Gulf Trail: 0.7 mi., 30 min.
  to Star Lake Trail: 0.9 mi. (1.4 km.), 35 min.
  to Madison Hut (via Star Lake Trail): 1.0 mi., 40 min.

Pine Link (AMC)
The Pine Link begins near the highest point of the Pinkham B (Dolly Copp) Rd. on the west side, directly opposite the private road to Pine Mtn., 2.4 mi. from US 2 and 1.9 mi. from NH 16. Near it are a spring and a small parking space.

The trail generally follows the crest of a northeast spur of Howker Ridge. In 1968 a fire below the outlook burned close to the south side of the trail, opening fine views east and south. Above the outlook the trail unites with Howker Ridge Trail at the spring south of the second Howk. For about 0.3 mi. the two trails coincide, running southwest through a group of small Howks. At the foot of the highest Howk the trails diverge, Howker Ridge Trail leading left for Mt. Madison summit. Pine Link, leading right, skirts the upper slopes of Bumpus Basin and crosses the Watson Path high on Gordon Ridge. It then contours around the cone of Mt. Madison, running nearly level—with fine views and great weather exposure—and joins the Osgood Trail, which descends on the left from Mt. Madison 30 yd. from Madison Hut.

Pine Link (map 6:E10-F9)
Distances (est.) from Pinkham B (Dolly Copp) Rd.

 to Howker Ridge Trail, lower junction: 2.3 mi., 2 hr. 20 min.

 to Watson Path: 3.2 mi., 3 hr. 15 min.

 to Madison Hut: 3.8 mi., 3 hr. 35 min.

Howker Ridge Trail (RMC)

This wild, rough trail leads from the Pinkham B (Dolly Copp) Rd. at the Randolph East parking area, 0.2 mi. south of US 2, to the Osgood Trail near the summit of Mt. Madison. It has good outlooks at different altitudes and passes three fine cascades.

Coinciding with the Randolph Path, it runs approximately 80 yd. west, turns south, crosses the railroad, and 30 yd. beyond diverges left (southeast) and leads to the west bank of Bumpus Brook, which it follows. The trail passes a cascade (Stairs Fall) that falls into the brook from the east, and at 0.7 mi. it passes Coosauk Fall, where Sylvan Way enters from the right. The trail continues a little west of the brook, and the Kelton Trail diverges right. About 1 mi. from the highway the Howker Ridge Trail turns east and crosses the brook at the foot of Hitchcock Fall, then rises steeply southeast. Howker Ridge curves right, partly enclosing the deep bowl-shaped valley called Bumpus Basin. The trail follows the crest of the ridge, on which there are several little peaks called the "Howks." The first is a long, narrow ridge covered with woods. In the col south of the first Howk is a spring (unreliable). From the second Howk there is a fine view in all directions, especially into Bumpus Basin. South of this Howk the Pine Link enters left (there is a spring on the Pine Link about 50 ft. to the east). The two trails coincide for about 0.3 mi., ascend among several Howks in a group, and separate again at the foot of the highest Howk, where Pine Link branches right. The Howker Ridge Trail climbs over the highest Howk (4311 ft.), descends a little southwest, then ascends steeply to the crest of Osgood Ridge, where it enters the Osgood Trail 0.3 mi. below the summit of Mt. Madison.

Howker Ridge Trail (map 6:E9-F9)
Distances (est.) from Pinkham B (Dolly Copp) Rd.

- **to** Sylvan Way: 0.7 mi., 30 min.
- **to** Hitchcock Fall: 1.0 mi., 50 min.
- **to** first Howk: 2.3 mi., 2 hr. 15 min.
- **to** second Howk: 3.0 mi., 2 hr. 55 min.
- **to** Pine Link, lower junction: 3.1 mi., 3 hr.
- **to** Osgood Trail: 4.1 mi. (6.6 km.), 4 hr. 10 min.
- **to** Mt. Madison summit (via Osgood Trail): 4.4 mi., 4 hr. 25 min.

Kelton Trail (RMC)

This path links the Howker Ridge Trail to the Valley Way, running nearly from Coosauk Fall to Salmacis Fall, and passing several outlooks.

It branches right from the Howker Ridge Trail about 0.8 mi. from the Pinkham B (Dolly Copp) Rd. It climbs to Kelton Crag, with some steep, slippery sections, then ascends near the northwest arete of the fingerlike north spur of Gordon Ridge, reaching an upper crag at the edge of a very old burn. From both crags there are restricted views; there is usually water between them on the right. Ascending, with good views east, the trail reaches the Overlook at the edge of the old burn, and runs west to the Upper

Inlook where the Inlook Trail enters right from Dome Rock. The Kelton Trail then runs south, nearly level but rough in places, through dense woods. It crosses Gordon Rill (reliable water) and Snyder Brook, and enters the Brookside 100 yd. below the foot of Salmacis Fall.

Kelton Trail (map 6:E9)
Distances (est.) from Howker Ridge Trail

to Kelton Crag: 0.3 mi., 20 min.

to Inlook Trail: 0.8 mi., 55 min.

to the Brookside: 1.5 mi. (2.4 km.), 1 hr. 20 min.

Inlook Trail (RMC)

This steep path starts at the junction of the Randolph Path and the Brookside east of Snyder Brook, and leads up to the Kelton Trail at the Upper Inlook near the crest of the finger of Gordon Ridge. There are good outlooks west, north, and east, and several "inlooks" up the valley of Snyder Brook to Mt. John Quincy Adams and Mt. Adams. The best outlook is at Dome Rock at the tip of the finger.

Inlook Trail (map 6:E9)
Distances from Randolph Path

to Dome Rock: 0.5 mi., 40 min.

to Kelton Trail: 0.7 mi. (1.1 km.), 45 min.

The Brookside (RMC)

This trail follows Snyder Brook, from the point where the Valley Way leaves the brook at 0.9 mi. from the Appalachia parking lot to the Watson Path 100 yd. south of Bruin Rock, and offers views of many cascades and pools. It branches left from the Valley Way about 30 yd. above the Beechwood Way, and crosses Snyder Brook on a wooden bridge in common with the Randolph Path. East of the brook the Randolph Path and the Inlook Trail diverge left. In 0.3 mi. the Brookside recrosses the brook, and climbs along the west bank at a moderate grade to its junction with the Kelton Trail, which enters from the left. The trail becomes steeper and rougher, passes Salmacis Fall, and ends at the Watson Path south of Bruin Rock. The brook between Salmacis and Bruin Rock is wild and beautiful, with cascades, mossy rocks, and fine forest.

The Brookside (map 6:E9)
Distance (est.) from the Valley Way
   to Watson Path: 1.3 mi. (2.1 km.), 1 hr. 20 min.

Watson Path (RMC)
The old Watson Path, completed by L. M. Watson in 1882, originally led from the Ravine House to the summit of Mt. Madison. The present path begins at the Scar Trail, leads across the Valley Way to Bruin Rock, and then follows the original route to the summit. It is an interesting route to Mt. Madison, but is steep, rough, and, on the northwest slopes above treeline, exposed to the weather. The cairns above treeline are not very prominent, and the trail may be hard to follow when visibility is poor.

Branching from the Scar Trail 0.3 mi. from Valley Way, it runs level about 0.2 mi. and crosses the Valley Way 2.4 mi. from the Appalachia parking area, then continues at an easy grade to Bruin Rock—a large, flat-topped boulder on the west bank of Snyder Brook. Here the Brookside enters, coming up the west bank of the stream. After the Lower Bruin branches to the right toward the Valley Way, the Watson Path crosses the brook at the foot of Duck Fall at 0.4 mi. East of the stream, the Watson Path soon attacks the steep flank of Gordon Ridge on a very steep and rough footway. At 1.0 mi. the trail emerges from the scrub onto the grassy, stony back of the ridge. It crosses Pine Link at 1.4 mi. and ascends to the summit of Mt. Madison over rough and shelving stones.

Watson Path (map 6:E9-F9)

Distances from Scar Trail

   to Valley Way: 0.2 mi., 5 min.

   to Pine Link: 1.4 mi., 1 hr. 30 min.

   to Mt. Madison summit: 1.7 mi. (2.7 km.), 2 hr.

Distance from Appalachia parking area

   to Mt. Madison summit (via Valley Way and Watson
      Path): 4.1 mi. (6.6 km.), 4 hr. 10 min.

Valley Way (WMNF)

This is the direct route from the Appalachia parking area
to Madison Hut, well sheltered almost to the door of the
hut. In bad weather it is the safest and easiest route to or
from the hut. Portions of its upper section have washed,
becoming rocky and rough. Signs for several of the trails
that branch from the Valley Way are set so far back from
the junctions that they are easy to miss.

The trail, in common with the Air Line, begins at the
Appalachia, and crosses the railroad to a fork. The Valley
Way leads left and the Air Line right across the power line
location. In a few yards, the Maple Walk diverges left, and
at 0.2 mi. Sylvan Way crosses. The trail enters the WMNF
at 0.3 mi., and at 0.5 mi. the Fallsway comes in on the left,
soon leaving left for Tama Fall and the Brookbank, then
reentering the Valley Way in a few yards—it is a short but
worthwhile loop.

The Valley Way leads nearer Snyder Brook and is soon
joined from the right by Beechwood Way. About 30 yd.
above this junction the Brookside diverges left, and the
Valley Way turns right and climbs 100 yd. to the crossing of
the Randolph Path at 0.9 mi. It then climbs at a comfortable grade high above Snyder Brook. At 2.2 mi. Scar Trail
branches right, and at 2.4 mi. the Watson Path crosses,
leading left to the summit of Mt. Madison. The Valley Way
slabs the rather steep slopes of Durand Ridge considerably

above the stream. At 2.7 mi. the Lower Bruin enters left, coming up from Bruin Rock and Duck Fall. At 3.1 mi. a path leads 0.1 mi. right to Valley Way Campsite (tent platforms), and soon the main trail passes a spring to the right of the trail. At 3.2 mi. the Upper Bruin branches steeply right, leading in 0.2 mi. to the Air Line at the lower end of the Knife-edge.

Now the Valley Way steepens and approaches nearer to Snyder Brook. High up in the scrub, the path swings right away from the brook, then swings back toward the stream and emerges from the scrub close to the stream, reaching a junction with the Air Line Cutoff 50 yd. below the hut.

Valley Way (map 6:E9-F9)
Distances (est.) from Appalachia parking area
   to Randolph Path crossing: 0.9 mi., 45 min.
   to Watson Path crossing: 2.4 mi., 2 hr. 10 min.
   to Upper Bruin junction: 3.2 mi., 3 hr. 5 min.
   to Madison Hut: 3.7 mi. (6.0 km.), 3 hr. 40 min.
   to Mt. Madison summit (via Osgood Trail): 4.2 mi. (6.8 km.), 4 hr. 10 min.

Lower Bruin (RMC)
This short trail branches right from the Watson Path on the west bank of Snyder Brook, near Bruin Rock, and climbs at a moderate grade to the Valley Way.

Lower Bruin (map 6:E9)
Distance (est.) from Watson Path
   to Valley Way: 0.3 mi. (0.5 km.), 20 min.

Upper Bruin (RMC)
This short but steep trail branches right from the Valley Way 3.2 mi. from Appalachia (sign very hard to see from Valley Way) and climbs to the Air Line above treeline, 3.1 mi. from Appalachia.

Upper Bruin (map 6:E9)
Distance (est.) from Valley Way
   to Air Line: 0.1 mi. (0.2 km.), 10 min.

Air Line (AMC)

This trail, completed in 1885, is the shortest route to Mt. Adams from a highway. It runs from the Appalachia parking area up Durand Ridge to the summit. The middle section is rather steep, and the section on the knife-edged crest of Durand Ridge is very exposed to weather but affords magnificent views.

The trail, in common with the Valley Way, begins at Appalachia and crosses the railroad to the power line clearing, where the Air Line leads right and Valley Way left. In 40 yd. the Link and the Amphibrach diverge right. The Air Line soon crosses Sylvan Way and, 0.6 mi. from the Appalachia parking area, crosses Beechwood Way and Beechwood Brook. At 0.8 mi. from Appalachia the Short Line diverges right, and at 0.9 mi. it enters the Randolph Path, coincides with it for 15 yd., then diverges left uphill. At 1.6 mi. there may be water in a spring 30 yd. left (east) of the path (sign). From here the path becomes very steep for 0.5 mi., then eases up and reaches an old clearing known as Camp Placid Stream (water unreliable) at 2.4 mi., where the Scar Trail enters left, coming up from the Valley Way.

At 3.0 mi. the Air Line emerges from the scrub, and at 3.1 mi. the Upper Bruin comes up left from the Valley Way. The Air Line now ascends over the bare, ledgy crest of Durand Ridge known as the "Knife-edge," passing over crags that drop off sharply into King Ravine on the right, and descend steeply but not precipitously into Snyder Glen on the left. At 3.2 mi., just south of the little peak called Needle Rock, the Chemin des Dames comes up from King Ravine. From several outlooks along the upper part of this ridge, one can look back down the ridge for a fine demonstration of the difference between the U-shaped glacial cirque of King Ravine on the left (west), and the ordinary V-shaped brook valley of Snyder Brook on the right (east). At 3.5 mi. the Air Line Cutoff leads left (southeast) 0.2 mi. through the scrub to Madison Hut, which is visible from this junction in clear weather. Water is found on this branch not far from the main path.

The Air Line now departs a little from the edge of the ravine, going left of the jutting crags at the ravine's southeast corner, and rises steeply. At 3.7 mi. it passes the Gateway of King Ravine, and the King Ravine Trail diverges right and plunges between two crags into that gulf. Here there is a striking view of Mt. Madison. In a few steps the path enters the Gulfside Trail, turns right, and coincides with it for a few yards, attaining the high plateau at the head of the ravine. Then the Air Line diverges to the left (southwest), passing west of Mt. John Quincy Adams, up a rough way over large, angular stones to the summit of Mt. Adams.

Air Line (map 6:E9-F9)
Distances from Appalachia parking area
  to Randolph Path: 0.9 mi., 50 min.
  to Scar Trail: 2.4 mi., 2 hr. 25 min.
  to Chemin des Dames: 3.2 mi., 3 hr. 10 min.
  to Air Line Cutoff: 3.5 mi., 3 hr. 30 min.
  to Gulfside Trail: 3.7 mi., 3 hr. 45 min.
  to Mt. Adams summit: 4.5 mi. (7.2 km.), 4 hr. 20 min.
  to Madison Hut (via Air Line Cutoff): 3.7 mi. (6.0 km.),
    3 hr. 40 min.

Scar Trail (RMC)
This trail runs from the Valley Way 2.0 mi. from Appalachia to the Air Line at Camp Placid Stream, an old clearing 2.4 mi. from Appalachia. It provides a route to Mt. Adams which includes the spectacular views from

Durand Ridge while avoiding the steepest section of the Air Line, and also has good outlooks of its own.

It diverges from the Valley Way, and in 0.2 mi. it divides. The Scar Loop, an alternative route to the right, goes over Durand Scar and another viewpoint, while the main trail leads left to the beginning of Watson Path, ascends to rejoin the loop, and continues to the Air Line.

Scar Trail (map 6:E9)
Distances (est.) from Valley Way
   to Durand Scar (via Scar Loop): 0.3 mi., 20 min.
   to Watson Path (via main trail): 0.4 mi., 25 min.
   to Air Line (via either route): 1.0 mi. (1.6 km.), 1 hr.
Distance (est.) from Appalachia parking area
   to Mt. Adams summit (via Valley Way, Scar Trail or Scar Loop, and Air Line): 5.1 mi., 4 hr. 50 min.

Air Line Cutoff (AMC)
This short trail provides a direct route, sheltered by scrub, from the Air Line high on Durand Ridge to the Valley Way just below Madison Hut.

Air Line Cutoff (map 6:F9)
Distance from Air Line
   to Madison Hut: 0.2 mi. (0.3 km.), 10 min.

Star Lake Trail (AMC)
This trail leads from Madison Hut to the summit of Mt. Adams, slabbing the southeast side of Mt. John Quincy Adams. It is often more sheltered from the wind than the Air Line, but is steep and rough, especially in the upper part, and may be difficult to follow on descent. It runs south from the hut, in common with the Parapet Trail, rising gently. In about 0.1 mi. the Parapet Trail branches to the left, passing east of Star Lake. The Star Lake Trail passes west of the lake and reaches the Adams–Madison col

about 0.3 mi. from the hut. Here the Buttress Trail diverges left and descends. The Star Lake Trail continues southwest on the steep southeast slope of John Quincy. There is usually water issuing from the rocks on the right. The trail continues to slab up the steep east slope of Mt. Adams to the crest of a minor easterly ridge, then turns right and follows that ridge to the summit.

Star Lake Trail (map 6:F9)
Distances (est.) from Madison Hut
- *to* Buttress Trail: 0.3 mi., 15 min.
- *to* Mt. Adams summit: 0.9 mi. (1.4 km.), 1 hr.

Short Line (RMC)

This graded path, leading from the Air Line to the King Ravine Trail below Mossy Fall, was made in 1899–1901 by J. Rayner Edmands. It offers easy access to the Randolph Path and to King Ravine from the Appalachia parking area.

The Short Line branches right from the Air Line 0.8 mi. from Appalachia. At 0.5 mi. it unites with the Randolph Path, coincides with it for 0.4 mi., then branches left and leads south up the valley of Cold Brook toward King Ravine, keeping a short distance east of the stream. At 2.8 mi. from Appalachia, the path joins the King Ravine Trail just below Mossy Fall.

Short Line (map 6:E9)
Distances (est.) from Air Line Junction
- *to* Randolph Path, lower junction: 0.5 mi., 30 min.
- *to* Randolph Path, upper junction: 0.9 mi., 50 min.
- *to* King Ravine Trail: 1.5 mi. (2.4 km.), 1 hr. 30 min.

King Ravine Trail (RMC)

This branch from Lowe's Path through King Ravine was made by Charles E. Lowe in 1876. It is very steep and rough on the headwall of the ravine, but is one of the most spectacular trails in the White Mtns., offering an overwhelming variety of wild and magnificent scenery. It is not a good trail to descend, on account of steep, rough, slippery footing, and extra time should be allowed for the roughness and the views. The trip to the floor of the ravine is worthwhile even if you do not ascend the headwall.

King Ravine Trail diverges left from Lowe's Path 1.8 mi. from US 2, and rises over a low swell of Nowell Ridge. At 0.8 mi. it crosses Spur Brook below some cascades, and in a few yards more it crosses the Randolph Path at its junction with the Amphibrach, a spot called the "Pentodoi." Skirting the east spur of Nowell Ridge, it enters the ravine and descends slightly, crosses a western branch of Cold Brook, goes across the lower floor of the ravine, and crosses the main stream. In 0.2 mi. more it is joined by the Short Line, the usual route of access from the Appalachia parking area, near the foot of Mossy Fall (last sure water). Just above this fall Cold Brook, already a good-sized stream, gushes from beneath the boulders that have fallen into the ravine.

So far the path has been fairly level, rising only 400 ft. in 1.5 mi.; but in the next 0.3 mi. it rises about 550 ft. and gains the upper floor of the ravine (3500 ft). The grandeur of the view of the ravine and to the north warrants a trip to the top of a bank of fallen rocks. The Chemin des Dames branches left here. From this point to the foot of the headwall, about 0.4 mi., the path is very strenuous, winding over and under boulders ranging up to the size of a small house. A shortcut called the "Elevated" avoids some of the main boulder-caves. The main trail, the "Subway," 550 ft. long, is more interesting and takes only a few minutes longer. The Great Gully Trail diverges right a little farther south. In a boulder-cave near the foot of the headwall, reached by a wet loop path, there is ice throughout the year. About 2.6 mi. from Lowe's Path the ascent of the headwall begins. It is very steep and rough, rising about 1300 ft. in 0.4 mi., over large blocks of rock, to the "Gateway"; here the trail issues from the ravine between two crags, and immediately joins the Air Line close to its junction with the Gulfside Trail. From the Gateway there is a striking view of Mt. Madison. Madison Hut is in sight, and can be reached by the Gulfside Trail, left. The summit of Mt. Adams is about 0.5 mi. farther, by the Air Line.

King Ravine Trail (map 6:E9-F9)
Distances (est.) from Lowe's Path
to Randolph Path: 0.9 mi., 40 min.
to Short Line: 1.6 mi., 1 hr. 10 min.
to foot of King Ravine headwall: 2.6 mi., 2 hr.
to Gulfside Trail: 3.0 mi. (4.8 km.), 3 hr.

Chemin des Dames (RMC)
This trail leads from the floor of King Ravine up its east wall, and joins the Air Line above treeline. It is the shortest route out of the ravine, but is very steep and rough, climbing up over large rocks; it is also a difficult trail to descend.

From the King Ravine Trail, it winds through scrub to the east side of the ravine, where it climbs steeply over blocks of talus, alternately through scrub and over slides. Reaching the foot of a cliff, it angles to the right and climbs south to join the Air Line in a shallow col.

Chemin des Dames (map 6:E9-F9)
Distance from King Ravine Trail
to Air Line Trail junction: 0.3 mi. (0.5 km.), 40 min.

Great Gully Trail (RMC)
This trail provides an alternative route between the floor of King Ravine and the Gulfside Trail, reaching the latter at Thunderstorm Junction. It is extremely steep and rough,

and, like the other trails in the ravine, especially difficult to descend. Leaving the King Ravine Trail, it leads up the southwest corner of King Ravine and makes some use of the gully, crossing the brook above a high fall. Near the top of the headwall is a spring (unreliable). After emerging from the ravine the trail runs south to the junction of the Gulfside Trail and Lowe's Path at Thunderstorm Junction.

Great Gully Trail (map 6:F9)
Distance (est.) from King Ravine Trail
to Gulfside Trail: 1.0 mi. (1.6 km.), 1 hr. 15 min.

Amphibrach (RMC)

This trail runs from the Appalachia parking area to Memorial Bridge, then swings south and parallels Cold Brook to the five-way junction with the Randolph Path and King Ravine Trail known as the "Pentodoi." The trail takes its unusual name from its marking when it was first made, about 1883: three blazes—short, long, and short. It is a good approach to King Ravine, or to any point reached via the Randolph Path or the Link; and also, via the Beechwood Way, to points reached by the Short Line, the Air Line, or the Valley Way. Its moderate grade and relative smoothness make it relatively less difficult for descent after dark. It is, in fact, one of the kindest trails to the feet in this region.

The Amphibrach, in common with the Link, diverges right from the Air Line about 40 yd. south of its junction with the Valley Way and 100 yd. south of the Appalachia parking area. It runs west, and at 0.7 mi. the Beechwood Way diverges left, and the Sylvan Way enters left just east of Cold Brook—which is crossed on Memorial Bridge. Memorial Bridge is a memorial to J. Rayner Edmands, Eugene B. Cook, and other pioneer pathmakers: King, Gordon, Lowe,

Watson, Peek, Hunt, Nowell, and Sargent. Cold Brook Fall is visible from the bridge, a short distance upstream.

In about 50 yd. the Link diverges right, and 30 yd. beyond a side trail branches left to the foot of Cold Brook Fall. The Amphibrach now follows the course of Cold Brook, ascending west of the stream but generally not in sight of the water, and enters the WMNF. At 1.6 mi., near the confluence of Spur Brook and Cold Brook, the Monaway diverges right. The Amphibrach crosses Spur Brook on the rocks, ascends the tongue of land between the two brooks, shortly diverges left (east), and climbs gradually. It crosses the Cliffway and at 2.6 mi. the Amphibrach ends at "Pentodoi."

Amphibrach (map 6:E9)
Distances from Appalachia parking area
   to Memorial Bridge: 0.7 mi., 25 min.
   to Monaway: 1.6 mi., 1 hr. 20 min.
   to Randolph Path and King Ravine Trail: 2.6 mi. (4.2 km.), 2 hr. 10 min.

Cliffway (RMC)

This path runs from the Link 1.9 mi. from the Appalachia parking area, crosses the Amphibrach, and ends at the Randolph Path at the west end of Sanders Bridge over Cold Brook, 2.1 mi. from Appalachia. Gradients are generally easy, and much of the trail is level, but there are several short, steep pitches, and the trail changes direction frequently. Leaving the Link, it crosses some of the overgrown cliffs and ledges of the low swell of Nowell Ridge. The best view is from White Cliff. Here the Ladderback Trail diverges left along the cliff top to the Monaway. A very short and obscure path, Along the Brink, leads from the Cliffway to the Ladderback Trail via the mossy brink of White Cliff. At King Cliff the Monaway diverges left. The

Cliffway then passes Spur Brook Fall, crosses Spur Brook and the Amphibrach, and ends at the Randolph Path.

Cliffway (map 6:E9)
Distances (est.) from the Link
to White Cliff: 0.7 mi., 30 min.
to Spur Brook Fall: 1.6 mi., 1 hr.
to Randolph Path: 2.0 mi. (3.2 km.), 1 hr. 15 min.

Monaway (RMC)
The Monaway leads from the Cliffway near King Cliff, past a junction with the Ladderback Trail, to the Amphibrach 50 yd. below its crossing of Spur Brook. It is a narrow woods path of moderate grade, except for a short, steep pitch between the Ladderback Trail and the Cliffway.

Monaway (map 6:E9)
Distance (est.) from Cliffway
to Amphibrach: 0.3 mi. (0.5 km.), 10 min.

Ladderback Trail (RMC)
The Ladderback Trail leads from the Cliffway at White Cliff to the Monaway. Fine views of the Randolph Valley can be obtained from the cliff.

Ladderback Trail (map 6:E9)
Distance (est.) from Cliffway
to Monaway: 0.2 mi. (0.3 km.), 5 min.

Spur Trail (RMC)
This trail leads from the Randolph Path just above its junction with the King Ravine Trail, up the east spur of the Nowell Ridge near the west edge of King Ravine, and ends at Lowe's Path close to Thunderstorm Junction. At several points there are views into King Ravine. The section known

as the New Spur proved too steep for the amount of use it received and has been abandoned.

The Spur Trail diverges south from the Randolph Path about 100 yd. west of its junction with the King Ravine Trail, just west of Spur Brook. In 0.3 mi. there is a short branch to Chandler Fall, and 0.3 mi. farther up the Hincks Trail to Gray Knob diverges right and the Spur Trail crosses to the east side of the brook, the last water until Crag Camp. It ascends the spur that forms the west wall of King Ravine and goes over the Lower Crag, giving one of the best views of the ravine and an outlook east and north. A little farther on, a short branch leads to the Upper Crag, near which Crag Camp is situated. Here the Gray Knob Trail leads west 0.4 mi. to Gray Knob.

The trail continues up the spur, but not so near the edge of the ravine. It soon enters the region of scrub and passes a side path that leads east to Knight's Castle, a crag at the edge of the ravine about 0.1 mi. from Spur Trail. Above this junction the trail leaves the scrub, ascends to the east of the crest of Nowell Ridge, and merges with Lowe's Path just below Thunderstorm Junction and the Gulfside Trail, 0.3 mi. below the summit of Mt. Adams.

Spur Trail (map 6:E9-F9)
Distances from Randolph Path

to Crag Camp: 0.8 mi., 1 hr. 5 min.

to Lowe's Path: 1.9 mi. (3.1 km.), 2 hr. 10 min.

Hincks Trail (RMC)

The Hincks Trail diverges right from the Spur Trail about 0.3 mi. above the Chandler Fall side path, immediately before the Spur Trail crosses Spur Brook. The trail climbs steeply through blowdown areas and around many washouts to Gray Knob. The trail is rough and may be difficult to follow on descent due to the washouts.

Hincks Trail (map 6:E9-F9)
Distance (est.) from Spur Trail
  to Gray Knob: 0.7 mi. (1.1 km.), 50 min.

Gray Knob Trail (RMC)

The Gray Knob Trail leads from the Spur Trail near Crag Camp to Gray Knob, and continues past Lowe's Path and the Perch Path to the Randolph Path just before its junction with the Israel Ridge Path. It provides a route from Crag Camp and Gray Knob to Edmands Col without loss of elevation, but is rough and offers little protection from the elements. From the Spur Trail it runs almost on contour 0.4 mi. to Gray Knob, and continues a very short distance and crosses Lowe's Path. A very short path called the Quay diverges right just before this junction to a ledge on Lowe's Path a short distance north of the Gray Knob Trail crossing. In another 0.4 mi. the Perch Path diverges right. Ascending slightly, the Gray Knob Trail joins the Randolph Path near its junction with Israel Ridge Path.

Gray Knob Trail (map 6:E9-F9)
Distances (est.) from Spur Trail
  to Gray Knob: 0.4 mi., 15 min.
  to Randolph Path: 1.4 mi. (2.3 km.), 1 hr.

Perch Path (RMC)

This path runs from the Gray Knob Trail across Randolph Path, past the Perch, and ends on Israel Ridge Path. It diverges right from the Gray Knob Trail about 0.3 mi. south of Gray Knob. It descends moderately and crosses the Randolph Path at 0.3 mi., soon passes the Perch and runs nearly level to the Randolph Path.

Perch Path (map 6:F9)
Distances from Gray Knob Trail
  to Randolph Path: 0.3 mi., 10 min.

to the Perch: 0.4 mi., 15 min.

to Randolph Path junction: 0.5 mi. (0.8 km.), 20 min.

Lowe's Path (AMC)

This trail, cut in 1875-76 by Charles E. Lowe and Dr. William G. Nowell from Lowe's house in Randolph to the summit of Mt. Adams, is the oldest of the mountain trails that lead from the Randolph valley.

The trail begins on the south side of US 2, 100 yd. west of Lowe's Store, where cars may be parked (small fee). It follows a broad wood road for 100 yd., then diverges right at a sign giving the history of the trail and passes through a logged area, crosses the railroad track and then the power lines. It ascends through woods at a moderate grade, at first toward the southwest then swinging more south, crosses several small brooks, bears left where it enters the former route, and at 1.7 mi. crosses the Link.

At 1.8 mi. the King Ravine Trail branches left. Lowe's Path continues to ascend, and at 2.5 mi. passes close to the Log Cabin. Here two short spur paths lead left to the Randolph Path, and the Cabin-Cascades Trail to the Israel Ridge Path in Cascade Ravine leaves on the right. Water is always found at the Log Cabin and midway between the cabin and treeline. Very steep climbing begins, and at 2.7 mi. Lowe's Path crosses the Randolph Path. At an outlook at 3.2 mi., the short path called the Quay diverges left to Gray Knob Trail, and 30 yd. farther the Gray Knob Trail crosses. The cabin at Gray Knob is 0.1 mi. left (east). The grade moderates somewhat after these junctions.

The rest of the trail is above treeline and much exposed to wind. Views are very fine. The trail ascends steadily to the summit known as Adams 4 (5348 ft.)—the culminating peak of Nowell Ridge at 4.1 mi., then descends a little, keeping to the left of Mt. Sam Adams. The Spur Trail enters left 100 yd. before Lowe's Path crosses the Gulfside

Trail at Thunderstorm Junction at 4.5 mi.; the Great Gully Trail also enters at Thunderstorm Junction. It climbs moderately over the jumbled rocks of the cone of Mt. Adams, the Israel Ridge Path enters right at 4.6 mi., and Lowe's Path reaches the summit of Mt. Adams at 4.8 mi.

Lowe's Path (map 6:E9-F9)
Distances from US 2 near Lowe's Store
to the Link: 1.7 mi., 1 hr. 25 min.
to King Ravine Trail: 1.8 mi., 1 hr. 30 min.
to Log Cabin: 2.5 mi., 2 hr. 10 min.
to Randolph Path: 2.7 mi., 2 hr. 25 min.
to Gray Knob Trail: 3.2 mi., 3 hr. 5 min.
to Adams 4 summit: 4.1 mi., 4 hr.
to Gulfside Trail: 4.5 mi., 4 hr. 20 min.
to Mt. Adams summit: 4.8 mi. (7.7 km.), 4 hr. 35 min.

Cabin–Cascades Trail (RMC)
One of the earliest AMC trails (1881), Cabin–Cascades Trail leads from the Log Cabin on Lowe's Path to the Israel Ridge Path near the cascades on Cascade Brook. It links the Log Cabin with the trails in the vicinity of Cascade Ravine, as well as the cascades themselves.

The trail begins at Lowe's Path 2.5 mi. from US 2, opposite the Log Cabin, runs gradually downhill in general, with frequent ups and downs, and is narrow and wet for the first 0.3 mi. It crosses two small streams, then descends gradually to Israel Ridge Path just above its upper junction with the Link, near the first cascade at the Link's crossing of Cascade Brook. Not far from here is the second cascade, which can be visited by taking the Israel Ridge Path uphill.

Cabin–Cascades Trail (map 6:E9-F9)
Distance from Lowe's Path
to Israel Ridge Path: 1.0 mi., 30 min.

Israel Ridge Path (RMC)

This trail runs from the Castle Trail 1.3 mi. from Bowman (on US 2, 1.0 mi. west of Lowe's Store) to the summit of Mt. Adams. It was constructed as a graded path by J. Rayner Edmands beginning in 1892. Although hurricanes and slides have severely damaged the original trail, and there have been many relocations, the upper part is still one of the finest and most beautiful of the Randolph trails. Some brook crossings may be difficult in high water.

From Bowman follow the Castle Trail for 1.3 mi. Here, the Israel Ridge Path branches left and at 0.1 mi. crosses to the east bank of the Israel River. It follows the river, then turns left up the bank at 0.4 mi., as the Castle Ravine Trail continues along the river. The Israel Ridge Path bears southeast up the slope of Nowell Ridge into Cascade Ravine, and at 1.2 mi. the Link enters left. The trails coincide for 50 yd., and then the Link diverges right to cross Cascade Brook—the cascades can be reached by following this trail for a short distance. In another 60 yd. the Cabin–Cascades Trail enters left from the Log Cabin. The Israel Ridge Path now enters virgin growth. From this point to treeline, the forest has never been disturbed by lumbering, though slides have done much damage.

The path continues to ascend on the north side of Cascade Brook to the head of the second cascade at 1.4 mi., where it crosses the brook, turns right downstream for a short distance, then turns left and climbs. It runs southwest, then southeast, making a large zigzag up the steep slope of Israel Ridge—sometimes known as Emerald Tongue—between Cascade and Castle ravines. Soon the path turns sharply east, and at 2.2 mi. Emerald Trail diverges right for 0.2 mi. to Emerald Bluff, a remarkable outlook, and continues steeply down into Castle Ravine. The Israel Ridge Path zigzags up a rather steep slope, and the Perch Path diverges left (east) at 2.4 mi. The main path turns sharply south and ascends to treeline, where it joins the Randolph Path at 2.8 mi. The junction of the Gray Knob Trail with the Randolph Path is a short distance to the left (north) at this point. For 0.1 mi. the paths coincide, then the Israel Ridge Path branches to the left and, curving east, ascends the southwest ridge of Mt. Adams and joins the Gulfside Trail at 3.3 mi., near Storm Lake. It coincides with the Gulfside for 0.5 mi., running northeast past Peabody Spring and south of Mt. Sam Adams, aiming for the Adams–Sam Adams col. At 3.8 mi., just before and in sight of the col (Thunderstorm Junction), the Israel Ridge Path branches right from the Gulfside Trail, and at 3.9 mi. enters Lowe's Path, which leads to the summit of Mt. Adams at 4.1 mi. The cairns between the Gulfside Trail and Lowe's Path are rather sketchy, so in poor visibility it might be easier to follow Lowe's Path from Thunderstorm Junction to the summit.

Israel Ridge Path (map 6:E8-F9)
Distances from Castle Trail
  to Castle Ravine Trail: 0.4 mi., 20 min.
  to the Link: 1.2 mi., 1 hr. 5 min.
  to Perch Path: 2.4 mi., 2 hr. 25 min.
  to Randolph Path, lower junction: 2.8 mi., 2 hr. 55 min.
  to Gulfside Trail: 3.3 mi., 3 hr. 20 min.
  to Mt. Adams summit: 4.1 mi. (6.6 km.), 4 hr. 5 min.
  to Edmands Col (via Randolph Path): 3.4 mi., 3 hr. 15 min.

Emerald Trail (RMC)
This trail begins on the Castle Ravine Trail and the Link, about 0.2 mi. southeast of their lower junction, and climbs a very steep and rough route to Emerald Bluff, a fine viewpoint, then runs about level to Israel Ridge Path. The fine forest above Castle Ravine makes it worth the effort. A

good loop can be made by way of the Castle Ravine Trail, Emerald Trail, and Israel Ridge Path.

The trail leaves the Castle Ravine Trail and the Link, which coincide in this area, and descends slightly, crosses several brooks, then ascends a steep and rough route to Emerald Bluff. Follow blazes carefully. The viewpoint is 25 yd. to the left on a side path, while the main trail bears right and runs level through high scrub for 0.1 mi. to the Israel Ridge Path 0.2 mi. below its junction with the Perch Path.

Emerald Trail (map 6:F9)
Distances (est.) from Castle Ravine Trail and the Link
   to Emerald Bluff: 0.6 mi., 40 min.
   to Israel Ridge Path: 0.7 mi. (1.1 km.), 45 min.

Castle Ravine Trail (RMC)

This trail runs from the Israel Ridge Path, about 1.7 mi. from Bowman on US 2 (via the Castle Trail and Israel Ridge Path), and leads through Castle Ravine to the Randolph Path near Edmands Col. This is a wild and beautiful ravine, but parts of the trail are very rough, and it is a difficult trail to descend. While it is reasonably well sheltered after the first section, it crosses a great deal of unstable talus on the headwall, making footing extremely poor, especially for descending or when the rocks are wet. Still, it must be considered as a potential escape route from Edmands Col. Some of the brook crossings may be very difficult at moderate to high water.

From Bowman follow the Castle Trail and the Israel Ridge Path to a point 1.7 mi. from Bowman. Here the Israel Ridge Path turns left up a slope, while the Castle Ravine Trail leads straight ahead near the river. It crosses to the west bank (difficult at high water, and not easy at other times) and soon reaches a point abreast of the Forks of Israel, where Cascade and Castle brooks unite to form

Israel River. The trail crosses to the east bank, passes a fine cascade, and recrosses to the west bank. In general, it follows the route of an old logging road, now almost imperceptible. After entering Castle Ravine, the trail crosses to the east bank and climbs at a moderate to steep grade high above the brook. At 1.4 mi. the Link enters from the left, and the two trails coincide for about 0.2 mi. to the junction with the Emerald Trail left (north) from Israel Ridge. They continue together for another 0.1 mi., then cross to the southwest side of the brook in a tract of cool virgin forest beloved of musca nigra. The Link then turns right while the Castle Ravine Trail continues up the ravine southwest of the brook. Close to the foot of the headwall it crosses again, and in a few yards reaches the place where Castle Brook emerges from under the mossy boulders that have fallen from the headwall. At the foot of the headwall, the trail turns left and mounts the steep slope to Roof Rock, under which it passes (last water). This is a good shelter from rain.

Rising very steeply southeast, with very rough footing, the trail soon winds up a patch of bare rocks, marked by small cairns and dashes of paint, reentering the scrub at a large cairn. In a few hundred feet it emerges from the scrub at the foot of a steep slide of very loose rock (use extreme care when descending). It ascends, marked by paint, to the top of the headwall, and crosses rocks and grass, marked by cairns, to Spaulding Spring, and joins the Randolph Path (sign) 0.1 mi. north of Edmands Col. Descending, follow Randolph Path north from the col to Spaulding Spring, then follow the line of cairns north.

Castle Ravine Trail (map 6:E8-F9)
Distances (est.) from Israel Ridge Path

   to Forks of Israel: 0.3 mi., 10 min.
   to the Link: 1.4 mi., 1 hr. 10 min.

to Emerald Trail: 1.6 mi., 1 hr. 20 min.
to Roof Rock: 2.0 mi., 1 hr. 40 min.
to Randolph Path: 2.7 mi. (4.3 km.), 2 hr. 40 min.

Castle Trail (AMC)

This trail follows the narrow, serrated ridge that runs northwest from Mt. Jefferson, providing magnificent views in a magnificent setting. In bad weather it can be a dangerous trail due to long and continuous exposure to the northwest winds. It was made in 1883–84 but most of the path has since been relocated.

It begins at Bowman on US 2, 3 mi. west of the Appalachia parking area and 4.2 mi. east of the junction of US 2 and NH 115. Park on the north side of the railroad, cross the track, and follow the right-hand driveway for 150 yd. to where the trail enters woods on the right (signs). The trail circles left, crosses a power line, and at 0.4 mi. crosses the Israel River (may be difficult at high water) at the site of an old footbridge.

At 1.3 mi. the Israel Ridge Path branches left (east) toward the brook. Last sure water is a short distance along this trail. The Castle Trail continues southeast, on the northeast flank of Mt. Bowman, and at 2.3 mi. it passes a very large boulder on the left and becomes much steeper for the next 0.5 mi. At 2.8 mi., near the saddle between Mt. Bowman and the Castellated Ridge, it becomes less steep. The view into the ravine left and toward Jefferson is quite spectacular. The trail dips slightly, then continues level along the ridge through thick growth. At 3.4 mi. it is crossed by the Link coming up left from Castle Ravine and leading right to the Caps Ridge Trail. The ridge becomes very narrow and the trail is steep and rough. After passing over two ledges with an outlook from each, it reaches the first and most prominent Castle (4360 ft.), 3.6 mi. from Bowman. The view is very fine. The trail leads on over several lesser crags and ascends as the Castellated Ridge joins the main mass of Mt. Jefferson. Above, the Cornice crosses, leading northeast to the Randolph Path near Edmands Col and south to the Caps Ridge and Gulfside trails. The Castle Trail continues to within a few yards of the summit of Mt. Jefferson, where it connects with the Mount Jefferson Loop and the Six Husbands and Caps Ridge trails.

Castle Trail (map 6:E8-F9)
Distances (est.) from Bowman
   to Israel Ridge Path: 1.3 mi., 50 min.
   to first Castle: 3.6 mi., 3 hr. 15 min.
   to Mt. Jefferson summit: 4.8 mi. (7.7 km.), 4 hr. 30 min.

Caps Ridge Trail (AMC)

The Caps Ridge Trail makes a direct ascent of Mt. Jefferson from the height-of-land on the Jefferson Notch Rd., at an elevation of 3008 ft. This is the highest trailhead on a public through road in the White Mtns. Because of this high start, it is possible to ascend Mt. Jefferson and Mt. Clay with less climbing than by other routes. (In the ascent of Mt. Washington from the Caps Ridge, the descent from Monticello Lawn to Sphinx Col mostly cancels out the advantage of the higher start in comparison to the Jewell Trail.) However, the trail is steep and rough, the upper part is very exposed to weather, and there are numerous ledges which require rock scrambling and are slippery when wet. Therefore the route is more strenuous than might be inferred from the relatively small distance and elevation gain.

The trail leaves the Jefferson Notch Rd. at a parking area and crosses a wet section on puncheons. The trail then steadily ascends the lower part of the ridge; at 1.0 mi. there is an outcrop of granite on the right which provides a fine view, particularly of the summit of Jefferson and the Caps

Ridge ahead. There are several potholes in this outcrop which are normally formed only by torrential streams. Such streams occur on high ridges like the Ridge of the Caps only during the melting of a glacier, so these potholes indicate to geologists that the continental ice sheet once covered this area.

About 100 yd. beyond this outcrop, the Link enters from the left, providing a link to the Castle Trail. The trail follows the narrow crest of the ridge, becoming steeper and rougher as it climbs up into scrub, and views become more and more frequent. At 1.5 mi. the trail reaches the lowest cap (4400 ft.) after a steep scramble up ledges, and the trail is entirely in the open from here on. The trail continues very steeply up the ridge to the highest cap (4830 ft.) at 1.8 mi., then continues to climb steeply as the ridge blends into the summit mass. At 2.1 mi. the Cornice enters left, providing a very rough route to the Castle Trail and Edmands Col, and then diverges right in 20 yd., providing an easy shortcut to Monticello Lawn and points to the south. The Caps Ridge Trail continues east, keeping a little south of the crest of the ridge, to the summit of Mt. Jefferson, then descends east 40 yd. to the base of the little summit cone, where it meets the Castle and Six Husbands trails and the Mount Jefferson Loop.

Caps Ridge Trail (map 6:F8-F9)
Distances from Jefferson Notch Rd.

to the Link: 1.1 mi., 55 min.

to lower Cap: 1.5 mi., 1 hr. 30 min.

to upper Cap: 1.9 mi., 1 hr. 50 min.

to Cornice: 2.1 mi., 2 hr. 5 min.

to Mt. Jefferson summit: 2.5 mi., 2 hr. 40 min.

to junction with Mount Jefferson Loop: 2.6 mi. (4.2 km.), 2 hr. 45 min.

to Gulfside Trail (via Cornice): 2.5 mi., 2 hr. 30 min.

to Mt. Washington summit (via Cornice and Gulfside Trail): 5.5 mi., 4 hr. 35 min.

Boundary Line Trail (WMNF)

This trail begins on the Jewell Trail 0.3 mi. from the new parking area on the Base Rd. 1.1 mi. from its junction with the Jefferson Notch Rd., and runs to the Jefferson Notch Rd. 1.5 mi. below the Caps Ridge Trail—providing a short-cut between the base of the Caps Ridge Trail and the Jewell Trail and the Ammonoosuc Ravine Trail (Section 1). It follows the straight boundary line between two unincorporated townships, and is nearly level. Leaving the Jewell Trail, it runs north approximately along a surveyor's line, crosses Clay Brook, and ends at the Jefferson Notch Rd.

Boundary Line Trail (map 6:F8)
Distances from Jewell Trail

to Jefferson Notch Rd.: 0.7 mi. (1.1 km.), 20 min.

to Caps Ridge Trail (via Jefferson Notch Rd.): 2.2 mi., 1 hr. 5 min.

Jewell Trail (WMNF)

This trail begins at the new parking area on the Base Rd., climbs the unnamed ridge that leads west from Mt. Clay, and ends at the Gulfside Trail high on the west slope of Mt. Clay, 0.3 mi. north of the Clay–Washington col. The grade is constant, but seldom steep, there are no rock scrambles, and the footing is generally very good. It provides the easiest route to Mt. Washington from the west, with a great length of ridge above treeline with fine views but full exposure to the weather, and no shelter between the summit and treeline. In bad weather, or if afternoon thunderstorms threaten, it is safer to descend via Lakes of the Clouds Hut and the Ammonoosuc Ravine Trail, despite the steep and slippery footing on the latter trail; descent by the

Jewell Trail is much easier. The trail is named for Sergeant W. S. Jewell, an observer for the Army Signal Corps on Mt. Washington, who perished on the Greeley expedition to the Arctic in 1884.

The trail enters the woods directly across the road from the parking area, crosses the Ammonoosuc River at 0.1 mi., then swings northeast and ascends at an easy grade. At 0.3 mi. the Boundary Line Trail diverges left, while the Jewell Trail continues up the crest of the low ridge between the Ammonoosuc River and Clay Brook, joining the old route of the trail at 0.9 mi. At this point it descends slightly to Clay Brook, crosses on a footbridge, then climbs northeast by switchbacks up the south flank of the ridge and winds around its west end. Avoiding the craggy crest, it slabs the north flank and comes out above treeline on the west slope of Mt. Clay. It zigzags up the slope of Mt. Clay and enters the Gulfside Trail 0.3 mi. northwest of the Clay–Washington col. For Mt. Washington, follow the Gulfside right. For Mt. Clay, scramble up the rocks above the junction.

Jewell Trail (map 6:F8-F9)
Distances from Base Rd. parking area
   to Clay Brook crossing: 1.0 mi., 40 min.
   to Gulfside Trail: 3.5 mi. (5.6 km.), 3 hr. 10 min.
   to Mt. Washington summit (via Gulfside Trail): 5.0 mi.,
     4 hr. 25 min.

Pine Mountain Road

This private automobile road to the summit of Pine Mtn. begins a little northwest of the highest point of the Pinkham B (Dolly Copp) Rd., 2.4 mi. from US 2 and 1.9 mi. from NH 16, and opposite the foot of Pine Link. It is closed to public vehicular use, but may be used as a foot trail to the summit. Hikers should watch for automobiles descending on this road. The Ledge Trail, a foot trail over the top of the south cliff, diverges from the road and runs to the summit; it is frequently used to make a loop over the summit. The views from the summit are fine, both to the much higher surrounding peaks and to the valleys of the Androscoggin, Moose, and Peabody rivers. The Douglas Horton Center, a center for renewal and education operated by the New Hampshire Conference of the United Church of Christ (Congregational), occupies a tract of 100 acres on the summit. The center (not open to the public) consists of six buildings and an outdoor chapel on the more precipitous northeast peak. Although camping is not permitted, day hikers are welcome to appreciate the views.

The road runs east from Pinkham B Rd. across the col, and turns northeast and north to ascend along the west flank of the mountain, where the Ledge Trail branches right to climb around the south cliff and so to the summit. About 1.4 mi. from the highway a side trail leads left to a good spring. Opposite this path a shortcut leads right to the summit. The road climbs to the saddle north of the main summit, and turns south to the summit.

Pine Mountain Road (map 6:E10)
Distances (est.) from Pinkham B Rd.

to Ledge Trail: 1.0 mi., 35 min.

to summit: 1.8 mi. (2.9 km.), 1 hr. 20 min.

to Pinkham B Rd. (loop via Ledge Trail with return via Pine Mountain Road): 3.4 mi. (5.5 km.), 2 hr. 5 min.

Ledge Trail (WMNF)

This trail runs to the summit from the Pine Mountain Road (private, closed to public vehicles), 1.0 mi. from the Pinkham B (Dolly Copp) Rd. It runs around the south cliff and gives beautiful views westward.

Ledge Trail (map 6:E10)
Distance (est.) from Pine Mountain Road

to summit: 0.6 mi. (1.0 km.), 35 min.

Town Line Brook Trail (RMC)

A good but steep path runs from Pinkham B (Dolly Copp) Rd., 1.4 mi. southeast of the railroad crossing, to Triple Falls. These three beautiful cascades on Town Line Brook are named Proteus, Erebus, and Evans. The watershed is steep and the rainwater runs off very rapidly, so the falls should be visited during or immediately after a rain.

Town Line Brook Trail (map 6:E10)
Distance from Pinkham B (Dolly Copp) Rd.
to Triple Falls: 0.2 mi., 15 min.

Sylvan Way (RMC)

The Sylvan Way leads from the Link at Memorial Bridge, 0.7 mi. from the Appalachia parking area, over Cold Brook to Howker Ridge Trail at Coosauk Fall. Leaving Memorial Bridge it passes Cold Brook Fall in a few yards. At 0.1 mi. Beechwood Way crosses. Sylvan Way crosses Air Line at 0.6 mi. and Valley Way at 0.7. Soon, at 0.8 mi., Fallsway crosses, and Maple Walk enters left. Sylvan Way then crosses Snyder Brook and immediately after, the Brookbank. Randolph Path crosses at 1.1 mi. from Memorial Bridge, and, after a gradual ascent, the Sylvan Way ends at Howker Ridge Trail.

Sylvan Way (map 6:E9)
Distance from Memorial Bridge
to Howker Ridge Trail: 1.7 mi. (2.7 km.), 1 hr.

Fallsway (RMC)

Fallsway is an alternative route to the first 0.6 mi. of the Valley Way, following close to Snyder Brook and passing several falls. From the east end of the Appalachia parking area it goes east for 60 yd., then turns right on a gravel road and crosses the railroad and power lines. Here the Brookbank diverges left as Fallsway enters the woods. At

0.3 mi. from the Appalachia parking area, the path passes Gordon Fall, and Gordon Fall Loop diverges right. In a few yards Sylvan Way crosses and Maple Walk enters. Lower and Upper Salroc Falls are passed, and soon Fallsway enters Valley Way below Tama Fall. In a few yards Fallsway leaves Valley Way and passes Tama Fall. Brookbank then enters, and Fallsway ends in a few yards at Valley Way, above Tama Fall.

Fallsway (map 6:E9)
Distance from Appalachia parking area

to Valley Way junction above Tama Fall: 0.6 mi. (1.0 km.), 30 min.

Brookbank (RMC)

Brookbank diverges from Fallsway near the railroad and rejoins Fallsway above Tama Fall. It leaves Fallsway at the edge of the woods just beyond the power lines, 0.1 mi. from the Appalachia parking lot, and runs parallel to the railroad for about 0.1 mi., then crosses Snyder Brook, turns sharp right (south), and enters the woods. It runs up the east side of the brook, passing Gordon Fall, Sylvan Way, Upper and Lower Salroc Falls, and Tama Fall. Above Tama Fall it recrosses the brook and reenters Fallsway.

Brookbank (map 6:E9)
Distance from lower junction with Fallsway

to upper junction with Fallsway: 0.6 mi. (1.0 km.), 30 min.

Maple Walk (RMC)

The Maple Walk diverges left from Valley Way a few yards from the Appalachia parking area and runs to the junction of Fallsway and Sylvan Way. Just before the latter junction, Gordon Fall Loop diverges left and in 60 yd. reaches Fallsway at Gordon Fall.

Maple Walk (map 6:E9)
Distance from Valley Way
   to Sylvan Way and Fallsway: 0.2 mi. (0.3 km.), 5 min.

Beechwood Way (RMC)

This path runs from the Amphibrach 0.5 mi. from the Air Line, to the Valley Way just below its junctions with the Brookside and the Randolph Path. It follows a good logging road with moderate gradients. It leaves the Amphibrach, crosses Sylvan Way at 0.2 mi., then the Air Line at 0.6 mi., and joins the Valley Way just below its junction with the Brookside.

Beechwood Way (map 6:E9)
Distance from Amphibrach
   to Valley Way: 0.8 mi. (1.3 km.), 40 min.

SECTION 3

The Franconia, Twin, and Willey Ranges

The Central Region of the White Mtns. is a great wooded area studded with fine peaks, with no through highways and only a few gravel roads near the edges. The vast expanses of unbroken forest compensate for mountains that are, except for the Franconia Ridge and the cliffs of Mt. Bond, generally less rugged than the Presidentials. The region is bordered on the west and northwest by US 3 (and I-93), on the north by US 302, on the east by NH 16, and on the south by the Kancamagus Highway (NH 112). Section 3 includes the west and northwest portion of the Central Region, including the Franconia Range, Twin Range, and Willey Range. Most of the Pemigewasset Wilderness is also covered here. It should be noted that in this Guide the term Pemigewasset Wilderness is used strictly to refer to the officially designated wilderness area. Section 3 is divided from the eastern portion of the Central Region (which is covered in Section 4) by the Wilderness Trail (described in the present section), and by a continuation of the line of the Wilderness Trail east from its terminus at Stillwater Junction, over the plateau between Mt. Bemis and Mt. Willey, to US 302 in Crawford Notch. There are only two points of contact between trails in these two sections: first, where the Cedar Brook Trail (Section 4) meets the Wilderness Trail, just east of the latter's crossing of the East Branch of the Pemigewasset River via a suspension bridge; and second, where the Carrigain Notch Trail (Section 4) meets the Wilderness Trail and Shoal Pond Trail at Stillwater Junction. All of Section 3 is covered by the AMC Franconia map (map 5).

In this section the Appalachian Trail follows the Liberty Spring Trail and the Franconia Ridge Trail over Little Haystack Mtn. and Mt. Lincoln to Mt. Lafayette. It then runs along the Garfield Ridge Trail, passing close to the summit of Mt. Garfield, to Galehead Hut. Following the Twinway over South Twin Mtn. and Mt. Guyot, and passing near the summit of Zealand Mtn., it reaches Zealand Falls Hut, then takes the Ethan Pond Trail to US 302 in Crawford Notch.

FRANCONIA NOTCH AND THE FLUME

Franconia Notch lies between the Franconia Range on the east, and the Kinsman Ridge and Cannon Mtn. on the west. The region includes many interesting and accessible natural features such as the Profile (Old Man of the Mountain); Indian Head; Profile, Echo, and Lonesome lakes; the Flume, Pool, and Basin. The Plume and Pool are described below; the others, which are west of US 3, are discussed in Section 5. From the Flume area north to Echo Lake, the valley bottom and lower slopes on both sides lie within Franconia Notch State Park. Construction of I-93 through Franconia Notch has compelled the relocations of the lower portions of many of the trails covered in this section; much of this work has been complete, and plans for the rest are fairly well developed. Information regarding the current status of all facets of the project will be available at the Flume Visitor Center at the south end of the park, and also at Lafayette Place and the Cannon Mtn. Tramway. Hiker parking will be available at the Flume Visitor Center and the Basin, Lafayette Place, and Old Man parking lots. There will be no parking at the Appalachian Trail crossing near the former Whitehouse Bridge, which is now reached by the Whitehouse Trail from the Flume Visitor Center. The AMC, USFS, and the NHDP maintain an information booth during the summer and on fall weekends at the Lafayette Place parking area to provide information about weather, trail conditions, facilities, and regulations.

The Flume is a narrow gorge—one of the best-known features in the Franconia region—that can be reached from the Flume Visitor Center by graded trails or by an NHDP bus. There is a network of graded trails that connect points of interest, and a boardwalk through the Flume itself. It is open to visitors 30 May–15 Oct.; there is an admission fee for the Flume and the Pool. In the Flume, one can see broad ledges worn smooth by the action of the water and scoured by an avalanche in June 1883, which swept away a famous suspended boulder. Avalanche Falls at the upper end is worth visiting. The Pool is an interesting pothole formation in the Pemigewasset River, over 100 ft. in diameter and 40 ft. deep; it can be reached by a path of about 0.5 mi. from the visitor center. In the winter this is an easy, popular, and beautiful area to walk in, and there is no admission fee; however, several of the boardwalks are removed, restricting access to some parts.

GEOGRAPHY

The Franconia Range and the Twin Range are two high ridges which form a great horseshoe enclosing the western lobe of the Pemigewasset Wilderness, that vast area drained by the East Branch of the Pemigewasset. At one time it was an untracked wilderness, then a wasteland logged almost to total devastation, often referred to as the "so-called Pemigewasset Wilderness"; a recent act of Congress establishing the Pemigewasset Wilderness has once again officially entitled it to the name of Wilderness. This western lobe is drained by Franconia and Lincoln brooks, which almost encircle the long wooded ridge called Owl's Head. Starting at the southwest end of the horseshoe and running almost due north, the main ridge rises over several lower mountains to the high peaks of the Franconia Range: Mts. Flume, Liberty, Little Haystack, Lincoln, and Lafayette, the high point on the ridge. Swinging around to the east, the ridge crosses Mt. Garfield, Galehead Mtn., and South Twin Mtn., passing the lowest point (other than the ends), about 3400 ft., between Garfield and Galehead. Rising again to South Twin, where a major spur ridge leads north to North Twin Mtn., the main ridge runs southeast to Mt. Guyot. Here another major spur, Zealand Ridge, runs east; before it comes to an abrupt end at Zealand Notch, another ridge runs north from it over the Little River Mtns., which consist of Mt. Hale and the Sugarloaves. From Mt. Guyot the main ridge runs south over Mt. Bond and the Bondcliff before dropping to the East Branch. To the east lies the Willey Range, forming the west wall of Crawford Notch and the east wall of the broad, flat eastern lobe of the Pemigewasset Wilderness. The Rosebrook Range is a low northwest spur of the Willey Range. South from the Willey Range is the broad plateau which connects the Willey Range to the Nancy Range and Mt. Carrigain. This plateau rises steeply from Crawford Notch, providing the highest waterfalls in the White Mtns., then inclines gradually into the Pemigewasset Wilderness.

The Franconia Range ranks second among the ranges of the White Mtns. in elevation only. Its sharp, narrow ridge contrasts strikingly with the broad, massive Presidential Range. Mt. Lafayette (5260 ft.) was called "Great Haystack" on Carrigain's map of 1816, but was renamed in honor of the Marquis de Lafayette in gratitude for his assistance in the War of Independence. The highest part of the ridge, from Mt. Lafayette over Mt. Lincoln (5089 ft.) to Little Haystack Mtn. (4760 ft.), extends well above treeline. **Caution.** The portion of the Franconia Ridge above treeline is fully exposed to bad weather and is dangerous in adverse conditions. In particular, due to the narrowness of the ridge, there is unusually high danger from thunderstorms, and the ridge should be avoided when electrical

storms appear to be brewing. This part of the ridge is a
Gothic masterpiece; especially when seen from the west
(particularly from North Kinsman), it suggests the ruins of
a gigantic medieval cathedral. The peaks along the high,
serrated ridge are like towers supported by soaring but-
tresses which rise from the floor of the notch. There is a
knife-edged segment of the ridge between Lincoln and Little Haystack, with several interesting rock formations. To
the south rise the sharp, ledgy peaks of Mt. Liberty (4459
ft.) and Mt. Flume (4328 ft.), which are connected to each
other and to Little Haystack Mtn. by a long, graceful
ridge. Both these peaks have very fine views in all directions, particularly to the east over Mt. Bond and the
Pemigewasset Wilderness. Eagle Cliff (3420 ft.), a northwesterly spur of Mt. Lafayette, is remarkable for its sheer
cliffs and the detached finger of rock—the Eaglet—which
can be seen from the vicinity of the Old Man of the Mountain parking area. At the south end of the range, the ledges
of Little Coolidge Mtn. (2421 ft.) overlook the town of
Lincoln. There is no maintained trail to the ledges, but they
can be reached by bushwhacking from Lincoln.

The Twin Range is connected to the Franconia Range by
the Garfield Ridge, which runs north from Lafayette, then
swings to the east and culminates in the fine rocky peak of
Mt. Garfield (4500 ft.). Garfield rises like a sphinx over the
valleys of Franconia and Lincoln brooks to the south, providing one of the finest views in the White Mtns., including
a spectacular panorama of the higher Franconias to the
south. After passing Galehead Mtn. (4024 ft.), a wooded
hump with a restricted but excellent view of the Franconias, the ridge reaches South Twin Mtn. (4902 ft.), where
the views from the open summit are similar to Garfield's,
and equally fine, but from a different perspective. The summit of North Twin is densely wooded, but ledges almost at
the summit on the west and a short distance northeast

provide magnificent views. A small but very prominent peak, Haystack Mtn. (2713 ft.), which is sometimes called the Nubble, rises sharply from the lower end of North Twin's north ridge.

The main ridge now swings southeast, then south, crossing the bare summits of Mts. Guyot (4580 ft.) and Bond (4698 ft.), and Bondcliff (4265 ft.), the fine series of crags and ledges southwest of Mt. Bond. These three peaks, in addition to the spur of Bond called West Bond (4540 ft.), command views that are unequalled in the White Mtns. for their expansive views of forests and mountains, with virtually no sign of roads or buildings. For example, from the summit of Mt. Bond only the summit buildings on Mt. Washington and the Loon Mtn. ski slopes give visible evidence of human intrusion. Mt. Guyot was named for Arnold Guyot, the geographer who made the first accurate map of the White Mtns. He named several peaks, such as Mt. Tripyramid. Wherever there were mountains to be explored, Guyot could be found—there are also mountains named for him in the Great Smoky Mtns. and the Sierra.

The high point of the Zealand Ridge, Zealand Mtn. (4260 ft.), is wooded and viewless, but there is a magnificent outlook from Zeacliff, overlooking Zealand Notch and the eastern part of the Pemigewasset Wilderness from the east end of the ridge. Originally called the New Zealand Valley, presumably owing to its remoteness, the name was shortened to Zealand for the convenience of the railroad and post office. Much of Zealand Notch and the area to the north was reduced to a jumble of seared rock and sterile soil by a series of intensely hot fires around 1900. It has now made a reasonably complete recovery, a remarkable and outstanding testimony to the infinite healing powers of nature. Nowhere else in New England is there a better example of regeneration after disaster. At the height-of-land in Zealand Notch is Zealand Pond, which is unique for its having beaver dams as well as outlets at both ends; its waters eventually flow to the sea by both the Merrimack and the Connecticut rivers.

The Little River Mtns., lying between the Zealand River and Little River, offer excellent and easily attained panoramas of the surrounding summits from Mt. Hale (4054 ft.), Middle Sugarloaf (2539 ft.), and North Sugarloaf (2310 ft.). Mt. Hale was named for the Rev. Edward Everett Hale, author of the patriotic tale, "The Man Without a Country."

The Willey Range is a high ridge that rises sharply out of Crawford Notch. The ridge is rather narrow, with steep sides, but its crest undulates for about 2.5 mi. with relatively broad summits and shallow cols. The main peaks (from south to north) are Mt. Willey (4302 ft.), Mt. Field (4326 ft.), named for Darby Field, and Mt. Tom (4047 ft.). All are wooded to the top, but Willey has fine outlooks to the east over Crawford Notch, and to the south into the eastern lobe of the Pemigewasset Wilderness. A westerly spur ends abruptly at Zealand Notch with the cliffs of Whitewall Mtn. (3410 ft.). Mt. Avalon (3450 ft.) and Mt. Willard (2850 ft.) are easterly spurs offering fine views for relatively little effort; in fact no other spot in the White Mtns. affords so grand a view as Mt. Willard for so little effort. The Rosebrook Range continues northwest from Mt. Tom over Mt. Echo (3084 ft.), Mt. Stickney (3070 ft.), Mt. Rosebrook (3007 ft.), and Mt. Oscar (2746 ft.). There are no hiking trails, but the summit ledges of Mt. Oscar, with magnificent views over the Zealand Valley, can be reached by following ski slopes of the Bretton Woods Ski Area close to the col between Mt. Oscar and Mt. Rosebrook. The ridge is then followed northwest without a maintained trail about 0.3 mi. to the ledges.

Arethusa Falls and Ripley Falls are situated on brooks which descend the steep west side of Crawford Notch; in times of high water, these waterfalls can be quite spectacular. Between them stands Frankenstein Cliff, named for George L. Frankenstein, an artist whose work in the White Mtns. was once well known. A network of trails connects them and affords the opportunity for a variety of shorter day hikes.

The main part of the Pemigewasset Wilderness north of the East Branch is divided into two lobes. The western lobe, enclosed by the Franconia and Twin ranges, is a relatively narrow valley surrounded by the two steep ranges, occupied mainly by Owl's Head Mtn. (4025 ft.), one of the more remote major peaks in the White Mtns., named for the shape of its south end. The summit is wooded, but the great western slide provides some very fine views up to the Franconia Ridge and the isolated valley of Lincoln Brook. The eastern lobe is broader, with no important mountains, but Thoreau Falls, Ethan Pond, and Shoal Pond are interesting features. This region was the site of the most extensive logging in the White Mtns.; the devastation that resulted led to part of the eastern lobe being commonly referred to as the Desolation region. The history of this logging, and of the railroads which made it possible, is recounted in C. Francis Belcher's *Logging Railroads of the White Mountains*, published by the AMC.

HUTS, SHELTERS, AND CAMPING

HUTS

Greenleaf Hut (AMC)

Greenleaf Hut is located at the junction of the Old Bridle Path and Greenleaf Trail on Mt. Lafayette, at about 4200 ft., overlooking Eagle Lake. It is reached from US 3 via the Greenleaf Trail (2.5 mi.) or Old Bridle Path (2.9 mi.), and is 1.1 mi. from the summit of Mt. Lafayette and 7.7 mi.

from Galehead Hut. The hut accommodates 36 guests, and is open to the public during the summer and fall.

Galehead Hut (AMC)

Galehead Hut, built in 1932, is located at about 3800 ft. on a little hump on the Garfield Ridge, near the Twinway and the Garfield Ridge, Frost, and Twin Brook trails. It is reached in 4.6 mi. from the Gale River Loop Rd. (FR 25 and FR 92) via the Gale River and Garfield Ridge trails. It accommodates 38 guests and is open to the public during the summer and fall.

Zealand Falls Hut (AMC)

This hut, built in 1932, is located at about 2700 ft. beside Zealand Falls on Whitewall Brook, at the north end of Zealand Notch, near the Twinway and the Zealand and Ethan Pond trails. It is reached from the Zealand Rd. via the Zealand Trail in 2.8 mi. The hut accommodates 36 guests and is open to the public in summer and fall, and on a caretaker basis in the winter.

Crawford Notch Hostel (AMC)

Low-cost, self-service lodging is available in historic Crawford Notch. The main hostel holds thirty people in one large bunkroom. There is also a kitchen, bathrooms, and a common area. Three adjacent cabins accommodate eight persons each.

The hostel is open to the public. AMC members receive a discount on lodging. Overnight lodging is available year-round. Reservations are encouraged. Guests must supply food and sleeping bags; stoves and cooking equipment are provided. The hostel is an excellent choice for families and small groups and offers a wide range of hiking and outdoor experiences.

For information concerning AMC Huts, including opening and closing schedules, contact Reservation Secretary, Pinkham Notch Camp, Box 298, Gorham, NH 03581 (603-466-2727).

CAMPING

Pemigewasset Wilderness

In this area, camping and fires are prohibited above treeline, within one-quarter mile of 13 Falls Campsite, Thoreau Falls, Galehead Hut, Guyot Campsite, or within one-quarter mile of the Wilderness Trail and the East Branch from the wilderness boundary (near the Franconia Brook Trail junction) to the Thoreau Falls Trail junction, except at designated sites. No campsite may be used by more than ten persons at any one time.

Restricted Use Areas

The WMNF has established a number of Restricted Use Areas (RUA's) where camping and wood or charcoal fires are prohibited from 1 May to 1 November. The specific areas are under continual review, and areas are added to or subtracted from the list in order to provide the greatest amount of protection to areas subject to damage by excessive camping, while imposing the lowest level of restrictions possible. Violation of regulations in RUA's is usually punished by fines. A general list of RUA's follows, but one should obtain a map of current RUA's from the WMNF.

(1) No camping is permitted above treeline (where trees are less than 8 ft. tall). The point where the restricted area begins is marked on most trails with small signs, but the absence of such signs should not be construed as proof of the legality of a site.

(2) No camping is permitted within one-quarter mile of most facilities such as huts, cabins, shelters, or tentsites,

except at the facility itself. No camping is permitted within one-quarter mile of Garfield Pond.

(3) No camping is permitted within 200 ft. of certain trails, except at designated sites. In 1986, designated trails included the Garfield Ridge Trail, the Twinway from Galehead Hut to the summit of South Twin, and those portions of the Greenleaf Trail, Old Bridle Path, Falling Waters Trail, and Liberty Spring Trail which are not in Franconia Notch State Park (where camping is absolutely prohibited). No camping is permitted within one-quarter mile of the Wilderness Trail or the East Branch from the Kancamagus Highway to the wilderness boundary and the Franconia Brook Trail junction, except at Franconia Brook Campsite.

Franconia Notch State Park

Camping and fires are prohibited in Franconia Notch State Park, except at Lafayette Place Campground (fee charged).

Established Trailside Campsites

Camp 16 Campsite (WMNF), located at the junction of the Wilderness and Bondcliff trails, has nine tent platforms.

13 Falls Campsite (WMNF), located at the junction of the Franconia Brook, Lincoln Brook, and Twin Brook trails, has six tent platforms. The former shelter has been removed.

Franconia Brook Campsite (WMNF) is located on the Wilderness Trail 2.8 mi. from the Kancamagus Highway, and has sixteen tent platforms. The former shelter is closed to camping.

Guyot Shelter (AMC), located on a spur path from the Bondcliff Trail between the Twinway and the summit of Mt. Bond, has an open log shelter accommodating twelve, with six tent platforms in addition. There is a fine spring that is reliable in summer but may not flow in the cold seasons. A caretaker is in charge during the summer months, and there is a fee.

Liberty Spring Campsite (AMC), located on the Liberty Spring Trail 0.3 mi. below its junction with the Franconia Ridge Trail, has twelve tent platforms. A caretaker is in charge during the summer months, and there is a fee. The former shelter has been removed.

Garfield Ridge Campsite (AMC), located on a short spur path from the Garfield Ridge Trail 0.4 mi. east of Mt. Garfield, has seven four-person tent platforms and one twelve-person shelter. A caretaker is in charge during the summer months, and there is a fee.

Ethan Pond Campsite (AMC) is located near the shore of Ethan Pond, about 2.8 mi. from the Willey House Station. There is a shelter (capacity eight) and tent platforms (capacity twenty). Water may be obtained where the side path crosses the inlet brook.

LIST OF TRAILS   MAP

THE TRAILS

Franconia Ridge Trail (AMC)

This trail follows the backbone of the ridge from the summit of Mt. Lafayette south, over Mt. Lincoln, Little Haystack Mtn., Mt. Liberty, and Mt. Flume, ending at a junction with the Flume Slide Trail and the Osseo Trail. From Lafayette to Little Haystack it is almost constantly exposed to the full force of any storms, and is dangerous in bad weather. It is also particularly exposed to lightning in thunderstorms. Much work has been done to define and stabilize the trail and to reduce erosion. Hikers are urged to stay on the trail to save the thin alpine soils and fragile vegetation. From Mt. Lafayette to the Liberty Spring Trail it is part of the Appalachian Trail.

Leaving the summit of Mt. Lafayette the trail descends rather steeply, and passes through a small scrub patch in the col, which might provide some shelter in bad weather. It then crosses a prominent hump, descends, then climbs to the summit of Mt. Lincoln at 1.0 mi. It descends sharply to the ridge between Mt. Lincoln and Little Haystack Mtn., which is very narrow with steep slopes on both sides; then it follows a nearly level ridge in the open to the junction on the right, at 1.7 mi., with the Falling Waters Trail just under the summit rock of Little Haystack Mtn.

The Franconia Ridge Trail continues to the south end of the Little Haystack summit ridge, enters the scrub and descends steeply over ledges for a short distance, then moderates and follows the long ridge to a junction right with the Liberty Spring Trail at 3.5 mi. There is water at

Liberty Spring Campsite, 0.3 mi. down this trail. The Franconia Ridge Trail ascends to the rocky summit of Mt. Liberty at 3.8 mi., reaching the summit from the east, then makes a hairpin turn and descends to the east just a few yards south of its ascent route. The descent is steep at first, then moderates, and the trail passes through the col and ascends to the open summit of Mt. Flume; it then descends along the edge of the west cliff, enters the woods, and ends 0.1 mi. south of the summit in a little col at the junction with the Osseo Trail straight ahead and the Flume Slide Trail on the right.

Franconia Ridge Trail (map 5:H5)
Distances from Mt. Lafayette summit
  to Mt. Lincoln summit: 1.0 mi., 40 min.
  to Falling Waters Trail: 1.7 mi., 1 hr.
  to Liberty Spring Trail: 3.5 mi., 2 hr.
  to Mt. Liberty summit: 3.8 mi., 2 hr. 15 min.
  to Mt. Flume summit: 4.9 mi., 3 hr.
  to Flume Slide Trail/Osseo Trail junction: 5.0 mi. (8.0 km.), 3 hr. 5 min.

Flume Slide Trail (AMC)

This trail runs from the Liberty Spring Trail about 0.5 mi. from its junction with the Cascade Brook and Whitehouse trails, to the Franconia Ridge Trail 0.1 mi. south of the summit of Mt. Flume. It is an extremely steep, rough trail, with polished slabs which are very slippery when wet. It is not recommended for descent, and its use is discouraged in wet weather when the ledges are potentially dangerous. Views from the trail itself are very limited. The route over the slide is marked by paint on the ledges.

The trail leaves the Liberty Spring Trail on an old logging road that contours to the right (south). After 0.1 mi. the trail swings left off the logging road in a more easterly direction and begins a gradual ascent of the southwest shoulder of Mt. Liberty, with occasional descents and rises. In about 100 yd. it crosses a small brook, and about 0.1 mi. farther crosses a slightly larger one. From this point the trail contours for 0.5 mi., until it crosses a large brook on stepping stones. After rising from the brookbed, the trail climbs gradually and swings slightly more to the east. It continues to rise gradually, crossing several brooks. After passing through a swampy area, the trail crosses a small brook and turns almost east. From this point the trail should be followed carefully, since it makes several brook crossings before leaving the area to ascend to the bottom of the slide. While on the slide be careful not to dislodge stones that might endanger climbers below, and beware of rockfall from above. Near the top, the trail enters the woods at the left and climbs steeply in about 0.3 mi. to the Franconia Ridge Trail, where the Franconia Ridge Trail leads left (north) and the Osseo Trail leads right (south).

Flume Slide Trail (map 5:H4-H5)
Distances (est.) from Liberty Spring Trail
   to foot of slide: 3.0 mi., 2 hr. 10 min.
   to Franconia Ridge Trail: 4.3 mi. (6.9 km.), 3 hr. 35 min.

Liberty Spring Trail (AMC)

This trail begins at the junction of the Whitehouse Trail and the Cascade Brook Trail (Section 5), reached from the Flume Visitor Center by the Whitehouse Trail. There is no longer any parking at the former Whitehouse Bridge site. It passes Liberty Spring Campsite and reaches the Franconia Ridge Trail 0.3 mi. north of Mt. Liberty. The trail ascends steadily and rather steeply at times, but the footing, while not smooth, is always reasonably good. It is part of the Appalachian Trail.

Almost immediately after the starting point the trail joins a bike path, crosses the Pemigewasset River on a bridge, then diverges right from the bike path and starts to climb. It slabs northeast through hardwood growth, and in about 0.4 mi. joins the old main logging road from the former Whitehouse mill and soon levels off. At 0.5 mi. Flume Slide Trail leaves right (south). The Liberty Spring Trail then bears left, crosses several brooks (one large), heads more southeast, then ascends moderately to a sharp left turn at 1.3 mi.

The trail now rises at a moderate grade for some distance, then turns right and climbs more steeply. In places the footing is rough. About 0.6 mi. above the sharp turn a side path leads left to water. Some distance farther the trail becomes less steep and soon reaches Liberty Spring Campsite (3800 ft.) (last sure water). The path next ascends fairly steeply through low evergreens and ends in 0.3 mi. at the Franconia Ridge Trail; turn left (north) for Mt. Lafayette, right (south) for Mt. Liberty.

Liberty Spring Trail (map 5:H4-H5)
Distances from Whitehouse Trail

to sharp left turn: 1.3 mi., 1 hr. 5 min.
to Liberty Spring Campsite: 2.4 mi., 2 hr. 25 min.
to Franconia Ridge Trail: 2.7 mi. (4.3 km.), 2 hr. 45 min.
to Mt. Liberty summit (via Franconia Ridge Trail): 3.0 mi. (4.8 km.), 3 hr.

Whitehouse Trail (AMC)

This trail connects the parking lot at the Flume Visitor Center with the Liberty Spring Trail and the Cascade Brook Trail (Section 5), near the former parking area site at Whitehouse Bridge (where there is no longer any parking). Thus it is the route to these trails for hikers who bring their cars to the area.

It leaves the parking lot and runs north parallel to the main road. Just before reaching the Pemigewasset River, it joins the bike path, the Cascade Brook Trail diverges left, and the Liberty Spring Trail continues across the river on a bridge and diverges right off the bike path on the other side.

Whitehouse Trail (map 5:H4)
Distance from Flume Visitor Center parking area
   to Liberty Spring Trail/Cascade Brook Trail: 0.8 mi. (1.3 km.), 25 min.

Falling Waters Trail (AMC)

This trail begins at the new Lafayette Place parking lots on each side of I-93, and climbs to the Franconia Ridge Trail at the summit of Little Haystack Mtn., passing numerous waterfalls in its lower part. It is steep and rough in parts, and better for ascent than descent, but not dangerous unless there is ice on the ledgy sections near the brook.

The trail leaves the parking lot on the east side (reached from the west side by a paved path 0.1 mi. long) near the hiker information booth, in common with the Old Bridle Path, passing through a clearing and entering the woods. In 0.2 mi. it turns sharp right from the Old Bridle Path and immediately crosses Walker Brook on a bridge, then leads away from the brook heading southeast and east. At 0.7 mi. it crosses Dry Brook (use care if water is high), turns left and follows up the south bank to a beautiful cascade known as Stairs Falls. Above the falls the trail passes beneath Sawteeth Ledges and crosses the brook to the north bank just below Swiftwater Falls, which descend 60 ft. in a shady glen. Continuing on the north bank, the trail rises on a graded switchback for a short distance to an old logging road, which rises gradually in the narrow gorge of Dry Brook. The trail leaves the old road at a steep embankment, ascends in graded sections to Cloudland Falls (80 ft.), and climbs steeply to a viewpoint overlooking the head of the falls and out over the valley toward Mt. Moosilauke on the skyline.

At the head of Cloudland Falls are two small 25-ft. falls practically facing each other. The one to the south, which emerges from the woods, is on the branch of Dry Brook that runs down from Little Haystack, while the other is on the Mt. Lincoln branch. The trail continues steeply on the north bank of the Mt. Lincoln branch, soon crosses to the south bank, crosses back to the north side, climbs to and follows an old logging road, and recrosses to the south bank at 1.6 mi. After a view (cut) to the west, the trail takes the left fork of an old logging road, diverges left again, and ascends a ridge via a series of switchbacks. At the south end of the last switchback, at 2.8 mi., a side trail leads south about 100 yd. to the northeast corner of Shining Rock.

This steep granite ledge is over 200 ft. high and nearly 800 ft. long, is usually covered with water from springs in the woods above, and, seen from a distance, shines like a mirror in the sunlight. From this point there are fine views north and west over Franconia Notch. **Caution**. Climbing Shining Rock without rock climbing equipment and training is extremely dangerous.

The main trail continues north for a short distance, turns right, and climbs in a nearly straight line to the summit of Little Haystack.

Falling Waters Trail (map 5:H4-H5)
Distances from Lafayette Place parking area
   to Dry Brook: 0.7 mi., 25 min.
   to Stairs Falls: 0.8 mi., 30 min.
   to Cloudland Falls: 1.3 mi., 1 hr. 5 min.
   to Shining Rock side path: 2.8 mi., 2 hr. 35 min.
   to Franconia Ridge Trail: 3.2 mi. (5.1 km.), 3 hr. 10 min.

Old Bridle Path (AMC)

This trail runs from the Lafayette Place parking lots on each side of I-93 to Greenleaf Hut, where it joins the Greenleaf Trail. It affords fine views into Walker Ravine from outlooks in the upper part of the trail. For much of its length it follows the route of a former bridle path.

The trail leaves the parking lot on the east side (reached from the west side by a paved path 0.1 mi. long) near the hiker information booth in common with the Falling Waters Trail, passing through a clearing and entering the woods. In 0.2 mi. the Falling Waters Trail turns sharp right and immediately crosses Walker Brook on a bridge, while the Old Bridle Path continues along the brook for 50 yd., then swings left away from the brook and starts to climb at a moderate grade. At 1.2 mi. it comes to the edge of the bank high above Walker Brook, then swings away again. At 1.6 mi. it makes a sharp left turn with rock steps at the edge of the ravine, where there is a glimpse of Mt. Lincoln through the trees, then turns right and soon gains the ridge. At 1.9 mi. the first of the spectacular outlooks from the brink of the ravine is reached, and there are several more in the next 0.1 mi. The trail begins to ascend the steep part of the ridge, sometimes called Agony Ridge. At 2.4 mi. there is an unmarked side path that diverges right, passes two fine outlooks, and rejoins the main trail 40 yd. above the lower junction. Still climbing, the trail passes a view to Cannon Mtn., Mt. Kinsman, and Mt. Moosilauke from a grassy spot, then crosses a small sag through a patch of dead trees and soon reaches Greenleaf Hut.

Old Bridle Path (map 5:H4-H5)
Distance from Lafayette Place parking area
   to sharp turn with rock steps: 1.6 mi., 1 hr. 25 min.
   to Greenleaf Hut: 2.9 mi. (4.7 km.), 2 hr. 40 min.

Greenleaf Trail (AMC)

This trail runs from the Old Man parking lot on the west side of I-93 to Greenleaf Hut, where the Old Bridle Path joins, and thence to the summit of Mt. Lafayette, where it ends at the junction of the Franconia Ridge and Garfield Ridge trails. According to current plans, the trailhead will eventually be moved to the Tramway parking lot, still on the west side of I-93. Until it reaches the hut, the trail is almost completely in the woods, with few views—except when it traverses Eagle Pass, a wild, narrow cleft between Eagle Cliff and the west buttress of Mt. Lafayette, which has many interesting cliff and rock formations.

From the parking lot, present plans call for it to follow the bike path under the highway. It passes a small pond and turns sharp right at a large boulder, then starts to climb through a rocky area, parallel to and sometimes in sight of I-93. Turning right at the edge of a slide at 0.7 mi., the trail climbs moderately, first straight, then by numerous switchbacks, to Eagle Pass at 1.3 mi. The path leads east nearly level through the pass, crosses a small overgrown gravel slide, then swings more south and rises by long switchbacks, slabbing a northwest shoulder over loose stones that are slippery in wet weather. It finally reaches the top of the shoulder and continues a short distance to Greenleaf Hut at 2.5 mi.

At the hut, the Old Bridle Path enters on the right from Lafayette Place. The Greenleaf Trail heads toward Lafayette, enters the scrub, and dips slightly, passing south of Eagle Lakes, two picturesque shallow tarns (the upper lake is rapidly becoming a bog). The trail rises, passing over several minor knobs, and at 3.0 mi. swings left after passing a sandy area on the right. It soon climbs above the scrub into the open and ascends at a moderate grade, sometimes on rock steps between stone walls. At 3.4 mi. the trail bears left around a ledge from which issues a remarkable, very small but fairly reliable spring on the right of the trail. Now the trail turns right and soon reaches the summit of Mt. Lafayette. Here the Garfield Ridge Trail leads north and then northeast to Mt. Garfield, Garfield Ridge Campsite, Galehead Hut, and the Twin Range. To the south the Franconia Ridge Trail leads to Liberty Spring Campsite or to the Kancamagus Highway via the Osseo Trail.

Greenleaf Trail (map 5:G4-H5)
Distances from Old Man parking area
to Eagle Pass: 1.3 mi., 1 hr. 10 min.
to Greenleaf Hut: 2.5 mi., 2 hr. 20 min.
to Mt. Lafayette summit: 3.6 mi. (5.9 km.), 3 hr. 30 min.

Skookumchuck Trail (WMNF)

This is a pleasant and less frequently used route from I-93 to the north ridge of Mt. Lafayette, 0.7 mi. below the summit. Present plans call for a new parking area to be constructed in 1987 on US 3 just south of its junction with NH 141, about 0.7 mi. north of the former trailhead, with a new segment of trail constructed to link the new parking area to the old trail. Until this is done, it may be very difficult to approach the lower end of this trail due to road construction in the area. Since cars will not be permitted to park (or even stop, except for emergencies) in the area of the old trailhead, the following description is based on the assumption that the trailhead will be moved to some point near the planned location.

Leaving the parking lot, the trail parallels the road for about 0.7 mi. and enters the old route. At 1.1 mi. it reaches the edge of Skookumchuck Brook and follows the brook. At 1.8 mi. it crosses a small tributary on a rock bridge, climbs steeply away from the brook, then continues up above the valley at a moderate grade through a fine stand of birch. At 2.5 mi. it passes a small brook (unreliable) and continues to a shoulder at 3.6 mi., where there is a glimpse of Lafayette's north peak ahead. After a short, easy descent, the trail slabs to the north at mostly easy grades, then emerges above treeline near its junction with the Garfield Ridge Trail.

Skookumchuck Trail (map 5:G4-G5)
Distances from US 3

   to Garfield Ridge Trail: 4.2 mi. (6.8 km.), 3 hr. 40 min.

   to Mt. Lafayette summit: 4.9 mi. (7.9 km.), 4 hr. 15 min.

Garfield Ridge Trail (AMC)

This trail traverses the high ridge joining Mt. Lafayette to South Twin Mtn., running from the summit of Lafayette to Galehead Hut, and passing near the summit of Mt. Garfield on the way. The footway is rough, and there are numerous minor gains and losses of elevation, so the trail is more difficult than would be inferred from a glance at the map. Extra time should be allowed, particularly by those with heavy packs.

The trail starts from the summit of Mt. Lafayette and runs north along the ridge and over the north peak to a junction on the left with the Skookumchuck Trail on a shoulder at 0.7 mi. Swinging northeast, the Garfield Ridge Trail descends steeply to timberline and continues nearly on the crest of the ridge. It passes over a series of knobs on a large hump, descends its rough end to a tangled col at 2.5 mi., then climbs gradually toward Mt. Garfield. At 3.0 mi., near the foot of Garfield's cone, it passes to the right (south) of Garfield Pond, then climbs steeply, with many rock steps, to its high point on Mt. Garfield at 3.5 mi.; the bare summit, with magnificent views, is 60 yd. right (south) over open rocks. The trail descends steeply to a junction at

3.7 mi., where the Garfield Trail bears left for US 3, while the Garfield Ridge Trail bears right and descends very steeply northeast and east. At 3.9 mi. a side trail leaves left to a fine outlook over the Franconia Brook valley at 120 yd. and the AMC Garfield Ridge Campsite at 200 yd. The main trail continues down, crosses a small brook, and reaches a major col at 4.4 mi., where the Franconia Brook Trail leaves right and descends to 13 Falls. From this junction the Garfield Ridge Trail jogs left and follows the ridge, sometimes north and sometimes south of the crest, alternately up and down. At 5.7 mi. the trail passes an outlook to Owl's Head Mtn., descends a steep pitch, and at 6.0 mi. the Gale River Trail enters from the left. The Garfield Ridge Trail slabs the slope of Galehead Mtn., then turns right and climbs to a junction with the Twinway 40 yd. from Galehead Hut; turn right for the hut.

Garfield Ridge Trail (map 5:H5-G6)
Distances from Mt. Lafayette summit

- *to* Mt. Garfield summit area: 3.5 mi., 2 hr. 30 min.
- *to* Garfield Ridge Campsite spur path: 3.9 mi., 3 hr. 15 min.
- *to* Franconia Brook Trail: 4.4 mi., 3 hr. 30 min.
- *to* Gale River Trail junction: 6.0 mi., 4 hr. 30 min.
- *to* Galehead Hut: 6.6 mi. (10.7 km.), 5 hr.

Garfield Trail (WMNF)

This trail runs from the Gale River Loop Rd. (FR 92) to the Garfield Ridge Trail 0.2 mi. east of the summit of Mt. Garfield. This summit is bare rock with magnificent views. The trail follows an old road used for access to the former fire tower, and its grades are easy to moderate. The trailhead is reached by leaving US 3 at a picnic area 0.3 mi. south of its intersection with Trudeau Rd. (often called "Five Corners," signed for Trudeau Rd. and for the Ammonoosuc District Ranger Station). Follow the Gale River Loop Rd. south 1.2 mi., swing left where the trail continues straight ahead, and cross the bridge to a parking lot on the right. (Straight ahead on this road it is 1.6 mi. to the trailhead for the Gale River Trail.) This trail lies within the watershed of a municipal water supply, and hikers and campers should exercise care not to pollute the streams.

The trail begins on the west side of the South Branch of the Gale River, follows a logging road along the river for 0.4 mi., then bears left and crosses the river. This crossing is difficult at high water, but it is possible to avoid it by bushwhacking along the east bank to or from the parking area. The trail climbs slowly away from the river, crosses Thompson Brook at 0.9 mi., then quickly crosses and recrosses Spruce Brook and heads generally south. At 2.8 mi. the trail crosses a ridge and descends slightly; there are many fine birches, particularly below the trail. It climbs by several sweeping switchbacks, enters the conifers and reaches a blowdown area at 4.1 mi. Here it turns sharp left, runs through an area of large conifers, and slabs around the east side of the cone of Mt. Garfield to a junction with the Garfield Ridge Trail, which enters from the left, ascending from Garfield Ridge Campsite. The summit of Garfield is reached in 0.2 mi. by following a very steep section of the Garfield Ridge Trail to its high point, then climbing over the rocks on the left for 60 yd.

Garfield Trail (map 5:G5)
Distance from Gale River Loop Rd. (FR 92)

   to Garfield Ridge Trail: 4.6 mi. (7.5 km.), 3 hr. 35 min.
   to Mt. Garfield summit (via Garfield Ridge Trail): 4.8 mi. (7.7 km.), 3 hr. 50 min.
   to Garfield Ridge Campsite (via Garfield Ridge Trail): 4.9 mi. (7.8 km.), 3 hr. 45 min.

Gale River Trail (WMNF)

This trail runs from the Gale River Loop Rd. (FR 92) to the Garfield Ridge Trail 0.6 mi. west of Galehead Hut. The trailhead is reached by leaving US 3 at its intersection with Trudeau Rd. (often called "Five Corners," signed for Trudeau Rd. and for the Ammonoosuc District Ranger Station). Follow the Gale River Rd. (FR 25) southeast, bearing left at 0.6 mi., then turn sharp right at 1.3 mi. on the Gale River Loop Rd. and continue to the parking area on the left at 1.6 mi. (Straight ahead on the road it is 1.6 mi. from here to the Garfield Trail parking lot.) This trail lies within the watershed of a municipal water supply, and hikers and campers should exercise care not to pollute the streams.

The trail enters the woods, soon descends a bank and crosses a tributary of the north branch, then turns right on an old logging road that climbs easily along the west side of the North Branch of the Gale River, some distance away from the stream. At 1.4 mi. it comes to the edge of the stream, crosses it on a bridge at 1.7 mi., and becomes somewhat rougher, with several bypasses of muddy sections and washouts. The trail passes through an old logging camp site, crosses a major tributary, and recrosses to the west side of the North Branch at 2.5 mi. on stepping stones (difficult only in very high water). After passing the gravel outwash of an overgrown slide, the trail emerges at 3.1 mi. on a gravel bank above the stream at the base of a slide, where there are fine views up the valley and toward the Twins. The trail now becomes constantly steeper and rougher, and ends with a fairly steep climb to the Garfield Ridge Trail.

Gale River Trail (map 5:G5-G6)
Distances from Gale River Loop Rd. (FR 92)

to Garfield Ridge Trail: 4.0 mi. (6.4 km.), 2 hr. 55 min.

to Galehead Hut (via Garfield Ridge Trail): 4.6 mi. (7.4 km.), 3 hr. 25 min.

Frost Trail (AMC)

This trail leads from Galehead Hut to the summit of Galehead Mtn. Leaving the hut clearing, it descends into a sag, then passes a junction left with the Twin Brook Trail, where the Frost Trail turns sharp right. After a short distance, it ascends a steep pitch, at the top of which a side path leads left 30 yd. to an excellent outlook over the Twin Brook valley. The trail continues at a moderate grade to the flat summit, where there is a good view of Mt. Garfield and the Franconia Ridge.

Frost Trail (map 5:G6)

Distance from Galehead Hut

to Galehead Mtn. summit: 0.5 mi. (0.8 km.), 25 min.

Twinway (AMC)

This trail extends from Galehead Hut to the junction of the Zealand Trail and the Ethan Pond Trail 0.2 mi. beyond Zealand Falls Hut. For its entire length it is part of the Appalachian Trail.

From Galehead Hut, the trail passes over a ledgy hump with an outlook right, descends through a sag, then climbs steadily and steeply up the cone of South Twin to the south knob of the summit at 0.8 mi. Here the North Twin Spur begins and goes straight ahead 40 yd. to the north knob, while the Twinway turns right (south), and descends along the ridge toward Mt. Guyot, with easy to moderate grades after an initial steep pitch below the summit. At 1.8 mi. the trail crosses a ledgy hump with a view ahead to Guyot and Carrigain, and back to South Twin. It then descends easily to the col, and climbs out of the scrub on the side of Guyot to a junction on the right with the Bondcliff Trail at 2.8 mi. Guyot Campsite is 0.8 mi. from this junction via the Bondcliff Trail and a spur path.

The Twinway now ascends in the open to the flat summit

of Guyot at 2.9 mi., and, reentering the woods, slowly descends the long ridge to Zealand, reaching the col at 3.9 mi. It climbs rather steeply, and, at 4.1 mi., a few yards before reaching the height-of-land, passes a side path left that runs nearly level 0.1 mi. to the true summit of Zealand Mtn. The main trail continues down the ridge, passes a ledge overlooking Zeacliff Pond at 5.1 mi., then descends a steep pitch, and in a sag at 5.3 mi. passes an unsigned side path that leads right to the shore of Zeacliff Pond in 0.1 mi. The main trail follows a ledgy ridge over a number of humps, passing the junction right with the Zeacliff Trail at 5.7 mi. It soon reaches a loop side path right, which passes over the magnificent Zeacliff outlook and rejoins the main trail 50 yd. east of its point of departure. Here the Twinway turns left and descends moderately through birch woods. At 6.9 mi. the trail crosses two branches of Whitewall Brook on ledges, and the Lend-a-Hand Trail enters on the left in 10 yd. The Twinway passes Zealand Falls Hut at 7.0 mi., descends steeply for a short distance, then crosses the outlet of Zealand Pond and reaches the grade of the old logging railroad, where the Zealand Trail turns left and the Ethan Pond Trail turns right, both on the railroad grade.

Twinway (map 5:G6-G7)
Distances from Galehead Hut
- *to* South Twin summit: 0.8 mi., 1 hr.
- *to* Bondcliff Trail: 2.8 mi., 2 hr. 5 min.
- *to* Zealand Mt. summit spur: 4.1 mi., 2 hr. 55 min.
- *to* Zeacliff outlook spur: 5.8 mi., 3 hr. 50 min.
- *to* Zealand Falls Hut: 7.0 mi., 4 hr. 25 min.
- *to* Ethan Pond Trail/Zealand Trail: 7.2 mi. (11.6 km.), 4 hr. 30 min.

North Twin Spur (AMC)
This trail connects the Twinway on the summit of South Twin with the North Twin Trail on the summit of North

Twin. It leaves the Twinway at the south knob of South Twin, crosses the north knob in 40 yd., and descends moderately to the fern-filled col at 0.8 mi. Then it ascends to the summit of North Twin, where the North Twin Trail enters straight ahead, and a spur path leads left 60 yd. to a fine outlook.

North Twin Spur (map 5:G6)
Distance from the Twinway

to North Twin summit: 1.3 mi. (2.0 km.), 50 min.

North Twin Trail (WMNF)

This trail runs from Haystack Rd. (FR 304) to the summit of North Twin. This road begins on US 3 just west of a large WMNF boundary sign, about 2.3 mi. west of Twin Mountain village, and runs south 2.5 mi. to a parking area just past its crossing of the Little River. The three crossings of the Little River on this trail are very difficult or impassable at high water; the third is the least difficult, and the first two may be avoided by staying on the east bank and bushwhacking along the river. This trail is in the watershed of a municipal water supply, and hikers and campers should take care not to pollute the streams.

The trail leaves the parking area and crosses the river three times, ascending easily on an old railroad grade with occasional bypasses. After the third crossing, at 1.9 mi., the trail begins to climb away from the river and railroad grade, crossing and recrossing a tributary brook. The long, steady climb continues, and at 3.5 mi. the trail becomes quite steep, reaching the ledgy end of the ridge at 4.0 mi. The trail now climbs easily, passes a superb outlook ledge at 4.2 mi., and reaches the summit of North Twin at 4.3 mi. The North Twin Spur continues straight ahead to South Twin, and a side path leads right 60 yd. to a fine outlook.

North Twin Trail (map 5:G6)
Distances from Haystack Rd.
  to third crossing of Little River: 1.9 mi., 1 hr. 15 min.
  to North Twin summit: 4.3 mi. (7.0 km.), 3 hr. 35 min.

Zeacliff Trail (AMC)

This trail runs from the Ethan Pond Trail 1.3 mi. south of its junction with Zealand Pond, to the Twinway 0.1 mi. west of the Zeacliff outlook. It is an attractive trail, but extremely steep and rough in parts, and not recommended for hikers with heavy packs. Practically all of it is in the Pemigewasset Wilderness.

The trail leaves the Ethan Pond Trail and descends east over open talus, then drops very steeply to cross Whitewall Brook at 0.2 mi. Soon it begins to climb very steeply, then at 0.6 mi. the grade eases up. Soon the trail reaches the top of the ridge, where it ascends gradually through a beautiful birch forest, then slabs left to a rock face at 1.1 mi. The main trail turns right and ascends steeply to the right of the rock face, while a rough and somewhat obscure loop path runs under the rock face, then swings right, passes an outlook toward Carrigain Notch, and rejoins the main trail. Above this point the trail ascends very steeply to the Twinway. Turn right for the Zeacliff outlook.

Zeacliff Trail (map 5:G7)
Distance from Ethan Pond Trail
  to Twinway: 1.4 mi. (2.3 km.), 1 hr. 30 min.

Zealand Trail (WMNF)

The Zealand Trail runs from the end of Zealand Rd. to a junction with the Ethan Pond Trail and the Twinway just below Zealand Falls Hut. It is reached by following Zealand Rd. (FR 16), which leaves US 302 at Zealand Campground, about 2.3 mi. east of Twin Mountain village.

Zealand Rd. is closed to public vehicular use from mid-November to mid-May. The Zealand Trail starts at a parking area just before the gate at 3.5 mi. from US 302. The Zealand Trail is relatively easy, following old railroad grade much of the way, and passing through an area of beaver swamps, meadows, and ponds. All major brook crossings are bridged.

Leaving the parking area, the trail follows the railroad grade, then a bypass that is somewhat rough. It then returns to the grade and approaches Zealand River at 0.8 mi., near some ledges in the stream. It continues on the west bank, then makes the first of several brook crossings at 1.5 mi. The trail now passes through an area of beaver activity, staying mostly on the railroad grade, and at 2.3 mi. the A–Z Trail enters left. The Zealand Trail skirts Zealand Pond and ends at 2.5 mi., where the Ethan Pond Trail continues straight ahead, and the Twinway turns right to Zealand Falls Hut, 0.2 mi. away.

Zealand Trail (map 5:G7)
Distances from end of Zealand Rd.

   to A–Z Trail: 2.3 mi., 1 hr. 20 min.

   to Ethan Pond Trail/Twinway junction: 2.5 mi. (4.1 km.), 1 hr. 30 min.

   to Zealand Falls Hut (via Twinway): 2.7 mi., 1 hr. 40 min.

Lend-a-Hand Trail (AMC)

This trail connects Zealand Falls Hut with the summit of Mt. Hale. The climbing is fairly easy but the footing is rather rough for a good part of its distance, since the trail has a great number of puncheons crossing a very wet section.

This trail diverges right (north) from the Twinway 0.1 mi. above Zealand Falls Hut and climbs steadily, crossing a small brook three times. After about 0.5 mi. the grade becomes easy in a long section with numerous puncheons, where small brooks flow in and through the trail. At 1.5 mi. the trail enters a scrubby, ledgy area and ascends moderately. In a rocky area at 1.9 mi. a rock 15 yd. right of the trail offers a fine view. At 2.4 mi. the trail climbs another rocky pitch and continues in dense conifers to the summit, where the Hale Brook Trail leaves east (right). Many of the rocks on this bare summit are reputed to be strongly magnetic.

Lend-a-Hand Trail (map 5:G7-G6)
Distance from Twinway

to Mt. Hale summit: 2.7 mi. (4.3 km.), 2 hr.

Hale Brook Trail (WMNF)

This trail climbs from Zealand Rd. (FR 16), at a parking area 2.5 mi. from US 302, to the bare summit of Mt. Hale, where there are excellent views. The trail is relatively easy, with moderate grades and good footing, and passes through very fine birch forest much of the way.

The trail leaves the parking area, crosses a cross-country ski trail, then ascends steadily to cross Hale Brook at 0.8 mi. It continues the steady climb, then swings left and slabs gradually on the steep slope above Hale Brook, which rises to meet and cross the trail at 1.3 mi. Now the trail ascends by several switchbacks, crossing a small brook at 1.7 mi. Still ascending, and curving gradually to the right, it enters the conifers and attains the summit from the east.

Hale Brook Trail (map 5:G7-G6)
Distance from Zealand Rd.

to Mt. Hale summit: 2.2 mi. (3.5 km.), 2 hr. 15 min.

Sugarloaf Trail (WMNF)

This trail ascends both North Sugarloaf and Middle Sugarloaf from Zealand Rd. (FR 16), just south of the bridge over the Zealand River 1.0 mi. from US 302. Parking is just north of the bridge.

Leaving the road, the Sugarloaf Trail follows the river for 0.2 mi., coinciding with the Trestle Trail, then swings left as the Trestle Trail continues along the river. After this junction the Sugarloaf Trail immediately crosses a snow-mobile trail and a dirt road, and climbs gradually, passing a few large boulders. At 0.7 mi. it makes an abrupt ascent to the col between North and Middle Sugarloaf. In this col, at 0.9 mi., the trail divides. The left branch leads 0.4 mi. to Middle Sugarloaf, a fine and rewarding viewpoint for a modest effort. The last part of this trail below the summit is very steep. The right branch descends slightly and then climbs 0.3 mi. to North Sugarloaf, where the summit ledges afford excellent views.

Sugarloaf Trail (map 5:F6)
Distances from Zealand Rd.
   to Middle Sugarloaf: 1.3 mi. (2.1 km.), 1 hr. 10 min.
   to North Sugarloaf: 1.2 mi. (1.9 km.), 1 hr.

Trestle Trail (WMNF)

This short loop trail begins and ends at the bridge over the Zealand River on Zealand Rd. (FR 16), 1.0 mi. from US 302. (Parking is at the north end of the bridge.) An information leaflet is usually available at the trailhead. It leaves the road at the south end of the bridge and follows the river, coinciding with the Sugarloaf Trail for 0.2 mi. After the Sugarloaf Trail diverges left, the Trestle Trail leads away from the river, crosses a snowmobile trail, passes a large rock, then turns sharp right and joins and follows the snowmobile trail for a short distance. Then the trail turns sharp right on an old railroad grade, crosses the river on a bridge at 0.5 mi., and soon enters Sugarloaf II Campground. After following the campground road for

0.1 mi., it reenters the woods and returns to Zealand Rd. at the north end of the bridge.

Trestle Trail (map 5:F6)
Distance of loop
from Zealand Rd.: 1.0 mi. (1.6 km.), 35 min.

Mount Willard Trail (AMC)

This path runs from the AMC's Crawford Depot information center to the ledges above the cliffs overlooking Crawford Notch. The upper part was formerly a carriage road, and the trail has easy grades, good footing, and magnificent views from the ledges.

From the Crawford Depot, on the west side of US 302 across from the north end of Saco Lake, this trail coincides with the Avalon Trail for 0.1 mi. The Mount Willard Trail turns left, runs level, and soon turns right to begin the ascent. In another 100 yd. the trail bears right, bypassing to the west a severely washed-out portion of the old carriage road. At 0.7 mi. Centennial Pool is reached on the right. Beyond this point the trail bears left, rejoining the old carriage road, which it follows the remaining 0.7 mi. to the ledges just east of the true summit.

Mount Willard Trail (map 5:G8)
Distance from Crawford Depot
to Mt. Willard summit: 1.4 mi. (2.3 km.), 1 hr. 10 min.

Avalon Trail (AMC)

This trail runs from the AMC's Crawford Depot information center to the Willey Range Trail 90 yd. north of the summit of Mt. Field, passing along the way a short spur path to the fine outlook on Mt. Avalon. Some parts are steep and rough, but not severely so.

The trail starts on the west side of US 302 at the Crawford Depot. After 0.1 mi. the Mount Willard Trail leaves left, and the Avalon Trail ascends gradually and soon crosses a brook. About 70 yd. beyond this crossing a loop path diverges left, passes by Beecher and Pearl cascades, and shortly rejoins the main trail. The main trail continues at an easy grade, recrosses the brook at 0.8 mi., and begins a moderate ascent. At 1.3 mi. the A–Z Trail to Zealand Falls Hut diverges right. The Avalon Trail soon begins to climb rather steeply, and at 1.8 mi., in the small col just below the Mt. Avalon summit, a short side path diverges left and climbs steeply 100 yd. to a fine viewpoint. The main trail passes through a flat, ledgy area, then climbs steadily, with restricted views to the northeast, and reaches the Willey Range Trail. For the summit of Mt. Field go left (south) 90 yd.

Avalon Trail (map 5:G8-G7)
Distances from Crawford Depot
to Mt. Avalon spur path: 1.8 mi., 1 hr. 40 min.
to Willey Range Trail: 2.8 mi. (4.5 km.), 2 hr. 35 min.

A–Z Trail (AMC)
This trail provides a route from US 302 at the Crawford Depot to Zealand Falls Hut, crossing the Willey Range at the Field–Tom col. It diverges right from the Avalon Trail 1.3 mi. from Crawford's, crosses a steep gully, then climbs steadily, slabbing along the side of the valley. At 0.6 mi. it crosses the brook and soon begins to climb more steeply, reaching the height-of-land at 1.0 mi., where the Mount Tom Spur diverges right. The trail starts to descend gradually, and in 80 yd. the Willey Range Trail enters on the left. The descent becomes steeper until Mt. Field Brook is crossed at 1.6 mi., then the trail continues descending at easy to moderate grades, passing through a logged area and crossing several small brooks, and reaches the Zealand

Trail 2.3 mi. from the end of Zealand Rd. Zealand Falls Hut is 0.5 mi. left via the Zealand Trail and Twinway.

A–Z Trail (map 5:G7)
Distances from Avalon Trail
   to Willey Range Trail: 1.0 mi., 1 hr.
   to Zealand Trail: 3.7 mi. (6.0 km.), 2 hr. 20 min.
   to Zealand Falls Hut (via Zealand Trail and Twinway):
      4.2 mi., 2 hr. 40 min.

Ethan Pond Trail (AMC)

This trail begins at the Willey House Station, reached by a paved road 0.3 mi. long which leaves the west side of US 302 directly opposite the Webster Cliff Trail, about 1 mi. south of the Willey House site. It ends at the junction of the Zealand Trail and the Twinway, 0.2 mi. below Zealand Falls Hut. It is part of the Appalachian Trail.

The trail begins in a parking area just below the railroad tracks, crosses the tracks just north of the station, and in 0.2 mi. the Arethusa–Ripley Falls Trail diverges left. It climbs steadily, then becomes more gradual, and at 1.3 mi. the Kedron Flume Trail enters right. At 1.6 mi. the Willey Range Trail leaves straight ahead, and the Ethan Pond Trail turns left and climbs steadily to the height-of-land at 2.1 mi., passing from Crawford Notch State Park into the WMNF. It enters and follows an old logging road down to a point close to the southeast corner of Ethan Pond (which is not visible from the trail), named for its discoverer, Ethan Allen Crawford. Here, at 2.6 mi. from Willey House Station, a side trail right leads in 250 yd. to Ethan Pond Campsite.

At 4.2 mi. one branch of the Shoal Pond Trail goes straight ahead, and the Ethan Pond Trail bears right. The main trail soon merges into a spur of the old Zealand Valley railroad, which it follows to the main line at 4.6 mi., where the other branch of the Shoal Pond Trail enters left. At 4.9 mi. the Ethan Pond Trail crosses the North Fork on a wooden bridge, and at 5.1 mi. the Thoreau Falls Trail diverges left to continue down the North Fork. The Ethan Pond Trail follows the old railroad grade on a gradual curve into Zealand Notch, with its spectacular, fire-scarred walls. As the trail crosses the talus slopes of Whitewall Mtn. it comes into the open with fine views, and at 5.9 mi., in the middle of this section, the Zeacliff Trail diverges left. The Ethan Pond Trail reenters the woods and continues on the railroad grade to the junction with the Zealand Trail and the Twinway. For Zealand Falls Hut turn sharp left onto the Twinway and follow it for 0.2 mi.

Ethan Pond Trail (map 5:H8-G7)
Distances from Willey House Station

- *to* Willey Range Trail: 1.6 mi., 1 hr. 25 min.
- *to* side trail to Ethan Pond Campsite: 2.6 mi., 2 hr. 5 min.
- *to* Shoal Pond Trail (west branch): 4.6 mi., 3 hr. 5 min.
- *to* Thoreau Falls Trail: 5.1 mi., 3 hr. 20 min.
- *to* Zeacliff Trail: 5.9 mi., 3 hr. 40 min.
- *to* Zealand Trail/Twinway: 7.2 mi. (11.6 km.), 4 hr. 20 min.
- *to* Zealand Falls Hut (via Zealand Trail and Twinway): 7.4 mi., 4 hr. 30 min.

Kedron Flume Trail (AMC)

This trail runs from the Willey House site on US 302, past Kedron Flume, an interesting cascade, to the Ethan Pond Trail 0.3 mi. south of its junction with the Willey Range Trail. As far as Kedron Flume, the trail has easy to moderate grades with good footing. Past the flume it is very steep and rough.

Leaving US 302 south of the buildings at the Willey

House site, the trail passes through a picnic area and enters the woods. In 0.4 mi. it crosses the railroad tracks, with a fine view of Mt. Willey. At 1.0 mi , after a short descent, it crosses Kedron Brook. Above is an interesting flume and below is a waterfall where there is an excellent outlook; use care on slippery rocks. Above here the trail makes a very steep and rough climb, following a small brook part of the way, then becomes easier as it approaches the Ethan Pond Trail.

Kedron Flume Trail (map 5:G8)
Distances from Willey House site
to Kedron Flume: 1.0 mi., 50 min.
to Ethan Pond Trail: 1.3 mi., 1 hr. 15 min.

Willey Range Trail (AMC)
This trail begins on the Ethan Pond Trail 1.6 mi. from the Willey House Station, then runs over the summits of Mt. Willey and Mt. Field to the A–Z Trail in the Field–Tom col. With the Ethan Pond, A–Z, and Avalon trails, it makes possible various trips over the range between Willey House Station, the Crawford Depot, and Zealand Falls Hut. The section on the south slope of Mt. Willey is very steep and rough.

The trail continues straight ahead where the Ethan Pond Trail turns left, crosses Kedron Brook in 100 yd., and at 0.2 mi. it turns sharp left and crosses a small brook. At 0.4 mi. it crosses another small brook and climbs a very steep and rough slope with several ladders and occasional outlooks. The best view is from the east outlook, near the summit, reached by an unsigned side path leading right 40 yd. below the summit cairn. The main trail reaches the summit at 1.1 mi., circles around to the south outlook, then descends gradually, keeping to the west side of the ridge. It loses only 300 ft. in altitude at its low point, then climbs to the summit of Mt. Field at 2.5 mi. About 90 yd. north of this summit the Avalon Trail diverges right, and the Willey Range Trail climbs over a small knob and descends gradually northwest to the A–Z Trail at 3.4 mi. in the Field–Tom col. Turn left for Zealand Falls Hut or right for the Mount Tom Spur, Crawford Depot, and US 302.

Willey Range Trail (map 5:G8–G7)
Distances from Ethan Pond Trail

 to Mt. Willey summit: 1.1 mi., 1 hr. 25 min.

 to Mt. Field summit: 2.5 mi., 2 hr. 15 min.

 to A–Z Trail: 3.4 mi. (5.6 km.), 2 hr. 45 min.

Mount Tom Spur (AMC)

This short trail runs from the A–Z Trail to the summit of Mt. Tom. It leaves the A–Z Trail at the height-of-land, 80 yd. east of the Willey Range Trail junction, and climbs at a moderate grade. At 0.3 mi. there is a good view from a blowdown patch, and the trail continues to a false summit, where it swings left and reaches the true summit in 60 yd.

Mount Tom Spur (map 5:G7)
Distance from A–Z Trail

 to Mt. Tom summit: 0.6 mi. (0.9 km.), 30 min.

Arethusa Falls Trail (NHDP)

From the Arethusa Falls parking lot on the west side of US 302, the trail crosses the railroad and leads left (south) for 50 yd., where it turns right into the woods. It follows old roads above the north bank of Bemis Brook until it crosses the brook shortly below the falls. These are over 200 ft. high, the highest in the state. The Bemis Brook Trail diverges left 0.3 mi. from US 302 and rejoins at 0.9 mi., providing an attractive alternative.

Arethusa Falls Trail (map 5:H8)
Distance (est.) from Arethusa Falls parking area
to Arethusa Falls: 1.3 mi. (2.1 km.), 1 hr. 5 min.

Bemis Brook Trail (NHDP)

This alternate route to Arethusa Falls departs left from the Arethusa Falls Trail 0.3 mi. from its start at the railroad, angles toward the brook, and then follows close to the brook. Passing Fawn Pool, Coliseum Falls, and the Bemis Brook Falls, it then climbs steeply up the bank to rejoin the Arethusa Falls Trail.

Bemis Brook Trail (map 5:H8)
Distance (est.) from leaving Arethusa Falls Trail
to rejoining Arethusa Falls Trail: 0.6 mi. (1.0 km.), 40 min.

Arethusa–Ripley Falls Trail (AMC/NHDP)

These two spectacular spots in Crawford Notch are connected by a trail that starts at the end of the Arethusa Falls Trail just below the falls. It immediately crosses the brook and slabs away from the falls up the side of the valley on a graded path. It then doubles back on the south side of a smaller brook, which it soon crosses. A rougher path leads northeast across several small watercourses to the plateau behind Frankenstein Cliff. Turning east, the trail shortly passes the junction of the Frankenstein Cliff Trail and again heads north across the plateau. With various views of Mt. Webster, Crawford Notch, and Mt. Willey, the trail drops gradually and then more steeply on switchbacks to Avalanche Brook at the foot of Ripley Falls, which are about 100 ft. high. In dry weather, the brook is rather low. The rocks just off the path near the falls are slippery and should be avoided. Crossing the brook at the foot of the falls, the path rises slightly to the east for 0.4 mi. to join the Ethan Pond Trail 0.2 mi. from the Willey House Station; continue straight ahead for that destination.

Arethusa–Ripley Falls Trail (map 5:H8)
Distances (est.) from Arethusa Falls
- *to* Frankenstein Cliff Trail: 1.0 mi., 45 min.
- *to* Ripley Falls: 2.1 mi., 1 hr. 20 min.
- *to* Ethan Pond Trail: 2.5 mi. (4.0 km.), 1 hr. 30 min.
- *to* Willey House Station: 2.7 mi. (4.3 km.), 1 hr. 35 min.

Frankenstein Cliff Trail (NHDP)

Frankenstein Cliff, a prominent feature from the highway, juts out from the tableland south of Mt. Willey and affords excellent views of the lower part of Crawford Notch.

The trail leaves the west side of US 302 just south of the bridge over the Saco River and south of the entrance to the Dry River Campground. It briefly follows an old logging road and then climbs to the Frankenstein Cutoff and passes under the Frankenstein railroad trestle near the south abutment. It continues on switchbacks and stone steplike formations through the woods beneath the cliffs and up to the ridge, rather steeply in places. It then passes through open hardwood forest, crossing a streambed where there is usually water. It passes through a fine area of spruce and balsam to an outlook similar to that on Mt. Willard, with a view south in the notch.

Leaving the outlook, the trail ascends gradually through a fine stand of spruce in a west-northwest direction, skirting the top of the cliffs, with views of the valley and Mt. Bemis, and passing just south of the summit marked "2451" on map 5. At one point there is a view of Arethusa Falls far up at the head of the valley. Near the height-of-land the trail levels off, then descends the ridge for a short distance, and winds gradually to where it meets the Arethusa–Ripley Falls Trail.

Frankenstein Cliff Trail (map 5:H8)
Distances (est.) from US 302
to railroad trestle: 0.2 ml., 10 min.
to Frankenstein Cliff: 0.9 mi., 55 min.
to Arethusa–Ripley Falls Trail: 1.8 mi. (2.9 km.), 1 hr. 30 min.

Frankenstein Cutoff (NHDP)

This connection between the Frankenstein Cliff Trail just below the trestle, and the Arethusa Falls Trail at its parking lot, follows below (east of) the railroad embankment. Trespassing on the railroad is strictly prohibited, as is use of the tracks as a footway. The trail provides a circuit, going up the trail to Arethusa Falls, recrossing Bemis Brook, continuing up the slope on the Arethusa–Ripley Falls Trail, bearing right on the Frankenstein Cliff Trail, descending to and under the railroad trestle to the cutoff, and then returning to the parking area.

Frankenstein Cutoff (map 5:H8)
Distance (est.) from Frankenstein Cliff
to Arethusa Falls parking area: 0.5 mi. (0.8 km.), 15 min.

Wilderness Trail (WMNF)

The Wilderness Trail extends from the Kancamagus Highway (NH 112) for 8.9 mi. up the valley of the East Branch of the Pemigewasset River. Numerous trails diverge from this central artery, leading to various parts of the Pemigewasset Wilderness and to the adjoining mountains. For most of its length, the Wilderness Trail follows the bed of a logging railroad, which last operated in 1948.

The Wilderness Trail leaves the Kancamagus Highway at a large parking area with an information booth, just east of the concrete bridge over the East Branch, 4.1 mi. from the information center station at the I-93 exit in Lincoln and about 0.3 mi. beyond the Hancock Campground. The trail crosses the East Branch on a suspension bridge and turns right on the railroad bed, climbing almost imperceptibly. At 1.4 mi. the Osseo Trail diverges left, and at 2.6 mi. the Black Pond Trail leaves left. The Franconia Brook Campsite is situated on the left at 2.8 mi. Just before the bridge across Franconia Brook, a side trail leads north up the brook 0.4 mi. to Franconia Falls, almost an acre in area and among the finest in the mountains.

The Wilderness Trail crosses Franconia Brook on a footbridge, and in about 50 yd., at 2.9 mi., the Franconia Brook Trail climbs the bank on the left (north). Swinging more to the east, the Wilderness Trail enters the Pemigewasset Wilderness, crosses a brook at 3.9 mi., and reaches the Camp 16 clearing, where there are tent platforms, at 4.7 mi. Here the Bondcliff Trail diverges left (north). The Wilderness Trail then crosses Black Brook on a bridge to the left of the old railroad bridge (which is the last railroad trestle still standing), and at 5.4 mi. crosses to the south bank of the East Branch on a 180-ft. suspension bridge. On the far side, the Cedar Brook Trail (see Section 4) branches to the right (southwest).

Continuing upstream from the bridge, the Wilderness Trail now skirts the end of the long north ridge of Mt. Hancock, and just after crossing a small slide it reaches North Fork Junction at 6.3 mi., where the Thoreau Falls Trail diverges left (north) and the Wilderness Trail continues straight ahead. At 7.2 mi. the trail diverges from the railroad grade (which crossed the river here), crosses Crystal Brook, and soon rejoins the railroad, which has recrossed. After passing through the clearing of Camp 18, the trail leaves the railroad for the last time at 8.0 mi., and follows a path along the bank which crosses a low, piney ridge, then descends to cross the Carrigain Branch, which may be difficult at high water, at 8.7 mi. Soon it reaches

Stillwater Junction, coming into the junction at a right angle to the stream. Here the Carrigain Notch Trail (Section 4) leads right (southeast) to Desolation Shelter and Sawyer River Rd., while the Shoal Pond Trail crosses the stream directly ahead at an old dam (no bridge). (Avoid the path angling left down to the stream, which is an abandoned section of the Wilderness Trail.)

Wilderness Trail (map 5:15-H7)
Distances from Kancamagus Highway

to Franconia Brook Trail: 2.9 mi., 1 hr. 30 min.

to Bondcliff Trail: 4.7 mi., 2 hr. 30 min.

to Cedar Brook Trail: 5.4 mi., 2 hr. 45 min.

to Thoreau Falls Trail: 6.3 mi., 3 hr. 10 min.

to Stillwater Junction: 8.9 mi. (14.3 km.), 4 hr. 30 min.

to Desolation Shelter (via Carrigain Notch Trail): 9.5 mi., 4 hr. 50 min.

Osseo Trail (AMC)

This trail connects the lower end of the Wilderness Trail with the south end of the Franconia Ridge, near Mt. Flume. It begins on the west side of the Wilderness Trail, 1.4 mi. north of the parking area on the Kancamagus Highway. It heads west, following a brook in a flat area, then climbs the bank to the right and soon enters a section of an old incline logging railroad grade at one of its switchbacks. It continues up the valley on the grade and old logging roads not far above the brook. At 2.0 mi. it turns right and climbs by switchbacks to the top of the ridge to the north above the valley, then ascends the ridge—winding at first, then climbing by zigzags as the ridge steepens. At the top of this section are several wooden staircases, and at 3.2 mi. a side path (sign) leads right to a "downlook" with a very fine view of Mt. Bond. Soon the trail reaches the top of the ridge, and becomes easy until it reaches the crest of

the Franconia Ridge in a very flat area at 3.7 mi. The trail
turns sharp right here and ascends to a junction with the
Flume Slide Trail on the left and the Franconia Ridge Trail
straight ahead.

Osseo Trail (map 5:H5)
Distance from Wilderness Trail

to Flume Slide Trail/Franconia Ridge Trail junction: 4.1
mi. (6.6 km.), 3 hr. 35 min.

Black Pond Trail (WMNF)

This short, easy trail leaves the Wilderness Trail 2.8 mi.
from the Kancamagus Highway and ends at Black Pond,
where there is an interesting view of the lower ridges of Mt.
Bond from the western shore. Diverging left (west) from
the Wilderness Trail, it first follows a former logging railroad spur, crosses a small brook after 50 yd., soon bears
left, skirts the north shore of an old ice pond, and then
turns right. In 0.2 mi. the trail emerges from the woods,
crosses the Camp 7 clearing, and approaches a brook (left).
Bearing slightly right up a moderate incline parallel to the
brook below, it then descends to cross the outlet brook
from Black Pond, which it follows for a short distance. It
recrosses at a boggy spot, then recrosses the outlet brook
for the last time, follows it to Black Pond, then skirts the
southwest side of the pond and ends.

Black Pond Trail (map 5:H6-H5)
Distance from Wilderness Trail

to Black Pond: 0.8 mi. (1.4 km.), 30 min.

Franconia Brook Trail (WMNF)

This trail runs from the Wilderness Trail, 2.9 mi. from
the Kancamagus Highway, to the Garfield Ridge Trail 0.9
mi. east of the summit of Mt. Garfield.

It diverges north from the Wilderness Trail at a point

about 50 yd. east of the footbridge across Franconia Brook, climbs a steep bank, and enters an old railroad grade. Soon it enters the Pemigewasset Wilderness. The trail crosses Camp 9 Brook twice, and at 1.0 mi. swings right off the railroad grade to bypass a section flooded by an enthusiastic beaver colony. The trail crosses Camp 9 Brook, rejoins the railroad grade, and continues to the junction with the Lincoln Brook Trail, which diverges left (west) at 1.7 mi.

The Franconia Brook Trail passes an open swamp on the right of the trail, and continues to ascend gradually on the old railroad grade, passing through clearings that mark the sites of Camps 10, 12, and 13. At 5.1 mi. it reaches 13 Falls, a beautiful waterfall and cascade. At this point the Franconia Brook Trail turns right, leaves the old railroad grade, and passes the 13 Falls Campsite. Here the Lincoln Brook Trail reenters from the left (west), and the Twin Brook Trail soon branches off to the right. The Franconia Brook Trail continues on an old logging road for about 0.5 mi., then crosses to the west side of the brook. Now climbing somewhat more steeply, it continues along old logging roads to the top of the ridge, where it ends at the Garfield Ridge Trail. Garfield Ridge Campsite is 0.6 mi. left (west) by the Garfield Ridge Trail and spur path; Galehead Hut is 2.2 mi. right.

Franconia Brook Trail (map 5:H6-G5)
Distances from Wilderness Trail
   to Lincoln Brook Trail: 1.7 mi., 55 min.
   to 13 Falls Campsite: 5.1 mi., 2 hr. 50 min.
   to Garfield Ridge Trail: 7.3 mi. (11.7 km.), 4 hr. 40 min.

Lincoln Brook Trail (WMNF)

This trail begins and ends on the Franconia Brook Trail. Together, these two trails make a complete circuit around the base of Owl's Head Mtn. The south junction is 1.7 mi.

north of the Wilderness Trail, and the north junction is at 13 Falls Campsite. Several of the brook crossings on this trail may be very difficult at high water.

Turning left (west) off the Franconia Brook Trail, the Lincoln Brook Trail leads southwest through the woods to join an old railroad bed just before the crossing of Franconia Brook at 0.5 mi. In another 0.4 mi. it crosses Lincoln Brook from the north to the south side. (These crossings, which may be particularly difficult at high water, can be avoided by bushwhacking along the west banks of Franconia and Lincoln brooks from Franconia Brook Falls, following old logging roads part of the way. Another possible route involves bushwhacking due north from the end of the Black Pond Trail; this route rises easily through open woods, then descends a rather steep bank just before reaching the Lincoln Brook Trail. The Franconia Falls route is easier going toward the Wilderness Trail, and the Black Pond route is easier coming from it. The Black Pond route requires careful use of map and compass.) Beyond the Lincoln Brook crossing, the Lincoln Brook Trail follows the brook upstream on a long northward curve. It crosses a small brook at 2.2 mi., then the larger Liberty Brook at 2.8 mi. Soon it enters the Camp 11 clearing, climbs left to avoid a mudhole, rejoins the road, and crosses Lincoln Brook (sometimes difficult) to the east side at 3.0 mi. At 3.4 mi. it traverses the base of an old slide from Owl's Head, then crosses Lincoln Brook again at 4.2 mi. and continues north, crossing a divide into the Franconia Brook drainage with some glimpses of the northern Franconia Range behind (west) and of Mt. Garfield to the north. Parts of the trail through and north of the divide are rough. From the divide the trail descends to cross a west fork of Franconia Brook at 6.5 mi., then bears sharp right and follows down the left bank of the brook, crossing the main stream and rejoining the Franconia Brook Trail at the 13 Falls Campsite.

Lincoln Brook Trail (map 5:H6-H5)
Distances from Franconia Brook Trail
   to Owl's Head slide: 3.4 mi., 2 hr. 15 min.
   to 13 Falls Campsite: 6.7 mi. (10.8 km.), 4 hr. 5 min.

Owl's Head Path

This unofficial, unmaintained path ascends the slide on the west side of the mountain, starting from the Lincoln Brook Trail at a cairn 3.4 mi. from Franconia Brook Trail (south junction) and 0.4 mi. beyond the second crossing of Lincoln Brook. (*Note.* Hikers often mistake the Liberty Brook crossing for a crossing of Lincoln Brook, and thus think they have already passed the Owl's Head slide when they arrive at the Lincoln Brook crossing, just before the slide. At the slide, you will be on the east side of the main brook.) The slide is very steep and rough, and though considerably overgrown it is still potentially dangerous because of loose rock and smooth ledges, especially when wet. Great care should be taken both ascending and descending. The way is often marked by cairns of varying size and visibility. In general, it is easier to climb on the south side, which is mostly ledge with good hand and foot holds, and descend on the north side, which is mostly loose gravel. (In other words, keep to the right.) At the top of the slide, 0.3 mi. and 700 ft. above the Lincoln Brook Trail, there is a small spring spurting from the rock like a fountain, just before the trail enters the woods. From the top of the slide, a well-trodden, unmaintained path climbs rather steeply up to the ridge, which is reached at 0.8 mi. Here the path swings left and runs with minor ups and downs to the wooded summit. Hikers who find the slide unappealing may be able to bushwhack up or down the steep slope to the north, parallel to the slide, through mostly open woods.

Owl's Head Path (map 5:H5)
Distance from Lincoln Brook Trail
   to Owl's Head summit: 1.0 mi. (1.5 km.), 1 hr. 15 min.
Distance from Kancamagus Highway
   to Owl's Head (via Wilderness Trail, Franconia Brook
   Trail, Lincoln Brook Trail, and slide): 9.0 mi. (14.4
   km.), 6 hr.

Twin Brook Trail (AMC)

This trail runs from 13 Falls Campsite to the Frost Trail
0.1 mi. from Galehead Hut. It diverges from the Franconia
Brook Trail at 13 Falls Campsite and rises gradually east-
northeast. At the start, take care to follow blazes at sharp
bends, avoiding several old logging roads. After about 0.4
mi., the trail swings more to the north and heads up the
valley of Twin Brook, keeping to the left (west) of the
brook, which is occasionally audible but not visible. After
traversing four distinct "knees" of Galehead Mtn. in the
next mile, the trail eventually climbs steeply to its terminus
on the Frost Trail. Turn right for Galehead Hut.

Twin Brook Trail (map 5:G5-G6)
Distances from 13 Falls Campsite
   to Frost Trail: 2.6 mi. (4.2 km.), 2 hr. 5 min.
   to Galehead Hut (via Frost Trail): 2.7 mi. (4.3 km.), 2
   hr. 10 min.

Bondcliff Trail (AMC)

This trail begins on the Wilderness Trail at Camp 16, 4.7
mi. from the Kancamagus Highway, ascends over Bondcliff
and Mt. Bond, and ends at the Twinway just west of the
summit of Mt. Guyot. It connects the Pemigewasset Wilderness with the high summits of the Twin Range. The long
section on Bondcliff and one shorter section on Guyot are

above treeline, with great exposure to the weather. The views from this trail are unsurpassed in the White Mtns.

Leaving the Wilderness Trail at Camp 16, the Bondcliff Trail runs level for 100 yd., then turns left and climbs a bank to a logging road. Soon it enters a relocated section (its relocation has eliminated four crossings of Black Brook). At 1.1 mi. it rejoins the logging road along the brook and ascends easily, though parts of the road are severely eroded. It crosses the brook four times; the second crossing, at 1.9 mi., provides the last sure water. At the third crossing, at 2.5 mi., the trail turns right across the brook, climbs a steep slope on rock steps, then swings left to another logging road and crosses a gravel bank. In a short distance it makes the last brook crossing in a steep, south-facing ravine; if the brook is dry here, water can often be found a short distance farther up in the streambed. The trail winds up a small "hanging" ridge that protrudes into the main ravine, then at 3.2 mi. swings left and begins a long slab up the steep slope on a logging road, heading back to the southwest. At 4.1 mi. the trail reaches the crest of Bondcliff's south ridge, swings north, and ascends the ridge to a short, somewhat difficult scramble up a ledge. Soon it breaks out of the scrub and climbs along the edge of the cliffs, with spectacular views, reaching the summit of Bondcliff at 4.4 mi. The trail runs above treeline for about a mile and is dangerous in bad weather. When visibility is poor or weather bad, stay well to the east of the edge of the precipices. The trail now descends the open ridge into a long, flat col, then ascends the steep slope of Mt. Bond, reentering scrubby woods about halfway up. At 5.6 mi. the trail passes just west of the summit of Mt. Bond, which commands a magnificent unrestricted view of the surrounding wilderness and mountains. The trail descends north, crossing a minor knob, then drops down rather steeply past the spur path to West Bond at 6.1 mi., and leaves the Pemigewasset Wilderness. It reaches the Bond–Guyot col at 6.3 mi., where a spur path descends right (east) 0.2 mi. and 250 ft. to Guyot Campsite and spring. It then ascends to the bare south summit of Mt. Guyot, and continues in the open 0.2 mi. to its junction with the Twinway 0.1 mi. west of the higher, but less open, north summit of Guyot. Go straight ahead here for the Twins and Galehead Hut, or turn right for Zealand Mtn. and Zealand Falls Hut.

Bondcliff Trail (map 5:H6-G6)
Distances from Wilderness Trail
  to Bondcliff summit: 4.4 mi., 3 hr. 35 min.
  to Mt. Bond summit: 5.6 mi., 4 hr. 30 min.
  to Guyot Campsite spur: 6.3 mi., 4 hr. 50 min.
  to Twinway: 6.9 mi. (11.1 km.), 5 hr. 25 min.

West Bond Spur (AMC)
This short path leaves the Bondcliff Trail 0.6 mi. north of the summit of Mt. Bond, and 0.2 mi. south of the spur to Guyot Campsite. It descends moderately for 0.3 mi. to the col, ascends moderately for a short distance, then climbs the steep cone to the summit, the most easterly of several small peaks on a ridge running east and west. Views are magnificent from this sharp rock peak, perched high above the valleys of an extensive wilderness area.

West Bond Spur (map 5:H6)
Distance from Bondcliff Trail
  to West Bond summit: 0.5 mi. (0.8 km.), 25 min.

Thoreau Falls Trail (WMNF)
This trail runs from the Wilderness Trail at North Fork Junction, 6.3 mi. from the Kancamagus Highway, past Thoreau Falls, to the Ethan Pond Trail roughly halfway between Ethan Pond Campsite and Zealand Falls Hut.

Much of it follows an old railroad grade, but there are a few rather steep and rough sections. Practically the entire trail is in the Pemigewasset Wilderness.

It diverges left (north) from the Wilderness Trail on a railroad bed and in about 0.4 mi. crosses the East Branch of the Pemigewasset on a 60-ft. bridge, then follows the railroad bed along the North Fork. At about 2.1 mi. it turns right on a bypass that leaves the railroad grade just before a brook crossing, climbs for about 0.5 mi., passes above a slide area, and descends to rejoin the railroad grade about 0.1 mi. above the point where the railroad has recrossed the brook. The Thoreau Falls Trail follows the railroad to its end and then a logging road for another 0.9 mi. Climbing steeply on a rough footpath to the right of the falls, it then crosses the North Fork at the top of Thoreau Falls, which are beautiful when there is a good flow of water. Leaving the stream, the trail soon ends at the Ethan Pond Trail, about 0.2 mi. north of the latter's bridge over the North Fork. Turn left for Zealand Falls Hut and right for Ethan Pond Shelter.

Thoreau Falls Trail (map 5:H6-G7)
Distance from Wilderness Trail
   to Ethan Pond Trail: 5.1 mi. (8.2 km.), 2 hr. 50 min.

Shoal Pond Trail (AMC)

This trail runs from its junction with the Wilderness Trail and Carrigain Notch Trail (See Section 4) at Stillwater Junction to the Ethan Pond Trail between Zealand Falls Hut and Ethan Pond Campsite. At Stillwater Junction, the trail leads across the East Branch on the foundation of an old dam (no bridge), turns left on the railroad bed, and almost immediately leaves right. Gaining another railroad bed, the trail crosses Shoal Pond Brook; this crossing may be difficult if the water is high. The trail follows the railroad to its end, where there is a pleasant pool to the right in the brook. It then follows logging roads, crossing Shoal Pond Brook from west to east, and after about another mile recrosses the brook. A short distance below Shoal Pond, the trail crosses the brook for the last time, from west to east. Because of beaver activity, the trail keeps away from the shore east of the pond. About 0.1 mi. north of Shoal Pond the trail forks; the right (east) fork leads through swampy terrain toward Ethan Pond Shelter, while the left (west) fork leads toward Zealand Falls Hut. By either fork, it is a little less than 0.8 mi. from the pond to the Ethan Pond Trail.

Shoal Pond Trail (map 5:H7-G7)
Distances (est.) from Stillwater Junction
  to Shoal Pond: 3.5 mi., 2 hr.
  to Ethan Pond Trail: 4.3 mi. (6.9 km.), 2 hr. 20 min.

SECTION 4

The Carrigain and Moat Regions

This section covers the eastern portion of the Central Region (that part not included in Section 3), consisting of the areas bounded on the north by US 302, on the east by NH 16, and on the south by the Kancamagus Highway (NH 112); at the western edge it includes all areas and trails south and east of the Wilderness Trail. For a more precise description of the western boundary of Section 4, see the first paragraph of Section 3. Section 4 includes Mt. Carrigain and Mt. Hancock, the lesser mountains which surround them, and the lower but interesting mountains which lie between the Saco and Swift rivers, principally Mt. Tremont and the Moat Range. No single AMC map covers the entire area; roughly speaking, the area to the west of Bear Notch Rd. is covered by the Franconia map (map 5), the majority of the area to the east by the Chocorua-Waterville map (map 4), and the northern edge of the eastern section by the Mt. Washington Range map (map 6).

The Appalachian Trail does not pass through this section.

GEOGRAPHY

Mt. Carrigain (4680 ft.) is the central and highest point of a mass of jumbled ridges on the divide between the East Branch of the Pemigewasset River and the Saco River and its tributary, the Swift River. It was named for Philip Carrigain, NH secretary of state from 1805 to 1810, who made a map of the whole state in 1816, including an early attempt to portray the White Mtn. region. He was one of the party that named Mts. Adams, Jefferson, Madison, and Monroe in 1820. The view from the observation tower on the summit takes in a wide area and includes most of the important peaks of the White Mtns.; Carrigain is one of the competitors for the title of the finest viewpoint in the White Mtns. The view from Signal Ridge, Carrigain's southeasterly spur, is also magnificent. The northeasterly spur, Vose Spur (3870 ft.), forms the west wall of Carrigain Notch, facing Mt. Lowell on the east; Vose Spur has no trails and its ascent without trail is quite difficult.

Mt. Hancock rises to the west of Mt. Carrigain. It is a long ridge with several summits, of which the most important are the North Peak (4403 ft.), the highest, and the South Peak (4274 ft.). Both peaks are wooded to the top, but there is an excellent outlook ledge near the summit of the North Peak, and a good but restricted outlook from the South Peak. At one time this was one of the most inaccessible mountains in the White Mtns., but it is now easily climbed. The ridge line joining Mt. Carrigain and Mt. Hancock has no trail, and travel along it is extremely difficult. The line along this ridge on maps is part of the Lincoln–Livermore town boundary. Carrigain Pond, a beautiful and remote mountain pond that is one of the higher sources of the Pemigewasset River, is just north of the ridge. The Captain (3530 ft.), located only 0.3 mi. from Carrigain Pond, is a striking little peak with sheer cliffs overlooking the Sawyer River valley; hidden at the end of this isolated valley, it can be seen from only a few places.

Mt. Lowell (3743 ft.), Mt. Anderson (3722 ft.), Mt. Nancy (3906 ft.), and Mt. Bemis (3706 ft.) are a group of peaks northeast of Carrigain Notch that lie on the watershed between the Saco and the East Branch of the Pemigewasset. The region is notable for its concentration of four ponds—Nancy, Norcross, Little Norcross, and Duck—at an altitude of about 3100 ft., and for a stand of virgin spruce, just south of Nancy Pond on the north slopes of Duck Pond Mtn. This is said to be one of the two largest remaining areas of virgin timber in the state, though the hurricane of 1938 did great damage. In October 1964, the USFS established in this region the 460-acre Nancy Brook Scenic Area, to be maintained as nearly as possible in an undisturbed condition.

Mt. Tremont (3384 ft.) is the highest of several lower peaks which rise in the region around Sawyer Pond, east of Bear Notch Rd. Tremont lies south of the big bend in the Saco River; it is a narrow ridge, running north and south, with three conspicuous summits, of which the south is the highest. Still farther south is a fourth summit, Owl's Cliff (2951 ft.). The main summit of Tremont has spectacular views to the south, west, and north; Owl's Cliff has a fine outlook to the south. Southwest of both Mt. Tremont and Sawyer Pond is Green's Cliff (2915 ft.), with cliffs on its south and east faces; it is very prominent from the overlooks on the eastern half of the Kancamagus Highway. Ledges near its summit provide interesting views, but there is no trail. Bartlett Haystack (3010 ft.), an aptly named mountain that has sometimes been called Mt. Silver Spring, is another interesting peak without trails, lying east of Mt. Tremont. A ledge just a few feet west of the summit, shaped like the prow of a ship, affords a magnificent view to the south, west, and north. It is a relatively easy bushwhack from Haystacks Rd. (FR 44), about 0.5 mi. west of Bear Notch Rd., and is one of the more rewarding objectives available to experienced hikers who wish to acquire the skills of navigation by map and compass. The WMNF Bartlett Experimental Forest occupies a large area on the slopes of Bartlett Haystack and Bear Mtn.

Moat Mtn. is a long ridge that rises impressively to the west of the Saco River nearly opposite North Conway. The whole ridge was burned over many decades ago, and all the major summits are still bare, with magnificent views; there are also numerous scattered outlooks along the wooded parts of the ridge. There has been some uncertainty about

the names of the summits in the range, but in this Guide
the peaks are called North Moat (3201 ft.), Middle Moat
(2802 ft.), and South Moat (2772 ft.). The peak at the apex
of the Red Ridge (2750 ft.) has sometimes also been called
Middle Moat. From North Moat a ridge runs west to Big
Attitash Mtn. (2936 ft.), sometimes called West Moat, then
the ridge passes over lesser summits of Big Attitash and
swings southwest to Table Mtn. (2710 ft.), which has fine
views to the south from several open ledges just below the
summit. Next the ridge swings west again to the trailless
Bear Mtn. (3217 ft.), which forms the east side of Bear
Notch. On the east side of the Moat Range are White
Horse Ledge (1470 ft.) and Cathedral Ledge (1150 ft.), two
detached bluffs which present impressive cliffs to the Saco
valley. An auto road ascends to the summit of Cathedral
Ledge. Farther to the north, Little Attitash Mtn. (2518 ft.)
is a trailless peak on a long, curving ridge which
extends northeast from Big Attitash to end in Humphrey's Ledge
(1470 ft.). Pitman's Arch, a shallow cave in the face of
Humphrey's Ledge, was once reached by a toll path that is
now completely overgrown.

CAMPING

Pemigewasset Wilderness

In this area, camping and fires are prohibited above treeline, within one-quarter mile of 13 Falls Campsite, Thoreau
Falls, Galehead Hut, Guyot Campsite, or within one-quarter mile of the Wilderness Trail and the East Branch from
the wilderness boundary (near the Franconia Brook Trail
junction) to the Thoreau Falls Trail junction, except at
designated sites. No campsite may be used by more than
ten persons at any one time.

Restricted Use Areas

The WMNF has established a number of Restricted Use Areas (RUA's) where camping and wood or charcoal fires are prohibited from 1 May to 1 November. The specific areas are under continual review, and areas are added to or subtracted from the list in order to provide the greatest amount of protection to areas subject to damage by excessive camping, while imposing the lowest level of restrictions possible. A general list of RUA's follows, but one should obtain a map of current RUA's from the WMNF.

(1) No camping is permitted above treeline (where trees are less than 8 ft. tall). The point where the restricted area begins is marked on most trails with small signs, but the absence of such signs should not be construed as proof of the legality of a site.

(2) No camping is permitted within one-quarter mile of most facilities such as huts, cabins, shelters, or tentsites, except at the facility itself. In this section, camping is also prohibited at Diana's Baths, on the Moat Mountain Trail. Camping is permitted at Desolation Shelter.

(3) No camping is permitted within 200 ft. of certain trails. In 1986, designated trails included the Sawyer Pond Trail from Sawyer River Rd. to the end of the quarter-mile Restricted Use Area around Sawyer Pond itself.

Established Trailside Campsites

Desolation Shelter (AMC) is located on the Carrigain Notch Trail beside Carrigain Branch, 0.6 mi. southeast of Stillwater Junction and the Wilderness Trail. It accommodates eight, and tenting at the site is permitted.

Sawyer Pond Campsite (WMNF) is located on Sawyer Pond, reached by the Sawyer Pond Trail. There are five tent platforms on the northwest side of the pond, and a shelter that accommodates eight.

ACCESS ROADS

Important access roads in this area include the Kancamagus Highway (NH 112), connecting I-93 and US 3 in Lincoln to NH 16 in Conway. It is now a regular state highway which is paved and well maintained, and open in winter except during the worst storms. Bear Notch Rd. runs 9.3 mi. from US 302 at the crossroads in Bartlett village to the Kancamagus Highway about 13 mi. west of Conway. It is paved, but not usually plowed in winter. North of Bear Mtn. Notch it closely follows the line of an old railroad, and magnificent outlooks have been cleared. The gravel Sawyer River Rd. (FR 34) begins on US 302 0.2 mi. north of the major bridge over Sawyer River, 1.6 mi. north of the Sawyer Rock picnic area, or 7.9 mi. south of the Willey House site in Crawford Notch State Park. There is no road sign except for a brown post with "FR 34" on it, and it is usually gated during the snow season.

LIST OF TRAILS   MAP

Trails in the Mount Carrigain Region

Signal Ridge Trail	5:18-H7
Carrigain Notch Trail	5:18-H7
Desolation Trail	5:H7
Nancy Pond Trail	5:H8-H7

Trails in the Mount Hancock Region

Cedar Brook Trail	5:16-H6
Hancock Notch Trail	5:16-I7
Hancock Loop Trail	5:16-I7
Sawyer River Trail	5:18-I7

Trails in the Mount Tremont Region

Church Pond Loop Trail	4:J8-I8
Sawyer Pond Trail	4:J8-I8
Rob Brook Trail	4:I9-I8

Brunel Trail	5:18
Mount Tremont Trail	5/6:18

Trails in the Moat Mountain Region

Boulder Loop Trail	4:I10
Moat Mountain Trail	4/6:I11-I10
Red Ridge Trail	4/6:I10
Attitash Trail	4/6:I9-I10

Trails on White Horse Ledge and Cathedral Ledge

White Horse Ledge Trail	4/6:I11-I10
Bryce Path	4/6:I11-I10
Bryce Link Path	4/6:I11
Red Ridge Link	4:I10

THE TRAILS

Signal Ridge Trail (WMNF)

This trail ascends from Sawyer River Rd. (FR 34), 2.0 mi. from US 302, to the summit of Mt. Carrigain by way of Signal Ridge. The trail begins on the right just before the bridge over Whiteface Brook; there is a parking lot on the left, just beyond the bridge. There is a crossing of Whiteface Brook, which may be difficult at high water, less than 0.2 mi. from the road; at such times it may be best to avoid the crossing by bushwhacking up the south bank of the brook. The trail climbs moderately for most of its distance, using old roads which once provided access to the firewarden's cabin. The views from the observation tower on the summit and from Signal Ridge are magnificent. The loop back to Sawyer River Rd. via the Desolation and Carrigain Notch trails is interesting, but much longer, rougher, and more difficult.

Leaving the road, the Signal Ridge Trail soon reaches and follows an old logging road which crosses Whiteface Brook at 0.2 mi., then follows the south bank of the attractive brook, passing small cascades and pools. At 0.8 mi. it

begins to climb steadily away from the brook, then levels
and crosses a flat divide. At 1.4 mi. Carrigain Brook Rd.
(FR 86), a grass-grown gravel logging road, crosses the trail
at a right angle. (This road is not passable by vehicles, but
can be followed south 1.6 mi. to Sawyer River Rd. about
0.3 mi. before the gate at the end of that road. There is a
difficult brook crossing just before Sawyer River Rd. is
reached.) At 1.7 mi. the Carrigain Notch Trail diverges
right toward Desolation Shelter and the Pemigewasset Wilderness, and the Signal Ridge Trail soon crosses Carrigain
Brook, which may be difficult at high water. The trail
passes an area of beaver activity, crosses a shallow brook,
and begins to ascend, gradually at first. At 2.4 mi. it turns
sharp left where an old road continues straight up the
valley. The trail slabs the end of a ridge, turns right to
climb, then turns sharp left again (arrow) at the site of an
old camp and slabs again.

At 2.8 mi. the Signal Ridge Trail turns sharp right into a
birch-lined straight section 1.0 mi. long which slabs steadily up the side of the valley, with occasional views to the
cliffs of Mt. Lowell across Carrigain Notch. At the end of
this section, the trail turns sharp left and zigzags up the
nose of Signal Ridge—through several areas which were
damaged by the windstorm of December 1980—reaching
the high point of the bare crest of the ridge at 4.5 mi.
Views are magnificent, particularly to the cliffs of Mt. Lowell across Carrigain Notch. The trail descends slightly, then
angles left around to the south slope of the summit cone,
climbing to the site of the old firewarden's cabin, where
there is a well (water unsafe to drink without treatment).
Bearing left from the small clearing, the trail soon swings
right and climbs steeply to the small sag between Carrigain's two summit knobs, then turns right and soon reaches
the summit. Here the Desolation Trail enters from the Pemigewasset Wilderness.

Signal Ridge Trail (map 5:I8-H7)

Distances from Sawyer River Rd.

to Carrigain Notch Trail junction: 1.7 mi., 1 hr. 5 min.

to Signal Ridge: 4.5 mi., 3 hr. 50 min.

to Mt. Carrigain summit: 5.0 mi. (8.1 km.), 4 hr. 15 min.

Carrigain Notch Trail (AMC)

This trail runs from the Signal Ridge Trail, 1.7 mi. from Sawyer River Rd., through Carrigain Notch and past Desolation Shelter, to the Wilderness and Shoal Pond trails (see Section 3) at Stillwater Junction.

It diverges right (north) from the Signal Ridge Trail and crosses Carrigain Brook in 60 yd.; care is required to find the trail on the opposite bank at this crossing, going either way. Continuing on logging roads at easy grades, it passes through an area of beaver activity, then several stony areas, and at 1.6 mi. turns left off the road to bypass a muddy section. Here, on the right of the trail, there is a view of the ledges of Vose Spur, which form the west side of Carrigain Notch. Soon returning to the road, the trail climbs more steeply, and at 2.3 mi. reaches its height-of-land well up on the west wall of the notch. Very soon it strikes and follows an old logging road on the north side of the notch and descends moderately, and at 3.1 mi. turns left off the logging road and follows a path through the woods, which avoids the wet sections of the old road. At 4.1 mi. the trail enters an old railroad grade and turns sharp left on it; the Nancy Pond Trail follows the grade to the right from this point. At 4.9 mi. the trail bears left off the railroad grade, and soon turns sharp right where the Desolation Trail continues straight across the brook. At 5.1 mi. it passes Desolation Shelter, then bears right away from the Carrigain Branch and reaches Stillwater Junction; here the Wilderness Trail turns sharp left, and the Shoal Pond Trail turns right across the East Branch of the Pemigewasset.

Carrigain Notch Trail (map 5:I8-H7)
Distances from Signal Ridge Trail

to Carrigain Notch: 2.3 mi., 1 hr. 30 min.

to Nancy Pond Trail: 4.1 mi., 2 hr. 25 min.

to Desolation Shelter: 5.1 mi., 2 hr. 55 min.

to Stillwater Junction: 5.7 mi. (9.2 km.), 3 hr. 15 min.

Desolation Trail (AMC)

This trail runs from the Carrigain Notch Trail about 0.2 mi. southwest of Desolation Shelter to the summit of Mt. Carrigain. The upper part of the trail is very steep and rough, and requires great care, particularly on the descent or with heavy packs. In either direction substantial extra time may be required. Practically all of the trail is in the Pemigewasset Wilderness.

The trail leaves the Carrigain Notch Trail at a sharp turn at the edge of a tributary of the Carrigain Branch, crosses the brook, follows a railroad grade for 60 yd., then diverges left and climbs moderately, at times on old logging roads. The trail climbs into a fine stand of birches and merges into an unusually straight old logging road on the west side of the ridge crest. For a long section of this road there is old telephone wire at the left edge of the trail, which presents a potential danger of tripping. The road crosses to the east side of the ridge and deteriorates, and at 1.3 mi. the road ends and the trail crosses a short section of slippery rock blocks. The trail continues through an area where many rock steps have been built, then swings directly up the slope into virgin woods, and climbs a very steep and rough section. The grade remains steep, but it gradually eases up and the footing slowly improves as the trail reaches the crest of the steep ridge. At 1.8 mi. the trail abruptly reaches the top of the steep section, swings left, and slabs easily around the cone to the last short steep pitch to the summit.

Desolation Trail (map 5:H7)
Distances from Carrigain Notch Trail

  to upper end of old logging road: 1.3 mi., 1 hr. 20 min.
  to Mt. Carrigain summit: 1.9 mi. (3.1 km.), 2 hr. 15 min.

Nancy Pond Trail (Camp Pasquaney/WMNF)

This trail begins on the west side of US 302, 2.8 mi. north of the Sawyer Rock picnic area and 6.7 mi. south of the Willey House site in Crawford Notch State Park. It passes Nancy Cascades and Nancy and Norcross ponds, and ends on the Carrigain Notch Trail 1.0 mi. north of Desolation Shelter.

Leaving US 302 it follows an assortment of paths and old roads, but is well marked with yellow paint and signs. It first follows a logging road for 250 yd., diverges left and crosses a small brook, then joins a logging road along Halfway Brook. Soon it turns right off the road and crosses Halfway Brook, and a woods road joins from the right (descending, bear right here). The trail continues to the WMNF boundary, marked by a large pile of red-painted stones, at 0.8 mi. Here it enters and follows an old logging road along Nancy Brook, crossing the brook on the rocks at 1.6 mi. (may be difficult at high water). It continues upstream on the road and passes the remains of Lucy Mill at 1.8 mi. Above here the road virtually disappears, and the trail ascends through a rough area of landslides, recrosses Nancy Brook, and soon reaches the foot of Nancy Cascades at 2.4 mi.

The trail turns sharp left at the cascades and ascends the steep slope by switchbacks, providing another outlook at the middle of the cascades, and passes near the top of the cascades, which are several hundred feet high, at 2.8 mi. (Snow may remain in this ravine quite late in the spring.) From the top of the cascades, the trail winds through the moss-carpeted virgin spruce forest, past a small overgrown tarn to the northeast shore of Nancy Pond (4 acres in area) at 3.4 mi. Continuing along the north shore, the trail crosses the swamp at the upper end and continues over the almost imperceptible height-of-land that divides Saco from Pemigewasset drainage, to Little Norcross Pond. Skirting the north shore, it then climbs over another small rise to Norcross Pond (7 acres in area). Again hugging the north shore, and crossing into the Pemigewasset Wilderness, it enters a logging road 25 yd. before reaching the ledgy natural dam at the west end of Norcross Pond at 4.3 mi. (In the reverse direction, turn right off the logging road 25 yd. from the ledgy dam and follow a path along the shore of the pond.) At the ledges there is a commanding view of Mt. Bond and the Twin Range, with the Franconias in the distance.

After crossing the stream at the outlet of Norcross Pond, the Nancy Pond Trail continues west on a logging road on a gradual descent, passing a spring (iron pipe) on the south side of the trail at 5.5 mi. At 6.0 mi. the trail veers right, crosses Norcross Brook on a bridge, and shortly reaches an old railroad bed and swings left onto it. At 6.4 mi. it crosses Anderson Brook on a bridge, and then passes along the south side of the Camp 19 clearing. At 6.8 mi. it turns left off the railroad grade and recrosses Norcross Brook. On the other side, it follows another railroad grade, bears right at a fork, crosses Notch Brook, and ends 25 yd. beyond the brook. Here the Carrigain Notch Trail enters sharp left from Sawyer River Rd., and continues straight ahead on the railroad grade to Desolation Shelter and Stillwater Junction.

Nancy Pond Trail (map 5:H8-H7)
Distances from US 302
to foot of Nancy Cascades: 2.4 mi., 1 hr. 55 min.
to Nancy Pond: 3.5 mi., 2 hr. 50 min.
to Norcross Pond outlet: 4.3 mi., 3 hr. 15 min.

to Carrigain Notch Trail: 7.1 mi. (11.4 km.), 4 hr. 40 min.

to Desolation Shelter (via Carrigain Notch Trail): 8.1 mi. (13.0 km.), 5 hr. 10 min.

Cedar Brook Trail (WMNF)

This trail runs from the Hancock Notch Trail, 1.7 mi. from the Kancamagus Highway, to the Wilderness Trail at the east end of the suspension bridge, 5.4 mi. from the Kancamagus Highway. With the Hancock Notch Trail, this trail affords the most direct route to Mt. Hancock. The five crossings of the North Fork of the Hancock Branch between the Hancock Notch Trail and the Hancock Loop Trail are difficult in high water; but two are easily bypassed, and the others can be avoided by bushwhacking along the east bank to the Hancock Loop Trail (which makes the sixth crossing soon after its divergence from the Cedar Brook Trail).

Leaving the Hancock Notch Trail, it immediately crosses a small brook, climbs moderately on an old logging road for about 0.2 mi., then crosses the North Fork of the Hancock Branch five times in 0.4 mi. The first two crossings are close together and can be avoided by following a well-beaten path on the near bank. Following logging roads past the upper three crossings, the trail passes the beginning of the Hancock Loop Trail at 0.7 mi., 150 yd. beyond the fifth crossing.

The Cedar Brook Trail climbs more steeply to the height-of-land between Mt. Hancock and Mt. Hitchcock at 1.4 mi., where it enters the Pemigewasset Wilderness, then descends on logging roads on the east side of the valley, crossing several brooks, and reaches the site of Camp 24A (sign) at 2.9 mi. It continues to descend on old roads, and at 4.1 mi. it descends a bank to the old logging railroad at the edge of Cedar Brook and turns sharp right on the railroad grade.

Soon it passes through the extensive clearings of Camp 24 and descends toward the East Branch of the Pemigewasset. At 5.5 mi. a grass-grown road, which follows the east and south banks of the East Branch from the Wilderness Trail parking lot, enters on the left (no sign). The Cedar Brook Trail swings to the east and joins the Wilderness Trail at the east end of the suspension bridge.

Cedar Brook Trail (map 5:I6-H6)
Distances from Hancock Notch Trail
to Hancock Loop Trail: 0.7 mi., 30 min.
to height-of-land: 1.4 mi., 1 hr.
to Camp 24A: 2.9 mi., 1 hr. 45 min.
to Camp 24: 4.3 mi., 2 hr. 30 min.
to Wilderness Trail: 6.1 mi. (9.7 km.), 3 hr. 20 min.

Hancock Notch Trail (WMNF)

This trail begins at the Kancamagus Highway at the hairpin turn, passes through Hancock Notch between Mt. Hancock and Mt. Huntington, then descends along the Sawyer River to the Sawyer River Trail. At the Kancamagus Highway terminus, parking is available at the Hancock Overlook just above the trailhead. With the Cedar Brook and Hancock Loop trails, this trail is the most popular route to Mt. Hancock. From the Kancamagus Highway to the Cedar Brook Trail, the Hancock Notch Trail is heavily used, wide, and easily followed; from the Cedar Brook Trail to the Sawyer River Trail, it is wet and rough, and in places requires care to follow.

Leaving the Kancamagus Highway, it follows a railroad bed, crossing a brook at 0.6 mi. and gradually approaching the North Fork of the Hancock Branch. The trail stays on the same side of the North Fork, and follows logging roads at an easy grade after the railroad bed crosses the river. Then the trail crosses two brooks in less than 0.1 mi. and soon reaches the junction with the Cedar Brook Trail at 1.7 mi. (For Mt. Hancock, turn left on this trail and cross a small brook.) The Hancock Notch Trail rises somewhat more steeply for about 0.8 mi. to the notch, which is flat and very wet. East of the notch it passes through a dense stand of spruce on a rougher footway, descending quite rapidly at times. Crossing to the north side of the Sawyer River, then back to the south, the trail then diverges from the river, passes by a beaver pond, and follows logging roads across a south branch of the river. Descending, the trail crosses the Sawyer River twice, at 5.3 mi. and 5.8 mi. (both crossings may be difficult at high water), and follows newer logging roads to its end at the Sawyer River Trail at Hayshed Field, an overgrown clearing 1.2 mi. from Sawyer River Rd.

Hancock Notch Trail (map 5:16-17)
Distances from Kancamagus Highway

 to Cedar Brook Trail: 1.7 mi., 1 hr.

 to Hancock Notch: 2.5 mi., 1 hr. 35 min.

 to Sawyer River Trail: 6.6 mi. (10.7 km.), 3 hr. 40 min.

Hancock Loop Trail (AMC)

This trail makes a loop over both main summits of Mt. Hancock. It is steep and rough, but well trodden and easy to follow. It is reached by following the Hancock Notch and Cedar Brook trails from the hairpin turn on the Kancamagus Highway for about 2.4 mi. Brook crossings on the Cedar Brook Trail may be difficult at high water.

Leaving the Cedar Brook Trail on the right (east) 150 yd. north of the fifth crossing of the North Branch of the Hancock Branch, the trail follows an old logging road and soon recrosses the main brook, then passes a steep, rocky brookbed and a wet area. Keeping south of the main brook, some distance away from it and considerably higher, the trail continues its gradual ascent and reaches the loop junction at 1.0 mi. from the start. From this point the circuit over the two main summits of Mt. Hancock can be made in either direction. From here the trail is divided into three segments for convenience: North Link, Ridge Link, and South Link.

North Link

The North Link diverges left from the logging road at the loop junction and descends at an angle. Soon it crosses a gravel brookbed, often dry, where the foot of the Arrow Slide is visible about 50 yd. to the left. The trail now climbs roughly parallel to the slide, first at a moderate grade slabbing the hillside, then straight up, very steep and rough. Near the top, the trail veers left and becomes less steep. At the wooded summit of North Hancock, a side path leads left a short distance to a fine view south to the Sandwich Range and Osceola, while the Ridge Link turns right.

Ridge Link

This path connects the summits of North and South Hancock. At the summit of North Hancock, it starts almost due north, passing a side path in 0.1 mi. that leads right about 40 yd. to a restricted view of Mt. Carrigain from a ledge thought to resemble Plymouth Rock. Then the Ridge Link curves right to the east, and then south, traverses the ridge with several minor ups and downs, and climbs the narrow ridge to the south peak at 1.3 mi.

South Link

From the loop junction, the South Link continues along the logging road for another 0.1 mi., where the road peters out and a trail swings right up the hillside. The climb to South Hancock is unrelievedly steep, crossing numerous old logging roads. (These are some of the roads which are so prominent as light green lines across the dark slope when seen from other peaks.) At the summit, the Ridge Link enters on the left (north), and a short path descends west to a fine viewpoint overlooking the Sawyer River valley.

Hancock Loop Trail (map 5:I6-I7)
Distances from Cedar Brook Trail
to loop junction: 1.0 mi., 50 min.
to North Hancock (via North Link): 1.8 mi., 1 hr. 50 min.
to South Hancock (via South Link): 1.4 mi., 1 hr. 30 min.

Distances of loop
from Cedar Brook Trail (in either direction): 4.5 mi. (7.3 km.), 3 hr. 30 min.
from Kancamagus Highway: 9.3 mi. (15.0 km.), 6 hr. 5 min.

Sawyer River Trail (WMNF)

This trail leads from Sawyer River Rd. (FR 34), at the end of the section open to public vehicular use about 4.0 mi. from US 302, to the Kancamagus Highway 3.1 mi. west of the Sabbaday Falls parking area and 0.6 mi. east of Lily Pond. Almost all the way it follows the bed of an old logging railroad at easy grades.

The trail follows the gravel road past the gate, and in 100 yd. the Sawyer Pond Trail turns left to cross Sawyer River on a footbridge. The Sawyer River Trail continues, taking the left of two gated gravel roads at a fork, crosses Sawyer River on the logging road bridge, and diverges right onto the old railroad grade 100 yd. beyond the bridge. (The gravel road can be followed 1.1 mi. to the junction of the Sawyer River Trail and Hancock Notch Trail at Hayshed Field, where it enters the Sawyer River Trail at a right angle; there are excellent views of Mt. Tremont and Mt. Carrigain from this road.) The railroad grade continues along the Sawyer River for 0.7 mi., then begins to swing to the south. It crosses a washed-out area and two brooks, and reaches the overgrown clearing called Hayshed Field at 1.2 mi., where the Hancock Notch Trail turns sharp right and the gravel road described above enters on the left. The Sawyer River Trail follows the old railroad bed across an imperceptible divide in the flat region west of Green's Cliff, passing several beaver swamps, and crosses Meadow Brook on a bridge at 2.5 mi. It follows the west bank of this stream for some distance before curving gradually southwest to cross the Swift River (which can be very difficult in high water) at 3.5 mi. The trail now ascends easily upstream along the river, then climbs the bank, bearing left twice, to the Kancamagus Highway.

Sawyer River Trail (map 5:I8-I7)
Distances from Sawyer River Rd.
   to Hancock Notch Trail: 1.2 mi., 40 min.
   to Kancamagus Highway: 3.8 mi. (6.1 km.), 2 hr.

Church Pond Loop Trail (WMNF)

This loop trail provides an interesting short hike with little climbing to Church Pond and surrounding bogs and woods. It is very wet at times, and the brook crossings can be quite difficult at high water. The trail begins in Passaconaway Campground on the Kancamagus Highway; best parking may be at the Downes Brook Trail on the south side of the highway.

This trail starts from the far end of the west loop road around Passaconaway Campground near Site 18 (sign) and crosses Downes Brook and the Swift River in rapid succession. Both these crossings may be difficult, and will often require wading. After about 0.1 mi. the loop junction is reached in the woods. It is 0.9 mi. to the pond by the left-hand path, or 1.3 mi. by the right-hand path.

Taking the left-hand path, the trail follows an old logging road, bears right, becomes a footpath, crosses two open bogs (wet footing), and emerges on a knoll overlooking Church Pond, where there are fine views. The trail continues through more varied terrain. Continue straight ahead at a junction with a cross-country ski trail, and the trail soon returns to the loop junction.

Church Pond Loop Trail (map 4:J8-I8)
Distance of loop
 from Passaconaway Campground: 2.4 mi. (3.9 km.), 1 hr. 15 min.

Sawyer Pond Trail (WMNF)

This trail begins at the Kancamagus Highway 0.6 mi. east of Passaconaway Campground and 1.4 mi. west of Bear Notch Rd., passes Sawyer Pond and its campsite, and ends at Sawyer River Rd. (FR 34), near the gate which ends public vehicular access at 4.0 mi. The crossing of the Swift River on the Kancamagus Highway end often requires wading, and can be difficult at high water. Grades are easy.

From the Kancamagus Highway, the trail passes through a clearing, angles right to the bank of Swift River, and fords the stream to a sand bar. It soon enters the woods, passes a cross-country ski trail right, and runs through a fine pine grove. At 0.7 mi. a cross-country ski trail enters on the left, and at 1.1 mi. the Brunel Trail diverges right. At 1.7 mi. the trail crosses a new gravel logging road, then skirts the west slope of Birch Hill, descends gently, and crosses a grass-grown logging road diagonally at 2.6 mi. It then comes close to a small brook, bears left away from it, passes over a flat divide, and descends to Sawyer Pond. As the pond is approached, there are a number of conflicting side paths; use care to stay on the correct path. At a point 15 yd. from the pond (good views), the trail turns left, crosses the outlet brook at 4.5 mi., and passes near the tent platforms of the Sawyer Pond campsite. In 0.1 mi. it passes a side path right 0.2 mi. to the shelter. It then descends gradually on an old logging road, and at 5.7 mi. turns sharp left off the road and recrosses the Sawyer Pond outlet brook. It then continues to the bank of Sawyer River, turns right across a footbridge, then turns right on the gravel extension of Sawyer River Rd. about 100 yd. from the gate.

Sawyer Pond Trail (map 4:J8-I8)
Distances from Kancamagus Highway
to Brunel Trail: 1.1 mi., 35 min.
to Sawyer Pond: 4.5 mi., 2 hr. 30 min.
to Sawyer River Rd.: 6.0 mi. (9.7 km.), 3 hr. 15 min.

Rob Brook Trail (WMNF)

This short, almost level trail follows old roads and a logging railroad grade through an area of attractive ponds and swamps, with much beaver activity and some good views. It begins on Rob Brook Rd. (FR 35), which leaves Bear Notch Rd. about 0.8 mi. north of the Kancamagus Highway. Most of the trail is dry, but some brook crossings (including several made on beaver dams) are difficult at high water and wet in normal conditions.

It leaves Rob Brook Rd. on the left (south) 0.6 mi. from Bear Notch Rd., descends easily on an old road, crosses an area of open bogs with a glimpse of Mt. Carrigain, then takes the right branch at a fork where both trails are marked as cross-country ski trails with blue diamonds. At 0.6 mi. it reaches an old railroad grade and turns sharp right onto it, as cross-country ski trails follow the grade to the left. Soon it joins Rob Brook and crosses it five times. At the third crossing, which is made on a long beaver dam, there is a fine view of Mt. Tremont and Owl's Cliff. Soon the Rob Brook Trail ends where the Brunel Trail enters sharp left and continues straight ahead on the railroad grade.

Rob Brook Trail (map 4;I9-I8)
Distance from Rob Brook Rd.
   to Brunel Trail: 1.8 mi. (2.9 km.), 55 min.

Brunel Trail (WMNF)

This trail runs from the Sawyer Pond Trail 1.1 mi. north of the Kancamagus Highway to the summit of Mt. Tremont. However, the most-used approach is via the WMNF Rob Brook Rd. (FR 35), which leaves Bear Notch Rd. about 0.8 mi. north of the Kancamagus Highway. Rob Brook Rd. is closed to public vehicular travel, but is an easy route to the point where the Brunel Trail departs from it, 2.6 mi. from Bear Notch Rd. Since the Brunel Trail south of this point is rather confusing where it crosses and recrosses Rob Brook Rd., and the ford of the Swift River near the start of the Sawyer Pond Trail is frequently difficult, Rob Brook Rd. from Bear Notch Rd. is usually the easier access route. Parts of the Brunel Trail are very steep and rough; since the footway is obscure in some areas, the yellow blazes must be followed with care. The views to the west from Mt. Tremont, and to the south from Owl's Cliff, are excellent.

The trail diverges right (northeast) from the Sawyer Pond Trail, and in 0.2 mi. it approaches the new extension of Rob Brook Rd. (Plans call for a possible relocation of the trail in this area, perhaps avoiding this part of the road; if in doubt, this road can be followed to the right until trail signs are seen.) At the present time the trail enters the road, turns right and follows it for 60 yd., diverges left, follows a path through the woods for 0.1 mi., then crosses the road diagonally; all junctions with the road are unmarked. The trail runs through the woods, crosses a grass-grown logging road, and reaches the old logging railroad bed at 0.7 mi. Here the Rob Brook Trail follows the railroad bed to the right, while the Brunel Trail turns left and follows the railroad bed to Rob Brook Rd. at 1.0 mi. The trail turns right onto the road, follows it for 0.2 mi., leaves it right, and crosses two small brooks. It then returns to the road and follows it right for another 0.1 mi. to the Albany–Bartlett town line (sign) at 1.3 mi., where the trail (sign) turns left off the road for the final time. This point is 2.6 mi. from Bear Notch Rd. via Rob Brook Rd.

Leaving Rob Brook Rd., the Brunel Trail passes through a stand of large conifers, and at 2.1 mi. it reaches and follows the edge of a logged area (follow blazes carefully). At 2.5 mi. it crosses a small brook, and soon passes several large boulders announcing the approach to the east end of Owl's Cliff. At 2.8 mi. the trail swings left and climbs a very steep section, then turns sharp right (arrow), and the grade moderates and finally becomes easy as the height-of-land is reached. At 3.2 mi. (1.9 mi. from Rob Brook Rd.) a spur path (sign) diverges left and climbs to a point just below the summit of Owl's Cliff, then descends slightly to a fine outlook ledge (dangerous if wet or icy), 0.2 mi. from the main trail. From the junction, the Brunel Trail descends easily into a col, then passes through a section where the footway is obscure (watch for blazes) and ascends very steeply; sections running straight up the slope alternate with old logging roads angling to the left. At 3.9 mi. (2.6 mi. from Rob Brook Rd.), the trail reaches the summit ledges of Mt. Tremont, where the Mount Tremont Trail enters from the north.

Brunel Trail (map 5:I8)
Distances from Sawyer Pond Trail
   to junction with Rob Brook Rd. at Albany–Bartlett town line: 1.3 mi., 45 min.

to Owl's Cliff spur: 3.2 mi., 2 hr. 20 min.

to Mt. Tremont summit: 3.9 mi. (6.3 km.), 3 hr. 5 min.

Distances from Bear Notch Rd.

to junction with Brunel Trail at Albany–Bartlett town line (via Rob Brook Rd.): 2.6 mi., 1 hr. 15 min.

to Mt. Tremont summit: 5.2 mi. (8.4 km.), 3 hr. 35 min.

Mount Tremont Trail (PEAOC)

This trail leaves the south side of US 302 0.5 mi. west of the Sawyer Rock picnic area and 0.1 mi. west of the bridge over Stony Brook, and climbs to the summit of Mt. Tremont, where there are fine views. The trail suffered some damage by blowdowns in the windstorm of December 1980, and following it in the affected areas requires care. It is covered by maps 5 and 6, but not by either one of them alone.

Leaving US 302, it soon reaches and follows the west side of Stony Brook. At 0.7 mi. it swings right, climbs steadily for 0.3 mi. to the top of the ridge, then levels off and crosses a recent logging road. In the next one-quarter mile there is much blowdown; follow the trail carefully. (It is relatively straight, so one should look for it to continue in the original line after bypassing a bad spot.)

At 1.5 mi. the trail crosses a branch of Stony Brook after a slight descent, then zigzags up the steep northeast side of the mountain at a moderate grade, crossing a rather sharp boundary between birch woods and virgin conifers at 2.4 mi. Reaching the ridge top, it passes an outlook on the right, and continues to the ledgy summit.

Mount Tremont Trail (maps 5/6:18)
Distance from US 302

to Mt. Tremont summit: 2.8 mi. (4.6 km.), 2 hr. 40 min.

Boulder Loop Trail (WMNF)

This is a loop trail from Dugway Rd. near the WMNF Covered Bridge Campground to ledges on a southwest spur of the Moat Range. It offers excellent views for a relatively modest effort. An interpretive leaflet, keyed to numbered stations along the trail, is usually available at the trailhead.

The trail leaves the north side of Dugway Rd. just west of the campground entrance, and at 0.1 mi. reaches the loop junction. The left branch soon passes a large boulder (left), then climbs gradually for a mile. At 1.2 mi. a spur trail right (south) leads 0.2 mi. to ledges, from which there is a fine view of Mt. Passaconaway, Mt. Chocorua, and Middle Sister. The main trail continues around ledges, descends toward Big Brook, continues right below the ledges, passes a boulder (left), and then returns to the loop junction, 0.1 mi. from Dugway Rd.

Boulder Loop Trail (map 4:I10)
Distances from Dugway Rd.

  to loop junction: 0.1 mi., 5 min.
  to ledge spur trail: 1.2 mi., 1 hr. 10 min.
  to Dugway Rd. (complete loop): 2.7 mi. (4.3 km.), 2 hr.

Moat Mountain Trail (WMNF)

This trail traverses the main ridge of Moat Mtn., providing magnificent views from numerous outlooks. Parts of the ridge are very exposed to weather, particularly the section that crosses Middle Moat and South Moat. The trail is covered by map 4 and map 6, but not by either one alone.

The south terminus of the trail is located on Dugway Rd. At the lights in Conway village, turn north (directly opposite NH 153) onto Passaconaway Rd., which becomes West Side Rd. Go left at a fork, then left on Still Rd., which becomes Dugway Rd. The Moat Mountain Trail leaves Dugway Rd. about 3.5 mi. from Conway (sign). Dugway

Rd. continues and joins the Kancamagus Highway near Blackberry Crossing Campground. The northeast terminus is reached from Conway village via Passaconaway Rd. and West Side Rd., or from North Conway by taking the road just north of the Eastern Slope Inn west across the Saco River to West Side Rd. Once on West Side Rd., drive north to a point 0.7 mi. north of the road to Cathedral Ledge, then turn left onto a gravel road between farm fields, and park there.

From the northeast terminus, continue on foot on the gravel road about 0.5 mi. to the clearing just below Diana's Baths mill site. The main path leaves the upper end of the clearing, close to the Baths, by a logging road, which follows the north bank of Lucy Brook for about 0.5 mi. and then forks (sign). Here the Red Ridge Trail turns left across the brook and continues to Red Ridge; the right branch is the Moat Mountain Trail to North Moat. The Moat Mountain Trail crosses a swampy area, following the south bank of Lucy Brook, then at 2.3 mi. turns abruptly left uphill, away from the stream (last sure water); the Attitash Trail continues straight ahead toward Big Attitash Mtn. The Moat Mountain Trail ascends through the woods, and at 2.7 mi. it passes through ledgy areas, reaching the first good outlook at 3.4 mi. It reaches a shoulder at 3.8 mi. and runs nearly level through a patch of larger trees, then climbs fairly steeply through decreasing scrub and increasing bare ledge to the summit of North Moat at 4.2 mi., where there is an unobstructed view in all directions.

From the summit of North Moat the trail descends sharply to the base of the cone, then easily along a shoulder with occasional views. At the end of the shoulder it drops steeply, passing over ledges which require some scrambling, then moderates and continues to a col in a fine spruce forest. Ascending again, it passes the junction with the Red Ridge Trail left (east) at 5.3 mi., just below several large rocks which provide good views. The trail descends to the major col on the ridge, then climbs up to low scrub followed by open ledges with continuous views, and passes east of the summit of Middle Moat (which can be reached in 80 yd. over open ledges) at 6.2 mi. The trail descends to a minor col with a patch of woods which would provide some shelter in a storm, then ascends to the summit of South Moat at 6.8 mi.

The trail then descends into scrub and gradually increasing numbers of beautiful red pines, with views decreasing in frequency. At 7.5 mi. the trail passes an outlook to Mt. Chocorua (probably the first outlook on the ascent from the south), and the trail becomes steep with rough footing. Below this the grade eases considerably, and at 8.3 mi. the trail passes the red-painted WMNF boundary and immediately becomes a well-defined logging road, with easy grade and footing. At 8.8 mi. it goes straight at a crossroads, then another road enters from the left (in the reverse direction, bear left at an arrow 0.2 mi. from Dugway Rd.), and the trail passes through a farmyard to Dugway Rd.

Moat Mountain Trail (maps 4/6:I11-I10)
Distances from West Side Rd.

to Diana's Baths: 0.5 mi., 15 min.
to Red Ridge Trail: 1.1 mi., 35 min.
to Attitash Trail: 2.3 mi., 1 hr. 20 min.
to North Moat summit: 4.2 mi., 3 hr. 25 min.
to Red Ridge Trail: 5.3 mi., 4 hr. 5 min.
to Middle Moat summit: 6.2 mi., 4 hr. 40 min.
to South Moat summit: 6.8 mi., 5 hr.
to Dugway Rd.: 9.1 mi. (14.7 km.), 6 hr. 10 min.

Red Ridge Trail (WMNF)

This trail leaves the Moat Mountain Trail 1.1 mi. from West Side Rd., ascends Red Ridge, with magnificent views, and rejoins the Moat Mountain Trail, at the unnamed peak 1.1 mi. south of the summit of North Moat. With the Moat Mountain Trail, it provides a very attractive loop over the open summit of North Moat. The trail is covered by map 4 and map 6, but not by either one alone.

This trail branches left (south) from the Moat Mountain Trail 0.6 mi. from Diana's Baths and immediately crosses Lucy Brook. It runs generally south up a gentle grade, reaching Red Ridge Link on the left in about 0.7 mi., then continues almost level, crossing an area of active logging where the trail must be followed with care. At about 1.5 mi. from the Moat Mountain Trail, the trail turns sharp right (west) just before a red-blazed WMNF boundary. An old road and an abandoned trail continue ahead. This area is covered with rounded stones, and a branch of Moat Brook flows underground here, at least in some periods. The trail follows the brookbed up for about 0.5 mi., then crosses the brook (last sure water) and ascends the wooded slope of Red Ridge, rather steeply for the first 0.3 mi. Passing alternately through scrub and over ledges, it emerges and winds up the crest of the bare ridge, with magnificent views, then rejoins the Moat Mountain Trail on the main Moat ridge at a rocky knob between North Moat and Middle Moat.

Red Ridge Trail (maps 4/6:110)
Distances from Moat Mountain Trail (lower junction)
to Red Ridge Link: 0.7 mi., 25 min.
to Moat Mountain Trail (upper junction): 3.6 mi. (5.8 km.), 2 hr. 50 min.

Attitash Trail (WMNF)
This trail runs from Bear Notch Rd., 2.7 mi. south of its junction with US 302 in Bartlett village, to the Moat Mountain Trail 2.3 mi. west of West Side Rd. There are

good views from the ledges of Table Mtn., but otherwise the trail is in the woods all the way, and some sections between Table Mtn. and Big Attitash Mtn. are obscure. The trail is covered by map 4 and map 6, but not by either one alone. It is also shown very accurately on the USGS Crawford Notch quad, along with several other trails which no longer exist.

Leaving the small parking area on Bear Notch Rd., follow a grass-grown gravel logging road, which crosses a major branch of Louisville Brook in about 120 yds. At 0.3 mi. the trail bears right on an older road as the gravel road bears left into a cleared area. The trail comes to the edge of Louisville Brook at 0.6 mi., at a small, ledgy cascade, then follows near the brook. In less than 0.1 mi. it turns left (arrow) at a logging road fork and ascends moderately to the col between Bear Mtn. and Table Mtn. at 1.3 mi. Here it turns sharp left and climbs more steeply, soon reaching the edge of the October 1984 burn, and crosses two ledges, with excellent views to the south and southwest. At 1.9 mi. it reaches its high point on Table Mtn., and passes somewhat south of the summit, with views available a short distance to the right from the edge of the south cliff.

From this point on the trail appears to be used more by moose than by humans, and is difficult to follow in some sections. It descends into a col at 2.5 mi., where there is a brook (unreliable), passes a ledgy spot with a glimpse of Mt. Carrigain, and soon climbs a very steep pitch to the main ridge of Big Attitash. From here the trail, which is somewhat obscure, runs on the ridge top or a bit to its north side until it passes very close to the summit of Big Attitash at 4.7 mi. It descends, rather steeply at times, into the valley of Lucy Brook, which is crossed seven times. The first crossing, at 5.9 mi., may be dry; some of the crossings may be difficult in high water. The trail follows an old logging road along the brook, and at some of the crossings (which are mostly marked with arrows) care must be used to pick up the trail on the opposite bank. At 7.2 mi. it reaches the junction with the Moat Mountain Trail, which can be followed right to North Moat or straight ahead to Diana's Baths and West Side Rd.

Attitash Trail (maps 4/6:I9-I10)
Distances from Bear Notch Rd.
to high point on Table Mtn.: 1.9 mi., 1 hr. 40 min.
to Big Attitash Mtn. summit: 4.7 mi., 3 hr. 35 min.
to Moat Mountain Trail: 7.2 mi. (11.6 km.), 4 hr. 40 min.

White Horse Ledge Trail (NHDP)

This trail, marked by yellow blazes, begins at the rear (east) of the parking lot at Echo Lake in Echo Lake–Cathedral Ledge State Park, ascends over the open summit of White Horse Ledge, and descends to the Bryce Path. (To reach Echo Lake–Cathedral Ledge State Park from North Conway, take the road just north of the Eastern Slope Inn, cross the Saco, bear left on West Side Rd., and soon enter the park on the right. There is a park map at the entrance gate.) The trail is covered by map 4 and map 6, but not by either one alone.

Shortly after leaving the parking lot, the west arm of the Echo Lake Trail turns off right at a sign, and the White Horse Ledge Trail continues straight ahead 0.4 mi. to the boulders at the south end of the ledge. After leveling off, it descends slightly, slabs the ridge, then climbs fairly steeply by switchbacks to join a woods road. It follows the road right, gradually ascending for about 0.5 mi. and circling well around to the southwest side of the mountain, to the junction with the Red Ridge Link. Here it turns sharp right, climbs sharply, then levels off and reaches the summit ledges, where there are excellent views, in 0.2 mi. The trail continues, turning sharp left, descends along the crest of the north ledge and through the woods to a junction (sign) with the Bryce Path. You can either follow the Bryce Path left to the top of Cathedral Ledge, or descend steeply to the right to the base and the Bryce Link Path, which leads back to Echo Lake.

White Horse Ledge Trail (maps 4/6:I11-I10)
Distances (est.) from Echo Lake parking area
  to Red Ridge Link: 1.5 mi., 1 hr. 10 min.
  to White Horse Ledge summit: 1.7 mi., 1 hr. 25 min.
  to Bryce Path junction: 2.3 mi. (3.7 km.), 1 hr. 40 min.
  to Echo Lake parking area (via Bryce Path): 2.9 mi., 2 hr.

Bryce Path (NHDP)

This trail runs from the Echo Lake parking lot to the summit of Cathedral Ledge. It is named for James, Viscount Bryce, who laid out the path in 1907 when he was British ambassador to the US. The trail is covered by map 4 and map 6, but not by either one alone.

It leaves the parking lot by following first the White Horse Ledge Trail, then the Lake Trail, which it leaves on the west shore of Echo Lake. It soon reaches a junction with the Bryce Link Path right from Cathedral Ledge Rd. and the rock climbers' trail to White Horse Ledge on the left. (The ledges are extremely dangerous; this trail is not maintained by the State Park Authority.) The Bryce Path turns right, passes near the foundation of an old sugar house, and climbs directly uphill with steep, rough footing for about 0.4 mi. It then bears right, then right again where the White Horse Trail leaves left. This right fork swings north through a flat, wooded upland, and after about 0.5 mi. comes directly to the south slope of Cathedral Ledge, which it ascends steeply to the summit.

Bryce Path (maps 4/6:I11-I10)
Distances (est.) from Echo Lake parking area
  to Bryce Link Path: 0.3 mi., 10 min.
  to White Horse Ledge Trail: 0.6 mi., 30 min.
  to Cathedral Ledge summit: 1.2 mi. (1.9 km.), 55 min.

Bryce Link Path (NHDP)

This path links the lower part of Cathedral Ledge Rd. to the Bryce Path from the Echo Lake parking area. The trail is covered by map 4 and map 6, but not by either one alone. At the park entrance on West Side Rd., a road leads west about 0.3 mi. to a fork. The right (north) fork is Cathedral Ledge Rd.—the automobile road to the summit of Cathedral Ledge. Take the left (south) fork to the edge of the woods and the parking area. The Bryce Link Path enters the woods, and passes trails merging in from the left. At 0.2 mi. it ends where the Bryce Path from Echo Lake comes in on the left and the rock climbers' trail up White Horse Ledge goes straight ahead.

Bryce Link Path (maps 4/6:I11)
Distance (est.) from parking area off Cathedral Ledge Rd.
  to Bryce Path: 0.2 mi. (0.3 km.), 5 min.

Red Ridge Link (NHDP)

This trail links the Red Ridge Trail with the White Horse Ledge Trail, offering a route to the top of White Horse Ledge from Diana's Baths, in combination with the Moat Mountain, Red Ridge, and White Horse Ledge trails. It is well marked by orange blazes. It leaves the Red Ridge Trail at a sign about 0.7 mi. from the Moat Mountain Trail and 1.8 mi. from West Side Rd. via the Moat Mountain Trail. It ascends through open hemlock forest and then younger growth at a moderate grade, and ends at the White Horse Ledge Trail 0.2 mi. below the summit ledges.

Red Ridge Link (map 4:I10)
Distance (est.) from Red Ridge Trail
  to White Horse Ledge Trail: 0.5 mi. (0.8 km.), 25 min.

SECTION 5

Cannon and Kinsman

This section covers Kinsman Mtn. and Cannon Mtn.; the lower peaks in the same range, principally Mt. Wolf, the Cannon Balls, and Mt. Pemigewasset; and several smaller mountains to the west and north, including Cooley Hill, Bald Mtn. and Artist's Bluff, and Mt. Agassiz. It is bounded on the east by I-93 and US 3, and on the south by NH 112 (Lost River Rd.). The entire section is covered by the AMC Franconia map (map 5).

Construction of I-93 through Franconia Notch is now well underway. Most of the changes which affect trails in this section have already been completed. The Profile Lake Trail, formerly described in this section, no longer exists; it has been superseded by a bike path that parallels I-93 for the entire route through the notch. Information concerning the progress of construction and related changes will be available at the Flume Visitor Center at the south end of the notch, and at Lafayette Place and the Tramway. Hiker information will be available at the information booth at the parking lot on the east side of I-93 at Lafayette Place; this information booth is normally open all summer and on weekends in the fall.

In this section the Appalachian Trail follows the Kinsman Ridge Trail from Kinsman Notch to Kinsman Junction (near Kinsman Pond), the Fishin' Jimmy Trail from Kinsman Junction to Lonesome Lake Hut, and the Cascade Brook Trail from Lonesome Lake Hut to I-93 approximately 1 mi. north of the Flume Visitor Center.

GEOGRAPHY

The heart of this region is the Cannon–Kinsman range. The northern half of the range is a high, well-defined ridge, of which Cannon Mtn. and the two peaks of Kinsman Mtn. are the most important summits. The southern half of the range is broad, with only one significant summit, Mt. Wolf.

At the north end of the range is Cannon Mtn. (4100 ft.). This dome-shaped mountain is famous for its magnificent profile, the Old Man of the Mountain, and for its imposing east cliff. It takes its name from a natural stone table, superimposed on a boulder, that resembles a cannon when seen from Profile Clearing. Three ledges, not in a vertical line, at the north end of the east cliff form the Great Stone Face immortalized by Nathaniel Hawthorne when viewed from the vicinity of Profile Lake. For some years state park personnel have protected the Old Man from the otherwise inexorable forces of ice and gravity by filling cracks with cement and maintaining a system of cables and turnbuckles. Cannon Mtn. has a major ski area, operated by the state, and an aerial tramway—recently constructed to replace the first such passenger tramway in North America—that extends from a valley station (1970 ft.) just off I-93 to a mountain station (4000 ft.) just below the main summit. The tramway is operated in the summer for tourists and in the winter for skiers. Hiking is not permitted on ski trails in the summer. Just northeast of Cannon Mtn. are Bald Mtn. (2340 ft.) and Artist's Bluff (2340 ft.), two small but very interesting peaks at the north end of Franconia Notch, offering excellent views for little exertion. Bald Mtn. is a striking miniature mountain with a bold, bare, rocky cone, while Artist's Bluff is a wooded dome with the fine cliff for which it is named on the southeast face.

On the ridge southwest of Cannon Mtn. are three humps called the Cannon Balls (east to west: 3769 ft., 3660 ft., and 3693 ft.). All are wooded, but the highest, the northeast Cannon Ball, affords good outlooks. Bridal

Veil Falls, one of the more attractive falls in the mountains, is located on Coppermine Brook in the ravine between Cannon Mtn. and the Cannon Balls on the north side of the ridge. Lonesome Lake (2740 ft.) is located on the high plateau which forms the floor of the ravine lying between Cannon Mtn. and the Cannon Balls, to the south of the ridge. Trails completely encircle the lake, which has excellent views from its shores. The whole area around the lake is in Franconia Notch State Park, and camping is not permitted.

Kinsman Mtn. lies south of the Cannon Balls, and its two peaks are the highest points on the ridge. North Kinsman (4293 ft.) is wooded, and its true summit is actually a pointed boulder, but ledges just to the east of the summit command magnificent views. The view of Mt. Lafayette and Mt. Lincoln across Franconia Notch is particularly impressive. South Kinsman (4358 ft.) has a broad, flat summit with two knobs of nearly equal height. The USGS Lincoln quad puts the summit elevation on the north knob, which is just off the main trail, but the south knob bears the cairn and is preferred by most hikers. Views are fine, but one must wander around the summit plateau to obtain the best outlooks. Kinsman Mtn. shelters two very beautiful mountain ponds: Kinsman Pond under the east cliffs of North Kinsman, and Harrington Pond under the bluff at the end of South Kinsman's south ridge. Two spurs of the Kinsman group are especially notable. On the west, Bald Peak (2470 ft.) is a flat, ledgy knob with good views, reached by a spur from the Mount Kinsman Trail. On the east, lying below the massive southeast ridge of South Kinsman, is Mt. Pemigewasset (2557 ft.), with its famous natural rock profile, the Indian Head; the ledgy summit commands excellent views for a modest effort.

South of Kinsman Mtn., only Mt. Wolf has much claim

to prominence. Its summit bears a ledge with an excellent view to the east and northeast. Although lacking in peaks, the southern part of the range does have several aquatic attractions, including Lost River, Gordon Pond and Gordon Fall, and Georgiana and Harvard falls. The Lost River Reservation, property of the SPNHF, lies about 5 mi. west of North Woodstock on NH 112 (Lost River Rd.). Lost River, one of the tributaries of Moosilauke Brook, flows for nearly 0.5 mi. through a series of caves and large potholes, for the most part underground. At one place it falls 20 ft. within one of the caves, and at another, known as Paradise Falls, 30 ft. in the open air. Trails, walks, and ladders make the caves accessible. In order to protect the forest and caves, in 1911 the SPNHF began to acquire the surrounding land, and it now owns about 770 acres bordering the highway on both sides for nearly 2.5 mi. The SPNHF maintains a nature garden, containing more than three hundred indigenous plants, and the Ecology Trail, which circles the inner parking lot area and provides information at numbered and marked sites described in a brochure provided by the SPNHF. The reservation is open from May through October; an admission fee is charged.

This section also includes several scattered peaks and trails. Mt. Agassiz (2369 ft.) is between Franconia and Bethlehem villages, and is reached by a paved road about 1 mi. long—formerly a toll auto road—which leaves NH 142 between those two villages. There is an excellent and extensive view from the summit. The former restaurant and observation tower are now a private residence, so hikers who visit the summit (on foot only) should exercise great care to respect the rights of the property owner. Cooley Hill (2485 ft.) is a wooded, viewless peak, but a trail built to its former fire tower has survived the loss of its reason for existence.

HUTS, SHELTERS, AND CAMPING

HUTS

Lonesome Lake Hut (AMC)

Lonesome Lake Hut, at about 2760 ft., is located on the west shore of Lonesome Lake, with superb views of the Franconia Range. The hut was built in 1964, replacing cabins on the northeast shore. It accommodates 46 and is open to the public from mid-June to mid-September. The hut may be reached by the Lonesome Lake Trail, the Cascade Brook Trail, the Fishin' Jimmy Trail from Kinsman Junction, or by the Dodge Cutoff from the Hi-Cannon Trail. Camping is not permitted around the hut or the lake.

For schedules and information contact Reservation Secretary, Pinkham Notch Camp, Box 298, Gorham, NH 03581 (603-466-2727).

CAMPING

Restricted Use Areas

As of 1986, there were no Restricted Use Areas in this section. Campers should still employ good camping practices.

Franconia Notch State Park

No camping is permitted in Franconia Notch State Park except at Lafayette Campground (fee charged). In this section, the areas included in the park consist mostly of the northeast slopes of Cannon Mtn., and the regions surrounding Lonesome Lake and extending east from the lake to I-93.

Established Trailside Campsites

Eliza Brook Shelter (AMC) is located on the Kinsman Ridge Trail at its crossing of Eliza Brook. Tent camping is permitted in the area.

Kinsman Pond Campsite (AMC), with a shelter and tent platforms, is located on Kinsman Pond near Kinsman Junction, where the Kinsman Ridge, Kinsman Pond, and Fishin' Jimmy trails meet. There is a caretaker in the summer and a fee is charged. Tent camping is permitted in the area.

Coppermine Shelter (WMNF) is located on the Coppermine Trail west of Bridal Veil Falls. Tent camping is permitted in the area.

LIST OF TRAILS   MAP

Trails on the West Side of the Range

Coppermine Trail	5:G3-H4
Mount Kinsman Trail	5:G3-H4
Reel Brook Trail	5:H3
Beech Hill Trail (abandoned)	5:H3-I3

Trails West of NH 116

Jericho Road Trail	5:H3
Cobble Hill Trail	5:H2

THE TRAILS

Kinsman Ridge Trail (AMC)

This trail follows the crest of the main ridge from the height-of-land on NH 112 in Kinsman Notch to the Old Man parking lot off I-93 in Franconia Notch. (There are plans to relocate the Franconia Notch trailhead to a new hiker parking lot near the Tramway, to be shared with the Greenleaf Trail.) From NH 112 to Kinsman Junction, it is part of the Appalachian Trail. For much of its length it is a more difficult route than one might infer from the map. Footing is often rough and there are many minor ups and downs. Hikers with heavy packs should allow considerable extra time for many parts of the trail. There is little water on or near the trail, and none that a cautious hiker will drink without treatment.

The trail leaves NH 112 just to the north of the height-of-land, about 0.5 mi. north of the Lost River entrance, and opposite the north terminus of the Beaver Brook Trail. It climbs a steep sidehill bearing gradually away from the road for 0.1 mi., and then swings right and climbs very steeply northeast, through the SPNHF Lost River Reservation. At 0.4 mi. the grade relaxes, and the trail soon crosses a swampy sag on puncheons and reaches a junction on the right, at 0.6 mi., with the Dilly Trail from Lost River. At

0.9 mi. it crosses the summit of a wooded knob and descends steeply by zigzags, soon passes a small stream (unreliable), and follows the ridge over several minor humps. At 2.4 mi. it passes the first of two good outlooks to the east, crosses a significant hump, and descends past a boulder to the right of the trail, with a view of Mt. Wolf ahead. At 3.3 mi. it passes over a stagnant brook at the low point of the trail in the ravine, then ascends 30 yd. to the junction where the Gordon Pond Trail enters on the right, 0.3 mi. from Gordon Pond.

The trail climbs by short, steep sections alternating with easy sections, crossing a small brook (reliable water) at 3.9 mi., and ascends to a point just below the summit of the west knob of Mt. Wolf. It descends slightly in a shallow sag, then climbs to a point near the summit of the east knob of Mt. Wolf, at 4.6 mi., where it makes a sharp left turn. Here a side path leads right 60 yd. to the summit of the east knob, where there is a fine view of the Franconias and the peaks to the east and southeast. The main trail now descends the east side of Wolf's north ridge at a moderate grade, but with a rough footway and numerous short ascents. At 6.0 mi. the trail turns left, runs almost level, and meets the Reel Brook Trail, which enters left at 6.5 mi., just south of the col between Mt. Wolf and Kinsman Mtn.—which was the original Kinsman Notch. The Kinsman Ridge Trail continues along the ridge top, crosses under the power lines at 7.0 mi., and descends to the bank of Eliza Brook at 7.5 mi., where a side path runs left 55 yd. to Eliza Brook Shelter.

The Kinsman Ridge Trail crosses Eliza Brook and in 50 yd. intersects a grass-grown gravel logging road and follows it to the left. (The points where the trail turns off this road, going in either direction, should be carefully watched for.) The trail follows the road for 0.3 mi., then turns left off it and follows a very scenic section of Eliza Brook, with several attractive cascades and pools. At 8.6 mi. the trail recrosses Eliza Brook and soon climbs rather steeply to cross the bog at the east end of Harrington Pond on puncheons. Here, at 8.9 mi., there is an interesting view of the shoulder of South Kinsman rising above the beautiful pond. (*Note.* The section of the trail between Harrington Pond and South Kinsman may require much extra time, particularly for those with heavy packs, and is also somewhat exposed to weather.) The trail continues at a moderate grade for 0.3 mi., then climbs a steep pitch, crosses a minor hump and a blowdown patch, then struggles up a very steep and rough pitch to an outlook where the climbing becomes somewhat easier, and climbs to the bare south knob of South Kinsman's summit, which is very exposed to the weather, at 9.9 mi.

From here the Kinsman Ridge Trail crosses a scrub-filled sag, passes west of the north knob of South Kinsman at 10.0 mi., and descends relatively easily to the col between South and North Kinsman at 10.5 mi. The trail now climbs steadily to a side path (sign) at 10.9 mi., which leads right 25 yd. to a fine outlook to the Franconias, and continues another 70 yd. to a ledge which looks directly down on Kinsman Pond. The true summit of North Kinsman is a pointed boulder on the right of the main trail, 30 yd. north of the outlook spur. The Kinsman Ridge Trail now descends steeply to the junction with the Mount Kinsman Trail on the left at 11.3 mi., and continues to Kinsman Junction at 11.5 mi. Here the Fishin' Jimmy Trail continues the Appalachian Trail to Lonesome Lake, and the Kinsman Pond Trail bears right, leading in 0.1 mi. to Kinsman Pond and Kinsman Pond Shelter.

The Kinsman Ridge Trail bears sharp left at Kinsman Junction, and soon rises abruptly 100 ft. to a hump (3812 ft.) on the ridge. It then continues to the Cannon Balls, the three humps that constitute the ridge leading to Cannon

Mtn. On top of the first (west) Cannon Ball there is a meadow, a little below which water may often be found on the trail. The trail descends sharply to a deep ravine, where water is usually found nearby. The trail slabs north of the second (middle) Cannon Ball and enters the next col with very little descent. After climbing over the third (northeast) Cannon Ball, with some views, it descends to the junction at 13.8 mi. with the Lonesome Lake Trail, which leads south 1.0 mi. to Lonesome Lake Hut (water can be found 0.2 mi. down this trail). In a short distance it reaches the low point in Coppermine Col, at the base of Cannon Mtn., then ascends Cannon Mtn., climbing very steeply among huge boulders. About 0.4 mi. below the summit the Hi-Cannon Trail enters right, and the Kinsman Ridge Trail soon enters the gravel Rim Trail, encountering a maze of trails in the summit area. At the true summit, to the left of the Rim Trail, there is an observation tower.

The Rim Trail continues around the edge of the summit plateau, and the Kinsman Ridge Trail diverges right where the Rim Trail turns left toward the tramway terminal. Descending the semi-open east flank of the main peak over rocks and ledges, then through scrub, it crosses a sag and ascends slightly to the east summit. At the point where it makes a right-angle turn left (north), a side trail, marked by occasional cairns, turns sharp right out upon the ledges to the southeast—with a good view of the Franconia Range—then, swinging around northeast and descending, leads in 300 yd. from the junction to the Cannon, an excellent viewpoint. The main trail soon drops steeply on a rough and rocky footway, improves somewhat in the lower half, and reaches the Old Man parking lot.

Ascending Cannon Mtn. from the Old Man parking lot, the trail climbs steeply, becoming steeper and rockier as it ascends. In a level area, at about 1.3 mi., a side path goes straight ahead to the ledges; here the main trail turns sharp right to cross over the east summit, pass through a sag, and climb to the Rim Trail.

Kinsman Ridge Trail (map 5:I3-G4)
Distances from NH 112 in Kinsman Notch
   to Dilly Trail: 0.6 mi., 45 min.
   to Gordon Pond Trail: 3.3 mi., 2 hr. 20 min.
   to Reel Brook Trail: 6.5 mi., 3 hr. 30 min.
   to Eliza Brook Shelter spur: 7.5 mi., 5 hr.
   to Harrington Pond: 8.9 mi., 6 hr. 15 min.
   to South Kinsman summit: 10.0 mi., 7 hr. 15 min.
   to North Kinsman summit: 10.9 mi., 7 hr. 50 min.
   to Mount Kinsman Trail: 11.3 mi., 8 hr. 5 min.
   to Kinsman Junction: 11.5 mi., 8 hr. 10 min.
   to Lonesome Lake Trail: 13.9 mi., 9 hr. 35 min.
   to Hi-Cannon Trail: 14.3 mi., 10 hr. 5 min.
   to Cannon Mtn. summit: 14.7 mi., 10 hr. 25 min.
   to side path to ledges: 15.4 mi., 10 hr. 45 min.
   to Old Man parking area: 16.7 mi. (26.9 km.), 11 hr. 25 min.
Distances from Old Man parking area
   to side path to ledges: 1.3 mi., 1 hr. 30 min.
   to Cannon Mtn. summit: 2.0 mi. (3.2 km.), 2 hr. 5 min.

Bald Mountain–Artist's Bluff Path (NHDP)

The two trailheads of this trail are located on NH 18 just west of its junction with I-93, north of Echo Lake. The west trailhead is at the edge of the large parking lot for the Roland Peabody Memorial Slope section of the Cannon Mtn. Ski Area, on the north side of NH 18 about 0.4 mi. from I-93. The east trailhead is on NH 18 opposite Echo Lake beach. Artist's Bluff and the summit of Bald Mtn. provide fine views for very little effort.

Leaving the Peabody Slopes parking lot, the trail follows an old carriage road and reaches the top of the ridge in about 0.3 mi. At this point a spur path diverges left and climbs the rocky cone of Bald Mtn., reaching the top in about 0.1 mi. About 10 yd. beyond the junction with the trail to Bald Mtn., the main trail turns right and proceeds over the Artist's Bluff ridge. It descends slightly to the top of a steep, gravelly gully, where an unmarked path diverges left to the top of Artist's Bluff. The main trail continues down the gully to NH 18.

Bald Mountain–Artist's Bluff Path (map 5:G4)
Distances (est.) from Peabody Slopes parking area
to fork in trail: 0.3 mi., 15 min.
to Echo Lake beach: 0.8 mi. (1.3 km.), 40 min.
to Bald Mtn. (via spur path): 0.4 mi., 25 min.

Lonesome Lake Trail (AMC)

This trail begins at the parking lot on the west side of I-93 at Lafayette Place and runs past Lonesome Lake to the Kinsman Ridge Trail at Coppermine Col. It follows the route of an old bridle path much of the way to Lonesome Lake, with excellent footing and easy to moderate grades. Beyond the lake it is of average difficulty.

The trail leaves the parking lot and follows signs through the campground. In a short distance the Pemi Trail diverges left, and the Lonesome Lake Trail begins to climb at a moderate grade. At 0.3 mi. a bridge crosses a small brook at a sharp left turn in the trail, and at 0.4 mi. the Hi-Cannon Trail leaves right. From this point the trail is a series of three long switchbacks, with a slight descent before reaching a junction at 1.2 mi. with the Cascade Brook Trail (left) and the Dodge Cutoff (right), near the shore of Lonesome Lake. For the shortest route to Lonesome Lake Hut, follow the Cascade Brook Trail. The former bridle path ends, and the Lonesome Lake Trail becomes a footpath that continues along the north shore.

For 0.2 mi. it coincides with the Around-Lonesome-Lake Trail, which then diverges left, leading in 0.3 mi. to Lonesome Lake Hut. The Lonesome Lake Trail continues north and west, soon begins to rise more steeply, and ends at the Kinsman Ridge Trail in Coppermine Col, 0.8 mi. southwest of the summit of Cannon Mtn.

Lonesome Lake Trail (map 5:H4)
Distances from Lafayette Place parking area (west side)
to Hi-Cannon Trail: 0.4 mi., 20 min.
to Cascade Brook Trail/Dodge Cutoff: 1.2 mi., 1 hr. 5 min.
to Lonesome Lake Hut (via Cascade Brook Trail and Fishin' Jimmy Trail): 1.5 mi., 1 hr. 15 min.
to Kinsman Ridge Trail: 2.3 mi. (3.7 km.), 2 hr.

Around-Lonesome-Lake Trail (AMC)

This trail encircles Lonesome Lake, making use of portions of other trails. It has fine views, especially of the Franconia Range. On occasion parts of this trail are inundated, especially those on the west shore.

Starting at the junction of the Lonesome Lake and Cascade Brook trails, it follows the latter south along the east shore, turns west and follows the Fishin' Jimmy Trail, crosses the outlet of the lake, and continues ahead where the Fishin' Jimmy Trail bears left to ascend to the hut. The trail continues north through the bogs along the west side of the lake (the only section not shared with another trail), crosses several inlet brooks, and meets the Lonesome Lake Trail shortly after entering the woods. Turn right on the Lonesome Lake Trail and continue to the junction with the Cascade Brook Trail, which completes the circuit.

Around-Lonesome-Lake Trail (map 5:H4)
Distance for complete loop
from any starting point: 0.8 mi. (1.3 km.), 25 min.

Hi-Cannon Trail (NHDP)

This trail begins at the Lonesome Lake Trail 0.4 mi. from Lafayette Place parking area, and ends on the Kinsman Ridge Trail 0.4 mi. south of the summit of Cannon Mtn. It is steep near Cliff House, somewhat rough at times, and potentially dangerous if there is ice on the ledges above Cliff House. It passes several fine viewpoints, particularly those overlooking Lonesome Lake.

The trail diverges right (west) from the Lonesome Lake Trail, and begins to ascend gradually by switchbacks. Watch carefully for a sharp right switchback at 0.1 mi., where an old logging road continues straight and rejoins the Lonesome Lake Trail. At 0.8 mi. the Dodge Cutoff from Lonesome Lake enters left at the top of a ridge. At 1.2 mi. there is a fine outlook across Franconia Notch and the area around Lafayette Campground, and 100 yd. farther the trail passes Cliff House (right)—a natural rock shelter—and ascends a ladder. It now passes along a cliff edge with three fine outlooks over Lonesome Lake in the next 0.2 mi. (*Note.* Use caution on the ledges.) Then the trail ascends moderately to the top of the ridge, turns right, and at 2.0 mi. ends at its junction with the Kinsman Ridge Trail. For the summit of Cannon Mtn. follow the Kinsman Ridge Trail right 0.4 mi.

Hi-Cannon Trail (map 5:H4)
Distances from Lonesome Lake Trail

to Dodge Cutoff: 0.8 mi., 50 min.

to Kinsman Ridge Trail: 2.0 mi. (3.2 km.), 2 hr. 10 min.

to Cannon Mtn. summit (via Kinsman Ridge Trail): 2.4 mi., 2 hr. 20 min.

Dodge Cutoff (NHDP)

This direct connection between the Hi-Cannon and Lonesome Lake trails provides a shortcut between Cannon

Mtn. and Lonesome Lake Hut. It was named in honor of Joe Dodge, a former manager of the AMC hut system.

It leaves the Hi-Cannon Trail 0.8 mi. above the junction of the Lonesome Lake and Hi-Cannon trails, and descends gradually (generally southwest) to a flat area, then crosses a small stream, a slight rise, and another flat area. It ends at the junction of the Lonesome Lake and Cascade Brook trails on the east shore of the lake, 0.3 mi. from Lonesome Lake Hut.

Dodge Cutoff (map 5:H4)

Distance from Hi-Cannon Trail

to Lonesome Lake Trail: 0.3 mi. (0.5 km.), 15 min.

Pemi Trail (NHDP)

This trail extends from the Lonesome Lake Trail just south of the Lafayette Place parking area to the Basin. Diverging left (south) from the Lonesome Lake Trail, it follows the west bank of the Pemigewasset River southward at an almost level grade and ends at the Basin.

Pemi Trail (map 5:H4)

Distance (est.) from Lonesome Lake Trail

to the Basin: 1.5 mi. (2.4 km.), 45 min.

Basin–Cascades Trail (NHDP)

This trail starts at the Basin (parking areas on either side of I-93) and ascends along the beautiful lower half of Cascade Brook, ending at the Cascade Brook Trail. From the Basin cross a bridge and go 25 yd. to a junction. Take the right path for 40 yd., passing a Basin–Cascades Trail sign, then turn left and approach Cascade Brook, remaining on the north bank. Informal side paths lead onto the smooth granite ledges, from which there are views of the Franconia Range across the notch. At about 0.4 mi. a rough side path leads down to a good view of Kinsman Falls, and 40 yd. farther up the main trail a path to the left leads to a view from the top of the falls. In another 0.1 mi. the main trail crosses a narrow bridge with a single handrail to the south bank of the brook and continues its gradual ascent. At about 0.9 mi. there are views of upper and lower Rocky Glen Falls. The trail turns left through a little box canyon and in 80 yd. meets the Cascade Brook Trail. For a good view of Rocky Glen Falls from above, return cautiously down the brook about 60 yd.

Basin–Cascades Trail (map 5:H4)
Distances from the Basin parking area (west side)

  to Kinsman Falls: 0.4 mi., 20 min.

  to Cascade Brook Trail: 1.0 mi. (1.6 km.), 45 min.

Cascade Brook Trail (AMC)

This trail, a link in the Appalachian Trail, leads from a junction with the Liberty Spring Trail at the former Whitehouse Bridge site on I-93 to Lonesome Lake. There is no parking at the Whitehouse Bridge site, which is reached in 0.8 mi. from the Flume Visitor Center hiker parking area via the Whitehouse Trail (see Section 3). It is a relatively easy trail, but the crossing of Cascade Brook may be difficult at high water.

From the junction with the Whitehouse and Liberty Spring trails, cross under I-93, turn left, then in 10 yd. turn right, entering the woods. The trail climbs at a moderate grade, crosses Whitehouse Brook in 0.2 mi., continues generally northwest, and reaches a junction at the edge of Cascade Brook, where the Basin–Cascades Trail enters right at 1.3 mi. About 60 yd. downstream on Cascade Brook are some beautiful cascades and pools. The Cascade Brook Trail immediately crosses Cascade Brook on the rocks (may be difficult), and continues to climb along the northeast bank. At 1.8 mi. the Kinsman Pond Trail diverges left, and from this point the Cascade Brook Trail

follows an old logging road to the junction with Fishin'
Jimmy Trail at the outlet of Lonesome Lake. Lonesome
Lake Hut is 120 yd. to the left. The Cascade Brook Trail
continues along the east side of the lake and ends at the
Lonesome Lake Trail in 0.2 mi.

Cascade Brook Trail (map 5:H4)
**Distances from Whitehouse Trail/Liberty Spring Trail
junction**

> *to* Basin–Cascades Trail: 1.3 mi., 50 min.
> *to* Kinsman Pond Trail: 1.8 mi., 1 hr. 20 min.
> *to* Fishin' Jimmy Trail: 2.7 mi., 2 hr.
> *to* Lonesome Lake Trail: 2.9 mi. (4.7 km.), 2 hr. 5 min.

Fishin' Jimmy Trail (AMC)

This trail, a link in the Appalachian Trail, leads from
Lonesome Lake to the Kinsman Ridge Trail at Kinsman
Junction, near Kinsman Pond. Parts of it are steep and
rough. It received its peculiar name from the chief charac-
ter in a story written by Annie Trumbull Slosson, which
takes its scene in this region.

Diverging from the Cascade Brook Trail at the south end
of Lonesome Lake, it crosses the outlet brook and passes
just to the south of Lonesome Lake Hut at 0.1 mi. It begins
to slab the ridge, rising sharply at 0.3 mi., then passing
over several ascents and descents. It passes a large rock
block (left) at 0.6 mi. and ascends, crossing reliable water
at 1.2 mi. Soon it climbs steeply, levels out at 1.6 mi.,
ascends over a ledge at 1.8 mi., and levels out again at 2.1
mi. It reaches Kinsman Junction and the Kinsman Ridge
Trail at 2.3 mi., 0.1 mi. north of Kinsman Pond Shelter.

Fishin' Jimmy Trail (map 5:H4)
Distances from Cascade Brook Trail

> *to* Lonesome Lake Hut: 0.1 mi., 5 min.
> *to* Kinsman Junction: 2.3 mi. (3.6 km.), 1 hr. 50 min.

Kinsman Pond Trail (AMC)

This trail runs to Kinsman Pond and Kinsman Junction from the Cascade Brook Trail 1.8 mi. from I-93 at the Whitehouse Bridge site, which is reached by following the Whitehouse Trail (Section 3) 0.8 mi. north from the Flume Visitor Center. The upper part of this trail is wet, steep, rocky, and very rough, sharing the footway at times with small brooks, making rocks slippery; it may be difficult to follow.

Leaving the Cascade Brook Trail, the trail crosses to the southwest side of the brook in 10 yd., and proceeds west by logging roads. Soon rising, it crosses a small brook at a cascade and reaches virgin forest near a brook. The trail swings northwest, crossing a brook (last reliable water), and at 1.9 mi. crosses the outlet of Kinsman Pond not far below the pond itself. It climbs over and around ledges on the east shore of the pond and passes Kinsman Pond Shelter, and in 0.1 mi. from the shelter meets the Kinsman Ridge and Fishin' Jimmy trails at Kinsman Junction. Kinsman Pond Shelter accommodates twelve. Water in this area is not potable unless treated.

Kinsman Pond Trail (map 5:H4)
Distance from Cascade Brook Trail
   to Kinsman Junction: 2.4 mi. (3.9 km.), 2 hr.

Mount Pemigewasset Trail (NHDP)

This trail runs from the Flume Visitor Center parking area to the summit of Mt. Pemigewasset (Indian Head), where excellent views are obtained with modest effort.

The trail crosses under I-93 and climbs moderately. At 0.9 mi. the trail approaches but does not cross a brook, and then ascends at a moderate grade, generally west and southwest. It approaches the summit from the north side, and is joined on the right by the Indian Head Trail just before reaching the open summit ledges.

Mount Pemigewasset Trail (map 5:H4)
Distance (est.) from Flume Visitor Center parking area
   to Mt. Pemigewasset summit: 1.4 mi. (2.3 km.), 1 hr. 15 min.

Indian Head Trail

This trail runs to the summit of Mt. Pemigewasset (Indian Head) from a parking area on the west side of US 3, 200 yd. south of the Indian Head Resort. The summit ledges afford excellent views.

The trail leaves the parking area, crosses under I-93, and ascends by easy grades through hardwoods, passes near the base of the cliffs on the south side that form the Indian Head, and then climbs a steep gully and approaches the summit from the west. The Mount Pemigewasset Trail joins left just below the summit ledges.

Indian Head Trail (map 5:H4)
Distance (est.) from US 3
   to Mt. Pemigewasset summit: 1.0 mi. (1.6 km.), 1 hr. 10 min.

Georgiana Falls Path

These falls on Harvard Brook are a series of cascades ending in a pool. The path is on private land and not officially maintained. It begins about 2.5 mi. north of North Woodstock on Hanson Farm Rd., which leaves the west side of US 3 opposite the Longhorn Restaurant, crosses Hanson Brook on a bridge, and reaches a parking area at about 0.1 mi. at the end of the pavement. Follow a dirt road through a tunnel under the northbound lanes of I-93, bear right, then left, through the tunnel under the southbound lanes. At about 0.5 mi., where the road bears right, the road enters the woods straight ahead and follows the north side of Harvard Brook for about 0.5 mi. The trail continues up the brook on sloping rocks, without markings, to Georgiana Falls. Above Georgiana Falls there is a series of cascades terminating in Harvard Falls about 0.5 mi. farther up the brook.

Georgiana Falls Path (map 5:I4)
Distance (est.) from Hanson Farm Rd.

    to Georgiana Falls: 1.3 mi. (2.1 km.), 1 hr.

Gordon Pond Trail (WMNF)

This trail runs from NH 112 1.7 mi. west of its junction with US 3 in North Woodstock to the Kinsman Ridge Trail south of Mt. Wolf, passing Gordon Fall and Gordon Pond. The trailhead on NH 112 is located opposite Govoni's Restaurant and Agassiz Basin (see Section 6); there are signs here in the summer but not at other times. Park just west of the buildings.

The trail (WMNF sign) follows the driveway through the buildings on the north side of NH 112 ("No Trespassing" signs do not apply to hikers who stay on the trail), and at 0.1 mi. it turns right at a crossroads and follows an old railroad grade. At 0.6 mi. it crosses under the power lines, soon crosses a gravel road, and at 1.1 mi. another road enters on the right. (In the opposite direction, bear right here; there may be an arrow pointing to the wrong branch.) At 1.6 mi. the trail approaches Gordon Pond Brook and a logging road crosses the brook, but the trail remains on the southwest bank and swings to the northwest to recross the power lines at 1.8 mi. The trail crosses Gordon Pond Brook (may be difficult at high water) at 2.0 mi. and continues along the north bank, crossing a tributary at 2.6 mi., and swings left to cross the main brook on a snowmobile bridge at 3.2 mi. The trail continues on an old road, becoming somewhat steeper, and crosses a minor ridge to the southerly branch of Gordon Pond Brook where it passes Gordon Fall. Crossing the brook on a ledge at the top of the fall at 3.7 mi., it soon recrosses, passes a very wet section of trail, then crosses Gordon Pond Brook at 4.4 mi. Just before it recrosses the main brook at 4.5 mi., unsigned paths lead right to the shore of the pond, where there is an interesting view of the steep face of Mt. Wolf. The trail itself does not come within sight of the pond, but continues on a level grade, bears left where an unsigned path enters right, and climbs easily to the Kinsman Ridge Trail.

Gordon Pond Trail (map 5:I4-I3)
Distances from NH 112
to Gordon Pond: 4.5 mi., 3 hr. 5 min.
to Kinsman Ridge Trail: 4.8 mi. (7.7 km.), 3 hr. 20 min.

Dilly Trail (SPNHF)
This trail, which runs from Lost River Reservation to the Kinsman Ridge Trail 0.6 mi. from NH 112, leaves the northeast corner of the dirt parking area (not the paved area directly beside NH 112) within the Lost River Reservation. At the trailhead there is a sign marked "Dilly Trail .75." The trail is well marked with white paint. At about 100 yd., it starts steeply up the cliffs and ledges overlooking the Lost River Reservation, which can be seen at about 0.1 mi. The trail climbs over ledges and begins a series of switchbacks at about 0.3 mi. It reaches the distinctive edge of the ridge at about 0.7 mi., where a branch trail right goes about 50 yd. east to a lookout over Lost River and to the mountains south of Kinsman Notch. The main trail turns sharp left (northwest), passing through open hardwoods and rising slightly, with views and glimpses of the

country to the northeast, and reaches the junction with the Kinsman Ridge Trail at about 0.8 mi.

Dilly Trail (map 5:I3)
Distances (est.) from Lost River Reservation parking lot
   to lookout over Lost River: 0.7 mi., 45 min.
   to Kinsman Ridge Trail: 0.8 mi., 50 min.

Coppermine Trail (WMNF)

This trail to Bridal Veil Falls is reached by Coppermine Rd., which leaves the east side of NH 116 3.4 mi. south of NH 18 in Franconia and 7.7 mi. north of NH 112 at Bungay Corner. The road is usually passable by automobiles for at least 0.5 mi., and possibly for 0.3 mi. more. The trail follows along the north side of Coppermine Brook, then crosses to the south side, ascends at a somewhat steeper grade, passes the WMNF Coppermine Shelter, and ends at the base of the Bridal Veil Falls.

Coppermine Trail (map 5:G3-H4)
Distance (est.) from NH 116
   to Bridal Veil Falls: 2.5 mi. (4.0 km.), 1 hr. 50 min.

Mount Kinsman Trail (WMNF)

This trail climbs to the Kinsman Ridge Trail 0.4 mi. north of North Kinsman, from the east side of NH 116 at the Franconia–Easton town line, about 4 mi. south of NH 18 in Franconia village and 2.0 mi. north of the Easton town hall. There is a sign for the town line a few yards north of the trail, but none for the trail itself, which follows a logging road at a prominent gate opposite a house. The trail climbs at moderate grades but is sparsely marked, and care is frequently required to follow it.

From the gate it follows a logging road which soon swings right, then bears right at a fork (arrow). Ascending easily, at times level, it passes a sugar house left at 0.6 mi., and at 1.1 mi. enters the WMNF, where a loop path left makes a short bypass of a wet section of road. The road, now distinctly older and steeper, crosses a substantial brook at 1.5 mi. at the site of the former Kinsman Cabin (which has been dismantled). At 1.8 mi. it crosses a small brook that falls over a mossy ledge to the left of the trail, then at 2.1 mi. crosses Flume Brook. Just over Flume Brook, a side path descends close to the brook bank for 150 yd. to small, steep-walled Kinsman Flume—a classic eroded dike—at the top of which an overhanging boulder presents a reasonable facsimile of a profile. The main trail continues on the road for another 70 yd., then turns sharp left, where a spur path 0.2 mi. long leads sharp right and makes an easy ascent to Bald Peak, a bare eminence with fine views crowning a west spur of Mt. Kinsman.

The axe-blazed trail now joins and follows Flume Brook, winding up the mountainside at easy to moderate grades, with good footing except for scattered steep pitches with rough footing. It crosses several small brooks and at 3.2 mi. climbs a ledge by means of a short ladder. Soon it swings right and angles upward to the right, then swings left and climbs straight up to the ridge top, where it meets the Kinsman Ridge Trail. For North and South Kinsman turn right; for Kinsman Pond turn left.

Mount Kinsman Trail (map 5:G3-H4)
Distances from NH 116

to Bald Peak spur trail: 2.1 mi., 1 hr. 45 min.

to Kinsman Ridge Trail: 3.7 mi. (5.9 km.), 3 hr. 20 min.

Reel Brook Trail (WMNF)

This trail ascends to the Kinsman Ridge Trail in the col between Mt. Wolf and South Kinsman (the original Kinsman Notch), 1.0 mi. south of Eliza Brook Shelter, from a gravel road which leaves NH 116 3.7 mi. north of the junction with NH 112 at Bungay Corner and 1.1 mi. south of the Easton town hall. The road, which is not plowed in winter, can be driven to a fork (hiker logo on post) at 0.6 mi. from NH 116, where the left branch leads to an open field (parking). The grades on this trail are moderate, but the footing is often very muddy. The Beech Hill Trail, which formerly continued along this road and led to NH 112 near Wildwood Campground, has been officially closed by the WMNF.

The trail enters the woods (sign) and follows a logging road southeast, parallel to but some distance northwest of Reel Brook. The trail crosses several brooks. At 1.2 mi. the road bears right and descends, and very shortly the trail diverges left, crosses a small brook, reaches a wide logging road at 1.3 mi., and turns left onto it. (In the opposite direction, this turn is potentially obscure; turn sharp right (arrow) 100 yd. after leaving power line clearing.) In 100 yd. the trail enters the power line clearing, crosses it on a diagonal (avoid path diverging left up along the lines), and reenters the woods. The old road crosses a tributary, then Reel Brook itself twice, and enters a newer logging road, which descends from the left just before the third and last crossing of Reel Brook at 1.9 mi. The trail now follows the logging road away from the brook; the road is very muddy, with numerous loose stones, and caution must be used, especially descending. It climbs moderately to a fork at 2.4 mi., where the main road swings left to the power lines, while the trail, with improved footing, forks right on another road. In another 100 yd. the trail diverges right off the logging road, which swings left. From here the trail climbs gradually to the Kinsman Ridge Trail.

Reel Brook Trail (map 5:H3)
Distance from road fork near field

to Kinsman Ridge Trail: 2.9 mi. (4.7 km.), 2 hr. 5 min.

Beech Hill Trail (WMNF)

This trail, which formerly ran from the Reel Brook Trail to NH 112 near Wildwood Campground, has been officially closed by the WMNF.

Jericho Road Trail (WMNF)

This trail ascends to the site of the Cooley Hill fire tower, from a point just north of the height-of-land on the west side of NH 116, about 1.5 mi. north of its junction with NH 112 at Bungay Corner. It was originally constructed as a horse trail, and mostly follows logging roads of varying ages. There are no views.

The trail follows a gated gravel logging road (FR 480) and continues straight on an older road at about 0.3 mi., where the newer branch road bears right. After about 1.0 mi., the road crosses a culvert and deteriorates. At about 2.0 mi., the road drops slightly into a sag, and comes to a corner distinctively marked with red-painted stones. Here the trail turns off the road and, marked by flagging and axe blazes, circles right and then climbs. It comes out on another old road, which it follows up the crest of the ridge to the summit of Cooley Hill, marked by the concrete piers of the old fire tower.

Jericho Road Trail (map 5:H3)

Distance (est.) from NH 116

to Cooley Hill: 3.3 mi. (5.3 km.), 2 hr. 30 min.

Cobble Hill Trail (WMNF)

This trail runs from NH 112 to the end of Mill Brook Rd. south of Landaff Center village. It follows old roads all the way, and there are no views. It leaves NH 112 at a point 0.1 mi. west of Woodsville Reservoir and follows an old road along the west side of Dearth Brook. At 0.7 mi. the abandoned South Landaff Rd. leaves left. The trail ascends grad-

ually north, crosses the height-of-land between Cobble Hill
and Moody Ledge, and descends to end at Mill Brook Rd.

Cobble Hill Trail (map 5:H2)
Distance from NH 112

　to Mill Brook Rd.: 3.5 mi. (5.6 km.), 2 hr.

SECTION 6

The Moosilauke Region

This section comprises Mt. Moosilauke and several lower ranges and peaks. These include the Benton Range and the Stinson–Carr–Kineo area. Also described in this section is the series of mountains rising to the east of the Connecticut River, over or near which the Appalachian Trail crosses on its way from Hanover to Glencliff. The latter group includes Moose Mtn., Smarts Mtn., Mt. Cube, and Webster Slide Mtn. The section is bounded on the north by NH 112, on the east by US 3 (and I-93), and on the south by a line which follows NH 25 west from Plymouth, then runs south on NH 118, then west again on US 4. This section is partly covered by the AMC Chocorua–Waterville map (map 4) and the AMC Franconia map (map 5). Moosilauke itself is covered on both maps. The Benton Range is partly on map 5, but better covered by the USGS East Haverhill quad. The Stinson–Carr–Kineo region is covered by map 4. The Moose–Smarts–Cube area is covered by USGS quads, and also by a map of the Appalachian Trail from Pomfret VT to Kinsman Notch published by the Dartmouth Outing Club (DOC).

In this section the Appalachian Trail (AT) follows trails of the DOC trail system from the Connecticut River at Hanover to the west flank of Moose Mtn., then over Holts Ledge, Smarts Mtn., Mt. Cube, and Mt. Mist, and past Webster Slide Mtn. to NH 25. Much of this part of the AT has been relocated, or will be in the near future. Updates on the DOC trails, including this part of the AT, may be obtained from Director of Trails and Shelters, Box 9, Robinson Hall, Dartmouth, NH 03755. From NH 25 the trail, still maintained by the DOC, follows the Town Line Trail, runs along North and South Rd. and Sanatorium Rd. for short distances, then follows the Glencliff Trail and Moosilauke Carriage Road, passing about 0.1 mi. southeast of the summit of Mt. Moosilauke, then descends on the Beaver Brook Trail to Kinsman Notch.

GEOGRAPHY

Mt. Moosilauke (4802 ft.) is the farthest west of White Mtn. peaks over 4000 ft., and the dominating peak of the region between Franconia Notch and the Connecticut River. There is disagreement over whether the name should be pronounced to rhyme with "rock" or with "rocky." At one time Moosilauke was commonly corrupted to "Moosehillock," but the name actually means "a bald place" and has no reference to large, antlered beasts. The bare summit, once the site of a stone lodge called the Tip-Top House, commands an extremely fine view over ridge after ridge of the White Mtns. to the east, and across the Connecticut valley to the west. It has several minor summits, the most important being the South Peak (4523 ft.), an excellent viewpoint that provides fine views into Tunnel Ravine that are denied to the main summit. To the north are two prominent wooded humps, the trailless Mt. Blue (4529 ft.), and Mt. Jim (4172 ft.), which form the ridge that encloses Jobildunk Ravine, a glacial cirque on the east side of the mountain through which the headwaters of the Baker River flow from their source in a bog which was once Deer Lake. The summit of Moosilauke is very exposed to weather, and there is no longer any shelter near the summit. A trail guide to Mt. Moosilauke, containing much information on the human and natural history of the mountain, has been published by the Environmental Studies Division of the DOC.

The Appalachian Trail between Hanover and Glencliff is never far from the divide between the Connecticut and Pemigewasset drainages, but the mountains which it passes near or over do not really form a range. Webster Slide Mtn. (2184 ft.) rises steeply above Wachipauka Pond, with excellent views, while nearby wooded Mt. Mist (2230 ft.) has a fine outlook. Mt. Cube (2909 ft.), located in Orford, has several fine viewpoints, and is one of the more rewarding small mountains in the region. Smarts Mtn. (3238 ft.), located in Lyme, affords interesting views of a less-known country from its abandoned fire tower. Holts Ledge (2110 ft.) has good views to the east and southeast. Moose Mtn. (North Peak, 2300 ft.; South Peak, 2290 ft.), is located in Hanover; the old Province Rd., laid out in 1772 to connect Governor Wentworth's residence in Wolfeboro with the Connecticut Valley towns, passes through the col between the two peaks. The South Peak is reached by a side path which leaves the Clark Pond Loop in the col, while the North Peak is currently trailless, but plans call for relocation of the Appalachian Trail to cross its summit.

The Benton Range is composed of Black Mtn. (2830 ft.), Sugarloaf Mtn. (2609 ft.), trailless Jeffers Mtn. (2994 ft.), Blueberry Mtn. (2662 ft.), and trailless Owls Head (1967 ft.). The views from Black, Sugarloaf, and Blueberry mountains are excellent.

Stinson Mtn. (2900 ft.), Carr Mtn. (3453 ft.), Rattlesnake Mtn. (1594 ft.), and trailless Mt. Kineo (3313 ft.) lie in the angle formed by the Pemigewasset and Baker rivers. Stinson Mtn. and Carr Mtn. offer excellent views from summits which once bore fire towers. In the northern part of the area is the site of the village of Peeling, a hill community which was the original settlement in the town of Woodstock, but was deserted about the time of the Civil War. Most of the area has grown up, and only traces of the village remain. Persons interested in visiting this region should contact the Pemigewasset Ranger District office in Plymouth for information.

Agassiz Basin is an interesting series of potholes on Moosilauke Brook next to NH 112, 1.6 mi. west of North Woodstock. The basin is next to Govoni's Restaurant, and there are signs during the summer season. There are two bridges across the gorge, connected by a short path on the south bank; the upper one reaches NH 112 on the porch of the restaurant. The entire loop is about 250 yd. long.

SHELTERS AND CAMPING

Restricted Use Areas

There are no Restricted Use Areas in this section.

Dartmouth College Land

No camping or fires are permitted on Dartmouth College land east and south of the summit of Moosilauke, roughly bounded by a line starting just south of Hurricane Mtn. and following the ridgeline over South Peak, Mt. Moosilauke, Mt. Blue, Mt. Jim, and Mt. Waternomee, and then south from Waternomee to NH 118.

Established Trailside Campsites

Velvet Rocks Shelter (DOC) is on the Appalachian Trail 1.5 mi. north of Hanover.

Moose Mountain Shelter (DOC) is on the Clark Pond Loop near Harris Junction, 0.5 mi. east of the Appalachian Trail.

Clark Pond Campsite (DOC) is located on the Clark Pond Loop at Clark Pond.

Trapper John Shelter (DOC) is near Holts Ledge, 14 mi. north of Hanover.

Smarts Shelter and Ranger Cabin (DOC) are both near Smarts Mtn. summit.

Cube Shelter (DOC) is on the Appalachian Trail just south of Mt. Cube.

Jeffers Brook Shelter (DOC) is located just off the Town Line Trail.

Beaver Brook Shelter (DOC) is located at the base of Beaver Brook Trail, 0.4 mi. from NH 112 in Kinsman Notch.

Three Ponds Shelter (WMNF) is located on a knoll above the middle pond on a side trail from the Three Ponds Trail.

ACCESS ROADS

The Ravine Lodge Rd., which is the access road to the DOC's Ravine Lodge (the lodge is not open to the public), leads to a trailhead where most of the trails on the southeastern part of Mt. Moosilauke begin. The road leaves NH 118 on the north, 5.8 mi. east of its northerly junction with NH 25 and 7.2 mi. west of its junction with NH 112. From NH 118 it is 1.6 mi. to the turnaround at the end of the road, where the trails begin at the upper left corner. The Tunnel Brook Rd. (FR 147) is reached by leaving NH 116 on the Noxon Rd., east of Benton village and just west of the Benton–Landaff town line, or by taking the road south from NH 112 0.5 mi. east of its easterly junction with NH 116. These two roads join at an acute angle, just west of a bridge over Tunnel Brook, and Tunnel Brook Rd. continues south from this junction. Hubbard Brook Rd. (FR 22) begins 1.1 mi. west of US 3 at West Campton and runs through the Hubbard Brook Experimental Forest.

LIST OF TRAILS	MAP
Trails on Mount Moosilauke	
Beaver Brook Trail	5:I3
Tunnel Brook Trail	5:I2
Benton Trail	5:I2-I3
Glencliff Trail	5:I2
Hurricane Trail	5:I3-I2
Moosilauke Carriage Road	5:J2-I2

THE TRAILS

Beaver Brook Trail (DOC)

This trail, which runs from NH 112 at the height-of-land in Kinsman Notch to the summit of Moosilauke, is a link in the Appalachian Trail. It passes the beautiful Beaver Brook

Cascades, but the section along the cascades is extremely steep and rough, making this trail the most arduous route to the summit in spite of its relatively short distance. In icy conditions it may be dangerous.

Leaving NH 112 directly opposite the Kinsman Ridge Trail, this trail crosses a bridge over Beaver Brook, swings to the left, recrosses the brook on a bridge, and at 0.3 mi. passes a side path which leads left in 100 yd. to Beaver Brook Shelter (DOC). The main trail ascends along Beaver Brook, soon rising very steeply past Beaver Brook Cascades, with many rock steps, wooden steps, and hand rungs. At 1.1 mi. the cascades end, and the trail bears left along a tributary and becomes progressively easier, eventually following old logging roads to the junction with the Asquam–Ridge Trail at 1.9 mi. Here the Asquam–Ridge Trail turns sharp left, while the Beaver Brook Trail bears right and ascends easily to the edge of Jobildunk Ravine. Here it proceeds with rough footing, contouring along the brink of the ravine, and passes several outlooks over the ravine. It then passes close to, but not within sight of, the bog which was once Deer Lake, crossing two small outlet brooks at 2.7 mi. Then the trail climbs moderately to the edge of treeline. Here, at a sign, the left branch of the trail, marked as the Appalachian Trail but hard to see for the first few yards, runs 0.1 mi. to the site of the old DOC cabin, where it meets the Gorge Brook Trail. The right branch of the Beaver Brook Trail climbs 110 yd. to the summit of Moosilauke.

Beaver Brook Trail (map 5:I3)
Distances from NH 112

to Asquam–Ridge Trail: 1.9 mi., 2 hr. 5 min.

to Mt. Moosilauke summit: 3.4 mi. (5.5 km.), 3 hr. 15 min.

Tunnel Brook Trail (WMNF)

This trail leads from the end of the maintained section of Tunnel Brook Rd. (FR 147), 2.4 mi. from its beginning, to North and South Rd. (FR 19). The central portion is subject to disruption by beaver activity, and short sections may be very wet or obscure. There are good views of beaver ponds and the slides on Mt. Clough.

Leaving the parking area at the end of Tunnel Brook Rd., the trail continues south on an old logging road, crosses Tunnel Brook at 0.8 mi., recrosses at 1.3 mi., and soon reaches an outlook to the slides on Mt. Clough. At 1.6 mi. it recrosses Tunnel Brook on a beaver dam (potentially wet and obscure), and at 1.9 mi. it reaches an open spot on the shore of Mud Pond, with a view up to the South Peak of Moosilauke. Soon it crosses the outwash from a slide and begins to descend on a logging road along Slide Brook, passing a reservoir at 3.3 mi., and crossing and recrossing the brook. At 4.2 mi. it crosses Jeffers Brook, passes a camp, and ends at North and South Rd. Care should be taken not to pollute Slide Brook, which is the water supply of the NH Home for the Elderly in Glencliff.

Tunnel Brook Trail (map 5:I2)
Distances from end of Tunnel Brook Rd.

to Mud Pond: 1.9 mi., 1 hr. 10 min.

to North and South Rd.: 4.4 mi. (7.1 km.), 2 hr. 25 min.

Benton Trail (WMNF)

This trail ascends to the summit of Mt. Moosilauke from the Tunnel Brook Rd. (FR 147), 1.6 mi. south of its beginning. It follows the route of an old bridle path, has moderate grades and good footing, and is probably the easiest route to the summit of Moosilauke.

The trail descends slightly from the parking lot to an old logging road, follows the road along Tunnel Brook for 0.1

mi., then crosses the brook (may be difficult at high water), and bears right on an old logging road, ascending the wooded spur which forms the south wall of Little Tunnel Ravine. At 1.3 mi. there is a splendid view to the left into the ravine. The trail passes a spring (sign) on the right at 2.2 mi., then soon turns sharp right and climbs at moderate grades through a beautiful evergreen forest to treeline, ascending the bare north ridge, marked by cairns, the last 0.2 mi. to the summit.

Benton Trail (map 5:I2-I3)
Distance from Tunnel Brook Rd.
to Mt. Moosilauke summit: 3.6 mi. (5.7 km.), 3 hr. 20 min.

Glencliff Trail (DOC)

This trail runs from Sanatorium Rd., 1.2 mi. from its junction with NH 25 in Glencliff village, to the Moosilauke Carriage Road just north of Moosilauke's South Peak. It is part of the Appalachian Trail. There is only one steep section, and the footing is generally good.

The trail leaves the road, passes a gate and enters a pasture, and soon crosses a small brook on a bridge. It joins a farm road (descending, bear left), then crosses a brook and follows a cart track along the left edge of a field. It enters the woods, and the Hurricane Trail immediately diverges right (east) at 0.4 mi. The Glencliff Trail ascends moderately on a logging road which gradually fades away, crossing several small brooks, to a restricted outlook from a blowdown patch at 2.0 mi. Soon the trail swings right, going straight up the slope, and at 2.5 mi. it becomes quite steep. At the top of the ridge it levels and reaches the junction with the spur path (sign), which leads right 0.2 mi. to the open summit of South Peak. In a few more steps it enters the Moosilauke Carriage Road; for the summit, turn left.

Glencliff Trail (map 5:I2)
Distances from Sanatorium Rd.
to Moosilauke Carriage Road: 3.0 mi., 3 hr.
to Mt. Moosilauke summit (via Moosilauke Carriage Road): 3.9 mi. (6.3 km.), 3 hr. 40 min.

Hurricane Trail (DOC)

This trail runs around the south end of Moosilauke, linking the low end of the Glencliff Trail, the lower part of the Moosilauke Carriage Road, and Ravine Lodge Rd. It makes possible a number of loop trips. East of the Moosilauke Carriage Road it is level and clear; some parts to the west are steep and rough.

The Hurricane Trail continues straight where the Gorge Brook Trail turns right, 0.2 mi. from Ravine Lodge Rd. It crosses Gorge Brook on a log bridge and descends to the bank of Baker River, where it picks up a logging road and follows it on a long curve away from the river. At 1.0 mi. it reaches the Moosilauke Carriage Road, coincides with it left (downhill) for 0.3 mi., crossing Big Brook on a bridge, then turns right (west) off the Moosilauke Carriage Road and follows a logging road into a small, moist clearing. Here it turns sharp left, follows Little Brook for a while, and reaches the height-of-land at 2.6 mi., then continues nearly level for 0.2 mi. as the trail passes north of the little hump called Hurricane Mtn. Then it descends, rather steeply at times, to the Glencliff Trail 0.4 mi. from Sanatorium Rd.

Hurricane Trail (map 5:I3-I2)
Distances from Gorge Brook Trail
to Moosilauke Carriage Road (upper junction): 1.0 mi., 30 min.
to Glencliff Trail: 4.3 mi. (6.9 km.), 2 hr. 35 min.

Moosilauke Carriage Road

This former carriage road runs to the summit of Moosilauke from Breezy Point, the site of the Moosilauke Inn. The road to Breezy Point leaves NH 118 2.5 mi. north of its junction with NH 25 (which is 1.0 mi. north of Warren village). Follow the road for 1.6 mi., just past the driveway to the Inn, and park where the road descends slightly (sign). Grades are easy but the footing is poor for several long sections.

Continuing on the dirt road, the trail enters a clearing at 0.3 mi., where the trail bears right at a sign ("MT TRAIL") and continues on a logging road with no markings. The Hurricane Trail enters left at 1.3 mi., and the trails cross Big Brook on a bridge, after which the Hurricane Trail diverges right to Ravine Lodge Rd. The trail now begins to climb by a series of switchbacks through a beautiful mature hardwood forest, with easy to moderate grades and excellent footing. At 3.1 mi. the Snapper Trail enters right, and soon the footing deteriorates, as the old road is severely washed out, with much loose rock, and at 4.2 mi. the Glencliff Trail enters left. A few steps left a spur trail leads 0.2 mi. to South Peak, a fine viewpoint. The old road, now part of the Appalachian Trail, continues along the ridge, with a narrow fringe of trees on each side. At 4.9 mi. it reaches treeline, where the Appalachian Trail diverges right on a cutoff path (no sign) running 0.2 mi. to the old cabin site, while the Moosilauke Carriage Road ascends the windswept ridge to the summit.

Moosilauke Carriage Road (map 5:J2-I2)
Distances from Breezy Point

to Snapper Trail: 3.1 mi., 2 hr. 25 min.

to Glencliff Trail: 4.2 mi., 3 hr. 30 min.

to Mt. Moosilauke summit: 5.1 mi. (8.3 km.), 4 hr. 5 min.

Gorge Brook Trail (DOC)

This trail runs from Ravine Lodge Rd. to the summit of Moosilauke. It is the shortest route to the summit, and well sheltered, but the middle section is very steep.

Leaving the turnaround at the end of Ravine Lodge Rd., it descends to the river and crosses it on a footbridge, and immediately turns left where the Asquam-Ridge Trail diverges right. At 0.2 mi. it turns sharp right as the Hurricane Trail continues straight, and at 0.3 mi. the Snapper Trail diverges left. The Gorge Brook Trail follows Gorge Brook, crossing it at 0.5 mi. and recrossing at 1.3 mi., both times on bridges. At 1.6 mi. it bears right and soon starts to climb very steeply and roughly up the slope away from the brook. Eventually the grade begins to moderate and views can be obtained between and over the small trees. The trail winds through scrub, with increasing open areas, reaches the old cabin site where the Appalachian Trail crosses, and in another 150 yd. gains the summit.

Gorge Brook Trail (map 5:J3-I3)
Distance from Ravine Lodge Rd.

to Mt. Moosilauke summit: 2.8 mi. (4.6 km.), 2 hr. 40 min.

Snapper Trail (DOC)

This trail, originally cut as a downhill ski trail, runs from the Gorge Brook Trail 0.3 mi. from Ravine Lodge Rd. to the Moosilauke Carriage Road 2.0 mi. below the summit of Moosilauke. It makes possible a number of loop hikes from Ravine Lodge Rd. Leaving the Gorge Brook Trail, it soon crosses Gorge Brook and another small brook on bridges, then ascends steadily, becoming steeper as it approaches the Carriage Road.

Snapper Trail (map 5:J3-I3)
Distance from Gorge Brook Trail
to Moosilauke Carriage Road: 1.0 mi. (1.6 km.), 1 hr.

Asquam–Ridge Trail (DOC)

This trail runs from the Gorge Brook Trail near Ravine Lodge Rd. to the Beaver Brook Trail on top of the Blue Ridge, providing a long but rather easy route to Moosilauke's summit.

It leaves the Gorge Brook Trail, turning sharp right just across the Baker River footbridge, and follows the west bank of the river. At 0.5 mi. it enters a logging road which comes from the end of Ravine Lodge Rd., continues along the river, crosses on a footbridge at 1.5 mi., and turns sharp right to ascend gradually. At 1.9 mi. the trail turns sharp left where the Al Merrill Loop from Ravine Lodge Rd. enters straight ahead, and follows another logging road very gradually upward. Eventually it encounters some steeper pitches, passes a few yards left of the wooded summit of Mt. Jim, then descends easily to the Beaver Brook Trail.

Asquam–Ridge Trail (map 5:J3-I3)
Distances from Gorge Brook Trail
to Beaver Brook Trail: 3.9 mi. (6.4 km.), 2 hr. 45 min.
to Mt. Moosilauke summit (via Beaver Brook Trail): 5.5 mi. (8.8 km.), 4 hr. 10 min.

Town Line Trail (DOC)

This trail, a short link in the Appalachian Trail, runs from NH 25 150 yd. north of the Wachipauka Pond Trail to North and South Rd. 0.1 mi. north of its junction with Sanatorium Rd. About 0.2 mi. from North and South Rd. a side trail runs north about 0.1 mi. to Jeffers Brook Shelter.

Town Line Trail (map 5:J2)
Distance from NH 25
  to North and South Rd.: 1.0 mi. (1.6 km.), 40 min.

Wachipauka Pond Trail (DOC)
This link in the Appalachian Trail, blazed in white, leaves NH 25, 1.4 mi. west of Glencliff and 150 yd. south of the Town Line Trail. It rises steeply, crosses Wyatt Hill, then descends west gradually to the north of Wachipauka Pond. The trail slabs the base of Webster Slide Mtn., and a spur trail to its summit leaves right. The main trail passes Hairy Root Spring, climbs Mt. Mist gradually, passes an excellent outlook east, crosses the wooded summit, and descends gradually to NH 25C. From here the Appalachian Trail continues over Ore Hill and passes through an abandoned mine, then continues to NH 25A. Relocations are in process between NH 25A and NH 25C.

Wachipauka Pond Trail (map 5:J2/DOC map)
Distances (est.) from NH 25
  to Webster Slide Mtn. spur path: 2.2 mi., 1 hr. 25 min.
  to NH 25C: 4.3 mi. (6.9 km.), 2 hr. 50 min.

Webster Slide Mountain Spur (DOC)
This mountain is ascended by a spur trail that leaves the Wachipauka Pond Trail right (north) about 2.2 mi. from NH 25, and follows an old wood road (former route of Appalachian Trail) for 0.2 mi., then turns sharp right and climbs rather steeply to the summit. The best view is a few steps down on the open ledges.

Webster Slide Mountain Spur (map 5:J1)
Distance (est.) from Wachipauka Pond Trail
  to Webster Slide Mtn. summit: 1.0 mi. (1.6 km.), 50 min.

Mount Cube Trail (DOC)

The Appalachian Trail crosses Mt. Cube, providing several fine outlooks. The northern end leaves NH 25A some distance east of the height-of-land, while the western end begins on Quinttown Rd., which leaves NH 25A 1.7 mi. west of the height-of-land and reaches the trail in about 1 mi.

Leaving NH 25A, the trail climbs at moderate to steep grades to the north knob, then continues with only slight descent to the higher south summit. It descends along the southwest ridge, then swings west and descends steadily, passing the Cube Shelter about 0.2 mi. before reaching Quinttown Rd.

Mount Cube Trail (DOC map)
Distances (est.) from NH 25A

to Mt. Cube summit: 1.5 mi., 1 hr. 30 min.

to Quinttown Rd.: 3.0 mi. (4.8 km.), 2 hr. 15 min.

Smarts Mountain Trail (DOC)

The Appalachian Trail crosses this mountain; the south end is on Cummins Pond Rd. (sometimes called Lyme-Dorchester Rd.) about 3 mi. east of Lyme Center, while the north end is at Quinttown, a crossroads reached in 2.0 mi. by a dirt road that leaves NH 25A on the right, about 1.5 mi. east of Orfordville. It may be possible to drive 0.8 mi. more on the road south from Quinttown and park at the second house (abandoned) on the right.

The Appalachian Trail—also called the Ranger Trail, since it is the old firewarden's trail—starts up a wood road, with a brook on the right (east). The road ends at a garage (2.0 mi.), and the trail turns right across the brook. The brook is later recrossed (last reliable water), and the grade steepens. There are occasional views to the south and west from the upper reaches of the trail. At the summit are the old fire tower, the warden's cabin (a DOC shelter), an open shelter, and the junction with the Clark Pond Loop. Potable water may be found 0.2 mi. north of the ranger cabin, to the right of the trail. The trail descends along the valley of Mousley Brook, joins the Quinttown Trail (DOC) which comes from Cummins Pond Rd., and soon crosses Mousley Brook, then passes a private cabin on the right and a shed on the left, and reaches the road south from Quinttown.

Smarts Mountain Trail (DOC map)
Distances (est.) from Cummins Pond Rd.
   to Smarts Mtn. summit: 3.5 mi., 2 hr. 45 min.
   to Quinttown Trail: 6.4 mi., 4 hr. 15 min.
   to Quinttown: 7.5 mi., 4 hr. 45 min.

Holts Ledge Trail (DOC)
Holts Ledge is crossed by the Appalachian Trail. The northern terminus is on Cummins Pond Rd., just east of the Dartmouth Skiway, and the south terminus is on Goose Pond Rd., 3.3 mi. east of NH 10.

Leaving Cummins Pond Rd., the trail ascends, much of the time parallel to a ski trail (do not hike on ski trail). At 1.5 mi. it passes a side path that leads in 0.2 mi. to Trapper John Shelter, and continues to ascend, turns sharp right at a fence and reaches the crest of Holts Ledge, where there are fine views. The trail descends, turning sharp right in 0.2 mi., then follows along a brook on a wood road, crosses the brook, passes a farmhouse, and turns left on a dirt road which it follows to Goose Pond Rd.

Holts Ledge Trail (DOC map)
Distances (est.) from Cummins Pond Rd.
   to Holts Ledge: 2.1 mi., 1 hr. 40 min.
   to Goose Pond Rd.: 4.1 mi., 2 hr. 40 min.

Clark Pond Loop (DOC)

This blue-blazed trail, much of which is an older route of the Appalachian Trail, provides an alternate route between Harris Junction (2.7 mi. from Etna–Hanover Center Rd.) and the summit of Smarts Mtn.

Leaving Harris Junction, the trail follows the old Wolfeboro Rd., crossing Moose Mtn. at the col between the North and South peaks, where a side path leads right to the summit of the South Peak. The main trail then passes Moose Mtn. Shelter, the Moose Mountain Inn, an old cemetery 0.1 mi. beyond, and continues straight along a dirt road toward Goose Pond. Descending, it soon crosses Marshall Brook at the north end of Goose Pond. At a road junction, it crosses onto a wood road, soon taking a sharp right. Ascending, it soon becomes a dirt road. The trail veers left from the road near the remains of an old farm, follows a telephone line across a field and, bearing right, reenters the woods. At 5.2 mi. it reaches an asphalt road, follows the road right for 0.5 mi., then turns sharp left on a dirt driveway. The trail turns right onto a wood road and follows it to the outlet of Clark Pond. It veers left and soon picks up another wood road, and bears left at a fork to Clark Pond. The trail follows the eastern edge of Clark Pond, and a sharp left will soon bring you to Clark Pond campsite. Water can be obtained from a stream to the east.

North of the campsite, the trail turns right (east) up a ridge, then right at the ridgetop to a semi-open field. Past this field the trail bears right onto another wood road. It renews its ascent, but soon descends toward a level wood road, where it turns left to follow the Mascoma River for 0.4 mi. It turns left again, following an irregular ridge through young alders, then descends gradually, crosses a boulder field, and continues along the side of the ridge. Upon reaching the valley floor the trail turns left onto a wood road. The road crosses the river and two tributaries, then crosses Cummins Pond Rd. and follows a trail through the woods that is somewhat difficult to follow due to deadfall. In 0.5 mi. it enters a good logging road and turns left on it, follows the road as it gradually fades away, and continues to the summit on a well-defined but sparsely blazed path.

Clark Pond Loop (DOC map)
Distances (est.) from Harris Junction
 to Clark Pond campsite: 8.3 mi., 4 hr. 30 min.
 to Cummins Pond Rd.: 13.2 mi., 7 hr.
 to Smarts Mtn. summit: 17.6 mi. (28.3 km.), 10 hr.

Blueberry Mountain Trail (WMNF)
This trail crosses the summit of Blueberry Mtn., affording good views. The east terminus is on North and South Rd. 0.8 mi. north of Sanatorium Rd., and the west terminus is reached by driving north from East Haverhill on Lime Kiln Rd., continuing straight at the junction at 1.5 mi., then continuing to the trail sign on the left at 2.3 mi., near a sugar house.

From the west terminus, the trail follows a good logging road past a steel gate, passes south of a sawmill, and ascends gradually, coming out on open ledges. It crosses the flat summit and descends into the woods to a logging road, which it follows to the parking lot at North and South Rd.

Blueberry Mountain Trail (map 5:I1-I2)
Distances from sugar house off Lime Kiln Rd.
 to Blueberry Mtn. summit: 3.0 mi., 2 hr. 25 min.
 to North and South Rd.: 4.5 mi. (7.2 km.), 3 hr. 10 min.

Black Mountain Trail (WMNF)
This trail ascends Black Mtn. from the north. From a four-way intersection in Benton village, follow the road which runs approximately south. At 0.8 mi. the road

swings west and becomes gravel. Continue to a place where a snowmobile trail branches right, where there is room to park. Continue on foot up the road, past a WMNF wooden gate, to a grassy clearing, where the trail leads south. It is well marked, and ascends at moderate grades to meet the Chippewa Trail a few feet west of the summit. The part of the trail that once continued south from here has been abandoned. Tipping Rock is a short distance east.

Black Mountain Trail (map 5:H1-I1)
Distance (est.) from road near wooden gate
   to Black Mtn. summit: 2.5 mi. (4.0 km.), 1 hr. 55 min.

Chippewa Trail (WMNF)

This trail reaches the summit of Black Mtn. from Lime Kiln Rd., which leaves NH 25 in East Haverhill, bears left at a major fork at 1.5 mi. and continues to a point 3.3 mi. from NH 25, where the trail begins on the left of a parking area. The trail crosses a barbed wire fence, soon descends a small slope, and crosses a wood road. The trail soon turns right on a logging road (left leads to old lime kilns), bears left at a fork, and then rises steadily to a pasture. It crosses the pasture, generally to the left, enters the woods, and begins the steep ascent toward the ledges. The trail is marked with yellow and white arrows and blazes. It ends at its junction with the Black Mountain Trail a few feet west of the summit.

Chippewa Trail (USGS East Haverhill quad)
Distance from parking area off Lime Kiln Rd.
   to Black Mountain Trail junction: 1.9 mi. (3.1 km.), 1 hr. 40 min.

Sugarloaf Trail

This trail ascends Sugarloaf Mtn.; it is not officially maintained and may be dangerous on the ledges, particularly in bad weather. To reach the trail, turn north off NH 25 in East Haverhill, follow Lime Kiln Rd., continue straight at 1.5 mi., then continue 0.8 mi. Turn left here and proceed to a garage on the right, then follow a dirt road right 0.6 mi. to a small parking area.

The trail leaves right, beyond an open pasture and a brook crossing, and follows through woods to an upper pasture. Keep right, and then sharp right across a brook (last water). The trail then slabs moderately to a high pasture, crosses through the middle, turns left at ledges, then bears right up a steep shoulder to the first of two ladders. Here the trail turns sharp right, continuing through woods (use care). The trail then ascends rather steeply to the summit. There are good views of the Benton Range and of Mt. Moosilauke, and the trail passes through varied stands of virgin timber on the ascent.

Sugarloaf Trail (USGS East Haverhill quad)
Distance (est.) from parking area
   to Sugarloaf Mtn. summit: 1.5 mi. (2.4 km.), 1 hr. 30 min.

Stinson Mountain Trail (WMNF)

This trail is reached by following Stinson Lake Rd. north from NH 25 in Rumney. At the foot of the lake, 5.0 mi. from NH 25, turn right uphill for 0.8 mi., then turn right again on the old Doe Town Rd. to a parking lot at 0.3 mi. on the left. The fire tower has been dismantled but fine views are still available in every direction except southwest. Metamorphosed strata make the summit ledge geologically interesting.

The trail leaves the parking lot and soon enters and follows an old farm road between stone walls. After passing a cellar hole left, it becomes steeper, entering a logging road at 0.9 mi., where it turns sharp left. At 1.1 mi. there is a junction. Take the right fork; left is the old tractor road to the summit, longer and less pleasant. The trail climbs by switchbacks and rejoins the old tractor road just below the summit (note left turn here on descent). From the summit a spur path leads southwest about 80 yd. to a view over Stinson Lake.

Stinson Mountain Trail (map 4:K3)
Distance from parking lot
 to Stinson Mtn. summit: 1.8 mi. (2.9 km.), 1 hr. 35 min.

Rattlesnake Mountain Trail (WMNF)

This trail begins on Buffalo Rd.—the road along the north bank of Baker River—2.5 mi. west of Rumney village at a small parking area with an historical marker. It ascends easily, then steeply, to the height-of-land at 0.8 mi. Here the summit ledges of Rattlesnake Mtn., with fine views over the Baker River valley, can be reached by following one of several informal paths south for about 0.2 mi. The main trail descends to Stinson Lake Rd. 0.4 mi. north of Rumney village, but trailhead access problems have caused the WMNF to suspend maintenance of the trail east of the ridge crest. Present plans call for the eastern section to be abandoned; the WMNF hopes to construct a loop path over the summit ledges and back to the parking lot.

Rattlesnake Mountain Trail (map 4:L2-L3)
Distance from Buffalo Rd.
 to crest of ridge: 0.8 mi. (1.3 km.), 45 min.

Stevens Brook Trail (WMNF)

This trail has been officially closed by the WMNF.

Carr Mountain Trail (WMNF)

This trail begins on the Three Ponds Trail 0.5 mi. from the new parking area on Stinson Lake Rd., ascends to a short spur trail to the summit of Carr Mtn., and descends to the old Warren–Wentworth highway 0.1 mi. south of the former state fish hatchery.

The trail diverges sharp left (south) from the Three Ponds Trail and fords Sucker Brook at 0.2 mi. (This crossing is difficult at high water, but can be avoided by following the Three Ponds Trail to its bridge over Sucker Brook, then returning back southeast along Sucker Brook on an old logging road to the Carr Mountain Trail. This route is about 0.8 mi. longer.) The trail then ascends to meet its former route (an old wood road) and continues a moderate ascent, leaving the wood road at 1.6 mi. and climbing rather steeply to the ridge top, passing at 2.9 mi. a side path left which reaches the summit in about 50 yd. The main trail descends, crosses a brook, and at 4.7 mi. enters a wood road which descends along Clifford Brook. It passes through a stone wall at 5.4 mi., passes a house on the right, and descends to the old Warren–Wentworth highway.

Carr Mountain Trail (map 4:K3-K2)
Distances from Three Ponds Trail
to Carr Mtn. summit side path: 2.9 mi., 2 hr. 30 min.
to old Warren–Wentworth highway: 6.3 mi. (10.1 km.), 4 hr. 10 min.

Three Ponds Trail (WMNF)

This trail starts on Stinson Lake Rd. at a new parking lot 1.9 mi. north of the foot of Stinson Lake, passes the attractive ponds, and crosses a low ridge to NH 118, 4.4 mi. northeast of its intersection with NH 25 about 1 mi. north of Warren village.

Leaving the parking lot, it passes junctions with the Mount Kineo Trail right at 0.1 mi. and the Carr Mountain Trail left at 0.5 mi. At 1.0 mi. it crosses Sucker Brook on a bridge and continues along the brook, crossing it three more times, without bridges. At 2.2 mi., a side path diverges right on the shore of the middle pond, passes Three Ponds Shelter on a knoll overlooking the pond, and rejoins the main trail. At 2.5 mi. the Donkey Hill Cutoff continues straight, while the Three Ponds Trail turns left across a brook on a beaver dam, picks up a logging road, and follows it to a point 80 yd. from the upper pond. Here the road continues to the edge of the pond, but the trail turns sharp left and starts to ascend. From here on it is much less heavily used and must be followed with some care. The trail enters a logging road, leaves it on a bypass around the swamp at Foxglove Pond, and crosses Brown Brook for the first of three times at 3.8 mi. The trail now climbs to the height-of-land at 5.1 mi., then descends, makes a hairpin turn right, and enters a system of logging roads, following them to the Hubbard Brook Trail 0.2 mi. east of NH 118.

Three Ponds Trail (map 4:K3-J3)
Distances from Stinson Lake Rd.
- *to* Three Ponds Shelter: 2.5 mi., 1 hr. 30 min.
- *to* height-of-land: 5.1 mi., 3 hr. 10 min.
- *to* Hubbard Brook Trail: 7.2 mi. (11.7 km.), 4 hr. 10 min.

Donkey Hill Cutoff (WMNF)
This trail links the Three Ponds Trail 2.5 mi. from the Stinson Lake Rd. parking area to the Mount Kineo Trail 1.7 mi. from the parking area, making possible a loop hike. It crosses several small ridges and follows the edge of an extensive beaver swamp for much of its distance.

Donkey Hill Cutoff (map 4:K3)
Distance from Three Ponds Trail
- *to* Mount Kineo Trail: 1.1 mi. (1.8 km.), 45 min.

Mount Kineo Trail (WMNF)

This trail begins on the Three Ponds Trail 0.1 mi. from the new parking lot on Stinson Lake Rd., crosses the ridge of Mt. Kineo almost a mile east of the true summit, and descends to a spur road off Hubbard Brook Rd. (FR 22) 6.3 mi. from US 3 in West Thornton. The part of this trail south of the ridge crest is an attractive woods walk.

Leaving the Three Ponds Trail, it proceeds north over several minor ups and downs and enters the old route of the trail (a logging road along Brown Brook) at 1.0 mi. The trail climbs along the attractive brook, and crosses it at 1.6 mi. on ledges, where the Donkey Hill Cutoff diverges left. The Mount Kineo Trail runs northwest along the edge of a large swamp, then at 2.3 mi. it swings right, away from the swamp, crosses several small brooks, and eventually climbs east, alternately slabbing on old logging roads and climbing straight up on steep, rough sections. At 3.9 mi. it crosses the ridge in a small col, then descends to an old logging road, which it follows through several extremely muddy stretches to a gravel spur road passable by cars, about 0.5 mi. from its junction with Hubbard Brook Rd. (sign).

Mount Kineo Trail (map 4:K3-J3)
Distances from Three Ponds Trail

to Donkey Hill Cutoff: 1.6 mi., 1 hr.
to height-of-land: 3.9 mi., 2 hr. 45 min.
to Hubbard Brook Rd. spur: 5.1 mi. (8.2 km.), 3 hr. 20 min.

Hubbard Brook Trail (WMNF)

This trail runs from Hubbard Brook Rd. (FR 22), at a hairpin turn across Hubbard Brook 7.6 mi. from US 3 in West Thornton, to NH 118 4.4 mi. northeast of the junction with NH 25, which is 1.0 mi. north of Warren village.

The trail is not easy to follow, and its only attractions are several beaver ponds.

Leaving the road, it soon passes a beaver pond where the trail is ill-defined, but by following the north bank the trail will be found where it enters the woods just above the north end of the pond. It crosses a low height-of-land at 0.9 mi. and descends on an assortment of logging roads and paths, crosses a beaver dam between two ponds, and enters a gravel logging road at 2.0 mi. ("HB" blazed into tree at junction). Soon it passes the Three Ponds Trail on the left and continues to NH 118.

Hubbard Brook Trail (map 4:J3)
Distance from Hubbard Brook Rd.
   to NH 118: 2.5 mi. (4.1 km.), 1 hr. 20 min.

Peaked Hill Pond Trail (WMNF)

This trail follows an active logging road to Peaked Hill Pond from US 3, north of exit 29 of I-93, at the 93 Motel. The footing on the road is poor, the area is heavily logged, and there are no views. The pond is on private property. From US 3, follow the road west under I-93, then bear right and park. Pass a steel gate at 0.6 mi., ascend gradually, and at a level area follow a path that soon regains the road, passes through a logging yard, and continues to the pond.

Peaked Hill Pond Trail (map 4:K4)
Distance from US 3
   to Peaked Hill Pond: 2.3 mi. (3.7 km.), 1 hr. 20 min.

Mount Cilley Trail (WMNF)

This trail has been officially closed by the WMNF.

SECTION 7

The Waterville Valley Region

This section covers the mountains which surround the valley of the Mad River, commonly called the Waterville Valley, including Mt. Tecumseh, Mt. Osceola, Mt. Tripyramid, Sandwich Mtn., and their subordinate peaks. This region is bounded on the north by the Kancamagus Highway; on the east by a line between the Sleeper Ridge and Mt. Whiteface; on the south by NH 113, Sandwich Notch Rd., and NH 49; and on the west by US 3. At the boundary between Section 7 and Section 8 (Chocorua and the Eastern Sandwich Range), the only points of contact between trails are at the junction of the Sleeper Trail (Section 7) with the Downes Brook Trail (Section 8), and at the junction of the Flat Mountain Pond Trail (Section 7) with the McCrillis Trail (Section 8). The entire section is covered by the AMC Chocorua–Waterville map (map 4).

ROAD ACCESS

Waterville Valley. From I-93 near Campton, NH 49 (Mad River Rd.) runs northeast beside the Mad River more than 11 mi. into the center of Waterville Valley, passing a group of lodges and condominiums and ending near the Waterville Valley library, Golf and Tennis Club, and the Snows Mtn. Ski Area and ski-touring center. At about 10.6 mi. from I-93 Tripoli Rd. turns sharp left, passing the road to the Mt. Tecumseh Ski Area at 1.3 mi., and shortly begins to follow the West Branch of the Mad River northwest to the height-of-land west of Waterville Valley (Thornton Gap, 2300 ft., the pass between Mts. Osceola and Tecumseh), and then westward to its end at NH 175 (East Side Rd.) and I-93 in Woodstock. The road is gravel except for paved sections on each end, narrow in places, and winding. Drive slowly and with caution. This road has not been plowed during the winter. A road runs west from the library about 0.8 mi. to Tripoli Rd. north of the ski area.

Sandwich Notch Rd. This interesting dirt road passes through a former farming region which has almost completely reverted to wilderness, and has recently been added to the WMNF. It runs northwest from Center Sandwich to NH 49 between Campton and Waterville Valley. The road is sound, but narrow, steep and rough, and very slow going; it is maintained this way to prevent it from becoming an attractive route for through traffic. Beede Falls (Cow Cave), in the Sandwich town park 3.4 mi. from Center Sandwich, is worth a visit. From NH 113 in Center Sandwich, take the road northwest from the village and keep left at 2.6 mi. where the right-hand road leads to Mead Base (Explorer Scout camp), trailhead for the Wentworth Trail to Mt. Israel. The road continues past trailheads for the Crawford–Ridgepole Trail at 3.9 mi., the Guinea Pond Trail at 5.7 mi., and the Algonquin Trail at 7.3 mi., and ends at NH 49 at 11.0 mi.

Sandwich area. Confusion sometimes results from the rather erratic behavior of NH 113 and NH 113A, its alternate route between North Sandwich and Tamworth. Both roads change direction frequently, and NH 113 unites with and diverges from NH 25 between its two junctions with NH 113A. It is therefore necessary to study very carefully directions to trailheads on the southeast slopes of the Sandwich Range. Whiteface Intervale Rd. leaves NH 113A about 3 mi. north of the western junction of NH 113 and NH 113A, where NH 113A bends from north-south to east-west. Bennett St. turns left from Whiteface Intervale Rd. 0.1 mi. from NH 113A, continues straight past a junction at 1.7 mi., where it becomes rougher, and ends at 2.4 mi. at Jose's (rhymes with doses) bridge.

GEOGRAPHY

Mt. Tecumseh (4003 ft.), named for the Shawnee leader, is the highest and northernmost summit of the ridges that form the west wall of the valley. Thornton Gap separates it from Mt. Osceola to the northeast; to the west and southwest, long ridges run out toward Woodstock and Thornton. On the end of the south ridge, the fine, rocky peak of Welch Mtn. (2605 ft.) overlooks the Campton meadows, and forms the west wall of the narrow south gateway to Waterville Valley through which the Mad River flows. The views from the open summit are excellent. Dickey Mtn. (2734 ft.) is close at hand to the northwest, with the best views from a fine, open ledge 0.2 mi. north of its summit.

Mt. Osceola (4340 ft.), the highest peak in the region, lies north of the valley. It was named for the great chief of the Seminole people. It is a narrow, steep-sided ridge, with a number of slides in its valleys, and is particularly impressive when seen from the outlooks along the west half of the Kancamagus Highway. Although the fire tower has been removed from its summit, it still commands magnificent views. Osceola has two subordinate peaks, the East Peak (4156 ft.) and the West Peak (4114 ft.). West of Osceola is the Scar Ridge (3774 ft.), which runs northwest parallel to the Hancock Branch and ends at the lower peaks above Lincoln, of which the most important is Loon Mtn. (3065 ft.), which can be ascended via the major ski area on its north slope. At the far west end is Russell Crag (1926 ft.), with interesting ledges but no trails; north of the crag is Russell Pond, with a WMNF campground that is reached by a paved road. To the east of Osceola is Mad River Notch, in which the Greeley Ponds are located, and across the notch is Mt. Kancamagus (3728 ft.), a trailless mass of rounded, wooded ridges, named for a Penacook sachem.

Mt. Tripyramid is the rugged and very picturesque

mountain that forms the east wall of Waterville Valley, and overlooks the Albany Intervale which lies to the north and east. It was named by the illustrious cartographer Arnold Guyot for the three pyramidal peaks that cap the narrow, steep-sided ridge. North Peak (4140 ft.) affords a sweeping view to the north which is gradually becoming overgrown. Middle Peak (4110 ft.), the most nearly symmetrical pyramid of the three, provides a view toward Passaconaway and Chocorua from the summit; two fine outlooks over the Waterville Valley toward Tecumseh and Osceola lie to the west of the trail near the summit. South Peak (4090 ft.) is viewless. From South Peak, the high, rolling Sleeper Ridge (West Peak, 3870 ft.; East Peak, 3850 ft.) connects Tripyramid with Mt. Whiteface. A major east spur called the Fool Killer (3570 ft.) blends into the main mass so well when viewed from a distance that incautious parties attempting to climb the mountain from the east, before the construction of the trails, often found themselves on top of that spur instead, separated from their goal by a long, scrubby ridge with deep valleys on either side.

Tripyramid is best known for its slides, great scars which are visible from long distances. The North Slide, which occurred during heavy rains in August 1885, is located on the northwest slope of North Peak. It exposed a great deal of bedrock that is geologically interesting, and is ascended mainly on steep ledges. The South Slide, which is located on the southwest face of the South Peak, fell in 1869 and is mostly gravel. Two smaller slides descend into the valley of Sabbaday Brook from the east face of Middle Peak. Tripyramid is steep and rugged, and all routes to its summits have at least one rough section. Consequently the mountain is more difficult to climb than a casual assessment of the altitude, distance, and elevation gain might suggest.

Sabbaday Falls, a picturesque small waterfall and pool formed by an eroded trap rock dike, is reached from Sabbaday Falls Picnic Area on the Kancamagus Highway by a graded gravel section of the Sabbaday Brook Trail.

Sandwich Mtn. (3993 ft.), sometimes called Sandwich Dome, is the westernmost major summit of the Sandwich Range and forms the south wall of the Waterville Valley. It looks over the lower Mad River to the west. On the south and southwest, Sandwich Notch separates it from the Campton and Holderness mountains. Sandwich Mtn. was once called Black Mtn., a name that has also been applied to its southwest spur (3500 ft.), which is ledgy with many fine outlooks, and to a nubble (2732 ft.) at the end of this spur. According to the USGS, the lower peak is entitled to the name. To the northeast, a high col separates Sandwich Mtn. from the long ridge of Flat Mtn. (3310 ft.) in Waterville; Pond Brook has cut a deep ravine between its east shoulder and the rounded Flat Mtn. (2950 ft.) in Sandwich. The two Flat Mtn. Ponds (2310 ft.) lie east of Sandwich Mtn. and west of Mt. Whiteface, between the two Flat Mtns.; the dam at their south end has united them, making one larger pond. The area is still recovering from lumbering begun in 1920 and an extensive fire in 1923. In the flat region south of Sandwich Mtn. lie a number of attractive ponds, including Guinea Pond and Black Mtn. Pond. South of these ponds is Mt. Israel (2630 ft.), which provides a fine panorama of the Sandwich Range from its north ledge, and offers great rewards for the modest effort required to reach it.

Jennings Peak (3460 ft.) and Noon Peak (2976 ft.) form a ridge running north toward Waterville Valley. Sandwich Mtn. has fine views north over the valley, but those from Jennings Peak are even better. Acteon Ridge runs from Jennings Peak to the west over sharp, bare Sachem Peak (2860 ft.) and ends in the open, rocky humps of Bald Knob (2300 ft.), which faces Welch Mtn. across the Mad River

Valley; this ridge is occasionally traversed, although there is no path.

CAMPING

Sandwich Range Wilderness

In this area camping and fires are prohibited above tree-line, and no campsite may be used by more than ten persons at one time.

Restricted Use Areas

The WMNF has established a number of Restricted Use Areas (RUA's) where camping and wood or charcoal fires are prohibited from 1 May to 1 November. The specific areas are under continual review, and areas are added to or subtracted from the list in order to provide the greatest amount of protection to areas subject to damage by excessive camping, while imposing the lowest level of restrictions possible. A general list of RUA's follows, but one should obtain a map of current RUA's from the WMNF.

(1) No camping is permitted above treeline (where trees are less than 8 ft. tall). The point where the restricted area begins is marked on most trails with small signs, but the absence of such signs should not be construed as proof of the legality of a site.

(2) No camping is permitted within one-quarter mile of most facilities such as huts, cabins, shelters, or tentsites, except at the facility itself.

(3) No camping is permitted, at any time of the year, within the Greeley Ponds Scenic Area or within one-quarter mile of the Greeley Ponds Trail from the north boundary of the scenic area to the Kancamagus Highway. No camping is permitted within one-quarter mile of the Sabbaday Falls Trail from the Kancamagus Highway to the Sandwich Range Wilderness boundary.

Established Trailside Campsites

Flat Mtn. Pond Shelter (WMNF) is located on the shore of Flat Mtn. Pond on the Flat Mountain Pond Trail. Tent camping is permitted in the area.

Black Mtn. Pond Shelter (WMNF) is located on the shore of Black Mtn. Pond on the Black Mountain Pond Trail. Tent camping is permitted in the area.

Gleason Trail	4:K7
Flat Mountain Pond Trail	4:K8-K7
Algonquin Trail	4:K6
Black Mountain Pond Trail	4:K7-K6
Guinea Pond Trail	4:K6-K7

Trails on Mount Israel

| Mead Trail | 4:K7 |
| Wentworth Trail | 4:L7-K7 |

THE TRAILS

Mount Tecumseh Trail (WMNF)

This trail starts at the Mt. Tecumseh Ski Area well to the right of the main lodge (as you face it), climbs the east slope of Tecumseh, then descends the northwest ridge to Tripoli Rd. (FR 30) 1.3 mi. west of the Mount Osceola Trail parking lot.

Starting at the ski area parking lot, the trail follows the south side of Tecumseh Brook for 0.4 mi., turns left up the bank, and comes out on the north edge of the ski slope, which it follows uphill for 80 yd. The trail enters the woods right and shortly returns to the north edge of the ski slopes, which it ascends with good views to the east. At a cairn and red arrow at 0.9 mi., the trail goes right into the woods on an old logging road, angling upward along the south side of the Tecumseh Brook valley, then climbs to a flat area where it turns right. Here, at 1.9 mi., the Sosman Trail from the top of the ski area enters from the left. In another 120 yd. the Sosman Trail forks left to ascend the summit from the west. The Mount Tecumseh Trail swings right, descends slightly, circling the steep cone, and finally climbs steeply to the summit from the north. The summit has good views, particularly to Mt. Osceola and Mt. Tripyramid.

The trail descends west, then swings northwest past an

excellent outlook, passes through a shallow col and ascends to the summit of the west ridge at 2.9 mi. It passes over numerous knobs, then descends to a col at 3.9 mi., where it turns right and slabs down the north slope of the ridge on an old logging road. Near the bottom it turns right, crosses Eastman Brook, and ends at Tripoli Rd.

Mount Tecumseh Trail (map 4:J6)
Distances from Mt. Tecumseh ski area parking lot
to Mt. Tecumseh summit: 2.2 mi. (3.6 km.), 2 hr. 10 min.
to Tripoli Rd.: 5.3 mi. (8.6 km.), 3 hr. 45 min.

Sosman Trail (WVAIA)

This trail connects the summit of Tecumseh with the top of the ski area. It leaves the summit to the southwest, switchbacks down the slope, and joins the Mount Tecumseh Trail at 0.2 mi. In 120 yd. it diverges right again and follows the ridge south, passing over a rocky hump with an interesting view of Tecumseh's summit cone, and comes out on a ledge at the top of the ski area. (To find the trail at the ski area, look for a yellow blaze on a white birch.) From here it is about 1.8 mi. to the base lodge via ski trails.

Sosman Trail (map 4:J6)
Distance from summit of Mt. Tecumseh
to top of ski area: 0.8 mi. (1.3 km.), 30 min.

Welch–Dickey Loop Trail (WVAIA)

This loop trail affords fine views for a modest effort. The section which ascends Welch Mtn. is also one of the first trails to be clear of snow in the spring. Some of the ledges may be slippery when wet. From NH 49, about 4.5 mi. from its junction with NH 175, Upper Mad River Rd. goes northwest across the Mad River, and in 0.7 mi. Orris Rd. diverges right ("Welch Mountain" sign). Follow this road for 0.6 mi. and take a short fork right to a parking area, where the trail begins. In 15 yd. the trail forks. The right branch, leading to Welch Mtn., shortly crosses a brook and follows its east side for about 0.5 mi., then turns sharp right and slabs south to reach the ledges on the south ridge of Welch Mtn. at 0.9 mi. from the start. From here the trail follows its older route over open ledges interspersed with jack pines and dwarf birches to the ledgy summit of Welch Mtn. at 1.9 mi.

From here the loop drops steeply to a wooded col, then rises, working to the left around a high rock slab. Just above this a branch trail leads right 0.2 mi. to the north outlook from an open ledge. The main loop continues over the summit of Dickey Mtn. at 2.4 mi. and descends another prominent ridge to the southwest, with many outlook ledges, entering the woods to stay at the base of a fine ledge at 3.2 mi. It continues to descend, then turns left onto a logging road with a cellar hole on the right, and soon reaches the loop junction and the parking lot.

Welch–Dickey Loop Trail (map 4:K5)
Distances from Orris Rd. parking area

    to Welch Mtn. summit: 1.9 mi., 1 hr. 45 min.

    to Dickey Mtn. summit: 2.4 mi., 2 hr. 10 min.

    to Orris Rd. parking area (complete loop): 4.4 mi. (7.0 km.), 3 hr. 10 min.

Short Walks (WVAIA)

A system of local trails is maintained in the valley. Trail information and a map, "Hiking Trails of the Waterville Valley," may be obtained at the service station on Tripoli Rd. opposite the Waterville Campground or at the "Jugtown" store. It should be noted that the hiking trails are frequently intersected by recently cut ski-touring trails, which are marked in black and yellow. A separate map of these is available locally.

Some of the most interesting walks are the Cascade Path, to a series of beautiful waterfalls on Cascade Brook (1.5 mi.); the River Path along the Mad River (about 1.3 mi.); to the Big Boulder on Slide Brook (1.0 mi.); to Fletcher's Cascade, off the Drake's Brook Trail (1.7 mi.); and to Greeley Ledges, between the Snows Mountain Trail and the top of Snows Mtn. ski slopes (0.8 mi.).

The Scaur, a rock outlook between Mad River and Slide Brook, with views north, south, and west, may be reached either by Kettles Path (1.0 mi.) from the Livermore Trail, or by the steeper Scaur Trail (0.5 mi.) from the Greeley Ponds Trail; the two routes join at the foot of the final climb to the outlook. On a shoulder of the East Peak of Osceola are the large Davis Boulders and Goodrich Rock (one of the largest glacial erratics in NH), reached by the Goodrich Rock Trail (1.0 mi.) from the Greeley Ponds Trail. The Flume, an attractive small gorge in the headwaters of Flume Brook (not to be confused with the Franconia Notch Flume), is reached by a side trail (1.8 mi.) from the Greeley Ponds Trail.

Snows Mountain Trail (WVAIA)

This trail follows the route of the former Woodbury Trail to the shoulder of Snows Mtn., follows the ridge south and east to the summit, and then descends the west slope of the mountain back to Waterville. *Note.* Due to projected residential and ski trail construction, parts of this trail may be difficult to follow.

The trail leaves the north end of the tennis courts, enters the woods, climbing steeply for 100 yd., then turns left onto a ski slope. It follows the chair lift to avoid residences. Above the houses it reenters the woods right, climbing for about another 0.3 mi., then leveling off. At 0.6 mi. a trail leaves left to Greeley Ledges and the top of the ski slope. At 1.1 mi. the Snows Mountain Trail reaches the end of the old Woodbury Trail section and turns right, climbing gradually to Snows Mtn. Outlook, which gives a good view west. The ascent continues, passing a large boulder with a northeast view. The trail levels out, then climbs to a high point of the ridge. At 1.8 mi. a side trail leads left 0.1 mi. to a ledge at the summit. The Snows Mountain Trail descends, passing additional viewpoints to the south and west, then continues gradually down the west slope of the mountain and ends on Upper Greeley Hill Rd., above the swimming pool at Waterville.

Snows Mountain Trail (map 4:J6)
Distances from Waterville library
to Snows Mtn. summit: 1.9 mi., 1 hr. 35 min.
to Upper Greeley Hill Rd.: 3.4 mi. (5.5 km.), 2 hr. 20 min.

Mount Osceola Trail (WMNF)
This trail runs from a parking area on Tripoli Rd. (FR 30), just west of the height-of-land in Thornton Gap 7.0 mi. from I-93, over Mt. Osceola and East Osceola, to the Greeley Ponds Trail at the height-of-land in Mad River Notch. The trail from Thornton Gap to the summit of Osceola is relatively easy, with moderate grades and good footing, but the section between East Osceola and Greeley Ponds Trail is extremely steep and rough.

The trail leaves Tripoli Rd. and climbs moderately, going east across the south slope of Breadtray Ridge. At 1.3 mi. it begins to climb by switchbacks toward the ridge top, and at 2.3 mi. crosses a small brook (unreliable) on a log bridge. The trail resumes its switchbacks, gains the summit ridge and turns right, and soon reaches the summit ledge at 3.2 mi., with excellent views. The trail turns left and descends, alternating flat stretches with steep, rocky descents. Just before reaching the main col it descends a steep chimney, which can be avoided by a detour to the left (north).

The trail passes the col at 3.8 mi. and climbs past a fine outlook on the left to the summit of East Osceola at 4.2 mi. The trail then crosses a lower knob, and descends steeply, then moderately, to a shoulder. At the top of a gully there is an outlook 25 yd. to the left, and the main trail descends the steep, loose gully, goes diagonally across a small, rocky slide with good views, and continues to descend very steeply past a sloping rockface, where it turns left. At 4.9 mi. it turns sharp left onto a newly constructed segment that descends moderately under the impressive cliffs of the north spur to the Greeley Ponds Trail.

Mount Osceola Trail (map 4:J6-I6)
Distances from Tripoli Rd.
to Mt. Osceola summit: 3.2 mi., 2 hr. 35 min.
to Mt. Osceola, East Peak: 4.2 mi., 3 hr. 20 min.
to Greeley Ponds Trail: 5.7 mi. (9.2 km.), 4 hr.

Greeley Ponds Trail (WMNF)

This trail runs from the Livermore Trail about 0.3 mi. from the parking area on Livermore Rd. (FR 53), past the Greeley Ponds, through Mad River Notch, and ends at the Kancamagus Highway 4.5 mi. east of the Wilderness Trail parking lot. It is crossed numerous times by a ski-touring trail marked with blue diamonds. Grades are easy, and the ponds are beautiful.

The trail leaves the Livermore Trail sharp left just after the first bridge beyond the Depot Camp clearing, and follows an old truck road past the Scaur Trail right at 0.7 mi. and the Goodrich Rock Trail left at 0.9 mi. The truck road ends at 1.1 mi., where the trail crosses Mad River on Knight's Bridge. At 1.2 mi. the Flume Path diverges right, and the trail soon crosses Flume Brook and passes an old logging camp. It continues across several small brooks and enters the Greeley Ponds Scenic Area at 2.6 mi. The trail soon crosses Mad River on a bridge and reaches the lower Greeley Pond at 2.9 mi., then the upper pond at 3.4 mi. An unmarked path crosses the upper pond outlet, passes a fine view on a small beach, and loops around the pond to rejoin the main trail in Mad River Notch. The main trail ascends easily to the notch, passing the Mount Osceola Trail left at the height-of-land at 3.8 mi., and descends over numerous brooks (all the difficult crossings are bridged) to the Kancamagus Highway.

Greeley Ponds Trail (map 4:J6-I6)
Distances from Livermore Trail

to lower Greeley Pond: 2.9 mi., 1 hr. 45 min.

to Mount Osceola Trail: 3.8 mi., 2 hr. 15 min.

to Kancamagus Highway: 5.1 mi. (8.2 km.), 2 hr. 55 min.

East Pond Trail (WMNF)

This trail runs north from Tripoli Rd. (FR 30), 5.4 mi. east of its intersection with I-93, to the Kancamagus Highway 3.7 mi. east of the Wilderness Trail parking lot. It passes scenic East Pond and crosses the pass between Mt. Osceola and Scar Ridge.

Leaving Tripoli Rd., it follows a gated gravel road and continues straight on an older road where the gravel road swings right. At 0.4 mi., near the site of the old Tripoli Mill, the Little East Pond Trail turns left on an old railroad grade, while the East Pond Trail continues ahead on a logging road. At 0.8 mi. it crosses East Pond Brook, and at 1.4 mi., near the point where the newly constructed East Pond Loop leaves left for Little East Pond, a side path leads right 40 yd. to the south shore of East Pond.

The trail swings left away from the pond and climbs moderately on old logging roads to the height-of-land at 2.2 mi., then descends steadily on logging roads, crossing Cheney Brook at 3.1 mi. and Pine Brook at 4.3 mi. Just after the latter crossing (which may be difficult at high water) the trail reaches an old logging railroad spur and follows it almost all the way to the Kancamagus Highway.

East Pond Trail (map 4:J5-I6)
Distances from Tripoli Rd.
   to East Pond: 1.4 mi., 1 hr. 5 min.
   to Kancamagus Highway: 5.1 mi. (8.2 km.), 3 hr. 15 min.

Little East Pond Trail (WMNF)

This trail leaves the East Pond Trail left (northwest), 0.4 mi. from Tripoli Rd. and follows an old railroad grade slightly uphill, crossing Clear Brook at 0.7 mi. then soon bears sharp right from the end of the railroad grade and continues at a moderate grade to Little East Pond, where it meets the East Pond Loop.

Little East Pond Trail (map 4:I6-I5)
Distance from East Pond Trail
   to Little East Pond: 1.7 mi. (2.8 km.), 1 hr. 10 min.

East Pond Loop (WMNF)

This new trail runs at a fairly level grade between East Pond and Little East Pond, making possible a loop trip which visits both ponds.

East Pond Loop (map 4:I6-I5)
Distance from East Pond
   to Little East Pond: 1.4 mi. (2.3 km.), 50 min.
Distance of complete loop to both ponds
   from Tripoli Rd.: 4.9 mi. (7.9 km.), 3 hr.

Livermore Trail (WMNF)

This trail runs from Waterville Valley to the Kancamagus Highway at Lily Pond. It once connected Waterville Valley to the Sawyer River logging railroad, which led to the now deserted village of Livermore on Sawyer River. The Livermore Trail consists of logging roads of various ages and conditions; the gravel southern section, from Tripoli Rd. to Flume Brook Camp, is also called Livermore Rd. (FR 53).

From the parking area on Livermore Rd., the trail follows a gated gravel road across a branch of Mad River. The Greeley Ponds Trail, another gravel road, diverges sharp left 40 yd. past the bridge. About 0.1 mi. past the first bridge the trail crosses Mad River on another bridge. In the next 2.0 mi. several of the WVAIA local paths intersect the trail: at 0.4 mi. from Depot Camp the Boulder Path diverges right; the Big Pines Path diverges left at 0.6 mi., and the Kettles Path diverges left at 0.8 mi.; at 1.7 mi. the Norway Rapids Trail diverges right, and the Cascade Path diverges right across a new logging bridge at 2.1 mi.

At 2.5 mi. the south end of the Mount Tripyramid Trail diverges right over Avalanche Brook to the South Slide and the Tripyramid peaks. After passing the site of Avalanche Camp to the left of the trail at 3.0 mi., where the road becomes more grass-grown, the trail reaches a hairpin turn to the left at 3.5 mi., where the north end of the Mount Tripyramid Trail diverges right for the difficult North Slide and the summits. At 3.7 mi. the Scaur Ridge Trail diverges right, offering a longer but safer and easier route to the summit of North Tripyramid. After climbing steadily for some distance, the trail crosses Flume Brook at 4.7 mi. and soon passes the clearing of Flume Brook Camp on the right of the trail, becoming wet and muddy at times.

At 4.9 mi. the gravel road ends in a clearing. The Livermore Trail bears slightly right on an older road (sign), and climbs gradually into the very flat Livermore Pass (2864 ft.) at 5.5 mi. It descends slowly at first, runs in a dry brookbed for a while, then descends rather steeply, slabbing down the wall of a deep, wooded gorge. At 5.9 mi. it crosses the brookbed at the bottom of the gorge. The trail descends moderately, crossing several brooks and logging roads, and reaches the Kancamagus Highway east of Kancamagus Pass at 8.1 mi.

Livermore Trail (map 4:J6-I7)
Distances from Livermore Rd. parking area

to south end, Mount Tripyramid Trail: 2.5 mi., 1 hr. 25 min.

to north end, Mount Tripyramid Trail: 3.5 mi., 2 hr. 10 min.

to crossing of Flume Brook: 4.7 mi., 2 hr. 55 min.

to Kancamagus Highway: 8.1 mi. (13.0 km.), 4 hr. 40 min.

Mount Tripyramid Trail (WVAIA)

This trail makes a loop over the three summits of Tripyramid from the Livermore Trail, and is usually done from north to south—in order to ascend the steep slabs of the North Slide and descend the loose gravel of the South Slide. The trail is almost entirely within the Sandwich Range Wilderness. The steep slabs of the North Slide are difficult, and dangerous in wet or icy conditions. The loose footing on the South Slide may also be hazardous when wet or icy. Ice may form on the North Slide early in the fall and remain well into the spring. In poor conditions the Scaur Ridge Trail is a safer alternative. Allow plenty of time for this steep, rough trip.

The north end of the loop leaves the Livermore Trail at a hairpin turn 3.5 mi. from the Livermore Rd. parking area (0.5 mi. beyond the Avalanche Camp clearing). The trail descends sharply for 50 yd. to cross Avalanche Brook (last reliable water), then ascends at a moderate grade, occasionally requiring some care to follow, and reaches the gravel outwash of the North Slide at about 0.5 mi. from the

Livermore Trail. It now becomes extremely steep, climbing about 1200 ft. in 0.5 mi. Follow paint blazes on the rocks. Soon the trail reaches the first slabs and views become steadily more extensive. At the top of the slide the trail turns left into the woods and, in 0.1 mi., the Pine Bend Brook Trail enters from the left 20 yd. below the summit of North Peak.

The Mount Tripyramid Trail and the Pine Bend Brook Trail now coincide. They cross over the summit of North Peak and descend at a moderate grade toward Middle Peak. Just north of the col between North and Middle peaks, the Sabbaday Brook Trail enters left from the Kancamagus Highway, and the Pine Bend Brook Trail ends. The Mount Tripyramid Trail crosses the col and makes a steep ascent of the cone of Middle Peak. There are two outlooks to the right of the trail near the true summit, which is a few yards left at the high point of the trail. The trail descends into the col between Middle and South peaks, then climbs moderately to the wooded summit of South Peak. From this summit the trail starts to descend steeply, and soon reaches the top of the South Slide. In another 60 yd. the Sleeper Trail to Mt. Whiteface diverges left at a sign. The descent to the foot of the slide at 3.0 mi. is steep, with poor footing. The trail now follows logging roads, crossing several small brooks; Cold Brook, the first sure water, is crossed at 4.1 mi. Continuing on old roads, the trail eventually crosses Avalanche Brook and ends 25 yd. farther on the Livermore Trail, 2.5 mi. from the Livermore Rd. parking area.

Mount Tripyramid Trail (map 4:J7)
Distances from Livermore Trail
  to summit of North Peak: 1.2 mi., 1 hr. 30 min.
  to Sabbaday Brook Trail: 1.7 mi., 1 hr. 45 min.
  to summit of Middle Peak: 2.0 mi., 2 hr.

to summit of South Peak: 2.4 mi., 2 hr. 15 min.
to Sleeper Trail: 2.6 mi., 2 hr. 20 min.
to Livermore Trail: 4.9 mi. (7.9 km.), 3 hr. 30 min.

Distance of complete loop
from Livermore Rd. parking area: 10.8 mi. (17.4 km.), 6 hr. 55 min.

Scaur Ridge Trail (WMNF)

This trail runs from the Livermore Trail to the Pine Bend Brook Trail, affording an easier, safer alternative route than the North Slide. It is almost entirely within the Sandwich Range Wilderness. It diverges right (east) from Livermore Trail 3.7 mi. from the Livermore Rd. parking area. Following an old logging road at a moderate grade, it crosses a small brook at 0.9 mi., and soon bears left off the road. Climbing somewhat more steeply, it turns right at 1.1 mi. and enters the Pine Bend Brook Trail at the top of a narrow ridge at 1.2 mi. The summit of North Tripyramid is 0.8 mi. to the right via the Pine Bend Brook Trail.

Scaur Ridge Trail (map 4:J7)
Distance from Livermore Trail
to Pine Bend Brook Trail: 1.2 mi. (1.9 km.), 1 hr. 5 min.
Distance of complete loop
from Livermore Rd. parking area (via Scaur Ridge Trail and South Slide): 11.9 mi., 7 hr. 15 min.

Pine Bend Brook Trail (WMNF)

This trail ascends North Tripyramid from the Kancamagus Highway 1.0 mi. west of the Sabbaday Falls Picnic Area. Parts of it are steep and rough.

The trail leaves the highway and very shortly turns sharp right onto the grade of the old Swift River logging railroad. After 0.1 mi., it turns sharp left off the railroad grade and follows Pine Bend Brook southwest on an old logging road, making three crossings of the brook. After the third crossing, at 1.3 mi., the trail begins to swing more to the west, entering the Sandwich Range Wilderness, and crosses several small tributaries and passes over a minor divide to a westerly branch of Pine Bend Brook, which it crosses and recrosses (last sure water). After crossing the brookbed again in a rocky section at 2.2 mi., the trail becomes rough and steep as it ascends along the north bank of the brook valley, then recrosses the brookbed and slabs steeply up an even steeper slope with poor footing. Soon it reaches and ascends a minor easterly ridge, with less difficult climbing. Shortly after reaching this ridge, there is a good view of Mt. Washington and the cliffs of Mt. Lowell. Eventually the trail reaches the ridge running from Tripyramid north to Scaur Peak, crosses it and descends slightly to the west side, then turns left and continues almost level to the junction on the right at 3.2 mi. with the Scaur Ridge Trail. Rising gradually on the very narrow wooded ridge, the trail provides occasional glimpses of the North Slide, then descends slightly. Soon it attacks the final steep, rough, and rocky climb to North Peak. The Mount Tripyramid Trail enters from the North Slide on the right 20 yd. below this summit. (There are good views from the top of the slide, 0.1 mi. from this junction via the Mount Tripyramid Trail.) The two trails coincide, passing the summit of North Peak and descending at a moderate grade to the junction with the Sabbaday Brook Trail just north of the col between North and Middle peaks.

Pine Bend Brook Trail (map 4:I7-J7)
Distances from Kancamagus Highway
to Scaur Ridge Trail: 3.2 mi., 2 hr. 40 min.
to summit of North Peak: 4.0 mi., 3 hr. 25 min.
to Sabbaday Brook Trail: 4.5 mi. (7.2 km.), 3 hr. 40 min.

Sabbaday Brook Trail (WMNF)

This trail begins at the Sabbaday Falls Picnic Area and ascends to the col between North Tripyramid and Middle Tripyramid. There are numerous brook crossings, which may be difficult at high water.

From the parking area follow a well-graded gravel path along the brook. A side path bears left and passes several viewpoints over Sabbaday Falls, rejoining at 0.3 mi., where the gravel path ends, and the trail continues on an old logging road with easy grades. At 0.5 mi. it crosses onto a small island in the brook and soon crosses back to the west bank. At 0.7 mi. the trail makes the first of three crossings of Sabbaday Brook in 0.2 mi. (All three may be difficult in high water, but the first two can be avoided by bushwhacking along the west bank, since they are only 0.1 mi. apart.) The trail enters the Sandwich Range Wilderness, and for nearly 2.0 mi. follows the old logging road on the east bank of Sabbaday Brook, then turns sharp right, descends briefly, and makes a fourth crossing of the brook at 2.8 mi. Above this the brook and trail swing to the west, then northwest, up the narrow valley between Tripyramid and the Fool Killer, climbing more steadily and crossing the brook twice more. The trail passes the base of a small slide on the Fool Killer, crosses the brook for the seventh and last time (last water) at 4.1 mi., and soon reenters the old route of the trail above a slide. From here it climbs steeply and is rough, with many rocks and roots. Finally it levels off and meets the Pine Bend Brook Trail and the Mount Tripyramid Trail just north of the col between North and Middle Tripyramid; turn right for North Peak (0.5 mi.) or left for Middle Peak (0.3 mi.).

Sabbaday Brook Trail (map 4:J8-J7)
Distances from Sabbaday Falls Picnic Area

  to fourth crossing of Sabbaday Brook: 2.8 mi., 1 hr. 50 min.

to Pine Bend Brook Trail/Mount Tripyramid Trail: 4.6 mi. (7.4 km.), 3 hr. 30 min.

Sleeper Trail (SSOC)

This trail connects Mt. Tripyramid with Mt. Whiteface and the eastern peaks of the Sandwich Range. It runs from the Downes Brook Trail (see Section 8) in the col between Mt. Whiteface and the Sleeper Ridge, over the high, double-domed Sleeper Ridge, to the Mount Tripyramid Trail high on the South Slide. It is entirely within the Sandwich Range Wilderness.

The trail leaves the Downes Brook Trail 0.9 mi. below the summit of Mt. Whiteface and skirts north of a swampy area. The only sure water is just north of the junction on the Downes Brook Trail. It soon begins to ascend the East Sleeper, and there are occasional views to the east and north through the trees. Passing 0.1 mi. left (southwest) of the summit of East Sleeper, the trail descends into the col between the Sleepers and passes close to the summit of West Sleeper through mature woods. After descending to the Tripyramid col the trail bears west and contours along South Tripyramid until it enters the easternmost of the two south slides. Small cairns and yellow blazes mark the winding route on the slide, as the trail climbs steeply about 100 yd. to reenter the woods on the opposite side. After 100 yd. through the wooded area the trail enters the large western slide, where it meets the Mount Tripyramid Trail. To locate the beginning of the trail on the Tripyramid Slide, look for a small sign at the far east edge of the slide, 60 yd. below its top.

Sleeper Trail (map 4:J7)
Distance (est.) from Downes Brook Trail
to Mount Tripyramid Trail: 2.8 mi. (4.5 km.), 2 hr

Sandwich Mountain Trail (WMNF)

This trail runs to the summit of Sandwich Mtn. from a parking lot just off NH 49, 0.4 mi. southwest of its junction with Tripoli Rd. There are fine views from several levels of the trail. It leaves the southwest corner of the parking lot, crosses Drakes Brook on a footbridge, and soon turns east and climbs steeply to Noon Peak at 1.7 mi. It then follows the curving, gradual ridge, covered with beautiful mosses, and passes several outlooks. There is a spring (unreliable) on the west side of the trail, which soon skirts the east slope of Jennings Peak. The Drakes Brook Trail enters left at 2.7 mi., and at 2.8 mi. a spur path leads right 0.2 mi. to the ledgy summit of Jennings Peak, which commands magnificent views. The trail enters the Sandwich Range Wilderness. The Smarts Brook Trail enters right at 3.3 mi., and the Sandwich Mountain Trail ascends moderately toward the summit of Sandwich Mtn. About 90 yd. below the summit the Algonquin Trail enters right, and 15 yd. below the summit the Bennett Street Trail enters right.

Sandwich Mountain Trail (map 4:J6-K7)
Distances from parking area off NH 49

   to Drakes Brook Trail: 2.7 mi., 2 hr. 15 min.
   to Sandwich Mtn. summit: 3.9 mi. (6.3 km.), 3 hr. 20 min.

Drakes Brook Trail (WMNF)

This trail leaves the same parking lot off NH 49 as the Sandwich Mountain Trail and rejoins that trail near Jennings Peak. The trail leaves north from the parking lot and follows a logging road for 0.4 mi. At this point the trail to Fletcher's Cascades continues up the road, and the Drakes Brook Trail diverges right and crosses Drakes Brook. The trail follows an old logging road, climbing away from the brook and returning to its bank several times. At 2.6 mi. it climbs by switchbacks up the west side of the ravine and joins the Sandwich Mountain Trail north of Jennings Peak, about 1.2 mi. from the summit of Sandwich Mtn.

Drakes Brook Trail (map 4:J6-K6)
Distances from parking area off NH 49
- *to* Sandwich Mountain Trail: 3.2 mi. (5.2 km.), 2 hr. 35 min.
- *to* Sandwich Mtn. summit (via Sandwich Mountain Trail): 4.4 mi. (7.1 km.), 3 hr.

Smarts Brook Trail (WMNF)

This trail follows the valley of Smarts Brook from NH 49 to the Sandwich Mountain Trail in the sag south of Jennings Peak. The valley is wild and pleasant, and the trail is relatively easy.

The trail leaves the east side of NH 49 from the south end of a parking area just northeast of the Smarts Brook bridge, crosses the brook on the highway bridge and immediately turns left and climbs a short distance to a logging road, which it follows left. After crossing the Tri-Town Trail (a cross-country ski trail), it joins a better road, and at 1.1 mi. passes a swimming hole left. Soon the Tri-Town Trail reenters on the right, and the Smarts Brook Trail turns sharp left to cross the brook on a bridge, then turns right and follows the brook, and recrosses at 1.6 mi. The trail enters the Sandwich Range Wilderness, crosses a tributary at 2.6 mi., and at 3.7 mi. passes several boulders. It then crosses the brook, and passes several more very large boulders in the next 0.4 mi. Soon it turns left and climbs by a long switchback to the ridge top, where it meets the Sandwich Mountain Trail.

Smarts Brook Trail (map 4:K6)
Distances from parking area on NH 49
- *to* pools in Smarts Brook: 1.1 mi., 40 min.

> *to* Sandwich Mountain Trail: 5.1 mi. (8.2 km.), 3 hr. 45 min.
>
> *to* Sandwich Mtn. summit (via Sandwich Mountain Trail): 5.7 mi. (9.2 km.), 4 hr. 25 min.

Bennett Street Trail (WODC)

This trail runs to the summit of Sandwich Mtn. from the Flat Mountain Pond Trail 0.3 mi. from Bennett St. at Jose's bridge. Its blue blazes should be followed with care.

From Jose's bridge, continue west on the Flat Mountain Pond Trail past a gate to a small clearing, where the Bennett Street Trail turns right. It follows a logging road along the southwest bank of Pond Brook, crossing several small streams, and at 0.6 mi. the Gleason Trail diverges left. It bears away from Pond Brook and follows a tributary, then at 1.6 mi. crosses the Flat Mountain Pond Trail, which at this point is an old railroad grade. The Bennett Street Trail ascends the bank and climbs steadily, entering the Sandwich Range Wilderness, and at 2.3 mi. turns right on a logging road. At 2.9 mi. it turns left off the logging road and at 3.5 mi. the Gleason Trail rejoins on the left. The trail soon turns left onto another old road at a point where there is an unreliable spring on a side path right, soon passing a spur path left (sign) to another unreliable spring. The trail now climbs to a junction with the Sandwich Mountain Trail; the summit is 15 yd. to the right.

Bennett Street Trail (map 4:K7)
Distance from Flat Mountain Pond Trail

> *to* Sandwich Mtn. summit: 4.0 mi. (6.4 km.), 3 hr. 25 min.

Gleason Trail (AMC)

This trail begins and ends on the Bennett Street Trail, providing an alternative route that is about 0.6 mi. shorter, but consequently steeper, to the summit of Sandwich Mtn.

The yellow blazes must be followed with care; the trail is rather steep, and footing may be poor when the trail is wet.

It diverges left from the Bennett Street Trail at 0.6 mi. (0.9 mi. from Jose's bridge) and ascends across a ledgy brook to cross the Flat Mountain Pond Trail (old railroad grade) at 0.5 mi. This junction is marked only by a small cairn and arrows. The trail soon turns left and enters the Sandwich Range Wilderness, climbs through a beautiful hardwood forest, then approaches a brook and turns right without crossing it at 1.0 mi. Soon it turns left onto a logging road, follows it for 40 yd., and turns right off it and continues rather steeply to the ridge top at 1.5 mi., where the trail levels off. It then ascends moderately to its upper junction with the Bennett Street Trail, 0.5 mi. below the summit of Sandwich Mtn.

Gleason Trail (map 4:K7)
Distance from lower junction with Bennett Street Trail
to upper junction with Bennett Street Trail: 2.2 mi. (3.6 km.), 2 hr. 15 min.

Flat Mountain Pond Trail (WMNF)

This trail runs to the ponds from Whiteface Intervale Rd. about 0.3 mi. north of its intersection with Bennett St., then descends to Bennett St. at Jose's bridge. It is an easy trail for most of its distance.

The trail leaves Whiteface Intervale Rd., just before the bridge over Whiteface River, on a gated logging road, crosses a beaver pond outlet with good views, bears left at a fork, and turns sharp right off the road at 0.6 mi. Soon it reaches an older, grassy logging road and follows it left. At 1.4 mi. it leaves this road right and descends gradually to Whiteface River, crossing the river on large rocks into the Sandwich Range Wilderness at 1.8 mi., and immediately picks up the former route of the trail, a logging road along the east bank. At 2.0 mi. the McCrillis Trail turns sharp

right up the bank, and the Flat Mountain Pond Trail continues to ascend along the river at comfortable grades, then
crosses a major branch at 3.6 mi. Continuing the ascent,
it passes over a small hump and descends to the edge of Flat
Mtn. Pond at 4.6 mi., where it enters the old railroad
grade. It follows the grade to a fork at the edge of the
major inlet brook; the trail follows the left fork across the
stream, while the right fork runs to the edge of a swampy
area. Continuing along the pond, the main trail soon diverges right to circle around an area in which the grade has
been flooded, passes a boulder with a view of Mt. Whiteface, and returns to the grade at 5.6 mi., leaving the Sandwich Range Wilderness. Here, 70 yd. straight ahead on a
spur path, is the Flat Mtn. Pond Shelter, worth visiting just
for the view across the pond. The main trail turns right on
the railroad grade and descends gradually into the valley of
Pond Brook.

At 6.7 mi. the grade makes a hairpin turn left at an old
beaver pond, soon crosses a small brook, passes a logging
camp site, and crosses the brook twice more. At 7.9 mi. the
trail crosses a major tributary, swings left, and at 8.0 mi.
the Bennett Street Trail crosses. After a wet section where
the railroad ties remain, the Gleason Trail crosses at 8.5
mi. (small cairn, arrow, yellow blazes, no sign). Both the
Bennett Street and Gleason trails can be used as shortcuts
to Jose's bridge. At 9.6 mi. the Guinea Pond Trail continues ahead on the railroad grade, while the Flat Mountain
Pond Trail turns left on a logging road, passes a gate, goes
through a small clearing, where the Bennett Street Trail
turns sharp left, and passes a second gate just before reaching the parking area at Jose's bridge.

Flat Mountain Pond Trail (map 4:K8-K7)
Distances from Whiteface Intervale Rd.
    to McCrillis Trail: 2.0 mi., 1 hr. 10 min.

to Flat Mtn. Pond Shelter spur path: 5.6 mi., 3 hr. 30 min.

to Guinea Pond Trail: 9.6 mi., 5 hr. 30 min.

to Josc's bridge: 10.5 mi. (16.9 km.), 5 hr. 55 min.

Algonquin Trail (SLA)

This trail ascends Sandwich Dome from Sandwich Notch Rd., and has many extensive views from open ledges on the southwest shoulder, sometimes called Black Mtn. The trail is steep and rough, with a few rock scrambles which can be avoided by side paths.

The trail leaves the north side of Sandwich Notch Rd. 1.5 mi. north of the power line along the Beebe River and 3.7 mi. south of NH 49. It follows an old logging road across a brook and past a small meadow, and at 0.9 mi., in a small clearing, turns left off the road (watch carefully for yellow blazes). Soon it begins to climb steeply, then moderates and passes through a ledgy area with two small brooks, then climbs steeply again to a col at 2.1 mi., where it enters the Sandwich Range Wilderness. Here it turns right, descends slightly, then attacks the west end of the ridge, climbing steeply with two rock pitches both of which can be avoided by side paths to the right; at the second, good views are missed unless one walks back to the ledges. The grade moderates, and at 2.8 mi. (3300 ft.) the Black Mountain Pond Trail enters right. The Algonquin Trail continues to ascend moderately, then descends steeply into a small col at 3.5 mi., and ascends moderately again to the Sandwich Mountain Trail 90 yd. below the summit.

Algonquin Trail (map 4:K6)
Distance from Sandwich Notch Rd.

to Sandwich Mountain Trail: 4.5 mi. (7.3 km.), 3 hr. 30 min.

Black Mountain Pond Trail (SLA)

This trail runs from the Guinea Pond Trail 1.6 mi. from Sandwich Notch Rd., past Black Mtn. Pond and its shelter, to the Algonquin Trail 1.8 mi. below the summit of Sandwich Mtn. Sections of the trail below Black Mtn. Pond are wet, and the part from the pond to the ridge is very steep and rough.

This trail leaves the north side of the Guinea Pond Trail almost opposite the Mead Trail, crosses Beebe River (may be difficult at high water), continues generally north to the west bank of Beebe River (which has turned north), and recrosses at a large beaver dam. At 0.8 mi. it crosses an overgrown gravel road that crosses the brook on the left side of the trail, and enters the Sandwich Range Wilderness. It continues to ascend easily, and at 2.4 mi. reaches the west edge of Black Mtn. Pond at the shelter. (The shelter and the area to the west are not within the Sandwich Range Wilderness.) It winds around in the woods near the pond, passing through a small stand of virgin spruce, then turns right and crosses a beaver dam with a small pond on the left, and begins the steep climb. About halfway up it reaches the first of several outlook ledges with good views south; views to the west increase as the trail works around toward the west end of the shoulder. At 3.3 mi. it passes a boulder cave, turns sharp right, and continues to the Algonquin Trail at 3300 ft. elevation.

Black Mountain Pond Trail (map 4:K7-K6)
Distances from Guinea Pond Trail

to Black Mtn. Pond Shelter: 2.4 mi., 1 hr. 35 min.

to Algonquin Trail: 3.5 mi. (5.6 km.), 2 hr. 45 min.

Guinea Pond Trail (WMNF)

This trail runs east from Sandwich Notch Rd. 5.7 mi. from Center Sandwich, just south of the bridge over Beebe

River, to the Flat Mountain Pond Trail 0.9 mi. from Bennett St. at Jose's bridge. It follows a gated road to the old railroad grade in a power line clearing, and follows the grade along Beebe River past numerous ponds and swamps. At 1.2 mi. it passes a second gate, and soon the trail turns right, then left on a road, to bypass a flooded section of the grade. Soon the trail runs through the woods to bypass a flooded section of the road, then rejoins the railroad grade and reaches the junctions with the Mead Trail right at 1.6 mi. and the Black Mountain Pond Trail left 10 yd. farther. Continuing east, the trail crosses a brook twice; in high water, follow a path along the south bank. The trail crosses another brook, and at 1.8 mi. a side path runs left 0.2 mi. to the shore of Guinea Pond. At 2.8 mi. the trail crosses a branch of Cold River (may be difficult at high water) and continues on the grade to the junction with the Flat Mountain Pond Trail, which enters right from Jose's bridge and follows the grade ahead to Flat Mtn. Pond.

Guinea Pond Trail (map 4:K6-K7)
Distances from Sandwich Notch Rd.
   to Mead Trail/Black Mountain Pond Trail: 1.6 mi., 50 min.
   to Flat Mountain Pond Trail: 4.0 mi. (6.4 km.), 2 hr. 5 min.

Mead Trail (SLA)
This trail ascends to the summit of Mt. Israel from the Guinea Pond Trail 1.6 mi. from Sandwich Notch Rd. It crosses a small ridge and a sag, then the power lines, and ascends along the ravine of a small brook, crossing it at 0.9 mi. It continues to ascend past a small spring (unreliable) to the Wentworth Trail; the summit ledge, with fine views, is 70 yd. left.

Mead Trail (map 4:K7)
Distance from Guinea Pond Trail
   to Wentworth Trail: 1.7 mi. (2.8 km.), 1 hr. 25 min.

Wentworth Trail (SLA)

This trail ascends Mt. Israel from Mead Base (Explorer Scout camp) off Sandwich Notch Rd. 2.6 mi. from Center Sandwich, and affords splendid views of the Lakes Region and the Sandwich Range.

Park in the field below the camp buildings, and enter the woods at left rear of the main camp building (sign). The trail, blazed in yellow, leads directly uphill, following an old cart path through an opening in a stone wall 0.3 mi. above the camp. It turns right, slabs the hillside above the wall, turns left, then turns right at a brookbed at 0.8 mi. Soon it begins to switchback up the slope, and at 1.5 mi. it passes a rock face right and a fine outlook 10 yd. left across Squam Lake and Lake Winnipesaukee. The trail reaches the ridge 100 yd. farther up, and climbing becomes easier, soon becoming almost level in a dense coniferous forest. Then the trail turns right at a ledge, with a good view north, near the summit of the west knob, and continues along the ridge to the junction with the Mead Trail left; the summit is a ledge 70 yd. past the junction.

Wentworth Trail (map 4:L7-K7)
Distance from Mead Base
   to Mt. Israel summit: 2.1 mi. (3.5 km.), 1 hr. 55 min.

Mount Chocorua and the Eastern Sandwich Range

This section covers trails on Mts. Chocorua, Paugus, Passaconaway, and Whiteface, and their subsidiary peaks and ridges. The region is bounded on the north by the Kancamagus Highway (NH 112), on the east by NH 16, on the south by NH 25, and on the west by a line between the Sleeper Ridge and Mt. Whiteface. At the boundary between Section 7 (The Waterville Valley Region) and Section 8, the only points of contact between trails are at the junction of the Sleeper Trail (Section 7) with the Downes Brook Trail (Section 8), and at the junction of the Flat Mountain Pond Trail (Section 7) and the McCrillis Trail (Section 8). The entire section is covered by the AMC Chocorua-Waterville map (map 4). The Chocorua Mountain Club (CMC), Wonalancet Outdoor Club (WODC), and the WMNF maintain most of the trails in this area. The CMC marks its trails with yellow paint and signs, while the WODC trails have blue paint and signs. The Chocorua-Paugus region is accurately shown on a contour map issued by the CMC (9th ed., 1976) with a panorama from Mt. Chocorua (available for $1 from the Chocorua Mountain Club, Chocorua, NH 03817). The trails in the Paugus-Passaconaway-Whiteface region are shown on a map issued by the WODC (1976).

GEOGRAPHY

The Sandwich Range extends about 30 mi. from Conway on the Saco River to Campton on the Pemigewasset, with summits of just over 4000 ft. rising abruptly about 3000 ft. from the lake country to the south. Although the range is not outstanding for its elevation—the North Peak of Mt.

Tripyramid, at 4140 ft., is its highest point–the mountains are nevertheless quite rugged, and their viewpoints offer interesting combinations of mountain, forest, and lake scenery.

Mt. Chocorua (3475 ft.), the picturesque rocky cone at the east end of the range, is reputedly one of the most frequently photographed mountains in the world. It has a substantial network of trails; several trails are very heavily used, but it is usually possible to avoid crowds (until the summit is reached) by taking less popular trails. The Piper Trail, Champney Falls Trail, and Liberty Trail are probably the most popular. Confusion sometimes occurs from the fact that several trails are considered to extend all the way to the summit, although they converge below the summit—which is reached by only one path. Thus a given segment of trail may bear several names at once, although in this Guide one trail usually is considered to end where two merge, and only two trails (the Piper Trail and the Brook Trail) are described as reaching the summit. In descending from the summit, go 50 yd. southwest on the only marked path, down a small gully to the first junction. The trails on the open rocks are marked with paint, and junctions are signed with WMNF signs or paint, or both.

Caution. The extensive areas of open ledge which make Chocorua so attractive also pose a very real danger. Many of the trails have ledges which are dangerous when wet or icy, and the summit and upper ledges are severely exposed to lightning during electrical storms. The safety of any untreated water source in this heavily used area is very doubtful. Although Chocorua is relatively low compared to other major White Mtn. peaks, its trailheads are also located at low elevations, and the substantial amount of climbing makes Chocorua a strenuous trip.

Three Sisters, a northern ridge of Mt. Chocorua, is nearly as high and also has bare summits. Middle Sister

(3330 ft.), the highest of the three, bears the remains of an old stone fire tower. White Ledge (2010 ft.) is a bluff just east of the Three Sisters, with a ledgy top from which there is a good view east. The ledgy south shoulder of Chocorua is called Bald Mtn. (2110 ft.). On the northwest side of the mountain is Champney Falls, named for Benjamin Champney (1817–1907), pioneer White Mountain artist. The falls are beautiful, when there is a good flow of water, but meager in dry seasons.

Mt. Paugus (3210 ft.), a low but rugged and shaggy mountain once aptly called "Old Shag," was named by Lucy Larcom for the Pequawket chief who led in the battle of Lovewell's Pond. There is no trail to the wooded true summit; all trails end at an overgrown ledge 0.3 mi. south. Paugus Pass (2210 ft.) is a pass on the ridge that connects Mt. Passaconaway and the Wonalancet Range on the west with Mt. Paugus.

Mt. Passaconaway (4060 ft.) is a graceful peak named for the great and legendary sachem ("Child of the Bear") of the Penacooks who ruled at the time the Pilgrims landed. It is densely wooded, but there is a good view into the Bowl from the true summit, and a fine outlook to the east and north from a ledge a short distance from the summit on the Walden Trail. A side path descends from the Walden Trail between the summit and the east outlook to the splendid, secluded north outlook. A major ridge extends southeast to Paugus Pass over two subpeaks, which give the mountain its characteristic steplike profile when viewed from the lake country to the south. Square Ledge (2690 ft.) is a bold, rocky promontory that is a northeast spur of the first subpeak. From the farther subpeak, which is sometimes called Mt. Hedgehog (3150 ft.), the Wonalancet Range runs south, consisting of Hibbard Mtn. (2910 ft.) and Mt. Wonalancet (2800 ft.); both peaks are wooded, with good outlook ledges. Wonalancet is named for a

Penacook sachem who was a son of Passaconaway. Another Hedgehog Mtn. (2530 ft.) is north of Passaconaway. This small but rugged mountain rises between Downes and Oliverian brooks and commands fine views over the Swift River Valley and up to Passaconaway; the best views are from ledges near the summit and on the east shoulder. Mt. Potash (2670 ft.) lies between Downes and Sabbaday brooks on its west. The summit is open and ledgy and affords excellent views of the surrounding mountains and valleys in all directions.

Mt. Whiteface (4010 ft.) doubtless received its name from the precipitous ledges south of its south summit. The true summit of the mountain is wooded, but the slightly lower south summit, 0.3 mi. south of the true summit, affords magnificent views from the bare ledge at the top of the precipices. Two lesser ridges run south on either side of the cliffs, while the backbone of the mountain runs north, then northeast, connecting it with Mt. Passaconaway. Sleeper Ridge on the northwest connects Whiteface to Mt. Tripyramid. East of Mt. Whiteface lies the Bowl, a secluded valley encircled by the main ridge of Mt. Whiteface and the south ridge of Mt. Passaconaway. This area has been reserved as a natural area, and is now included within the Sandwich Range Wilderness.

West of Whiteface the range sprawls; one major ridge continues northwest over the Sleeper Ridge to Tripyramid, then ends at Livermore Pass. West of this high pass lies the mountain mass composed of peaks such as Kancamagus, Osceola, Scar Ridge, and Tecumseh; these have not been traditionally regarded as part of the Sandwich Range, although connected with it. Another major ridge runs southwest over Sandwich Dome and soon loses its definition as it descends to the Campton mountains and toward the Squam Range. Everything west of the Whiteface–Sleeper Ridge col is covered in Section 7.

CAMPING

Sandwich Range Wilderness

In this area camping and fires are prohibited above tree-line, and no campsite may be used by more than ten persons at one time.

Restricted Use Areas

The WMNF has established a number of Restricted Use Areas (RUA's) where camping and wood or charcoal fires are prohibited from 1 May to 1 November. The specific areas are under continual review, and areas are added to or subtracted from the list in order to provide the greatest amount of protection to areas subject to damage by excessive camping, while imposing the lowest level of restrictions possible. A general list of RUA's follows, but one should obtain a map of current RUA's from the WMNF.

(1) No camping is permitted above treeline (where trees are less than 8 ft. tall). The point where the restricted area begins is marked on most trails with small signs, but the absence of such signs should not be construed as proof of the legality of a site.

(2) No camping is permitted within one-quarter mile of most facilities such as huts, cabins, shelters, or tentsites, except at the facility itself.

(3) No camping is permitted within 200 ft. of certain trails. In 1986, designated trails included the Champney Falls Trail up to the boundary of the Mt. Chocorua RUA.

(4) No camping is permitted at any time of the year on the upper part of Mt. Chocorua, except at Camp Penacook and Jim Liberty Cabin. Campfires are prohibited even at these sites.

Established Trailside Campsites

Camp Penacook (WMNF), located on a spur path off the Piper Trail on Mt. Chocorua, is an open shelter that accommodates six to eight, with a tent platform that also accommodates six to eight. There is water nearby.

Jim Liberty Cabin (WMNF) is located on a ledgy hump 0.5 mi. below the summit of Mt. Chocorua. The water source is scanty in dry weather.

Old Shag Camp (CMC), on Mt. Paugus, has been removed.

Camp Rich (WODC) is on the southwest side of Mt. Passaconaway on the Dicey's Mill Trail at about 3500 ft. elevation. It is an open log shelter for eight. Wilderness policies will probably require its eventual removal.

Camp Shehadi (WODC) is an open shelter for six at the junction of the Rollins and Downes Brook trails, 0.1 mi. north of the south summit of Mt. Whiteface. Wilderness policies will probably require its eventual removal. The nearest reliable water is 0.9 mi. down the Downes Brook Trail.

Camp Heermance (WODC) is an open shelter accommodating six in a partially sheltered spot near the summit of Mt. Whiteface, about 20 yd. north of an unreliable spring (water unreliable) near the top of the Blueberry Ledge Trail. Wilderness policies will probably require its eventual removal. The original shelter at this site was built in 1912. The nearest reliable water is 1.0 mi. down the Downes Brook Trail.

ROAD ACCESS

Confusion sometimes results from the rather erratic behavior of NH 113 and its alternate route between North Sandwich and Tamworth, NH 113A. Both roads change direction frequently, and NH 113 unites with and diverges from NH 25 between its two junctions with NH 113A. It is therefore necessary to study very carefully directions to trailheads on the southeast slopes of the Sandwich Range.

Whiteface Intervale Rd. leaves NH 113A about 3.0 mi.

north of the western junction of NH 113 and NH 113A, where NH 113A bends from north-south to east-west. Bennett St. turns left from Whiteface Intervale Rd. 0.1 mi. from NH 113A, continues straight past a junction at 1.7 mi., where it becomes rougher, and ends at 2.4 mi. at Jose's (rhymes with doses) bridge.

Ferncroft Rd. leaves NH 113A at Wonalancet village, at a right angle turn in the main highway. It shortly passes the Wonalancet post office, and at 0.5 mi. a gravel road (FR 337) turns right 0.1 mi. to a parking area. No parking is permitted farther up Ferncroft Rd.

Fowler's Mill Rd. runs between NH 16 (at the bridge that crosses the south end of Chocorua Lake, about 1.5 mi. north of Chocorua village), and NH 113A (3.3 mi. north of the eastern junction of NH 113 and NH 113A in Tamworth, and just north of the bridge over Paugus Brook). Paugus Mill Rd. (FR 68) branches north (sign) from Fowler's Mill Rd. 1.3 mi. east of NH 113A, and runs to a parking area at 0.7 mi., beyond which the road is closed to vehicles.

LIST OF TRAILS   MAP

THE TRAILS

Champney Falls Trail (WMNF)

This trail runs from the Kancamagus Highway, 11.5 mi. from NH 16 in Conway, to the Piper Trail in the flat saddle between Chocorua and the Three Sisters. Champney Falls are attractive, and the trail has moderate grades all the way.

Leaving the parking area, the trail soon crosses Twin Brook on a footbridge, turns right, and proceeds south with easy grades, mostly on an old logging road, to Champney Brook. At 1.4 mi. a loop path 0.4 mi. long diverges left to Pitcher Falls and Champney Falls. The main trail passes an outlook north, the loop path rejoins at 1.7 mi., and the steady ascent continues. At 2.4 mi. the trail reaches the first of several switchbacks, and at 3.0 mi. the Champney Falls Cutoff diverges left toward Middle Sister. Soon the Champney Falls Trail reaches the ledgy saddle, where there is an outlook on a side path right, then passes the junction left with the Middle Sister Trail, and in another 80 yd. ends at its junction with the Piper Trail, 0.6 mi. from the summit of Chocorua.

Champney Falls Trail (map 4:J9)
Distances from Kancamagus Highway

to Champney Falls loop: 1.4 mi., 1 hr.
to Piper Trail: 3.2 mi., 2 hr. 35 min.
to Mt. Chocorua summit (via Piper Trail): 3.8 mi. (6.1 km.), 3 hr. 5 min.

Champney Falls Cutoff

This short trail leads from the Champney Falls Trail, 3.0 mi. from the Kancamagus Highway, to the col between Middle Sister and First Sister, giving access to the fine views from the old tower site on Middle Sister. Leaving the Champney Falls Trail, it follows an old road past an outlook ledge, then swings right and soon reaches the Middle Sister Trail.

Champney Falls Cutoff (map 4:J9)
Distance from Champney Falls Trail
   to Middle Sister Trail: 0.3 mi. (0.5 km.), 15 min.

White Ledge Loop Trail (WMNF)

This loop trail to White Ledge has two entrance routes. The main one is at White Ledge Campground; the alternative one leaves NH 16 opposite Pine Knoll Camp, about 0.5 mi. northeast of White Ledge Campground, and follows an old town road 0.5 mi. to the east branch of the trail, 0.6 mi. from the campground.

The main trail diverges right from the main campground road and forks at 0.3 mi. The east branch goes right across a small brook, runs to the junction with the alternative route at 0.6 mi., soon bears left in an open area and climbs steadily to the height-of-land east of the main bluff of White Ledge at 1.3 mi. The trail now descends, and at 2.0 mi. it turns sharp left in an overgrown pasture and climbs moderately up the east end of White Ledge to the summit at 2.7 mi., where there is a good view east. The trail descends past an outlook to Chocorua, then turns sharp left at 3.7 mi. and reaches the loop junction at 4.1 mi.

White Ledge Loop Trail (map 4:J10)
Distances from White Ledge Campground
   to loop junction: 0.3 mi., 10 min.
   to White Ledge summit (via east branch): 2.7 mi., 2 hr. 5 min.
   to White Ledge summit (via west branch): 1.7 mi., 1 hr. 30 min.
   to White Ledge Campground (complete loop): 4.4 mi. (7.1 km.), 2 hr. 55 min.

Middle Sister Trail (WMNF)

This trail runs from NH 16 at the WMNF White Ledge Campground over the Three Sisters, and ends at the Champney Falls Trail in the saddle between the Sisters and Chocorua. It provides good views.

The trailhead is on the left branch of the campground road. Park in the parking lot at the campground picnic area. The trail diverges west from the left branch road 100 yd. south of the junction and follows a lumber road over the flat col between Chocorua and White Ledge. It crosses Hobbs Brook at 1.8 mi., in an area damaged by the December 1980 windstorm, then climbs more steeply to the col between the Three Sisters ridge and Blue Mtn. at 3.2 mi., where the trail turns sharp left and ascends the northeast spur of the Third Sister, with several good outlooks. At 4.1 mi. the Carter Ledge Trail enters on the left, and the Middle Sister Trail crosses the ledgy summit of Third Sister and a small dip beyond, then reaches the summit of the Middle Sister at 4.4 mi. The trail continues across ledges marked by paint, passes the Champney Falls Cutoff right, and continues ahead over First Sister to its terminus on the Champney Falls Trail. From here it is 80 yd. (left) to the Piper Trail, then 0.6 mi. to the summit of Mt. Chocorua.

Middle Sister Trail (map 4:J10-J9)
Distances from White Ledge Campground

to Middle Sister summit: 4.4 mi., 3 hr. 30 min.
to Champney Falls Trail: 4.9 mi. (7.9 km.), 3 hr. 50 min.

Carter Ledge Trail (WMNF)

This trail provides an attractive alternative route to Middle Sister from White Ledge Campground, or (via Nickerson Ledge Trail) from the Piper Trail. Carter Ledge, an interesting objective in its own right, is a fine open ledge, with views of Chocorua and one of three colonies of Jack Pine *(Pinus banksiana)* in the White Mtns.

Park in the picnic area parking space, and follow the left branch road in the campground 70 yd. beyond the beginning of Middle Sister Trail. Here the trail leaves the road and climbs moderately to the long southeast ridge of Carter Ledge, meeting the Nickerson Ledge Trail, which enters left at 2.0 mi. Soon the trail ascends a steep, gravelly slope, turns right at an outlook to Chocorua, passes through the Jack Pine stand and reaches the summit of the ledge at 2.8 mi. It passes through a sag, then works its way up the ledgy slope of Third Sister, steeply at times, and reaches the Middle Sister Trail 0.3 mi. northeast of Middle Sister.

Carter Ledge Trail (map 4:J10-J9)
Distances from White Ledge Campground
  to Nickerson Ledge Trail: 2.0 mi., 1 hr. 30 min.
  to Middle Sister Trail: 3.7 mi. (6.0 km.), 3 hr. 5 min.

Piper Trail (WMNF)
This popular trail to Chocorua from NH 16, first blazed by Joshua Piper, begins behind the Piper Trail Cabins and Restaurant (sign, fee for parking). It leads across an open field, enters the woods, and follows a logging road across the WMNF boundary at 0.6 mi. The Weetamoo Trail diverges left at 0.8 mi., and the Nickerson Ledge Trail diverges right at 1.4 mi. After crossing Chocorua River (a small brook at this point) at 2.0 mi., the trail then ascends moderately past a cleared outlook to Carter Ledge, goes over a series of switchbacks, stone steps, and paving, and at 3.1 mi. a spur path diverges left 0.2 mi. to Camp Penacook (open shelter, tent platform, water). The main trail turns sharp right and ascends, with more stone steps and paving, soon reaching open ledges with spectacular views to the north, east, and south. The Champney Falls Trail enters right at 3.9 mi., and in another 0.2 mi. the West Side Trail (sometimes considered, and signed as, a

part of the Liberty Trail) enters on the right. The Piper Trail, marked with yellow paint, continues over open ledges to the summit. In bad weather it may be safer to use the West Side and Brook trails to reach the summit, since the Piper Trail crosses a ledge at the foot of a minor northern crag which may be dangerous in wet or windy conditions.

Piper Trail (map 4:J10-J9)
Distances from NH 16
- *to* Nickerson Ledge Trail: 1.4 mi., 1 hr.
- *to* Chocorua River crossing: 2.0 mi., 1 hr. 25 min.
- *to* Camp Penacook spur trail: 3.1 mi., 2 hr. 25 min.
- *to* Champney Falls Trail: 3.9 mi., 3 hr. 10 min.
- *to* Mt. Chocorua summit: 4.5 mi. (7.2 km.), 3 hr. 35 min.

Nickerson Ledge Trail (WMNF)

This trail connects the Piper Trail with Carter Ledge Trail and Middle Sister, making possible loop hikes that include the attractive ledges on the northeast part of the mountain. It leaves the Piper Trail 1.4 mi. from NH 16 and climbs rather steeply 0.2 mi. to Nickerson Ledge, which has a restricted view of the summit of Chocorua, then continues with a gradual ascent to the Carter Ledge Trail 2.0 mi. above White Ledge Campground.

Nickerson Ledge Trail (map 4:J10)
Distance from Piper Trail
- *to* Carter Ledge Trail: 0.8 mi. (1.3 km.), 35 min.

Weetamoo Trail (CMC)

This trail connects the lower part of the Piper Trail, 0.8 mi. from NH 16, with the Hammond Trail well up on Bald Mtn., and gives access to the ledges of the south ridge of Chocorua from the Piper Trail.

The trail diverges left from the Piper Trail and crosses

Chocorua River at 0.4 mi., then leaves the river and crosses a logged area, passes a small brook (last sure water) at 1.0 mi., passes an outlook to Chocorua and reaches Weetamoo Rock, an immense boulder, at 1.7 mi. The trail ends at the Hammond Trail, 2.0 mi. from the summit of Mt. Chocorua.

Weetamoo Trail (map 4:J10-J9)
Distance from Piper Trail
   to Hammond Trail: 1.9 mi., 1 hr. 35 min.

Hammond Trail (CMC)

This trail provides a route up Bald Mtn., the ledgy south ridge of Mt. Chocorua. The trailhead is on a dirt road that leaves NH 16 on the left (west) 3.0 mi. north of the junction with NH 113 in Chocorua village, directly opposite a large boulder; parking is on the right 0.4 mi. from NH 16.

The trail leaves the parking area, crosses Stony Brook, passes the WMNF boundary, then recrosses Stony Brook. At 0.8 mi. the trail crosses a logging road, then climbs steadily to the crest of Bald Mtn. at 1.9 mi. It crosses a sag, then ascends along the ridge. At 2.1 mi. the Weetamoo Trail enters right, and the Hammond Trail passes over several humps to its end at the junction with the Liberty Trail 1.1 mi. from the summit of Mt. Chocorua.

Hammond Trail (map 4:J10-J9)
Distances from parking area off NH 16
   to Bald Mtn.: 1.9 mi., 1 hr. 45 min.
   to Liberty Trail: 3.0 mi., 2 hr. 40 min.

Liberty Trail (WMNF)

This is the easiest route to Chocorua from the southwest. It begins at the parking area just before the gate on Paugus Mill Rd. (FR 68). This is a very old path which was improved somewhat by James Liberty in 1887, and further developed as a toll bridle path by David Knowles and Newell Forrest in 1892. Knowles built the two-story Peak House in 1892, which was blown down in September 1915. The stone stable was rebuilt by the CMC in 1924 and named the Jim Liberty Shelter. This lasted till 1932, when the spring winds blew off the roof, and in 1934 the WMNF replaced it with an enclosed cabin with bunks.

The Liberty Trail follows a gated side road that branches right just before the gate on the main road (which continues to the Bolles and Brook trails), and ascends at a steady, moderate grade, mostly along the route of the former bridle path. It crosses Durrell Brook at 1.1 mi., and at 2.7 mi. it reaches the ridge top, where the Hammond Trail enters right. The Liberty Trail crosses a hump, descends into the sag beyond, then climbs to Jim Liberty Cabin at 3.3 mi., where a red-blazed side path leads right 0.1 mi. to a mediocre water source. The Liberty Trail swings to the left (west) at the foot of a ledge and follows the old bridle path, which was often blasted out of the rock. It circles around the southwest side of the cone with a moderate ascent and meets the Brook Trail on a ledge at 3.6 mi., 10 yd. before the Bee Line Trail enters the Brook Trail. The summit of Mt. Chocorua is 0.2 mi. farther via the Brook Trail. The summit can be avoided during bad weather by following the West Side Trail, which enters 25 yd. beyond the Bee Line Trail and runs north around the west side of the summit cone to the Piper Trail.

Liberty Trail (map 4:J9)
Distances from Paugus Mill Rd. parking area
to Hammond Trail: 2.7 mi., 2 hr. 10 min.
to Jim Liberty Cabin: 3.3 mi., 2 hr. 40 min.
to Brook Trail: 3.6 mi., 3 hr. 5 min.
to Mt. Chocorua summit (via Brook Trail): 3.9 mi. (6.2 km.), 3 hr. 20 min.

West Side Trail (WMNF)

This trail runs from the Piper Trail 0.4 mi. north of the summit of Chocorua to the ledge where the Liberty, Brook, and Bee Line trails join. It has easy grades and is well sheltered, and affords a route for avoiding the summit rocks in bad weather. It has been signed as the Liberty Trail at times in the past. It leaves the Piper Trail in a flat area north of the summit and circles the west side of the cone to the Brook Trail, 25 yd. above its junction with the Bee Line Trail.

West Side Trail (map 4:J9)

Distance from Piper Trail

    to Brook Trail: 0.5 mi. (0.7 km.), 20 min.

Brook Trail (CMC)

This trail runs from the parking area at the end of Paugus Mill Rd. (FR 68) to the summit of Chocorua. It was cut by the country people to avoid paying a toll on the Liberty Trail. High up, it ascends steep ledges with excellent views, but is more difficult than the Liberty Trail and potentially dangerous in wet or icy conditions. An excellent loop trip can be made by ascending the Brook Trail and descending the Liberty Trail.

From the parking area on Paugus Mill Rd., continue past the gate north on the gravel road. After 0.1 mi. the Bolles Trail diverges left, and at 0.4 mi., just before the bridge over Claybank Brook, the Brook Trail turns right off the gravel road. It follows the south bank of the brook, passes a junction left with the Bickford Path, and climbs well above the brook. At 1.8 mi. the trail returns to the brook at a tiny waterfall, and finally crosses it at 2.5 mi. The trail steepens, and the first ledge is reached at 3.0 mi. Now the trail climbs the steep, open ledges of the Farlow Ridge, where it is marked with cairns and yellow paint. At 3.4 mi. the Liberty

Trail comes in on the right, and the Bee Line Trail comes in 10 yd. beyond on the left on the same ledge. In about 25 yd. the West Side Trail, a bad weather summit bypass, turns left (north), and the Brook Trail climbs steeply east over the ledges, then swings northeast (left) to the junction where the Piper Trail enters left (sign). The two trails climb east to the summit through a small gully.

Brook Trail (map 4:J9)
Distances from Paugus Mill Rd. parking area
   to Claybank Brook crossing: 2.5 mi., 1 hr. 45 min.
   to Liberty Trail: 3.4 mi., 2 hr. 50 min.
   to Mt. Chocorua summit: 3.6 mi. (5.9 km.), 3 hr. 5 min.

Bee Line Trail (CMC)
This trail runs from the Old Paugus Trail on the south ridge of Mt. Paugus to the Brook Trail on the upper west ledges of Mt. Chocorua, linking the two summits almost by a bee line. On the upper part of Chocorua the trail is very rough, with poor footing, and there are steep ledges which may be difficult or dangerous when wet or icy.

The trail leaves the Brook Trail on a ledge below the summit of Chocorua, 10 yd. north of the junction of the Brook and Liberty trails. In 100 yd. it makes a sharp right turn on a ledge (follow with care), and descends very steeply, partly in the track of a slide. At 0.9 mi. the trail crosses a brook in a steep ravine, becomes somewhat less steep, recrosses the brook and follows it on an old logging road, and reaches the Bolles Trail at 1.9 mi. This point is 2.0 mi. from the Paugus Mill Rd. parking area via the Bolles Trail.

The Bee Line Trail now crosses Paugus Brook, enters the Sandwich Range Wilderness, and runs over a narrow ridge. At 2.2 mi. the Bee Line Cutoff departs left (southeast), and the Bee Line Trail crosses a small brook and climbs steeply up the side of the mountain, making some use of old lumber roads, to the Old Paugus Trail near the top of the ridge.

Bee Line Trail (map 4:J9)
Distances from Brook Trail/Liberty Trail junction
   to Bolles Trail: 1.9 mi., 1 hr.
   to Old Paugus Trail: 3.0 mi. (4.8 km.), 2 hr. 5 min.

Bee Line Cutoff (CMC)

This trail provides a shortcut to the Bee Line Trail to Mt. Paugus from the Paugus Mill Rd. parking area. It is almost entirely within the Sandwich Range Wilderness. It diverges northwest from the Bolles Trail 1.2 mi. from the parking area and follows an old lumber road to the Bee Line Trail, 0.2 mi. west of the junction of the Bee Line and Bolles trails.

Bee Line Cutoff (map 4:J9)
Distance from Bolles Trail
   to Bee Line Trail: 0.6 mi. (1.0 km.), 20 min.

Bolles Trail (WMNF)

This trail connects the Paugus Mill Rd. (FR 68) parking lot with the Champney Falls Trail parking lot on the Kancamagus Highway, passing between Mt. Chocorua and Mt. Paugus, and using old logging roads most of the way. It is named for Frank Bolles, who reopened a very old road in 1891 and called it the "Lost Trail." South of the height-of-land, the majority of the trail is in or near the Sandwich Range Wilderness.

The Bolles Trail diverges from the Brook Trail (which here is a gravel logging road) 0.1 mi. north of the Paugus Mill Rd. parking lot. At 0.2 mi. it crosses Paugus Brook (may be difficult at high water) and at 0.5 mi. the Old Paugus Trail and Bickford Path enter left. In 90 yd. the Bickford Path diverges right. Soon the Bolles Trail passes the huge Paugus Mill sawdust pile (left), and at 1.1 mi. the Bee Line Cutoff diverges left. The Bolles Trail now crosses two branches of Paugus Brook (avoid herd path on west bank at second brook, where bridge has been washed out of position). At 1.9 mi. the Bee Line Trail crosses, and at 2.6 mi. the Bolles Trail recrosses Paugus Brook, turns right in an old logging camp (trail requires care to follow here due to berry bush growth), and soon begins to climb more steeply through a sandy area to the height-of-land at 3.7 mi. The trail then descends steeply to Twin Brook, crosses it twelve times, and reaches the Kancamagus Highway just past the west end of the Champney Falls Trail parking lot.

Bolles Trail (map 4:J9)
Distances from Brook Trail
to Bickford Path/Old Paugus Trail: 0.5 mi., 20 min.
to Bee Line Trail: 1.9 mi., 1 hr. 10 min.
to Kancamagus Highway: 5.7 mi. (9.2 km.), 3 hr. 30 min.

Bickford Path (WODC)
This trail runs from NH 113A 1.1 mi. east of Wonalancet to the lower part of the Brook Trail, offering a walking route from Wonalancet to the Old Paugus, Bolles, and Brook trails to Mt. Chocorua and Mt. Paugus. The trail's blue blazes must be followed with care due to lack of an obvious footway.

The trail leaves NH 113A and ascends easily on an old logging road, passes behind two camps, and descends easily to a field with a private home at 0.7 mi. Turning left at the horse corral, it reenters the woods at the east edge of the field, soon enters the WMNF, climbs moderately to a ridge top, and descends on the other side. The Old Paugus Trail enters left 20 yd. west of Whitin Brook, and the two trails cross the brook and meet the Bolles Trail at 2.0 mi. The Bickford Path turns left (north) on the Bolles Trail for 90 yd., then turns right (east), crosses Paugus Brook, and soon reaches a logging road (road leads to right to Paugus Mill Rd. parking area). The path turns left and follows the road for about 0.1 mi., then turns right (turns poorly marked), descends easily, and crosses Claybank Brook to the Brook Trail, where the Bickford Path ends.

Bickford Path (map 4:K9-J9)
Distances from NH 113A
  to Bolles Trail: 2.0 mi., 1 hr. 15 min.
  to Brook Trail: 2.5 mi. (4.0 km.), 1 hr. 30 min.

Old Paugus Trail (CMC)

This trail runs to the summit of Mt. Paugus from the Bolles Trail 0.7 mi. from the Paugus Mill Rd. parking area. It is almost entirely within the Sandwich Range Wilderness. Portions of the trail are very steep and rough, with poor footing, and may be dangerous in wet or icy conditions.

The trail leaves the Bolles Trail along with the Bickford Path, crosses Whitin Brook, then Bickford Path diverges left 20 yd. beyond the brook. The Old Paugus Trail continues along Whitin Brook, crosses it at 0.7 mi., then turns right at 1.0 mi. as the Whitin Brook Trail continues straight ahead along the brook. The trail now climbs steeply, passes a junction left with the Big Rock Cave Trail at 1.3 mi., climbs a steep gully, then swings right along the base of a rock face, and climbs steadily through a spruce forest to the junction right with the Bee Line Trail at 2.1 mi. It then ascends sharply, passes an outlook right (sign), then eases up, passes the site of the former Old Shag Camp (now removed), crosses a small brook, and climbs to the south knob. Here the Old Paugus Trail ends and the Lawrence Trail continues ahead.

Old Paugus Trail (map 4:J9)
Distances from Bolles Trail
to Bee Line Trail: 2.1 mi., 1 hr. 50 min.
to Lawrence Trail: 2.8 mi. (4.5 km.), 2 hr. 30 min.

Whitin Brook Trail (CMC)

This trail runs from the Old Paugus Trail to the Cabin Trail and gives access to points in the vicinity of Paugus Pass from the Paugus Mill Rd. parking area. It must be followed with care, particularly at the crossings of Whitin Brook; some of the bridges over this brook are unsafe. It is almost entirely within the Sandwich Range Wilderness.

The trail continues along Whitin Brook where the Old Paugus Trail turns right upslope, 1.0 mi. above the junction of the Old Paugus and Bolles trails. In 0.2 mi. the Big Rock Cave Trail crosses, then the Whitin Brook Trail crosses the brook three times. After the last crossing, at 0.7 mi., the trail swings left away from the brook and climbs through spruce woods to the Cabin Trail, 0.4 mi. south of its junction with the Lawrence Trail.

Whitin Brook Trail (map 4:J9-J8)
Distance from Old Paugus Trail
to Cabin Trail: 1.6 mi. (2.5 km.), 1 hr. 15 min.

Big Rock Cave Trail (WODC)

This trail runs from the Cabin Trail 0.3 mi. from NH 113A over the flat ridge of Mt. Mexico to the Whitin Brook and Old Paugus trails. It provides easy access to Big Rock Cave, an interesting boulder cave that invites exploration.

Diverging right from the Cabin Trail, it ascends moderately on an old logging road which fades away to a trail, reaching the very flat summit of Mt. Mexico at 1.1 mi. and entering the Sandwich Range Wilderness. From here it descends moderately, then steeply, and passes Big Rock Cave (right) at 1.6 mi. It then crosses Whitin Brook (may be difficult at high water) and the Whitin Brook Trail at 1.7 mi., and climbs to its end at the Old Paugus Trail.

Big Rock Cave Trail (map 4:K8-J9)
Distances from Cabin Trail
  to Big Rock Cave: 1.6 mi., 1 hr. 10 min.
  to Old Paugus Trail: 2.1 mi. (3.4 km.), 1 hr. 35 min.

Cabin Trail (WODC)

This trail runs from NH 113A 0.5 mi. east of Wonalancet to the Lawrence Trail 0.3 mi. east of Paugus Pass. It starts on a driveway, passes a house, and at 0.3 mi. the Big Rock Cave Trail diverges right. The Cabin Trail ascends easily on a logging road over several small brooks to the height-of-land at 2.2 mi., where the Whitin Brook Trail enters right. The Cabin Trail stays to the east side of Whitin Ridge, passes two outlooks to Mt. Paugus, and ends at the Lawrence Trail just inside the Sandwich Range Wilderness.

Cabin Trail (map 4:K8-J8)
Distances from NH 113A
  to Whitin Brook Trail: 2.2 mi., 1 hr. 40 min.
  to Lawrence Trail: 2.7 mi. (4.3 km.), 2 hr.

Lawrence Trail (WODC)

This trail runs from the junction of the Old Mast Road and the Walden and Square Ledge trails, 2.0 mi. from the Ferncroft Rd. parking area (via the Old Mast Road), to the junction with the Old Paugus Trail on the south knob of Mt. Paugus. Sections of it are extremely steep and rough, with poor footing. It is entirely within the Sandwich Range Wilderness.

The trail leaves the multiple junction at the north end of the Old Mast Road, and descends slightly into Paugus Pass at 0.3 mi., where it is joined on the left (north) by the

Oliverian Brook Trail from the Kancamagus Highway and on the right (south) by the Kelley Trail from Ferncroft. The Lawrence Trail climbs to a knob at 0.6 mi. where the Cabin Trail enters right. It then descends to the southeast side of the ridge at the base of the Overhang, passes along the face of high, wooded cliffs, and ascends a very steep and rough slope to an outlook to Mt. Paugus at 0.9 mi. The trail then descends steeply into a hollow and crosses two small brooks. It climbs steeply again, crosses another brook, and continues at a moderate grade to the south knob of Mt. Paugus, where the Old Paugus Trail continues ahead.

Lawrence Trail (map 4:J8-J9)
Distance from Old Mast Road
   to Old Paugus Trail: 2.1 mi. (3.4 km.), 1 hr. 40 min.

Kelley Trail (WODC)

This trail runs from the Ferncroft Rd. parking area to the Lawrence and Oliverian Brook trails at Paugus Pass, through an interesting ravine. The upper part of the trail is rough, with poor footing and numerous slippery rocks.

It leaves the Ferncroft Rd. parking area and follows a gated gravel logging road (FR 337), bearing right where the Old Mast Road bears left. In 0.2 mi. the Gordon Path leaves right (sign), and at 0.5 mi. the Kelley Trail diverges left from the gravel road, crosses a branch of the road at a brook crossing, and follows the brook. In about 0.5 mi. the trail begins to climb above the brook, then returns to the brook at the top of a small cascade. It now crosses the brook (or its dry bed) five times, then climbs steeply out of a small box ravine and soon reaches Paugus Pass, just inside the Sandwich Range Wilderness.

Kelley Trail (map 4:K8-J8)
Distance from Ferncroft Rd. parking area
   to Lawrence Trail: 2.2 mi. (3.6 km.), 1 hr. 40 min.

Oliverian Brook Trail (WMNF)

This trail runs from the Kancamagus Highway 1.0 mi. west of Bear Notch Rd. to the Lawrence and Kelley trails at Paugus Pass. Much of the trail, particularly south of the Passaconaway Cutoff, is very wet.

The trail runs along the west side of Oliverian Brook, crosses an old railroad bed and a recent logging road, then joins an old railroad grade and follows it for nearly 0.5 mi. At 1.2 mi. it turns left off the railroad grade, and at 2.0 mi. the Passaconaway Cutoff diverges right (southwest). The Oliverian Brook Trail continues south and crosses a major tributary at 2.3 mi., then the main brook at 2.8 mi. Soon it crosses a side channel of the main brook to an island, then crosses the main channel, and reaches the junction right with the Square Ledge Branch Trail at 3.4 mi., shortly after the crossing of Square Ledge Brook. The trail then enters the Sandwich Range Wilderness, crosses Oliverian Brook, climbs up on the bank above the brook, then recrosses on a bridge and continues to climb along the brook to Paugus Pass.

Oliverian Brook Trail (map 4:J8)
Distances from Kancamagus Highway
  to Passaconaway Cutoff: 2.0 mi., 1 hr. 5 min.
  to Square Ledge Branch Trail: 3.4 mi., 2 hr.
  to Paugus Pass: 4.4 mi. (7.1 km.), 2 hr. 40 min.

Old Mast Road (WODC)

This trail runs from the Ferncroft Rd. parking area to the junction with the Walden, Square Ledge, and Lawrence trails 0.3 mi. west of Paugus Pass. The original road was reputedly built for hauling out the tallest timbers as masts for the British navy.

Leaving the parking area, the trail takes the left-hand road (the right is the Kelley Trail). At 0.1 mi. the Wonalancet Range Trail diverges left, just before the bridge over Spring Brook. Soon the WMNF boundary is crossed, and at 0.9 mi. the trail crosses a recent logging road, then soon enters another and follows it for 0.1 mi. The trail continues to climb, then levels, passes a small brook left, and ends at the multiple junction, just inside the Sandwich Range Wilderness.

Old Mast Road (map 4:K8-J8)
Distance from Ferncroft Rd. parking area
    to Lawrence Trail/Walden Trail/Square Ledge Trail: 2.0 mi. (3.2 km.), 1 hr. 35 min.

Dicey's Mill Trail (WODC)
This trail ascends Mt. Passaconaway from the Ferncroft Rd. parking area, with moderate grades and good footing. It was the earliest trail to be laid out on the mountain.

From the parking area, return to Ferncroft Rd. and turn right, following the gravel road past Squirrel Bridge, where the Blueberry Ledge Trail turns left. Pass a gate (not intended to keep out hikers) and a house, and continue on the road, which becomes a logging road. About 40 yd. before the trail enters the WMNF and Sandwich Range Wilderness at 0.8 mi., a marked path left crosses Wonalancet River to the Blueberry Ledge Cutoff on the opposite bank. Soon the trail swings right and steepens, then the grade becomes easy again and continues to the junction left with the Wiggin Trail at 1.9 mi. At 2.3 mi. the Dicey's Mill Trail crosses the river, passes a large boulder, and begins a long slabbing ascent along the side of a ridge, following an old logging road at a moderate grade through hardwoods, with occasional views of the Wonalancet Range. At the ridge top, at 3.7 mi., the Rollins Trail from Mt. Whiteface enters left. The Dicey's Mill Trail then climbs through a rough, wet section, crosses a small brook, and reaches the junction at 3.9 mi. where the East Loop continues straight. Here the Dicey's Mill Trail turns left, passes Camp Rich (25 yd. left on a side trail), and climbs, steeply at times, to join the Walden Trail. The summit and south outlook are 40 yd. right on a spur path, while the Walden Trail leads 90 yd. to the east outlook.

Dicey's Mill Trail (map 4:K8-J8)
Distances from Ferncroft Rd. parking area
to Wiggin Trail: 1.9 mi., 1 hr. 20 min.
to Rollins Trail: 3.7 mi., 2 hr. 55 min.
to Mt. Passaconaway summit: 4.6 mi. (7.3 km.), 3 hr. 45 min.

East Loop (WODC)
This very short trail begins at the Dicey's Mill Trail near the small brook, just below Camp Rich, and descends slightly to the base of the final ascent of Mt. Passaconaway on the Walden Trail. It is entirely within the Sandwich Range Wilderness.

East Loop (map 4:J8)
Distance from Dicey's Mill Trail
to Walden Trail: 0.2 mi. (0.4 km.), 10 min.

Walden Trail (WODC)
This trail ascends Mt. Passaconaway from the junction of the Old Mast Road and the Square Ledge and Lawrence trails via the southeast ridge. It is a more interesting but longer and rougher route to Passaconaway from Ferncroft Rd. (via the Old Mast Road) than the direct Dicey's Mill Trail. It is almost entirely within the Sandwich Range Wilderness.

The trail runs northwest from the Old Mast Road up a very steep slope with poor footing. At the top of the shoulder the grade eases and the trail crosses a minor knob and a

sag, then climbs again and passes a side path that leads
right 20 yd. to a view of Mt. Washington. At 0.7 mi. it
passes the large boulder that is the true summit of Mt.
Hedgehog, and at 0.9 mi. the Wonalancet Range Trail enters left. The Walden Trail now descends steeply to a col,
follows along a brookbed (possible water) for 50 yd., then
climbs very steeply again over the next subpeak, descends
easily to a col, and climbs gradually to the junction right
with the Square Ledge Trail at 2.1 mi. The trail now starts
to slab around the south face of the mountain, and at 2.2
mi. the East Loop continues straight where the Walden
Trail swings right and climbs steeply to the east outlook.
The junction with the Dicey's Mill Trail is 90 yd. beyond
the outlook, and the summit is 40 yd. left from that junction. Between the east outlook and the Dicey's Mill Trail a
side path descends right 0.3 mi. to a fine north outlook.

Walden Trail (map 4:J8)
Distances from Old Mast Road
  to Square Ledge Trail: 2.1 mi., 1 hr. 40 min.
  to Mt. Passaconaway summit: 2.8 mi. (4.5 km.), 2 hr. 30
    min.

Wonalancet Range Trail (WODC)
This trail ascends from the Old Mast Road, 0.1 mi. from
the Ferncroft Rd. parking area, over the Wonalancet Range
to the Walden Trail west of Mt. Hedgehog. There are good
views from ledges on the way, and the trail offers an alternative, but longer and rougher, route to Mt. Passaconaway
from Ferncroft.

The trail diverges left from the Old Mast Road just
before the bridge over Spring Brook, and crosses a logging
road on a steep bank, runs through a flat area, then passes
a logged area, crossing a gravel road at 0.7 mi. At 1.3 mi. it
starts to climb steeply, crosses a fine outlook ledge, then

swings around to the south edge of Mt. Wonalancet and
turns north to cross the summit at 1.8 mi. The trail descends to a col, entering the Sandwich Range Wilderness,
and then climbs to the summit of Mt. Hibbard, where there
is an outlook west at 2.7 mi. It continues to ascend moderately, then descends slightly to the junction with the
Walden Trail.

Wonalancet Range Trail (map 4:K8-J8)
Distances from Old Mast Road
> *to* Mt. Wonalancet summit: 1.8 mi., 1 hr. 40 min.
> *to* Walden Trail: 3.2 mi. (5.1 km.), 2 hr. 40 min.

Passaconaway Cutoff (WMNF)

This trail provides the shortest route to Mt. Passacona-
way from the north, running from the Oliverian Brook
Trail, 2.0 mi. from the Kancamagus Highway, to the
Square Ledge Trail (and thence to the summit via the
Walden Trail). Leaving the Oliverian Brook Trail, the cut-
off follows an old logging road, crosses a brook at 0.5 mi.,
then runs above the brook to the junction with the Square
Ledge Trail.

Passaconaway Cutoff (map 4:J8)
Distance from Oliverian Brook Trail
> *to* Square Ledge Trail: 1.7 mi. (2.8 km.), 1 hr. 25 min.

Distance from Kancamagus Highway
> *to* Mt. Passaconaway summit (via Oliverian Brook,
> Square Ledge, and Walden trails): 5.2 mi. (8.3 km.), 4
> hr.

Square Ledge Trail (WODC)

This trail runs from the junction of the Old Mast Road
and the Walden and Lawrence trails, over Square Ledge, to

the Walden Trail just below the summit cone of Mt. Passaconaway. It is within the Sandwich Range Wilderness from the multiple junction to the Passaconaway Cutoff.

From the multiple junction, it descends from the height-of-land, crossing two small brooks, and at 0.9 mi., just before the second brook, the Square Ledge Branch Trail diverges right (east) to join the Oliverian Brook Trail. A short distance farther, the main trail makes a sharp turn left (west) to ascend the ledge. It bears east for a short distance, then climbs very steeply to the shoulder. A spur leads off the trail 20 yd. to a ledge with a fine view across the valley. Leaving the ledge, the trail ascends to the wooded summit of the ledge, and then descends to the junction right with the Passaconaway Cutoff at 1.9 mi. The Square Ledge Trail turns sharp left, crosses a dip, passes through an old logging camp site, and crosses a small slide. The trail now becomes steep as it climbs to the Walden Trail.

Square Ledge Trail (map 4:J8)
Distances from Old Mast Road/Lawrence Trail/Walden Trail

to Passaconaway Cutoff: 1.9 mi., 1 hr. 15 min.
to Walden Trail: 2.6 mi. (4.2 km.), 1 hr. 55 min.

Square Ledge Branch Trail (WODC)

This short trail begins on the Oliverian Brook Trail 3.4 mi. from the Kancamagus Highway, and runs to the Square Ledge Trail below the steep section that ascends the ledge. It is used to make a loop over Square Ledge from the Kancamagus Highway.

Square Ledge Branch Trail (map 4:J8)
Distance from Oliverian Brook Trail
to Square Ledge Trail: 0.5 mi. (0.8 km.), 25 min.

UNH Trail (WMNF)

This loop trail to the ledges of Hedgehog Mtn. begins on the south side of the Kancamagus Highway 0.2 mi. east of the WMNF Passaconaway Campground. It offers fine views for a modest effort. It was named for the UNH Forestry Camp which was formerly located nearby.

The trail follows a logging road from the highway 0.1 mi. south to a loop junction. The left branch follows a logging road, climbing moderately, and crosses a small brook at 1.6 mi. The trail shortly swings left to a view north and east, then bears right to reach the east ledges at 2.1 mi., with fine views south and east. The trail then runs along the top of the cliffs on the south face, enters the woods under the steep, ledgy south side of the main peak, and bears gradually toward the north onto the west slope of the peak, which it climbs in a short series of switchbacks to the summit of Hedgehog Mtn. at 3.0 mi. The trail then descends steadily, and makes a left turn at 3.7 mi., where a side path leads 60 yd. right to Allen's Ledge and its restricted view. The main trail descends to a logging road, turns right on it, and follows it to the loop junction.

UNH Trail (map 4:J8)
Distances from Kancamagus Highway

> to east ledges: 2.1 mi., 1 hr. 40 min.
> to Hedgehog Mtn. summit: 3.0 mi., 2 hr. 15 min.
> to Kancamagus Highway (complete loop): 4.9 mi. (7.9 km.), 3 hr. 15 min.

Mount Potash Trail (WMNF)

This trail ascends to the open ledges of Mt. Potash from the Downes Brook Trail, 0.2 mi. from the Kancamagus Highway almost directly opposite the entrance to the Passaconaway Campground.

The trail turns sharp right off the Downes Brook Trail, heads generally southwest, and crosses Downes Brook (may be difficult) at 0.1 mi. After crossing the brook, the trail turns sharp left and soon crosses a logging road. At 0.9 mi. it turns sharp left and climbs to a fine outlook ledge at 1.2 mi., then turns sharp right into the woods, and continues to the summit. The route over the open ledges below the summit is marked with yellow paint. In descending, use caution in following the marked route on the rock slabs just below the summit.

Mount Potash Trail (map 4:J8)
Distance from Downes Brook Trail
  to Mt. Potash summit: 1.7 mi., 1 hr. 40 min.

Rollins Trail (WODC)

This trail runs along the high ridge that connects Mt. Whiteface to Mt. Passaconaway. It begins on the Downes Brook Trail at Camp Shehadi, in the col between the true summit and the open south summit of Whiteface, and ends on the Dicey's Mill Trail 0.2 mi. below Camp Rich. On the ridge of Mt. Whiteface some sections are steep and rough. It is entirely within the Sandwich Range Wilderness.

From the Downes Brook Trail in the col, it climbs north rather steeply, then runs along the ridge crest to the true summit (no marking) of Mt. Whiteface at 0.2 mi. It continues along the narrow ridge, with outlooks to the east across the Bowl, descending gradually with occasional steep pitches to the Whiteface–Passaconaway col. The trail then slabs onto the south face of Passaconaway, ascends slightly, and meets the Dicey's Mill Trail.

Rollins Trail (map 4:J8)
Distance from Downes Brook Trail
  to Dicey's Mill Trail: 2.3 mi. (3.7 km.), 1 hr. 15 min.

Blueberry Ledge Trail (WODC)

This trail, which was opened in 1899, ascends Mt. White-face—ending on the lower south summit—from the Fern-croft Rd. parking area. The trail is very scenic, but the upper part is steep, and though wooden steps have been placed and rock steps blasted, it is still difficult, particu-larly on the descent, and is dangerous in icy conditions.

From the parking area, return to Ferncroft Rd. and follow it to Squirrel Bridge at 0.3 mi., where the Dicey's Mill Trail continues straight ahead. The Blueberry Ledge Trail turns left across the bridge and follows a private gravel road, avoiding driveways, then diverges left into the woods where the road curves right. Here, at 0.5 mi., the Pasture Path to Mt. Katherine leaves left. In 0.1 mi. the trail joins an old road, and the Blueberry Ledge Cutoff diverges right to follow the bank of Wonalancet River. The trail crosses into the WMNF and Sandwich Range Wilder-ness, and at 0.9 mi. it continues straight where the McCril-lis Path to Whiteface Intervale Rd.—not to be confused with the McCrillis Trail to Mt. Whiteface—follows the old road sharp left. The Blueberry Ledge Trail passes through a flat area, ascends moderately, and at 1.6 mi. reaches the bottom of the ledges (views very limited) and ascends to the top of the ledges, where there is a view of the Ossipee Range. The trail reenters the woods, and the Blueberry Ledge Cutoff immediately rejoins right at 2.0 mi. It climbs gently through open hardwoods and then rises steeply past Wonalancet Outlook to the top of the ridge, drops slightly into a hollow, then ascends slightly to a junction with the Wiggin Trail on the right at 3.2 mi. Now the trail climbs moderately, then swings sharp right at an outlook at 3.6 mi., climbs a ledge by means of wooden steps, and contin-ues along the steep, rough, rocky ridge, with several excel-lent viewpoints. At the top of the ridge it passes a spur path to Camp Heermance, then joins the Downes Brook and

McCrillis trails just north of the ledges of the lower south summit. The true summit is 0.3 mi. farther north via the Downes Brook and Rollins trails.

Blueberry Ledge Trail (map 4:K8-J8)
Distances from Ferncroft Rd. parking area

to Blueberry Ledge Cutoff, upper junction: 2.0 mi., 1 hr. 30 min.

to McCrillis Trail/Downes Brook Trail: 3.9 mi. (6.2 km.), 3 hr. 25 min.

Blueberry Ledge Cutoff (WODC)

This trail begins and ends on the Blueberry Ledge Trail, and provides a walk along the Wonalancet River as an alternative to the viewless ledges. It is equal in distance, but somewhat rougher than the parallel section of the Blueberry Ledge Trail.

It leaves the Blueberry Ledge Trail 0.6 mi. from the Ferncroft Rd. parking area, and descends slightly to the river bank. At 0.3 mi. the Dicey's Mill Trail lies just across the river; an old logging road crosses the river at this point and the Blueberry Ledge Cutoff follows it upstream into the Sandwich Range Wilderness. The trail soon climbs a small ridge and returns to the bank high above the brook, then swings away from the brook, meets and follows a small tributary, then swings right and climbs steeply to the bottom of the upper ledge. Marked by cairns and paint it climbs parallel to the Blueberry Ledge Trail, enters the woods at the top of the ledge, then swings left to meet the Blueberry Ledge Trail.

Blueberry Ledge Cutoff (map 4:K8)
Distances from Blueberry Ledge Trail, lower junction

to Blueberry Ledge Trail, upper junction: 1.4 mi. (2.3 km.), 1 hr. 10 min.

Wiggin Trail (WODC)

This trail, cut in 1895 and nicknamed "The Fire Escape," connects the Dicey's Mill Trail 1.9 mi. from the Ferncroft Rd. parking area with the Blueberry Ledge Trail just below the upper ledges. It is steep and rough, and lies entirely within the Sandwich Range Wilderness.

Leaving the Dicey's Mill Trail, it crosses Wonalancet River (may be difficult at high water), bears left and ascends a little knoll, crosses a small brook, and bears right. It tends to angle to the right as it climbs. Eventually it reaches the Blueberry Ledge Trail just north of a small hollow.

Wiggin Trail (map 4:J8)
Distance from Dicey's Mill Trail
   to Blueberry Ledge Trail: 1.1 mi. (1.8 km.), 1 hr. 15 min.

McCrillis Trail (WMNF)

This trail ascends Mt. Whiteface—ending at the lower south summit—from the Flat Mountain Pond Trail (see Section 7), 2.0 mi. from Whiteface Intervale Rd. It is steep and rough, but sheltered, and entirely within the Sandwich Range Wilderness. Do not confuse this trail with the McCrillis Path, which runs from Whiteface Intervale Rd. to the Blueberry Ledge Trail.

Leaving the Flat Mountain Pond Trail on the east bank of Whiteface River, it ascends a bank, then runs east nearly level to intersect the former route, an old logging road, at 0.4 mi. Turning left on this road, it climbs moderately, passing through a wet area, and at 2.0 mi. begins to climb steeply. At 2.6 mi. it passes the first of several outlooks, some of which provide good views onto the "white face." The trail reenters the woods, climbs steeply again, and finally climbs along the edge of the southwest ledges (use caution) to the Downes Brook and Blueberry Ledge trails

just north of the ledges of the lower south summit. The
true summit is 0.3 mi. farther north via the Downes Brook
and Rollins trails. (Descending, walk from the highest rock
southwest along the edge of the ledges.)

McCrillis Trail (map 4:K8-J8)
Distances from Flat Mountain Pond Trail
  to base of steep climb: 2.0 mi., 1 hr. 35 min.
  to Downes Brook Trail/Blueberry Ledge Trail: 3.2 mi.
  (5.1 km.), 3 hr.

McCrillis Path (WODC)
This trail follows old roads from the Blueberry Ledge
Trail, 0.9 mi. from the Ferncroft Rd. parking area, to
Whiteface Intervale Rd. Do not confuse it with the McCrillis Trail to Mt. Whiteface. Its grades are mostly easy. It
leaves the Blueberry Ledge Trail left, following the old
road, and climbs to the height-of-land. Tilton Spring Path
leaves left at 0.2 mi., there is a small cellar hole on the right
at 0.8 mi., and the trail enters recent logging at 1.1 mi. A
branch road enters on the right at 1.3 mi., just across
Tewksberry Brook (eastbound, bear right across brook),
and at 2.1 mi. the road reaches the edge of a very wet open
meadow (markings end at a faded old sign 30 yd. back).
Turn right on a gravel road and follow it to a gravel pit,
bear left, turn left on another gravel road at an intersection, and reach Whiteface Intervale Rd. just east of Whiteface Auto Body. The trailhead for the Flat Mountain Pond
Trail is 0.6 mi. to the right (west, then south).

McCrillis Path (map 4:K8)
Distance from Blueberry Ledge Trail
  to Whiteface Intervale Rd.: 2.3 mi. (3.8 km.), 1 hr. 15
  min.

Downes Brook Trail (WMNF)

This trail ascends Mt. Whiteface—ending at the lower south summit—from the Kancamagus Highway almost directly opposite Passaconaway Campground. It crosses Downes Brook ten times, and a few crossings may be difficult at high water.

Leaving the Kancamagus Highway, the trail follows an old logging road along Downes Brook. At 0.2 mi. the Mount Potash Trail diverges right, and at 0.7 mi. the trail makes the first of four crossings of Downes Brook in a span of 0.6 mi. At 2.2 mi. it crosses an extensive gravel outwash, crosses the main brook twice more, and passes through an old logging camp at 2.9 mi. After three more crossings, there are views of the slides on the steep slope of Mt. Whiteface across the valley, and the trail crosses the brook for the last time in the flat col between Sleeper Ridge and Mt. Whiteface. Here, at 5.1 mi., just before a swampy area, the Sleeper Trail (see Section 7) leaves right, and the Downes Brook Trail turns left and climbs moderately to the col between the true summit and the bare south summit of Mt. Whiteface at 6.0 mi. Here, at Camp Shehadi, the Rollins Trail leaves left (north), passing over the true summit of Whiteface at 0.2 mi., and continuing toward Mt. Passaconaway. The Downes Brook Trail turns right, climbs a short, steep pitch, and soon ends at the junction with the Blueberry Ledge and McCrillis trails just north of the bare ledges of the south summit.

Downes Brook Trail (map 4:J8)
Distances from Kancamagus Highway
to Sleeper Trail junction: 5.1 mi., 3 hr. 40 min.
to McCrillis Trail/Blueberry Ledge Trail: 6.1 mi. (9.8 km.), 4 hr. 25 min.

Shorter Paths in the Ferncroft Area (WODC)

These trails are not as well-beaten as the more important paths, and must be followed with care. The Gordon Path (1.0 mi.) runs from the Kelley Trail 0.2 mi. from the Ferncroft Rd. parking area to NH 113A, 0.3 mi. west of the trailhead for the Cabin and Big Rock Cave trails. The Pasture Path (1.1 mi.) runs from the Blueberry Ledge Trail 0.5 mi. from the Ferncroft Rd. parking area, past Tilton Spring at 0.6 mi., to the summit of Mt. Katherine, a broad ledge with restricted views. The Red Path (0.6 mi.) runs from the Wonalancet post office to Tilton Spring. The Tilton Spring Path (0.9 mi.), rather difficult to follow at times, runs from Tilton Spring to the McCrillis Path 0.2 mi. from the Blueberry Ledge Trail.

The Carter and Baldface Ranges

This section covers the Carter–Moriah Range, the Baldface Range, the valley of the Wild River, which lies between them, and the lower mountains on the long ridges which extend south from the two major ranges. The major peaks in the area are: in the Carter–Moriah Range, Wildcat Mtn., Carter Dome, Mt. Hight, South Carter Mtn., Middle Carter Mtn., Mt. Moriah, and Shelburne Moriah Mtn.; in the Baldface Range, North Baldface, South Baldface, West Royce Mtn., and East Royce Mtn.; in the southern part, Black Mtn., North and South Doublehead, Kearsarge North, and Black Cap. The area is bounded on the west by NH 16, on the north by US 2, and on the east and south by ME 113/NH 113 (which crosses the state line several times). Many trails in this section coincide with or intersect cross-country ski trails, and care must be taken to distinguish one from the other. Almost the entire area is covered by the AMC Carter–Mahoosuc map (map 7); the exception is the Green Hills of Conway range at the far south end of the region, which is covered by the USGS North Conway quad.

In this section the Appalachian Trail begins at NH 16 opposite Pinkham Notch Camp and follows the Lost Pond, Wildcat Ridge, Nineteen-Mile Brook, Carter–Moriah, Kenduskeag, and Rattle River trails to US 2 east of Gorham. It crosses the summits of Wildcat Mtn., Carter Dome, Mt. Hight, South Carter Mtn., and Middle Carter Mtn., and near the summit of Mt. Moriah.

GEOGRAPHY

The Carter–Moriah Range would be a great deal more prominent among White Mtn. ranges were it not for those neighbors which rise 1500 ft. higher across Pinkham

Notch. On a ridge about 10 mi. long there are eight significant peaks over 4000 ft., and the wild and spectacular Carter Notch. Mt. Hight and Shelburne Moriah Mtn. command the finest views in the range, while those from Carter Dome and Mt. Moriah are also excellent. To the east the range overlooks the broad, forested valley of the Wild River and the rocky peaks of the Baldface group, and far beyond lies the Atlantic which reflects the sun on the southeast horizon behind Sebago Lake on clear midmornings.

Wildcat Mtn. is the most southerly mountain in the range. Of its numerous summits, the highest is the one nearest to Carter Notch; its five most prominent summits are designated, from east to west: A Peak (4422 ft.), B Peak (4330 ft.), C Peak (4298 ft.), D Peak (4010 ft.), and E Peak (4041 ft.). The mountain is heavily wooded, but there are magnificent outlook ledges on the Wildcat Ridge Trail west of E Peak, a lookout tower with extensive views on D Peak near the top of the Wildcat Ski Area, a good view east to the Baldface area from C Peak, and fine views straight down into Carter Notch from A Peak.

Carter Notch, the deep cleft between Carter Dome and Wildcat Mtn., includes some of the finest scenery in this region. In the notch are the two small, beautiful Carter Lakes. The actual notch (3388 ft.) is north of the lakes, but the Rampart, a barrier of rocks, rises on the south side, so that the lakes are totally enclosed and their outlet is forced to run underground. Above the lakes the impressive cliffs of Wildcat Mtn. rise vertically nearly 1000 ft. to the west, and to the east Carter Dome rises steeply, with the immense boulder called Pulpit Rock jutting out above the notch. Large sections of the cliffs on each side have fallen into the notch to form caves that are interesting to explore, and where ice sometimes remains well through the summer. A rough trail over the Rampart leaves the Wildcat River Trail about 100 yd. south of Carter Notch Hut and runs east over the huge rocks, where there is a good view toward Jackson and many boulder-caves that invite exploration (use caution).

Carter Dome (4832 ft.) once bore a fire tower on its flat, scrub-fringed summit. There are excellent views in most directions from open areas in the vicinity of the summit. Mt. Hight (4675 ft.) is a bare rock peak with the best views in the range. South Carter Mtn. (4430 ft.) is wooded with no views. Middle Carter Mtn. (4610 ft.) is wooded, but there are good outlooks from various points along its ridge crest, including a good view of the Presidentials 70 yd. north of the summit. North Carter Mtn. (4530 ft.) has views from its summit and from ledges along the ridge north and south of the summit; the best views are east to the Baldface Range. Imp Mtn. (3730 ft.) is a trailless north spur of North Carter. Imp Profile (3165 ft.) is a fine cliff on a west spur of North Carter. The profile is best seen from the Pinkham B (Dolly Copp) Rd. at the monument marking the site of the Dolly Copp house.

Mt. Moriah (4049 ft.) has fine views in all directions from its ledgy summit block. Mt. Surprise (2194 ft.) is a northwest spur of Moriah that offers restricted views. Mt. Evans (1443 ft.) is a low north spur of the Moriah group which, for comparatively little effort, affords fine views of Mt. Washington and the Northern Peaks and good views up and down the Androscoggin River and across to the Mahoosuc Range. Shelburne Moriah Mtn. (3735 ft.) offers magnificent views—surpassed in this range only by Mt. Hight—from acres of flat ledges at the summit and outlooks on its southwest ridge.

The Baldface–Royce Range extends southwest from Evans Notch, between the Wild River and the Cold River. The summits are relatively low, but so are the valleys, and thus the mountains rise impressively high above their bases. The highest peaks in the range are North Baldface (3591 ft.)

and South Baldface (3569 ft.); their upper slopes were swept by fire in 1903 and the resulting great expanses of open ledge make the circuit over these peaks one of the finest trips in the White Mtns. With Eagle Crag (3030 ft.), a northeast buttress, these peaks enclose a cirquelike valley on their east. To the southwest are Sable Mtn. (3490 ft.) and Chandler Mtn. (3329 ft.), wooded and trailless, and to the southeast is Eastman Mtn. (2936 ft.), which affords fine views from its ledgy summit.

A ridge descends northeast from Eagle Crag over Mt. Meader (2782 ft.), which has ledgy outlooks, to the Basin Rim, where there are fine views from the brink of a cliff, then ascends to the Royces. West Royce Mtn. (3210 ft.), with good views to the east and southeast from a ledge near the summit, is located in NH, and East Royce Mtn. (3114 ft.), with good views in nearly all directions, is in ME; the state line crosses slightly to the east of the col between them.

A number of lower mountains rise from the ridges which extend south from the main ranges. Spruce Mtn. (2272), which is trailless, and Eagle Mtn. (1615 ft.), are small peaks on a south ridge of Wildcat Mtn. Eagle Mtn. has a path and views from the summit. Black Mtn. (3303 ft.), which lies across Perkins Notch from Carter Dome, is a long ridge with seven summits (more or less). Only the southernmost summit, the Knoll (1910 ft.), and a knob (2758 ft.) in the middle of the ridge, offer good views. North Doublehead (3050 ft.), with a cabin on the summit and good outlooks east and west near the summit, and South Doublehead (2938 ft.), with good views from several ledges, form a small, sharp ridge southeast of Black Mtn. Southwest of Doublehead is the low range composed of Thorn Mtn. (2287 ft.) and Tin Mtn (2030 ft.); the former trail on Thorn Mtn. has been closed. East of Doublehead lie the valleys of Slippery Brook and the East Branch of the Saco. In the valley of Slippery Brook is Mountain Pond, a crescent-shaped body of water about three-quarters of a mile long by half a mile wide, entirely surrounded by woods and overlooked by Baldface, Mt. Shaw, and Doublehead.

Kearsarge North (3268 ft.), sometimes called Mt. Pequawket, rises above Intervale. The summit bears an abandoned fire tower that is in good condition, and the views are magnificent in all directions; this is one of the finest viewpoints in the White Mtns. Bartlett Mtn. (2661 ft.) is a shoulder extending westward toward Intervale; it has no trails, but has a number of ledges that invite exploration. Running south from Kearsarge North are the Green Hills of Conway: Hurricane Mtn. (2101 ft.), Black Cap (2370 ft.), Peaked Mtn. (1734 ft.), Middle Mtn. (1850 ft.), Cranmore Mtn. (1690 ft.), and Rattlesnake Mtn. (1590 ft.). Only Hurricane Mtn., Black Cap, and Peaked Mtn. have trails, although Cranmore Mtn. can be ascended via ski trails; all four, especially Black Cap and Peaked Mtn., have fine views. There is a range of trailless hills extending northeast from Kearsarge North, of which the most prominent is Mt. Shaw (2566 ft.).

HUTS, SHELTERS, AND CAMPING

Carter Notch Hut (AMC)

The AMC constructed this stone hut in 1914. It is located at 3288 ft. elevation, about 60 yd. south of the smaller lake, at the southern terminus of the Nineteen-Mile Brook Trail and the northern terminus of the Wildcat River Trail. The hut, with two bunkhouses, accommodates forty. It is open from mid-June to mid-September, and in the winter on a caretaker basis.

For current information and schedule, contact Reservation Secretary, Pinkham Notch Camp, Box 298, Gorham, NH 03581 (603-466-2727).

CAMPING

Restricted Use Areas

The WMNF has established a number of Restricted Use Areas (RUA's) where camping and wood or charcoal fires are prohibited from 1 May to 1 November. The specific areas are under continual review, and areas are added to or subtracted from the list in order to provide the greatest amount of protection to areas subject to damage by excessive camping, while imposing the lowest level of restrictions possible. A general list of RUA's follows, but one should obtain a map of current RUA's from the WMNF.

(1) No camping is permitted above treeline (where trees are less than 8 ft. tall). The point where the restricted area begins is marked on most trails with small signs, but the absence of such signs should not be construed as proof of the legality of a site. The area around the summit of Carter Dome is under this restriction.

(2) No camping is permitted within one-quarter mile of most facilities such as huts, cabins, shelters, or tentsites, except at the facility itself. In this section, only Carter Notch Hut and Imp Campsite, plus the area around Zeta Pass, have this restriction. Tent camping is permitted at other shelters and cabins.

(3) No camping is permitted within 200 ft. of certain trails. In 1986, designated trails included the Lost Pond Trail.

Established Trailside Campsites

Imp Campsite (AMC) is located on a spur path from the Carter–Moriah Trail between Moriah and North Carter. There is a shelter and tentsites. In summer there is a caretaker, and a fee is charged. Water is found in a nearby brook.

Rattle River Shelter (WMNF) is located on the Rattle River Trail 1.7 mi. from US 2.

Spruce Brook Shelter (WMNF) is located on the Wild River Trail about 3.2 mi. from Wild River Campground.

Perkins Notch Shelter (WMNF) is located on the southeast side of Wild River, just south of the No-Ketchum Pond, with bunk space for six.

Blue Brook Shelter (WMNF) is located on the Black Angel Trail (and a branch trail connecting to the Basin Trail) 0.3 mi. east of Rim Junction.

Baldface Shelter (WMNF) is located on the Baldface Circle Trail, just below the ledges on South Baldface. The water source near the shelter may not be reliable.

Province Pond Shelter (WMNF) is located on the Province Brook Trail at Province Pond.

Mountain Pond Shelter (WMNF) is located on the Mountain Pond Loop Trail at Mountain Pond.

Doublehead Cabin (WMNF) is located at the summit of North Doublehead, with bunks for eight. There is no water nearby.

Black Mountain Cabin (WMNF) is located on the Black Mountain Ski Trail. It has bunks for eight. There is no water near the cabin or on the trail.

LIST OF TRAILS   MAP

Trails on Ridge and West Slopes of Carter Range

Wildcat Ridge Trail	7:G9-F10
Lost Pond Trail	7:F9-G9
Square Ledge Trail	7:F9-F10
Thompson Falls Trail	7:F10
Carter–Moriah Trail	7:E10-F10
Nineteen-Mile Brook Trail	7:F10
Carter Dome Trail	7:F10
Imp Trail	7:F10

| North Carter Trail | 7:F10 |
| Stony Brook Trail | 7:E10-F11 |

Trails on Ridge and North Slopes of Moriah Group

Kenduskeag Trail	7:E11-E12
Rattle River Trail	7:E11
Mount Evans Path	7:E11
Shelburne Trail	7:E12-F12

Trails of the Wild River Valley

Wild River Trail	7:F12-G10
Hastings Trail	7:E13-E12
Highwater Trail	7:E13-F11
Burnt Mill Brook Trail	7:F12
Moriah Brook Trail	7:F12-F11
Black Angel Trail	7:F12-F10
Basin Trail	7:F12
Eagle Link	7:F11-F12

Trails on East Side of Baldface–Royce Range

Royce Trail	7:F12
Royce Connector Trail	7:F12
East Royce Trail	7:F13-F12
Laughing Lion Trail	7:F12
Basin Rim Trail	7:F12
Mount Meader Trail	7:G12-F12
Meader Ridge Trail	7:F12
Baldface Circle Trail	7:G12
Bicknell Ridge Trail	7:G12
Baldface Knob Trail	7:G12
Eastman Mountain Trail	7:G12
Slippery Brook Trail	7:G12-G11
Bradley Brook Trail [abandoned]	

Trails in the East Branch Region

Mountain Pond Loop Trail	7:G11
East Branch Trail	7:H11-G11
Bald Land Trail	7:G11

THE TRAILS

Wildcat Ridge Trail (AMC)

This trail runs from the Glen Ellis Falls parking lot on NH 16, over the numerous summits of Wildcat Mtn., to the Nineteen-Mile Brook Trail 0.3 mi. north of Carter Notch Hut. It is more commonly entered by the Lost Pond Trail from Pinkham Notch Camp, which avoids the often difficult crossing of the Ellis River; from the Lost Pond Trail to Carter Notch it is a part of the Appalachian Trail. The sections from the Lost Pond Trail to E Peak and from A Peak to Carter Notch are very steep and rough, and there are several ups and downs along the trail that make it somewhat more difficult than one might infer from a casual glance at the map or the distance summary. Hikers with heavy packs should allow substantial extra time. The section between NH 16 and E Peak may be dangerous when wet or icy.

The trail starts on the east side of NH 16 opposite the parking area for Glen Ellis Falls, and leads east across the stream (may be very difficult) to a target. At 0.1 mi. the Lost Pond Trail enters left, and the trail shortly begins the very steep climb up the end of the ridge (use care on all ledge areas), crossing two open ledges, both with fine views of Mt. Washington across Pinkham Notch. At 0.9 mi. it passes a level, open ledge with fine views south, dips slightly, then resumes the climb. At 1.2 mi. a side path (sign) leads left to a spring, and at 1.5 mi. the main trail climbs to the top of a steep ledge with a superb view of the southeast face of Mt. Washington. The trail continues to climb over several knobs and passes 3 yd. left of the summit of E Peak at 1.9 mi., then descends to the summit station of the Wildcat Ski Area in the col at 2.1 mi. From here the easiest ski trails (those farthest to the north) descend to the base lodge in 2.6 mi.

The trail climbs to the summit of D Peak, where there is an observation tower; an easier trail maintained by the ski area parallels this segment to the west. The Wildcat Ridge Trail next descends into Wildcat Col, the deepest col on the main ridge, at 2.5 mi. It passes over a small hogback and through a second sag, then begins the climb to C Peak over several "steps"—fairly steep climbs interspersed with level sections. There is a good outlook east from C Peak, at 3.3 mi., followed by a significant descent into a col and a climb to B Peak, then a shallower col and an easy climb to A Peak at 4.2 mi. As the trail turns left near this summit there is a spur path that leads right 20 yd. to a spectacular view into Carter Notch. The trail now descends rather steeply to the Nineteen-Mile Brook Trail at the height-of-land in Carter Notch. For Carter Notch Hut, turn right (south).

Wildcat Ridge Trail (map 7:G9-F10)
Distances from NH 16

to summit of E Peak: 1.9 mi., 2 hr. 15 min.

to Wildcat Col: 2.5 mi., 2 hr. 45 min.

to summit of C Peak: 3.3 mi., 3 hr. 30 min.

to summit of A Peak: 4.2 mi., 4 hr. 35 min.

to Nineteen-Mile Brook Trail: 5.0 mi. (8.0 km.), 5 hr.

Lost Pond Trail (AMC)

This trail runs from Pinkham Notch Camp to the lower end of the Wildcat Ridge Trail, and is part of the Appalachian Trail. It avoids the difficult and sometimes dangerous crossing of the Ellis River at the beginning of the Wildcat Ridge Trail. It leaves NH 16 opposite Pinkham Notch Camp, crosses a bridge over the Ellis River, and turns south at the end of the bridge, where the Square Ledge Trail turns left. The Lost Pond Trail follows the Ellis River, which is soon joined by the larger Cutler River. The trail follows the east bank, then leaves it and climbs at a moderate grade to Lost Pond at 0.5 mi. It follows the east shore with good views, descends slightly, and joins the Wildcat Ridge Trail.

Lost Pond Trail (map 7:F9-G9)
Distance from NH 16

to Wildcat Ridge Trail: 0.9 mi. (1.5 km.), 30 min.

Square Ledge Trail (AMC)

This trail diverges left from the Lost Pond Trail at the east end of the footbridge crossing Ellis River, where the latter trail turns south. It ascends in about 0.1 mi. to a ledge which, though overgrown, offers a fine view of Pinkham Notch Camp. The trail then continues north and joins a cross-country ski trail heading northeast to a clearing, where it turns right (east) and climbs moderately, passing Hangover Rock. It then climbs to the base of Square Ledge and ascends steeply via a V-slot about 50 yd. to an outlook that has excellent views of Pinkham Notch and Mt. Washington.

Square Ledge Trail (map 7:F9-F10)
Distance (est.) from Lost Pond Trail
  to Square Ledge: 0.5 mi. (0.8 km.), 30 min.

Thompson Falls Trail (WMNF)

This trail runs from the Wildcat Ski Area to Thompson Falls, a series of high falls on a brook flowing from Wildcat Mtn. Except in wet seasons, the brook is apt to be rather low, but the falls are well worth visiting for the excellent views of Mt. Washington and its ravines from the large, sloping ledges that the brook flows over.

From the Wildcat Ski Area parking area, cross the bridge to the east side, turn left and follow the Nature Trail north; continue ahead where a branch leaves left at 0.1 mi. and also where a loop leaves right and returns. Leaving the Nature Trail, the trail to the falls crosses a small stream and a maintenance road. It then leads up the south side of the brook to the foot of the first fall, crosses to the north side above the fall, bears right, and continues up the brook for another 0.3 mi.

Thompson Falls Trail (map 7:F10)
Distance from Wildcat Ski Area
  to end of trail: 0.8 mi. (1.3 km.), 40 min.

Carter-Moriah Trail (AMC)

This trail runs 13.8 mi. from Gorham to Carter Notch, following the crest of the Carter Range. The trailhead at

Gorham is reached by following US 2 east from Gorham about 0.5 mi., then taking a sharp right just past the bridge and railroad track crossing and following a paved road about 0.5 mi. to the turnaround at its end. (On foot from Gorham follow the road that leaves the east side of NH 16 just south of the railroad tracks. Bear right in 0.1 mi. on Mill St., and in 0.1 mi. more a path left leads across the Peabody River on a footbridge. Turn right here and follow the road to its end where the trail enters the woods left.) From the Kenduskeag Trail near the summit of Mt. Moriah to Carter Notch it is part of the Appalachian Trail. Water is very scarce on the trail.

Part I. Gorham to Mount Moriah

The trail follows a logging road up a steep bank, then climbs moderately past a clear-cut, bears right, then left along the edge of another clear-cut, and ascends through open hardwoods. At 2.0 mi. an open ledge to the right affords good views, and the trail soon passes to the right of the insignificant summit of Mt. Surprise and its tiny box canyon. The trail soon becomes steeper and climbs over ledges which have excellent views. The trail stays near the ridge top, but winds from side to side, occasionally dipping below the crest. At 4.2 mi. there is a glimpse of Moriah's summit ahead, and at 4.5 mi. a spur path leads right 50 yd. to the ledgy summit of Mt. Moriah, which affords excellent views.

Part II. Mount Moriah to North Carter

From the Mt. Moriah summit spur trail junction, two routes descend the ledges of the Moriah summit block. The right-hand one is probably easier, but both are rock scrambles, and are dangerous when icy (in which case it may be better to bushwhack through the woods). By either route, it is less than 100 yd. to the junction where the Kenduskeag

Trail turns left, then right, toward Shelburne Moriah Mtn. Here the Carter–Moriah Trail turns right (southwest). From this junction south it is part of the Appalachian Trail and has white blazes. It follows the ridge crest south through woods and over an open knob, then descends moderately to excellent outlooks from the south cliffs, and reaches the col at 5.9 mi. Here the Moriah Brook Trail enters left and the Carter–Moriah Trail turns right and follows a boardwalk. In 40 yd. the Stony Brook Trail enters straight ahead, and the Carter–Moriah Trail turns left. It continues with several minor ups and downs, crosses some ledges, and at 6.6 mi. a spur trail descends right 0.2 mi. to Imp Campsite, where there is a shelter, tent platforms, and water. The trail crosses a small brook, passes through a wet area, ascending on the plateau south of Imp Mtn., and at 7.7 mi. begins a rather steep and rough climb to North Carter Mtn., which is reached at 8.2 mi.

Part III. North Carter to Zeta Pass

The path continues south, passes a fine outlook, and winds along the crest of the ridge. At 8.5 mi. the North Carter Trail enters right, and the trail continues over numerous ledgy humps and boggy depressions. The best views in this area are from the ledgy hump called Mt. Lethe, to the left of the trail. A good outlook to the Presidentials is passed 70 yd. before the trail reaches the wooded summit of Middle Carter Mtn. (sign) at 9.1 mi. The trail then descends easily, passes an open area with a view west, ascends a short, steep ledge, and reaches the col between Middle and South Carter at 10.0 mi. It then ascends to a point 10 yd. left (east) of the summit of South Carter (sign) at 10.4 mi., and descends gradually, with occasional steeper sections, to Zeta Pass, where it makes a short ascent to the junction right with the Carter Dome

Trail at 11.2 mi. There may be water on a side path from the Carter Dome Trail 80 yd. below this junction.

Part IV. Zeta Pass to Carter Notch

The two trails climb easily to the south for 0.2 mi., then the Carter Dome Trail continues ahead, and the Carter–Moriah Trail turns left and climbs rather steeply up to the summit of Mt. Hight at 11.8 mi. At this bare summit are the best views in the range. The trail makes a very sharp right turn, and caution must be exercised to stay on the trail if visibility is poor, particularly northbound, since a beaten path continues north from the summit. (Compass bearings from the summit are: southbound, 240° magnetic; northbound, 290° magnetic.) The trail passes through a col and the Carter Dome Trail reenters right at 12.2 mi. In another 25 yd. the Black Angel Trail enters left, and the Carter–Moriah Trail climbs steadily to the summit of Carter Dome at 12.6 mi., where the Rainbow Trail enters left. The trail descends moderately, passing a side path at 13.1 mi. that leads right 60 yd. to a fine spring. At 13.5 mi. a side path leads 30 yd. left to an excellent outlook over Carter Notch. Soon the trail begins to descend very steeply to Carter Notch, ending on the Nineteen-Mile Brook Trail at the shore of the larger Carter Lake. Carter Notch Hut is 0.1 mi. left.

Carter–Moriah Trail (map 7:E10-F10)
Distances from Gorham trailhead

to Mt. Moriah summit: 4.5 mi., 3 hr. 50 min.

to Moriah Brook and Stony Brook trails: 5.9 mi., 4 hr. 35 min.

to Imp Shelter spur trail: 6.6 mi., 5 hr. 5 min.

to North Carter Trail: 8.5 mi., 6 hr. 40 min.

to Middle Carter summit: 9.1 mi., 7 hr. 5 min.

to South Carter summit: 10.4 mi., 7 hr. 50 min.

to Zeta Pass: 11.2 mi., 8 hr. 20 min.
to Mt. Hight summit: 11.8 mi., 9 hr.
to Black Angel Trail: 12.2 mi., 9 hr. 15 min.
to Carter Dome summit: 12.6 mi., 9 hr. 35 min.
to Nineteen-Mile Brook Trail: 13.8 mi. (22.2 km.), 10 hr. 10 min.

Nineteen-Mile Brook Trail (WMNF)

This trail runs from NH 16 about 1 mi. north of the Mt. Washington Auto Rd. to Carter Notch Hut, and is the easiest route to the hut. Sections of the trail close to the brook bank sometimes become dangerously icy in the cold seasons.

Leaving NH 16, the trail follows the northeast bank of Nineteen-Mile Brook on the remains of an old road, and the Nineteen-Mile Brook Link Trail enters on the left from the Great Gulf parking area. At 1.2 mi. it passes a dam in the brook, and at 1.9 mi. the Carter Dome Trail diverges left for Zeta Pass. The Nineteen-Mile Brook Trail crosses a tributary on a footbridge, and at 2.2 mi. crosses another brook at a small cascade, also on a footbridge. At 3.1 mi. the trail crosses a small brook and begins to ascend more steeply to the height-of-land at 3.6 mi., where the Wildcat Ridge Trail diverges right (west), and a side path leads left to a view of the Rampart. The Nineteen-Mile Brook Trail drops steeply to the larger Carter Lake, passes the Carter–Moriah Trail left at 3.8 mi., crosses between the lakes, and reaches Carter Notch Hut and the junction with the Wildcat River Trail.

Nineteen-Mile Brook Trail (map 7:F10)
Distances from NH 16
to Carter Dome Trail: 1.9 mi., 1 hr. 25 min.
to Wildcat Ridge Trail: 3.6 mi., 2 hr. 45 min.
to Carter Notch Hut: 3.8 mi. (6.2 km.), 2 hr. 55 min.

Carter Dome Trail (WMNF)

This trail runs from the Nineteen-Mile Brook Trail 1.9 mi. from NH 16 to Zeta Pass and the summit of Carter Dome, following the route of an old road that served the long-dismantled fire tower that once stood on Carter Dome. Grades are steady and moderate all the way.

Leaving the Nineteen-Mile Brook Trail, it follows a tributary brook, crossing it at 0.5 mi. and recrossing at 0.8 mi. At the latter crossing it swings left, then in 50 yd. turns sharp right and ascends by a series of seven switchbacks, passing a good spring left at 1.1 mi., and passing questionable water right (sign) 80 yd. below the junction with the Carter-Moriah Trail at Zeta Pass at 1.9 mi. The Carter Dome Trail coincides with the Carter-Moriah Trail to the right (south), then at 2.1 mi. the Carter-Moriah Trail turns left to Mt. Hight—good views, but steep and exposed to weather—while the sheltered Carter Dome Trail continues its steady ascent. At 2.7 mi. the Carter-Moriah Trail reenters from the left, the Black Angel Trail enters from the left in 25 yd. more, and the Carter Dome and Carter-Moriah trails coincide to the junction with the Rainbow Trail at the summit of Carter Dome.

Carter Dome Trail (map 7:F10)
Distances from Nineteen-Mile Brook Trail
> *to* Zeta Pass: 1.9 mi., 1 hr. 45 min.
> *to* Carter Dome summit: 3.1 mi. (5.0 km.), 2 hr. 50 min.

Imp Trail (WMNF)

This trail makes a loop over the cliff which bears the Imp Profile, providing fine views. The ends of the loop are about 0.3 mi. apart on NH 16, with the north end about 2.6 mi. north of the Mt. Washington Auto Rd. and 5.4 mi. south of Gorham.

The north branch of the trail heads east up the south side of the Imp Brook valley, through a pleasant stand of hemlocks, then crosses the brook at 0.8 mi. It slabs north up to a ridge, and follows its crest, nearly level for some distance. The trail slabs more steeply up the north side of the ridge and continues nearly to the bottom of a ravine northeast of the cliff, then turns right and circles steeply to the viewpoint at 2.2 mi.

From the cliff, the trail skirts the edge of the Imp Brook ravine and crosses a large brook in about 0.3 mi. Becoming somewhat rough, it continues generally south to the junction with the North Carter Trail left at 3.1 mi., then passes the site of an old logging camp. The Imp Trail turns right and descends a logging road generally southwest, and, just before reaching Cowboy Brook, turns northwest. After crossing another brook, in about 0.8 mi., it follows an old logging road north down to cross a small brook; it then immediately crosses a larger brook, turns sharp left, runs west-southwest about level for 75 yd., and ends at NH 16.

Imp Trail (map 7:F10)
Distances from northern terminus on NH 16
to viewpoint: 2.2 mi., 1 hr. 55 min.
to North Carter Trail: 3.1 mi., 2 hr. 35 min.
to southern terminus on NH 16: 6.0 mi. (9.7 km.), 4 hr. 10 min.

North Carter Trail (WMNF)
The trail leaves the south branch of Imp Trail 2.9 mi. from NH 16, just above an old logging camp site. It follows an old logging road, and at 0.3 mi. turns right on another old road. At 0.5 mi. it leaves the road sharp left and climbs more steeply to the Carter-Moriah Trail 0.3 mi. south of the summit of North Carter.

North Carter Trail (map 7:F10)
Distance from Imp Trail
   to Carter–Moriah Trail: 1.2 mi. (1.9 km.), 1 hr. 15 min.

Stony Brook Trail (WMNF)

This trail leaves NH 16 on a gravel road just south of the bridge over the Peabody River, about 2 mi. south of Gorham (park in small area behind trail sign; do not drive up road). It ends in the col between North Carter and Moriah. This trail is the best access to the beautiful south ledges of Mt. Moriah. The lower part of the trail is unattractive and has been disrupted by new housing construction at the beginning, and by logging farther along. Follow trail markings with great care, and be alert for changes from this description.

From NH 16 the trail follows the gravel road, bearing left at 0.1 mi., and passing a camp and a chain gate at 0.3 mi. The trail keeps left at a gravel pit at 0.4 mi., and bears right at a fork at 0.9 mi. (blue blazes and arrow may be hard to see). The trail follows a logging road which becomes less obvious as it ascends moderately, and at 2.3 mi. the trail crosses Stony Brook at a pleasant small cascade and pool, and begins to climb more steeply. At 3.1 mi. it crosses a small brook on a mossy ledge and climbs steadily to the ridge and the Carter–Moriah Trail.

Stony Brook Trail (map 7:E10-F11)
Distance from NH 16
   to Carter–Moriah Trail: 3.6 mi. (5.8 km.), 2 hr. 55 min.

Kenduskeag Trail (WMNF)

This trail runs from the Carter–Moriah Trail near the summit of Mt. Moriah to the Shelburne Trail in the col between Shelburne Moriah Mtn. and Howe Peak, 4.5 mi. south of US 2. Named by an Abenaki word meaning "a pleasant walk," it provides excellent views from the ledges of Shelburne Moriah. From Mt. Moriah to the Rattle River Trail it is part of the Appalachian Trail.

From the trail junction below the summit ledges of Mt. Moriah, the trail turns sharp right in 15 yd. and runs over a lesser summit, then descends steeply past an outlook, moderates, and continues the descent to the junction with the Rattle River Trail at 1.4 mi. The trail now climbs over a section of knobs and ledges, with fine views, to the flat, ledgy summit of Shelburne Moriah Mtn. at 2.6 mi. The upper part of this section of trail is very exposed to weather—in fact, more so than any other part of the Carter–Moriah Range. The trail descends steadily to a sharp, narrow col at 3.2 mi., then climbs over two knolls with views, and ends at the Shelburne Trail.

Kenduskeag Trail (map 7:E11-E12)
Distances from Carter–Moriah Trail

to Rattle River Trail: 1.4 mi., 45 min.

to Shelburne Moriah Mtn. summit: 2.6 mi., 1 hr. 35 min.

to Shelburne Trail: 4.1 mi. (6.5 km.), 2 hr. 25 min.

Rattle River Trail (WMNF)

This trail runs to the Kenduskeag Trail in the Moriah–Shelburne Moriah col from US 2 near the east end of the bridge over Rattle River, about 300 yd. east of the North Rd. intersection and 3.0 mi. east of Gorham. It is a part of the Appalachian Trail.

From US 2 it leads generally south, following a logging road on the east side of the stream. A snowmobile trail enters right at 0.3 mi., the trails cross a tributary at 0.6 mi., and soon the snowmobile trail leaves left. At 1.7 mi. the Rattle River Trail passes the WMNF Rattle River Shelter (left), and soon crosses Rattle River (may be difficult at high water), then crosses back over its westerly branch. At 3.2 mi. it again crosses the river, and starts to climb steadily. It passes a small cascade left at 3.7 mi., and soon bears away from the brook and climbs steeply to the ridge top, where it meets the Kenduskeag Trail.

Rattle River Trail (map 7:E11)

Distances from US 2

to Rattle River Shelter: 1.7 mi., 1 hr. 5 min.

to Kenduskeag Trail: 4.3 mi. (6.9 km.), 3 hr. 25 min.

Mount Evans Path

This short path ascends little Mt. Evans, beginning on US 2 0.1 mi. west of the sign for Shadow Pool and 0.8 mi. west of the Rattle River Trail parking area. For a modest effort, there are fine views from its ledges of Mt. Washington and the Northern Peaks, and good views up and down the Androscoggin River and across to the Mahoosuc Range. It is on private property, and the road is posted against vehicular entry.

Follow a dirt road marked by a small trail sign, high in a tree and hard to see. In about 120 yd. there is a yarding area for lumbering operations beyond the power line clearing; bearing right, follow the road out the southwest corner of this area. In about 100 yd., the road reaches a small spring and branches. Follow the less-used left branch for another 100 yd. and again branch left, crossing the stream a second time. The trail now climbs and reaches the crest of a narrow ridge in about 50 yd. Turn right to follow the crest south through a logged area. A short distance above the top of the ridge and near the summit the trail steepens and divides, the left branch (obscure) leading to the lookout on the Mahoosuc Range and the valley below. The right branch (straight ahead) goes to a western ledge that affords the best view of the Northern Peaks; the summit is reached left over open ledges. The top is composed of smooth ledges with scattered conifers and a large boulder that is, perhaps, the actual summit.

Mount Evans Path (map 7:F11)
Distance from US 2
   to Mt. Evans summit: 0.7 mi. (1.1 km.), 35 min.

Shelburne Trail (WMNF)

This trail begins on US 2, passes through the col between Shelburne Moriah Mtn. and Howe Peak, and descends to Wild River Rd. It begins on US 2 about 9 mi. east of Gorham at the west end of an abandoned wayside area immediately west of the ME/NH border. Go about 0.1 mi. into this area and take a good dirt road (FR 95) right for 0.9 mi. to a gate. At the Wild River end it leaves Wild River Rd. (FR 12) 0.6 mi. north of Wild River Campground and fords the river, which can be difficult even at moderate water levels. For this reason the trail is often approached via the Wild River Trail, the Moriah Brook Trail bridge, and the Highwater Trail.

The trail follows the continuation of FR 95 past the gate (follow with care in this area of active logging) and turns left off the main road shortly after the first bridge. At 2.7 mi. it reaches the junction with the former route and begins to climb. At 4.6 mi. the trail crosses a very small stream twice, and shortly reaches the height-of-land, where it meets the eastern terminus of the Kenduskeag Trail. (For Shelburne Moriah Mtn. follow this trail right.) The Shelburne Trail continues over the height-of-land and descends steadily, crosses a brook and enters an old logging road. It then turns sharp left at 6.8 mi. onto another logging road, which it follows east down the valley of Bull Brook, soon crossing a branch of the brook. At 7.6 mi. the Highwater Trail enters from the right (south) and leaves on the left (north) 10 yd. farther on. This junction may be poorly signed. To avoid the Wild River crossing, follow the Highwater Trail south to the Moriah Brook Trail bridge. The main trail continues straight across a dry channel and fords Wild River to Wild River Rd.

Shelburne Trail (map 7:E12-F12)
Distances from gate on FR 95
  to Kenduskeag Trail: 4.3 mi., 3 hr. 5 min.
  to Wild River Rd.: 7.5 mi. (12.0 km.), 4 hr. 40 min.

Wild River Trail (WMNF)

This trail begins at the end of Wild River Rd. (FR 12) at Wild River Campground, runs along the Wild River valley to Perkins Notch, and descends to the Wildcat River Trail between Carter Notch Rd. and Carter Notch. Wild River Rd. leaves ME 113 just south of the bridge over Evans Brook at Hastings and runs 5.7 mi. to the campground, where there is a fork. Follow the right branch to a parking area.

The trail follows an old logging railroad bed which continues Wild River Rd. generally southwest on the southeast bank of Wild River. At 0.3 mi. the Moriah Brook Trail leaves right to cross the river on a bridge, and at 2.7 mi. the Black Angel Trail enters left and coincides with the Wild River Trail as both turn west and cross to the northwest side of Wild River on Spider Bridge. Just across the bridge the Highwater Trail from Hastings enters right and the Wild River and Black Angel trails turn left. In 0.1 mi. the Black Angel Trail diverges right for Carter Dome. The Wild River Trail continues generally southwest, passes Spruce Brook Shelter (right), then crosses Spruce Brook. Just before crossing Red Brook (may be difficult at high water), it leaves the old railroad bed and bears right. About 0.6 mi. after crossing Red Brook the Eagle Link leaves left for Eagle Crag, and in another 0.4 mi. the trail crosses to the south bank of Wild River. About 0.5 mi. beyond this crossing the East Branch Trail leaves left. The Wild River Trail soon crosses the Wild River to the north bank, and recrosses for the last time in about 0.4 mi.

The trail skirts the south side of No-Ketchum Pond, passes the WMNF Perkins Notch Shelter, heads more west, and begins a gradual climb into Perkins Notch. About 0.8 mi. beyond the shelter the Rainbow Trail leaves right for Carter Dome, and about 0.6 mi. farther the Bog Brook Trail leaves left for Carter Notch Rd. From this junction the trail descends gradually through the woods and ends at the Wildcat River Trail.

Wild River Trail (map 7:F12-G10)
Distances from Wild River Campground parking area
to Moriah Brook Trail: 0.3 mi., 10 min.
to Spider Bridge: 2.7 mi., 1 hr. 30 min.
to Eagle Link: 5.0 mi., 3 hr. 10 min.
to East Branch Trail: 6.4 mi., 3 hr. 50 min.
to Perkins Notch Shelter: 6.7 mi., 4 hr.
to Rainbow Trail: 7.5 mi., 4 hr. 30 min.
to Bog Brook Trail: 8.2 mi., 4 hr. 50 min.
to Wildcat River Trail: 9.4 mi. (15.1 km.), 5 hr. 30 min.

Hastings Trail (WMNF)
This trail starts at a parking lot at the junction of ME 113 and Wild River Rd. (FR 12) about 100 yd. south of Evans Brook bridge at the deserted logging village of Hastings. It follows logging roads to its terminus on US 2, 60 yd. inside the east end of an abandoned wayside area immediately west of the ME/NH border, about 9.2 mi. east of Gorham and 2.0 mi. west of Gilead ME.

From Wild River Rd. it crosses Wild River on the 180-ft. suspension footbridge. On the west bank the Highwater Trail leaves left, heading up the northwest side of the river.

The Hastings Trail enters the woods on a logging road running generally north. After passing the remains of an old telephone line, it follows an old, narrow logging road, then descends (right) onto an old, broad logging road for about 0.3 mi., and (right) onto a private dirt road for about 0.4 mi. to the old wayside area.

Hastings Trail (map 7:E13-E12)
Distance from Hastings
to US 2: 2.6 mi. (4.1 km.), 1 hr. 20 min.

Highwater Trail (WMNF)

This trail runs along the northwest side of Wild River from Hastings on ME 113 to the Wild River Trail at the west end of Spider Bridge, providing a means of avoiding unbridged crossings of the Wild River, which are frequently very difficult. Most of the way it follows old logging roads with easy grades, close to the river.

It leaves the Hastings Trail left (south) at the west end of the suspension bridge, across from the parking lot at Hastings. It follows an old logging road that bears away from the river at about 0.8 mi. In another 0.5 mi. the trail bears left from the logging road, crosses into NH and continues up the river. Heading generally southwest, it crosses Martins Brook and 1.0 mi. beyond follows a logging road to cross the Shelburne Trail. The trail then crosses Bull Brook and in about 1.0 mi. reaches the footbridge where the Moriah Brook Trail crosses Wild River. It joins the Moriah Brook Trail, the trails turn sharp right in 0.1 mi., and 0.3 mi. farther the Highwater Trail leaves the Moriah Brook Trail (left) and crosses Moriah Brook. The trail continues on top of a steep bank, then crosses and follows logging roads, each for a short distance. It crosses Cypress Brook and 0.1 mi. beyond ends near Spider Bridge at the coinciding Black Angel and Wild River trails.

Highwater Trail (map 7:E13-F11)
Distances from Hastings Trail
   to Martins Brook: 3.7 mi., 1 hr. 50 min.
   to Shelburne Trail: 5.0 mi., 2 hr. 40 min.
   to Moriah Brook Trail: 6.1 mi., 3 hr. 10 min.
   to Wild River Trail/Black Angel Trail: 8.9 mi. (14.3
      km.), 4 hr. 45 min.

Burnt Mill Brook Trail (WMNF)

This trail ascends from Wild River Rd. (FR 12), 2.7 mi.
south of ME 113, to the Royce Trail in the col between East
Royce Mtn. and West Royce Mtn. From Wild River Rd. the
trail ascends logging roads south for 1.2 mi. and then bears
southeast, climbing more steeply and crossing the brook
three times, and reaches the col between the Royces, where
it meets the Royce Trail.

Burnt Mill Brook Trail (map 7:F12)
Distance (est.) from Wild River Rd.
   to Royce Trail: 2.0 mi. (3.2 km.), 1 hr. 50 min.

Moriah Brook Trail (WMNF)

This trail ascends to the col between Mt. Moriah and
North Carter from the Wild River Trail 0.3 mi. south of
Wild River Campground. It is an attractive trail, passing
Moriah Gorge, traversing fine birch woods which have
grown up after fires, and providing fine views up to the
impressive south cliffs of Moriah.

The trail leaves right from the Wild River Trail and in 75
yd. crosses the Wild River on a footbridge, where the Highwater Trail joins right. The trail turns left and follows the
river bank about 0.1 mi., then turns sharp right and generally follows the course of the former lumber railroad up
Moriah Brook, and at 0.4 mi. the Highwater Trail leaves
left. At 1.4 mi. the Moriah Brook Trail crosses Moriah
Brook (may be difficult at high water); the gorge down-

stream from this crossing merits exploration. The trail follows the south bank of the brook, then recrosses at 2.8 mi., and in another 0.4 mi. passes some attractive cascades and pools, crosses a ledge, then crosses a branch of Moriah Brook just above the confluence with the main brook. The trail continues through birch woods and crosses the main brook four more times, the last crossing in a boulder area below a small cascade at 4.7 mi. The trail becomes rather wet, and winds through almost pure stands of white birch below the impressive south cliffs of Mt. Moriah, then climbs to the col and the Carter–Moriah Trail.

Moriah Brook Trail (map 7:F12-F11)
Distance from Wild River Trail
 to Carter–Moriah Trail: 5.5 mi. (8.8 km.), 3 hr. 45 min.

Black Angel Trail (WMNF)

This trail begins at Rim Junction—where the Basin and Basin Rim trails cross—descends to cross the Wild River on Spider Bridge along with the Wild River Trail, then climbs to the Carter–Moriah Trail 0.4 mi. north of Carter Dome.

Leaving Rim Junction, it descends gradually southwest 0.5 mi. to the Blue Brook Shelter, where a branch trail runs north for 0.3 mi. to connect with the Basin Trail 0.3 mi. west of Rim Junction. From Blue Brook Shelter the Black Angel Trail ascends moderately west and passes through a col, then descends to an old logging road and follows it generally west for 1.4 mi. down the Cedar Brook valley, remaining on the north side of the stream and making several obvious shortcuts at curves. The trail then leaves the logging road, turns more north, and joins the Wild River Trail to cross Wild River on Spider Bridge. Just across the bridge the Highwater Trail leaves right for Hastings, and the Black Angel and Wild River trails continue ahead. The Black Angel Trail diverges right in 0.1 mi., and rises slowly through open woods. About 1.5 mi. up from the Wild River the grade steepens; at 2.2 mi. the trail crosses the north branch of Spruce Brook, and about 0.5 mi. beyond enters virgin timber. The grade lessens as the trail slabs the east slope of Mt. Hight, passes lookout points on its south-southeast slope, turns southwest, and ends at the Carter-Moriah Trail.

Black Angel Trail (map 7:F12-F10)
Distances from Rim Junction
- *to* Blue Brook Shelter: 0.5 mi., 15 min.
- *to* Spider Bridge: 2.7 mi., 1 hr. 40 min.
- *to* Carter-Moriah Trail: 7.5 mi. (12.1 km.), 5 hr. 35 min.

Basin Trail (WMNF)

This trail runs from Wild River Campground to Basin Pond (0.7 mi. from NH 113, near Cold River Campground) through the low point in the ridge connecting Mt. Meader to West Royce, giving easy access to the magnificent views along the brink of the cliffs.

Leaving the parking area at Wild River Campground, it follows an old lumber road. At 0.4 mi., where the road swings right, the trail continues straight ahead and soon approaches the southwest bank of Blue Brook, which it follows for about 0.8 mi. At 1.3 mi. it crosses the brook at the foot of a pretty cascade and then follows the northeast bank, passing opposite a very striking cliff to the south of the brook. The trail leaves Blue Brook, crosses another small brook, then climbs somewhat more steeply. At 2.0 mi. a side trail branches right 0.3 mi. to Blue Brook Shelter and the Black Angel Trail, and the Basin Trail soon crosses the Basin Rim Trail and meets the Black Angel Trail at Rim Junction. Follow the Basin Rim Trail north for less than 0.3 mi. to reach a fine viewpoint at the top of the cliff that overhangs the Basin.

The trail now descends very steeply along the south side and foot of a great cliff, and crosses a wide, stony brook. In 0.3 mi. more it passes the upper end of a loop path that leads right 0.3 mi. to Hermit Falls, then returns to the main trail 0.2 mi. below its point of departure. The Basin Trail descends to an old logging road and turns right on it, and passes the lower junction with the Hermit Falls loop on the right, 1.0 mi. from the Basin Pond parking area. The main trail follows the road across two small brooks and a small clearing, enters and follows a newer road to a point about 0.3 mi. from the parking area, then leaves it, crosses numerous brooks, and reaches the parking area.

Basin Trail (map 7:F12)
Distances from Wild River Campground
to Rim Junction: 2.2 mi., 1 hr. 30 min.
to Hermit Falls loop path, lower junction: 3.5 mi., 2 hr. 10 min.
to Basin Pond parking area: 4.5 mi. (7.2 km.), 2 hr. 40 min.

Eagle Link (AMC)
This trail runs from the Wild River Trail 5.0 mi. southwest of Wild River Campground to the junction with the Baldface Circle and Meader Ridge trails 0.2 mi. south of Eagle Crag. It leaves the Wild River Trail and soon crosses Wild River (may be difficult at high water), then bears sharp right and ascends generally east at a moderate grade. It crosses a large brook, slabs the north slope of North Baldface, and ends at the junction of the Baldface Circle and Meader Ridge trails.

Eagle Link (map 7:F11-F12)
Distances from Wild River Trail
to Baldface Circle Trail/Meader Ridge Trail: 2.4 mi. (3.9 km.), 1 hr. 45 min.

Royce Trail (AMC)

This trail runs to the summit of West Royce Mtn. from the west side of ME 113, about 0.3 mi. north of the access road to the WMNF Cold River Campground. Leaving ME 113, it follows a narrow road about 0.3 mi. Cross the Cold River, and bear right on the trail, which is blazed in blue. In 1.1 mi. the trail crosses and recrosses the river, then, crossing the south branch of Mad River, it rises more steeply and soon passes Mad River Falls. A side trail leads left 25 yd. to a viewpoint. The trail becomes rather rough, with large boulders, and rises steeply under the imposing ledges for which East Royce is famous. At 1.0 mi. from the falls, the Laughing Lion Trail enters right, and at a height-of-land 0.2 mi. beyond, after a very steep ascent, the Royce Connector Trail to East Royce branches right. The Royce Trail bears left at this junction and descends somewhat, then climbs to the height-of-land between the Royces, where the Burnt Mill Brook Trail to Wild River Rd. bears right while the Royce Trail turns abruptly left (west) and ascends the steep wall of the col. It then continues by easy grades over ledges and through stunted spruce to the summit, where it meets the Basin Rim Trail.

Royce Trail (map 7:F12)

Distances from ME 113

to Mad River Falls: 1.6 mi., 1 hr.

to Laughing Lion Trail: 2.6 mi., 2 hr.

to Royce Connector Trail: 2.8 mi., 2 hr. 25 min.

to West Royce Mtn. summit: 4.0 mi. (6.4 km.), 3 hr. 30 min.

Royce Connector Trail (AMC)

This short trail connects the Royce Trail and the East Royce Trail, permitting the ascent of either Royce from either trail, and providing good views from ledges along the way.

Royce Connector Trail (map 7:F12)
Distance from Royce Trail
  to East Royce Trail: 0.2 mi. (0.3 km.), 5 min.

East Royce Trail (AMC)

This trail climbs rather steeply to East Royce Mtn. from the west side of ME 113 just north of the height-of-land. Leaving the highway, it immediately crosses Evans Brook and ascends steeply, crossing several other brooks in the first 0.5 mi. At the final brook crossing at 1.0 mi. the Royce Connector Trail to the Royce Trail for West Royce enters from the left. The East Royce Trail emerges on open ledges at about 1.1 mi., reaches an open subsidiary summit at 1.3 mi., and the true summit, also bare, is 0.1 mi. farther. A spur trail can be followed over several more ledges to a large open ledge with a beautiful outlook to the north and west.

East Royce Trail (map 7:F13-F12)
Distance from ME 113
  to East Royce Mtn. summit: 1.4 mi. (2.3 km.), 1 hr. 30 min.

Laughing Lion Trail (CTA)

This trail begins on the west side of ME 113, just north of a roadside picnic area and about 2.3 mi. north of the road to Cold River Campground, and ends on the Royce Trail. It descends in a northerly direction to Cold River, then ascends steeply, mostly west and southwest, with occasional fine views down the valley. The trail continues north, mostly at a steep grade, leveling off just before it ends at the Royce Trail.

Laughing Lion Trail (map 7:F12)
Distances from ME 113
  to Royce Trail: 1.0 mi. (1.6 km.), 1 hr.

Basin Rim Trail (AMC)

This trail runs along the ridge which runs from Mt. Meader—on the east knob at the junction with the Mount Meader and Meader Ridge trails—to the summit of West Royce Mtn., where it meets the Royce Trail. It has fine views, particularly at the top of the cliff that forms the wall of the Basin.

The trail leaves the east knob of Mt. Meader and descends north over the ledges. Just after crossing a small brook, it reaches a col, then slabs the east side of a prominent hump called Ragged Jacket. The trail soon descends steeply from ledge to ledge down the north slope to the lowest point of the ridge (1870 ft.), then rises gradually over ledges to Rim Junction, passing a magnificent viewpoint at the edge of the cliffs on the east. At Rim Junction it crosses the Basin Trail, and the Black Angel Trail also enters. In about 0.3 mi. there is a view east over the great cliff of the Basin Rim. Passing west of the prominent southeast knee of West Royce, the trail climbs, with only short intervening descents, passes a small brook (unreliable), and ends at the summit of West Royce Mtn.

Basin Rim Trail (map 7:F12)
Distances from Mount Meader Trail/Meader Ridge Trail
to Rim Junction: 1.2 mi., 40 min.
to West Royce Mtn. summit: 3.7 mi. (6.0 km.), 2 hr. 35 min.

Mount Meader Trail (AMC)

This trail runs from the west side of NH 113, about 0.5 mi. north of the entrance to the Baldface Circle Trail, to a junction with the Meader Ridge and Basin Rim trails on the ridge crest at an easterly knob of Mt. Meader.

From NH 113 it follows a logging road (do not block entrance) that stays on the north side of Mill Brook, and at about 0.8 mi. passes a side path left which goes about 0.2 mi. to Brickett Falls and then returns to the main trail. The trail continues about 1.0 mi. mostly on an old road, then bears right and begins a steep climb of about 0.5 mi. up the heel of the ridge. Coming out on open ledges with fine views, it reaches the east knob of Mt. Meader in 0.2 mi.

Mount Meader Trail (map 7:G12-F12)
Distance from NH 113
   to Meader Ridge Trail: 2.9 mi. (4.7 km.), 2 hr. 25 min.

Meader Ridge Trail (AMC)

This trail runs along the ridge crest from a junction with the Mount Meader and Basin Rim trails on the east knob of Mt. Meader, to a junction with the Baldface Circle Trail and Eagle Link, 0.2 mi. south of Eagle Crag.

From the east knob of Mt. Meader the trail descends slightly in a southwest direction and in 0.2 mi. reaches the true summit of Mt. Meader. Descending again, with a small intervening ascent, it passes several good viewpoints to the east. At a sign, a short side path to the west leads up to a large open ledge with fine views to the west. The Meader Ridge Trail passes the deepest col of the ridge 0.4 mi. from the summit and crosses a fairly reliable small brook; sometimes there is also water upstream a short distance in a swampy place called the Bear Traps. The trail then climbs about 0.5 mi. to an intermediate peak and descends 0.3 mi. to another col. Climbing again, it emerges from timberline in 0.4 mi., passes over the summit of Eagle Crag, and then descends slightly 0.2 mi. to meet the Baldface Circle Trail and Eagle Link.

Meader Ridge Trail (map 7:F12)
Distances from Mount Meader Trail/Basin Rim Trail
   to Baldface Circle Trail/Eagle Link: 2.0 mi. (3.2 km.), 1 hr. 15 min.

Baldface Circle Trail (AMC)

This trail makes a loop over North and South Baldface from NH 113, about 0.2 mi. north of the driveway to the AMC Cold River Camp. It is one of the most attractive trips in the White Mtns., with about 4 mi. of open ledge with unobstructed views.

Leaving NH 113, the trail passes a junction left with the Slippery Brook Trail at 0.3 mi., and reaches Circle Junction at 0.7 mi., where a side path leads north 0.1 mi. to Emerald Pool. From here, the trail is described in a clockwise direction—up South Baldface, over to North Baldface, and down Eagle Crag—but the circuit in the reverse direction is equally fine.

From Circle Junction the trail runs southwest, then turns south, crosses a brook, and climbs to an old logging road which it follows for almost 1.0 mi. At 0.4 mi. from Circle Junction a loop path leads left 0.3 mi. to Chandler Gorge and rejoins the main trail 0.1 mi. above its departure point. About 2.0 mi. from Circle Junction the trail swings around the south side of Spruce Knoll to Last Chance Spring (unreliable) and South Baldface Shelter. From here the trail climbs the very steep ledges, marked by cairns and paint, for about 0.5 mi. On the broad shoulder below the summit of South Baldface, the Baldface Knob Trail enters left (south). The Baldface Circle Trail then ascends to the summit of South Baldface and, bearing right, follows a broad ridge, mostly in the open, to the summit of North Baldface. Descending from North Baldface the trail turns more northeast and again follows a broad, open ridge toward Eagle Crag. In 0.9 mi. from the summit of North Baldface, the Bicknell Ridge Trail leaves right, providing a scenic alternative route to NH 113. Just 0.3 mi. beyond this point the Eagle Link leaves left (west) for Wild River Trail, the Meader Ridge Trail continues straight ahead (north) for Eagle Crag and Mt. Meader, and the Baldface Circle Trail turns sharp right and descends steeply on ledges, passing water (unreliable in dry seasons) 0.6 mi. below Eagle Link. At 1.7 mi. from Eagle Link, a side path leads right to cross the brook (use caution) above Eagle Cascade and climbs to the Bicknell Ridge Trail. At 2.4 mi. from Eagle Link the trail crosses a branch of Charles Brook, and 0.1 mi. farther the Bicknell Ridge Trail enters right. The trail descends steadily through a hardwood forest, follows Charles Brook past Mossy Slide (right), then crosses to the south bank of the brook, and reaches Circle Junction.

Baldface Circle Trail (map 7:G12)
Distances from NH 113
to Circle Junction: 0.7 mi., 25 min.
to South Baldface Shelter: 2.5 mi., 2 hr.
to Baldface Knob Trail: 3.1 mi., 2 hr. 50 min.
to South Baldface summit: 3.6 mi., 3 hr. 20 min.
to North Baldface summit: 4.7 mi., 4 hr.
to Eagle Link/Meader Ridge Trail: 5.9 mi., 4 hr. 40 min.
to Bicknell Ridge Trail, lower junction: 7.6 mi., 5 hr. 30 min.
to Circle Junction (loop): 8.9 mi., 6 hr. 10 min.
to NH 113: 9.6 mi. (15.4 km.), 6 hr. 30 min.

Bicknell Ridge Trail (CTA)
This trail begins on the north branch of the Baldface Circle Trail 1.3 mi. from NH 113 and ends on the same trail 0.9 mi. north of North Baldface. Diverging from the Baldface Circle Trail, it immediately crosses Charles Brook, and ascends gradually through second-growth hardwood. After about 1.0 mi., it turns more west, rises more rapidly along the south side of Bicknell Ridge, and, just before the first ledges, crosses a brookbed where there is usually water among the boulders. Soon the trail emerges on the open ledges, and a side path enters right

from Eagle Cascade and the Baldface Circle Trail. Above this junction the trail mostly travels over broad, open ledges with excellent views to the ridge top, where it rejoins the Baldface Circle Trail.

Bicknell Ridge Trail (map 7:G12)
Distances from Baldface Circle Trail (lower junction)
to Eagle Cascade side path: 1.4 mi., 1 hr. 20 min.
to Baldface Circle Trail, upper junction: 2.4 mi. (3.9 km.), 2 hr. 30 min.

Baldface Knob Trail (WMNF)

This trail, in combination with the Slippery Brook Trail, provides an alternative route to South Baldface which avoids the steep ledges on the Baldface Circle Trail. It begins at the Slippery Brook Trail in the col between Eastman Mtn. and South Baldface, opposite the beginning of the Eastman Mountain Trail, then climbs to Baldface Knob and continues along the open ridge to the Baldface Circle Trail on the shoulder below the summit of South Baldface.

Baldface Knob Trail (map 7:G12)
Distance (est.) from Slippery Brook Trail
to Baldface Circle Trail: 0.7 mi. (1.1 km.), 35 min.

Eastman Mountain Trail (CTA)

This trail ascends Eastman Mtn. from the Slippery Brook Trail at the height-of-land in the col between Eastman Mtn. and South Baldface, opposite the lower terminus of the Baldface Knob Trail. The trail first descends slightly then rises quite steeply, onto the north ridge, where outlook points provide fine views of South Baldface and Sable Mtn. It continues generally southeast to the summit, which has a rewarding view in all directions.

Eastman Mountain Trail (map 7:G12)
Distance (est.) from Slippery Brook Trail
  to Eastman Mtn. summit: 0.8 mi. (1.3 km.), 40 min.

Slippery Brook Trail (WMNF)

This trail runs from the Baldface Circle Trail 0.3 mi. from NH 113 through the col between South Baldface and Eastman Mtn. to Slippery Brook Rd. (FR 17, called Town Hall Rd. at its southern end), 7.2 mi. from NH 16A.

Leaving the Baldface Circle Trail, it soon crosses a branch of Chandler Brook, ascends generally southwest through woods, crosses another branch brook, and crosses the col between South Baldface and Eastman, where the Baldface Knob Trail leaves right (north) for South Baldface and the Eastman Mountain Trail leaves left (south). The Slippery Brook Trail soon descends to Slippery Brook, which it crosses six times. Shortly after the last crossing, at a clearing, it passes the junction left with the abandoned Bradley Brook Trail. The trail stays on the east bank, crosses a logging road, and ends at Slippery Brook Rd., 200 yd. north of the gate. (In the reverse direction, it diverges left from the road north of the gate.)

Slippery Brook Trail (map 7:G12-G11)
Distances (est.) from Baldface Circle Trail
  to Baldface Knob Trail/Eastman Mountain Trail: 3.0 mi., 2 hr. 35 min.
  to last crossing of Slippery Brook: 5.0 mi., 3 hr. 35 min.
  to Slippery Brook Rd.: 7.0 mi. (11.3 km.), 4 hr. 35 min.

Bradley Brook Trail (WMNF)

This trail has been officially closed by the WMNF.

Mountain Pond Loop Trail (WMNF)

This trail begins on Slippery Brook Rd. (FR 17, called Town Hall Rd. at its southern end), 6.8 mi. from NH 16A. East of Mountain Pond the former route of the trail has been officially closed by the WMNF, and the cabin formerly at the pond has been removed. At 0.3 mi. from the road, there is a fork; bearing left, the trail reaches the Mountain Pond Shelter in another 0.6 mi., then continues around the pond and returns to the fork, crossing the outlet brook, which may be difficult in high water.

Mountain Pond Loop Trail (map 7:G11)
Distance (est.) from Slippery Brook Rd.
of complete loop: 2.6 mi. (4.2 km.), 1 hr. 25 min.

East Branch Trail (WMNF)

This trail begins on Slippery Brook Rd. (FR 17, the southern part is called Town Hall Rd.), 5.2 mi. from NH 16A and just south of the junction with East Branch Rd. (FR 38). It follows the East Branch of the Saco River, then crosses a height-of-land and ends on the Wild River Trail at the foot of the hill east of Perkins Notch, 0.3 mi. east of Perkins Notch Shelter. It is very muddy south of the height-of-land, at times difficult to follow, and the three crossings of the East Branch are hard at normal water levels and would be hazardous at high water.

Leaving Slippery Brook Rd., the trail descends to cross Slippery Brook, then enters and follows an old railroad bed on the east side of the East Branch. At 2.0 mi. it crosses East Branch Rd., then crosses the East Branch three times (difficult); the last crossing is at a stretch of still water, and in a few yards East Branch Rd. enters left and ends. The trail then crosses Gulf Brook, leaves the railroad bed within 0.1 mi., and follows old logging roads. About 1.3 mi. north of the end of East Branch Rd., the trail crosses

Black Brook and shortly bears northwest away from the river, then climbs by easy grades to a divide between Black Mtn. and a prominent southwest spur of North Baldface. The logging road dwindles to a trail, passes through a patch of spruce, and descends 0.3 mi. to its junction with the Wild River Trail on the south bank of Wild River.

East Branch Trail (map 7:H11-G11)
Distances (est.) from Slippery Brook Rd.

to crossing of East Branch Rd.: 2.0 mi., 1 hr. 10 min.
to end of East Branch Rd.: 3.3 mi., 1 hr. 50 min.
to height-of-land: 6.6 mi., 4 hr.
to Wild River Trail: 8.0 mi. (12.9 km.), 4 hr. 40 min.

Bald Land Trail (WMNF)

This trail follows an old roadway from Black Mtn. Rd. to the East Branch through the divide between Black Mtn. and North Doublehead. It is marked in parts as a cross-country ski trail and crosses several other ski trails. The west trailhead is reached in 3.0 mi. from NH 16 in Jackson by following NH 16B to Dundee Rd., taking the latter past Black Mtn. Ski Area, then bearing left uphill on Black Mtn. Rd. to a small parking area on the right. The east trailhead is 0.2 mi. from the end of East Branch Rd. (FR 38), a branch of Slippery Brook Rd. (FR 17).

The trail passes a gate and follows the East Pasture (ski) Trail for 0.3 mi., then diverges right (sign), crosses Great Brook and follows an old road with a stone wall on the right. At 0.7 mi. it leaves the stone wall at a slight uphill grade and turns more to the northeast. (Avoid an abandoned ski-touring trail diverging left.) Continue along the edge of an overgrown pasture, reenter the woods, and bear right at a fork, then turn left (sign). In 100 yd. more the trail reaches the height-of-land, bears right into the woods, and begins a long, moderate descent, crossing another ski trail just before it reaches East Branch Rd.

Bald Land Trail (map 7:G11)
Distance from Black Mtn. Rd.
  to East Branch Rd.: 2.4 mi. (3.9 km.), 1 hr. 25 min.

Rainbow Trail (WMNF)

This trail climbs to the summit of Carter Dome from the Wild River Trail in Perkins Notch about 0.8 mi. west of the Perkins Notch Shelter near No-Ketchum Pond. After leaving the Wild River Trail, it passes through a sag, then ascends steadily on the southeast slope of Carter Dome. At 1.5 mi. it passes just east of the summit of a southerly knob, and runs in the open, with fine views, into a sag, then climbs moderately to the Carter–Moriah Trail at the summit of Carter Dome.

Rainbow Trail (map 7:G11-F10)
Distance from Wild River Trail
  to south knob: 1.5 mi., 1 hr. 40 min.
  to Carter Dome summit: 2.5 mi. (4.0 km.), 2 hr. 25 min.

Bog Brook Trail (WMNF)

This trail begins at a small parking area on Carter Notch Rd., about 3.0 mi. from NH 16B just west of its sharp turn at the crossing of Wildcat Brook. It ends on the Wild River Trail 1.5 mi. west of Perkins Notch Shelter. Some brook crossings may be difficult at high water.

The trail follows a dirt road (sign) past a camp and bears right off the road into the woods (marked here by blue diamonds) at a turnaround at the WMNF boundary. Running nearly level, it crosses Wildcat Brook, then another brook, and then the Wildcat River, a tributary of Wildcat Brook. In 60 yd. the Wildcat River Trail continues straight ahead, while the Bog Brook Trail diverges right. The trail now ascends moderately, crossing a gravel logging road (FR 233) which leads (to the left) back to Carter Notch Rd. The trail then follows Bog Brook through a wet area, crossing and recrossing the brook, to the Wild River Trail.

Bog Brook Trail (map 7:G10)
Distances from Carter Notch Rd.

to Wildcat River Trail: 0.7 mi., 25 min.

to Wild River Trail: 2.8 mi. (4.5 km.), 1 hr. 45 min.

Wildcat River Trail (AMC)

This trail runs to Carter Notch Hut from the Bog Brook Trail, just east of the Wildcat River crossing 0.7 mi. from Carter Notch Rd. Brook crossings may be difficult at high water.

From the Bog Brook Trail junction, the trail follows the east bank of Wildcat River, crossing a gravel logging road (FR 233) which leads back (to the left) to Carter Notch Rd. At 1.0 mi. the trail crosses Bog Brook, and the Wild River Trail enters right at 1.9 mi. Soon the trail crosses Wildcat River, turns sharp right in 100 yd., and continues to ascend at a moderate grade. It climbs toward Carter Notch, passes a side trail right that leads to the rocks of the Rampart, and in 100 yd. more reaches Carter Notch Hut and the junction with the Nineteen-Mile Brook Trail.

Wildcat River Trail (map 7:G10-F10)
Distances from Bog Brook Trail

to Bog Brook crossing: 1.0 mi., 40 min.

to Wild River Trail: 1.9 mi., 1 hr. 15 min.

to Carter Notch Hut: 3.6 mi. (5.8 km.), 2 hr. 40 min.

Hutmen's Trail (HA)

This trail crosses the flat ridge between Spruce Mtn. on the south and Wildcat Mtn. on the north, running from NH 16 to NH 16B. There are plans to relocate this trail,

and at the present time the trail can be followed from the
NH 16 terminus—4.2 mi. north of Jackson and 5.6 mi.
south of Pinkham Notch Camp—only as far as Marsh
Brook, just east of the ridge crest. The old description of
the trail to this point is reprinted here, but this too may
change. The new location of the NH 16B trailhead has not
yet been determined. Hikers wishing to use this trail should
check at Pinkham Notch Camp for details.

The trail crosses a small field, begins to ascend the moderately steep west slope of Spruce Mtn., and shortly approaches a small brook (right). After about 0.4 mi. it
begins to level, bears away (left) from the brook, turns
more north, and shortly crosses another brook on a bridge.
The trail then goes through an old spruce and softwood
area, nearly level, bears right (east) as it reaches the height-
of-land, and passes along the south edge of an old pasture
(left). It continues on a level grade for another 0.3 mi.
through the woods, then begins to descend at a moderate
grade to Marsh Brook.

Hutmen's Trail (map 7:G10)
Distances (est.) from NH 16
   to Marsh Brook: 1.5 mi., 1 hr. 5 min.
   to NH 16B (via former route): 2.3 mi. (3.5 km.), 1 hr. 30
   min.

Hall's Ledge Trail (HA)
This trail starts on the east side of NH 16, just south of the
bridge over the Ellis River, 5.2 mi. north of the covered
bridge in Jackson. Use the Rocky Branch Trail parking lot,
0.1 mi. north of the NH 16 bridge. The trail ends on Carter
Notch Rd. 0.1 mi. north of the Bog Brook Trail parking
area.

From NH 16, follow the river a short distance, then veer
right uphill toward an overgrown field. Turn right, follow-

ing cairns, then turn left uphill into woods and ascend to a high bank overlooking a brook. To this point the trail is marked with yellow blazes. It bears away from the brook and in about 0.1 mi. begins a short, steep ascent. From the top of this rise it runs generally north and northeast through fine woods with intervals of level stretches and slight rises, then ascends moderately through a section of spruce a short distance below the ledge. The ledge, on the left, is small and overgrown; at the end of a straight, almost level stretch of about 100 yd., Mt. Washington, Boott Spur, and the Gulf of Slides may be seen through the trees.

Beginning 50 yd. beyond Hall's Ledge—following cairns which have been placed where old logging roads came together—the trail descends to Carter Notch Rd. From the first cairn the logging road descends slightly, passes a fine outlook toward Mt. Washington, shortly bears right uphill, then left; at 0.4 mi., at a sharp right turn, it begins a long descent. The road passes the Wildcat Reservation plaque (right), and a side road enters right about 0.3 mi. beyond. From this point the road descends about 0.7 mi. to end at Carter Notch Rd.

Hall's Ledge Trail (map 7:G10)
Distances (est.) from NH 16

to Hall's Ledge: 1.6 mi., 1 hr. 40 min.
to Wildcat Reservation plaque: 2.4 mi., 2 hr. 5 min.
to Carter Notch Rd.: 4.2 mi. (6.7 km.), 3 hr.

Black Mountain Ski Trail (WMNF)

This trail to Black Mountain Cabin and a knob (2758 ft.) on the ridge of Black Mtn. that provides fine views, begins at a sign on Carter Notch Rd. 3.7 mi. from Wentworth Hall in Jackson. There is no water on the trail. It follows a dirt road, then enters the woods and continues steadily uphill to the cabin. Continuing to the left of the cabin, the trail reaches a fork in 0.3 mi. A short distance to the left is the summit of the knob, with fine views to Mt. Washington, Wildcat Mtn., and Carter Notch. Straight ahead is the East Pasture (ski) Trail; a short distance down this trail, an unmarked trail turns right and returns to the cabin.

Black Mountain Ski Trail (map 7:G10)
Distance (est.) from Carter Notch Rd.
   to cabin: 1.4 mi., 1 hr. 25 min.
   to summit of knob: 1.7 mi. (2.7 km.), 1 hr. 40 min.

Eagle Mountain Path

Eagle Mtn. is a small peak that can be climbed from NH 16B, 0.8 mi. from Wentworth Hall in Jackson, by a path which starts in the parking lot behind the Eagle Mtn. House. Start uphill on a dirt road, and soon turn right and pass a large pump house on the right. The road becomes older, then becomes a path, and ascends to an open swampy area. Cairns mark the way along the right side of the swamp and into the woods, where the climbing becomes steeper. After passing a large boulder on the right, turn left uphill by switchbacks. At the summit there is a large cairn, and a splendid view a few steps south.

Eagle Mountain Path (map 7:G10)
Distance (est.) from NH 16B
   to summit of Eagle Mtn.: 1.0 mi. (1.6 km.), 50 min.

Doublehead Ski Trail (WMNF)

This trail ascends North Doublehead from the east (left) side of Dundee Rd. 2.9 mi. from NH 16 at the Jackson covered bridge. Take NH 16B, turn right on Dundee Rd., bear right over the bridge and continue to the parking area. The trail enters the woods, swings left, and becomes steeper. At 0.6 mi. it bears slightly left where the Old Path leaves right. The ski trail ascends by a zigzag route on the

west slope of North Doublehead, terminating at the
WMNF Doublehead Cabin on the summit. The nearest
water is alongside the trail about halfway down. Beyond
the cabin, a path leads in 30 yd. to a good view east,
overlooking Mountain Pond.

Doublehead Ski Trail (map 7:H11-G11)
Distance from Dundee Rd.
  to North Doublehead summit: 1.8 mi. (2.9 km.), 1 hr. 40
    min.

Old Path (JCC)
This trail ascends to North Doublehead from the
Doublehead Ski Trail, 0.6 mi. from Dundee Rd. It diverges
right and passes a brook left in 50 yd., rises at a moderate
grade for about 0.1 mi., then steepens somewhat until it
reaches the height-of-land in the col between the peaks at
0.6 mi. Here the New Path enters right, and the Old Path
turns left and ascends moderately, then more steeply, passing a side path left to a splendid view west. In a short
distance it reaches the summit of North Doublehead, the
cabin, and the Doublehead Ski Trail.

Old Path (map 7:H11-G11)
Distance (est.) from Doublehead Ski Trail
  to North Doublehead summit: 1.0 mi. (1.6 km.), 1 hr.

New Path (JCC)
This trail ascends South Doublehead and continues to
the col between South and North Doublehead, where it
meets the Old Path. It starts on Dundee Rd., 3.4 mi. from
NH 16 at the Jackson covered bridge and 0.5 mi. beyond
the parking area for the Doublehead Ski Trail. It is marked
with cairns, and is steep in its upper half.

The trail declines slightly as it leaves the road and in 60
yd. bears right, then left, and follows a logging road at a

slight upgrade. At 0.3 mi. from the road bear left and in about 100 yd. descend slightly and cross a small brook. Proceed uphill for 100 yd. and bear right at a cairn. About 0.2 mi. from this point the trail crosses a small, almost flat, ledge, and crosses a smaller ledge a short distance beyond. From here the trail begins the steep climb to South Doublehead, approaching it from the southeast slope. It meets the ridge path at a point between two open ledges. The summit of South Doublehead, with a view, is right; the New Path turns left, crosses a fine outlook ledge, and descends slightly to meet the Old Path in the col to the north.

New Path (map 7:H11)
Distances (est.) from Dundee Rd.
to South Doublehead: 1.3 mi., 1 hr. 25 min.
to Old Path: 1.5 mi. (2.4 km.), 1 hr. 30 min.

Mount Kearsarge North Trail (WMNF)
This trail ascends Kearsarge North from the north side of Hurricane Mtn. Rd., 1.5 mi. east of NH 16 near the state highway rest area at Intervale. It is a relatively easy trail to the magnificent views of Kearsarge North, but the total climb of 2700 ft. should not be underestimated.

Leaving the road, it runs level for a short distance, then climbs rather easily past a summer residence, on an old road well up on the bank above a brook. At 1.1 mi. it passes several boulders and the old road starts to become rougher. It climbs steadily into a ledgy area, where there are views to Mt. Chocorua and Moat Mtn., crosses the crest of the ridge connecting Kearsarge North to Bartlett Mtn. at 2.4 mi., swings right, and ascends mostly along the north side of the ridge. At 2.9 mi. the trail makes a sharp right turn at a steep spot, then slabs around to the west edge of the summit ledges and climbs to the tower.

Mount Kearsarge North Trail (map 7:I11-H11)
Distances from Hurricane Mtn. Rd.
to boulders: 1.1 mi., 55 min.
to crest of ridge: 2.4 mi., 2 hr. 15 min.
to Mt. Kearsarge North summit: 3.1 mi. (5.0 km.), 2 hr. 50 min.

Weeks Brook Trail (WMNF)

This trail ascends Kearsarge North from South Chatham Rd., 5.2 mi. from ME 113 in North Fryeburg ME and 0.1 mi. north of the east terminus of Hurricane Mtn. Rd. Following the trail requires some care, particularly in the part near the road and in the upper part.

The trail leaves the main road on a private driveway near a house on the south side of a branch of Weeks Brook. It crosses the brook (arrow) at 0.1 mi. to a clearing, where it follows the north side of the brook on another logging road. (In high water use a bridge about 50 yd. upstream from the marked crossing.) At 0.4 mi. the trail crosses into the WMNF and reaches a clearing at 1.2 mi., where it bears slightly right, then reenters the woods. The road quickly becomes distinctly older and rougher, and begins to climb gradually, then moderately, to Shingle Pond. At 2.8 mi. the trail makes its closest approach to the pond, which has been visible for some time. At 3.2 mi. the trail reaches Weeks Brook, then soon crosses on a ledge and follows the north bank of the attractive brook, crossing and recrossing a branch several times. It enters an open boggy area at 4.0 mi., where the trail turns sharp left at a sign. The trail makes a winding ascent (watch for arrows), first moderately, then steeply, enters low scrub and blueberries, passes a fine view east as it turns sharp right, then soon reaches a ledge with views south, from which the fire tower is visible. From here to the summit the trail may be slightly obscure but the direction is obvious (however, follow trail with extreme care when descending). On the summit it meets the Mount Kearsarge North Trail from Hurricane Mtn. Rd.

Weeks Brook Trail (map 7:I12-H11)
Distance from South Chatham Rd.

to Kearsarge North summit: 4.9 mi. (7.8 km.), 3 hr. 50 min.

Province Brook Trail (WMNF)

This trail provides an easy hike to Province Pond, where there is a WMNF shelter. North of the shelter the former route of the trail has been officially closed by the WMNF. The trail begins at the end of Peaked Hill Rd. (FR 450) 2.6 mi. from South Chatham Rd. Peaked Hill Rd. leaves South Chatham Rd. 4.4 mi. from ME 113 in North Fryeburg ME and 0.9 mi. north of the east end of Hurricane Mtn. Rd.

The trail leaves the north end of Peaked Hill Rd. and heads northwest up Province Brook, crosses the brook shortly before reaching Province Pond, and ends at Province Pond Shelter.

Province Brook Trail (map 7:H12)
Distance from north end of Peaked Hill Rd.

to Province Pond Shelter: 1.6 mi. (2.6 km.), 1 hr.

Hurricane Mountain Path

The trail to the summit of Hurricane Mtn. leaves the north side of Hurricane Mtn. Rd. 3.7 mi. east of NH 16 and 0.1 mi. west of the height-of-land, diagonally opposite the Black Cap Path. Follow an old road for about 0.3 mi., then bear right onto the trail and follow cairns that lead to open ledges and the north end of the wooded summit.

Hurricane Mountain Path (map 7:I12)
Distance (est.) from Hurricane Mtn. Rd.

to Hurricane Mtn. summit: 0.5 mi. (0.8 km.), 25 min.

Black Cap Path

The orange-blazed path to the bare summit of Black Cap, which affords the best views in the Green Hills range, leaves the south side of Hurricane Mtn. Rd. 3.7 mi. from NH 16 and 0.1 mi. west of the height-of-land, at a sign. It passes through spruce, then beech forest; a trail leaves right for Cranmore Mtn. at 0.9 mi., and the Black Cap Path soon reaches the summit ledges.

Black Cap Path (USGS North Conway quad)
Distance (est.) from Hurricane Mtn. Rd.
  to Black Cap Mtn. summit: 1.2 mi. (1.9 km.), 55 min.

Peaked Mountain Path

This sharp, rocky knoll, bare except for a few small pines, affords good views. From NH 16 in North Conway, take Artist's Falls Rd. (across from the Millbrook House) for 0.5 mi., then turn right on Woodland Rd. for 0.9 mi. to its end at a small reservoir (parking). The start of the trail is marked by a cairn below the fence on the downhill side of the reservoir. In 25 yd. it crosses the brook at a small flume, continues straight ahead for a few yards, then bears sharp left and continues straight ahead, ascending fairly steeply to the top of the first ledges. Here, at a large cairn and a 6 ft. rectangular boulder, a loop trail to the ledges diverges sharp right, marked by ribbons and cairns, while the main trail continues straight ahead.

The ledge loop is by far the more attractive way to ascend. It follows along the top of the ledges for about 0.3 mi., then ascends left through a narrow belt of woods, climbing steeply to the top of a shoulder of the mountain. Continue right along an almost level grassy shelf, turning abruptly left through a wooded hollow, where the loop intersects the main trail—which enters at a right angle, marked by a double set of ribbons. Continue straight ahead to climb steeply to the "Peak," where there are views south and west. On returning down the main trail from the loop junction, in 0.2 mi. look for a conical "smashed" boulder 6 ft. high, where another loop trail, marked by ribbons and cairns, can be taken to the right. This trail is less steep than the ascent route, connecting with an old logging road in about 0.3 mi. Bear left here. After crossing Artist Falls Brook, bear left at a logging road junction to return to the starting point.

Peaked Mountain Path (USGS North Conway quad)
Distance (est.) from Woodland Rd.
  to Peaked Mtn. summit: 2.0 mi. (3.2 km.), 1 hr. 35 min.

Speckled Mountain Region

This section comprises the mountains and trails east of Evans Notch and the valley of the Cold River, almost all contained within the WMNF. The section is bounded on the west by ME 113/NH 113, and on the north by US 2. Except for a sliver of land near North Chatham NH, the entire section lies in ME. The area suffered a destructive windstorm in December 1980; all trails have now been reopened, but some may pose route-finding problems for several more years, due to undergrowth in the areas where the forest canopy is gone. The AMC Carter–Mahoosuc map (map 7) covers the entire area, except for the trails on Albany Mtn., which are covered by the USGS East Stoneham quad.

The Appalachian Trail does not pass through this section.

GEOGRAPHY

The major part of this region is occupied by a jumbled mass of ridges with numerous ledges; although the peaks are not high, they offer a variety of fine walks.

Speckled Mtn. (2906 ft.) is the highest peak of the region. It is one of at least three mountains in ME that have been known by this name. The summit's open ledges have excellent views in all directions. Mt. Caribou (2828 ft.)—called Calabo in the Walling map of Oxford County (1853)—is the second highest peak in the area. It has a bare, ledgy summit that affords excellent views. Albany Mtn. (1910 ft.) has open summit ledges with excellent views in all directions. Blueberry Mtn. (1781 ft.) is a long, flat spur running southwest from Speckled Mtn. The top is mostly one big ledge, with sparse and stunted trees. Numerous open spaces afford excellent views, especially from the southwest ledges on the summit. Between Blueberry Mtn. and the west ridge of

Speckled Mtn., Bickford Brook passes two sets of flumes, falls, and boulders of unusual beauty.

Deer Hill (1220 ft.), often called Big Deer, is located south of Speckled Mtn. and east of Cold River. The views from the east and south ledges are excellent. Little Deer Hill (about 1000 ft.), a lower hill west of Deer Hill that rises only about 600 ft. above the valley, gives fine views of the valley and the Baldfaces from its summit ledges. Pine Hill (about 1200 ft.) and Lord Hill (about 1200 ft.) are southeast of Deer Hill, and their open ledges and pastures afford interesting views.

The Roost (1374 ft.) is a small hill near Hastings, with open ledges which afford fine views of the Wild River valley, the Evans Brook valley, and many mountains.

CAMPING

Restricted Use Areas

There were no RUA's in this region in 1986.

Established Trailside Campsites

Caribou Shelter (WMNF) is located on the Caribou Trail northeast of the summit of Mt. Caribou. The spring nearby is not reliable.

LIST OF TRAILS	MAP
Trails to the North and East of Speckled Mountain	
Roost Trail	7:E13
Wheeler Brook Trail	7:E13
Caribou Trail	7:E13-E14
Mud Brook Trail	7:F13-E13
Haystack Notch Trail	7:F13-E14
Albany Notch Trail	USGS
Albany Mountain Trail	USGS

Trails on Speckled Mountain

Trails South of Speckled Mountain

THE TRAILS

Roost Trail (WMNF)

This trail ascends the Roost from the east side of ME 113, near the junction with Wild River Rd. at Hastings. It ascends a steep bank for 30 yd., then bears right (east) and ascends gradually along a wooded ridge, crosses a brook at 0.3 mi., rises somewhat more steeply at its upper end, and emerges on a small rock ledge. A side trail descends east through woods to spacious open ledges, where the views are excellent. The main trail continues, descends generally southeast at a moderate grade, crosses a small brook, and swings back west on an old road to return to ME 113 just south of the upper (south) bridge over Evans Brook at Hastings.

Roost Trail (map 7:E13)
Distances (est.) from ME 113 at Hastings
  to the Roost: 0.5 mi., 25 min.
  to ME 113, south trailhead: 1.3 mi. (2.1 km.), 50 min.

Wheeler Brook Trail (WMNF)

This trail begins on the south side of US 2 about 2.3 mi. east of the junction of ME 113 and US 2. It ends at Little Lary Brook Rd. (FR 8), 1.3 mi. from its junction with ME 113, 7.0 mi. north of the road to Cold River Campground, and 3.5 mi. south of the junction of US 2 and ME 113.

From US 2, it follows the west side of Wheeler Brook, crosses the brook several times, and, keeping generally to an old logging road, rises about 1400 ft. to its highest point on the northwest slope of Peabody Mtn. (there is no trail to the wooded summit). The trail descends generally southwest and ends at Little Lary Brook Rd. Because of logging activities, care should be exercised in following the trail at the south end, especially when starting from this end, since the first 400 yd. or so of the trail have been obliterated.

Wheeler Brook Trail (map 7:E13)
Distances (est.) from US 3

to Little Lary Brook Rd.: 3.4 mi. (5.5 km.), 2 hr. 30 min.

to ME 113 (via Little Lary Brook Rd.): 4.7 mi., 3 hr. 40 min.

Caribou Trail (WMNF)

This trail begins on the east side of ME 113 about 6.4 mi. north of the road to Cold River Campground. There is parking space for several cars at the trailhead. The trail ends at Bog Rd. (FR 6), which leads about 3 mi. to US 2, 1.5 mi. west of West Bethel. (Sign at junction of Bog Rd. and US 2 reads "STEAM RAILROADIANA.")

From ME 113, the trail immediately crosses Morrison Brook (may be difficult at high water) and follows it for about 2.3 mi., crossing and recrossing several times. One crossing, at 1.6 mi., is at the head of Kees Falls, a 25-ft. waterfall. The trail levels off at the height-of-land as it crosses the col between Gammon Mtn. and Mt. Caribou. Here the Mud Brook Trail leaves right for the summit of Mt. Caribou, passing Caribou Shelter and Caribou Spring (unreliable) in 0.3 mi. The Caribou Trail continues ahead at the junction, descends more rapidly, turns northeast toward the valley of Bog Brook, east of Peabody Mtn., and ends at Bog Rd.

Caribou Trail (map 7:E13-E14)
Distances from ME 113

to Mud Brook Trail: 2.7 mi., 2 hr. 10 min.

to Mt. Caribou summit (via Mud Brook Trail): 3.2 mi., 2 hr. 35 min.

to Bog Rd.: 5.2 mi. (8.4 km.), 3 hr. 25 min.

Mud Brook Trail (WMNF)

This trail begins on ME 113, 5.7 mi. north of the road to Cold River Campground, 0.7 mi. south of the trail-head for the Caribou Trail, 2.0 mi. south of the bridge at Hastings, and just north of the Mud Brook bridge. It passes over the summit of Mt. Caribou and ends at the Caribou Trail. Despite its ominous name, the footing on the trail is good.

From ME 113, it runs generally east along the north side of Mud Brook, rising gradually for 1.8 mi., then crosses a branch brook and swings more steeply left (north). The trail crosses several smaller brooks and, 1.0 mi. from the beginning of the steep ascent, comes out on a small, bare knob with excellent views east. There is a short descent into a small ravine, then the trail emerges above timberline and crosses ledges for about 0.3 mi. to the summit of Mt. Caribou. It descends north, passes Caribou Spring (unreliable) left and Caribou Shelter right 70 yd. farther, and meets the Caribou Trail in the col.

Mud Brook Trail (map 7:F13-E13)
Distances from ME 113

to Mt. Caribou summit: 3.1 mi., 2 hr. 30 min.

to Caribou Trail: 3.6 mi. (5.8 km.), 2 hr. 45 min.

Haystack Notch Trail (WMNF)

This trail starts on the east side of ME 113, 4.8 mi. north of the road to Cold River Campground. It runs generally east, with easy footing and little climbing, through Haystack Notch and down the valley of the West Branch of the Pleasant River. Here it meets the Miles Notch Trail at an old road heading northeast that continues to a paved road that leads generally north to West Bethel on US 2, across from the post office.

Haystack Notch Trail (map 7:F13-E14)
Distance from ME 113

to Miles Notch Trail: 5.2 mi. (8.4 km.), 3 hr.

Albany Notch Trail (WMNF)

From US 2 at West Bethel, opposite the post office, go south on the unmarked road which becomes FR 7, then take FR 18, following signs for Crocker Pond Campground. About 5.5 mi. from US 2 and 0.5 mi. before the campground, the trail leaves right (southwest). Park off the road. The trail is wide and almost level for 1.0 mi. At 0.6 mi., just before a small brook crossing, the Albany Mountain Trail leaves left (south). The Albany Notch Trail ascends to the height-of-land. Beyond there, at 1.7 mi., another trail goes left (east) and connects with the Albany Mountain Trail. The Albany Notch Trail continues south to old wood roads and ME 5.

Albany Notch Trail (USGS East Stoneham quad)
Distance (est.) from FR 18

to ME 5: 3.8 mi. (6.1 km.), 1 hr. 55 min.

Albany Mountain Trail (WMNF)

This trail ascends Albany Mtn. on its north slope, from the Albany Notch Trail 0.6 mi. from FR 18. About 0.5 mi. below the summit, a trail branches right (west), leading in 0.5 mi. to the Albany Notch Trail on the south side of the notch. The Albany Mountain Trail continues ahead and shortly enters the open summit area. From this point the trail is well cairned and leads directly to the summit. (There are many side paths made by blueberry pickers.)

Albany Mountain Trail (USGS East Stoneham quad)
Distance (est.) from Albany Notch Trail
   to Albany Mtn. summit: 1.4 mi. (2.3 km.), 1 hr. 10 min.

Miles Notch Trail (WMNF)

This trail begins at the same point as the Great Brook Trail. From ME 5 in North Lovell ME, go northwest for 1.9 mi. on a road marked "Evergreen Valley." Turn right on a road just before a bridge, with the sign "F & R Ames" at the corner; the trailhead is 1.5 mi. from this corner. The north terminus, shared with the Haystack Notch Trail, is on an old road that leads west from the road that runs south from West Bethel on US 2, across from the post office.

From the south terminus, the trail leads generally north and, after about 0.3 mi., turns abruptly left on a blue-blazed trail. It climbs for about a mile, then again makes an abrupt left turn, leaving the blue blazes. The trail crosses a branch of Beaver Brook, becomes much steeper after another mile, and passes through Miles Notch, where the Red Rock Trail leaves left (west) for the summit of Speckled Mtn. From Miles Notch it descends along Miles Brook to the terminus of the Haystack Notch Trail.

Miles Notch Trail (map 7:F14-E14)
Distances from south terminus
   to Red Rock Trail: 3.7 mi., 2 hr. 20 min.
   to north terminus: 6.1 mi. (9.8 km.), 3 hr. 35 min.

Blueberry Ridge Trail (CTA)

This trail begins and ends on the Bickford Brook Trail, leaving at a sign 0.6 mi. from its trailhead at the Brickett Place on ME 113, and rejoining 0.5 mi. below the summit of Speckled Mtn. (The Blueberry Ridge Trail may also be reached from Shell Pond Rd. via the Stone House or White Cairn trails.) It descends to cross Bickford Brook, then ascends southeast to an open area just over the crest of Blueberry Ridge, where the White Cairn Trail leaves right. The Stone House Trail enters on the right 0.2 mi. farther, only a few steps beyond the top of Blueberry Mtn. An overlook loop 0.5 mi. long, with excellent views to the south, leaves the Blueberry Ridge Trail shortly after the White Cairn Trail junction and rejoins it shortly before the Stone House Trail junction. From the junction with the Stone House Trail, marked by signs and a large cairn, the Blueberry Ridge Trail to Speckled Mtn. bears left and descends to a spring (unreliable) a short distance from the trail on the left (north). The trail turns sharp right here, continues over ledges marked by cairns, through occasional patches of woods, and over several humps. Above the top of the Rattlesnake Brook ravine the trail ends at the Bickford Brook Trail in a shallow col about 0.5 mi. below the summit of Speckled Mtn. The Bickford Brook Trail leads somewhat more steeply through woods and over ledges to the rocky top.

Blueberry Ridge Trail (map 7:F13)
Distances from Bickford Brook Trail, lower junction
- *to* Blueberry Mtn. and Stone House Trail: 0.9 mi., 50 min.
- *to* Bickford Brook Trail, upper junction: 3.1 mi., 2 hr. 20 min.

Bickford Brook Trail (WMNF)

This trail extends from the Brickett Place on ME 113, 0.2 mi. north of the road to Cold River Campground, to

the top of Speckled Mtn. The trail enters the woods near
the garage, the WMNF service road to Speckled Mtn.
enters left at 0.3 mi., and the two coincide for about 2.5
mi. In 0.4 mi. the Blueberry Ridge Trail leaves right (east)
for Bickford Slides. Another path leaves right 0.2 mi.
farther for the upper end of the Slides, forming a loop. A
third path to the Upper Slides leaves right 0.2 mi. farther
and descends on the high bank of the gorge to the second
path, then continues to the Blueberry Ridge Trail. The
Bickford Brook Trail crosses a branch of the brook, then
bears slightly left and ascends more steeply. Farther up
on the ridge the Spruce Hill Trail enters left. The trail
then passes west and north of the summit of Ames Mtn.
and into the col between Ames Mtn. and Speckled Mtn.,
where the Blueberry Ridge Trail rejoins right. The trail
then continues upward about 0.5 mi. more to the summit.

Bickford Brook Trail (map 7:F12-F13)
Distances from ME 113

to Blueberry Ridge Trail, lower junction: 0.6 mi., 35
min.
to Spruce Hill Trail: 2.8 mi., 2 hr. 20 min.
to Blueberry Ridge Trail, upper junction: 3.5 mi., 2 hr.
45 min.
to Speckled Mtn. summit: 4.1 mi. (6.6 km.), 3 hr. 10
min.

Spruce Hill Trail (WMNF)

This trail runs from the east side of ME 113, opposite the
East Royce Trail and 3.0 mi. north of the road to Cold
River Campground, to the Bickford Brook Trail, with
which it forms the shortest route to Speckled Mtn. It ascends generally southeast through woods, with excellent
views of Evans Notch, to the summit of Spruce Hill, de-

scends to a subsidiary col, then climbs to connect with the Bickford Brook Trail.

Spruce Hill Trail (map 7:F13)
Distances from ME 113
to Bickford Brook Trail: 1.8 mi. (2.9 km.), 1 hr. 25 min.
to Speckled Mtn. summit (via Bickford Brook Trail): 3.1 mi., 2 hr. 15 min.

Cold Brook Trail (WMNF)
This trail ascends Speckled Mtn. from a trailhead reached from ME 5 in North Lovell ME. Follow a road with the sign "Evergreen Valley" for 2.0 mi., taking the first right after a bridge with the Evergreen Valley sign, and continue 0.4 mi. farther. The WMNF sign is on the paved road, but a gravel road may be followed for 0.5 mi. to a parking area. The road becomes rougher, and in 0.2 mi. turns left (gate).

The next 1.0 mi. is on a muddy road, circling on contour to a cabin marked "Sugar Hill," the Duncan McIntosh House. Continuing ahead on the road, take the left fork, then the right. The trail descends for 0.1 mi. to a brook, crossing it just above a fork. The trail climbs and circles along the farther branch, passes west of Sugarloaf Mtn., and ascends the south side of Speckled Mtn., passing a junction left with the "Link Trail" from the Evergreen Valley Ski Area. It emerges on open ledges about 1.5 mi. south of the summit. With excellent views for the next mile, the trail continues to the summit.

Cold Brook Trail (map 7:F14-F13)
Distance from trailhead parking area
to Speckled Mtn. summit: 4.7 mi. (7.6 km.), 3 hr. 30 min.

Red Rock Trail (WMNF)

This trail ascends to Speckled Mtn. from the Miles Notch Trail in Miles Notch, affording fine views of the surrounding mountains. It leaves the Miles Notch Trail, bears northwest, then shortly west, and ascends Red Rock Mtn. It then follows the ridge, with several ups and downs, to Butters Mtn. In the next col, the Great Brook Trail diverges southeast, descending to West Stoneham. The Red Rock Trail then turns south, soon crosses the summit of Durgin Mtn., and bears southwest to the summit of Speckled Mtn. There is a spring near the trail about 0.1 mi. east of the summit.

Red Rock Trail (map 7:F14-F13)
Distances from Miles Notch Trail

to Great Brook Trail: 3.3 mi., 2 hr.

to Speckled Mtn. summit: 5.5 mi. (8.8 km.), 3 hr. 40 min.

Great Brook Trail (WMNF)

This trail ascends to the Red Rock Trail east of Speckled Mtn., beginning at the same point as the Miles Notch Trail. From ME 5 in North Lovell ME, go northwest for 1.9 mi. on a road marked "Evergreen Valley." Turn right on a road just before a bridge, with the sign "F & R Ames" at the corner; the trailhead is 1.5 mi. from this corner.

The trail continues up the old road about 1.5 mi. through open woods and crosses Great Brook. It leaves the old road and follows Great Brook, mostly northwest, becoming steeper in the last 0.5 mi., reaches the ridge, and joins the Red Rock Trail in the col between Butters Mtn. and Durgin Mtn.

Great Brook Trail (map 7:F14-F13)
Distances (est.) from trailhead

to Red Rock Trail: 3.8 mi., 2 hr. 40 min.

to Speckled Mtn. summit (via Red Rock Trail): 6.0 mi. (9.7 km.), 4 hr. 20 min.

Stone House Trail (CTA)

This trail and the White Cairn Trail are reached from Shell Pond Rd., which leaves NH 113 on the east side 0.7 mi. north of the AMC Cold River Camp. A padlocked steel gate on Shell Pond Rd. 1.1 mi. in from NH 113 makes it necessary to park cars at that point.

The trail leaves left 0.5 mi. beyond the gate, east of an open shed, follows a logging road, and approaches Rattlesnake Brook. Off-trail is Rattlesnake Flume, a gorge worth visiting. At a point 0.2 mi. upstream from the flume, the logging road bears uphill left, and the trail continues straight ahead. Just beyond, a side trail descends right about 150 yd. to Rattlesnake Pool, at the foot of a small cascade. In about 0.3 mi. the main trail bears left on a still older logging road and at 1.0 mi. begins to climb, straight and steep, generally northwest, to the top of the ridge, where it ends at the Blueberry Ridge Trail, only a few steps from the top of Blueberry Mtn. For Speckled Mtn., turn left.

Stone House Trail (map 7:F13)

Distances from Shell Pond Rd.

to Rattlesnake Flume: 0.2 mi., 10 min.

to Blueberry Mtn. summit: 1.3 mi. (2.1 km.), 1 hr. 15 min.

White Cairn Trail (CTA)

This trail provides access to the open ledge on Blueberry Mtn. and, with the Stone House Trail, makes an easy half-day circuit. The trail leaves Shell Pond Rd. at a small clearing 0.2 mi. beyond the locked gate. It follows old logging roads north and west to an upland meadow, then climbs steeply up the right (east) margin of the cliffs seen from the road, to a broad view of the Baldfaces and Royces. Following the crest of the cliffs to the west, the trail turns north, traversing open ledges and scrub growth along a line of cairns to end at a junction with the Blueberry Ledge Trail, 0.2 mi. west of the upper terminus of the Stone House Trail. A loop trail from the Blueberry Ledge Trail, near its junction with this trail, also affords fine views.

White Cairn Trail (map 7:F13)
Distances (est.) from Shell Pond Rd.
to top of cliffs: 1.0 mi., 1 hr.
to Blueberry Ridge Trail: 1.5 mi., 1 hr. 30 min.

Shell Pond Trail (WMNF)

This trail begins at the gate on Shell Pond Rd., 1.1 mi. from NH 113, and follows the road for another 0.5 mi. to the Stone House (left). Continue along the edge of the field, bearing into the woods shortly before the field ends. The logging road crosses Rattlesnake Brook in about 0.4 mi., passing north (not within sight) of Shell Pond; there is no trail to Shell Pond itself. After crossing another inlet brook, the trail bears left off the logging road, ascends gradually, and ends at Deer Hill Rd. (FR 9) 3.5 mi. from NH 113.

Shell Pond Trail (map 7:F13-G13)
Distance (est.) from gate on Shell Pond Rd.
to Deer Hill Rd.: 1.8 mi. (2.9 km.), 1 hr.

Horseshoe Pond Trail (CTA)

This trail, blazed with bright yellow paint, starts from Deer Hill Rd. (FR 9), 4.7 mi. from NH 113, at a small parking area at a curve in the road, where the pond is visible. It descends moderately past the Styles grave, which is enclosed by a stone wall, enters a recent logging road and turns right on it. In a few steps, a loop path leaves left for the northwest shore of Horseshoe Pond. The main trail continues on the logging road for 300 yd., then leaves right at a cairn and ascends on skid roads through the clear-cut resulting from the timber salvage operations after the 1980 windstorm, following cairns and overgrown skid roads back into the woods to the old trail. The loop path from the pond rejoins at an incipient apple orchard, and the main trail ascends to the Pine–Lord loop path north of Lord Hill.

Horseshoe Pond Trail (map 7:G13)
Distance (est.) from Deer Hill Rd.
   to Pine–Lord loop path: 1.1 mi. (1.8 km.), 50 min.

Paths to Big Deer Hill and Little Deer Hill (CTA)

The Leach Link Trail leaves Shell Pond Rd. just east of the bridge over Cold River, and runs 1.1 mi. to the dam at the AMC Cold River Camp, where one can also enter the trail. From here the Leach Link Trail continues along the river, while the path to Little Deer Hill runs level for a short distance, then rises slowly, crosses a logging road, and climbs at a moderate grade through the woods. It crosses two open ledges with views of the valley, then ascends through a short woods section before reaching the open summit of Little Deer 0.6 mi. from the dam. As an alternative, one can continue along the Leach Link Trail and ascend Little Deer via the recently reopened Ledge Trail, which passes interesting ledges and a cave, but is very steep and rough, dangerous in icy conditions, and not recommended for descent.

At the summit of Little Deer one has a choice of several routes. One can descend on the steep path that runs south from the summit and, turning right at the base of the hill, return to the starting point via the Leach Link Trail. Another path leads east from the northeast corner of the

summit ledge and descends into the col. The trail then
ascends gradually, generally east, to the Big Deer summit at
1.4 mi. from Cold River Camp. A few steps east of the
summit there is a viewpoint, and 0.3 mi. south the trail
crosses another outlook, then descends through woods. A
branch trail leaves left (southeast) and runs to Deer Hill
Rd. 1.4 mi. from NH 113, and a side path runs left from
this branch trail to Deer Hill Spring ("Bubbling Spring"),
an interesting shallow pool with air bubbles rising through
a small, light-colored sand area. Just beyond this junction
the trail swings right (west) and for a short distance passes
through scrub in an old clear-cut area. It descends through
woods, crosses an old road, then a small brook in a shallow
gully, shortly bears left, then sharp left at a junction, where
the south path to Little Deer Hill turns right. From this
junction the trail runs nearly level out to the Leach Link
Trail on the east side of the Cold River.

Paths to Pine Hill and Lord Hill (CTA)

The loop path to these hills was formerly called the
Conant Trail. From NH 113 take Deer Hill Rd. (FR 9) 1.4
mi., then turn right and park. The path runs east (left at
crossroads) across Colton Brook on a bridge—Colton Dam
is located several hundred yards to the right from here—
and soon divides. From here the path makes a loop (total
distance approximately 5 mi.). To the right, the trail follows a logging road 0.6 mi. to a level spot near an old cellar
hole, then turns left on a logging road, then immediately
left again. The trail turns left again and ascends Pine Hill,
rather steeply at times, passing a fine ledge part of the way
up, and reaches the summit, which has a good view north.
The trail descends northeast, turns right into the woods
and runs east, then turns north and passes through the
cutover area, and crosses Bradley Brook in the col. It then
climbs over an old road, passes an outlook over Horseshoe

Pond, and reaches ledges near the summit of Lord Hill. It turns right and descends into the cutover area, then turns left at the junction right with the Horseshoe Pond Trail. The trail slabs the south side of Harndon Hill, past a cellar hole, to Harndon Hill Rd., then shortly enters a logging road, which leads back to the loop junction.

SECTION 11

Mahoosuc Range Area

This section includes the region along the ME/NH border which lies east and north of the Androscoggin River, as it runs south from Lake Umbagog near Errol to Gorham then swings east from Gorham to Bethel ME. It is bounded by NH 16 on the west, by US 2 on the south, and by NH 26/ME 26 on the northeast. The backbone of the region is the Mahoosuc Range, which rises from the east bank of the river above Berlin and Gorham, runs east, then gradually swings toward the north to its far end at Grafton Notch. This section covers the main Mahoosuc Range and all the trails on it, but does not cover some of the routes on eastern spurs of the range which lie wholly within ME. Such mountains and routes are covered in the *AMC Maine Mountain Guide*. The most important peaks in the Mahoosuc Range are Old Speck Mtn., Mahoosuc Arm, Goose Eye Mtn., Mt. Carlo, Mt. Success, Cascade Mtn., and Mt. Hayes. The region is completely covered by the AMC Carter–Mahoosuc map (map 7).

In this section the Appalachian Trail begins at the trailhead of the Rattle River Trail (Section 9) on US 2, follows the highway west 0.2 mi. to North Rd., then follows North Rd. for 0.5 mi., crossing the Androscoggin, and turns left on Hogan Rd. for 0.2 mi. to the Centennial Trail. It then follows the Centennial Trail, the Mahoosuc Trail, and the Old Speck Trail to Grafton Notch, the limit of the area covered in this Guide; the Baldpate Mountain Trail continues on the opposite side of the notch. In its course through the Mahoosucs, the Appalachian Trail crosses the summits of Cascade Mtn., Mt. Success, and Mt. Carlo, and near the summits of Mt. Hayes, Goose Eye Mtn., Mahoosuc Arm, and Old Speck Mtn.

GEOGRAPHY

The southern part of the Mahoosuc Range is a broad, ledgy, lumpy ridge, with numerous spurs extending south toward the Androscoggin valley. The main peaks, from west to east, are Mt. Hayes (2555 ft.), Cascade Mtn. (2631 ft.), Bald Cap (3065 ft.) and its two subsidiary peaks (all three trailless), Bald Cap Peak (2795 ft.) and North Bald Cap (2893 ft.). The northern part of the range is higher and narrower, with a well-defined ridge crest and two long subsidiary ridges running southeast toward the Androscoggin and Bear rivers; between these subsidiary ridges flows the Sunday River. The main peaks, from southwest to northeast, are Mt. Success (3565 ft.), Mt. Carlo (3565 ft.), the three peaks of Goose Eye Mtn. (West Peak, the highest, 3870 ft.; East Peak, 3794 ft.; North Peak, 3690 ft.), Fulling Mill Mtn. (North Peak, 3450 ft.), Mahoosuc Mtn. (3490 ft.), Mahoosuc Arm (3790 ft.), and Old Speck Mtn. (4180 ft.). Old Speck is the third highest mountain in ME; its name distinguishes it from the several other Speckled (with ledges) mountains in the general area. Mt. Success is named for the unincorporated township in which it is located, and Mt. Carlo is named for a dog. The origin of Goose Eye Mtn.'s peculiar name is in doubt; the most plausible explanation maintains that the geese in their flights south from the Rangeley Lakes appear almost to graze its summit, and it is, therefore, "goose high."

The views from Goose Eye, a striking rock peak, are among the best in the White Mtns., and most of the other peaks have fine views, either from the summits or from the numerous open ledges scattered throughout the range. There are several fine mountain ponds, including Speck Pond, one of the highest ponds in ME, Gentian Pond, Dream Lake, and Page Pond. The most remarkable feature of the range is Mahoosuc Notch, where the trail winds around and under huge fragments of rock which have fallen from the cliffs of Mahoosuc Mtn. to the northwest; Fulling Mill Mtn. forms the southeast wall.

The Alpine Cascades on Cascade Brook, which flows from the northwest slope of Cascade Mtn., are an attractive sight except in dry seasons. They can be approached from the gravel road along the railroad tracks on the east side of the Androscoggin, probably best reached from NH 16 by crossing the river at the highway bridge just south of Berlin. Follow the road south along the railroad. Nearly opposite the Cascade Mill of the James River Co., a footpath diverges left across the tracks, then divides into three paths; the right branch leads about 100 yd. to the foot of Cascade Falls.

From the major peaks of the southern part of the range, ridges run toward the Androscoggin, bearing interesting smaller peaks. Among these mountains are Middle Mtn. (2010 ft.), Mt. Crag (1412 ft.), Mt. Ingalls (2242 ft.), Mt. Cabot (1512 ft.), and Crow's Nest (1287 ft.). There are also two interesting waterfalls on the south side of the range. Dryad Fall is reached by the Dryad Fall Trail. Lary Flume is a wild chasm that resembles the Ice Gulch and Devil's Hopyard, with many boulder caves and one fissure cave. There is no trail, but experienced climbers have followed the brook that may be reached by bushwhacking east where the Austin Brook Trail begins its last 0.5 mi. of ascent to Gentian Pond.

ACCESS ROADS

Success Pond Rd. runs from Berlin to Success Pond, about 14 mi. The entrance to the road may be reached from NH 16 by crossing the Androscoggin River on the bridge at the traffic lights north of the city proper. Turn right (south) 0.2 mi. from NH 16 onto Hutchins St., which jogs left in

0.4 mi., crosses a railroad track, then turns right to resume its original direction. At 0.8 mi. (1.0 mi. from NH 16) turn left onto a gravel road where, in 1986, there was a large sign reading "OHRV PARKING ½ MILE." The road passes through a bulldozed yard with huge wood piles; watch out for large trucks, especially those entering from the right. The first part of the road has frequently been difficult to distinguish from branch roads, but once past this area, it is well defined. The road is not generally open to public vehicular use in winter. Trailheads are marked only with small AMC standard trail signs, often at old diverging logging roads with no well-defined parking area, so one must look for them carefully. The lower parts of the trails originating on this road have been disrupted frequently in the past by construction of new logging roads; great care is necessary to follow the proper roads, ascending or descending.

North Rd. provides access to the trails on the south side of the Mahoosuc Range. This road leaves US 2 about 2.8 mi. east of its easterly junction with NH 16 in Gorham, and crosses the Androscoggin River on the Lead Mine Bridge; the Appalachian Trail follows this part of the road. North Rd. then swings east and runs along the north side of the river to rejoin US 2 just north of Bethel ME. Bridges connect North Rd. and US 2 at the villages of Shelburne NH and Gilead ME.

CAMPING

Land in this section is owned by the state of ME and by the James River Co. and other private interests. Hiking is permitted through their courtesy. No part of this section is included in the WMNF. Camping and wood fires are prohibited by state laws except at authorized sites (shelters and Trident Col).

Trident Col Campsite (AMC) is on a side path from the Mahoosuc Trail in Trident Col. There are sites for four tents. Water is available about 50 yd. below (west of) the site.

Gentian Pond Campsite (AMC) on Gentian Pond has a large shelter and tentsites.

Carlo Col Shelter (AMC) is located on the Carlo Col Trail, 0.3 mi. below the Mahoosuc Trail at Carlo Col.

Full Goose Shelter (AMC) is located on the Mahoosuc Trail between Fulling Mill Mtn. and Goose Eye Mtn. There is a spring 30 yd. east of the shelter.

Speck Pond Campsite (AMC), located at Speck Pond on the Mahoosuc Trail, includes a shelter and tent platforms. There has been a caretaker present in the summer, and a fee is charged.

LIST OF TRAILS   MAP

THE TRAILS

Mahoosuc Trail (AMC)

This AMC trail extends the entire length of the range, from Gorham NH to the summit of Old Speck. Beyond its junction with the Centennial Trail, the Mahoosuc Trail is a link in the Appalachian Trail. Camping is limited to the tentsites at Trident Col and to the four shelters: Gentian Pond (with tentsites), Carlo Col, Full Goose, and Speck Pond (which also has tent platforms). The sites may have a caretaker, in which case a fee is charged. Water is scarce, particularly in dry weather, and its purity is always in question. This is a rugged trail—particularly for those with heavy packs—with many ledges, some of them steep, and numerous minor humps and cols. Many ledges are slippery when wet. Mahoosuc Notch is regarded by many who have hiked the entire length of the Appalachian Trail as the most difficult mile. It can be hazardous in wet or icy conditions and can remain impassable through the end of May. Do not be deceived by the relatively low elevations; this trail is among the most rugged of its kind in the White Mtns.

Part I. Gorham to Centennial Trail

To reach the trail, cross the Androscoggin River by the footbridge under the Boston & Maine Railroad bridge, 1.3 mi. north of the Gorham post office on NH 16. On the east bank, follow the road to the right (southeast) along the river for 0.6 mi., then cross the canal through the open upper level of the powerhouse (left of entrance). Beyond, keep straight ahead about 100 yd. to the woods at the east end of the dam, where the trail sign will be found. The trail is sparsely blazed in blue. Turn left and follow an old road north along the side of the canal for 125 yd., and then turn right uphill; at 0.2 mi. from this turn the trail crosses the overgrown clearing beneath a power line, then bears right and reaches but does not cross a brook, and follows it closely for 100 yd. It ascends at only a slight grade for about 0.3 mi. to a side path that leads right 0.2 mi. to Mascot Pond, just below the cliffs seen prominently from Gorham. The Mahoosuc Trail crosses a woods road (crossing poorly marked), then ascends a brook valley, which it crosses and recrosses four times. At 2.5 mi. it passes Popsy Spring on the left, climbs steeply, and emerges on the southwest side of the flat, ledgy summit of Mt. Hayes. An unmarked footway leads a few yards right to the best viewpoint south over the valley. A cairn marks the true summit of Mt. Hayes. The trail descends 0.2 mi. to the junction on the right with the Centennial Trail, on open ledges with good views north.

Part II. Centennial Trail to Gentian Pond

From here north the Mahoosuc Trail is part of the Appalachian Trail, marked with white blazes. It descends north to the col between Mt. Hayes and Cascade Mtn. (There is sometimes water in this area.) The trail then ascends Cascade Mtn. by a southwest ridge, over ledges and large fallen rocks, emerging on the bare summit ledge. It turns back sharply into the woods, descending gradually with occasional upgrades to the east end of the mountain, then enters a fine forest and descends rapidly beside cliffs and ledges to Trident Col. A side path leads left about 200 yd. to Trident Col campsite, with space for four tents. Water is available about 50 yd. below (west of) the site. The bare ledges of the rocky cone to the east of Trident Col repay a scramble to the top; a route ascends between two large cairns near the tentsite side path.

The trail descends rather steeply to the southeast, and slabs the ridge past the foot of this cone, of a second similar peak, and of the peak just west of Page Pond, which together form the Trident. Following a logging road except where it bypasses wet spots, the trail crosses three or four brooks, at least one of which should have water. At a sign it turns left from the logging road and ascends to Page Pond. The trail passes the south end of the pond, crosses a beaver dam, and climbs gradually, then steeply, to the summit of Wocket Ledge, a spur from Bald Cap. The fine view from some ledges 200 yd. south of the summit, reached by a side trail, should not be missed. The Mahoosuc Trail descends east, crosses the upper left branch of Peabody Brook, then climbs around the nose of a small ridge and descends gradually to the head of Dream Lake. The trail bears left here, then right around the north end of the lake and crosses the inlet brook. Just beyond, the Peabody Brook Trail leaves right.

From the Peabody Brook Trail junction, the Mahoosuc Trail follows a lumber road left 100 yd. It soon recrosses the inlet brook, passes over a slight divide into the watershed of Austin Brook, ascends through some swampy places, and descends to Moss Pond. It continues past the west shore of the pond and follows an old logging road down the outlet brook. About 0.3 mi. below Moss Pond the trail turns abruptly right downhill from the logging road to Gentian Pond, skirts the southwest shore of the pond, crosses a small brook first, then soon drops to cross the outlet brook. A few yards beyond are the Gentian Pond Shelter (capacity twenty) and tentsites, and the Austin Brook Trail diverges right for North Rd. in Shelburne.

Part III. Gentian Pond to Carlo Col

From Gentian Pond Shelter the trail climbs about 0.5 mi. to the top of the steep ridge whose ledges overlook the pond from the east, then descends more gradually. About 0.5 mi. farther it passes through a col, climbs over two steep humps, with water in the col beyond the second hump, and then begins to ascend the southwest side of Mt. Success. The grade is steep and the footing is rough for about the next 0.5 mi. The trail climbs over open ledges with an outlook to the southwest, passes through a belt of high scrub, and finally comes out on the summit of Mt. Success.

The trail turns sharp left here and descends through scrub, then forest, to the sag between Mt. Success and a northern subpeak, where the Success Trail enters left. The main trail climbs slightly, slabs the southeast side of the subpeak, and then descends to the steep-sided major col between Mt. Success and Mt. Carlo. The trail then rises steadily, passes the ME/NH border signs, and in 0.5 mi. more descends steeply past a fine outlook ledge into the little box ravine called Carlo Col. The Carlo Col Trail from Success Pond Rd. enters left here, and the Carlo Col Shelter is located at the head of a small brook about 0.3 mi. down the Carlo Col Trail.

Part IV. Carlo Col to Mahoosuc Notch

From Carlo Col the trail climbs steadily to the bare southwest summit of Mt. Carlo, where there is an excellent view. It then passes a lower knob to the northeast, and descends through a mountain meadow, where there is a fine view of Goose Eye Mtn. ahead, to the col, where there is sometimes water. The trail turns more north and climbs steeply to a ledgy knoll below Goose Eye, then climbs steeply again to the narrow ridge of the main peak of Goose Eye Mtn. Use care on the ledges. At the ridge top the Goose Eye Trail branches sharp left, reaching the open summit, with spectacular views, in 0.1 mi., and continuing to Success Pond Rd. Here the Mahoosuc Trail turns sharply to the right (east) and follows the ridge crest through mixed ledge and scrub to the col, then climbs steeply through woods and open areas to the bare summit of the East Peak of Goose Eye Mtn. Here it turns sharp north down the bare ridge, and enters the scrub at the east side of the open space. Beyond the col the trail runs in the open nearly to the foot of the North Peak, except for two interesting box ravines, where there is often water. At the foot of the North Peak the trail passes through a patch of woods, then climbs directly to the summit. Here it turns east along the ridge crest and swings northeast down the steep slope, winding through several patches of scrub. At the foot of the steep slope it enters the woods, slabs the west face of the ridge, and descends to the col. Full Goose Shelter is located on a shelf here; there is a spring 30 yd. behind (east of) the shelter. The trail then turns sharp left and ascends, coming into the open about 0.3 mi. below the summit of the South Peak of Fulling Mill Mtn. At this peak the trail turns sharp left, runs a few hundred yards through a meadow, and descends northwest through woods, first gradually then steeply, to the head of Mahoosuc Notch. Here the Notch Trail to Success Pond Rd. diverges sharply left (southwest).

Part V. Mahoosuc Notch to Grafton Notch

From the head of Mahoosuc Notch the trail turns sharp right (northeast) and descends the length of the narrow notch along a rough footway, passing through a number of boulder caverns, some with narrow openings where progress will be slow and where ice remains into the summer. The trail is blazed on the rocks with white paint. **Caution.** Great care should be exercised in the notch on account of slippery rocks and dangerous holes, and the notch may be impassable through early June because of snow, even with snowshoes. Heavy backpacks will impede progress considerably.

At the lower end of the notch the trail leaves the brook, bears left, ascends gradually and, after slabbing the east end of Mahoosuc Mtn. for about 0.5 mi., follows up the valley of Notch 2, then crosses to the north side of the brook. The trail then ascends, winds along rocks and ledges, and climbs through fine forest, in general slabbing the ridge of Mahoosuc Arm at a very steep angle. A little more than halfway up it passes the head of a little flume, in which there is sometimes water. On the flat summit ledges near the top of Mahoosuc Arm the May Cutoff diverges left and passes over the true summit to the Speck Pond Trail. The Mahoosuc Trail follows the open, winding ridge for about 0.5 mi., southeast, northeast, and north, then drops steeply about 0.3 mi. to Speck Pond (3430 ft.), one of the highest ponds in ME, bordered with thick woods. The trail crosses the outlet brook and continues around the east side of the pond about 0.3 mi. to Speck Pond Campsite (in summer, there is a caretaker and a fee for overnight camping). The Speck Pond Trail descends from here to Success Pond Rd.

The trail then climbs about 0.3 mi. to the southeast end of the next hump on the ridge, passes over it, and slabs the east face of a second small hump. In the gully beyond, a few yards east of the trail, there is a spring. The trail climbs to the open shoulder of Old Speck; the footway is definite up this open ridge, and hikers need only stay on the crest. Near the top of the shoulder the trail bears right, reenters the woods, and follows the wooded crest with blue blazes that mark the boundary of Grafton Notch State Park. The Old Speck Trail, which continues the Appalachian Trail north, diverges left to Grafton Notch, and in 0.3 mi. more the Mahoosuc Trail reaches the summit and observation tower.

Mahoosuc Trail (map 7:E10-C13)
Distances from NH 16, Gorham
- *to* Mt. Hayes summit; 3.1 mi., 2 hr. 20 min.
- *to* Centennial Trail: 3.3 mi., 2 hr. 25 min.
- *to* Cascade Mtn. summit: 5.2 mi., 3 hr. 35 min.
- *to* Trident Col: 6.6 mi., 4 hr. 20 min.
- *to* Page Pond: 7.4 mi., 5 hr.
- *to* Wocket Ledge: 8.1 mi., 5 hr. 50 min.
- *to* Dream Lake, inlet brook crossing: 9.2 mi., 6 hr. 20 min.
- *to* Gentian Pond Shelter: 11.4 mi., 8 hr.
- *to* Mt. Success summit: 14.3 mi., 10 hr. 50 min.
- *to* Success Trail: 14.9 mi., 11 hr. 20 min.
- *to* Carlo Col Trail: 16.8 mi., 13 hr. 20 min.
- *to* Mt. Carlo: 17.2 mi., 13 hr. 50 min.
- *to* Goose Eye Trail: 18.7 mi., 15 hr. 20 min.
- *to* Goose Eye Mtn., East Peak: 19.0 mi., 15 hr. 45 min.
- *to* Goose Eye Mtn., North Peak: 20.0 mi., 16 hr. 5 min.
- *to* Full Goose Shelter: 21.1 mi., 16 hr. 35 min.
- *to* Notch Trail: 22.7 mi., 17 hr. 30 min.
- *to* foot of Mahoosuc Notch: 23.7 mi., 19 hr. 20 min.
- *to* Mahoosuc Arm summit: 25.2 mi., 21 hr.
- *to* Speck Pond Shelter: 26.1 mi., 21 hr. 40 min.
- *to* Old Speck Trail junction: 26.9 mi., 22 hr. 45 min.
- *to* Old Speck Mtn. summit: 27.2 mi. (43.8 km.), 23 hr.

Success Trail (AMC)

This trail ascends to the Mahoosuc Trail 0.6 mi. north of Mt. Success, from Success Pond Rd. 5.4 mi. from Hutchins St. The trail sign is easy to miss. The trail follows a logging road, bears right at a fork at 0.1 mi., and passes straight through a clearing, entering the woods at a sign in 0.4 mi. Soon the trail starts to climb steadily on the road, and at 1.4 mi. reaches the upper edge of an area of small second-growth trees, swings right, and ascends more steeply. At 1.6 mi. a loop path 0.3 mi. long diverges right to a spectacular ledge outlook with fine views of the Presidentials and the mountains of the North Country. In a little over 100 yd. the upper end of the loop path rejoins, and the main trail ascends to a ridge crest, from which it descends very gradually to a brook (unreliable) at an old logging camp site. The trail now makes an easy climb up a shallow ravine, part of the way in the bed of a small (unreliable) brook (follow paint blazes carefully), and soon reaches the Mahoosuc Trail at the main ridge crest.

Success Trail (map 7:D12)
Distances from Success Pond Rd.

to Mahoosuc Trail: 2.4 mi. (3.8 km.), 2 hr.

to Mt. Success summit (via Mahoosuc Trail): 3.0 mi., 2 hr. 30 min.

Carlo Col Trail (AMC)

This trail ascends to the Mahoosuc Trail at the small box ravine called Carlo Col; it leaves Success Pond Rd. in common with the Goose Eye Trail about 8.2 mi. from Hutchins St. From the road the two trails angle to the left, and in 100 yd. the Carlo Col Trail diverges sharp right 50 yd. to a broad logging road, which it follows east for 0.8 mi., with little gain in elevation. Turning left off the road at a log yard, the trail immediately crosses the main brook, continues near it for about 0.3 mi., then turns obliquely left away from the brook and follows a branch road with a steeper rise. It crosses back to the south, over the north and south branches of the main brook, and bends east up the rather steep south bank of the south branch. Avoiding several false crossings of this brook, it climbs to Carlo Col Shelter (last water for several miles). Continuing up the dry ravine, the trail ends at the Mahoosuc Trail about 0.3 mi. beyond the shelter. There is a fine outlook ledge a short distance to the right (west) on the Mahoosuc Trail.

Carlo Col Trail (map 7:C12-C13)
Distance from Success Pond Rd.

to Mahoosuc Trail: 2.6 mi. (4.1 km.), 2 hr. 5 min.

Goose Eye Trail (AMC)

This trail ascends Goose Eye Mtn. from Success Pond Rd. 8.2 mi. from Hutchins St., and reaches the Mahoosuc Trail 0.1 mi. beyond the summit. The trail leaves the road in common with the Carlo Col Trail, angling to the left, and in 100 yd. the Carlo Col Trail diverges sharp right. The Goose Eye Trail follows an old logging road, crosses two brooks, and enters a more recent gravel road which comes in from the right (descending, bear right). In 100 yd. it diverges right (watch carefully for sign) from the gravel road, passes through a clear-cut area, crosses a wet section, and at 1.4 mi. it reaches the yellow-blazed ME/NH state line. The trail slabs at a moderate grade up the south side of a ridge through fine hardwoods, climbs more steeply uphill, then becomes gradual at the crest of the ridge; at 2.6 mi. there is a glimpse of the peak of Goose Eye ahead. The trail ascends moderately along the north side of the ridge, then ascends steeply, scrambling up a difficult ledge that may be dangerous if wet or icy, then comes out on the open ledges below the summit. From the summit, which has magnificent views in all directions, the trail continues 0.1 mi. to the Mahoosuc Trail, which turns right (southbound) and runs straight ahead (northbound).

Goose Eye Trail (map 7:C12-C13)
Distances from Success Pond Rd.

to Goose Eye Mtn. summit: 3.1 mi., 2 hr. 40 min.

to Mahoosuc Trail: 3.2 mi. (5.2 km.), 2 hr. 45 min.

Notch Trail (AMC)

This trail ascends to the southwest end of Mahoosuc Notch from a spur road that leaves Success Pond Rd. 10.9 mi. from Hutchins St., in an area of active logging. The spur road crosses two bridges, and the trail proper begins at 0.6 mi. at a sign and follows a logging road into the woods. (It may be possible to drive to this point.)

The trail ascends easily, following logging roads much of the way, with bypasses at some of the wetter spots, along a slow-running brook with many signs of beaver activity. At the height-of-land it meets the Mahoosuc Trail. Turn left for the notch; very soon the valley, which has been an ordinary one, changes sharply to a chamber formation, and the high cliffs of the notch, which have not been visible at all on the lower part of the trail, come into sight.

Notch Trail (map 7:C12-C13)

Distance (est.) from Success Pond Rd.

to Mahoosuc Trail: 2.8 mi. (4.5 km.), 1 hr. 45 min.

Speck Pond Trail (AMC)

This trail ascends to Speck Pond from Success Pond Rd.; take the right fork of the road about 11.5 mi. from Hutchins St., and continue 0.9 mi. to the trailhead. The trail leaves the road, enters the woods, and follows the north side of a small brook for 1.5 mi. It then swings left away from the brook, climbs rather steeply at times, passes a relatively level section, then climbs very steeply to the junction with the May Cutoff, which leads over the true summit of Mahoosuc Arm to the Mahoosuc Trail. The Speck Pond Trail passes an excellent outlook over the pond and up to Old Speck, then descends steeply to the pond, and reaches the campsite and the Mahoosuc Trail.

Speck Pond Trail (map 7:C12-C13)
Distance (est.) from Success Pond Rd.
   to Speck Pond Campsite: 3.7 mi. (6.0 km.), 3 hr.

May Cutoff (AMC)

This short trail runs from the Speck Pond Trail to the Mahoosuc Trail, across the true summit of Mahoosuc Arm, with only minor ups and downs.

May Cutoff (map 7:C13)
Distance (est.) from Speck Pond Trail
   to Mahoosuc Trail: 0.3 mi. (0.5 km.), 10 min.

Old Speck Trail (AMC)

This trail, part of the Appalachian Trail, ascends Old Speck Mtn. from a well-signed parking area on ME 26 at the height-of-land in Grafton Notch. From the north side of the parking lot follow the left trail; the right trail goes to Baldpate Mtn. In 0.1 mi., the Eyebrow Trail leaves right to circle an 800-ft. cliff shaped like an eyebrow. The Old Speck Trail crosses a brook and soon begins to climb, following a series of switchbacks to approach the falls on Cascade Brook. Above the falls the trail, now heading more north, crosses the brook for the last time (last water), and 0.1 mi. farther passes the upper terminus of the Eyebrow Trail on the right. The main trail bears left, ascends gradually to the north ridge, where it bears more left, and follows the ridge, which has views southwest. At about 3300 ft. the trail turns southeast toward the summit, and at about 3600 ft. the Link Trail diverges left. The Old Speck Trail turns more south and ascends to its end at the Mahoosuc Trail. The flat, wooded summit of Old Speck, where an observation tower affords fine views, is 0.3 mi. left (west); Speck Pond Shelter is 1.2 mi. to the right.

Old Speck Trail (map 7:B13-C13)
Distances from ME 26

   to Eyebrow Trail, upper junction: 1.2 mi., 1 hr. 5 min.

   to Link Trail: 3.1 mi., 2 hr. 40 min.

   to Mahoosuc Trail: 3.5 mi. (5.6 km.), 3 hr. 10 min.

   to Old Speck Mtn. summit (via Mahoosuc Trail): 3.8 mi., 3 hr. 20 min.

Link Trail

This trail descends very steeply from the Old Speck Trail, 3.1 mi. from ME 26, to the site of the firewarden's cabin, giving access to the East Spur Trail, which provides an attractive loop trip.

Link Trail (map 7:C13)
Distance (est.) from Old Speck Trail

   to East Spur Trail: 0.3 mi. (0.5 km.), 15 min.

East Spur Trail

This trail ascends the east spur of Old Speck; it is steeper and rougher than the Old Speck Trail, and harder to follow, but has much better views. It is not recommended in bad weather. From the site of the old firewarden's cabin, reached from the Old Speck Trail via the Link Trail, it crosses the brook, ascends steeply, then turns sharp left and slabs southeast to open ledges. It continues through open areas and woods to a large boulder left, where the trail turns sharp right. The trail climbs up to a small, rock promontory and continues to ascend through a mixture of rock and scrub to the Mahoosuc Trail in a small clearing 30 yd. north of the summit of Old Speck Mtn.

East Spur Trail (map 7:C13)
Distance (est.) from Link Trail

   to Old Speck Mtn. summit: 1.0 mi. (1.6 km.), 1 hr.

Eyebrow Trail

This trail provides an alternative route to the lower part of the Old Speck Trail, passing over the edge of the cliff called the Eyebrow, which overlooks Grafton Notch. The trail leaves the Old Speck Trail on the right 0.1 mi. from the parking area off ME 26. It turns right at the base of a rock face, crosses a rock slide, and turns sharp left, then ascends steadily, bearing right where a side path leaves straight ahead for an outlook. Soon the trail runs at a moderate grade along the top of the cliff, with good views, descends to an outlook, then runs mostly level to the Old Speck Trail.

Eyebrow Trail (map 7:B13)
Distance (est.) from Old Speck Trail, lower junction
   to Old Speck Trail, upper junction: 1.4 mi. (2.3 km.), 1 hr. 10 min.

Centennial Trail (AMC)

This trail, a part of the Appalachian Trail, begins on Hogan Rd.; this dirt road turns west from North Rd. north of its crossing of the Androscoggin River, just before it swings abruptly to the east. There is a small parking area 0.3 mi. from North Rd., and parking is also permitted at the junction of North Rd. and Hogan Rd.; in any case, do not block the road. The Centennial Trail was constructed by the AMC in 1976, its centennial year.

From the parking area on Hogan Rd., the trail runs generally northwest. After 50 yd. it bears left up a steep bank into the woods, levels off, and reaches the first of many stone steps in 0.1 mi. The trail ascends rather steeply, then more gradually, with a limited view of the Androscoggin River. It turns left onto a woods road and crosses a brook at about 1.2 mi. (last water). The trail then crosses a logging road and at 1.6 mi. turns sharp right; the ledge to the left has fine views of the Moriahs and Mt. Washington.

The trail climbs steeply, past a second good outlook right, to a ridge crest, and soon descends into a small valley, then ascends to open ledges with a fine view of the Mahoosuc Range and the Androscoggin valley to the right. At 3.3 mi. the trail reaches an easterly summit of Mt. Hayes, where there is an excellent view of the Carter–Moriah Range and Northern Presidentials from open ledges. The trail descends slightly, then ascends across a series of open ledges to end at the Mahoosuc Trail at 3.7 mi. The summit of Mt. Hayes is 0.2 mi. left, with fine views. The Appalachian Trail turns right (north) on the Mahoosuc Trail.

Centennial Trail (map 7:E11-D11)
Distance from Hogan Rd.
  to Mahoosuc Trail: 3.7 mi. (6.0 km.), 2 hr. 35 min.

Peabody Brook Trail (AMC)

This trail ascends to the Mahoosuc Trail at Dream Lake from North Rd., 1.3 mi. east of US 2. Overnight parking is not permitted at the base of this trail.

The trail follows a logging road between two houses and bears right at a fork. It continues north along the brook and bears left at a fork at 0.8 mi., soon becomes a trail, and begins to ascend moderately. At 1.2 mi. a path leaves left and descends about 0.5 mi. to Giant Falls. The trail rises more steeply, and at 1.5 mi. there is a good view (left) of Mt. Washington and Mt. Adams through open trees. The trail climbs a short ladder just beyond. About 0.5 mi. farther, it crosses the east branch of the brook, then recrosses in 0.3 mi. From here the trail is nearly level, and enters a rather broad open area, making a sharp left turn in about 0.4 mi. Soon Dream Lake is seen left. The Dryad Fall Trail leaves right 0.2 mi. beyond the sharp turn, and the Peabody Brook Trail ends 120 yd. farther at the Mahoosuc Trail.

Peabody Brook Trail (map 7:E11-D11)
Distance from North Rd.
  to Mahoosuc Trail: 3.1 mi. (4.9 km.), 2 hr. 20 min.

Austin Brook Trail (AMC)

This trail ascends to the Mahoosuc Trail at Gentian Pond from North Rd., 0.6 mi. west of Meadow Rd. (which crosses the Androscoggin at Shelburne village). There is limited parking on the south side of the road. The trail passes through a turnstile on private land and follows the west side of Austin Brook, passing between the garage (left) and a summer camp called "The Wigwam" (right) about 0.3 mi. from the road. Then the trail turns sharp left, ascends a small bank, and continues about 0.5 mi. to Austin Brook, which it crosses to reach Mill Brook Rd., a gated logging road. Turn left on the logging road, and continue past a brook crossing to the junction left with the Dryad Fall Trail. About 0.3 mi. farther, take the left fork of the road. The Austin Brook Trail continues along the logging road, which soon turns sharp right. From this point follow arrows at branch roads, bearing right. In about 0.8 mi. the trail crosses the brook that drains Gentian Pond, crosses a clearing, enters a logging road, soon bears left away from it, and begins the rather steep climb of about 0.5 mi. to the Mahoosuc Trail at Gentian Pond Shelter.

Austin Brook Trail (map 7:E12-D12)
Distance from North Rd.
  to Gentian Pond: 3.3 mi. (5.3 km.), 2 hr. 30 min.

Dryad Fall Trail (AMC)

This trail runs from the Austin Brook Trail to the Peabody Brook Trail near Dream Lake, passing Dryad Fall, one of the highest cascades in the mountains—particularly interesting for a few days after a rainstorm, since its several cascades fall at least 300 ft. over steep ledges. The trail is blazed in yellow, and may be somewhat difficult to follow, since it is used very little. It leaves the Austin Brook Trail on the left about 2.0 mi. from North Rd., just past the second brook crossing. It gradually ascends old logging roads through woods for about 0.5 mi., then drops down (right) to Dryad Brook, which it follows nearly to the base of the falls. Rocks in the vicinity of the falls are very slippery and hazardous. From here the trail climbs steeply northeast of the falls. After rising several hundred feet, with good views of the falls, the trail bears right and joins a logging road. It ascends left on this road, which soon meets another logging road. It follows this road left, crossing Dryad Brook above the falls and climbing left. The trail then heads generally west for 0.8 mi., until it slabs off obliquely right. From here almost to Dream Lake it goes through woods, generally west, rising at a moderate grade. At the crest of the ridge the trail again meets a logging road, then descends to end at the Peabody Brook Trail about 100 yd. from the Mahoosuc Trail. (Descending, watch carefully for where the trail turns down steeply right off the logging road above the falls.)

Dryad Fall Trail (map 7:D12-D11)
Distances (est.) from Austin Brook Trail
to Dryad Fall: 0.8 mi., 45 min.
to Peabody Brook Trail: 1.5 mi. (2.5 km.), 1 hr. 25 min.

Scudder Trail
This trail, blazed red and white, provides access to the ledges and summit of Mt. Ingalls. It begins on Mill Brook Rd., a gated logging road which leaves North Rd. about 50 yd. west of Meadow Rd. (the road which crosses the Androscoggin on a bridge from Shelburne village). It diverges from Mill Brook Rd. on the second road right, 0.5 mi.

from North Rd., crosses the Yellow Trail and shortly enters an open area. Bearing left, the trail continues as a woods road to a sign on the right, where another road climbs to the Ingalls–Cabot col and the Judson Pond Trail. The Scudder Trail turns sharp left at the col and soon comes out on a ledge on the west side of the ridge, with views over the Androscoggin valley. The trail climbs back eastward, passing the blue blazes of a Boise-Cascade Co. boundary in a ravine beneath a high cliff. The trail wanders back and forth, emerging on open ledges on both sides of the ridge, and finally circles an extensive ledge with views southwest. It then climbs 150 yd. to the wooded summit of Mt. Ingalls. A herd path, axe blazed with some white paint markings, leads down 0.3 mi. to a scenic mountain tarn.

Scudder Trail (map 7:E12-D12)
Distances (est.) from Mill Brook Rd.

    to Ingalls–Cabot col: 1.3 mi., 55 min.
    to lower ledges: 1.5 mi., 1 hr. 5 min.
    to upper ledges: 2.5 mi., 1 hr. 55 min.
    to Mt. Ingalls summit: 3.0 mi. (4.8 km.), 2 hr. 20 min.

Middle Mountain

Follow a woods road that leaves North Rd. on the north just east of Gates Brook, 2.4 mi. from the west junction of North Rd. and US 2. Continue on this road for about 0.8 mi., past a trail right that leads to Mt. Crag at 0.4 mi., then take a left branch that leads up the ravine between First Mtn. and Middle Mtn., at one point making a sharp left turn up a blowdown-strewn gully. The trail, blazed yellow, is not to be confused with large yellow boundary markings on the woods road and on the summit trail. Just before the height-of-land, the trail turns off the road right and climbs, at first steeply, along the ridge to the bare summit of Middle Mtn., where there are fine views.

Mount Crag

This small mountain is easily climbed and offers a fine view up and down the Androscoggin valley. It has two trails.

(1) Take the road described for the ascent of Middle Mtn. A trail leaves this road 0.4 mi. from North Rd., on the right, and climbs steeply to the ledges.

(2) Follow the Austin Brook Trail about 0.3 mi. in from North Rd., then go left on the Yellow Trail to Mt. Crag. The Yellow Trail gives convenient access to the Austin Brook Trail and Mt. Crag from the Philbrook Farm Inn on North Rd. It leads west from the north end of the access road behind the cottages connected with the inn. The trail coincides with the Red Trail to Mt. Cabot for 50 yd., then branches left and leads west on a practically level grade. It crosses several woods roads, Scudder Trail, Mill Brook Rd., Austin Brook, and the Austin Brook Trail, then heads generally northwest to the summit of Mt. Crag, going through an extensive lumbered area (but it is easy to follow).

Mount Cabot and Crow's Nest

This range runs south and southeast from Mt. Ingalls. Several trails, distinguished by color, start from the access road at the Philbrook Farm Inn on North Rd. The easternmost is the White Trail, which leads to Crow's Nest. The Blue and Red trails both lead to the summit of Mt. Cabot, making a loop trip possible. The Yellow Trail slabs west to Mt. Crag and provides access to Mt. Ingalls via the Scudder Trail.

The *White Trail* is best reached from the dirt road east of the Philbrook Farm Inn that starts immediately west of the fire pond. Follow this road to the first cottage, where the White Trail turns right by a large rock. Shortly, the Wiggin Rock Trail (Orange Trail) leaves left while the White Trail climbs east along an old logging road for a mile, passing through a recently logged area (follow blazes carefully). Leaving the logging road, it makes a short, steep ascent to the wooded summit. The trail ends a few yards farther at a limited viewpoint to the northeast.

The *Wiggin Rock Trail (Orange Trail)* climbs from its junction with the White Trail for about 0.3 mi. to Wiggin Rock, a small ledge with a view southeast across the Androscoggin valley. Beyond the viewpoint, the trail drops steeply for about 0.3 mi. to the Blue Trail.

The *Blue Trail* starts from the gravel road immediately to the west of the Philbrook Farm Inn, follows a good wood road, and passes the Orange (Wiggin Rock) Trail on the right. Shortly before this road reaches an old reservoir, the Blue Trail turns right on a badly eroded road. The Blue Trail continues much of the way on logging roads at an easy grade to a boundary marker, beyond which the trail climbs more steeply for about 0.3 mi. to the summit and the Red Trail. The summit is wooded, but a ledge on the right shortly before the summit gives a view east, and an orange-blazed trail from the summit leads left to an open ledge with views southwest.

The *Red Trail* bears left from the Blue Trail on the access road west of the Philbrook Farm Inn, coinciding with the Yellow Trail for 50 yd., then diverges left. It continues on a series of logging roads, passes an orange-blazed trail to a viewpoint (Mary's Aerie) on the right, crosses a small brook, circles around, and finally climbs steeply to approach Mt. Cabot from the north. The Judson Pond Trail leads left (downhill) shortly before the Red Trail reaches the summit and the junction with the Blue Trail. (See Blue Trail for views.)

The *Judson Pond Trail* (which no longer reaches Judson Pond, due to logging activity in that region) is an orange-blazed connecting trail that diverges from the Red Trail 0.1 mi. northwest of the summit of Mt. Cabot, and in 0.2 mi. reaches the Ingalls–Cabot col and the junction with the Scudder Trail. Beyond this point the trail has been abandoned.

The North Country

As C. F. Belcher comments (*Appalachia* XXXIII:37), referring to the Kilkenny, "this area has built up a legend of isolation and mystery . . . even though for years it has been the intimate hunting and fishing preserve of those living nearby and a knowing few"—and a source of income for the wood products industries and their employees and suppliers. These remarks apply, with emphasis, to the entire North Country. The appearance of wilderness masks the active presence of logging operations, and the lack of marked and signed trails disguises the extensive network of paths known very well to local woodsmen.

From the Presidential Range this vast wooded region extends 65 mi. north to the Canadian border. It varies in width from 25 mi. at the southern end to less than 15 at Pittsburg. Its natural boundaries are the Israel and Moose rivers on the south, the Androscoggin and Magalloway rivers on the east, and the Connecticut River on the west.

In the southern quarter of this region, south of the Upper Ammonoosuc River and NH 110 and NH 110A, between the towns of Groveton and Milan, the mountains are still relatively high—two just over 4000 ft.—and grouped compactly into ranges, like those farther south. Above this line lies the true North Country, a region very similar to the adjacent section of ME. The mountains are lower—very few exceed 3500 ft.—and most have wooded summits. The noteworthy peaks, for example the Percys, Mt. Magalloway, and Rump Mtn., are scattered, separated by long stretches of less interesting terrain. Although the main backbone of the White Mtns.—the divide between the Connecticut River and the streams and lakes to the east—continues north through this country all the way to the Canadian border, it is for the most part illdefined, with no outstanding summits. Except for Dixville Notch, there is little rugged mountain scenery, although there are several large lakes.

South of the Upper Ammonoosuc, good public roads are always within a reasonable distance, and the interior, most of which is within the WMNF, has a well-developed trail system. In the great tract to the north, however, only a few mountains, even those over 3000 ft., have trails, and these are not regularly maintained by any organization.

There are three main highways in this most northerly section. US 3 follows the Connecticut valley to its uppermost headwaters beyond the Connecticut Lakes, on the Canadian border. An alternate road between Colebrook and Pittsburg is NH 145. On the east side of the state, NH 16, which continues as ME 16, accompanies the Androscoggin and Magalloway rivers north to the outlet of Lake Aziscohos, then swings east to the Rangeley Lakes. NH 26, the only east-west road north of the Upper Ammonoosuc, crosses from Errol to Colebrook through Dixville Notch.

Even public secondary roads are few and short, although the paper companies have constructed an intricate system of good main-haul gravel roads. Many of these have gates or are restricted, and on all of them heavy log trucks have the right of way. These roads are not signed, and the lack of striking landmarks makes travel on them confusing for the inexperienced. The scarcity of settlements and confusing river drainages make the usual advice about following a stream when lost inadvisable. Competent woodsmen will find pleasure in the area's remoteness, but should clear their plans with the landowners in advance. In general, camping and fires are prohibited throughout the region.

Because this northern section is managed for the continuous production of timber, roads and trails may change radically from one year to the next. Obtain specific information about current conditions in advance. The following contact people may be of help: District Ranger Gary Carr, Androscoggin District, WMNF, Gorham; NH Fish and Game District Chief Jeffrey Gray, West Milan; NH District Forest Rangers Richard Belmore, Lancaster, and Burham Judd, Pittsburg; and Berlin Fish Hatchery Superintendent Warren Ingram, York Pond.

Contacts for the chief landowners are, International Paper: Neil McGinness, Stratford, and Tom Eubanks, Augusta ME; Champion International: Donald Tase, West Stewartstown; Boise Cascade: Mike Brown or Sumner Burgess, Woods Department, Rumford ME; James River: Elwood Haines, Groveton, and Rick Mackin, Berlin; Diamond International: Jim Andritz, Groveton. For the Dartmouth College Grant, contact Nelson Ham at the Second College Grant gatehouse or Earl Jette, Dartmouth College, Hanover.

LIST OF TRAILS   MAP

THE CHERRY–DARTMOUTH RANGE

Cherry Mtn. is a prominent mountain located in the town of Carroll, west of the Presidential Range. The highest peak is Mt. Martha (3573 ft.), which has good outlooks from the summit area, although the former fire tower has been dismantled. A northern spur, Owl's Head (3258 ft.), has a spectacular view from a fine ledge just south of the wooded summit. The Dartmouth Range is a ridge with numerous humps running southwest to northeast, lying between Cherry Mtn. and the Presidentials. The range is completely trailless; Mt. Dartmouth (3727 ft.) and Mt. Deception (3671 ft.) are the most important summits. Cherry Mtn. Rd. (FR 14), 6.9 mi. long, runs from US 302 about 0.8 mi. west of the Fabyan Motel to the junction of NH 115 and NH 115A, passing through the high notch that separates the two mountain masses. Refer to map 8, Pilot.

Cherry Mountain Trail (WMNF)

This trail leaves NH 115 1.9 mi. from its junction with US 3, opposite Lennon Rd. Starting as a recent logging road, it passes straight through the log yard at 0.3 mi. and continues straight ahead at 0.5 mi., where another road diverges right. In 0.7 mi. it becomes a footpath on an old roadbed, climbing higher above the brook that it parallels, and passing a spring left at 1.1 mi. At 1.5 mi. the trail reaches the ridge crest, where a spur turns left and climbs 0.2 mi. to the summit of Mt. Martha, where it meets Martha's Mile.

The Cherry Mountain Trail turns right and descends moderately on an old road with excellent footing, and in 1.5 mi. from the junction with the summit spur the Black Brook Trail leaves right (south) for US 302. The Cherry Mountain Trail continues down the slope and ends at Cherry Mtn. Rd. (which is narrow—use care) just north of its height-of-land, 3.2 mi. from US 302 and 3.7 mi. from NH 115.

Cherry Mountain Trail (map 8:F6-F7)
Distances from NH 115

to Mt. Martha summit spur trail: 1.7 mi., 1 hr. 45 min.

to Mt. Martha summit (via spur trail): 1.9 mi., 1 hr. 55 min.

to Black Brook Trail: 3.3 mi., 2 hr. 30 min.

to Cherry Mtn. Rd.: 5.2 mi. (8.4 km.), 3 hr. 30 min.

Black Brook Trail (WMNF)

This trail, which is used lightly and marked sparsely, leads north from a small parking area on the north side of US 302, about 0.4 mi. west of the Zealand Campground and 1.9 mi. east of US 3. It immediately crosses the Maine Central Railroad, and follows old logging roads at moderate grades through hardwoods. Eventually it crosses the height-of-land on a southerly spur of Cherry Mtn., and descends a short distance to the Cherry Mountain Trail, 1.8 mi. below the summit and 1.9 mi. above Cherry Mtn. Rd.

Black Brook Trail (map 8:F6-F7)
Distance from parking area off US 302

to Cherry Mountain Trail: 3.4 mi. (5.5 km.), 2 hr. 30 min.

Owl's Head Trail (RMC)

This trail ascends to the fine outlook on Owl's Head. It begins on NH 115 at the Stanley Slide historical marker, 5.9 mi. from the junction with US 3 and 0.7 mi. from the junction with NH 115A. The trail immediately steps over Slide Brook and runs through the woods, dropping into the trench from the 1885 landslide at 0.7 mi. It enters the old route of the trail, and crosses a gravel logging road into a region which has been recently logged, requiring great care in following the trail along skid roads and through second growth. At the top of the logged area the trail turns sharp right into the overgrown track of the slide, where footing is slippery and poor. The trail reaches the ridge above the slide and continues steeply to the summit, where Martha's Mile continues across the magnificent outlook ledge and on to Mt. Martha.

Owl's Head Trail (map 8:E7)
Distance from NH 115
to Owl's Head summit: 1.9 mi. (3.1 km.), 2 hr.

Martha's Mile

Martha's Mile is a link trail between the summits of Mt. Martha and Owl's Head. It leaves the ledge at the summit of Owl's Head, swings north, then sharp left, and descends a very short, steep pitch. It then descends easily to a col and climbs moderately, with excellent footing, to the summit of Mt. Martha.

Martha's Mile (map 8:E7-F6)
Distance from Owl's Head
to Mt. Martha summit: 0.8 mi. (1.3 km.), 40 min.

Pondicherry Wildlife Refuge

This fine 300-acre refuge, located mostly in Jefferson with a few acres in Whitefield, is a National Natural Landmark. It consists of Big Cherry Pond (about 90 acres) and Little Cherry Pond (about 25 acres). As "Great Ponds," these are in the custody of the state. Surrounding each are bands of open bog and bog-swamp forest belonging to the Audubon Society of NH.

"Pondicherry" is the old name for Cherry Pond and nearby Cherry Mtn. The refuge is managed jointly by the NH Fish and Game Department and Audubon. Fishing is allowed, but not hunting or trapping. At least fifty kinds of water birds and an unusual variety of mammals have been recorded in the refuge, and several uncommon species of both water and land birds nest there. Pondicherry is also interesting for its vegetation and its spectacular views of the Presidential Range. Best access is east from Whitefield Airport by either the old B&M Railroad right-of-way, which is driveable, and tracks beyond, or the old Maine Central right-of-way off the road from the airport to NH 115.

CRESCENT RANGE

The Crescent Range lies north of US 2 and west of NH 16 in the towns of Jefferson, Randolph, and Berlin. The chief summits, west to east, are Boy (Bois) Mtn., Mt. Randolph, Mt. Crescent, Black Crescent Mtn., Mt. Jericho, and Mt. Forist. In addition to map 8, refer to the Randolph Mountain Club map of the Randolph valley and the Northern Peaks, and to the USGS Mt. Washington and Gorham quadrangles.

Active lumbering and residential developments on the south slopes may intrude on some of the following trails. Watch carefully for markers and signs, and inquire locally for further information. A snowmachine trail network which runs generally north of the ridge line may provide access to Mt. Forist, Mt. Jericho, and possibly other points.

Boy (Bois) Mountain (2220 ft.)

Boy (Bois) Mtn. is located east of Jefferson Highlands. An open ledge near the summit provides an easily accessible view of the northern Presidential Range.

The trail is maintained by the Carter-Bridgman family, and leaves the highway 1.3 mi. east of the junction of US 2 with NH 115A. Park on the terrace south of the highway, west of the road to Jefferson Notch (now closed to traffic), and not in the driveway to the Carter estate. There is no sign at the road. Go up the dirt drive between the garden and the raspberry patch and pass between the house and barn. From this point signs and arrows mark the path.

Boy Mountain (map 8:E8)
Distance from US 2
   to Boy Mtn. summit: 0.7 mi. (1.1 km.), 40 min.

Local Paths in Randolph

The town of Randolph consists of two sections. A lower section lies along Durand Rd. (the former US 2), in the Moose River valley, and an upper section is situated on Randolph Hill, a plateau extending southeast from the foot of Mt. Crescent, reached by Mt. Crescent Rd. Lowe's Store and the Ravine House site are in the lower section and the Mt. Crescent House site is in the upper section. On the south slope of the hill, connecting the two sections of the town and providing access from various points to major mountain trails, is a well-developed network of paths, maintained by the Randolph Mountain Club (RMC). These are described in detail in the RMC publication *Randolph Paths* and are shown on that club's map of the Randolph valley and the Northern Peaks.

Lookout Ledge (2240 ft.)

This granite cliff on a knob of the southeast ridge of Mt. Randolph gives one of the best views of the floor of King Ravine and its rock glacier, with moderate effort. It is reached by the Pasture Path, Ledge Trail, Sargent Path, Vyron D. Lowe Trail and Crescent Ridge Trail. The ledge is on private property. No fires are permitted.

Vyron D. Lowe Trail (RMC)

This path ascends from the vicinity of Lowe's Store and Cabins, near the west end of Durand Rd., to Lookout Ledge.

Entering the woods north of Durand Rd. just east of Lowe's Cabins (sign), the trail parallels the road, then ascends, crossing a number of logging roads and logged areas. At 1.8 mi. it joins the Crescent Ridge Trail. Turn right (east) for Lookout Ledge.

Vyron D. Lowe Trail (map 8:E9)
Distance from Durand Rd.

to Lookout Ledge: 1.9 mi. (3.0 km.), 1 hr. 25 min.

Sargent Path

This is the most direct route to Lookout Ledge, as well as the steepest. It is maintained by the Cutter family. Leave Durand Rd. at the sign "1916" opposite a dark red cottage 0.8 mi. west of the Ravine House site and 0.9 mi. east of Randolph Spring. The path rises steadily to the ledge, where it meets the Ledge and Crescent Ridge trails. This trail is little used, but well blazed, and it can be followed with caution.

Sargent Path (map 8:E9)
Distance from Durand Rd.

to Lookout Ledge: 0.8 mi. (1.3 km.), 50 min.

Ledge Trail (RMC)

Leading from the Ravine House site to Lookout Ledge, this trail forms a steep but direct route to the outlook. At the west end of the hotel site, look for a trail sign on the driveway. Follow blazes across a rocky slope above which the "Eusden" house is visible. The trail soon leaves the yard and, rising steadily northwest, climbs through deep and beautiful woods to the notch at 0.7 mi., where the

Notchway diverges right for Randolph Hill. The Ledge Trail turns sharp left, steepens, and leaves the woods to follow an overgrown lumber road through second growth, where it shortly intersects the Pasture Path at 1.1 mi. The trail reenters the woods, climbs steeply over some rocks, and descends slightly, passing the Eyrie, a small outlook, and continues on a few yards to end at the Crescent Ridge Trail. Just below is Lookout Ledge.

Ledge Trail (map 8:E9)
Distance from Ravine House site
   to Lookout Ledge: 1.3 mi. (2.1 km.), 1 hr. 10 min.

Pasture Path (RMC)

This trail leads from Randolph Hill Rd. to the Ledge Trail. The Pasture Path begins at Randolph Hill Rd. about 0.1 mi. above Stearns Rd. and runs west through old pastures and woods, using parts of Stearns Rd., Glover Spring Rd., and High Acres Rd., passing the Diagonal, Wood Path, EZ Way, and Bee Line. Below High Acres, the path leaves High Acres Rd., passes through ancient forest and then light woods. Grassy Lane diverges right, and the Pasture Path enters young second growth and turns sharp left. The Notchway diverges here, and the Pasture Path continues across several tributaries of Carlton Brook and ascends to meet the Ledge Trail below Lookout Ledge.

Pasture Path (map 8:E9)
Distances from Randolph Hill Rd.
   to Glover Spring Rd.: 1.2 mi., 40 min.
   to Notchway: 1.9 mi. (3.1 km.), 1 hr. 5 min.
   to Lookout Ledge (via Ledge Trail): 2.8 mi., 1 hr. 40 min.

Notchway (RMC)

This connecting path leads 0.9 mi. from the Ledge Trail to the Pasture Path about 0.5 mi. west of the Mt. Crescent House site. The Notchway leaves the Ledge Trail at the notch, ascends slightly, passes through a lumbered area, an old forest, and a swamp, crosses three tributaries of Carlton Brook, and then rises. Here the trail has been relocated. Follow arrows left to a logging road and from there to the Pasture Path.

Notchway (map 8:E9)
Distance from Ledge Trail
 to Pasture Path: 0.4 mi. (0.6 km.), 20 min.

Mount Crescent (3230 ft.)

Mt. Crescent, northwest of Randolph Hill, derives its name from the shape of the summit. It is ascended by the Mount Crescent and Crescent Ridge trails.

Mount Crescent Trail (RMC)

This trail begins at Randolph Hill Rd. about 0.3 mi. west of the Mt. Crescent House site, opposite the head of Grassy Lane. Do not park here; leave cars at the Mt. Crescent House site. The trail coincides for 0.1 mi. with Cook Path, which then branches right. The Mount Crescent Trail continues on the logging road for another 0.1 mi. to the junction with the Carlton Notch Trail, where it turns right and begins to ascend the mountain.

At 0.3 mi. from Randolph Hill Rd., the Boothman Spring Cutoff enters from the Mt. Crescent House site, and the main trail steepens. At 0.7 mi. it passes Castleview Loop, which leads in about 50 yd. to Castleview Rock. At 1.1 mi. the Crescent Ridge Trail branches right for the north summit of Mt. Crescent. The Mount Crescent Trail continues left (northwest) to the south viewpoint and then to the south summit of Mt. Crescent, where there is a glimpse of the Northern Peaks. The path continues for 0.2 mi. to the north summit, also wooded, from which the Pliny and Pilot ranges can be seen across the broad valley of the Upper Ammonoosuc. The trail ends here, at the second junction with Crescent Ridge Trail. An alternate way to the upper part of Mt. Crescent is via the Crescent Ridge Trail.

Mount Crescent Trail (map 8:E9)
Distance from Randolph Hill Rd.

to Mt. Crescent, north summit: 1.7 mi. (2.7 km.), 1 hr. 40 min.

Crescent Ridge Trail (RMC)

This trail branches right from the Mount Crescent Trail 1.1 mi. from Randolph Hill Rd. and crosses the east flank of the mountain. From there it turns west and climbs directly to the north outlook, where it again meets the Mount Crescent Trail. Continuing southwest, it descends gradually, crossing Carlton Brook, to Carlton Notch, where it crosses the Carlton Notch Trail. The Crescent Ridge Trail then follows a ridge that extends to the southwest, passing Lafayette View, an outlook with an excellent view of King Ravine and Mts. Madison, Adams, and Jefferson. The trail then descends into the col south of Mt. Crescent, crosses the headwaters of a branch of Carlton Brook, and climbs to the summit of Mt. Randolph. From here the trail descends steeply on an old lumber road to the Ledge Trail just above Lookout Ledge.

Crescent Ridge Trail (map 8:E9)
Distances from Randolph Hill Rd.

to Mt. Crescent, north outlook (via Mount Crescent Trail): 1.8 mi., 1 hr. 35 min.

to Carlton Notch Trail: 2.5 mi., 2 hr.

to Lafayette View: 3.3 mi., 2 hr. 25 min.
to Mt. Randolph summit: 3.9 mi., 2 hr. 55 min.
to Lookout Ledge: 4.8 mi. (7.7 km.), 3 hr. 30 min.

Castleview Loop (RMC)

The Castleview Loop diverges left from the Mount Crescent Trail 0.7 mi. from Randolph Hill Rd. In a few feet a side trail leads left to Castleview Rock, an interesting boulder. The main trail descends gently through light woods, passing Castleview Ledge, which is named for its unique view of the Castellated Ridge of Mt. Jefferson. Entering thick forest, the loop then descends steeply and in about 0.3 mi. ends at the Carlton Notch Trail near the Mt. Crescent Water Co. Reservoir.

Castleview Loop (map 8:E9)
Distance from Mount Crescent Trail
to Carlton Notch Trail: 0.4 mi. (0.6 km.), 15 min.

Carlton Notch Trail (RMC)

The Carlton Notch Trail leads from the Mount Crescent Trail through the col between Mt. Randolph and Mt. Crescent to the Pond of Safety. This trail is not heavily used and may be obscure.

The trail starts on the Mount Crescent Trail 0.1 mi. above its junction with the Cook Path, and 0.2 mi. from Randolph Hill Rd. The Mount Crescent Trail turns right at this point, and the Carlton Notch Trail continues straight ahead. The trail rises gently on an old logging road, passing the Mt. Crescent Water Co. reservoir and the Castleview Loop (right) at 0.7 mi. from Randolph Hill Rd. It then ascends steeply for about a mile to Carlton Notch, where it crosses the Crescent Ridge Trail.

From Carlton Notch the trail descends via a series of old logging roads, with many wet areas, gradually swinging west to join the Pond of Safety Trail from the Kilkenny area and Stag Hollow Rd. from Jefferson. Turn left (southwest) for 200 yd. to a road leading right (northwest) for another 350 yd. to the Pond of Safety. Turn right (northeast) for Bog Dam Rd. in the Kilkenny.

Carlton Notch Trail (map 8:E9-E8)
Distances from Randolph Hill Rd.
  to Carlton Notch: 1.7 mi., 1 hr. 20 min.
  to Stag Hollow Rd.: 4.0 mi. (6.5 km.), 2 hr. 30 min.
  to Pond of Safety (via Stag Hollow Rd.): 4.3 mi., 2 hr. 40 min.

Boothman Spring Cutoff (RMC)

This shortcut gives access to the Ice Gulch and Mt. Crescent from the Mt. Crescent House site on Randolph Hill Rd., a good starting point with parking space. The trail is level throughout, leading from the old hotel driveway (sign), through a field, then into the woods. At 0.2 mi. from the end of the field, the cutoff passes Boothman Spring. At 0.4 mi. it crosses the Cook Path to the Ice Gulch, then a lumber road, and ends at the Mount Crescent Trail.

Boothman Spring Cutoff (map 8:E9)
Distance from Mt. Crescent House site
  to Mount Crescent Trail: 0.5 mi. (0.8 km.), 20 min.

Ice Gulch

The Ice Gulch is a deep cut on the southeast slope of the Crescent Range, between Mt. Crescent and Black Crescent Mtn. The bed of the gulch is strewn with great boulders that lie in picturesque confusion, similar in many respects to those scattered over the floor of King Ravine. Among the boulders are many caves, some with perpetual ice. Springs and the melting ice form the headwaters of Moose Brook.

Two paths lead to the gulch: Cook Path to the head, and Ice Gulch Path to the foot and from there through the gulch. A short trail, Peboamauk Loop, follows Moose Brook below the Ice Gulch, past Peboamauk Fall and several fine springs back to Ice Gulch Path.

Cook Path (RMC)

This trail begins on Randolph Hill Rd. opposite Grassy Lane, about 0.3 mi. west of the Mt. Crescent House site. Do not leave cars here; park at the Mt. Crescent House site. The trail coincides with the Mount Crescent Trail for about 0.1 mi., then branches right, passing an old trail, and then at 0.4 mi. the Boothman Spring Cutoff, a shortcut from the Mt. Crescent House site. It ascends and then descends to the head of Ice Gulch, where it ends. The Ice Gulch Path begins here and descends through the Ice Gulch. Follow signs.

Cook Path (map 8:E9-D9)
Distance from Randolph Hill Rd.
   to head of Ice Gulch, Ice Gulch Path: 2.6 mi. (4.2 km.), 2 hrs.

Ice Gulch Path (RMC)

This path is the descent route from Cook Path through the Ice Gulch and back to Randolph Hill Rd.

From the head of the Ice Gulch, the descent is steep to the "Vestibule," where there is an excellent spring. **Caution:** The way down the gulch is rough and hikers should be careful. Allow ample time; there are no exits from the ravine in the mile between the "Vestibule" and Fairy Spring. The general direction is southeast, with views toward Gorham and down the gulch. At the foot of the gulch the trail passes Fairy Spring on the right (west). Just below the spring the Peboamauk Loop enters from the left, coming up the brook from Peboamauk Fall. The Ice Gulch Path turns right, climbs the west bank of the ravine and heads south across several wet areas to the "Marked Birch." Here it bears right and the Peboamauk Loop leaves left. The Ice Gulch Path runs southwest for about 2.0 mi., crossing three major brooks and a woods road, and ends at Sky View Farm on Randolph Hill Rd. about 0.4 mi. east of the Mt. Crescent House site.

Ice Gulch Path (map 8:E9-D9)
Distances from head of Ice Gulch
  to site of "Marked Birch": 1.4 mi., 1 hr.
  to Randolph Hill Rd.: 3.4 mi. (5.5 km.), 2 hr.

Peboamauk Loop (RMC)

This loop of the Ice Gulch Path passes a fine cascade and travels beside a pleasant stream. On the ascent, after branching right from the Ice Gulch Path, the trail descends steeply to Peboamauk Fall ("Winter's Home"), then rises steeply and follows Moose Brook for about 0.3 mi., ending at the foot of the Ice Gulch just below Fairy Spring, where it reenters the Ice Gulch Path.

Peboamauk Loop (map 8:E9)
Distance from Ice Gulch Path, lower junction
  to Ice Gulch Path, upper junction: 0.3 mi. (0.5 km.), 15 min.

Black Crescent Mountain (3264 ft.)

There are no trails on this mountain, located north-northeast of Mt. Crescent. It can be ascended from the head of the Ice Gulch, or from the high point on the Cook Path by logging roads. The upper part of a large slide on the south side of the mountain has an excellent view.

Mount Jericho (2487 ft.)

Mt. Jericho lies at the east end of the Crescent Range, just west of Berlin NH. Like many northern mountains, its summit was bared by the forest fires of the early 1900s. Now partially overgrown, it still offers a fine view east to the Mahoosucs and an obstructed view of the Carter Range, the northern Presidentials, and the Tinker Brook valley. There is no trail to the summit; however, snowmachine routes lead through the sag between Mt. Jericho and Mt. Forist. To ascend, follow NH 110 from its junction with NH 16 in Berlin about 0.5 mi. to Second Ave. Turn left (south) on Second Ave. and go to the end of the street, then turn right (west) on Haskell St. to its end (60 yd.) Park here, but avoid blocking either the driveways to the adjacent houses or the start of the trail straight ahead.

Enter an open way through the woods and proceed west 0.4 mi. to an intersection with a snowmachine trail (signs). Turn right (north) and continue up the valley of an intermittent brook, crossing it several times. At about 1.0 mi., in a wet area, turn left (west) on an old logging road. This area is marked with several snowmachine trail signs. In about 0.2 mi. an intermittent stream gully is crossed. There are a number of red blazes marking a property boundary in this vicinity. Turn left (southwest) and bushwhack up the north side of the streambed for about 0.5 mi. into the slight depression between the two summits. Go right (northwest) to the higher and more open summit. There is also a view from the lower summit.

Mount Jericho (map 8:D10)
Distance from Haskell St.

to summit: 2.2 mi. (3.6 km.), 2 hr.

Mount Forist (2046 ft.)

Locally known as Elephant Mtn. because of its shape as seen from Berlin, Mt. Forist was named for Merrill C. Forist, an early settler. (Note that the name of this mountain is spelled incorrectly on the USGS Berlin quadrangle.) There are several approaches to the summit on the elephant's "head," or to the outlook on its "rear end." One of

the better ways follows NH 110 from its junction with NH
16 in Berlin about 0.5 mi. to Madigan St. At this point you
will see the ledges directly ahead. Follow Madigan St. to its
upper end, where the trail begins. Follow the trail for about
50 yd. to the base of the cliff (trail may be obscure), turn
left and follow the base about 50 yd. to an old slide, now
mostly overgrown. The trail leads up the mountain at a
rather steep angle to a point about halfway between the
elephant's head and its tail. Bear left and follow the trail to
the summit on the "head," where there is a good view of
Berlin and the Androscoggin valley toward Gorham.

Mount Forist (map 8:D10)
Distance (est.) from Madigan St., Berlin
   to summit: 0.6 mi. (1.0 km.), 1 hr. 15 min.

PLINY AND PILOT RANGES

These are essentially one mountain mass, extending north
and south between the Israel and Upper Ammonoosuc rivers
just east of Lancaster. The Pliny Range forms the semicircular southern end of this mass; its chief summits are Mt. Starr
King, Mt. Waumbek, and Mt. Weeks. Across Willard Notch
from Mt. Weeks, the Pilot Range begins, including Terrace
Mtn., Mt. Cabot—the highest peak in the entire North
Country—Mt. Mary, and Hutchins Mtn., often known as
Mt. Pilot. A spur that extends northeast from Mt. Cabot
carries The Bulge and The Horn.

Refer to the AMC Pilot map (map 8), to the USGS Mt.
Washington and Percy quadrangles, or to the Starr King-
Waumbek section of the RMC map of the Randolph valley
and the Northern Peaks.

Mount Starr King (3913 ft.)

Named for Thomas Starr King, author of "The White
Hills," this mountain is located northeast of Jefferson vil-

lage. The summit is wooded, but views have been cleared in several directions. The Starr King Trail reaches the summit from the village of Jefferson.

Mount Waumbek (4005 ft.)

Immediately east of Mt. Starr King, Mt. Waumbek is the highest point of the Pliny Range. It was formerly called Pliny Major. The Starr King Trail leads to the summit.

Starr King Trail (RMC/WMNF)

The trail leaves US 2 at a WMNF sign on the north side of the highway 0.2 mi. east of its junction with NH 115A. Park on the south side of US 2, 100 yd. west of the trailhead, in the area near the Waumbek swimming pool. Parking is prohibited along US 2 and on the private road at the start of the trail.

Start up this road, avoiding right branches leading to private houses, and pass a small reservoir (left) at 0.3 mi. and then, in another 0.2 mi., the stone foundations of a springhouse (right). The road deteriorates into a logging road, which the trail follows uphill for about 0.3 mi. The trail then turns right off the road and climbs the west slope of the mountain for almost 0.8 mi., then turns north to traverse the west flank for about 1.0 mi. The trail passes two springs (left down and then right up) about three quarters of the way over this section.

Leaving the traverse, the trail turns right and climbs to the summit in another 150 yd. The trail continues another 60 yd. to an excellent cleared viewpoint south and west, the site of a former shelter. From this point the route to Mt. Waumbek winds southeast and then east along the ridge, descending slightly to the col, from which it rises for about 0.7 mi. to the wooded summit, from which there are limited views.

Starr King Trail (map 8:D7)
Distances from US 2
    to beginning of traverse: 1.6 mi., 1 hr. 35 min.
    to Mt. Starr King summit: 2.8 mi. (4.5 km.), 2 hr. 40 min.
    to Mt. Waumbek summit: 3.8 mi. (6.1 km.) 3 hr. 20 min.

Mount Weeks

Located northeast of Mt. Waumbek, this mountain has three distinct peaks. The North Peak (3890 ft.) may be climbed from the height-of-land in Willard Notch (see York Pond Trail). There is no trail and the summit is wooded with no views.

The South Peak (3885 ft.) may be climbed from North Weeks by following the ridge or from the south by following a route up Priscilla Brook. (The Priscilla Brook trail has been abandoned and the route is now obscure.) Again, there is no trail to the summit, but there is a view to the north.

Terrace Mountain (3640 ft.)

Northwest of Mt. Weeks and south of Mt. Cabot, Terrace Mtn. is named for its appearance when seen from the west. There is no longer any trace of the former trail crossing the summits between Bunnell and Willard notches.

Mount Cabot (4170 ft.)

Located north of Bunnell Notch, the summit of Mt. Cabot is wooded with no views. Outlooks east and west have been cleared from the site of the former fire tower, 0.3 mi. southeast of the true summit, and there are excellent views from the ledges above Bunnell Notch.

Mount Cabot Trail (WMNF)

In addition to ascending Mt. Cabot, this trail provides access to the York Pond Trail and to the Kilkenny Ridge

Trail. From the junction of US 2 and NH 116 just west of the village of Jefferson, go west 0.3 mi. to North Rd. Turn right (north) for 2.3 mi. to Gore Rd., turning right again for 1.7 mi. to Pleasant Valley Rd. In 0.8 mi. turn right on Arthur White Rd. to the parking area (sign) about 50 yd. before the end of the road at "Heath's Gate." Do not block the road or the driveway. From Heath's Gate, the Mount Cabot Trail follows a logging road through a clear-cut area (1986) 0.4 mi. to the Kilkenny logging railroad bed. The York Pond Trail to York Pond and the Berlin Fish Hatchery by way of Willard Notch begins here, going right (southeast) along the railroad bed.

The Mount Cabot Trail continues ahead on a good road. After another 0.4 mi. the road ends and the trail becomes a footway for 1.4 mi. to the Bunnell Brook crossing. After climbing north to northeast from the brook, the trail swings southeast to a southwest-facing outlook in 0.6 mi. and to the south-facing "Bunnell Rock" in another 100 yd. From here the trail turns northeast again and climbs through evergreens, with two switchbacks, to a cabin maintained by the Jefferson Boy Scouts. Beyond (sign), the trail leads north to the open area where the fire tower was formerly located (views), through a shallow sag, then gradually up to the true summit (sign). The Kilkenny Ridge Trail begins here, leading over The Bulge to Unknown Pond in 2.8 mi. and to South Pond in 9.7 mi. A side trail right (east) 0.2 mi. beyond the cabin leads steeply downhill 250 yd. to a spring. The sign "Bishop–Leavitt Spring Trail" recognizes two former firewardens who staffed the Mt. Cabot fire tower.

Mount Cabot Trail (map 8:D7-C8)
Distances from Heath's Gate
   to York Pond Trail: 0.4 mi., 15 min.
   to Bunnell Brook crossing: 2.2 mi., 1 hr. 35 min.

to outlook (Bunnell Rock): 2.9 mi., 2 hr. 20 min.
to cabin: 3.5 mi., 2 hr. 55 min.
to Mt. Cabot summit: 3.9 mi. (6.2 km.), 3 hr. 5 min.

The Bulge (3920 ft.) and The Horn (3905 ft.)

These peaks lie just north of Mt. Cabot in the Pilot Range. They are reached via the Kilkenny Ridge Trail, which follows the ridge that joins them to Mt. Cabot. The Bulge is wooded with no views, while The Horn is a jumble of bare rocks with views in all directions. The Kilkenny Ridge Trail (described in the Kilkenny section) passes over The Bulge, and a side trail leads from it to The Horn.

Hutchins Mountain (3710 ft.)

Hutchins Mtn., on the USGS Percy quadrangle, also called Mt. Pilot, was named after Alpheus Hutchins, an early settler. It lies at the northwest end of the Pilot Range, separated from Mt. Cabot by Mt. Mary and several unnamed peaks. To ascend, take the road from Grange to Groveton via Lost Nation. Near the foot of Hutchins Mtn., the paved road turns sharp left and a dirt road goes right, crossing Cummings Brook. This is private land; do not block road, driveway, or parking areas. From this point, the route goes up the southeast side of Cummings Brook for about 1.5 mi. to the basin below the summit (see USGS map). Cross the brook and ascend to the southwest ridge of the mountain, which can then be followed to the higher of the two summits. It is possible to follow the Pilot ridge southeast over Mt. Mary to join the Kilkenny Ridge Trail between Mt. Cabot and The Bulge.

KILKENNY DISTRICT

The "Kilkenny" includes the area drained by the head-waters of the Upper Ammonoosuc River, north of the Cres-

cent Range, east of the Pliny–Pilot Range, and south of
NH 110. It includes all of the unincorporated town of
Kilkenny along with sizeable chunks of Berlin, Milan, Randolph, Stark, and some of Jefferson and Lancaster. It is
sometimes referred to as the Kilkenny Wilderness, wild in
the sense that it lacks hikers' amenities. Hunters and fishermen are especially attracted to the Kilkenny, as are others
who enjoy the sense of being far from the crowds. Those
who expect to find their trails groomed and manicured are
doomed to disappointment, and possibly to the inconve-
nience of getting lost.

Historically this region has been a major timber harvest
area and many of the features of interest reflect past and
present logging activity both on private inholdings and on
the National Forest lands which are managed for multiple
use.

The trails in this section generally follow an extensive
network of old, older, and ancient logging roads or railroads. Primary trails are blazed with yellow paint. The
visual environment on the maintained trails has generally
been screened from logging activity, but the longer view
often includes vegetational diversity resulting from timber
harvest and reforestation, and access roads may be in
evidence. As a result of the variety of vegetation types,
chances are excellent that one will see many kinds of native
wildlife.

The Kilkenny Ridge Trail links some of the attractions of
this area, including the Devil's Hopyard, Rogers Ledge,
The Horn and The Bulge, and Mt. Cabot. There are
backcountry campsites at Rogers Ledge and Unknown
Pond.

The center of this area is accessible by York Pond Rd.
(FR 13) to the Berlin Fish Hatchery at York Pond, and by
Bog Dam Rd. (FR 15), which makes a 15.5 mi. loop south
of York Pond. Bog Dam Rd. follows the earlier Upper

Ammonoosuc Trail and logging road network, passing the
sites of several former logging camps. With the present
Upper Ammonoosuc Trail and the Landing Camp Trail, it
provides access to the site of Bog Dam, built to provide a
"head" of water for the spring logging drives and later
used as a town water supply.

York Pond Rd. leaves NH 110 7.4 mi. northwest of its
beginning at NH 16 in Berlin. There is a gate at the Berlin
Fish Hatchery that is locked from 4 PM to 8 AM. Hikers
who plan to leave cars at the trailheads west of this gate
should make prior arrangements with the hatchery
(449-3412), with Supt. Warren Ingram (449-2533), or with
Foreman Royce Benedict (449-2541). Foot travel is not restricted.

This is a backcountry area in which trails are maintained
only once annually. It is advisable to check with the Androscoggin District Office in Gorham (466-2713) for current status. Refer to AMC Pilot map (map 8), to the USGS
Percy quadrangle, and to the USFS map of the WMNF.

South Pond Recreation Area (WMNF)

A picnic and swimming area is operated by the WMNF
at South Pond, south of NH 110 in Stark. There is no
camping here. This is the northern terminus of the
Kilkenny Ridge Trail. The access road to South Pond Recreation Area is gated and may be closed from 8:30 PM to
9:00 AM, and at times when the picnic area is not open.
Foot travel is always permitted. Check with the Androscoggin District Office of the WMNF (466-2713) for details.

Devil's Hopyard

This picturesque gorge on a brook that empties into
South Pond resembles the Ice Gulch in Randolph, but is
shorter and narrower. The small side stream is for the most
part completely out of sight beneath moss-covered boul-

ders, while ledges overhang the path. (Use caution where rocks are wet and covered with moss.)

Devil's Hopyard Trail (WMNF)

The trail begins at the South Pond Recreation Area. It coincides with the Kilkenny Ridge Trail, which leads south from the picnic area, skirting the west side of the pond and crosses a brook in 0.6 mi. After passing an abandoned route, the Devil's Hopyard Trail shortly diverges right (west) from the Kilkenny Ridge Trail (sign). At 0.8 mi. it crosses the brook to the north side. In the next 0.1 mi. the trail enters the Hopyard and after about 0.3 mi. rises steeply at its west end. Be careful in this section since the rocks are slippery. This is a dead-end trail.

Devil's Hopyard Trail (map 8:B8)
Distances from South Pond
  to end of trail: 1.2 mi. (2.0 km.), 40 min.

Rogers Ledge (2945 ft.)

Rogers Ledge, in the northern tip of the town of Kilkenny, is about 3.5 mi. northwest of York Pond. The entire southwest face of the ledge is a cliff, and the view from the top includes the Kilkenny area, the Pilot Range, the Mahoosucs, and the Presidential Range. It may be reached from South Pond by the Kilkenny Ridge Trail or from the York Pond Fish Hatchery by the Mill Brook Trail and the Kilkenny Ridge Trail.

Kilkenny Ridge Trail (WMNF)

The Kilkenny Ridge Trail runs from South Pond Recreation Area to the summit of Mt. Cabot. From the parking lot at South Pond, go right (south) toward the lakeshore, following the sign to Devil's Hopyard. At 0.7 mi. the Hopyard trail diverges right (west) and the Kilkenny Ridge

Trail continues straight ahead. It crosses two brooks on
bridges, and runs southeast and south following old logging roads. At 2.5 mi. the trail bears sharp right (west),
crossing from one logging road to another, then resumes its
generally southerly course. At 3.2 mi. the town boundary
between Stark and Kilkenny is crossed. At 3.4 mi. the grade
steepens and at 4.1 mi. Rogers Ledge is reached.

From the south-facing ledge the view south toward the
Presidential Range includes the Androscoggin River valley,
the Mahoosuc Range, the entire Kilkenny basin, and the
northern shoulder of Mt. Cabot. This ledge was named in
honor of Major Robert Rogers, leader of Rogers's Rangers
in the French and Indian Wars. From the viewpoint, the
trail swings east around the ledge and, passing a side path
to a backcountry campsite at 0.5 mi., descends in 0.6 mi.
to a junction with Mill Brook Trail. This junction is 4.6 mi.
from South Pond. The trail continues west, passing a beaver pond at 5.4 mi., and at 6.0 mi. begins the steady ascent
to the ridge east of Unknown Pond. It reaches the crest of
the ridge at 6.5 mi. and descends to the pond at 6.9 mi. The
Unknown Pond Trail enters from the left (south) and coincides for 100 yd. then diverges right (north) toward Stark.

The Kilkenny Ridge Trail continues around the north
shore of the pond. Crossing two small brooks, it swings
north around the end of the ridge, and in 0.6 mi. begins
the climb to the sag between The Bulge and The Horn,
which it reaches in another mile. A side trail leads left
(east) 0.3 mi. to the open rocks of The Horn, from which
there are extensive views. The Kilkenny Ridge Trail turns
right (west) and ascends to the wooded summit of The
Bulge, drops to the saddle, and climbs to Mt. Cabot. There
are no signs on this trail beyond Unknown Pond, but there
are yellow blazes and the footway is clear. From the summit
of Cabot the Mount Cabot Trail descends to East Lancaster.

Kilkenny Ridge Trail (map 8:B8-C8)
Distances from South Pond Recreation Area
   to Rogers Ledge: 4.1 mi., 2 hr. 55 min.
   to Mill Brook Trail: 4.6 mi., 3 hr. 15 min.
   to Unknown Pond: 6.9 mi., 4 hr. 45 min.
   to the side trail to The Horn: 8.5 mi., 5 hr. 55 min.
   to The Bulge: 8.8 mi., 6 hr. 5 min.
   to Mt. Cabot summit: 9.7 mi. (15.5 km.), 6 hr. 35 min.
   to Heath's Gate (via Mount Cabot Trail): 13.5 mi. (21.8 km.), 8 hr. 35 min.

West Milan Trail (WMNF)

This trail leaves York Pond Rd. (FR 13) just west of the bridge over the Upper Ammonoosuc River, 1.8 mi. from NH 110. Much of the first 0.8 mi. passes through private land logged in 1986; attention to trail signs and paint blazes is advised. The Berlin–Milan town line and a small stream are crossed in this section. The trail crosses Fogg Brook just after leaving the logged area, Fifield Brook at 1.7 mi., and Higgins Brook at 3.8 mi. A logging road enters left (west) at 4.3 mi. and in another 0.1 mi. the trail reaches the WMNF gate on Spruceville Rd. This road runs north 1.5 mi. to NH 110. Turn right (east) for West Milan.

West Milan Trail (map 8:C9)
Distance from York Pond Rd.
   to Spruceville Rd.: 4.5 mi. (7.2 km.) 2 hr. 15 min.

Mill Brook Trail (WMNF)

Formerly a through route from Stark village to York Pond, the north section of this trail has been abandoned by the WMNF from the height-of-land to Stark. Beaver activity and logging have obscured the footway north of its intersection with the Kilkenny Ridge Trail. From the Berlin Fish Hatchery at York Pond, go north behind the main hatchery building, and follow signs and arrows across Cold Brook to pick up an old logging road on the east side of the brook. (The start may be obscure; ask at the hatchery for directions.) The trail ascends along Cold Brook for about 1.3 mi. then diverges right (east) up a side stream. It crosses the Berlin–Milan town boundary at 1.7 mi. and the Milan–Kilkenny boundary at 2.7 mi. Just north of the height-of-land, the trail ends at the Kilkenny Ridge Trail. Turn right (east) for Rogers Ledge and left (west) for Unknown Pond.

Mill Brook Trail (map 8:C8)
Distance from York Pond Rd.
　to Kilkenny Ridge Trail: 3.9 mi. (6.2 km.), 2 hr. 25 min.

Unknown Pond Trail (WMNF)

The trail begins on York Pond Rd. 2.0 mi. west of the hatchery gate (sign) between a small pond and a beaver swamp. It continues northwest, crossing the brook at 1.9 mi. (About 70 yd. beyond, it crosses a tributary which flows from a small tarn under the ledges southeast of The Horn.) Crossing the main stream again at 2.1 mi., the trail soon begins the ascent to Unknown Pond, which it reaches at 3.2 mi. There are backcountry campsites and a pit toilet here.

The trail swings east around the pond, joining the Kilkenny Ridge Trail at the southeast corner, and coincides with it for about 100 yd. to the northeast corner of the pond. Here the Kilkenny Ridge Trail swings west toward Mt. Cabot and the Unknown Pond Trail goes north toward Mill Brook Rd. in Stark. From the pond, the trail crosses a wet area and descends steeply for a mile, then more gradually, soon crossing the Kilkenny–Stark town line. It traverses the slope east of Mill Brook and ends at Mill Brook Rd. (FR 11) in 2.2 mi. Turn right (east). This road is gated

0.8 mi. north of this intersection; the gate is 3.8 mi. south of NH 110. There is a sign (hiker symbol) on NH 110 at the beginning of Mill Brook Rd., and a sign ("Trail" with arrow) at the gate. There is a WMNF sign at the point where the trail leaves the forest road, just east of a bridge across Mill Brook.

Unknown Pond Trail (map 8:D8-C8)
Distances from York Pond Rd.

  to stream crossing: 1.8 mi., 1 hr. 15 min.
  to Unknown Pond: 3.2 mi. (5.2 km.), 2 hr. 20 min.
  to Mill Brook Rd.: 5.5 mi., 3 hr. 30 min.
  to WMNF gate: 6.3 mi. (10.2 km.), 3 hr. 55 min.
  to NH 110: 10.1 mi., 5 hr. 50 min.

York Pond Trail (WMNF)

This trail leaves the end of York Pond Rd. (FR 13) and, following old logging roads, passes through Willard Notch and then follows the Kilkenny logging railroad bed to East Lancaster. It is blazed with yellow paint.

From the fish hatchery gate at York Pond, continue west 2.2 mi. on York Pond Rd. to a fenced raceway. The trailhead (sign) is on the road to the left. The entrance to the trail is gated, but foot travel is not restricted. The York Pond Trail follows a good gravel road for 0.2 mi., then diverges left (arrow). In a few hundred yards it crosses a small dam, then continues up the south side of the brook, crossing two branches. At 0.9 mi. it begins to swing up a hardwood ridge, crossing a well-defined old logging road. At 2.4 mi. it reaches its highest point. The trail slabs the south side of the notch, rising and falling twice, and remaining well above the floor of the notch. It then descends gradually through several swampy areas and crosses three streams. At 5.6 mi. it crosses the WMNF boundary and at 6.6 mi. the Tekwood Rd. down Garland Brook diverges left (west). The trail continues, now in a northwesterly direction until it joins the Mount Cabot Trail at 7.0 mi. Turn left (west) for East Lancaster; turn right (east) for Mt. Cabot. The trail reaches the parking area at Heath's Gate (the former White's farm) at 7.4 mi.

York Pond Trail (map 8:D8-D7)
Distances from York Pond trailhead
to high point of trail: 2.4 mi., 1 hr. 45 min.
to WMNF boundary: 5.6 mi., 3 hr. 20 min.
to Mount Cabot Trail: 7.0 mi., 4 hr.
to Heath's Gate: 7.4 mi. (11.9 km.), 4 hr. 15 min.

Pond of Safety

This small but attractive pond lies north of the Crescent Range in the town of Randolph. It derived its name from an incident during the American Revolution. Several local men, who had joined the Continental army, differed with the authorities as to the terms of their enlistment. They retired to this isolated region to hunt and fish, and remained out of reach until there was no further danger that they might be apprehended as deserters. The pond has continued to be a place of refuge from the woes of civilization for fishermen, hunters, cross-country skiers, and snowmobilers.

It may be reached from the Kilkenny area by the WMNF Pond of Safety Trail, from Randolph Hill by the Carlton Notch Trail, and from Jefferson by Stag Hollow Rd. This latter is passable by four-wheel-drive vehicle.

Pond of Safety Trail (WMNF)

This trail leaves Bog Dam Rd. (FR 15) 7.9 mi. south of its eastern junction with York Pond Rd. (FR 13). From Bog Dam Rd., the trail follows a good logging road (gated), crossing a branch of the Upper Ammonoosuc River at 0.1

mi. At 0.5 mi. it intersects the state snowmachine trail and turns right (west) toward Pond of Safety. There may be signs at this point.

Rising gradually, the trail bears west and southwest on a good logging road to a junction at 1.7 mi., where the trail turns left (southeast). There are snowmachine signs and an obscure Forest Service arrow at this junction. This point is roughly the high point on the low ridge which the trail crosses. From here the trail, on an increasingly good logging road, descends through several clearings to a building at 2.5 mi. The road goes left (east) at this point, passes the intersection (obscure) with the Carlton Notch Trail at 2.9 mi., crosses a brook, and joins Stag Hollow Rd., which leads to Jefferson. At 3.0 mi. a road right (west) leads 0.2 mi. to a clearing from which a path right (north) descends to the Pond of Safety shore.

Pond of Safety Trail (map 8:D9-E8)
Distance from Bog Dam Rd.
to Carlton Notch Trail: 2.9 mi., 1 hr. 45 min.
to side trail to pond: 3.0 mi. (4.8 km.), 1 hr. 45 min.
to Ingerson Rd. (via Stag Hollow Rd.): 6.8 mi., 3 hr. 45 min.
to Randolph (via Carlton Notch Trail): 7.0 mi., 4 hr. 45 min.

Upper Ammonoosuc Trail (WMNF)

This trail, a remnant of a former through route from Jefferson to Milan, leaves the west side of Bog Dam Rd. (FR 15) 4.1 mi. south of its eastern junction with York Pond Rd. It leads generally southwest, crosses a brook at 0.5 mi., and reaches the site of Bog Dam at 0.9 mi. (There is a clearing here, and a pool in the river, but the dam which formerly provided a "head" of water for river driving each spring is gone.) At 1.7 mi. the Landing Camp

Trail diverges left (east). In about 0.2 mi. the trail crosses the Upper Ammonoosuc River and in another 0.3 mi. crosses Keenan Brook. It then rises and ends at Bog Dam Rd. 5.3 mi. south of its westerly junction with York Pond Rd.

Upper Ammonoosuc Trail (map 8:D9-D8)
Distances from Bog Dam Rd. (east)

  to Landing Camp Trail: 1.7 mi., 50 min.

  to Bog Dam Rd. (west): 2.7 mi. (4.4 km.), 1 hr. 20 min.

Landing Camp Trail (WMNF)

This trail links the Upper Ammonoosuc Trail with Bog Dam Rd. and is part of an old trail that connected Bog Dam with Randolph through Hunter's Pass. It leaves Bog Dam Rd. 6.2 mi. south of its eastern junction with York Pond Rd. (This vicinity is the site of the former logging Camp 19.) Descending gradually, the trail passes the open site of the former Camp 18, crosses three small streams, rises over a knoll, and descends to run nearly level for about 0.4 mi. to its end on the Upper Ammonoosuc Trail.

Landing Camp Trail (map 8:D9)
Distances from Bog Dam Rd.

  to Camp 18 site: 0.4 mi., 15 min.

  to Upper Ammonoosuc Trail: 1.9 mi. (3.0 km.), 55 min.

UPPER AMMONOOSUC REGION

The mountains in this section, in the vicinity of the village of Stark, have attractive views from their summits. They are on private land, and do not have maintained trails.

Percy Peaks

These two peaks, north of Stark on the Upper Ammonoosuc River, are the most conspicuous mountains in the northern view from Mt. Washington. The summit of the North Peak (3418 ft.) is bare, except for low scrub; that of the South Peak (3220 ft.) is wooded, but there are several good viewpoints. Refer to the USGS Percy quadrangle. The trails described below are on North Percy; there are no trails to the South Peak, but an obscure footway with some flags leads from the col between the peaks to the south summit.

West Side Trail

This is not a maintained trail, though it gets sufficient use that the footway is clear and major obstructions are removed. The route was laid out by Bob and Miriam Underhill, both noted rock climbers, who delighted in finding short but challenging routes to good viewpoints.

A short, direct route up North Percy from the west, the trail must be followed with some care. The upper slabs are steep and exposed. Although this is not a rock climb in the technical sense, use of hands is required. Extreme caution is advised in wet weather. Leaving NH 110 2.1 mi. east of Groveton, go north on Emerson Rd. 2.2 mi. to Emerson School Corner (so marked on the USGS map; there is no longer a school here). The paved road turns sharp right (east) and a gravel road turns left. The gravel road north is Nash Stream Rd., owned and maintained by Diamond International (sign). This road is closed from spring thaw through Memorial Day weekend. Watch for heavy logging traffic and park cars off the travel lanes. Follow this road for 2.7 mi. to a large rock on the east side of the road (several cairns). There may or may not be a sign here. The trail leaves in the vicinity of this rock, crosses a small wet area, and joins a logging road in a few yards.

The trail follows logging roads generally parallel to, and north of, Slide Brook for 0.6 mi. Here the trail approaches the brook and then bears left up the north bank and follows the ridge above the main stream for 0.4 mi. It crosses a small gully, turns left, and begins to climb more steeply. The beginning of the slabs is reached in 0.2 mi. and the Notch Trail junction in another 0.1 mi. This lower section of the slabs is mossy and extremely slippery when wet. Stay right (south) of the slabs below the trail junction, ignoring some blazes painted on the rock (these were placed in an unusually dry year).

About 80 yd. above the Notch Trail junction, the trail crosses the slab (very slippery) and then continues to follow it uphill. In this section, follow paint blazes carefully and beware of wet spots. (Note. In this section some of the blazes are above the route; look ahead for the line of travel. Avoid getting out on the slabs to the right (south) of the route, as these get progressively steeper.) As the trail climbs higher, the slabs are steeper and less wet, and views begin to appear. The summit is reached at 1.7 mi. from the road. (In descending, head southwest from the summit cairn and watch for paint blazes.)

West Side Trail (map 8:B7)
Distances from Nash Stream Rd.

to Notch Trail: 1.2 mi., 1 hr. 10 min.

to North Percy summit: 1.7 mi. (2.7 km.), 1 hr. 55 min.

Notch Trail

This trail, an alternative to the West Side Trail, avoids the steep, exposed slabs near the summit. It is recommended in wet weather or for those who prefer not to deal with the steep rock. It diverges right (south) from the West Side Trail 0.1 mi. above the base of the first open slab (sign) and traverses several ledges, staying north of the low point in the notch. Toward the east side of the notch a flagged route to South Percy leads right (south). Leaving the notch, the trail ascends along a rocky outcrop with increasingly wide views. It comes out into the open and follows blazes and cairns to the summit, from which there are good views in all directions.

Notch Trail (map 8:B7)
Distance from West Side Trail
  to North Percy summit: 1.0 mi. (1.6 km.), 1 hr.

Sugarloaf Mountain (3701 ft.)
East of North Stratford, at the head of Nash Stream, this summit commands an extensive view, particularly of the Percy Peaks. Refer to the USGS Percy and Guildhall quadrangles. Blue Mtn. (3723 ft.), a trailless peak in the same mountain mass, is the highest peak in NH outside the WMNF.

Sugarloaf Trail
The summit trail is a logging road that ascends the east side of the mountain by a direct route. It begins on Nash Stream Rd. 8.4 mi. from Emerson Rd. This point is 80 yd. beyond the crossing of the main Nash Stream. Park off the road in a grassy area. The trail (no signs) passes south of a camp, crosses a small brook, and continues through an open field. It then enters the woods and swings northwest, ascending at a steady grade to the firewarden's cabins (abandoned) at 1.6 mi. A short distance above the cabins, near a spring, the trail divides. The right branch climbs to the ridge north of the summit, turns left (south), and reaches the summit in 0.5 mi. The left branch also reaches the summit, is 0.1 mi. shorter, steeper, and has several blowdowns across it. The former fire tower has been removed.

Sugarloaf Trail (USGS Percy quad)
Distances from Nash Stream Rd.
to warden's cabins: 1.6 mi., 1 hr. 35 min.
to Sugarloaf Mtn. summit: 2.1 mi. (3.4 km.), 2 hr. 10 min.

Devil's Slide (1700 ft.)

This sheer cliff west of Stark rises 740 ft. above the valley. From NH 110 take Stark Rd. across the covered bridge, go left (west) and cross the railroad tracks. There is no trail, but logging roads may possibly be followed from here to the summit. Ask locally for current directions.

ANDROSCOGGIN HEADWATERS

North of Berlin and east of the main height-of-land lies a region of rivers and lakes which are of special interest to fishermen and canoeists. Among these waterways are a few hills from which the view is worth the visit. Much of this land is in private hands, with gates on the access roads. Chief landowners are Dartmouth College and Boise Cascade Corporation. Both are hospitable to hikers, but do not usually permit vehicular traffic over their roads. This, and the considerable distances involved, limit access to the region. The Thirteen Mile Woods, along the Androscoggin River between Milan and Errol, is managed by a consortium of landowners and state agencies. This provides a scenic drive along the river, access to fishing and canoeing, and a public campground at Mollidgewock.

Signal Mountain Trail

Signal Mtn. (2673 ft.) is west-southwest of Errol. It is no longer possible to ascend the fire tower, from which there was a good view. Refer to the USGS Errol quadrangle.

From NH 16 in the Thirteen Mile Woods on the Androscoggin River between Dummer and Errol, turn west on a gravel road that enters 0.1 mi. south of the steel bridge at Seven Islands. This is the road to Millsfield Pond, and it passes south of Signal Mtn. At 5.4 mi. from NH 16 go right (north) at a sharp fork (snowmachine signs), then left after 0.2 mi. Continue 1.0 mi. to a grassy turnout (snowmachine sign: "Signal Mt."). The path follows the snowmachine route to the summit. At 1.0 mi. there is a three-forked junction; take the left (east) fork (sign). The trail reaches the ridge from the northeast and swings west and southwest toward the summit. At 1.4 mi. take a left fork (sign). The old foot trail (right) is not used and is obscure. There is a view of Millsfield Pond from behind the cabin site. The lower steps have been removed from the fire tower and the tower itself is scheduled for removal.

Signal Mountain Trail (USGS Errol quad)
Distance from turnout
  to Signal Mtn. summit: 1.7 mi. (2.7 km.), 1 hr. 20 min.

Second College Grant

Far to the north of Hanover, above the headwaters of the Androscoggin River, lies the Second College Grant, given to Dartmouth College "for the assistance of indigent students." On this grant between Errol NH and Wilsons Mills ME the Swift Diamond and the Dead Diamond come together to form the Diamond River, which then enters the Magalloway River from the west. This in turn joins the Androscoggin River at Umbagog Lake. Branches of the Dead Diamond extend well up into the Connecticut Lakes region. Refer to the USGS Errol quadrangle. Immediately below the confluence of its two branches, the Diamond enters a wild and beautiful gorge cut between the Diamond Peaks on the north and Mt. Dustan on the south. This valley is served by a private logging road, open to walkers but not to vehicles without a permit.

At 9.0 mi. north of Errol, or 0.5 mi. west of the ME/NH state line, a gravel road leaves NH 16 on the west near a small cemetery. The College Grant gatehouse is reached in 1.0 mi. Hikers may leave their cars here, cross the Diamond on a logging bridge, and proceed up through the gorge. Good viewpoints are reached in about 0.5 mi., the Dartmouth Peaks Camp at 1.1 mi., and the Management Center at 1.5 mi. Hellgate, another scenic gorge, is reached 12.5 mi. from the gatehouse. The latter gets its name from the trouble riverdrivers had getting their logs through the narrow gorge without jamming. A path has been cut from the Management Center to the ledges on the Diamond Peaks. Other short paths to points of interest have also been opened. For further information, call Nelson Ham, the gatekeeper (482-3225), or write to Earl Jette, Director of Outdoor Programs, Dartmouth College, PO Box 9, Hanover NH 03755.

Diamond Peaks Trail

The Diamond Peaks (2071 ft.), between the Dead Diamond and Magalloway rivers, comprise a nearly semicircular ridge. Their attractive feature is a high cliff on the concave side of the ridge, facing south. There are a number of viewpoints from the cliff. The trail begins across the road from the Dartmouth Management Center, on the north side of the clearing. It crosses a cutover area, then enters the woods and begins to ascend. At about 0.3 mi. a side trail leads left 100 yd. to Alice Ledge, with a view of the Management Center area. The main trail turns gradually more south and climbs over the long West Peak, with several good outlooks, descends slightly, and climbs to the sharp east summit, where there is another viewpoint. Beyond this point the trail is not maintained and is obscure.

Diamond Peaks Trail (USGS Errol quad)
Distance from the Management Center
  to Diamond Peaks, east summit: 1.1 mi. (1.8 km.), 55
  min.

DIXVILLE REGION

The mountains in the vicinity of Dixville Notch are relatively low and have no open summits. There are no maintained trails to Cave Mtn. (3185 ft.), Mt. Abeniki (2780 ft.), or Mt. Sanguinari (2746 ft.). Snowmachine trails provide access to Dixville Peak (3482 ft.) and footpaths provide access to Table Rock on Mt. Gloriette (2780 ft.) and traverse the ridge north of the notch on Mt. Sanguinari. The Balsams Hotel has a guide to paths in the notch, available in summer from the information booth on NH 26 just across from the hotel entrance road.

Dixville Notch (1990 ft.)

Between Mt. Sanguinari (north) and Mt. Gloriette (south), with the Mohawk River flowing west and Clear Stream east, the Notch itself is less than 2 mi. in length, with a steep grade on each side, and is only wide enough to admit the highway. The cliff formations, formed of vertical strata, are impressively jagged. South from the highest point, high up on the cliffs, one can see the formation known as the Profile.

Just west of the high point, on the north side of the road, is Lake Gloriette (1871 ft.), an artificial lake formed from the headwaters of the Mohawk River. It is part of the grounds of the Balsams Hotel, which owns most of the land west of the height-of-land on both sides of the road. The management maintains a number of summer and winter trails, some suitable for horse travel. Part of their operation is the Wilderness Ski Area on the west slopes of

Dixville Peak. Cross-country ski and snowmachine trails are also part of this complex.

From a parking area just east of Lake Gloriette there is a trail to Table Rock, from which a panoramic view of the notch may be obtained. About 1 mi. east of the Balsams, near a picnic area north of the highway, is a small but attractive flume (sign). The trail is very short. Another path from this point, the Sanguinari Ridge Trail, traverses the cliffs north of the notch and ends at the road near Lake Gloriette. A little farther east on the south side of the highway is a second picnic area from which a slightly longer trail leads to Huntingdon Cascades.

Mt. Gloriette (2780 ft.)

Forming the south side of the notch, this mountain includes the rock formations Table Rock, Old King, Third Cliff, and Profile Cliff. There are paths to all of them, but only that to Table Rock is clearly signed.

Table Rock (2540 ft.)

This cliff juts out from the north side of Mt. Gloriette, south of the highway. Formed of vertical slabs, it is less than 10 ft. wide at its narrowest point and extends over 100 ft. from the shoulder of the mountain. The view is extensive. The most direct approach is from a parking area in the heart of the notch.

Table Rock Trail

Beginning at a sign in the parking area east of Lake Gloriette, the path ascends steeply for about 0.2 mi. to the ridge, turns right and in a few yards emerges onto the "Table." The vertical drop is about 700 ft. A branch path to the left (east), at the point where the trail meets the crest of the ridge, passes a cleft known as the Ice Cave and approaches the cliffs known as Old King, Third Cliff, and

Profile Cliff. There are no signs, and several intersecting footways. Another trail to Table Rock starts from NH 26 0.6 mi. east of its junction with the Wilderness Ski Area access road. This trail is considerably less steep than the direct route and is marked with small signs, beginning at the edge of the woods off the highway. There are several intersecting paths in this area and caution should be used, particularly in descending, as the signs are placed for ascent only. In descending, enter the woods above Table Rock, avoid a path west, and take the next right (west) fork.

Table Rock Trail (USGS Dixville quad)
Distances to Table Rock
from parking area: 0.3 mi. (0.5 km.), 30 min.
from NH 26 near ski area access road: 0.7 mi. (1.1 km.), 40 min.

Dixville Peak (3482 ft.)

Dixville Peak is the highest mountain in the vicinity of Dixville Notch and is wooded to the summit. It is accessible by snowmachine trails. A route from the vicinity of Table Rock along the ridge to the peak, shown on the USGS map, is now obscure. Inquire at the Balsams Hotel information booth.

Mount Sanguinari (2748 ft.)

This mountain forms the north wall of Dixville Notch. Its name derives from the color of its cliffs at sunset. The Sanguinari Ridge Trail does not go to the summit.

Sanguinari Ridge Trail

This trail starts at the Flume Brook picnic area of the Dixville Notch State Wayside, a rest area on the north side of NH 26 east of the height-of-land. It climbs a scenic ridge, following an old 1920s trail in places, as well as the blue-blazed state park boundary. The trail is mostly through balsam and spruce forests, with some hardwoods. Along the ridge crest and overlooking the notch are outlook points with views of Table Rock and Old King cliffs, and toward Errol and the Mahoosuc Range. The most spectacular view is from a rocky pinnacle 1.0 mi. west of the picnic area overlooking Lake Gloriette and the Balsams Hotel. The trail descends past Index Rock by graded switchbacks to the entrance road at the Balsams Hotel. It is marked with long pale yellow paint blazes and directional signs.

Sanguinari Ridge Trail (USGS Dixville quad)
Distance from the Flume Brook picnic area
　to the Balsams Hotel entrance road: 1.5 mi. (2.4 km.), 1
　hr. 40 min.

CONNECTICUT LAKES REGION

Some 10 mi. above Colebrook, the Connecticut River valley bends northeast and, just beyond the village of Beecher Falls VT, comes wholly within NH. Between its source near the Canadian line and the village of Pittsburg, the river passes through a chain of lakes of increasing size, numbered first to fourth in upstream order from the south. A high dam at Pittsburg created Lake Francis—the lowest lake in the series, it is below First Lake—and dams are responsible for the present size of both First and Second lakes. First Lake, 5.5 mi. long and 2.5 mi. wide at its broadest, and Lake Francis are the largest bodies of water in NH north of the Presidential Range. US 3 passes close to all of the lakes except Fourth, crossing the river from west to east between Second and Third lakes, and eventually entering Canada. It is the only road of any consequence in the region. Refer to USGS Second Lake, Indian Stream, and Moose Bog quadrangles.

Much of the land in the Connecticut Lakes Region, including Mt. Magalloway, Deer Mtn., and Fourth Connecticut Lake, is privately owned. While the owners do not discourage the use of their lands for hiking, they do request that these activities be limited to the daylight hours. Overnight camping and open fires are prohibited. Use of registered vehicles is limited to those roads which are not gated and not posted for road closure. Use of ATVs is prohibited at all times.

Mount Magalloway (3360 ft.)

Located east of First Connecticut Lake, this peak overlooks the Middle Branch of the Dead Diamond River. Turn southeast from US 3 just northeast of Coon Brook, 4.7 mi. from the First Connecticut dam. Drive on a gravel road 1.4 mi. to the Connecticut River bridge. Take the main road straight ahead beyond the bridge, following small signs ("Lookout Tower"). This is a main-haul logging road on which loaded trucks have the right of way. Pass two side roads (right) and at 5.3 mi. from US 3, after crossing the height-of-land, turn right. There are signs at this turn, but they are not clearly visible as you approach the intersection. At 1.6 mi. from this intersection there is a clear-cut area. Signs point out the trail to the fire tower. Park so as not to block the road ahead, which is used by woods equipment but is not open to unauthorized vehicles.

Mount Magalloway Trail

The trail begins at an open loading area and crosses an extensive clearing, heading toward Mt. Magalloway. It is signed and marked with orange tape. In the clear-cut area, it is crossed by several logging tracks and is swampy in part. Entering the woods, it crosses a small stream and heads generally southeast through a wet area. It then enters a woods road and turns left (east). Note this point for the return trip. The road ends in a grassy area, from which a faint track runs east, and the trail, now a rougher road, runs southeast. At a sign, a very faint logging road diverges right (south). Just beyond this point the trail passes a cabin. Beyond the cabin, the rough track passes a spring and ascends steeply to the summit, reaching the fire tower in 0.7 mi. There are excellent views southeast toward Aziscohos Lake and northeast to Rump Mtn. A short trail behind the warden's cabin leads to the top of the ledges, from which there is also a good view.

Mount Magalloway Trail (USGS Second Connecticut Lake quad)

Distances from parking area

to cabin: 1.1 mi., 35 min.

to fire tower and Mt. Magalloway summit: 1.8 mi. (2.9 km.), 1 hr. 20 min.

Bobcat Trail

The Bobcat Trail parallels the Mount Magalloway Trail, following the ridge west of the fire tower. It is probably easier to locate from the summit than from below. At the point where the track from the summit begins to drop steeply, the Bobcat Trail diverges left. It is not signed and the footway may be obscure. There are some blazed trees and, a few hundred feet from the junction, there is a sign ("Bobcat Outlook"). The path follows the crest of the ridge through softwoods, descends the end of the ridge to a high col, turns right (northeast) and continues to descend steeply. At the foot of the grade, the path enters a swampy area, following a very faint logging road, and rejoins the woods road near the turnaround below the cabin. This point is marked by two signs, both of which point to the main trail. The Bobcat Trail is steep, but more attractive than the rather badly eroded main trail.

Bobcat Trail (USGS Second Connecticut Lake quad)
Distances from fire tower
to upper end of Bobcat Trail: 0.1 mi., 5 min.
to lower end of trail: 0.5 mi. (0.8 km.), 15 min.

Deer Mountain (3005 ft.)

Located west of the Connecticut River, between Second and Third lakes, Deer Mtn. has no view from its summit. The fire tower and warden's camp were removed in 1985.

Deer Mountain Trail

The lower section of this trail has been much disturbed by logging and much of the rest of the mountain is to be cut in 1986–87. Ask at Moose Falls Campground for current conditions.

Leave US 3 on a gravel logging road just south of Moose Falls Campground. This is just south of the northernmost highway bridge across the Connecticut River. Go west 0.6 mi. to a cleared area. This has grown up with scrub; there may be orange tapes near the road and at the upper edge of the open area. Follow a route across the clearing aiming toward the northwest corner. A skid road runs generally in the right direction. After entering the woods, in the next 0.6 mi. bear right at three forks, crossing the stream three times. Watch for orange and blue tape, and signs of an old telephone line. At 0.6 mi. from the gravel road, go left (west) just before the main skid road enters a large clearcut area; the sign here is not obvious. The trail passes a good spring about a mile beyond this point and the site of the former warden's cabin in another 0.3 mi. The fire tower was 0.3 mi. beyond.

Deer Mountain Trail (USGS Second Connecticut Lake quad)

Distances from US 3

to warden's cabin site: 2.6 mi., 1 hr. 45 min.

to fire tower site: 2.9 mi. (4.7 km.), 1 hr. 55 min.

Fourth Connecticut Lake (2605 ft.)

This little pond, northwest of Third Lake and just south of the Canadian line, is the ultimate source of the Connecticut River. Once considered as remote a spot as the mountains had to offer, it is now accessible from US 3. From the US Customs station at the border on US 3, follow the international boundary uphill to the west (left). The boundary is a wide swath cut through the forest and marked at irregular intervals by brass discs set in concrete. It is cleared at ten-year intervals, more or less, and some of the markers are not readily visible. At marker 484-15 (0.6 mi. from the road) enter the woods (left), bearing south-southwest. The lake will be found in 0.1 mi. There is a snowmachine sign here and the route is marked with orange tape. There is no obvious footway. Paths which diverge into the woods from markers 484-13 and 484-14 may also be followed. All intersect before the lake is reached.

Fourth Connecticut Lake (USGS Second Connecticut Lake quad)

Distance from US Customs station

to Fourth Lake: 0.7 mi. (1.1 km.), 40 min.

Rump Mountain (3647 ft.)

Located in ME just east of the NH border, 7.0 mi. south of the Canadian line, Rump Mtn. was formerly known as Mt. Carmel, or Camel's Rump from its appearance from the southwest. This attractive but remote mountain has views of three states and Quebec province, and in clear weather, possibly of Katahdin. Rump Mtn. is on land now owned by the Boise Cascade Corporation. Although the company does not object to hikers crossing their lands, there are restrictions on vehicle travel and camping. Contact the corporation Woods Department, Rumford ME or its district forester in West Milan NH.

Cardigan and Kearsarge

This section includes Mt. Cardigan and its subsidiary peaks, and Plymouth Mtn., Ragged Mtn., and Mt. Kearsarge. It is bounded on the north by US 4, NH 118, and NH 25; on the east by I-93; and on the southwest by I-89. The AMC Cardigan map (map 2) covers the Cardigan area; Plymouth Mtn. is on the USGS Holderness quad, and Mt. Kearsarge and Ragged Mtn. are on the USGS Mt. Kearsarge quad.

LIST OF TRAILS   MAP

Trails on Ragged Mountain

Ragged Mountain Paths   USGS

Trails on Mount Kearsarge

Wilmot Trail   USGS
Warner Trail   USGS

MOUNT CARDIGAN

The outstanding peak of west central NH, Mt. Cardigan is located in Orange (near Canaan) and Alexandria (near Bristol). Excellent views are available from the steep-sided rock dome of "Old Baldy" itself, as well as from the South Peak—also noted for its blueberries in season—and from Firescrew, the north peak, named for a spiral of fire and smoke that rose from it during the conflagration in 1855, which denuded the upper slopes of the mountain. Though relatively low, Cardigan provides a great variety of terrain, from low hardwood forests to the wind-swept summit. Its trails vary from gentle woods walks, to the West Ridge Trail (a traditional first "big mountain climb" for children), to the Holt Trail, with upper ledges that constitute one of the more difficult scrambles among the regular hiking trails in New England. From the east, a fine circuit can be made by ascending Cardigan by the Holt, Cathedral Forest, and Clark trails—or by taking the much more challenging Holt Trail all the way—and returning over Firescrew via the Mowglis and Manning trails.

Most of the mountain is within a state reservation of over 5000 acres. Adjacent to the park is the AMC's 1000-acre Cardigan Reservation, which occupies much of "Shem Valley" and portions of the east slopes of the mountain. The AMC Cardigan Lodge, which has a main lodge, a cottage, a campground, and "Hi-Cabin," provides meals and lodging to the public during the summer season. A trail map, showing hiking and ski trails, is available at the

lodge. Nearby Newfound Lake, with Wellington State
Park, offers swimming, boating, and fishing. For reservations contact the Manager, AMC Cardigan Lodge, RFD,
Bristol, NH 03222 (603-744-8011). The usual approach is
from Bristol, easily accessible from I-93. Turn left (west)
from NH 3A at the stone church at the foot of Newfound
Lake, continue straight ahead through the crossroad at 1.9
mi., bear right at 3.1 mi., and turn left at 6.3 mi. At 7.4 mi.
from the church, turn right on a gravel road, then bear
right at 7.5 mi. at the "Red Schoolhouse," and continue to
the lodge at 8.9 mi. This road is plowed in winter, but must
be driven with great care.

While many of the trails on Mt. Cardigan are heavily
used and well beaten, others, noted in the individual descriptions, are lightly used, sparsely marked, and receive
little maintenance. Such trails may be difficult to follow if
not recently maintained, in the early part of the season
when a footway is not clearly established, or in the fall
when covered by leaves. Although these trails are not recommended for the inexperienced, they may be followed
fairly readily by experienced hikers, although one should
carry map and compass, keep track of one's location on
the map, and carefully follow whatever markings do exist.

THE TRAILS

West Ridge Trail (NHDP)

This is the main trail to Mt. Cardigan from the west, and
the shortest and easiest route to the summit. From NH 118
about 0.5 mi. north of Canaan, turn right at a large Cardigan State Park sign. Bear right 2.7 mi. from NH 118,
shortly after crossing Orange Brook. At 3.4 mi. bear left to
a parking area at 4.1 mi., where there are picnic tables and
restrooms.

The well-beaten trail starts at a sign in the parking area. It crosses a service road, and just beyond, at 0.4 mi., the South Ridge Trail diverges right at a sharp turn in the West Ridge Trail. The trail passes a well and a brook, both left, climbs to a junction with the Skyland Trail right, then crosses a rustic bridge and reaches the Hermitage, a small open shelter at 1.0 mi. At the shelter the Hurricane Gap Trail diverges right (no sign) for Hi-Cabin and the Clark Trail (water 200 yd. above shelter on Hurricane Gap Trail), and shortly beyond, a branch of the South Ridge Trail leads right to the warden's cabin. From here the West Ridge Trail ascends marked ledges to join the Clark Trail just below the summit.

West Ridge Trail (map 2)
Distance from Cardigan State Park parking area
   to Mt. Cardigan summit: 1.4 mi. (2.3 km.), 1 hr. 15 min.

South Ridge Trail
This trail provides access to Mt. Cardigan, South Peak, and Rimrock, and also makes possible a scenic loop in combination with the West Ridge Trail. It diverges right from the West Ridge Trail 0.4 mi. from the State Park parking area, crosses a brook and climbs, rather steeply at times, to Rimrock, where it crosses the Skyland Trail at 0.7 mi. (Descending, follow the left of two lines of cairns on the ledge below Rimrock.) The trail continues across marked ledges, passing the summit of South Peak at 1.0 mi., where a poorly marked spur descends to the Hurricane Gap Trail. The South Ridge Trail turns left and descends to cross the Hurricane Gap Trail, then turns sharp right at a junction (left is the branch trail to the West Ridge Trail at the Hermitage shelter, 0.2 mi.), and continues to the warden's cabin, where it ends at the Clark Trail.

South Ridge Trail (map 2)
Distance from West Ridge Trail
   to Clark Trail: 1.3 mi. (2.1 km.), 1 hr.
Distance from Cardigan State Park parking area
   for complete loop (via West Ridge, Clark, and South
   Ridge trails): 3.4 mi. (5.4 km.), 2 hr. 30 min.

Orange Cove Trail

This trail provides a direct approach from the west to
Mowglis Trail, Cilley's Cave, Hanging Rocks, and Crag
Shelter. Follow directions above for West Ridge Trail, but
bear left 2.7 mi. from NH 118, immediately after crossing
Orange Brook. Follow this road 1.2 mi. to end of pavement. This trail (no sign) is the old Groton–Orange road
and is easily followed. It passes the State Park boundary,
bears left at a fork, and climbs easily past a large beaver
pond at 1.0 mi. to end at the Mowglis Trail in the col
between Cilley's Cave and Cataloochee Mtn. The Mowglis
Trail continues straight ahead on the old road to Groton,
or sharp right to Cilley's Cave and Mt. Cardigan.

Orange Cove Trail (map 2)
Distance from end of paved road
   to Mowglis Trail: 1.6 mi. (2.5 km.), 1 hr.

Mowglis Trail

This trail has been maintained by Camp Mowglis on
Newfound Lake since 1921. From Hebron village on the
north end of the lake follow signs to Sculptured Rocks
State Geological Site on the Cockermouth River, an interesting glacial gorge with potholes and a popular picnic spot
with a swimming hole. Continue 1.0 mi. farther on Sculptured Rocks Rd. to a point just beyond the white bridge
over Atwell Brook. The trail (no sign) follows the old Gro-

ton–Orange road, which forks left and follows Atwell Brook, ascending at a moderate grade. It may be possible to drive 1.4 mi. to a logging road fork, where the trail keeps right on the old road. The trail ascends past the State Park boundary at 2.4 mi., to a junction with the Orange Cove Trail at 3.5 mi. in the col between Cilley's Cave and Cataloochee Mtn. Here the Orange Cove Trail continues ahead on the old road, while the Mowglis Trail turns left and climbs briefly to a junction with the Elwell Trail at 3.7 mi. Soon after this junction a spur trail (sign) leads left 80 yd. to Cilley's Cave, a lonely, rocky retreat, where it is said a hermit once lived, and about 0.3 mi. farther another spur leads left to Hanging Rocks.

Hanging Rocks is an interesting glacial formation that forms a natural shelter. About 100 yd. from the Mowglis Trail the spur forks. The right fork leads 0.1 mi. across the top of the ledge, with a fine view east, and the left fork descends 0.1 mi. among the rocks at the foot of the ledge. There is a steep connecting link at the far end of these two paths.

The Mowglis Trail then ascends more steeply past Crag Shelter—an open shelter accommodating fifteen, maintained by Camp Mowglis—at 4.6 mi. to an outlook north, where the trail turns sharp right and climbs to the summit of Firescrew at 5.1 mi., where it meets the Manning Trail. It descends across wide ledges deeply marked by glacial action, passes a side trail left (0.2 mi. long, 200-ft. descent) to Grotto Cave and a smaller boulder cave, marked by a sign painted on the rocks, then ascends steeply to the summit of Mt. Cardigan.

Mowglis Trail (map 2)
Distance from Sculptured Rocks Rd.
to Mt. Cardigan summit: 5.7 mi. (9.2 km.), 4 hr.

Elwell Trail

This trail extends over 10 mi. from Newfound Lake to
the Mowglis Trail, 2.0 mi. north of Mt. Cardigan. It is
named in honor of Col. Alcott Farrar Elwell, who directed
Camp Mowglis for fifty years and helped develop many of
the trails in this region. The trail begins on West Shore Rd.
directly opposite the entrance to Wellington State Park. At
0.5 mi. it passes a spur trail that leads left 0.2 mi. to Goose
Pond, crosses the open summit of Little Sugarloaf at 0.8
mi., continues along the ridge, and finally climbs steeply to
the summit of Sugarloaf at 1.7 mi. About 100 yd. past this
summit the trail turns sharp left, descends steeply, then
runs fairly level across the old Hebron–Alexandria turn-
pike.

It then climbs by steep switchbacks, with rough footing,
to the summit ridge of Bear Mtn., where there are several
fine outlooks across Newfound Lake. The Elwell Trail continues along the ridge, passes under power lines, and
crosses the Welton Falls Trail at 4.8 mi. It ascends gradually with occasional steep pitches, past several fine outlooks, to the summit of Oregon Mtn. The trail descends
sharply to a junction with the Carter Gibbs Trail (right)
and the Old Dicey Road (left) at 7.9 mi.; then crosses a
brook and climbs gradually to the summit of Mowglis Mtn.
at 8.9 mi., where there is a tablet honoring Camp Mowglis
on the right. It descends again to the next col at 9.9 mi.,
where the Back 80 Trail diverges left for Cardigan Lodge,
then climbs fairly steeply to a spur trail leading left 130 yd.
to Cilley's Cave (sign), and descends slightly to end at the
Mowglis Trail. Between Mowglis Mtn. and the Back 80
Trail junction the trail must be followed with care.

Elwell Trail (map 2)
Distance from West Shore Rd.
  to Mowglis Trail: 10.6 mi. (17 km.), 7 hr. 15 min.

Carter Gibbs Trail

This trail leaves Sculptured Rocks Rd. (small sign 50 yd. in) at a small gravel turnout on the south side, 0.2 mi. east of the Sculptured Rocks parking area. It may be possible to drive the first 1.1 mi. It follows a gravel road for about 0.5 mi., then turns left where a right fork crosses Dane Brook on a snowmobile bridge. In another 0.3 mi. it bears right at a fork and follows an old logging road that gradually peters out. The trail then climbs more steeply to the height-of-land between Oregon Mtn. and Mowglis Mtn., where a side path (sign) leads right 0.2 mi. to an outlook on Carter's Knob. The main trail then descends sharply 0.3 mi. to the Elwell Trail opposite the upper terminus of the Old Dicey Road.

Carter Gibbs Trail (map 2)
Distance from Sculptured Rocks Rd.
  to Elwell Trail: 3.0 mi. (4.8 km.), 2 hr. 15 min.

Welton Falls Trail

This trail, now quite difficult to follow south of the ridge top, provides a route from Hebron to the Elwell Trail and Welton Falls Rd. The trail diverges left from Hobart Hill Rd. 0.8 mi. from the village square in Hebron. The only sign at the trailhead is a small Mowglis Trail marker. The trail follows an old road across a brook through a ruined farm, makes a sharp right turn in a log yard, then slabs the hillside to another old road. It turns left and ascends this road, passing under power lines, and crosses the Elwell Trail at the top of the ridge at 1.5 mi. Descending, and becoming obscure, it soon joins old logging roads and follows them past a ruined camp, where it crosses a road diagonally to an overgrown field. Becoming a trail again, it descends across a brook, on and off old roads, and continues to a gravel road at the edge of a field (parking). The gravel road continues to Welton Falls Rd. just north of the bridge over Fowler River. This point can also be reached by following the route described for Cardigan Lodge. Bear right 6.3 mi. from the stone church and continue 0.8 mi., just across the bridge.

Welton Falls Trail (map 2)
Distance from Hobart Hill Rd.
   to Welton Falls Rd.: 3.3 mi. (5.3 km.), 2 hr.

Old Dicey Road
Follow the route described above for Cardigan Lodge but bear right 6.3 mi. from the stone church. Follow the road for another 1.2 mi. Where the good road turns sharp right uphill, continue straight ahead another 0.1 mi. to a parking area at a washed-out bridge. Follow the road, which is the Old Dicey Road, across a brook. At 0.2 mi. the Manning Trail diverges left on a cart track, while the Old Dicey Road continues to a clearing at 1.1 mi. Here the Back 80 Loop continues straight ahead, and the Old Dicey Road turns right and climbs past an old shack and cellar hole, along a small brook, to end at the Elwell Trail opposite the south terminus of the Carter Gibbs Trail.

Old Dicey Road (map 2)
Distance from parking area
   to Elwell Trail: 2.0 mi. (3.3 km.), 1 hr. 30 min.

Back 80 Loop
This short trail connects the Old Dicey Road with the Back 80 Trail and makes possible a circuit to Welton Falls from Cardigan Lodge. It follows an old road straight ahead from the clearing where the Old Dicey Road turns right, then bears left to cross two brooks within a short distance, and ascends across another brook and the 93Z Ski Trail to meet the Back 80 Trail at a cellar hole.

Back 80 Loop (map 2)
Distance from Old Dicey Road
   to Back 80 Trail: 0.8 mi. (1.2 km.), 35 min.

Back 80 Trail

This trail diverges right from the Holt Trail about 100 yd. west of Cardigan Lodge and follows an old logging road. At 0.3 mi. the Short Circuit Ski Trail diverges right, and about 0.5 mi. farther the trail turns sharp right, where the Alleeway Ski Trail turns left, and reaches a cellar hole. The trail to the right is the Back 80 Loop to Welton Falls; the Back 80 Trail turns left (follow the trail with care from here on). It crosses the 93Z Ski Trail, then a brook at a scenic little waterfall. It turns sharp left at 1.2 mi. at a corner post at the east corner of Back 80 Lot and runs along the northern corner of the lot. The trail goes around a flowage from a beaver dam, which may force a detour through the woods, passes a junction at 1.8 mi. with the Duke's Link Ski Trail, then turns sharp right, crosses a brook, turns left, and follows the brook and the edge of another beaver pond to the back corner post (marked Draper-NHFS-AMC). The trail then ascends gradually across a brook to end at the Elwell Trail in the col between Mowglis Mtn. and Cilley's Cave.

Back 80 Trail (map 2)
Distance from Holt Trail
   to Elwell Trail: 2.4 mi. (3.9 km.), 1 hr. 30 min.

Manning Trail

This trail was constructed by the AMC as a memorial to the three Manning brothers, Robert, Charles, and Francis, who were killed by a train during a blizzard in 1924 while hiking on a section of track near Glencliff which was often used as a shortcut between DOC trails. The trail diverges left from the Old Dicey Road 0.2 mi. from the parking area near the washed-out bridge on Welton Falls Rd., follows a cart path to the Fowler River, crosses on stones, and enters the Welton Falls Reservation (NHDP). It continues up-river to a deep, mossy ravine and the main falls. There are many attractive falls and rapids, as well as spectacular potholes, above and below the main falls. From Welton Falls the trail climbs and descends many small ridges, usually in sight of the river, to a junction with the Hiawata Trail at 1.1 mi. The Manning Trail turns right at this junction, crosses the river without a bridge (difficult at high water) and ascends to a plateau, where it passes through a planted grove of spruces. It crosses the 93Z Ski Trail, then descends through a picnic area to Cardigan Lodge. (To reach the Manning Trail from the lodge, ascend through a picnic area to the road at right of the fireplace.)

The Manning Trail continues past the lodge, coincides with the Holt Trail for 0.3 mi., then diverges right, passes the old Holt cellar hole, turns right at an arrow, and climbs through the woods to the first ledges. It passes a small brook, then climbs again to a great open ledge where the Duke's Ski Trail enters right, then diverges right at the head of the ledge. The Manning Trail turns left through scrubby woods, ascending at times steeply, until it reaches ledges where the Duke's rejoins from the right. The trail follows cairns and paint markings across flat ledges to the cairn where it ends at the Mowglis Trail, just below the summit of Firescrew. Mt. Cardigan summit is to the left on Mowglis Trail.

Manning Trail (map 2)
Distances from Old Dicey Road
  to Cardigan Lodge: 1.6 mi., 1 hr.
  to Mowglis Trail: 4.0 mi. (6.4 km.), 3 hr.

Distance from Cardigan Lodge
   to Mt. Cardigan summit (via Manning Trail and Mowglis Trail): 3.0 mi. (4.8 km.), 2 hr. 30 min.

Hiawata Trail

This trail connects the Manning Trail with Shem Valley
Rd. 0.4 mi. east of the lodge (sign), and is used at high
water to avoid the difficult crossing of Fowler River on the
Manning Trail to Welton Falls.

Hiawata Trail (map 2)
Distance from Shem Valley Rd.
   to Manning Trail: 0.3 mi. (0.5 km.), 10 min.

Holt Trail

This is the shortest, but far from the easiest, route from
Cardigan Lodge to the summit of Mt. Cardigan. The upper
ledges are very steep, and the scramble up these ledges is
more difficult than any other trail in this section, and dangerous in wet or icy conditions. The trail is maintained by
Camp Mowglis and named for the camp's founder, Elizabeth Ford Holt.

From Cardigan Lodge the Holt Trail follows a gravel
road to a junction with the Manning Trail, then a lumber
road almost to the Bailey Brook bridge. There it diverges
right, and the Alexandria Ski Trail continues straight. The
Holt Trail stays on the north bank of the brook, then
crosses at the head of Elizabeth Falls to rejoin the Alexandria Ski Trail near Grand Junction. The Cathedral Forest
Trail (Holt-Clark Cutoff) diverges left, providing an easier
ascent of Mt. Cardigan via Cathedral Forest and the Clark
Trail. The Alexandria Ski Trail also diverges left here, and
shortly beyond the Alleeway Ski Trail diverges right. The
Holt Trail continues along Bailey Brook to a point directly
under the summit, climbs steeply on a rocky path through

woods, then emerges on open ledges and makes a rapid, sporty, and very steep ascent over marked ledges to the summit.

Holt Trail (map 2)
Distances from Cardigan Lodge
    to Grand Junction: 1.1 mi., 35 min.
    to Mt. Cardigan summit: 2.2 mi. (3.6 km.), 2 hr.

Cathedral Forest Trail (Holt-Clark Cutoff)
This trail leads left from the Holt Trail at Grand Junction and ascends to the Clark Trail in the Cathedral Forest, providing the easiest route to the summit of Cardigan from the east. About 100 yd. above the junction the Vistamont Trail branches left to Orange Mtn. Ascending in graded switchbacks past the huge dead trunk of the Giant of the Forest, the trail joins the Clark Trail at a large cairn.

Cathedral Forest Trail (map 2)
Distances from Holt Trail, Grand Junction
    to Clark Trail: 0.6 mi., 30 min.
    to Mt. Cardigan summit (via Holt, Cathedral Forest, and Clark trails): 2.6 mi. (4.2 km.), 2 hr. 10 min.

Clark Trail
The official beginning of this trail is on Shem Valley Rd. 0.6 mi. east of Cardigan Lodge, but most hikers will find it more convenient to enter via the Woodland Trail from Cardigan Lodge. The trail proper starts at the top of a ledgy ridge, opposite "Shim Knoll," and follows a rough dirt road left (sign: "Williams") past a summer residence. At 0.5 mi., just over Clark Brook, the Woodland Trail enters right. The two trails together ascend a logging road at a moderate grade, and at 1.1 mi. the Woodland Trail turns sharp left on the logging road, and the Clark Trail contin-

ues straight ahead on an older road. It passes an old cellar hole, enters the state reservation at a level grade in a beautiful forest, then climbs rather steeply to cross the Vistamont Trail at 1.9 mi. The grade becomes more gradual, and the Clark Trail reaches the Cathedral Forest, where the Cathedral Forest Trail enters from the right at 2.2 mi. As the trail continues a moderate ascent, the Alexandria Ski Trail enters right near P. J. Ledge, and 30 yd. farther the Hurricane Gap Trail leaves left for Hi-Cabin and the Hermitage Shelter. The Clark Trail continues past a side trail left that leads to a spring and Hi-Cabin, then climbs on ledges and through scrub to the warden's cabin at 2.9 mi., where it meets the South Ridge Trail. Turning right, it follows marked ledges steeply to the summit.

Clark Trail (map 2)
Distance from Shem Valley Rd.
to Mt. Cardigan summit: 3.1 mi. (5 km.), 2 hr. 30 min.

Hurricane Gap Trail

This Trail connects the east and west sides of the mountain through the col between Cardigan and South Peak. It leaves the Clark Trail just above P. J. Ledge, passes an unsigned spur right to a spring, then reaches the AMC Hi-Cabin, where another spur trail leads right 60 yd. to the spring and 40 yd. farther to the Clark Trail. It climbs past a spur that leads 0.1 mi. left to South Peak, then crosses the South Ridge Trail at 0.4 mi. at the height-of-land, and descends to the West Ridge Trail at the Hermitage. (Reliable water is found on the Hurricane Gap Trail 200 yd. above the Hermitage.)

Hurricane Gap Trail (map 2)
Distance from Clark Trail
to West Ridge Trail: 0.6 mi. (0.9 km.), 30 min.

Vistamont Trail

This trail connects the Holt Trail with the Skyland Trail at Orange Mtn. (sometimes also called Gilman Mtn.). It leaves the Cathedral Forest Trail left about 100 yd. above Grand Junction and rises over a low ridge, where it crosses the Clark Trail at 0.6 mi. It then drops to cross a branch of Clark Brook, and ascends by switchbacks up the east spur of Orange Mtn., climbing moderately on open ledges to the Skyland Trail 80 yd. southeast of the rocky summit, where there are fine views.

Vistamont Trail (map 2)
Distance from Cathedral Forest Trail
  to Skyland Trail: 1.6 mi. (2.6 km.), 1 hr. 20 min.

Woodland Trail (Skyland Cutoff)

The trail runs from Cardigan Lodge to the Skyland Trail near the summit of Church Mtn. It leaves the parking lot to the left of the pond, crosses the outlet brook on a bridge, and passes the east entrance of the Kimball Ski Trail. It continues through woods past the Brock Farm cellar hole and field, then turns right on the Clark Trail at 0.6 mi. At 1.2 mi. it diverges sharp left on a logging road and descends across a brook, and climbs to a large beaver pond at 2.1 mi. From here on the trail is harder to follow and great care must be used. It ascends along the inlet brook, crosses it, and doubles back along the edge of the pond, then climbs moderately past a corner post marked "Draper" in a boggy area near a large boulder. Finally it rises more steeply to end at the Skyland Trail at the northwest shoulder of Church Mtn.

Woodland Trail (map 2)
Distance from Cardigan Lodge
  to Skyland Trail: 3.3 mi. (5.2 km.), 2 hr. 15 min.

Skyland Trail

This trail runs from Alexandria Four Corners to the West Ridge Trail just below the Hermitage. It follows the western and southern boundaries of Shem Valley, and in 4.5 mi. crosses five of the six peaks that extend south and southeast from Cardigan summit. It is lightly marked for much of its distance and, particularly between Brown Mtn. and Orange Mtn., must be followed with great care. It is, however, a very scenic route.

The trail starts at Alexandria Four Corners, reached by following signs from the stone church at the foot of Newfound Lake to Alexandria village. Continue through the village on the main road, which turns sharp right, then left, pass under the power lines and then, as the main road turns sharp left for Danbury, continue straight ahead for about 4.0 mi. to the corner (sign: "Rosie's Rd."). Best parking is here; do not block roads above.

The trail follows the road right (north) from the corner and soon bears left at a fork. At about 0.3 mi. it turns sharp left (arrow) on a short road to a clearing, and ascends moderately to the edge of a logged area and a house. It climbs almost to the wooded summit of Brown Mtn., then turns left and crosses the col to the summit of Church Mtn. (2290 ft.) at 1.1 mi., where there is an outlook. It continues past a junction (right) at 1.3 mi. with the Woodland Trail coming from Cardigan Lodge, then follows the ridge top over Grafton Knob (2210 ft.) to Crane Mtn. (2430 ft.) at 2.1 mi., with good views from several ledges near the summit. The Skyland Trail continues to Orange Mtn. (2630 ft.) at 3.3 mi., where the Vistamont Trail enters 80 yd. before the summit. There are fine views from the summit ledges. The trail descends to a col, then climbs fairly steeply to Rimrock at 4.3 mi., where it crosses the South Ridge Trail. It descends along a ledge (follow the right of two lines of cairns) and soon enters the West Ridge Trail just below the Hermitage Shelter.

Skyland Trail (map 2)
Distance from Alexandria Four Corners
   to West Ridge Trail: 4.6 mi. (7.3 km.), 3 hr. 15 min.

Ski Trails at Cardigan Lodge

The AMC maintains a number of ski trails in the woods around Cardigan Lodge, in addition to the hiking trails, many of which are also skiable. A map available at the lodge shows most of these trails and their ratings, which range from novice cross-country to expert alpine terrain on the ledges of Cardigan and Firescrew. Some of these trails were cut as alpine trails in the days before modern tows became common. Ski trails are not maintained for summer use, and hikers are requested not to use them.

PLYMOUTH MOUNTAIN

Plymouth Mtn. (2187 ft.) lies in Plymouth, northeast of Newfound Lake. The true summit is wooded, but nearby open ledges afford excellent views. Refer to the USGS Holderness quadrangle.

Plymouth Mountain Trail

At the crossroads on NH 3A near the head of Newfound Lake, where the lake shore road to Hebron village runs west, go east on Pike Hill Rd. and bear left at the first fork. Since the road may be impassable beyond, this is probably the best spot to park. In another 1.1 mi., after the second bridge over a brook, the trail leaves right on an old logging road (sign). It is marked with Camp Mowglis stencilled signs. It crosses a brook (follow trail with care), follows another old road upward, and turns sharp left where a branch trail enters right. (Descending, turn sharp right here where the branch trail, marked by a Mowglis sign, goes almost straight ahead.) The trail ascends to an outlook over Newfound Lake, becomes less steep, crosses a false summit, and climbs to the true summit (sign). From here an open ledge 30 yd. straight ahead (east) provides fine views of Franconia Notch and the White Mtns., while a line of cairns leads right (southwest) to an outlook over Newfound Lake to Mt. Cardigan.

Plymouth Mountain Trail (USGS Holderness quad)
Distances from US 3A
   to start of foot trail: 1.4 mi., 1 hr.
   to Plymouth Mtn. summit: 2.9 mi. (4.6 km.), 2 hr. 15 min.

RAGGED MOUNTAIN

Ragged Mtn. (2250 ft.) lies in the towns of Andover and Danbury. The name is apt, since it is a large, irregular, rugged mass, most of which is heavily wooded. There are several peaks of nearly equal height with numerous ledgy outlooks. The Bulkhead (1910 ft.) is a precipitous buttress on the east side. The Ragged Mtn. Ski Area, which has not operated for several years, is on the slightly lower west peak. Refer to the USGS Mt. Kearsarge quadrangle.

Ragged Mountain Paths

The mountain has a number of trails, which seem to go through regular cycles of decline and rebirth. The best approach is from the old ski area, reached from NH 104 in Danbury. Continue on the dirt road east near the ski area parking lot. After crossing Gulf Brook on a snowmobile bridge 0.5 mi. from the ski area, turn right on a logging road. This road continues well up on the mountain, where it becomes a trail and climbs south-southeast nearly to the ridge, then very steeply to the Old Top.

Another route leaves the summit of the West Peak, ascended by the ski trails, which are becoming somewhat overgrown. From the summit follow the easternmost ski trail. After about 0.3 mi. it makes a sharp left down the top of the ridge, and Wilson's Wonder (ski) Trail (to Proctor Academy) veers right. Take Wilson's Wonder as it drops downhill for 10 yd., then circles back southeast, dropping to the western dip of the col between the West Peak and the West Top.

There is a well-blazed trail along the ridge, about 1.1 mi. long, which leaves from the Wilson's Wonder Trail in the western col, descends slightly, climbs steeply, then moderately to where both paths rejoin, just east of the West Top ("West Peak" on some signs), which has fine views south. The ridge path continues past a trail junction, then past another junction with a logging road—which descends past a spur trail to Balanced Rock to join the Wilson's Wonder trail to Proctor. The ridge trail then ascends past a spring to the summit (restricted views) and continues to the "Old Top," which has the finest views on the mountain.

MOUNT KEARSARGE

Mt. Kearsarge (2937 ft.) is located in Warner, Wilmot, Andover, and Salisbury. It has a bare summit with fine views in all directions. Mt. Kearsarge probably was discovered shortly after the Pilgrims landed. On a seventeenth-century map (Gardner's) it appears as "Carasarga," but since Carrigain's map of 1816 "Kearsarge" has remained the accepted spelling. On the summit there is a fire tower and an airways beacon, on separate prominent ledges about 30 yd. apart, and a fire warden's cabin near the tower. Refer to the USGS Mt. Kearsarge quadrangle.

Wilmot (Northside) Trail

From NH 11 between Wilmot Flat and Elkins, take Kearsarge Valley Rd. south, then follow signs to Winslow State Park and the site of the old Winslow House (caretaker's cabin, picnic area, water, and parking space; modest admission fee). The trail starts from the parking area to the left of a service garage. It is well beaten and marked with red paint. The trail crosses under power lines and climbs moderately to a fork. (The left branch rejoins above and is slightly shorter but rougher.) The right branch climbs more steeply past Halfway Rock, slabs upward to an outlook north, then turns south and ascends over bare ledges, marked with orange paint, to the summit.

Wilmot Trail (USGS Mt. Kearsarge quad)
Distance from parking area, Winslow State Park
  to Mt. Kearsarge summit: 1.1 mi. (1.8 km.), 1 hr. 5 min.

Warner (Southside) Trail

Leave NH 103 in Warner and follow signs to the toll gate at Rollins State Park. A small fee is charged, and the gate is often closed on weekdays before Memorial Day and after Labor Day. There is a picnic area with tables, fireplaces, and water. The road then mainly follows the route of the old carriage road along the crest of Mission Ridge and ends at a parking area 3.7 mi. above the toll gate. There are more picnic tables and fireplaces here, but no water.

The trail follows the old carriage road, now badly eroded, to a ledge with a fine view. (An unsigned, red-blazed trail, 0.1 mi. longer and rough, bypasses the worst section of the old road to the right and rejoins at the outlook.) The trail then swings left and rises to the foot of the summit ledges, where there are toilets. An orange-blazed trail diverges sharp right, a direct route to the warden's cabin. The main trail, blazed in silver, continues across the ledges to the beacon and tower.

From the west end of the parking area, an unsigned trail starts as a cart track to the foot of the ledges and, marked with red paint on the rocks, climbs steeply to the top. Faded paint blazes lead along sparsely wooded ledges toward the tower, then to the main trail just below the beacon.

Warner Trail (USGS Mt. Kearsarge quad)
Distance from parking area, Rollins State Park
to Mt. Kearsarge summit: 0.6 mi. (1.0 km.), 25 min.

Monadnock and Southwestern New Hampshire

This section covers the area west of the Merrimack River and south of I-89. Mt. Monadnock is by far the best known and most popular peak in the area. Other peaks include the Pack Monadnocks, Temple Mtn., and Barrett Mtn. on the Wapack Trail; the Uncanoonuc Mtns. in Goffstown, Crotched Mtn. in Francestown, and Sunapee Mtn. in Newbury. Monadnock itself is covered by the AMC Grand Monadnock map (map 1), and there is a two-page map of the Wapack Trail in this section; other mountains are covered by USGS quadrangles as indicated in their descriptions. In addition to the areas for which trails are described in this section, mention should be made of Pisgah State Park in Chesterfield, Hinsdale, and Winchester. This undeveloped park contains 13,000 acres within which there is great opportunity for exploration.

LIST OF TRAILS	MAP
Trails on Mount Monadnock	
White Arrow Trail	1
Dublin Path	1
Pumpelly Trail	1
White Dot Trail	1
White Cross Trail	1
Harling Trail	1
Cascade Link	1
Spellman Trail	1
Birchtoft Trail	1
Marlboro Trail	1
Halfway House Region Paths	1

MOUNT MONADNOCK

Mt. Monadnock (3165 ft.), also called Grand Monadnock, lies in Jaffrey and Dublin, about 10 mi. north of the NH/MA border. It is an isolated mountain rising 1500 to 2000 ft. above the surrounding country. The upper 500 ft. is open ledge, bared by a series of forest fires which culminated around 1820. Mt. Washington is sometimes visible when it has snow cover. There are several major trails to the summit and a network of connecting and secondary trails on the east, south, and west sides of the main peak. The condition of some of these secondary trails varies from year to year; it may be advisable to inquire about the condition of secondary trails from State Park personnel.

The public reservation on the mountain now comprises about 5000 contiguous acres cooperatively administered by the state, the town of Jaffrey, the Association to Protect Mt. Monadnock, and the SPNHF. At the Monadnock State Park, just off Memorial Rd., the state maintains picnic grounds, a parking lot, and a public campground (fees charged for each). Camping is not permitted anywhere on the mountain, except at the state park campground. Dogs are not allowed anywhere in the state park.

A former toll road, now closed to automobiles, is still

open for hikers. It leaves NH 124 near the height-of-land, 5.0 mi. west of Jaffrey and about 4 mi. east of Troy, and climbs about 1.3 mi. to the site where a hotel, the Halfway House, formerly stood on the west flank of the south ridge at about 2100 ft. The White Arrow Trail—the most direct route to the summit from this area—and many other trails start near the Halfway House site, which is a good base for circuit trips.

Monadnock is reputedly one of the most frequently climbed mountains in the world. It has occasionally been ascended by several thousand hikers on one day. It would be wise to regard any water source on this mountain with extreme suspicion.

White Arrow Trail

One of the oldest routes to the summit, this trail continues along from the end of the toll road at the site of the Halfway House. It is marked by painted white arrows. It runs north, crosses a brook, passes through the former picnic grounds and, bearing slightly east, immediately begins to climb steeply through the woods on a broad, rocky way. In about 0.3 mi. Quarter-Way Spring is passed, and the trail climbs to treeline. It bears left here and starts to ascend the ledges. Just below the last stretch to the summit there is an interesting scramble up an inclined chimney. Emerging from this narrow gully, the trail turns right for the summit a few yards away.

White Arrow Trail (map 1)
Distance from Halfway House site
   to Mt. Monadnock summit: 1.0 mi. (1.6 km.), 1 hr.

Dublin Path (SPNHF)

From the flagpole in Dublin go west on NH 101 (Main St.). At 0.4 mi. bear left on Old Marlboro Rd. At 2.5 mi.

go left downhill on Old Troy Rd., through a crossroad, to a small clearing on the right at 4.0 mi., where there is parking space. (Beyond the houses at 3.4 mi. the road becomes narrow and poor; it may be impassable when muddy.) The trail, marked with white D's, starts opposite the clearing and climbs to the tip of the ridge, passing a spring at 1.0 mi. It follows the ridge over slabs, passes another spring at the foot of a rock at 1.8 mi., and emerges above timberline. The Marlboro Trail joins just beyond a prominent cap of rock, a false summit. The Dublin Path continues to meet the White Arrow Trail 50 yd. below the true summit.

Dublin Path (map 1)
Distance from Old Troy Rd.
   to Mt. Monadnock summit: 2.2 mi. (3.5 km.), 2 hr.

Pumpelly Trail (SPNHF and AMC)
Follow NH 101 (Main St.) west from Dublin and turn left on Old Marlboro Rd. (sign). The trail leaves the road left at 0.4 mi., opposite a log cabin on the pond, 75 yd. east of where the road reaches the shore. The trailhead is marked with a wooden sign on a post. The trail is wide for 120 yd., then turns right into a narrow path through a stone wall (small cairn and sign). It crosses the summit of Oak Hill then turns right and mounts the steep north end of Dublin Ridge. There is a spring on the south side of the trail near the foot of the steep pitch. The trail zigzags up and emerges on the open shoulder of the mountain about 2.0 mi. from the summit. For about the first 0.3 mi. on the ridge, the trail winds among the rocks and scrubby spruces and firs, always following the ridge top. About 1.0 mi. from the summit, it comes out on bare, glaciated rocks. For the remaining distance it is marked by large cairns. From a saddle (2700 ft.) at 2.8 mi., about 0.3 mi. north of

the dominant summit on the ridge, a line of cairns and yellow blazes that leads left is the Cascade Link, a direct descent toward the reservation and Jaffrey.

The Pumpelly Trail continues along the ridge. Just before it reaches the Sarcophagus, a huge rectangular boulder in plain view, the Spellman Trail enters left at 3.5 mi. About 0.3 mi. beyond the Sarcophagus the Red Spot–Old Ski Trail enters left and, soon after, a northeast extension of the Smith Connecting Trail, marked with yellow spots and cairns, leaves left for the White Dot and White Cross trails and from there to Bald Rock and into the complex of trails that radiate from the Halfway House site. The Pumpelly Trail, marked by cairns, continues over ledges to the summit. Glacial striations are plainly visible on many of the ledges.

(Descending, look for a large white arrow on summit rock marked Pumpelly Trail. There are few cairns for the first 200 yd. and care must be taken to locate the first one. In several cases cairns are rather small.)

Pumpelly Trail (map 1)
Distance (est.) from Old Marlboro Rd.

> to Mt. Monadnock summit: 4.5 mi. (7.3 km.), 3 hr. 30 min.

White Dot and White Cross Trails

These two trails have a common origin, coincide for their first 0.8 mi., then separate, but rejoin for the last 0.3 mi. to the summit. Both trails start on a broad jeep road near the warden's office at the west end of Poole Memorial Rd. in Monadnock State Park. They descend slightly and cross a small brook. At about 0.6 mi. the Spruce Link, a cutoff that rejoins the White Cross Trail above Falcon Spring, leaves left. The White Dot and White Cross trails then climb gradually 0.2 mi. through woods to a junction with

the Cascade Link at Falcon Spring at 0.7 mi. The White
Dot Trail is steeper, but not appreciably shorter than the
White Cross. Views from the White Cross are more inter-
esting.

The White Dot Trail goes straight from the Falcon
Spring junction, northwest up the steep ridge, and emerges
in about 0.5 mi. on the bare plateau near treeline. It crosses
an old trail that runs north to the Red Spot Trail, then
climbs the ledges through meager evergreens badly damaged by a forest fire. Another branch trail connecting with
the Red Spot Trail leaves right 100 yd. farther, and 200 yd.
beyond, the White Dot Trail crosses the Smith Connecting
Trail, which circles the east side of the summit cone from
the Halfway House site to the Pumpelly Trail. In a few feet
the south branch of the Red Spot Trail enters right, and the
White Dot rejoins the White Cross Trail at 1.8 mi. to
continue up slanting ledges to the summit.

The White Cross Trail leaves left at Falcon Spring junction and slabs gradually uphill behind the spring. In a short
distance the Spruce Link enters on the left and the White
Cross Trail turns sharply right and starts to climb at moderate grades over boulders left by an old slide. It passes
through an old burn (fine views back to the east and south
across a ravine called Dingle Dell) and finally reaches the
flat southeast shoulder. It soon emerges from sparse evergreens on the ledges. The Smith Connecting Trail crosses,
and a few feet farther the White Cross rejoins the White
Dot Trail at 1.9 mi. to continue to the summit. Above this
junction the trail is most frequently marked with white dots
rather than white crosses.

White Dot Trail (map 1)
Distance from Poole Memorial Rd.
  to Mt. Monadnock summit: 2.0 mi. (3.2 km.), 1 hr. 45
  min.

White Cross Trail (map 1)
Distance from Poole Memorial Rd.
  to Mt. Monadnock summit: 2.1 mi. (3.4 km.), 1 hr. 45 min.

Harling Trail (SPNHF)

This trail begins on Dublin Rd. in Jaffrey, just north of the second of two brooks that are about 0.5 mi. north of the Monadnock Bible Conference, formerly called "the Ark." The beginning of the trail, not signed, is now a private drive to a new residence. Please do not obstruct the driveway. There is room for two or three cars to park opposite the trail entrance. The trail follows a logging road, bearing left before the house, across partially cut-over land. About 0.5 mi. from the highway the logging road veers right, but the trail stays west on the traces of an old woods road, marked by small cairns. It reaches the Cascade Link a short distance north of the Falcon Spring junction. At the junction, follow the Cascade Link right for the Red Spot, Spellman, and Pumpelly trails.

Harling Trail (map 1)
Distance from Dublin Rd.
  to Cascade Link: 1.1 mi. (1.7 km.), 50 min.

Cascade Link (AMC)

This trail runs between Falcon Spring junction and the Pumpelly Trail, slabbing gradually upward, south to north. With the Pumpelly Trail, it is an interesting descent from the summit to the state park. With either the Spellman Trail or the Red Spot Trail it offers the sportiest and most varied ascents from the east side of the mountain.

The Cascade Link starts at the Falcon Spring junction, reached by the White Dot and White Cross trails. It runs northeast, descends slightly, and passes through spruce woods to a brook and the little cascades for which this trail is named. At about 0.3 mi. it crosses the brook and climbs gradually along its east side, rising about 300 ft. before it leaves the brook. The trail winds over some ledges in thick woods. About 0.3 mi. from the brook crossing, just before an old east-west stone wall, the Birchtoft Trail enters right and, 100 ft. beyond, the Red Spot leaves left for Dublin Ridge and the Pumpelly Trail. About 100 yd. beyond the wall the Spellman Trail leaves left. About 0.1 mi. beyond the wall, the Cascade Link turns left over a knob with a wide view. It passes through woods across a small brook, which it follows closely along the east bank to where the brook rises, close to the boundary between Dublin and Jaffrey. From there, prominent cairns mark the Cascade Link over open ledges to a saddle on the Dublin Ridge (2700 ft.), where it ends at the Pumpelly Trail. (The Pumpelly Trail is a picturesque descent with many outlooks. It is marked with yellow paint blazes.)

Cascade Link (map 1)
Distance from Falcon Spring
   to Pumpelly Trail: 1.5 mi. (2.5 km.), 1 hr. 30 min.

Spellman Trail

This trail runs from the Cascade Link and makes the steepest (700 ft. in about 0.5 mi.) climb on the mountain, up to the Pumpelly Trail just north of the Sarcophagus. The Spellman Trail is a good scramble in its middle section, with excellent views back to the east. This trail is difficult to follow when snow covers the white dots that mark the route on the rocks, because in winding about to avoid the worst ledges, the trail does not always follow a clear line.

Spellman Trail (map 1)
Distance from Cascade Link
   to Pumpelly Trail: 0.5 mi. (0.8 km.), 40 min.

Birchtoft Trail

This trail leaves the Monadnock Recreation Area located on Dublin Rd. 1 mi. north of Poole Memorial Rd. The Monadnock Recreation Area campground is privately owned; there is a parking fee, and hikers are requested to register at the lodge office. Follow the recreation area entrance road a short distance. Turn left on the first driveway and follow it 100 yd. to the shore of Gilson Pond (parking). The trail (sign) skirts the east and south shores of the pond and ascends by easy grades to end at the Cascade Link, 30 yd. south of its junction with the Red Spot Trail.

Birchtoft Trail (map 1)

Distance (est.) from Gilson Pond

   to Cascade Link: 2.0 mi. (3.2 km.), 1 hr. 25 min.

Marlboro Trail (SPNHF)

This is one of the oldest trails to the summit, dating to 1850 or earlier. Follow NH 124 west from Jaffrey, past roads to Monadnock State Park and the Halfway House site. Take the first dirt road on the right, 0.6 mi. west of Perkins Pond. Follow this road 0.7 mi. to a small clearing on the left and an old cellar hole (parking). The trail follows a woods road for about 0.5 mi. to an east-west wall, then up the steep nose of the ridge to the open ledges. It is marked with cairns and white M's to its junction with the Dublin Path, about 0.3 mi. west of the summit. The Marian Trail leaves the Marlboro Trail on the right at the ledges known as the Stone House (2350 ft.), 0.3 mi. from the Marlboro Trail–Dublin Path junction.

Marlboro Trail (map 1)

Distance from parking area, road west of Perkins Pond

   to Dublin Path: 2.2 mi. (3.5 km.), 2 hr.

Halfway House Site Region

There are good, varied walks here. One of the finest scenic trails on Mt. Monadnock is the *Cliff Walk,* marked with white C's, which runs along the south and east edge of the south ridge, from Hello Rock to Bald Rock, past splendid viewpoints—notably Thoreau's Seat, Emerson's Seat, and What Cheer Point—and historical points such as the Graphite Mine (left), which was in operation about 1850. Several paths lead up to the Cliff Walk from the Halfway House site. Two are the Hello Rock and Thoreau trails, which leave the Halfway House clearing at the southeast corner between the road and Moses Spring. The *Hello Rock Trail* ascends gradually to Hello Rock through a fine forest. A few yards from the start the *Thoreau Trail* diverges left and leads north to the Cliff Walk Trail. Hello Rock may also be reached from the south via the *Cliff View Trail,* which leaves the Parker Trail about 0.3 mi. from the toll road.

Bald Rock is the bare peak on the south ridge of Monadnock; its highest point is a pointed boulder inscribed "Kiasticuticus Peak." From Bald Rock, the *Smith Connecting Trail,* marked with yellow S's, descends a short distance, soon passes Coffee Pot Corner, and shortly reaches the "Four Spots," a trail junction. The Smith Connecting Trail goes right at this junction, eventually crosses the White Cross Trail, then the White Dot Trail, and ends at the Pumpelly Trail. The trail that forks left at the Four Spots junction climbs with little grade to join the Sidefoot Trail, which soon reaches the White Arrow Trail.

The *Sidefoot Trail* is an excellent alternative to the lower part of the White Arrow Trail and avoids some of the heavy traffic on that trail. To reach the Sidefoot Trail, climb the bank at the left of the Halfway House clearing and follow a path a few yards into the woods to a trail junction. The Sidefoot Trail leaves left at this junction to join the White Arrow Trail at Halfway Spring. (Distance from Halfway House site to White Arrow Trail junction: 0.5 mi.) Three trails in close succession—the *Do Drop Trail,* the *Noble Trail,* and the *Hedgehog Trail* (name not on old sign)—leave to the right of the Sidefoot Trail and climb steeply to the Cliff Walk. The *Chipmunk Trail* runs from the Do Drop Trail to the Thoreau Trail.

The *Fairy Spring Trail* leaves the former picnic grounds at the north end of the Halfway House clearing and climbs to the peak of Monte Rosa, past the foundation of Fassett's "Mountain House" and Fairy Spring. Turn right (left leads back to picnic grounds, signed *Monte Rosa Trail*), then bear left (right leads directly to the Tooth), and ascend Monte Rosa. The trail then descends steeply to the Tooth, a large pointed boulder, and continues to the *Smith Summit Trail* (white dots), which leads gradually around the west side to the summit in slightly more than 0.5 mi.; a short side trail to the top of the "Black Precipice" (sign) soon leaves to the right, providing a view of the "Amphitheater." The *Mossy Brook Trail* leads west from the toll road about 0.3 mi. below the Halfway House site, crosses the Metacomet–Monadnock Trail, and then a short but steep connecting trail to the right (east) leads to Monte Rosa. The *Marian Trail* leaves this junction, then turns sharp right near the Bear Pit, a depression to the west so named because a bear was once reputedly trapped in the quagmire. The Marian Trail continues about 0.8 mi. to the Marlboro Trail at the Stone House. A rewarding round trip to the summit combines the Cliff Walk with the Monte Rosa trails.

Parker Trail (SPNHF)

This trail begins at Monadnock State Park on the west side of the outlet brook from the reservoir and heads west across the south slope of the mountain. It maintains a gentle grade and provides easy walking through heavy woods. It joins the toll road about 0.5 mi. below the Half-way House site. This trail has signs at both ends and is blazed with yellow paint.

Parker Trail (map 1)
Distance from west side of reservoir outlet brook
  to toll road: 1.6 mi. (2.6 km.), 40 min.

Lost Farm Trail

This trail branches right from the Parker Trail 0.3 mi. from the state park and leads in 1.1 mi. to Emerson's Seat on the Cliff Walk Trail. A fine circuit walk from the park headquarters combines this trail with the Cliff Walk, the Smith Connecting Trail, and either the White Cross or the White Dot trails.

Lost Farm Trail (map 1)
Distance from Parker Trail
  to Cliff Walk Trail: 1.1 mi. (1.8 km.), 45 min.

METACOMET–MONADNOCK TRAIL

This trail, 160 mi. long, begins in the Hanging Hills of Meriden CT, and runs north along the trap rock ridge that borders the Connecticut River. It traverses Mt. Tom and the Holyoke Range, passes over the Northfield Hills, Mt. Grace, Little Monadnock, and Gap Mtn., and terminates at Grand Monadnock. The NH section, marked by white rectangular paint blazes, is easy to follow. The 1984 edition of the trail guide, published by the Berkshire Chapter of the AMC, is available from the AMC.

MONADNOCK–SUNAPEE GREENWAY

The SPNHF and AMC cooperatively maintain this continuous trail which runs for over 50 mi., mostly along ridge tops, between these two major peaks in southwest NH. Because a large part of this trail is located on private property, users should be particularly aware of their status as guests and avoid thoughtless behavior which could jeopardize this privilege. A guide to the Monadnock–Sunapee Greenway is available from the AMC or the SPNHF.

WAPACK TRAIL

This is for the most part a skyline trail that follows the ridge of the Wapack Range for approximately 21 mi. It runs from Watatic Mtn. in Ashburnham MA, over Barrett and Temple mountains and across the Pack Monadnocks in NH. There are many open ledges with fine views, and the spruce forest is similar to that of a more northern region. The trail is blazed with yellow triangles and marked by cairns on open ledges. An organization named "Friends of the Wapack" has been instituted to protect and maintain the trail (PO Box 106, Greenville NH 03048).

Section I. Watatic Mountain

There are three approaches from the south to the start of the Wapack Trail:

(1) The trail leaves from MA 119, 0.7 mi. west of the MA 101 junction northeast of Ashburnham. It climbs steeply, following power and telephone lines to the summit tower on Watatic Mtn., which has a sweeping view. The trail descends northwest through spruce woods that are a state bird sanctuary, then crosses pastures over Nutting Hill to a junction near cellar holes (obscured by bushes) that mark the Nutting Place, settled by James Spaulding just before

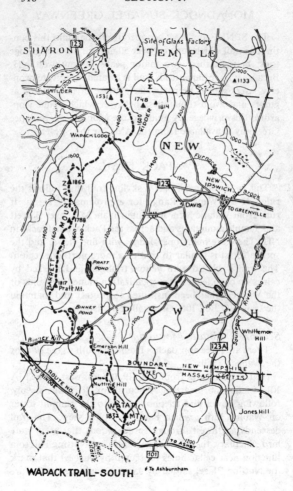

WAPACK TRAIL-SOUTH

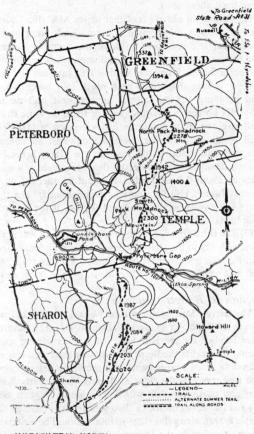

WAPACK TRAIL-NORTH

the Revolution and continued by his son-in-law, Jonas Nutting, until about 1840.

(2) Follow an old ski trail that leaves MA 119, 1.5 mi. west of the MA 101 junction. The trail leads along an old road (bear left at a fork) up through overgrown pastures and spruce forest to the trail junction on Nutting Hill near the cellar holes. From the Nutting Hill junction the trail follows a long-abandoned road north into beech woods and in about 0.5 mi. crosses an east-west wall on the MA/NH border. A few yards west of the trail, close to the wall, are two stone monuments, one erected in 1834. The trail continues north for about 0.3 mi. past an obscure junction with another old road on the right, bears left slightly downhill (west by north), then turns right at a small clearing about 0.3 mi. farther. In about another 0.5 mi. it reaches Binney Hill Rd. (no longer maintained). The trail turns left (west) on this road and follows it for 300 yd., then bears right (north).

(3) The third approach is to follow Binney Hill Rd. north from MA 119 to the trail junction described above. Binney Hill Rd. can be driven for only about 0.3 mi. in from MA 119, and parking is limited because of private residences.

Section II. Barrett Mountain

The Barrett Mtn. section of the Wapack Trail runs from Binney Hill Rd. to Wapack Lodge on NH 123. Shortly after leaving Binney Hill Rd., the trail crosses a small brook, then skirts the Binney Ponds near their west shores. (Flooding from beaver dams may require a detour here.) The trail traverses the ridge of Barrett Mtn., nearly 3 mi. long and partly wooded, with four summits (highest 1881 ft.) and numerous outlooks. Two private trails intersect the Wapack Trail along this ridge so hikers should be especially careful to identify the Wapack Trail at any junctions. In the saddle between the third and fourth summits, the trail crosses the location of one of the oldest roads from MA to the hill towns, "The Boston Road," built in 1753. The trail ascends an outlying knoll, then descends to Wapack Lodge, located on NH 123 on the site of a house built in 1776 by Deacon John Brown of Concord MA. (Accommodations and meals are not available, and the lodge is no longer identified by a sign.)

Section III. Kidder Mountain

The Wapack Trail next crosses the lower western slopes of Kidder Mtn. From Wapack Lodge it crosses the highway and enters the woods opposite the lodge driveway. In about 0.6 mi. the trail turns left on an old roadway with bordering stone walls and crosses under a power line 150 yd. beyond. (A poor, blue-blazed side trail leads right from here along the power lines, then left into the woods to the summit of Kidder Mtn., about 1.5 mi.) The Wapack Trail descends to a junction with a gravel road from the left at a pond on the right. It turns right onto a woods road, crosses the pond outlet, and ascends gradually to the Wildcat Hill–Conant Hill saddle, where there is an old homestead to the right. The trail ascends gradually, still on the old roadway, crosses the beaver pond outlet on the right at 0.6 mi. and a stream at about 1.0 mi., and in another 130 yd. reaches a junction with Sharon Rd.

Section IV. Temple Mountain

The trail continues straight ahead along Sharon Rd. for 0.4 mi., bears right at a fork, then turns right 30 yd. beyond to follow a dirt road for a short distance before entering the woods. (From Sharon Rd. north the trail passes through private land known as Avelinda Forest. Please observe the no fires—no smoking rules posted in the forest.) The trail then ascends the south end of Temple Mtn., which has several bare summits—but the highest,

Holt Peak (2084 ft.), is broad, wooded, and viewless. A short distance south of Holt Peak, the trail crosses a stone wall, then turns sharp left and parallels the wall a short distance before climbing to the summit. (An alternate route, marked by old red blazes, continues straight ahead beyond the wall, swings to the east of the summit, and rejoins the main trail about 0.3 mi. north of the summit.) The trail follows the ridge, which has wide views, especially toward Grand Monadnock. Stone monuments mark the Sharon–Temple town line, which also follows this ridge. From the north summit the trail descends through the Temple Mtn. Ski Area to NH 101 in Peterboro Gap, a few yards east of the road up South Pack Monadnock, which leaves NH 101 at the height-of-land.

Section V. Pack Monadnock

This extended ridge culminates in two open peaks, Pack Monadnock (2310 ft.), usually called South Pack Monadnock, and North Pack (2278 ft.); "pack" is an Indian word meaning "little." It lies between Peterborough and Temple NH, and is a well-known landmark in southern NH and eastern MA. On the summit of South Pack is a small state reservation, General James Miller Park. (To reach the park, drive up the road that starts at the parking lot located just off NH 101, about 100 yd. west of the Temple Mtn. parking lot.)

The Wapack Trail crosses NH 101 just east of the state park sign, enters the woods, and reaches a trail junction 25 yd. east of the parking area (sign, "Foot Trails," at east end of area). The blue-blazed trail right is the former route of the Wapack Trail. (It slabs the east side of the mountain, then climbs moderately past two radio towers to the automobile road just below the summit at a small sign, "Parking Lot." Continuing north from the summit road—sign, "Wapack"—it joins the present Wapack Trail, which enters left at remnants of the Peterborough Merchants' cairn.)

The official Wapack Trail is substantially more difficult than the former route, particularly for descent, and may be obscure. It continues north from the trail junction near the parking area, crosses the automobile road and immediately attacks a steep ledge. Turning northwest, it skirts the crest of ledges with views southwest and passes two crevice caves. The trail turns east through woods and over ledges, crosses a hollow, and slabs north parallel to the automobile road through a beautiful hemlock forest. It ascends to the Peterborough Merchants' cairn and the junction with the former Wapack Trail on a ledge 0.1 mi. north of the South Pack summit. (In this area a trail marked with yellow C's is encountered several times.)

The Wapack Trail leads down the wooded north slope past a spring, over the semiopen "Middle Peak" to another spring, where it turns sharp right and ascends directly to the summit of North Pack. This ledgy peak provides fine views of central NH, the Contoocook River valley, and, on a clear day, of Mt. Washington and other White Mtn. peaks. The trail descends north, northwest, then north again through overgrown pastures, and ends at Old Mountain Rd., 2.6 mi. west of NH 31 (via Old Mountain Rd. to Russell Station Rd.).

Wapack Trail
Distances from MA 119 west of Ashby MA

to Watatic Mtn. summit: 0.5 mi., 30 min.

to road at the south foot of Barrett Mtn.: 2.6 mi., 2 hr.

to Barrett Mtn., south summit: 4.5 mi., 3 hr. 15 min.

to Barrett Mtn., middle summit: 5.6 mi., 4 hr.

to Barrett Mtn., north summit: 7.0 mi., 5 hr.

to NH 123: 8.5 mi., 6 hr.

to road at south foot of Temple Mtn.: 10.8 mi., 7 hr.

to Temple Mtn., main summit (Holt Peak): 13.5 mi., 9 hr.

to NH 101: 15.5 mi., 10 hr. 15 min

to South Pack Monadnock summit: 17 mi., 11 hr. 30 min.

to North Pack Monadnock summit: 19.5 mi., 12 hr. 45 min.

to Old Mountain Rd.: 21.0 mi. (33.6 km.), 13 hr. 45 min.

UNCANOONUC MOUNTAINS

This twin-peaked mountain is situated in Goffstown, prominently visible from many points around Manchester. Refer to the USGS Pinardville quadrangle. The South Mtn. (1315 ft.) has a forest of communications towers, a paved road, and the remains of a cable railway grade, but there is no route which can be recommended to foot travelers at this time. The North Mtn. (1324 ft.) has two paths, which are not officially maintained.

From NH 114 in Goffstown, just east of the junction with NH 13, follow Mountain Rd. south and bear left at 0.9 mi. The trailhead (somewhat hard to find) is on the right at 1.4 mi. The trail is marked with white circles. It passes through a stone wall and in front of a small cave. It climbs steeply through a fine hemlock forest, then moderates, passes an outlook and approaches the summit, passing a side path which leads down to a view of Manchester.

At 0.4 mi. from the start of the first trail, just beyond Goffstown Water Works Rd., turn right on a woods road. In a depression near a shed, climb a bank right, and follow a white-blazed trail that leads moderately then steeply to a jeep trail at a large scrub pine just southwest of the summit.

Uncanoonuc Mountains, North Mountain
(USGS Pinardville quad)
Distances to summit
from trailhead via first trail: 0.6 mi. (1.0 km.), 40 min.

from trailhead via second trail: 0.7 mi. (1.2 km.), 40 min.

CROTCHED MOUNTAIN

Crotched Mtn. (2050 ft.) is in Francestown and Bennington, with a south spur in Greenfield. The fire tower on the summit is now abandoned and probably unsafe to climb, but there are excellent views from scattered ledges around the summit. Refer to the USGS Peterborough and Hillsboro quadrangles.

Greenfield Trail (CU)

From NH 31 0.9 mi. north of Greenfield, follow a road with the sign "Crotched Mountain Rehabilitation Center." Pass Gilbert Verney Dr. on the right 1.4 mi. from NH 31 and park 0.1 mi. farther where there is a gated road on the left. ("No Trespassing" signs do not apply to hikers.) There is no trail sign, but the trail is a gravel road. Take a left fork almost immediately, then bear left at a sign, and continue on this road through overgrown blueberry barrens. Shortly after entering larger trees, take the left fork (sign) where the road ends. The trail continues to Lookout Rock, which has an excellent view west and south and an impressive view of Mt. Monadnock. The Bennington Trail soon enters left at a stone wall, and the two trails coincide to the summit.

Greenfield Trail
(USGS Peterborough and Hillsboro quads)
Distances from parking area
  to Bennington Trail: 1.4 mi., 1 hr 5 min.
  to Crotched Mtn. summit: 1.8 mi. (2.9 km.), 1 hr. 20 min.

Bennington Trail (CU)

From NH 31, 1.6 mi. south of Bennington, take the road with signs "Summus Mons Campground" and "Mountain Rd." for 0.5 mi. to the campground entrance. The trail follows a dirt road right (sign), which may be passable for cars for 0.2 mi. The trail turns sharp right here (sign) and follows an old logging road to a double cairn and sign, where it turns left. Follow it with care. It passes a spring, then begins to climb more steeply to a junction with the Greenfield Trail. The two trails then coincide to the summit.

Bennington Trail
(USGS Peterborough and Hillsboro quads)

Distances from campground entrance

   to Greenfield Trail: 1.2 mi., 1 hr.

   to Crotched Mtn. summit: 1.6 mi. (2.5 km.), 1 hr. 20 min.

Francestown Trail (CU)

This trail begins at the Crotched Mtn. Ski Area, off NH 47 west of Francestown. It starts as a driveway to the left of the lodge, just above the novice slope (sign, "Sugar Run" on building). It goes left of the equipment garage and becomes a service road, which crosses under the chair lift and circles back to the top of the lift, then climbs to the base of a wooden stairway that leads to the summit.

Francestown Trail
(USGS Peterborough and Hillsboro quad)

Distance from ski area base

   to Crotched Mtn. summit: 1.2 mi. (1.9 km.), 1 hr.

SUNAPEE MOUNTAIN

This irregular, massive mountain (2730 ft.) is in Newbury at the south end of Lake Sunapee. The mountain is heavily wooded, but Lake Solitude near its summit is unique for its high elevation, remoteness, and beauty of setting. Nearby are cliffs that rise 300 ft. to White Ledge, where there is a fine view southeast over the wild country of the Merrimack–Connecticut watershed. Refer to the USGS Sunapee quadrangle.

Mt. Sunapee State Park is on NH 103, 7 mi. east of Newport. There is a state-owned ski area on the north slope of the mountain; a hikers' map is available at the lodge. The mountain is easily climbed via the ski slopes (about 1.5 mi.). It is the northern terminus of the Monadnock–Sunapee Greenway. A trail, part of the Greenway, leads from the summit 1.6 mi. to Lake Solitude and connects to the Andrews Brook Trail from the east and to the Five Summers Trail from Pillsbury State Park in Washington.

The Lakes Region and Southeastern New Hampshire

This section covers the Squam Range near Squam Lake, the Belknap and Ossipee ranges near Lake Winnipesaukee, the Blue Hills and the Pawtuckaway Mountains to the south of the big lakes, and several scattered mountains, including Green Mtn. in Effingham. Most of the Squam Range and the Rattlesnakes are covered by the AMC Chocorua–Waterville map (map 4); the remaining mountains are covered by USGS maps as indicated in the descriptions. In addition to areas with trails described in this section, Bear Brook State Park (9300 acres) in Allenstown should be mentioned as an area with hiking opportunities.

Try-Me Trail	USGS
Ridge Trail	USGS
Flintlock Trail	USGS
Blue Dot Trail	USGS
Green Trail	USGS
Red Trail	USGS
East Gilford Trail	USGS
Piper Trail	USGS
Piper Cutoff	USGS

Trail on Green Mountain

| Green Mountain Trail | USGS |

Trail on Blue Job Mountain

| Blue Job Mountain Trail | USGS |

Trails in the Pawtuckaway Mountains

Mountain Trail	USGS
North Mountain Trail	USGS
Middle Mountain Trail	USGS

SQUAM LAKE AREA

In the vicinity of Squam Lake, the low peaks of the Squam Range and the Rattlesnakes to the north and Red Hill to the east have excellent views, combining lakes and mountains. Most of the trails are maintained by the Squam Lakes Association and are blazed with yellow paint. Refer to map 4, Chocorua–Waterville, and the USGS Squam Mtns. quadrangle. *The SLA Trails Guide* (1973) and a detailed map of the area by Bradford Washburn are available from the Squam Lakes Association, Plymouth NH 03264.

THE RATTLESNAKES

West Rattlesnake (1260 ft.) and East Rattlesnake (1289 ft.) are two low mountains near the north end of Squam

Lake. The summits are very easily climbed and the views are rewarding for the small effort involved. West Rattlesnake has fine views to the south and west from its southwest cliff. East Rattlesnake has a more limited but still excellent view over Squam Lake.

Rattlesnake Paths (SLA)

The *Old Bridle Path* is the easiest route to the West Rattlesnake outlooks. It leaves NH 113 between Center Sandwich and Holderness, 0.5 mi. northeast of the road to Rockywold and Deephaven camps and opposite the entrance to the Mount Morgan Trail (parking area). It follows an old cart road 0.9 mi. to the summit. Descending, the entrance to this trail is slightly northwest of the cliffs.

The *Ramsey Trail* is a much steeper route to West Rattlesnake. It leaves the road to Rockywold and Deephaven camps, 0.7 mi. from NH 113 and 90 yd. east of the entrance to the camps, along with the Undercut Trail (sign), which has another entrance almost opposite the camp entrance. In 0.1 mi. there is a crossroads, where the Ramsey Trail takes a sharp right and climbs steeply 0.4 mi. to a point just north of the summit cliffs (no sign at top). Left at the crossroads is the alternate route 0.1 mi. to the road; the *Undercut Trail* continues straight ahead 0.9 mi. (follow markings very carefully) to NH 113 0.1 mi. west of the Old Bridle Path parking area.

The *Pasture Trail* leads to West Rattlesnake from the road to Rockywold and Deephaven camps 0.9 mi. from NH 113. Park in the small area to the right before the first gate. The trailhead is 100 yd. east of the gate. Start on a road to the left, then turn right past Pinehurst Farm buildings. At 0.2 mi. the East Rattlesnake and Five Finger Point trails diverge right, and in 15 yd. the Pasture Trail bears left where the Col Trail continues straight ahead. The cliffs are reached at 0.6 mi. from the gate after a moderate ascent.

The *Col Trail* continues straight where the Pasture Trail bears left 0.2 mi. from the gate on the road to Rockywold and Deephaven camps. In 0.3 mi. it joins the Ridge Trail, follows it right for 30 yd., then turns left (sign, "Saddle"), passes over the height-of-land and descends (follow with care) to the edge of a beaver swamp. It enters an old road and turns left, then bears right to a gravel road, 0.7 mi. from the Ridge Trail junction. This trailhead is reached in 0.2 mi. from NH 113, 0.3 mi. east of the Holderness–Sandwich town line.

The *Ridge Trail* connects West and East Rattlesnake. It begins just northeast of the cliffs of West Rattlesnake and descends gradually. At 0.4 mi. the Col Trail comes in from the right, and just beyond leaves again to the left. The Ridge Trail ascends, and the East Rattlesnake Trail enters right at 0.8 mi. The Ridge Trail reaches the outlook ledge at 0.9 mi., and continues to the summit and the Butterworth Trail at 1.0 mi.

The *East Rattlesnake Trail* branches right from the Pasture Trail 0.2 mi. from the gate. In 25 yd. the Five Finger Point Trail continues straight ahead. The East Rattlesnake Trail turns left and ascends steadily 0.4 mi. to the Ridge Trail, 0.1 mi. west of the outlook. The *Five Finger Point Trail* runs on a slight downgrade for 0.7 mi., to a loop path 1.3 mi. long which circles around the edge of Five Finger Point, with several interesting viewpoints.

The *Butterworth Trail* leads to East Rattlesnake from Metcalf Rd., which leaves NH 113 0.7 mi. east of the Holderness–Sandwich town line. The trail leaves Metcalf Rd. on the right 0.5 mi. from NH 113, and climbs moderately 0.7 mi. to the summit. The viewpoint is 0.1 mi. farther via the Ridge Trail.

SQUAM RANGE

The Squam Range is a long ridge that stretches from Sandwich Notch Rd. to Holderness, northwest of NH 113 and roughly parallel to it. The most frequently climbed peaks are Mt. Morgan (2220 ft.) and Mt. Percival (2212 ft.). A very attractive circuit can be made by ascending the Mount Percival Trail, following the Crawford–Ridgepole Trail along the ridge, and descending on the Mount Morgan Trail.

"Old Highway" Trail (SLA)

At 1.3 mi. northeast of Holderness and 0.1 mi. beyond a sand pit, NH 113 turns right and this trail continues straight. A century ago, it was the main highway. The western portion is no longer passable by four-wheel-drive vehicles. It leads to the Prescott Trail and Old Mountain Road.

Prescott Trail (SLA)

This trail to Mt. Livermore (1500 ft.) turns left off the "Old Highway" Trail 0.8 mi. from NH 113, just beyond an old cemetery. It follows a logging road, then turns off it to the left, and turns right uphill. At 1.5 mi. a cutoff trail to the right leads directly to the summit. Beyond, the main trail climbs switchbacks over a low ridge and descends to the Crawford–Ridgepole Trail, which enters left at 1.8 mi. From this point the two trails ascend together via switchbacks for 0.4 mi. Just below the summit they turn sharp right and ascend steeply to the summit, where there is a view over Squam Lake.

Descending, the Crawford–Ridgepole Trail heading south and the Prescott Trail leave the summit together, descend to the west along an old stone wall, and turn left

onto an old bridle trail. After 0.4 mi. the Crawford–
Ridgepole Trail leaves on the right. From the top, the cutoff descends steeply to the east.

Prescott Trail (map 4:L6)
Distance from "Old Highway" Trail
   to Crawford–Ridgepole Trail: 1.0 mi. (1.6 km.), 45 min.

Old Mountain Road (SLA-Webster)

This trail leads up from the "Old Highway" Trail, 1.1
mi. from its western end at NH 113, to the Crawford–
Ridgepole Trail at the low point between Mt. Livermore
and Mt. Webster.

Old Mountain Road (map 4:L6)
Distance from "Old Highway" Trail
   to Crawford–Ridgepole Trail: 0.9 mi. (1.4 km.), 30 min.

Mount Morgan Trail (SLA)

This trail leaves the west side of NH 113, 0.5 mi. northeast of the road leading to Rockywold and Deephaven
camps. From the small clearing (parking), the trail follows
a logging road, turning off left almost immediately. The
trail bears right at a fork and soon begins the steeper ascent
of the southeast slope of the mountain. At 1.7 mi. the
Crawford–Ridgepole Trail leaves left for Mt. Webster (this
section may be obscure). The Mount Morgan Trail continues to a junction with the Crawford–Ridgepole Trail from
Mt. Percival. Here a side trail leads left to the clifftop
viewpoint and summit.

Mount Morgan Trail (map 4:L6)
Distance from NH 113
   to Mt. Morgan summit: 2.1 mi. (3.4 km.), 1 hr. 30 min

Mount Percival Trail (SLA)

The trail leaves the north side of NH 113, 0.3 mi. northeast of the Mount Morgan Trail parking area (best place to park). It follows a logging road past a gate to a log yard, then enters the woods, forking right off a logging road. The trail follows a generally northwest direction, and becomes steep at 1.6 mi., climbing past a fine view of Squam Lake to the summit.

Mount Percival Trail (map 4:L6)

Distance from NH 113

to Mt. Percival summit: 1.9 mi. (3.1 km.), 1 hr. 30 min.

Doublehead Trail (SLA)

This trail descends from the Crawford–Ridgepole Trail to NH 113, 3.3 mi. from Center Sandwich and 2.7 mi. east of the Mount Morgan Trail. It leaves the Crawford–Ridgepole Trail to the south 100 yd. west of the summit of East Doublehead. The trail descends over some ledges with fine views. It passes through a stone wall at 0.7 mi. and another at 1.0 mi. After passing through an area of recent logging activity, at 1.4 mi. the trail turns left (east) on an old road bordered by stone walls and follows it to NH 113.

Doublehead Trail (map 4:L6)

Distance from Crawford–Ridgepole Trail

to NH 113: 2.4 mi. (3.9 km.), 1 hr. 15 min.

Crawford–Ridgepole Trail (SLA)

This trail follows the backbone of the Squam Range, from Sandwich Notch to Mt. Morgan. The continuation to Holderness has become somewhat overgrown. Except for the segment between Percival and Morgan, the trail is used infrequently, despite fine views in the Squam–Doublehead section.

The trail starts on Sandwich Notch Rd. 0.5 mi. beyond

Beede Falls (Cow Cave) and 2.0 mi. from the power line along the Beebe River. From the road (sign) it ascends steeply, crosses an unnamed wooded peak, and continues along the ridge to Doublehead (2158 ft.). Just beyond the East Peak, at 2.1 mi., the trail turns right and descends where the Doublehead Trail diverges left past a viewpoint and down to NH 113. Continuing much of the way over open ledges, the Crawford–Ridgepole Trail passes a side trail to Uncle Paul's Potholes at 3.1 mi. and crosses Mt. Squam (2223 ft.), where there is a fine view from the east summit. The trail continues to the Mount Percival Trail and Mt. Percival at 4.5 mi., passes just west of the actual high point of the range, and continues to the Mount Morgan Trail at 5.4 mi. Side trails lead right to the Mt. Morgan summit and to a clifftop viewpoint.

To continue, descend the Mount Morgan Trail for 0.4 mi. Here the Crawford–Ridgepole Trail turns right for Mt. Webster. The Mt. Webster section was overgrown and obscure in 1985. The trail continues past two viewpoints overlooking the lake, reaches a junction with the Old Mountain Road, and continues 0.4 mi. to the summit of Mt. Livermore (view). The trail descends west from Mt. Livermore along a stone wall, branches right from the Prescott Trail and crosses two streams near a low col before rising again over a spur of Cotton Mtn. The lower half of the southeast slope down to NH 113 is a sand pit. The trail continues west and south to Mt. Fayal (1050 ft.), where it joins the Gephart Trail just northwest of the summit. The Gephart (west) and Davison (east) trails both connect Mt. Fayal to the Science Center of NH at the intersection of US 3 and NH 113 in Holderness.

Crawford–Ridgepole Trail (map 4:L6)
Distances from Sandwich Notch Rd.
  to West Doublehead summit: 2.2 mi., 2 hr.

   to Mt. Squam, east summit: 3.2 mi., 2 hr. 30 min.
   to Mt. Percival summit: 4.5 mi., 3 hr. 30 min.
   to Mt. Morgan summit: 5.5 mi., 4 hr.
   to Mt. Livermore summit: 10.0 mi. (16.1 km.), 6 hr. 30
   min.

RED HILL

Located north of Center Harbor, Red Hill (2029 ft.) provides fine views of lakes and mountains, especially of Squam Lake, from a fire tower. Refer to map 4, Chocorua-Waterville, and the USGS Winnipesaukee and Chocorua quadrangles.

Eagle Cliff Trail (SLA)

From the junction of NH 25 and NH 25B in Center Harbor, follow Bean Rd. for 5.2 mi. The entrance is difficult to see from the road: it is a path through a thicket in a depression just north of a red farmhouse. It climbs through an overgrown field, enters the woods, and ascends steeply to Eagle Cliff at 0.4 mi. From the upper ledge, the trail enters the woods and continues along the ridge to the fire tower on Red Hill. There is a limited view from the top of the first knoll at 0.7 mi. The trail descends steeply to a col, crosses another knoll, and shortly begins to ascend steadily through fine woods. It levels out and meets the Red Hill Trail just below the summit of Red Hill. Descending, the trail to Eagle Cliff diverges right from the Red Hill Trail (road) just below the firewarden's cabin (sign).

Eagle Cliff Trail (map 4:L7)
Distance from Bean Rd.
   to Red Hill fire tower: 2.3 mi. (3.7 km.), 2 hr.

Red Hill Trail

In Center Harbor at the junction of NH 25 and NH 25B, go northwest on Bean Rd. After 1.4 mi. take Silbey Rd. (sign for fire lookout) to a parking lot at a gated jeep road (no sign for trail). The trail, a jeep road, soon makes a sharp right turn uphill and crosses a brook in about 0.3 mi. At 0.4 mi. it swings left around a cellar hole. At 1.0 mi. there is a piped spring left. The Eagle Cliff Trail enters left just before the firewarden's cabin on Red Hill.

Red Hill Trail (map 4:L7)

Distance from parking area

to Red Hill summit: 1.7 mi. (2.7 km.), 1 hr. 15 min.

OSSIPEE MOUNTAINS

These mountains, located just north of Lake Winnipesaukee, occupy a nearly circular tract about 9 mi. in diameter. Mt. Shaw (2990 ft.), the highest of the Ossipees, is accessible from NH 171. Refer to map 4, Chocorua-Waterville. Also see the USGS Chocorua, Ossipee Lake, Winnipesaukee, and Wolfeboro quadrangles, which corner near the center of the Ossipee Mountains. The Chocorua and Winnipesaukee quadrangles show (rather inaccurately in some cases) the locations of many of the old carriage roads of the Plant Estate, now called Castle in the Clouds. There are no regularly maintained hiking trails on the range. The two trails described below are the most easily followed of several paths; others may be encountered, but are not blazed well enough to be followed by persons not familiar with them.

Mount Shaw Trail

The trail begins at a dirt road on the north side of NH 171, 3.9 mi. east of the junction of NH 109 and NH 171, 3.8

mi. west of Tuftonboro, 9.7 mi. west of the junction of NH
171 and NH 28 in Ossipee, and just east of a road from
Melvin Village and a bridge over Fields Brook. The trail
must be followed very carefully as it is blazed irregularly in
dark red, which is sometimes difficult to see. In addition, it
is overgrown in places and has suffered much blowdown
recently.

The trail follows the dirt road north 0.3 mi. to a hemlock
grove (left); there is a waterfall on the left. The trail de-
tours above the stream around a washout, then bears left
and follows the stream. It divides at 0.7 mi., bearing right,
then keeping right after passing through an old logging
camp clearing. It again divides at 0.9 mi., bears left and
goes through a deep cut. The trail again bears left at 1.1
mi. and then leaves the road at 1.4 mi., following the east
bank of Fields Brook and bearing right at a cairn. It
crosses to the west bank very shortly and at 1.8 mi. returns
to the east bank, which is the last crossing and last sure
water. Soon it climbs steeply out of the ravine to join an
old carriage road at 2.5 mi., turns right and passes a side
trail (right), which leads in 0.3 mi. to an open knob
(Black Snout, not the same as Black Snout Mtn.) with a
good view over Lake Winnipesaukee. The Mount Shaw
Trail continues on the carriage road and reaches the summit at 3.5 mi.

Mount Shaw Trail (USGS Winnipesaukee quad)
Distance from NH 171
   to Mt. Shaw summit: 3.5 mi. (5.6 km.), 2 hr. 45 min.

Bald Knob Trail

The trail begins on NH 171, at the Moultonboro-
Tuftonboro town line, about 0.5 mi. west of the Mount
Shaw trailhead at the Fields Brook bridge. Follow the dirt
road into a gravel pit. Facing Bald Knob, descend to the

lower right corner of the pit (northeast), bearing left, and in 40 yd. turn sharp left onto a dirt road. This road crosses a wet area and bears right as the road enters the woods. The trail, blazed in yellow, ascends steeply over rough and eroded terrain, reaching the first ledge at 0.7 mi. It passes more ledges with excellent vistas and then goes again into the woods, through boulders, and heads pretty much north, traveling at a less steep grade. The trail then turns south, scrambles up through a wide V in the rock, and meets an old carriage road turnaround before reaching Bald Knob with its fine views of Lake Winnipesaukee.

Bald Knob Trail (USGS Winnipesaukee quad)
Distance from NH 171
to Bald Knob: 1.0 mi. (1.6 km.), 1 hr.

MOUNT MAJOR

This 1784-ft. mountain is located in Alton, east of the Belknap Mtns. It has excellent views over Lake Winnipesaukee. Refer to the USGS Winnipesaukee quadrangle. The trail begins at a parking area (large sign) on NH 11, 4.2 mi. north of Alton Bay and 1.7 mi. from the NH 11 junction with NH 11D. The trail follows a lumber road west for 0.7 mi., then diverges sharp left on a path marked with dark-blue paint. It climbs steeply through second growth and over ledges to the ruins of a stone hut at the top. At several points there are one or more alternate paths, all of which lead to the summit.

Mount Major Trail (USGS Winnipesaukee quad)
Distance from NH 11
to Mt. Major summit: 1.5 mi. (2.4 km.), 1 hr. 20 min.

THE BELKNAP RANGE

The Belknap Mtns. are an isolated range in the town of Gilford. The principal peaks, from north to south, are Mt. Rowe (1670 ft.), Gunstock Mtn. (2250 ft.), Belknap Mtn. (2384 ft.), and Piper Mtn. (2030 ft.). A fire tower on Belknap and an observation tower on Gunstock, as well as numerous scattered ledges on all the peaks, provide fine views of Lake Winnipesaukee, the Ossipee and Sandwich ranges, and Mt. Washington. Principal trailheads are at the Gunstock Recreation Area (east side) and Belknap Carriage Rd. (west side). The East Gilford Trail also ascends from the east. Paths along the ridge connect all four summits. Refer to the USGS Winnipesaukee quadrangle.

Gunstock Recreation Area

This is a four-season recreation area off NH 11A, operated by Belknap County. It includes a major downhill ski area located on Mt. Rowe and Gunstock Mtn., and a 420-site campground. Ellacoya State Beach on Lake Winnipesaukee is nearby. The chair lift on Gunstock Mtn. operates on weekends and holidays in summer. A map of hiking trails is available at the base lodge.

Belknap Carriage Road

To reach this road, which provides access to all the trails on the west side of the Belknap Range, leave NH 11A at Gilford village and follow Belknap Mtn. Rd. south, bearing left at 0.8 mi. and right at 1.4 mi. At 2.4 mi. the Belknap Carriage Rd. forks left and leads to a parking area. Various relatively easy loop hikes may be made from this trailhead. For the Green, Red, and Blue Dot trails, follow the road up to the firewarden's garage (signs on wall). The Piper Cutoff is a short distance down the road.

Try-Me Trail

This trail ascends Mt. Rowe from the Gunstock parking area. Go right under the single chair lift, ascend the novice slope, pass around a fence, and follow a ski trail to the top of the lift just below the summit. The Ridge Trail begins at the summit. In descending, take ski trail to the left from the lift station.

Try-Me Trail (USGS Winnipesaukee quad)
Distance from Gunstock parking area
  to Mt. Rowe summit: 0.9 mi. (1.4 km.), 50 min.

Ridge Trail

From the summit of Mt. Rowe, this blue-blazed trail follows the ridge south, crossing ledges and blueberry fields through the saddle, ascends to a ski trail, and soon joins the Flintlock Trail at 0.7 mi. (Descending, turn left on ski trail at Ridge Trail sign, then shortly follow the arrow left into the woods.) The Ridge and Flintlock trails coincide to the summit of Gunstock Mtn. along the right edge of the ski trails. From the summit, at 1.6 mi., the Ridge Trail continues south on the right edge of the ski trails, then turns right into woods (watch carefully for arrow) and descends to the col, where the Blue Dot Trail enters right at 2.0 mi. It then ascends Belknap Mtn. and ends at the Red Trail just before the summit.

Ridge Trail (USGS Winnipesaukee quad)
Distance from Mt. Rowe summit
  to Belknap Mtn. summit: 2.5 mi. (4.1 km.), 1 hr. 50 min.

Flintlock Trail

This trail ascends Gunstock Mtn. from the Gunstock parking area. Go left (south) to a large stone fireplace (trail signs). This trail follows a service road that curves right upward and crosses under the chair lift. The Ridge Trail enters as a ski trail from the right at 0.8 mi., and the trails coincide to the Gunstock Mtn. summit, always keeping to the right on ski trails. Descending, keep to the left edge of the ski trails until the Ridge Trail enters (sign), then bear right on the service road.

Flintlock Trail (USGS Winnipesaukee quad)
Distance from Gunstock parking area
  to Gunstock Mtn. summit: 1.7 mi. (2.7 km.), 1 hr. 30 min.

Blue Dot Trail

This trail runs from Belknap Carriage Rd. to the Belknap–Gunstock col, from which either peak may be ascended via the Ridge Trail. It follows the road past the Red and Green trails, descends slightly to cross a brook, then diverges right and climbs the Ridge Trail.

Blue Dot Trail (USGS Winnipesaukee quad)
Distance from Belknap Carriage Rd. parking area
  to Ridge Trail: 0.6 mi. (1.0 km.), 25 min.

Green Trail

This trail from Belknap Carriage Rd. is the shortest route to Belknap Mtn., but is rather rough. It leaves the road behind the garage and crosses a service road and telephone line. There are several alternate paths (including the road), any of which may be followed to the warden's cabin, where there is a well, and to the tower at the summit.

Green Trail (USGS Winnipesaukee quad)
Distance from Belknap Carriage Rd. parking area
  to Belknap Mtn. summit: 0.7 mi. (1.1 km.), 40 min.

Red Trail

This less steep, more scenic route from Belknap Carriage Rd. to the summit of Belknap Mtn. leaves the road just beyond the Green Trail and climbs past a good outlook (west) to the summit.

Red Trail (USGS Winnipesaukee quad)
Distance from Belknap Carriage Rd. parking area
   to Belknap Mtn. summit: 0.8 mi. (1.3 km.), 45 min.

East Gilford Trail

To reach this trail—perhaps the most attractive on the range—turn right off NH 11A on Bickford Rd., 1.7 mi. south of the Gunstock Recreation Area road. Turn left on Wood Rd. and park near junction. The trail (sign) follows a cart track at the left of the house at the end of the road, circles around to the right, and bears right at a fork. Halfway up, near a brook on the right, the trail turns sharp left and climbs more steeply to the first outlook over Lake Winnipesaukee. It then continues at a moderate grade, mostly on ledges, and joins the Piper Trail; the two trails coincide for the final 0.2 mi. to the Belknap Mtn. summit.

East Gilford Trail (USGS Winnipesaukee quad)
Distance from Wood Rd.
   to Belknap Mtn. summit: 2.1 mi. (3.4 km.), 1 hr. 40 min.

Piper Trail

A continuation of the Ridge Trail, this white-blazed trail leaves the summit of Belknap Mtn. together with the East Gilford Trail, then diverges right and drops to the Belknap–Piper col. This part of the trail must be followed with care. At the col at 0.8 mi. the Piper Cutoff comes in right from Belknap Carriage Rd. The Piper Trail ascends along the ridge of Piper Mtn. and ends at a large cairn; the true summit is 0.2 mi. south across open blueberry fields.

Piper Trail (USGS Winnipesaukee quad)
Distance from Belknap Mtn. summit
   to Piper Mtn., true summit: 1.5 mi. (2.4 km.), 50 min.

Piper Cutoff

This well-beaten but unsigned trail (yellow-blazed at present) leaves Belknap Carriage Rd. below the last bridge at a yellow-blazed birch, then climbs to meet the Piper Trail in the Belknap–Piper col. Either peak may be ascended via the Piper Trail.

Piper Cutoff (USGS Winnipesaukee quad)
Distance from Belknap Carriage Rd. parking area
   to Piper Trail: 0.4 mi. (0.6 km.), 20 min.

GREEN MOUNTAIN

Green Mtn. (1907 ft.) is an isolated hill in the town of Effingham. The state owns 15 acres on the summit, which has a 50-ft. fire tower with an extended view. Refer to the USGS Ossipee Lake quadrangle.

From the junction of NH 25 and NH 153 northbound in Effingham Falls, follow NH 25 west for 0.2 mi., then turn left at a church (fire lookout sign). Follow this road south for 1.0 mi., then turn left again on High Watch Rd., then left again in 0.2 mi. at a T junction. The trail (a road closed by a chain) is 1.2 mi. farther on the right, just past High Watch Learning Center. The trail ascends moderately on this road to a fenced utility building, then climbs more steeply to the Green Mtn. summit.

Green Mountain Trail (USGS Ossipee Lake quad)
Distance from High Watch Rd.
  to Green Mtn. summit: 1.4 mi. (2.2 km.), 1 hr. 15 min.

BLUE JOB MOUNTAIN

Blue Job Mtn. (1356 ft.) is part of the Blue Hill Range, located in Strafford and Farmington. There are excellent views from a fire tower on the summit. Refer to the USGS Alton quadrangle.

The trail begins on Crown Point Rd., 5.6 mi. from NH 202A, just past the end of the blacktop. Crown Point Rd. leaves NH 202A at Glenn's Garage, 5.4 mi. east from its junction with NH 126 in Center Strafford, or 2.8 mi. west of its junction with NH 202 near Rochester. There is both a shaded foot trail and a cart track through blueberry fields to the summit.

Blue Job Mountain Trail (USGS Alton quad)
Distance from parking area
  to Blue Job Mtn. summit: 0.5 mi. (0.8 km.), 25 min.

PAWTUCKAWAY MOUNTAINS

The Pawtuckaways in Nottingham comprise a group of three parallel ridges—North Mtn. (995 ft.), Middle Mtn. (845 ft.), and South Mtn. (885 ft.)—all contained within Pawtuckaway State Park (5535 acres). Refer to the USGS Mt. Pawtuckaway quadrangle. The easiest road access to the mountains is from the state park off NH 156, but walking distances are much longer. Trails are reached by following the road toward the beach, passing a toll booth (fee charged in summer), and then passing a pond left. Trail maps are usually available at the State Park Visitors Center.

The mountains may also be reached from NH 107 between Deerfield and Raymond, 3.2 mi. north of NH 101 Business Loop, where there is a fire lookout sign. The road leads east, becoming gravel after 0.9 mi. Bear right at 1.2 mi., and reach the south junction of a loop road (Reservation Rd.) at 2.3 mi. This road is rough and at times eroded, but walking distances are shorter.

For the South Mtn. and Middle Mtn. continue straight for 0.2 mi., then bear left (sign, "Lookout Tower") 0.8 mi. to the former location of the ranger's camp, where there is a tiny, old graveyard. The Mountain Trail from the main part of the state park enters just ahead at a small parking area on the right, and the path to the South Mtn. tower (described below under Mountain Trail) leaves the parking area on the right.

Mountain Trail (NHDP)

This trail, the easiest route to South Mtn. from the main part of Pawtuckaway State Park, leaves the park road just past the toll booth and pond at location signed #2 (keyed to park trail map). It passes a chain gate and runs along the edge of the pond. At 0.5 mi. it bears right where the Round Pond Trail (a less clear route to Reservation Rd.) continues ahead. Bear right at junction at 1.9 mi. (left goes to Reservation Rd.), and reach Reservation Rd. at the parking area near the site of the firewarden's camp at 2.5 mi. From here the path climbs steeply to open summit ledges. At a small service building just below the summit, where the trail turns sharp right, a side trail turns left to an old well and continues to the "Devil's Staircase" (or "Indian Steps") and open ledges north-northwest of the tower.

Mountain Trail (USGS Mt. Pawtuckaway quad)
Distance from state park road
    to summit tower, South Mtn.: 2.9 mi. (4.7 km.), 2 hr.

Distance from Reservation Rd.
   to summit tower, South Mtn.: 0.4 mi. (0.7 km.), 20 min.

Boulder Natural Area and North Mountain Trail (NHDP)

In the valley east of North Mtn. there is an extraordinary collection of huge boulders and several other unusual and interesting rock formations. From the former location of the firewarden's camp continue 0.8 mi. to the north loop junction (1.3 mi. left from the south loop junction), then bear right (at location signed #6) for another 0.5 mi. As the road bears upward to the right, there are two obscure trailheads on the left. The trail to the boulders runs under a large fallen tree with "BOULDERS" carved into it by a chain saw. The trail, blazed in white, descends gradually 0.2 mi. to the boulders. Just beyond the boulders the trail turns sharp left at a junction (sign on tree, "Dead Pond"). Straight ahead from this junction (sign, "Lower Slab") a blazed trail leads around a beaver pond and past some rock formations to the road; turn right on the road to loop back to the starting point. The main trail runs to Dead Pond at 0.6 mi., turns left and climbs steeply to the Devil's Den (a crevice in the rocks to the left of the trail) and an outlook right. From here the trail slabs steeply up the north side of the ridge and, marked with cairns, continues roughly along the top to a small col below boulder cliffs. It climbs a switchback to an outlook where there is a Public Service Company reflector, then continues along the ridge to the overgrown summit.

North Mountain Trail (USGS Mt. Pawtuckaway quad)
Distance from trailhead
   to North Mtn. summit: 1.5 mi. (2.5 km.), 1 hr. 15 min.

Middle Mountain Trail (NHDP)

The trail to Middle Mtn. begins on an old road just south of the site of the old firewarden's camp. Grades are mostly moderate, and the trail runs through old fields past stone walls to ledges with good outlooks southwest.

Middle Mountain Trail (USGS Mt. Pawtuckaway quad)
Distance from Reservation Rd.

  to Middle Mtn. summit: 1.0 mi. (1.6 km.), 50 min.

APPENDIX A

Four Thousand Footers

The Four Thousand Footer Club was formed in 1957 to bring together hikers who had traveled to some of the less frequently visited sections of the White Mtns. In 1957, such peaks as Hancock, Owl's Head, and West Bond were trailless and practically never climbed. Other listed peaks with trails were seldom climbed, and the problem of over-use was unknown, except in the Presidentials and Franconias. Today the Four Thousand Footer Club is composed of active hikers whose travels in the mountains have made them familiar with many different sections of the White Mountain backcountry, and with the problems which threaten to degrade the mountain experience that we have all been privileged to enjoy. The Four Thousand Footer Committee hopes that this broadened experience of the varied beauties of our beloved peaks and forests will encourage our members to work for the preservation and wise use of wild country, so that it may be enjoyed and passed on to future generations undiminished.

The Four Thousand Footer Club recognizes three lists of peaks: the White Mountain Four Thousand Footers, the New England Four Thousand Footers, and the New England Hundred Highest Peaks. To qualify for membership, a hiker must climb on foot to and from each summit on the list. Applicants need not be AMC members, although the Committee strongly urges all hikers who make considerable use of the trails to contribute to their maintenance in some manner. Membership in the AMC is one of the most effective means of assisting these efforts.

If you are seriously interested in becoming a member of the Four Thousand Footer Club, please send a self-addressed, stamped envelope to the Four Thousand Footer Committee, Appalachian Mountain Club, 5 Joy

Street, Boston MA 02108, and details will be sent to you. After climbing each Four Thousand Footer, please record the date of the ascent, companions, if any, and other remarks.

Criteria for mountains on the official list are: (1) each peak must be 4000 ft. high, and (2) each peak must rise 200 ft. above the low point of its connecting ridge with a higher neighbor. The latter qualification eliminates such peaks as Clay, Franklin, North Carter, Guyot, Little Haystack, South Tripyramid, Lethe, Blue, and Jim. All 48 Four Thousand Footers are reached by well-defined trails, although the path to Owl's Head and some short spur trails to other summits are not officially maintained.

Following are the official lists of the Four Thousand Footers in NH, ME, and VT. Applicants for the White Mountain Four Thousand Footer Club must climb all 48 peaks in NH, while applicants for the New England Four Thousand Footer Club must climb the twelve peaks in ME and the five in VT as well. The New England Hundred Highest Club list includes a substantial number of peaks without trails, of which two are on private land where advance permission to enter is required. Peaks on this list for which routes are described in this Guide include: Sandwich Mtn. (3993 ft.), with several trails in Section 7; the Horn (3905 ft.), on the Kilkenny Ridge Trail; the East Sleeper (3850 ft.), just off the Sleeper Trail; and the Northeast Cannon Ball (3769 ft.), on the Kinsman Ridge Trail. A copy of the full list and related information can be obtained by sending a self-addressed, stamped envelope to the Committee at the address above.

On the following lists, elevations have been obtained from the latest USGS maps, some of which are now metric, requiring conversion from meters to feet. Where no exact elevation is given on the map, the elevation has been estimated by adding half the contour interval to the highest

contour shown on the map; elevations so obtained are
marked on the list with an asterisk.

FOUR THOUSAND FOOTERS IN NEW HAMPSHIRE

	Mountain	Elevation (feet)	(meters)	Date Climbed
1.	Washington	6288	1917	____
2.	Adams	5774	1760	____
3.	Jefferson	5712	1741	____
4.	Monroe	5384*	1641*	____
5.	Madison	5367	1636	____
6.	Lafayette	5260*	1603*	____
7.	Lincoln	5089	1551	____
8.	South Twin	4902	1494	____
9.	Carter Dome	4832	1473	____
10.	Moosilauke	4802	1464	____
11.	Eisenhower	4761	1451	____
12.	North Twin	4761	1451	____
13.	Bond	4698	1432	____
14.	Carrigain	4680	1426	____
15.	Middle Carter	4610*	1405*	____
16.	West Bond	4540*	1384*	____
17.	Garfield	4500*	1372*	____
18.	Liberty	4459	1359	____
19.	South Carter	4430*	1350*	____
20.	Wildcat	4422	1348	____
21.	Hancock	4403	1342	____
22.	South Kinsman	4358	1328	____
23.	Osceola	4340*	1323*	____

	Mountain	Elevation		Date
		(feet)	(meters)	Climbed
24.	Flume	4328	1319	___
25.	Field	4326	1319	___
26.	Pierce (Clinton)	4310	1314	___
27.	Willey	4302	1311	___
28.	North Kinsman	4293	1309	___
29.	South Hancock	4274	1303	___
30.	Bondcliff	4265	1300	___
31.	Zealand	4260*	1298*	___
32.	Cabot	4170*	1271*	___
33.	East Osceola	4156	1267	___
34.	North Tripyramid	4140	1262	___
35.	Middle Tripyramid	4110	1253	___
36.	Cannon	4100*	1250*	___
37.	Passaconaway	4060	1237	___
38.	Hale	4054	1236	___
39.	Jackson	4052	1235	___
40.	Moriah	4049	1234	___
41.	Tom	4047	1234	___
42.	Wildcat E	4041	1232	___
43.	Owl's Head	4025	1227	___
44.	Galehead	4024	1227	___
45.	Whiteface	4010*	1222*	___
46.	Waumbek	4006	1221	___
47.	Isolation	4005	1221	___
48.	Tecumseh	4003	1220	___

FOUR THOUSAND FOOTERS IN MAINE

	Mountain	Elevation (feet)	(meters)	Date Climbed
1.	Katahdin, Baxter Peak	5267	1605	___
2.	Katahdin, Hamlin Peak	4751	1448	___
3.	Sugarloaf	4250*	1295*	___
4.	Old Speck	4180	1274	___
5.	Crocker	4168	1270	___
6.	Bigelow, West Peak	4150	1265	___
7.	North Brother	4143	1263	___
8.	Saddleback	4116	1255	___
9.	Bigelow, Avery Peak	4088	1246	___
10.	Abraham	4049	1234	___
11.	Saddleback, the Horn	4023	1226	___
12.	South Crocker	4010*	1222*	___

FOUR THOUSAND FOOTERS IN VERMONT

	Mountain	Elevation (feet)	(meters)	Date Climbed
1.	Mansfield	4393	1339	___
2.	Killington	4235	1291	___
3.	Camel's Hump	4083	1244	___
4.	Ellen	4083	1244	___
5.	Abraham	4006	1221	___

About the Appalachian Mountain Club

The Appalachian Mountain Club (AMC), organized in 1876, has taken a leading part in efforts to preserve the beauty and economic value of the mountains and forests and to promote backcountry research and education. It has built and maintains many   foot trails and shelters in New Hampshire and Maine, and publishes *Appalachia Journal* (a semiannual magazine), a monthly *Appalachia Bulletin,* guidebooks, and other books relating to outdoor recreation and the environment. The AMC invites all who love the woods and mountains and wish to contribute to their protection to join the club. Membership is open to the public upon completion of an application form and payment of annual dues. Information on membership may be obtained by writing or telephoning AMC headquarters, 5 Joy St., Boston, MA 02108 (617-523-0636). Here an information center and library are open to the public Monday through Friday, 9 AM to 5 PM. The information center is a resource for questions about trails and camping, and sells guidebooks and books on outdoor recreation published by the AMC and others. Information is also available from the AMC at Pinkham Notch Camp (603-466-2727), 7 AM to 10 PM seven days a week, at the Old Bridle Path trailhead in Franconia Notch on summer days, at AMC huts during their operating season, and from the caretakers of shelter sites.

Club-sponsored lectures, meetings, and social gatherings are held in Boston and many other locations. The AMC also sponsors weekly outings and longer excursions, including some to foreign countries. Chapters in Maine, eastern New York, the Catskills, greater Philadelphia (Delaware Valley Chapter), New Hampshire, Connecticut, Rhode Island (Narragansett Chapter), Vermont, Washington DC, and Massachusetts (Worcester, Boston, Southeastern Massachusetts, and Berkshire chapters) also hold outings and meetings. There are opportunities to participate in trail clearing, skiing, canoeing, rock climbing, and other outdoor activities, in addition to hiking.

The AMC operates eight huts spaced a day's hike apart along the Appalachian Trail, staffed by young men and women who pack in much of the food and supplies. Hearty meals prepared by the crew are served family-style at specific hours; bunks, blankets, and pillows are provided. All huts are open from mid-June through Labor Day. Many huts are open during the spring and fall on a caretaker basis. During caretaker season, the hut stove and utensils are available for use, but each guest must bring a sleeping bag and food. Zealand Falls and Carter Notch remain open, on a caretaker basis, through the winter. In addition the AMC operates Pinkham Notch Camp and Crawford Hostel, and provides a hiker shuttle between Pinkham Notch Camp and major trailheads throughout the WMNF daily from mid-June through Labor Day. All these facilities are open to the public; AMC members receive a discount on lodging. Reservations and deposits are necessary to guarantee space. For complete information, write or call Reservations, AMC Pinkham Notch Camp, Box 298, Gorham, NH 03581 (603-466-2727).

AMC TRAILS

Development, construction, and maintenance of backcountry trails and facilities have been a major focus of the AMC's public-service efforts since the Club's inception. Today, through thirteen chapters, numerous camps, and its trails program, the AMC is responsible for maintaining and managing nearly 1000 mi. of trails, including over 250 mi. of the Appalachian Trail, many miles of ski trails, and more than twenty shelters and tent sites throughout the Northeast. The largest portion of these is in the White Mtns. area of NH and ME, where the AMC maintains over 100 hiking trails with an aggregate length of some 350 mi.

As a well-known and respected authority on hiking trails, the AMC works cooperatively with many federal, state, and local agencies, corporate and private landowners, and numerous other trail clubs and outdoor organizations.

AMC trails are maintained through the coordinated efforts of many people who volunteer their labor or contribute financial support, and the trails program staff and seasonal crew. Most of the difficult major construction projects are handled by the AMC trail crew, based in the White Mtns., which began operations in 1917 and is probably the oldest professional crew in the nation. Hikers who have benefited from the trails can help maintain them by donating their time for various projects and regularly scheduled volunteer trips with the AMC chapters. For hikers who are willing to assume responsibility for regular light maintenance of a trail, there is an Adopt-a-Trail Program.

For more information on any aspect of the Club's trail and shelter efforts, contact AMC Trails Program, Pinkham Notch Camp, Box 298, Gorham, NH 03581, or AMC Trails Program, 5 Joy St., Boston, MA 02108. Comments on the AMC's trail work and information on problems you encounter when hiking or camping are always welcome.

Glossary

For abbreviations see page xxx.

blaze	a trail marking on a tree or rock painted and/or cut
blazed	marked with paint on trees or rocks (blazes)
bluff	a high bank or hill with a cliff face over-looking a valley
boggy	muddy, swampy
boulder	large, detached, somewhat rounded rock
box canyon	rock formation with vertical walls and flat bottom
bushwhack	to hike through woods or brush without a trail
buttress	a rock mass projecting outward from a mountain or hill
cairn	pile of rocks to mark trail
cataract	waterfall
cirque	upper end of valley with half-bowl shape (scoured by glacier)
cliff	high, steep rock face
col	low point on a ridge between two mountains; saddle
crag	rugged, often overhanging rock eminence
grade	steepness of trail or road; ratio of vertical to horizontal distance

graded trail	well-constructed trail with smoothed footway
gulf	a cirque
gully	small, steep-sided valley
headwall	steep slope at the head of a valley, especially a cirque
height-of-land	saddle, col, or highest point reached by a trail or road
knob	a rounded, minor summit
lean-to	shelter
ledge	a large, smooth body of rock; or, but not usually in this book, a horizontal shelf across a cliff
ledgy	having exposed ledges, usually giving views
outcrops	large rocks projecting out of the soil
plateau	high, flat area
potable (water)	fit to drink
ravine	steep-sided valley
ridge	highest spine joining two or more mountains, or leading up to a mountain
runoff brook	a brook usually dry except shortly after rain, or snow melt
saddle	lowest, flattish part of ridge connecting two mountains; col
scrub	low spruce or fir trees near treeline

shelter	building, usually of wood, with roof and 3 or 4 sides, for camping
shoulder	point where rising ridge levels off or descends slightly before rising higher to a summit
a *slab (n.)*	a smooth, somewhat steeply sloping ledge
to *slab (v.)*	to walk across a slope
slide	steep slope where a landslide has carried away soil and vegetation
spur	a minor summit projecting from a larger one
spur trail	a side path off a main trail
strata	layers of rock
summit	highest point on a mountain; or, point higher than any other point in its neighborhood
switchback	zigzag in a trail to make a steep slope easier
tarn	a small pond, often at high elevation, or with no outlet
timberline	elevation that marks the upper limit of commercial timber
treeline	elevation above which trees do not grow

List of Trails

Note: Trails marked by an asterisk do not have a separate description, but are discussed or mentioned in groups or within other trails' descriptions.

A

B

560

C

S

INDEX

A

B

C

D

P

NOTES

NOTES

NOTES

NOTES

NOTES